ROTH FAMILY FOUNDATION

Music in America Imprint

Michael P. Roth

and Sukey Garcetti

have endowed this

imprint to honor the

memory of their parents,

Julia and Harry Roth,

whose deep love of music

they wish to share

with others.

The Danger of Music

The publisher gratefully acknowledges the generous support of the Music in America Endowment Fund of the University of California Press Foundation, which was established by a major gift from Sukey and Gil Garcetti, Michael Roth, and the Roth Family Foundation.

The Danger of Music

and Other Anti-Utopian Essays

Richard Taruskin

UNIVERSITY OF CALIFORNIA PRESS

Berkeley   Los Angeles   London

University of California Press, one of the most distinguished
university presses in the United States, enriches lives around the
world by advancing scholarship in the humanities, social sciences,
and natural sciences. Its activities are supported by the UC Press
Foundation and by philanthropic contributions from individuals
and institutions. For more information, visit www.ucpress.edu.

University of California Press
Berkeley and Los Angeles, California

University of California Press, Ltd.
London, England

© 2009 by The Regents of the University of California

Library of Congress Cataloging-in-Publication Data

Taruskin, Richard.
    The danger of music and other anti-utopian essays / Richard
Taruskin.
        p.   cm. — (Roth Family Foundation Music in America
imprint)
    Includes bibliographical references and index.
    ISBN 978-0-520-24977-6 (cloth : alk. paper)
    1. Musical criticism.   I. New York times.   II. Title.
    ML3785.T36   2009
    780.9—dc22   2007052244

Manufactured in the United States of America

18   17   16   15   14   13   12   11   10   09
10   9   8   7   6   5   4   3   2   1

This book is printed on Natures Book, which contains 50%
post-consumer waste and meets the minimum requirements of
ANSI/NISO Z39.48-1992 (R 1997) (*Permanence of Paper*).

To James Oestreich and Leon Wieseltier,
my co-perpetrators

*Intellectual life floats ethereally, like a fragrant cloud rising
from fermentation, above the reality of the worldly activities which
make up the lives of the peoples, governed by the will; alongside
world history there goes, guiltless and not stained with blood,
the history of philosophy, science, and the arts.*
—ARTHUR SCHOPENHAUER, *Parerga i Paralipomena* (1851)

Not.

CONTENTS

Preface

Against Utopia

For the past twenty years and more I have led a double life as a writer on music—or so they tell me. Ever since meeting James Oestreich and joining his stable of writers at *Opus* magazine (where my first article appeared in the issue of April 1985), I have written books, articles, and reviews both for scholarly venues and readerships and for . . . well, what's the opposite of scholarly? Unscholarly? I hope not. Popular? Not if sales are the measure. General interest? Would that it were so. No, the word most frequently used to describe venues and readerships in contrast to scholarly ones is *public.* I have been appearing in the "public press" as commentator and critic, which makes me an aspiring "public intellectual."

There are many who insist that the roles of public intellectual and academic are incompatible. The loudest such voice has been that of Russell Jacoby, whose *The Last Intellectuals: American Culture in the Age of Academe,* published by Basic Books in 1987, came out just when I was beginning to write for the *New Republic,* a magazine that was not only public, but not even specifically musical, and where as an academic musicologist I was supposedly even farther from home. Jacoby's book attracted my attention with its thesis that academic mores had eviscerated the American intellectual tradition, and that there were no successors to the generation of public intellectuals— Edmund Wilson, Lewis Mumford, C. Wright Mills (to list Jacoby's brightest luminaries)—who lived *la vie de bohème,* wrote forcefully and intelligibly for a wide nonprofessional readership, and offered a precious alternative to conformist thinking.

Jacoby's book was attacked as nostalgic, and (as I will be noting in due course) his subsequent writings have substantiated the charge to some degree. And one inconsistency in his argument was glaring. I remembered C. Wright Mills from my years as a student at Columbia, where he was a mainstay of the sociology department. He was an academic *as well as* a public intellectual. And so were Daniel Bell (also at Columbia in my day), John Kenneth Galbraith (a Harvard titan), and many of the others Jacoby praised. Clearly one *could* be both—couldn't one? Couldn't I aspire to a public role without compromising—or worse, being compromised by—my academic status? Jacoby's answer was that the men he was eulogizing may have ended up in the academy, but they were not formed there. That distinction was what saved them and condemned the likes of me. I could never aspire to their role because I had been fatally reared in a cozy insider world that imposed constraints on me that I would never fully comprehend, hence never escape.

Perhaps it was true, since at the outset I didn't see what the necessary difference was between academic and public writing. I did not like professional jargon any more than Jacoby seemed to like it, and I always found it a pleasant challenge, when the task called for it, to write seriously about music without using the technical vocabulary of the trade. It's true that when I became involved in heavy debate some opponents tried to besmirch me by associating me with the academic profession—to the Shostakovich groupies on the DSCH-list I was always "the Professor" or (worse) "the good Professor"—and on the other side there were those (Professor Leo Treitler, for example) who tried to belittle me for my "journalistic romps." But that was just politics, no? Just "othering," the last (or first) resort of the bigot.

In fact, I found that there were just as many journalists (Jim Oestreich himself, to begin with, both at *Opus* and, later, at the *New York Times*) who valued my academic status as a source of hard-won authority, and just as many academics (including, I'm happy to say, most of my colleagues in the Berkeley faculty and administration) who relished my public activities and thought, as I did, that it enhanced our collective image and influence in the world. For my part I have always talked up the idea of dual citizenship among my colleagues and, in particular, my pupils, and have encouraged (and, occasionally, facilitated) their public endeavors.

But there is indeed a difference between the roles, not insurmountable yet real enough, and it came home to me early. My fledgling years as a public writer coincided with a momentous historical watershed: the "fall of Communism" and the "end of the cold war." I put these phrases in scare quotes because they are both obvious exaggerations. There are powerful Communist governments left in the world, and to speak of the fall of Communism is about the most flagrant example one can find these days of Eurocentrism. And cold war attitudes certainly persist, both in academia and in the wider world of ideas. In fact, it was my journalistic activities that opened my eyes to that persistence. So these activities have been of great benefit to me even in my role as academic scholar, not only because they taught me how to write, but also because they allowed me, to a certain extent, an outsider's perspective on my home base and, by defamiliarizing it, enabled me to see aspects of it that (just as Jacoby had maintained) I had been conditioned to ignore. And yet, I thought (and think), the fact that I was vouchsafed that new perspective, however partially or haphazardly, and was transformed by it, effectively refuted Jacoby's fatalistic thesis.

What I learned was the extent to which my thinking, reflecting that of my profession, had been conditioned by utopianism.

.   .   .

To whatever extent the "fall of Communism" was real, it reflected disillusionment with utopian thinking. And living through that heady moment (a two-year moment lasting from the breaching of the Berlin Wall in 1989 to the dissolution of the Soviet Union in 1991) prompted further reflection on the relationship between utopian politics and other forms of utopian thinking, including two centuries' worth of thinking about music and the other arts. By 1989 I had already had something like four years' experience writing for public media, and I had been reacting with less than full consciousness to what I came to perceive as the biggest difference between public and academic writing.

Public writing is always tied to real-life occasions and experience, while academic writing does not have to be (and is often valued for its freedom from such ties). One cannot write "theoretically" in the public press without a practical "hook": a book or recording to review, a concert to promote, an event or pronouncement on which to comment. It is reactive writing, a response to a stimulus from without. The hook always keeps one in touch with a surrounding reality that one is not allowed to ignore. Such conditions are inimical to utopian thinking; for even if one is inclined to utopianism, any discrepancy between the nature of one's thought and the conditions to which one is reacting—any victory, that is, of ideology over observation—is likely to show up and temper one's inclinations.

Writing in the public sphere thus brought more fully to my consciousness the utopian underpinnings of much (most?) academic thought than would otherwise have been the case, made me sensitive to its blindnesses, its hypocrisies and the reasons for its ineffectualness, and set me consciously against it. Whatever impact my journalistic activity has had on my scholarly work, and through it on the wider world of scholarship, has been an anti-utopian impact.

What, then, is utopianism, and why am I against it? Recalling Thomas More's original coinage—the word *utopia* means "noplace"—it is obviously an orientation away from reality toward . . . what? Something different? Something better? What could be wrong with that?

In the wake of the events of 1989–91, it is a widespread perception that utopianism correlates alarmingly with intolerance. Certainly both Communism and Nazism imagined alternative realities and tried to get the actual world to conform to their visions, justifying all coercive means that would vouchsafe the overridingly precious ends. The Communist vision was grounded in ideals of social justice with which liberals tend to identify, while the Nazi vision was grounded in eugenicist ideals from which liberals recoil. But neither vision brooked deviation or dissent, and both brought forth monstrosities between which there is little point choosing. Utopianism, it would appear, always entailed a body count.

Against this perception there have been strong challenges. The equation is sometimes held to be a false converse. If totalitarianism is utopian, it does not necessarily follow that utopianism is totalitarian. Perhaps there are benign utopianisms. Nostalgic Marxists or ex-Marxists (Russell Jacoby, in his subsequent books, prominent among them) often say that while the Communist vision, however it may have been skewed in practice, was unquestionably a vision of a better world, the Nazi vision had no humanitarian component and therefore should not be called utopian.

But what utopians envision is not a better world. It is a perfect world—or in Kant's two-centuries-old formulation, "a perfectly constituted state"—that utopians wish to bring about. And that is what makes them dangerous, because if perfection is the aim, and compromise taboo, there will always be a shortfall to correct—a human shortfall. There will always be those whose presence mars your idea of perfection or mine, and if you or I really believe that we have the means of perfecting the world, you may feel justified in doing away with me, or I with you. When communism "fell," the intellectual world divided into two camps: those who said it was time to go back to the drawing board and those who said it was time to get rid of drawing boards. I am utterly of the latter persuasion, and have been devoting myself wholly—both as scholar and as journalist—to the destruction of drawing boards, that is, the hubristic fantasy that people can design a perfect world and then, at whatever cost, bring it into being.

Russell Jacoby had it right in another book, *The End of Utopia,* when he wrote that "someone who believes in utopias is widely considered out to lunch or out to kill."[1] The trouble is that he still wants to salvage utopianism, and thinks that by distinguishing "blueprint" utopianism, the kind that kills, from "iconoclastic" utopianism, he can reclaim the idea from the stigma. But "iconoclastic," implying the violent destruction of images (and by metaphorical extension, the debunking of sacrosanct ideas), is the wrong word for what Jacoby advocates. He means "aniconic"—a utopianism that, in keeping with Jewish religious tradition, makes no graven image of its endgame, contains no description of the perfect world it dreams about. But while aniconic utopians may not be out to kill, they are still out to lunch. The dream of perfection, more alluring than any reality, leads to a sterile sociopolitical snobbery.

Russell Jacoby himself can illustrate. In his latest book, still banging a teakettle for utopia, he complains that the students he now teaches (unlike his own generation of students, whom he romanticizes) lack the sort of imagination it takes to envision utopia. His main argument, particularly redolent of the utopianism of T. W. Adorno, is first enunciated as a question:

> Is it possible that imagination—the source of utopian speculation—has lost its vigor? That a relentless barrage of prefabricated "images" from movies and advertising has shackled its linguistic and factual offspring, "imagination"? Has imagination become unimaginative—or rather practical and realistic? The topic is difficult to circumscribe and my concerns resist proof. I offer only suggestive evidence. I sometimes teach a course on utopianism. The students arrive on the verdant California campus in various colors and sizes but generally with the easy smile and open gaze of those to whom life has been good. I allot time for students to sketch out their own utopias. They come up with laudable ideas—universal health care with choice of doctors; free higher education; clean parks; ecological vehicles—but very little that is out of the ordinary. Their boldest dreams could be realized by a comprehensive welfare state.[2]

Good for them! Their teacher's contempt for their practicality and unglamorous decency is contemptible. They are seeking betterment, not perfection. They may yet achieve something worthwhile even as Jacoby goes on kvetching from the sidelines, for while they may have given up on utopia, they have not given up on social progress. Indeed, the idea of incremental progress without a determinate endpoint—what Hans Blumenberg calls "infinite progress"—is the best alternative, and the best defense, against the blandishments of utopian thinking. "The idea of infinite progress," he writes,

> has a safeguarding function for the actual individual and for each actual generation in history. If there were an immanent final goal of history, then those who believe they know it and claim to promote its attainment would be legitimized in using all the others who do not know it and cannot promote it as mere means. Infinite progress does make each present relative to its future, but at the same time it renders every absolute claim untenable. This idea of progress corresponds more than anything else to the only regulative principle that can make history humanly bearable, which is that all dealings must be so constituted that through them people do not become mere means.[3]

Those, like Jacoby's students, who believe in human progress without believing in perfectibility or teleology will seek the best for their fellow human beings without being tempted to enslave them.

Jacoby's narcissistic contempt for what is unsexy and attainable resembles the contempt so many music critics (not only academics, but all who have accepted academic standards) entertain toward musicians who try to write good music (not "great music") and give good performances (not "great performances"), and who define the good in terms that relate to their actual, real-world audiences. There is the nexus between political utopianism and the kind that infests the world of classical music, and there is my reason for so passionately opposing the latter, even in the absence of a body count.

For there are casualties even so, and the main one has been the toll utopianism has taken on the value of classical music to and in contemporary culture. The most militant expression I know of never-say-die musical utopianism in the face of its manifest failure came unexpectedly from Arthur Berger, one of the gentlest of men, and a composer whose music I have always admired and enjoyed. Reacting belatedly to the "postmodernism" of such apostate modernists as George Rochberg, Berger counseled fortitude. He reminded his readers of some of earlier "radical shifts in music's evolution," such as the one around 1600, "when monody emerged to take the place of polyphony":

> It required a century and a half before the implications of that revolution began to be realized in the time of Mozart and Haydn. Monteverdi was the central figure in that reform—very loosely, what Schoenberg was to us. By 1650, after Monteverdi's death, the scene was quiet. It was a period of waiting for some significant developments of the experiments of 1600. . . . The point is that after Monteverdi, composers nurtured the new monody for over a century until it was ready to flower in the wondrous manifestations of the Classical era. This is how we should be nurturing the trends that some disdainfully call "modernist."[4]

This is the sort of wistful utopianism one associates with Chekhov's country doctors, who look dreamily toward a paradise for their grandchildren's grandchildren and write off their present suffering on that account. Even if today's new music scene is, er, "quiet," we must endure its hollowness stoically for the sake of some wondrous manifestation that may or may not flower forth in the future. In the most literal sense, since it advocates the *keeping* of an endangered flame, it is in its very utopianism the most conservative conceivable position, even though its advocates still delude themselves with the belief that they are keeping faith with revolutionary ideals. Comparisons with the Soviet order in its dotage are really unavoidable. As Sasha Chorny put it in "Descendants," a wonderful anti-Utopian (and implicitly anti-Soviet) poem that Dmitry Shostakovich set as one of *Five Satires,* op. 109 (1960), "I want a little light / *For myself, while I am alive.*" The italics were his.

The essays collected here cover a wide range of contemporary musical activity—composition, performance, criticism, historiography—and I have not attempted to impose any greater uniformity on them than their occasional nature warrants. Instead I have grouped them by venue: first a fairly large selection of *feuilletons* written for the cramped confines of the *New York Times* Sunday music page; then a smaller group of longer essays written for the *New Republic* (including two that, for reasons explained in the postscript to chapter 1, were published elsewhere); and finally the smallest group, consisting of critical essays and reviews that appeared in professional journals or self-identified musicological publications and reflect more insularly professional concerns while still using language accessible to interested nonprofessional readers. Within each group the pieces are ordered by simple chronology, and the whole is sandwiched between two texts originally delivered orally and published here for the first time.

What they all have in common is a spirit of protest against the utopian ideas, all corruptions of romanticism, that have isolated classical music from audiences and contributed to its precipitate decline as a cultural force in twentieth-century society. The pieces in this collection were written in most cases to bring unpleasant thoughts to consciousness and to stir up debate; and when debate became noteworthy it is reported in a postscript. In a couple of instances the articles have been slightly updated for their appearance here. In every such case the alterations are signaled.

The ideas against which these essays inveigh include the demand that performers sacrifice communication with their audience to sterile criteria of correctness (not always in the name of "historical" practice), the notion that esthetic considerations outweigh or outrank ethical ones (relieving musicians of the onus of ethical behavior), and the doctrine that composers owe their greatest debt not to the society in which they live but to the history of their art (and that historians are there to ratify and enforce it). To put it in utopian terms, in the name of autonomy and authenticity classical music has indeed become, to a degree once literally unthinkable, the music of noplace, composed for nobody and performed for nobody. In every case names are named (which is what has led to most of the bitterest controversy), not for the sake of scandal, but because it is always necessary to show that one is not arguing with straw men.

Indeed, the hold of utopia on real-world academic music thinking continues with little abatement. In November 2005, enjoying a year's sabbatical, I dropped in on the national meeting of the Society of Music Theory, an organization of which I am a rather passive member, just to see what was up, and what I saw appalled me. The best-attended papers were in almost every case devoted to purely speculative or hypothetical theoretical systems. One offered a general theory of atonal voice leading (replete with "laws") that was based on no existing musical practice but rather (as is inevitable in utopia) on a radically simplified imaginary practice that offered nothing to composers. Another paper proposed a theory that encompassed all possible chords in a single harmonic system, only proving for the nth time that totalism is the dependable enemy of pertinence.

Nobody claims that such ideas are useful, but why are they considered even interesting? My best guess is that they offer the reassurance of artistic or scholarly autonomy to those who cannot afford to subject their work to a cost-benefit analysis. But such reckonings are necessary, however agonizing, if serious music is to regain a respectable place even in the academy, to say nothing of the wider world. The idea of esthetic autonomy—initially a reaction to the nineteenth-century social emancipation (or, perhaps more accurately, the social abandonment) of the artist—has metamorphosed over the course of two centuries from a lifesaving into a life-threatening measure. That metamorphosis, entailing social divorce and moral irresponsibility, is the implicit subject matter of this book. The implicit anti-utopian aim of the book is to abet the reestablishment of a healthy musical ecology that can support—and is willing to support—noncommercial as well as commercial artistic endeavors. Whether the twenty-first century will witness such a renewal is anyone's guess. This book is one musical citizen's implicitly optimistic contribution to the project.

NOTES

1. Russell Jacoby, *The End of Utopia: Politics and Culture in an Age of Apathy* (New York: Basic Books, 1999), xi.

2. Russell Jacoby, *Picture Imperfect: Utopian Thought for an Anti-Utopian Age* (New York: Columbia University Press, 2005), xiv.

3. Hans Blumenberg, *The Legitimacy of the Modern Age*, trans. Robert M. Wallace (Cambridge, Mass.: MIT Press, 1983), 35; quoted in Karol Berger, *Bach's Cycle, Mozart's Arrow: An Essay on the Origins of Musical Modernity* (Berkeley: University of California Press, 2007), 164–65.

4. Arthur Berger, "Is There a Postmodern Music?" *Boston Review* (April 1987); rpt. in Arthur Berger, *Reflections of an American Composer* (Berkeley: University of California Press, 2002), 107.

Et in Arcadia Ego

Or, I Didn't Know I Was Such a Pessimist until I Wrote This Thing

I must begin by thanking the organizers of this conference—and Prof. Lawrence Lipking in particular, who actually tendered the invitation—for so unexpectedly asking me to speak today on the future of "music," which in my case is to say Western classical music, the only music about which I am qualified to pontificate. I say "unexpectedly" because exercises like your Chicago Seminars, which call themselves catholic or universal or interdisciplinary, tend so often to exclude music, or rather to forget it. Marginalism has always been the fate of serious musicians in our society, and it has become even worse lately, now that classical music has had to move over and share precious space at the margins of our pulsing musical commerce with jazz, once thought to be America's premiere contribution to world culture, but now decisively displaced by rock and newer forms of pop. You may not remember it, but no musician of my generation will ever forget Major General Lewis Hershey, head of the Selective Service System, telling reporters at the height of the Vietnam War how his organization functioned as an instrument of social engineering, and choosing music as his prime example of what was socially expendable.

I don't mean to complain, but serious musicians seem to be getting more expendable by the hour. (And since I don't see any sign of this abating I guess that's my first prediction.) One of my most dismal memories of two decades–plus at Columbia University is the annual effort the music department made to nominate the aging, now deceased Roger Sessions for an honorary degree, only to see an ephemeral parade of Bubbles, Mannies, Itzies, and Pinkies honored by the trustees of our liberal arts institution, where musical performance was

Originally delivered as an address at the Chicago Seminars on the Future, 13 April 1989. Published here for the first time.

not even taught as a major subject, and where every year the music department turned out its half-dozen superbly equipped yet socially useless and barely employable PhDs in composition. Music, to the Columbia trustees, as to the majority of educated Americans, was expensive entertainment, nothing more.

Or even less: the "general interest" magazines have been dropping serious music like a hot ocarina. The *New Yorker,* under its new management, has shown its appreciation of the fact that it employs the most distinguished music critic in the English-speaking world by putting in a pop reviewer to compete with him and reducing his space by half. The *Atlantic Monthly* pays attention now only to pop, with an occasional nostalgic look at old-time jazz. Does anyone even remember that *Harpers* once had a regular classical record review column? As for *The Nation,* it shows its concern for classical music by employing an opinionated, outlandishly incompetent amateur to babble about it from time to time, meanwhile making sure that its pop reviewer is technically qualified and satisfactory, and regularly featured.

The fact is, outside of its designated incubators serious music is no longer regarded today as something serious, or worth discussing, or even worth preserving except in gaudy metropolitan mausoleums. You can be a fully educated person in our society with no training or even significant exposure to music as an art, and never be made to feel a lack. So my simple answer to the question, "What is the future of music as an art?" is "What future?"

What have we done to deserve this? I think I know. Can we turn the situation around? I'm far less sure that I know, but I'm willing to share my thoughts with you, and eager to hear yours.

One of my most recent experiences in a career that has lately turned from fairly esoteric performance and more or less pure scholarship to encompass more public forms of writing has given me a deeper understanding of the problems facing music and the other arts in our society. The reasons for this change in my professional orientation have had to do partly with the fortuities of opportunity and with the need to feed a growing family, but also with an increasing frustration at the marginalism of which I have been speaking, and a wish to set an example for my professional colleagues of what we might do to counteract it. Both within the musical-intellectual community and without I have been raising my voice against the sterile formalism that still reigns among musicians, and against the mindless attitudes about music that prevail outside of the profession. A lot of what I have written has been deliberately provocative; and what it has provoked both from within and from without has shown me how unexpectedly close is the relationship between the formalism and the mindlessness. They are both surface manifestations of the same centuries-old cultural assumptions—assumptions that may have arisen in the first place as a lifesaving measure for music but which now threaten its existence.

During the past year [1988] I have written two fairly extended pieces for the *New Republic* (and let me gratefully except that magazine from my general lament about musical coverage in the nonspecialized press). The first was a review of a book about music in fascist Italy [chapter 31 in the present collection] that exhibited a blatant double standard. The author was very strict—overly strict, I thought—in his condemnation of all sorts of minor Italian composers who groveled before Mussolini and sought to turn the fascist cultural bureaucracy to their opportunistic advantage. And yet when dealing with the fascist allegiances of many more important modern musical figures, including some of the greatest, the author bent over backwards to excuse them. This led me inevitably to a consideration of the appeal of fascism between the wars to so many modern artists and some reflections on the affinities between aspects of musical modernism and aspects of totalitarian ideology.

The other piece, a revision of an essay originally written for the San Francisco Opera's program book, concerned Shostakovich's once-banned opera *The Lady Macbeth of the Mtsensk District*. Partly in reaction to the romanticized image of the composer as heroic political resister, I ventured to point out that the opera embodies a hideous moral inversion, and one, moreover, that is not at all incongruent with those perpetrated in other walks of Soviet life in the horrible period of the first Five Year Plan.

I will admit that such blunt moralizing is not the subtlest of critical modes, or the one in which I would have necessarily chosen to couch either of these pieces if I had had no polemical agenda. But I was frankly unprepared for the abusive mail that came pouring in in response to them. Clearly, I had violated some major taboos.

It was the formalists who chiefly responded to the first piece. A prominent American composer complained that "nowhere in Taruskin's article is there the faintest suggestion that an artist can have any motivation whatever in his choice of technical means and artistic styles other than a political one, or one that can at least be politically evaluated." He turned the tables on me by claiming that my attitude was no different from "the whole methodology of National Socialist (as well as Stalinist) musicology." Another composer challenged me to specify which notes and rests in Stravinsky's music were inherently fascist.

This sort of dare, depressingly common, is as good an illustration as any of the infantile mental level at which musical formalism operates in our overly professionalized musical culture. The only form of discourse recognized as legitimate is the most atomistic sort of analysis, one that precludes a priori any inquiry of intellectual substance. Of my first respondent's charges I won't bother to answer the explicit one; I was hardly attempting an inventory of all possible artistic motivations. But I do think that his implication—to wit, that artistic decisions are exempt from political evaluation—merits diagnosis as a very advanced extrapolation from the myth of musical autonomy, which holds that, since works of musical art are no longer directly involved with social activities such as worship, dancing, or labor, hence composing music is no longer a social activity, or one that bears on any aspect of life as socially experienced.

Composers who regard themselves in this way have effectively marginalized themselves. Meanwhile, it is not for any of us to say by what standards our actions may be evaluated, whether political, psychological, or esthetic. Self-exemption in advance is immediately to be evaluated as an act of arrogance and irresponsibility. It is an act composers in our society are trained to perform, and one that is in fact expected of them.

This I found out from the responses to my second piece, the one on Shostakovich, which chiefly attracted the mindless. Again, for merely raising the question of moral responsibility in a composer I was cast as a villain. "With a musicologist like Taruskin who needs an Ayatollah?" one reader wanted to know. Another was "struck by the resemblance between Stalin's and Taruskin's views of Shostakovich; the difference between them is that Stalin writes better." My favorite was a one-sentence letter that I can quote in its entirety: "Regarding Richard Taruskin's unrelentingly severe judgment of Katerina's [i.e., the heroine's] morality, I would be interested to know how he would 'judge' Mozart and Don Giovanni's morality?"

The writer of that last letter obviously never sat through *Don Giovanni* to the end, or else he would have known that Mozart judged his character severely enough, for his was a time when social convention demanded a judgment, however hypocritical we may now adjudge that demand. Social convention today demands the opposite—that nothing that goes on in "art" be judged from any standpoint other than the "esthetic," which is usually just a euphemism for the assertion of one's casual tastes or one's unexamined snobberies.

What my respondents have taught me is that one of the fundamental dogmas of our enlightened culture is that art is innocuous. "High art," that is—for we all know how vigilant many members of society are about the messages our popular musics convey. In their vigilance they are demonstrating the greater vitality of pop culture, in which, we are told, the vital stream of romanticism still trickles.[1] Our serious musicians have mainly given up on the romantic project—or so they fondly imagine—and are regarded by our society not as shamans or prophets but at best as comedians, at worst as cranks. In no case is a serious composer really regarded as a serious person in our society, nor are his works taken seriously, if we may measure seriousness by the amount of opposition they may arouse. If high art is bracketed off from life by its absolutism and autonomy, it can by definition administer no shocks, issue no threat, convey no message. Well-dressed audiences are trained to pay high prices to watch the antics of Shostakovich's multiple murderess yet think about nothing except the quality of her singing voice. If it is pointed out to them just what it is they have been witnessing, only then do they scream bloody murder.

It is the price, a cynic will say, of freedom. And there is unfortunately a grain of truth in the proposition that creative freedom varies inversely with the social value of the artistic product. For Confucius any change in musical practice was a sign of social disintegration and therefore to be forbidden. Today styles change weekly and no one cares. My own experience as an exchange student in the Soviet Union showed me vividly that where the practice of art is attended with risk artists know a kind of honor—or a kind of ignominy—we in the liberal West cannot imagine. Art, over there, was cherished and, above all, known in a way we can scarce imagine, either. I was there to research the operas of a certain Alexander Serov, a composer who died in the 1870s, and whose works, with one exception, did not survive the Revolution. I was very impressed to find that one of my friends in Russia, then an economics student, later a leader in computer education, knew all of them by name, and could even tell me something about their plots. I was positively amazed when the concierge of his apartment building could do the same.

In the West, a century-long tradition of reckless, socially irresponsible, and self-absorbed avant-garde behavior, supported by the dogma that art is the concern of artists only and coupled with an ever-increasing passivity on the part of an audience that is deprived by its education and by the growth of the recording industry of participatory skills in music, has led to the extreme apathy that threatens the continued existence of art music in our culture. And yet anyone who questions the dogma of autonomy, harmful though it has become, is immediately and unthinkingly branded an enemy of art.

I am coming to exactly the opposite conclusion. Art must be saved from the dogma. And while saying this I concede to my critics—I do not shrink from it—that a step away from our culture's apathy toward art and artists is a step in the direction of Auschwitz and the Gulag. But that is only because the fulcrum lies between the unbalanced extremes. It is a step toward balance that I am seeking and trying, through my critical activities, to further. Whatever few little signs that a trend toward balance may be taking shape, and they are far from unequivocal, are the cheeriest news I can bring you today.

What shall bring a change about? Utopian proposals and prescriptions have become commonplace. Several recent books—by John Blacking, an ethnomusicologist; by Christopher Small, a music educator; and most noisily by Jacques Attali, an economist; and a few others—have attempted to diagnose our musical malaise and to project the means of curing it.[2] The etiology of the disease is typically seen in terms of radical cleavages: between producer and consumer; between the elite and the mass; between subject and object, process and product, knowing and doing. Notions of high art and canon are routinely deplored and condemned. The cure is sought in wholeness: spontaneous participation, mass creativity, communal improvisation. Third-world cultures, notably African, are held up as models. Radical educational reform is urged.

Well, we can certainly do with a bit of educational reform. That is unquestionably where public funding for the arts should go, in my opinion. I would simplify the prescription: let's bring music—practical music, singing and playing (and reading), not just passive appreciation, and certainly not surveys or cultural smorgasbords—back into elementary and secondary education. That would give serious music a chance in our culture—and by "serious music" I mean the kind that requires a bit of memory involvement and cognitive skill, that inculcates truly music-based expectations and responses, and induces truly musical joys and satisfactions, regardless of where it comes from or what kind of instruments are involved. It could be Bach, it could be jazz; it could be Beethoven, it could be West African drumming; it could be Brahms, it could be Indian ragas, so long as competent and committed teachers may be found and exacting standards are set, whether or not they're met. But giving every kid a computer with built-in sound synthesizer and sequencer and sending the little darling off to invent music for himself (to cite one modest proposal I recently read) will only retard his discovery of music; and "world music" show-and-tell is worse than useless. I saw in the paper just yesterday that the president of the Juilliard School has put just such a course in place in his conservatory. "I want students to be ready to deal knowledgeably with the future," he was quoted as saying, "and that is the future."[3] Well, those are just the words of a politician running scared. That's not the future. That's nowhere.

If you want to see music thrive in our future, then everyone in our society should be allowed to learn what it is to think in music, not just think about it. It can only be because singing and playing and reading music remain part of the educational experience of every British schoolchild—or did before Thatcher, anyway—that classical record sales in Great Britain are roughly equal in gross volume to sales in America; and this despite the fact that the United Kingdom has only a third of our population, its per capita income is lower, and record prices there are higher. California kids used to get such training, my students at Berkeley tell me, before the great tax revolt of 1978 ("Prop 13") took hold. But of course music is always going to be the first item trimmed from any budget. Right, General Hershey?

The more sweeping proposals of Blacking, Small, Attali, and the rest are beyond what I take to be the bounds of serious practical discussion. For one thing, they are pervaded with neoprimitivism, imperialism's no less patronizing inverse mode. For another, like most utopian programs they are largely destructive, and I continue to believe that babies may yet be lurking in the bathwater. I am not ready to scrap our traditional repertory just yet, and before I'm done I'll tell you why. But my main objection to utopian prescriptions for musical reeducation is that they are really aimed at more fundamental constituents of our culture—things like literacy, market economics, division of labor, technology—things from which music cannot be so easily extricated and tinkered with by mere fiat. To think that it can is only to marginalize it and trivialize it anew. And, of course, like all liberals I am generally suspicious of utopia builders, for today's utopian is tomorrow's totalitarian. Change we cannot bring about through consensus is change we ought not undertake. You'll not find me brandishing an ax, my abusive correspondents notwithstanding, and any postprandial ax-brandishers today will find in me a ready opponent.

Thus, in spite of all nostalgic blandishments and good intentions, I believe we have to take it for granted that, in the foreseeable future, Western music will continue to consist in the main of the products of a composing and performing elite. These products will continue to be disseminated among and consumed by a nonproducing audience in ways that resemble those familiar means of public dissemination and mechanical reproduction that have been described and variously hailed and deplored since the days of Benjamin and Adorno. The best and most practical way of improving the supply, as I've been saying, is to go to work on the demand. But Jacques Attali's "Age of Composition," in which the art of music shall be miraculously removed from the institutions of specialized musical training and "returned" to all members of society, is not about to dawn, nor could it without force and iniquity. For who shall do the removing and returning? And what wily view of society is this that claims to be all-encompassing yet obviously excludes musicians as we know them now?

.   .   .

So where are we headed? To give you an honest answer I need to inform you even better than I already have as to where I'm coming from. If you are properly to evaluate my view of the future as it relates to the present, I must locate the present for you with respect to the past. In fact, it's one of the most useful things I could do today, for the usual telling of the story of music in the twentieth century—the academic telling, at any rate—is a barefaced pack of lies, or at best evasions, brought on by adherence to a quaint nineteenth-century view of history as straightforward linear progress. I am rather ashamed to admit before my present audience that most musicians still believe in this ancient doctrine even after all its ghastly consequences in the twentieth century, but believe it they do, especially the composers of yesterday's avant-garde, who today occupy the most conspicuous seats of power.

The history of music in the twentieth, the most violent of centuries, has not been a straight line but a zigzag. To be exact, there have been two zigs and an equal number of zags. They arose not merely in response or "reaction" to one another or to the music of the immediate past, but in response to the same hopes and horrors that have shaped the rest of human aspiration and endeavor. We are now living in the Second Zag, which will surely take us to century's end and beyond. That is my main premise, my main prediction, if you like.

What I call zigs are periods of optimism, of belief in boundless possibilities. The First Zig was really the continuation unto culmination of the romantic afflatus. Every nineteenth-century agony and ecstasy was maximalized in the years immediately preceding World War I through a zealous intensification of expressive and technical means. Those who were able and unafraid to bring this afflatus to the brink of apparent chaos—Schoenberg in *Erwartung*, Stravinsky in *Le Sacre du printemps*—were the geniuses of the age.

It was the Great War, of course, and the revolutions that followed in its wake, that produced the First Zag, or pessimistic retrenchment. Faced with real chaos, artists stopped playing with the idea. The project now became one of salvage. The First Zig was bracketed and rejected, along with the whole solipsistic era to which it had been appended, as artists sought refuge in ideas of certainty and stability, ideas of order. The composer of *Le Sacre du printemps* became the great neoclassicist and self-proclaimed antimodernist of the twenties and thirties, while the composer of *Erwartung* formulated one of the most orderly systems of composition of this or any age, and used it to compose little gavottes and gigues. He used it, as Stravinsky used his more obvious eighteenth-century mannerisms, to recapture what T. E. Hulme called "the dry hardness which you get in the classics."[4] Civilization was at stake, and for its sake individual talents (as T. S. Eliot averred) gladly sacrificed their personalities. They have not been recovered since.

As the Great War had given rise to the First Zag, the "Good War" (as you call it in Chicago) provoked the Second Zig, a great new burst of optimistic maximalism. Science won that war, you will recall, and in its aftermath enjoyed an unprecedented prestige. In music as everywhere else, the immediate post–World War II period was the age of technocrats, personified in music by two whose names have become emblems in America: Milton Babbitt and John Cage. Seeming antipodes (and behaving at the time very much like adversaries), they stood in several crucial ways on virtually the same ground, and defined the Second Zig in tandem.

As musicians of the interwar Zag had bracketed the First Zig and claimed kinship with its imaginary antithesis, the age of classicism, so musicians of the Second Zig bracketed the Zag. Zig called unto Zig. On the surface this led to some rather anomalous evaluations, especially as regarded the figures who had both zigged and zagged. Postwar ziggers reviled the neoclassic Stravinsky even as they worshiped *Le Sacre du printemps*. And, even as he worshiped the composer of *Erwartung*, the young Pierre Boulez, technocrat par excellence, came to bury the Schoenberg of the gigues and gavottes with a notorious journalistic blast.

This equivocation reflected a more serious one. There was no real kinship between the First Zig and the Second. Or rather, the kinship was of precisely the same order as obtained between the First Zag and the imaginary eighteenth century to which it had appealed for validation. Continuity was asserted for the sake of legitimacy, but means and ends had irrevocably altered. Maximalism of expressive purpose was replaced by an even more seductive maximalism—that of technical innovation. Never before were creative musicians so obsessed with métier.

American academics will recall this as the period of the great debate over the PhD in composition, when it was successfully argued that technically advanced musical composition could be regarded as a form of scientific research. To achieve such a status, of course, it had to give up all pretense to the kind of subjectivity normally associated with the arts. But this was no great loss, for composers had no more secure a sense of self in the shadows of Auschwitz and Hiroshima than anyone else. Indeed, contempt for the whole idea of individual self-expression was the one thing musicians of the postwar Zig could inherit directly from the interwar Zag. Originality, as much a requirement as ever, was now to be asserted, not in terms of arbitrary, self-dramatizing "inspiration," but in the form of rational and explicable technical advances that could be tested and duplicated by the musical-scientific community at large, every member of which had an obligation to advance the march of ever-burgeoning technical progress. The goal was to bring as much as possible in a musical composition under strictly rational control. This was known in those days as "responsible" composition.

The paradoxical result of this extreme rationalization of composition method was the introduction of an unprecedented degree of perceived, and even actual, fortuity into the product thus achieved. As Ernst Krenek put it in a famous confession:

> The composer has come to distrust his inspiration because it is not really as innocent as it was supposed to be, but rather conditioned by a tremendous body of recollection, tradition, training, and experience. In order to avoid the dictations of such ghosts, he prefers to set up an impersonal mechanism which will furnish, according to premeditated patterns, unpredictable situations. . . . The unexpected happens by necessity. The surprise is built in.[5]

Although they made so much franker and more deliberate a use of indeterminacy as to create an apparent rift with "total serialists" like Babbitt or Boulez, John Cage and his cohort were also scientists of a sort. They liked to call their work "experimental." Here is how Christian Wolff, a pupil of Cage's, described their aims: "One finds a concern for a kind of objectivity, almost anonymity—sound come into its own. The 'music' is a resultant existing simply in the sounds we hear, given no impulse by expressions of self or personality."[6] What enraged the more rationalistic technocrats was the fact that the other group's methods were so easy and permissive. As Charles Wuorinen, a protégé of Babbitt's, sniffed: "How can you make a revolution when the revolution before last has already said that anything goes?"[7]

The answer to that question seems in retrospect only too obvious. One of its most concise formulations has been given by a recent composer who defines his style as "writing in repetitive structures with very reduced pitch relationships, a steady eighth-note beat, and a static dynamic level."[8] The answer to "anything goes," naturally, is "hardly anything goes": reduce, restrict, pull back, eliminate. "You just have to tear everything down and begin again," says another recent composer. "It's a kind of re-education in music, and I think it's the beginning of a new music."[9] Obviously, we have come to the Second Zag, the one through which we are living now.

As before, as always, movements toward retrenchment are born out of pessimism, out of a sense of no-can-do. The unlimited technical advances and structural complexities in which composers reveled during the Second Zig have been cried down as deluded in the light of modern cognitive psychology and structural linguistics. There may be no limit to what the conceptualizing mind may devise, on this view, but there do seem to be limits on perceptual comprehension. Fred Lerdahl, a composer who has been especially involved with research into these questions, has confidently predicted that "the music of the future will emerge less from twentieth-century progressivist esthetics than from newly acquired knowledge of the structure of musical perception and cognition."[10] My impulse is to endorse this prediction, but all I can honestly state is a hope. Meanwhile, the fact that unregenerate ziggers have been outspokenly unwilling to accept such constraints has led to their discreditation not only by the civilian population but also to a large extent within the profession.

As before, there has been a bracketing. This time it has taken the deadliest form of all—canonization. The ziggers have been placed kicking and screaming in the pantheon, while the zaggers have busied themselves charting the future of music. As one shrewd critic has noted, only somewhat hyperbolically, "Milton Babbitt has gone from pariah to old master in the space of two years," dating the transformation from the award of his MacArthur Fellowship. John Cage, even as I speak, is occupying the august Norton chair of poetry at Harvard, doing his best to *épater* a new bourgeoisie—and with some success, to judge from the rumors I've been hearing, but not among the musicians there, who look on and smile in comfortable recognition. When I went to school one spoke of Babbitt with fear and of Cage with loathing. I can remember Otto Luening, my old composition teacher and the mildest of men, snarling at the mention of Cage ("What's he up to now, that enfant terrible of fifty?"). At seventy-seven Cage threatens no one, angers no one, and neither does the seventy-three-year-old Babbitt. Along with their numberless epigones, they have become irrelevant to the contemporary music scene.

Philip Glass, the composer whose prescription for retrenchment I quoted a moment ago, is the one who gets snarled at now. His music, outwardly so simple and unprepossessing, threatens and angers more than any other music being written now. What better evidence do we need of its potency? Or of its relevance to any discussion of the future of music. Along with confreres and competitors like Steve Reich and, more recently (and, as I'll suggest, more equivocally), John Adams, Glass has at last shattered the old myth of the Frankfurt School. Whatever one may think of it, and whatever it may say about the state of our culture, the music of Glass and Reich represents a style that is undeniably at once avant-garde and popular.

Its popularity, especially with audiences hitherto or traditionally indifferent to "classical" music, is a simple fact. What needs defense is the proposition that it is avant-garde. Its partial reliance on the normative vocabulary of conventional "tonal" music—its consonant harmonies, its diatonic motives, its triads, its major and minor scales, its endless arpeggios—has led to the charge that it is a cynical revival of outmoded easy idioms. Yet its syntax is by no means the normal syntax of conventional tonal music. The chords may be familiar, but they are arranged in sequences that are not only unfamiliar, but nonprogressive and hence inimical to the teleological assumptions on which tonal harmony is based. By neutralizing the forward thrust of harmony, this music seems to stanch the flow of time itself. In other words, the music is just as "post-Renaissance," to use Leonard B. Meyer's term, as the "experimental" music of the Second Zig.

Glass calls his music non-narrative. Reich, echoing Cage, speaks of process instead of product; but very much unlike Cage, he sees virtue in predictability and seeks a total determinacy. "Once the process is set up and loaded," he says, "it runs by itself."[11] It is just another way of achieving what all the postwar avant-gardists have sought: namely, the death of the self. As Reich has written, "While performing and listening to gradual musical processes one can participate in a particular liberating and impersonal kind of ritual. Focusing in on the musical process makes possible that shift of attention away from *he* and *she* and *you* and *me* outwards toward *it*."[12] The reason for the simple triadic vocabulary, let me suggest, is the need to avoid distraction. The composers of the Second Zag have sought to bracket pitch structure as an object of attention or site of contention. Given the development of Western music since the seventeenth century, there could hardly be a more radical act than that.

Because it uses instruments (electronic organs and keyboard synthesizers, for example) that are widely employed in commercial pop music, the music of these composers is often written off as a variety of pop music itself. Yet all of the composers who employ the repetitive style were trained as classical musicians and came to the style by way of more traditional classical ones. The repetitive style is a revolt from within, not a conquest from without; that is why I see it as a true Zag. Still, its use of pop instruments (and sometimes pop performers, too) and its "crossover" appeal do testify to countercultural origins and hence to the new music's cultural significance.

Those who called what went on in the sixties "modernism in the streets" completely misread what they were observing. What went up from the streets in the sixties was a call to desist. By the eighties the call has reached into every citadel of the musical establishment and into the cultural avant-garde, and it has led to the virtual abandonment of the modernist project as pursued by the musicians of the Second Zig. Anyone who has recently served on a composition search committee can vouch for this.

The reaction has taken many forms. What they all have in common is a fundamental impulse to dehistoricize, which seems closely related to the antiteleological structure of the music itself, and to transcend or deconstruct traditional stylistic and generic categories, particularly as regards high versus popular culture. Composers, especially young composers, often speak of a new freedom of choice. That is heartening, of course, but it could also be described as an exacerbated, even a narcissistic fragmentation, which, as many have pointed out, not only "diminishes the chances of a quality mass art,"[13] but in fact makes quality ever more difficult to discern. And anyone who has served on a recent composer search knows that, too.

The most obvious implementation of the project is out-and-out stylistic pastiche or collage, especially of styles that have remained popular with audiences while whole parades of modern idioms have come and gone. It would be easy to write off this sort of "composing in the past tense" as mere pandering, were it not for the fact that it makes defenders of high modernism so furious. Once again I cite the ability to enrage as a mark of cultural authenticity. Not even John Rockwell, the *New York Times* culture maven who prides himself on being the most omnivorous critic in the West, hesitates to condemn what has become known, erroneously, as neoromanticism. George Rochberg's opera *The Confidence Man,* written in this style, incited Andrew Porter, the *New Yorker*'s critic and normally a model of unflappable urbanity, into a hair-raising loss of cool. Like many others, Porter suspects Rochberg and those who share his predilections of harboring a neoconservative agenda. "His works could become cultural fodder for the New Right: Down with progressive thought! Down with progressive music!" the critic ranted.[14] What such music is really saying, though, and it's a message that needs to be heard, is, "Down with the narrative of progress!"

The impulse to dehierarchize musical styles and genres, and the concomitant proliferation of eclectic practices, has been much celebrated. John Schaefer, who runs the *New Sounds* program on public radio in New York, has published an engrossing book of the same name in which he attempts to classify and make comprehensible this new explosion of fringe activity, almost all of which he sees as a sign of new musical health.[15] Besides the so-called minimalism of Glass, Reich, et al. (I would prefer to call it pattern-and-process music, P&P for short), he devotes chapters to a dozen other trends that cross the usual frontiers between high culture and low, classical and folk, East and West, electronic and acoustic. The same kind of eclectic diversity is found in the repertoire of the punk-attired Kronos Quartet, by now the highest-paid ensemble in the history of chamber music. I characterize them so in order to remind you that they are not necessarily doing what they do entirely for their health, as the saying goes, or for the health of the culture. The music biz stands ready as ever to co-opt anyone's success, and the academy stands ready as ever to turn today's counterculture into tomorrow's orthodoxy. Both projects, in fact, are well along. Let me merely note the quickness with which all this mind-boggling diversity has been subsumed under a typically mind-numbing academic shibboleth. Ladies and gentlemen, I give you "postmodernism." And you can have it. And perhaps you'll tell me what it means.

.   .   .

But maybe I'm too readily skeptical. Let me quote to you some inspiriting words by Susan McClary, the feminist critic, who has emerged as the most rosy-eyed champion of what I have been calling the Second Zag. She sees in it not only the ineluctable wave of the future, but to a large degree a happy and so far unthreatened fait accompli:

> The new styles challenge the ideology of the rigorous, autonomous, elitist music produced in universities for seminars. They call into question the institutions of academic training and taxonomies, of orchestras and opera houses, of recording and funding networks.
> Many of the principal figures in these new styles come from groups traditionally marginalized, who are defined by the mainstream as noise anyway, and who thus have been in particularly good positions to observe the oppressive nature of the reigning order. Women, for instance, are not only strongly represented in these new modes of Composition—they are frequently leaders, which has never before been the case in Western "art" music. . . . Some individuals composing new kinds of music were originally associated with other media . . . or have found their most responsive audiences among dancers and visual artists. All are people who managed not to be silenced by the institutional framework, who are dedicated to injecting back into music the noise of the body, of the visual, of emotions, and of gender. . . . The traditional taxonomic distinction between high and popular culture becomes irrelevant in the eclectic blends characteristic of this new music. . . . A new breed of music critic has begun to articulate the way the world looks (and sounds) without the distortion of that distinction.[16]

And yet, and yet . . . *Et in Arcadia ego*. Even in Arcadia a spiritual death may lurk. What makes the music McClary describes so seductive? In what does its appeal to audiences consist? Ransom Wilson, an American flutist and conductor, has recounted his conversion to P&P at one of the great watershed events in the history of the Second Zag, the performance in 1976 of Philip Glass's five-hour opera, *Einstein on the Beach,* at the Metropolitan Opera House:

> There were no intermissions. The work continued relentlessly in its grip on all of us in that packed house. Suddenly, at a point some four hours into the opera there occurred a completely unexpected harmonic and rhythmic modulation, coupled with a huge jump in the decibel level. People in the audience began to scream with delight and I remember well that my entire body was covered with goose bumps.[17]

So much one may elicit from a pithed frog, and—if you remember your high school biology class—under conditions that are not dissimilar. Philip Glass, indeed, speaks frankly of eliciting a "biological" response from his audience. Here are his own words on the opera whose effects Wilson described:

> I decided that I would try to write a piece that left the audience standing, and I've almost never played that music without seeing everyone leave his seat; it's the strangest thing, almost biological. In fact, sometimes I've done concerts where I've played the Spaceship [i.e., the *Einstein* finale], and then as an encore played the last part of the Spaceship, and the same thing happens again.[18]

But no, there is nothing strange about this: it's basic behavior-modification therapy, and so far from spontaneous or liberating, it is calculated authoritarian manipulation. I find it sinister. My first contact with P&P came in June 1983 (yes, I'd been avoiding it) at a little festival sponsored by the New York Philharmonic and organized by the orchestra's then composer-in-residence, Jacob Druckman, around the theme "Since 1968—A New Romanticism?" Druckman's keynote essay in the program spoke optimistically of the "re-emergence of . . . Dionysian qualities: sensuality, mystery, nostalgia, ecstasy, transcendency." What I heard, in John Adams's *Grand Pianola Music,* was an attempt to reduce me to an autonomic nervous system. My body responded to the programmed thrills and chills even as my mind protested. I, too, felt gooseflesh—and, I'll admit, gooseflesh at a new-music concert was indeed a novelty. But it was a gooseflesh brought about not by way of evocation or epiphany but by anesthetizing the conscious mind and then administering a series of galvanic shocks. For me the experience was frightening. What had won so many over left me feeling diminished and degraded. And I guess I'm sounding like old man Adorno in spite of myself.

Are Scylla and Charybdis all that's left? Do we have no other choice than a choice of dehumanizations? On the one hand there is a music, increasingly under attack, that makes its appeal exclusively to the cerebral cortex. On the other hand there is a music, increasingly successful, that speaks, if I may put it so, directly to the medulla and the ganglia. Is there any music being written today that addresses an integrated personality, a whole human being?

Very little, I'm bound to say. Recognition of this sad fact has been one of the chief impulses behind the movement toward pastiche. The last musical style to combine or integrate an intellectual and a visceral appeal, many are convinced, was that of expressionism, and they are also convinced that only functional harmonic relations (a.k.a. "tonality") offers the possibility of such an integration. It is also one of the reasons why, incidentally, so much insignificant nineteenth-century music is being revived. Where the sixties witnessed the great discovery of Charles Ives, the eighties have witnessed the discovery of Horatio Parker, the teacher Ives rebelled against, along with all of his genteel Boston contemporaries. This resurrection of the *pompiers* is the true neoconservative movement in music today, if anything is.

I cannot see how such pastiche-cum-revival can possibly offer an avenue to the future or a means of reintegrating or rehumanizing our music. Pastiche imposes the worst constraints of all on such a project, for a successful simulacrum demands—indeed, implies—a transparent creator. I myself once restored half of an incompletely preserved fifteenth-century isorhythmic motet so that a choir I directed might perform it. To test my work I challenged the group to detect my contributions. They inevitably fixed on whatever stood out as unconventional or eccentric or interesting in the music—and of course that was the work of the original composer (and the reason I wanted to perform the piece). I had covered myself well, supplying no more than what any old Anonymus might have come up with. And that is why the "neoromantic" music of the late twentieth century has been by and large so unsatisfactory. It is the work of nineteenth-century Anons.

Besides, the romantic idiom that is being so staidly revived in the concert hall can hardly be reassociated there with the figure of the unreconstructed pantheistic, solipsistic, primitivistic romantic artist. That id-flaunting figure has been thoroughly preempted by now by the popular culture, and endlessly parodied in the movies where, as we know, an unbroken tradition of neoromantic tonal music has continued to thrive, in a line from Korngold through Tiomkin to John Williams. It seems unlikely that any composer will write freshly enough in the style at this late date to redeem it from the academy on the one hand and from kitsch appropriations on the other. The mere musician who stands before you today will not presume to tell you why our selves cannot be so easily reintegrated at the end of the fallen, Freud-infested twentieth century, but he can tell you that mere musicians are not going to accomplish the reconstitution single-handedly.

·   ·   ·

So these are among the reasons why not only the public for serious music but also to an unprecedented extent the musical profession itself has been losing faith and interest in the work of "serious" living composers, and why serious music seems for now irrevocably confined to the margins of our cultural life. My ultimate prediction this morning is not too happy. The foreseeable future of Western classical music, in my opinion, may not lie with its creators at all but with its curators. This is something that goes far beyond neoconservative revivals. The evidence is all around us that what is truly "hot" in music today, and where the liveliest creative energies are being expended, is not the project of decanonizing and rehumanizing our musical culture but that of finding radical approaches to the canonical works of the past.

An American composer recently complained that the so-called authenticity movement was "the one musical activity these days which has the passion of the new." He added that "the latest step forward in authentic performance practice draws the sort of attention previously reserved for new music," and, he concluded, "if you want to think there's some sour grapes there you're absolutely right."[19] The music page of the Sunday *New York Times* on the very day I happened to be writing this echoed these remarks: "Why," a banner asked, "does the audience for new works shrink as interest in early music grows?"[20] As in the case of P&P, what tends to baffle most is that this growth has encompassed audiences not traditionally interested in the classics.

Now "early music," as I suppose most people must realize by now, does not merely mean old music in this context, but a general philosophy of performing music. The stated objective is to perform any music in a fashion that approximates as closely as possible the performing conditions that obtained when the music was written. This historical verisimilitude is what is usually termed "authenticity" by the movement's apologists. In practice, as has become increasingly evident as the early music movement has encroached on the nineteenth century, it has actually meant performing all music in a style first promulgated by Stravinsky and other neoclassicists in the 1920s but equally characteristic of all the subsequent twentieth-century zigs and zags. In fact, a recognizable and consistent twentieth-century style of performance is the one thing that links practically all post–World War I styles of composition, whether Stravinsky's, Babbitt's, Cage's, or Glass's. Often called an "objective" style, it can be described by recalling Glass's definition of his music as always having a steady beat and a static dynamic. Modified to take Babbitt's serialized dynamics into account, wherein louds and softs, while thoroughly mixed, nevertheless succeed one another according to a predetermined (hence static) sequence, the portrayal will do as an all-purpose description of twentieth-century performance—streamlined, geometrical, and dehumanized. It describes "early music" performances of Bach, Mozart, and Beethoven equally well, despite the fact that contemporaneous performance practice for these composers was demonstrably altogether different. What "early music" performers are doing, then, is performing Bach, Mozart, or Beethoven as if they were Stravinsky, Babbitt, or Glass.

Thus "early music," though its pretension to "authenticity" is easily refuted, is nonetheless a profoundly authentic expression of our time—for better or worse. That, rather than its pretensions, is what gives it its vitality and its viability, and why its present project of encroachment on later and later repertories is destined to continue and succeed. Eventually we will be performing the music of the whole nineteenth century as if it were twentieth-century music. And then we will at last have the kind of authentic performance practice that gives practitioners a sense of their own cultural identity, which is what authenticity is—or should be—all about. Yet can anyone doubt for a moment that, were there a contemporary repertory to which audiences could relate the way audiences could once relate to new music, there would never have been the need for "early music"?

And if there were a viable repertory of new and timely operas, would we need to revamp old ones in the meretricious ways we read about daily in the newspapers? Actually, of course, the revampings are not travesties at all—they are a way of reclaiming the past for the present at a time when the present seems unable to replace the past. And though it may look paradoxical on the surface, it is absolutely logical (or at least consistent with the viewpoint I am developing) that the same productions (those by Peter Sellars, for example) that seem the most outrageous on the stage are the very ones most likely to have "original instruments" and all the rest of the authentistic equipage in the pit.

Many have come to look upon Sellars as the savior of opera. For Andrew Porter, Sellars "makes everyone who goes to see any of his productions feel that opera is the most important and most telling and trenchant art-form that we have."[21] Therefore when Sellars teamed up with John Adams—whose later work has combined traits of so-called minimalism with elements of so-called neoromanticism, making him perhaps the most comprehensively representative composer of the Second Zag—it was an event that raised hopes. It was a stroke of pure genius to base their opera on the figure of Richard Nixon, for this not only ensured a publicity bonanza but also completely short-circuited discussion of the work on its artistic merits. I do not propose to weigh them here. But *Nixon in China* will surely have many imitators—Sellars and Adams themselves are planning a sequel—and perhaps we are in for a revival of the short-lived genre known as *Zeitoper* that flourished in the Germany of the Weimar Republic, only based not on contemporary archetypes in the Brechtian fashion but on real people in the news. I'm sure an opera on Jim and Tammy Bakker is in the works (we've already had one on Jimmy Swaggart right here in Chicago, although it was irrelevantly tied for some reason to the libretto and music of Wagner's *Tannhäuser*). Who else? Ed Koch? Jesse Jackson? Charles and Di?

I look forward to these and other works of this kind, not for the sake of their timeliness or relevance, but because if they are provocative enough the new Zeitopers might at last succeed in reinjecting values other than esthetic ones into our public discussion of music, which will help music mean something to us again. The next Sellars-Adams piece is slated to deal with the hijacking of the *Achille Lauro* and the murder of Leon Klinghoffer. If, as there seems to be every reason to expect, the work will romanticize its cast of characters the way *Nixon in China* romanticized Mao Zedong and Zhou Enlai, we can look forward to some furious moral censure of a work of musical theater, something the world has hardly seen since the days when Stalin vilified poor Lady Macbeth of Mtsensk. I hope by now you will understand that it is not because I am a Stalinist that I can foresee nothing more beneficial to opera and to music generally than that sort of attention. An excess of esthetic autonomy has to all intents and purposes killed music in the twentieth century. A bit of old-fashioned ethical and political consternation may be just what it takes to revive it for the twenty-first.

POSTSCRIPT, 2008

I thought this previously unpublished public lecture (frequently rebroadcast on Chicago public television in the early 1990s, I'm told) would make an appropriate opening to this collection because it states explicitly the anti-utopian subtext that implicitly unites all the essays in the book, and because it brings consideration of composition and performance into explicit conjunction.

Needless to say, it has proved no more infallible than any other blanket prediction of its kind, nor, after nearly two decades, do I feel anywhere nearly as pessimistic. The reasons for my pessimism in 1989 had a lot to do with a factor I allowed to go unmentioned: the folding of *Opus* magazine, where I had been a contributing editor, after just four years as the best classical music journal in America. I was banking then on the *New Republic,* which remained hospitable to my writing for the next decade or more, but which, following a corporate sale (just as in the case of *Opus*), went abruptly into dumb-down mode where arts coverage was concerned. Two of the essays in this collection (chapters 35 and 36) were written in 2002 for the *New Republic* in the expectation that I would resume regular contributions there after having finished *The Oxford History of Western Music;* but instead, at the behest of the new owners, *TNR* hired a pop critic and declared my work too specialized in its appeal. I trust it was his own embarrassment at that turn of events, which involved the unremunerated killing of a piece that was already edited and scheduled to run, that induced Leon Wieseltier, *TNR*'s literary editor, to take such insulting leave of me with the remark that it was about time the magazine covered the music its readers actually listened to. (Since then the magazine has been sold again, and I am *persona grata* once more, as chapter 37 will attest.)

But I did not despair the way I did when *Opus* folded. Partly this was because Jim Oestreich, the old *Opus* editor, had taken over as the *New York*

Times's classical music editor (at first on Sundays, later for the weekday edition as well) and succeeded against the apparent odds not only in dramatically raising the standard of classical music coverage in America's newspaper of record, but of actually increasing its extent and then holding the fort against attempts (chiefly by Howell Raines, the paper's ill-fated executive editor, and Jodi Kantor, Raines's handpicked Arts and Leisure czar) to cut it back again and dumb it down. And I am particularly heartened that in Alex Ross the *New Yorker* now has its finest music critic ever—a critic with his finger on the pulse of what is genuinely new in music, not (like his predecessors, Andrew Porter and Paul Griffiths) what was new in days of old, and the knack of discerning, describing, and abetting its quality, all on a tight deadline. That renewed excellence in coverage has coincided with the unexpected, albeit limited, resurgence of vitality in classical music that is described and partly accounted for in chapter 15, in which Steve Reich is given an evaluation more in keeping with his stature, and chapter 35, a more skeptical but still benevolent assessment of a commercially successful strain of contemporary classical music, whose impending emergence could only be very dimly sensed in 1989. So there is new reason for what politicians call guarded optimism, and some of the later pieces in this collection reflect it. (Still and all, I do feel entitled to a little credit for foreseeing the scandal that attended *The Death of Klinghoffer*, although I had no way of foreseeing the role I would be playing, via chapter 26, in what might be called its second act.)

The résumé of the twentieth century's zigs and zags reflects the way I was teaching the subject in the late 1980s. Although I now find the account far too schematic and insufficiently nuanced (neglecting, as it does, so many exceptional figures among whom Edgar Varèse and Conlon Nancarrow are only the most obvious), it does provide the general framework around which I have structured my detailed treatment of twentieth-century music history in the fourth and fifth volumes of *The Oxford History of Western Music* (though without the zigzag terminology). Schematic accounts do have their value. For one thing, they are memorable, as I found out in fall 2005, when a member of the audience at a symposium, "Musical Historiographies," organized by Elaine Sisman as her Presidential Forum at the national meeting of the American Musicological Society, asked me—to my surprise and slight discomfiture—to comment on my old and never-published scheme. I realized then that, simplistic though it might be, it did serve at least to counter the alternative (and all-too-successful) simplistic account, that of steady linear progress.

NOTES

1. See Robert Pattison, *The Triumph of Vulgarity: Rock Music in the Mirror of Romanticism* (New York: Oxford University Press, 1987).

2. John Blacking, *How Musical Is Man?* (Seattle: University of Washington Press, 1973); Christopher Small, *Music-Education-Society* (London: John Calder, 1977); Jacques Attali, *Noise,* trans. Brian Massumi (Minneapolis: University of Minnesota Press, 1985).

3. Joseph Berger, "Ibn Batuta and Sitar Challenging Columbus and Piano in Schools," *New York Times,* 12 April 1989.

4. T. E. Hulme, *Speculations,* ed. Herbert Read (London: Routledge and Kegan Paul, 1936), 126–27.

5. "Extents and Limits of Serial Technique," in *Problems of Modern Music,* ed. Paul Henry Lang (New York: W. W. Norton, 1962), 90–91.

6. Quoted in John Cage, *Silence* (Cambridge, Mass.: MIT Press, 1966), 68.

7. Elliott Schwartz and Barney Childs, eds., *Contemporary Composers on Contemporary Music* (New York: Holt, Rinehart and Winston, 1967), 371.

8. Philip Glass, quoted in Cole Gagne and Tracy Caras, *Soundpieces: Interviews with American Composers* (Metuchen, N.J.: Scarecrow Press, 1982), 213.

9. Terry Riley, quoted in John Schaefer, *New Sounds* (New York: Harper & Row, 1987), 82.

10. Fred Lerdahl, "Cognitive Constraints on Compositional Systems," in *Generative Processes in Music,* ed. John A. Sloboda (Oxford: Clarendon Press, 1988), 257.

11. Steve Reich, *Writings about Music* (Halifax: Press of the Nova Scotia College of Art and Design, 1974), 9.

12. Ibid., 11.

13. John Rockwell, *All American Music* (New York: Summit Books, 1987), 233.

14. Andrew Porter, *Musical Events* (New York: Summit Books, 1987), 292.

15. See note 9.

16. Afterword to Attali, *Noise,* 157–58.

17. Notes accompanying EMI-Angel album DS-37340.

18. Gagne and Caras, *Soundpieces,* 216.

19. Quoted in Nicholas Kenyon, Introduction to *Authenticity and Early Music,* 1.

20. Donal Henahan, "Music View," *New York Times,* 26 March 1989, Arts and Leisure, 23.

21. *Tempo,* no. 167 (December 1988): 30.

2

Only Time Will Cover the Taint

The fact that pork is not kosher is no reflection on the pigs. Orthodox Jews avoid pig meat not because it tastes bad (how would they know?), or because it is bad for you (just look at the Cossacks), or even because pigs live in pigsties. They avoid it because unlike, for example, the meat of grasshoppers, it is forbidden, taboo, "tref"—the reverse of holy. The ban sanctifies its observers.

Similarly, the fact that many Israelis do not want to hear Wagner's music in their concert halls does not merely reflect on Wagner or his ugly personal beliefs. If an artist's anti-Semitism were enough to render his work tref, there would be precious little art in Israel. Among Russian composers, for example, only two famous ones seem *not* to have been anti-Semites. Rimsky-Korsakov gave classical proof of his tolerance for Jews by not only allowing but practically forcing his daughter to marry one (the composer Maximilian Steinberg); and Shostakovich, as a creative artist in Stalin's Russia, made common cause with other victims of oppression by working Jewish themes into several compositions.

Otherwise, take your pick of bigots. Chaikovsky? "Lots of filthy Yids"—in Russian, *zhidy*—"and the revolting atmosphere they take with them everywhere" spoiled train travel for him, he casually informed his adoring patroness. Stravinsky? A recently auctioned letter of his complains about a 1919 New York production of *Petrushka* by a trio of unauthorized "Israelites" (one of them Pierre Monteux, to whose efforts Stravinsky owed a large part of his early fame), heaping special scorn on the "horrible Jew-kraut sets" ("des horribles décors judéo-boches").

First published in the *New York Times*, 26 January 1992. Copyright © 2008 The New York Times Company. Reprinted by permission.

Musorgsky's anti-Semitism inhabits not only his letters but also his works. His suite *Pictures at an Exhibition* contains a well-known portrayal of "Two Jews, Rich and Poor." That, however, was not Musorgsky's title (it was invented after his death by his biographer, Vladimir Stasov), and his portrait was of one Jew, not two. The unsanitized title is known but rarely if ever transcribed correctly. Here it is, right off a photograph of the composer's manuscript: "'Samuel' Goldenberg und 'Schmuÿle.'" Note the quotation marks: they point up the repetition of the given name, first in Germanized form, then in the original Yiddish. The contrast embedded in title and music alike is thus a brazen insult: No matter how dignified or sophisticated or Europeanized a zhid's exterior, Musorgsky is telling us, winking, on the inside he is a jabbering, pestering little "Schmuÿle."

I'm sure the Israel Philharmonic has played *Pictures at an Exhibition* (in the philo-Semite Ravel's orchestration), and will continue to do so. And even if someone should notice this column and lodge a protest, nobody is going to call for a moratorium on *Boris Godunov* or *Khovanshchina*. And that is simply because Musorgsky is dead. It is his works that live and continue to affect our lives.

That is why defending Wagner against the unforeseen consequences of his anti-Semitism completely misses the point in our current fraught debates. We cannot punish the man now, nor can we earn his gratitude. To be sure, he was not responsible for the Nazis any more than Musorgsky was responsible for the tsar's pogroms. But if tsar or commissar had made Musorgsky the rallying point of a chauvinist campaign, and used his *Pictures* to justify the extermination of "Christ-killers," we might feel differently—not only about the *Pictures,* but about the operas as well.

Wagner's music was used by the Nazis in this way, and that is why it is tref to Holocaust survivors. Their objection to it is a symbolic act, sanctifying the memory of something that, in the opinion of many, it is not yet time to forget. Such an act deserves respect. And none of this would be in any way changed if Wagner the man should turn out to have been a secret lover of Jews, or even a Jew himself.

It does no good to argue that the music itself is inherently nonpolitical and nonracist. The music does not now exist, nor has it ever existed, in a social vacuum. Its meanings are not self-contained. They are inscribed not only by its creator, but by its users, Nazi and Jew alike. Leonard Bernstein has written that "the 'Horst Wessel Lied' may have been a Nazi hymn, but divorced from its words it's just a pretty song." Can we divorce it from its words? No more than we can follow the friendly sorcerer's recipe for turning lead into gold (melt and stir for three hours without thinking of the word *rhinoceros*). To say we should try is like asking, "But aside from that, Mrs. Lincoln, how was the show?"

It does no honor to Wagner's music to reduce it all to the level of "just a pretty song," which is the only way it can be rid of its taint before time and memory have done their slow, inevitable work. As long as some music somewhere is considered tref, we have not forgotten that music is a powerful form of persuasion that does work in the world, a serious art that possesses ethical force and exacts ethical responsibilities. (Nor have all musicians given in to the careerism that argues, with Daniel Barenboim, in favor of Wagner merely for the sake of a credential.) Let Wagner remain tref in Israel, and let the controversies rage. Far better that than curtailing moral controversy in the specious name of "the music itself" and letting Wagner become, in Israel's concert life as everywhere else, just another mild narcotic.

POSTSCRIPT, 2008

Even Shostakovich, it seems, may have been susceptible to the "taint." (Nu, who isn't?) Later in 1992, *Muzïkal' naya akademiya*, the post-Soviet successor journal to *Sovetskaya muzïka*, the organ of the Union of Soviet Composers, carried an interview with Solomon Volkov, author of *Testimony*, the faked memoirs of Shostakovich published in 1979.[1] Volkov told his interlocutor that before emigrating in 1976, while he was still an editor at *Sovetskaya muzïka*, he participated in an inspection of the literary remains of Valerian Mikhailovich Bogdanov-Berezovsky (1903–71), a minor composer but an important Leningrad critic, with whom Shostakovich had been close in the 1920s. In one of Bogdanov-Berezovsky's diaries, Volkov recalled finding an account of a visit by the sixteen-year-old "Mitya" Shostakovich during which the two of them complained about *zasil' ye zhidov*, "Jew dominance," in the arts.

Volkov has been caught in so many lies that it may be hard to accept anything from him as true. Even here, it could be argued, he might have had an ulterior motive—proving that he was not a hagiographer, for example— that could have tempted him to fabricate such a story. But it might be useful to admit it as true so as to test our response to the knowledge. Is there any point in holding it against a composer who later performed so many acts of risky solidarity with his Jewish colleagues? Surely not. But at the same time we are cautioned by such knowledge against thinking that all humanity can be sorted into two boxes in this way, any more than in any other, or that any such act of sorting gives us the right to an absolute moral judgment.

As to the matter of performing Wagner in Israel, it is important to keep it in mind that there is no legal ban against it. One can hear Wagner on Israeli radio, one can find Wagner in record stores, one is free to program the "Ride of the Valkyries" as a ring tone on one's cell phone. The "ban" is a voluntary abstinence on the part of the Israel Philharmonic in deference to members of its audience, who insist vocally on their right to a Wagner-free existence when other orchestras or musicians perform in front of them. There will be more to say about this, and about Daniel Barenboim's attempts to overcome the informal interdiction, in chapter 26.

NOTE

1. Galina Drubachevskaya, "Zdes' chelovek sgorel" (Here a Man Burned Up), *Muzïkal' naya akademiya,* no. 3 (1992): 3–14.

3

"Nationalism"
Colonialism in Disguise?

On page 1 of the *Times* recently, there was a report of lethal violence against peacekeepers in Somalia. Page 2 told of new threats to Middle East peace talks. Page 3 had several accounts of atrocities and hopelessness in Bosnia. Page 4 brought news of extreme hardship in the Caucasus as a result of territorial hostilities and ethnic separatism.

And on the arts page there was a rosy dispatch from a music critic attending a Dvořák festival in Spillville, Iowa, all about what a marvelous thing nationalism is.

You could not hope for a better illustration of what makes classical music seem so quaint and irrelevant to today's world, so barren of intellectual interest, so deserving of relegation to upscale consumer culture and academic backwaters. The ossification of its repertory has been accompanied by an ossification of attitudes. Both repertory and attitudes are nostalgic throwbacks to an imagined prelapsarian age preceding World War I, the original nationalist disaster.

The pretext for all the Dvořák fever, both in Spillville and now at Bard College, in Annandale-on-Hudson, New York, is the centennial of the "New World" Symphony, composed in New York during Dvořák's first year as director of Jeannette Thurber's National Conservatory of Music. Dvořák intended the work as an object lesson to his American pupils on how they might achieve an authentic American school of composition. As quoted by the critic Henry Krehbiel, Dvořák urged that they submit the indigenous musics of their country, namely Indian melodies and Negro spirituals, "to beautiful treatment in the higher forms of art." That was his "nationalist" creed,

First published in the *New York Times*, 22 August 1993. Copyright © 2008 The New York Times Company. Reprinted by permission.

and as a Bohemian subject of the Austrian crown, he practiced what he preached.

But as usual, what is most significant about this prescription is what it allowed to go unsaid. The "higher forms of art" that would justify and canonize the national were themselves considered not national but universal—or, to put it as a modern linguist would, "unmarked." Yet they were national all along. They were German. Mrs. Thurber's conservatory, like all nineteenth-century conservatories outside the German-speaking lands, was an agency of musical colonialism. Dvořák was brought in to direct it not as a Bohemian or a nationalist but as a master of the unmarked mother tongue.

Like other colonialisms, this one sought justification in the claim that it could develop local resources better than the natives unaided. Like other colonialisms, it maintained itself by manufacturing and administering ersatz "national" traditions that reinforced dependence on the mother country. The benign picturesque "nationalism" Dvořák preached and practiced was of this type—a matter of superficially "marking" received techniques, forms, and media with regionalisms (drones, "horn fifths," polkas in place of minuets), as one might don a native holiday costume.

But colonialist "nationalism" was a double bind. Dvořák's Bohemianisms were at once the vehicle of his international appeal (as a "naïf") and the guarantee of his secondary status vis-à-vis natural-born Universals (say, Brahms). Without the native costume, a "peripheral" composer could never achieve even secondary canonical rank, but with it he could never achieve more. If this was true for the mentor, how much truer would it be for the Americans whose "tradition" Dvořák purported to establish.

And so it has turned out. Nationalism, in music as elsewhere in the twentieth century, has been a curse and a straitjacket. Some American composers have successfully traded on it the way Dvořák did, particularly a greatly gifted left-leaning homosexual Jew from Brooklyn (a pupil of a Dvořák pupil), who managed to confect out of Paris and Stravinsky an ingratiating white-bread-of-the-prairie idiom that could be applied ad libitum to the higher forms of art. (But then, refused permission to relinquish his invented regionalisms, Aaron Copland ended his career embittered.) More often nationalism has been an invidious normative or exclusionary standard, a means of critical ethnic cleansing by which the legitimacy of American composers who do not choose to don a Stetson or grow an Afro can be impugned. (What business did Ellen Zwilich have vying with Mahler for a seat at the grown-ups' table? He's not part of her background, says the same critic whose report from Spillville got me started on this tirade.)

But the demand that American composers—or any others—reflect their immediate geographic and temporal background (that is, stay put in their place) is not only patronizing or authoritarian. It betrays an altogether anachronistic idea of what anybody's immediate background is in an age when all the world's music, along with the music of all of history, is instantly available, electronically, to one and all. That does not mean that all must now partake in what Olivier Messiaen once called "the international gray on gray." That, thankfully, is another anachronism, albeit of more recent vintage. The present, and the foreseeable future, is an era of idiolects. No one has a place to stay put in anymore, and beware of those who say that they do (or worse, that you do).

"We are all individual music cultures," as the ethnomusicologist Mark Slobin puts it, coexisting in a "fascinating counterpoint of near and far, large and small, neighborhood and national, home and away." The most boring thing American composers could do, and the most regressive, would be to heed the advice from Spillville and at this late date "obey" Dvořák's "command that Americans be Americans."

POSTSCRIPT, 2008

In terms of words elicited per words put forth, this turned out unexpectedly, yet beyond doubt, to be the most contentious piece I have ever published. *Times* readers hated it, but academics hailed it, and it has had some influence within musicology. Responses to it filled the *Times*'s Arts and Leisure mailbag on September 12. The correspondents were a very interesting and distinguished group.

Peter M. Alexander, a consultant to the Spillville celebration of the "New World" Symphony, claimed (citing Harmut Schick, who spoke in Spillville) that the work "can be interpreted as a specific rejection of the German model," and that (citing Michael Beckerman) afterwards Dvořák forsook the symphony in favor of the tone poem, a "lesser" genre and an un-German one. Balderdash. The tone poem (or, as Dvořák knew it, the symphonic poem) may have been pioneered by Liszt, a Hungarian, but it was immediately claimed by the so-called New German School, musicians who saw Wagner, Liszt, and Berlioz as the harbingers of the music of the future. (Prof. Beckerman certainly knew that; he couldn't have intended what Mr. Alexander understood him to have said.) The "New World" Symphony embodied a symphonic approach that Brahms, who hated the "futurists" as much as he revered the earlier German tradition, admired to the point of begging Dvořák to accept the directorship of the Vienna Conservatory in order to thwart a Brucknerian takeover. But at the same time the "New World" imported Wagnerian leitmotif technique into the symphonic domain in order to do justice to its hidden program adapted from Longfellow's "Song of Hiawatha." Dvořák was singularly endowed with the ability to synthesize the two German traditions—the "classical" and the "futurist"—and *this* was far more likely the basis of his appeal to Jeannette Thurber than Mr. Alexander's notion that "he came from outside the predominant German culture." He did no such thing, and saw no contradiction between his Czech heritage and the German musical culture in which he was trained to the point of mastery, any more than he saw a contradiction between his Czech ethnicity and his loyalty to the Habsburg crown. The conflicts we now imagine he must have felt were of much later vintage.

The composer Ben Yarmolinsky advised me to "think of Falla, Mussorgsky, Bartok—even Chopin" before condemning nationalism in music. Vivian Perlis, the distinguished oral historian who collaborated with Aaron Copland on his memoirs, chided me for ignoring all of "Copland's music that has nothing at all to do with Americana," citing such modernist works as the Piano Variations. "A more interesting and accurate slant on Copland and nationalism," she went on, "would be to examine why the public, not the composer, chose (and continues to choose) his Americana works over the other." But that *was* my slant. The lack of success Copland had with the public after he had given up Americana for twelve-tone music seriously depressed and silenced him, as many of his friends have noted—most particularly Leonard Bernstein, in a heartrending "Intimate Sketch" he published in *High Fidelity* magazine on the occasion of Copland's seventieth birthday in November 1970. That was what I meant when I wrote that Copland had been "refused permission to relinquish his invented regionalisms." It was the audience, certainly not I, who refused him.

Benson D. Scotch, a Vermont lawyer and lobbyist for the American Civil Liberties Union who had attended the Spillville events, was the first of many over the years to take umbrage at receiving "a homily on intolerance from someone referring to Aaron Copland as a 'left-leaning homosexual Jew from Brooklyn.'" But I share two of the four traits I attributed to Copland; I do not consider the others to be defects; and I certainly meant no disrespect, although I will admit to some rhetorical cunning in formulating the thought so bluntly. What I wished to call attention to was the artfulness—the "constructedness" as we nowadays say in the classroom—of Copland's Americanist persona. It seems a miracle—and a testimonial to the nature of creative genius—that someone quadruply removed from the all-American stereotype (indeed quintuply if you count his Paris training) should have nevertheless found what everyone has been persuaded to regard as the quintessential means of its "authentic" musical representation. It shows that those means are not "essential" at all, and that authenticity is a matter of perception, not "reality." All of which, I should think, is an implicit blow against bigotry.

My heart did sink a bit, though, as Mr. Scotch's letter reached its peroration: "The best chicken noodle soup in Spillville," he wrote,

> was provided by the Lutheran Church from a nearby town. Saturday morning's parade was full of sunshine and easy humor, but it was also a tribute to what we make of diversity in the United States, when we are at our best: pride in national

dance, music and costumes, yes, but a pride that is shared, explained and integrated into a triptych of other cultures and experiences.

I kept wondering, as my wife and I stood on Church Street in Spillville, how things might have developed in Bosnia if someone had thought of such festivals a few generations ago and Serbs, Croats and Muslims cheered at each other's parades, ate each other's version of filled pastries and made it their business to learn what each other's costumes meant.

It was that sort of condescending sentimentality I had uppermost in mind when I crafted the tiny reply that the *Times* allowed me: "National character in music, the Spillville festival, Dvořák and Aaron Copland have all received spirited defense. None of them was under attack in my essay, which was concerned with ill-considered critical standards, and with the nostalgic cultural mythology that these letters continue to exemplify."

4

Why Do They All Hate Horowitz?

The names of Vladimir Horowitz and Peter Ilyich Chaikovsky have often been linked, not least by the pianist's unequaled affinity for the composer's First Concerto. But what seems of especial moment this year—when a significant portion of Horowitz's recorded legacy has been reissued on CD by Sony Classical (with twenty-two more CDs coming next month from BMG), and when Chaikovsky's death centennial is being so studiously ignored—is that both are giants to whom Lilliputians inveterately condescend.

In the aftermath of the Mozart year, Chaikovsky's neglect can only seem a favor, but it is nevertheless peculiar. It defines his special place—one might even say his special importance. Hans Keller, magnificent curmudgeon that he was, captured it best: "Tchaikovsky, though wholeheartedly accepted by naïve music lovers and sophisticated composers alike, is still suspected by the West's intellectual lower middle class."

A little less coyly, this means that resistance to Chaikovsky, like most snobbery, arises out of a self-protective need. Putting down what is popular is an easy way to assert an anxious connoisseurship, but those secure in their perceptions can afford to recognize originality and expressive power even when it is not cloaked in crowd-excluding difficulty. The dismissive posture, Keller implied, is revealing not of Chaikovsky but of those who assume it.

Horowitz is a similar touchstone. Like Chaikovsky, he will always remain an easy target for those in need of one. As with Chaikovsky, it is difficult to write approvingly about him without falling into a defensive tone. But it might be useful to go on the offensive for a change, and analyze the nature

First published in the *New York Times*, 28 November 1993. Copyright © 2008 The New York Times Company. Reprinted by permission.

of the critical hostility he inspires. It will tell us a great deal about our classical-music culture and the clichés that undergird it.

So let's begin right at the top, with the *New Grove Dictionary of Music and Musicians.* Its entry on the pianist ends with a mean insult, the only such comment in the whole twenty-volume compendium of standard lore and data, and a flagrant lapse of tone. "Horowitz," it reads, "illustrates that an astounding instrumental gift carries no guarantee about musical under-standing."

To insinuate a lack of understanding is to suppose that the insinuator lacks it not. So the question fairly arises, what sort of musical understanding is it that Michael Steinberg, the author of the article, possesses but that is denied to Vladimir Horowitz? The answer, as it happens, is right in the article: Horowitz, we are told, "conceives of interpretation not as the reification of the composer's ideas, but as an essentially independent activity; in Schu-mann's 'Träumerei,' for example, he places the high points anywhere except where Schumann placed them."

How to unpack this? It is, first of all, entirely inferential. Horowitz never announced any such conception of interpretation. On the contrary, in a widely publicized remark he made shortly before his "Historic Return" to the concert stage in 1965 (as the record marketers are calling it), Horowitz swore belief "in the absolute supremacy of the composer." But both Mr. Steinberg's assertion and Horowitz's are only ploys. To profess subservience to the com-poser, whether it is done by a performer or by a critic, is to claim the Creator's authority for oneself. Everybody does it. Nobody has it (not even the com-poser, once the composing is done).

As to the specific case Mr. Steinberg cites, one can easily test it with the new records. "Träumerei" (Dreaming), the seventh little piece in Schu-mann's *Scenes of Childhood,* was a Horowitz specialty. The Sony reissues con-tain two renditions of it. One is a Columbia studio recording of the whole cycle from 1962; the other is an encore in "The Legendary 1968 TV Concert."

Where did Schumann "place the high points"? It is hard to know what Mr. Steinberg is talking about. There is only one dynamic marking in the entire twenty-four-measure piece, a *piano* at the very beginning (repeated in the last measure, suggesting that some other, unspecified thing has intervened). Or does Mr. Steinberg mean melodic high points? The distinctive melodic idea that binds the piece together consists of a rising arpeggio, the last note of which is repeated as a syncopation and held long. These long notes are con-spicuously and literally "high," all right, and they are hardly something that a performer will alter.

The interesting question, and possibly the one Mr. Steinberg had in mind, concerns the relationship between the dynamics (gradations of loud-ness) and the long high notes. And here Horowitz seems to have noticed something that eluded his critic. The melodic ascents, with one exception (not coincidentally, perhaps, the highest), are marked with crescendos, but the crescendos end with the arpeggios, just short of the long notes.

Here is where Horowitz worked his inimitable, infuriating magic. He plays the long repetitions not as the "natural" culminations Mr. Steinberg evidently expected but as preternatural echoes, responses from the dream world. And, with a control of touch and pedal that was his alone, he allows the supporting harmonies to steal in as a soft blur under the loudening melodic ascent, clearing only to reveal the faery answer. That Mr. Steinberg chose to censure precisely this is a scandal. What so affronted him?

What affronted him was the performer's creative initiative, and that is a lamentable litany of Horowitz abuse. "There is a text," Tim Page intoned, reviewing Harold Schonberg's recent biography of the pianist in the *New Republic*, "and there must be a coherent interpretation," which is to say, "a linear statement." "No good composer," he wrote, "builds according to passing whim, and it is frivolous for an interpreter to play that way."

These bromides and shalt-nots are a tired old story, thoroughly debased as critical currency. (I can hear Horowitz snorting "ProWINcial!" in rejoinder.) But they are not as old as Mr. Page may think. They go back no further than Stravinsky's high-hat holy war against "interpretation," on behalf of what he called "execution," defined as "the strict putting into effect of an explicit will that contains nothing beyond what it specifically commands." Thus, it is not enough scrupulously to observe what is written (as Horowitz did as often as anybody, and better than most; just listen to the staccato bass notes supporting the legato accompanying arpeggios in Schumann's *Arabeske,* another specialty available more than once in the Sony CDs). One must add nothing to what one (or, more democratically, to what we all) can see.

What this implies, of course, is that guiltless performances, like happy families, are ideally alike. (Mr. Page even says so outright. "Music," he warns, "is not like Heraclitus's river.") And that defines the critic's role in a way that makes it very easy: the critic is there to facilitate standardization by enforcing fidelity to scripture.

The same critics who do this are always lamenting the uniformity of the younger crop of performers, little realizing that they, along with contest juries, are chiefly responsible for producing it. For theirs is an esthetic of control, useful perhaps for disciplining the behavior of small children but not that of artists. Mr. Page's banal notions of "decorum" are nothing but a brake on artistic development. To Horowitz such strictures stopped being relevant somewhere between his circumcision and his bar mitzvah.

Besides, before Stravinsky (whose motives are worth a look, but not today), such simplistic notions of "text" never corresponded to any composer's idea of the score he produced. For no composer before Stravinsky, cockeyed optimist that he was, ever had so unrealistic a notion of what notation can accomplish. And that is why composers are of all performers the likeliest to make free with the written score. They know better than anyone else that as the critic Carolyn Abbate has put it with fabulous succinctness, "the text of music is a performance." Just listen to Debussy's Debussy or Prokofieff's Prokofieff. Rachmaninoff, Horowitz's mentor, liked to reprise the funeral march in Chopin's Second Sonata fortissimo instead of piano, the way Chopin notated ("performed") it. He was following the example of Anton Rubinstein, another charismatic performing composer, and some editors (Athur Friedheim for one) actually changed the score to conform to the tradition thus introduced.

One does not necessarily advocate such measures. But the fact that they were taken shows our contemporary esthetic of textual literalism to be a modern prejudice. Far from a self-evident verity to which all artists worthy of the name must inevitably subscribe, it is just a manifestation of modern existential anxiety. Music used to be regarded, in fact, exactly like a Heraclitean river: enduring works had histories that only began with their composition. Their traditions, maintained by authoritative performers, ensured that they would change over time and remain ever new.

Horowitz lived into the puritanical age of which his father-in-law, Arturo Toscanini, was a prophet. So he never dared follow Rachmaninoff's example (as his reading of the Chopin sonata on Sony attests). But it is he who now attracts the aggression the older man's forbidding creative majesty deterred.

And yet Horowitz's refusal to be limited by the limitations of texts is not the whole story. In itself it would never have called forth such critical wrath. For strange to say, many of the same critics who work hard to discredit Horowitz adulate Glenn Gould, an even loftier tamperer with texts. Why the double standard? Because Gould epitomized monastic unworldiness and intellectual abstraction, whereas Horowitz was urbane and visceral. Even more to the point, Gould upgraded modernist disregard of the audience to the point of anhedonia, while Horowitz aimed to please. All of which is to say that of the two, Gould was by far the truer romantic.

After hearing the first Bayreuth "Ring" in 1876, Chaikovsky confided his disgust with it to his brother. Before, composers tried to please the public, he complained, but now all they wanted to do was torment it. No wonder we condescend to Chaikovsky. He refused to condescend to us. In fact, he identified with us, his potential listeners and judges, testing his compositions on himself to see whether they moved him. (One way of pleasing your audience, after all, is to give it a good cry.)

Rachmaninoff, too, trusted and considered those who paid to hear him. He matter-of-factly confided, in a late letter to his friend Nikolai Medtner, that he let the coughing in the hall regulate the length of his *Variations on a Theme of Corelli*. ("When the coughing increases, I leave out the next variation. If there is no coughing, I play them in order. At one small-town concert, I forget where, they coughed so, that I only played 10 variations out of 20. The record so far is 18 variations, in New York.") Even the man Stravinsky derided as "a six-foot scowl" believed in, and lived by, Jules Renard's old precept that "art is no excuse for boring people." Horowitz, whose famous smile went ear to ear, and who could not claim a composer's prestige, felt the brunt of a dispensation in which respect for the public became in itself unrespectable.

"Horowitz is mainly attuned to people," Joseph Horowitz sniffed in the *Musical Quarterly* shortly after the pianist's death in 1989, whereas a proper artist "evokes a condition of artistic solitude." In his zeal to expose Horowitz's disastrously "skewed attention," the critic resorted to purely visual evidence from a film in which the pianist performed Chopin's B-minor Scherzo. (The acoustic evidence is in the Sony series, alternately a ride on the wind's back and an uncanny shimmer.) "At the close," Mr. Horowitz noted, "waiting for the penultimate chord to clock its six beats, Horowitz is already clowning, teasing the composer with goggling, gargoyle eyes. Impatient for the final chord to finish, he turns to his audience, begging a response." (The "audience" here consisted entirely of one man, the record producer.)

This is contrasted with a videotape of Claudio Arrau, whom the critic venerates, because "as far as one can tell, he sounds the final chords with his eyes closed." The clincher for Arrau is the comment, quoted reverently, "I've become indifferent to whether I please an audience or not."

How we love to be scorned. How eagerly we are taken in. And don't our idols know it. How refreshing is Horowitz's honest detachment, his frank acknowledgment that a musical performance is . . . well, a performance. A Soviet-born ethnographer told me of a field expedition she once undertook in the Russian north, collecting ritual laments, a folk genre that involves the realistic (and contagious) simulation of sobbing, wailing, and panting. Her finest informant had a whole roomful of onlookers bawling, including the collector herself, when she interrupted her performance to cock a wink and ask, "How'm I doing?" She, like Horowitz, was an artist.

So was Arrau, of course, but he preferred to pander to naive audience (and, as we see, critical) expectation and disguise his artifice as sincerity. Another who did so, according to an old and no doubt spurious tale, was Myra Hess, whose page-turner was mystifed, during an afternoon run-through, by the penciled marking "L.U." at various spots in the score where nothing special seemed to happen. At the performance that night, however, when the pianist came to the spots so marked, she *looked up* heavenward. But of course we forgive her. We want to be fooled. We want to believe that the artistic expression that moves us is the spontaneous groundswell of human feeling. (But, mind, in strict conformity with the score.)

Wishing it won't make it so, and Horowitz thought we were grown up enough to know that. He thought we were mature enough to revel along with him in his artifice. His was the most self-aware, most sophisticated kind of art, and he did us the honor of assuming we were as sophisticated as he was, and as aware of his awareness. He made no mistake where the naive listeners and the professionals were concerned. But there will always be that lower middle class.

POSTSCRIPT, 2008

Particularly gratifying was the response this piece elicited from pianists, the "professionals" I had uppermost in mind at the conclusion. Byron Janis, a Horowitz pupil, Barbara Nissman, a Prokofieff and Ginastera specialist, and Peter Nero were only the most famous of many to send cheering thanks. Harold Schonberg, too, favored me with a letter, which gives me a pretext here to pay tribute to him. He may have been an exasperating enemy of new music, good and bad alike, but he was a matchless connoisseur of romantic piano playing, and the only true connoisseur of anything ever to write daily music criticism during the period of my musical education. I learned an enormous amount from him, especially from his 1959 handbook, *The Collector's Chopin and Schumann,* which, no matter how out of date as a guide to record collecting, remains a wonderful guide to great piano playing and well worth an Amazon search.

Shortly before his death, Schonberg was commissioned to write the article that replaced Michael Steinberg's on Horowitz in the revised *New Grove Dictionary.* It was one of the last things he wrote, and if this piece had anything to do with its commissioning, I can rejoice in having done a good deed with it. "As a pianist [Horowitz] was unique," one may now read in the most authoritative English-language reference source. "It was not only a matter of an awesome technique. At its best his playing had infinite degrees of colour, and a sonority that could well have been unparalleled." And, "A future revisionist period may pay more attention to Horowitz's performances of Mozart, which many have derided as unstylistic. . . . It could well be that Horowitz's flexible and expressive approach to Mozart will eventually be recognized as in some sense more authentic than the work of so many late 20th-century 'authenticists.'" This prediction, I am happy to say, is coming true. Finally, "In any case, the position of Vladimir Horowitz as one of the supreme pianists in history cannot be challenged." Or rather, it can be, but only at the risk of one's own reputation as a connoisseur.

Tim Page has never recovered from this exposure of his pretension, and I have since become, along with Horowitz, one of his bêtes noires. In a show of bravado, he reprinted his review of Schonberg's biography (as "Vladimir Horowitz: A Dissent") in *Tim Page on Music* (Portland: Amadeus Press, 2002) with a preface bragging of its "inspiring a long denunciation in *The New York Times* Arts and Leisure section." And yet readers who care to compare the text in that book with my "denunciation" will not find the passages I quoted. Mr. Page removed them. His shame is my victory.

But his remarks were not the most shameful contribution to this debate. That came from Robert Holzel, who wrote in to the *Times* in the spirit of Glenn Plaskin's 1983 "pathography" (as Joyce Carol Oates would say) of Horowitz. Taking up my comparison with Chaikovsky, he noted an "elusive irony," whereby "what could seem so accessible, often sunny on its surface, could so much belie the troubled man who produced it." Oh dear, what can that matter be? The answer came later, when, taking up the comparisons with Gould and Arrau, he dismissed them, too, as belonging "more to the Horowitz camp—no pun intended." That could be the springboard for another, harsher, article.

5

Optimism amid the Rubble

"It is good to know how not to know how much one is knowing," Stefan Wolpe told an audience of young California composers in 1959. New York's most idiosyncratic serialist, a former dadaist approaching his seventh decade, was trying to keep them young at a time when modern music was going gray.

In its immediate context the Gertrude Stein-ish aphorism was playful shoptalk aimed against the unbending rationalism that then defined musical seriousness. Don't become self-consciously obsessed with technique, Wolpe urged, or rely on the rules and routines you've been taught. ("When art promises you this sort of reliability," he cautioned, "drop it.") And for heaven's sake, don't put your education on display. Instead, "mix surprise and enigma, magic and shock, intelligence and abandon, form and anti-form." Only by freeing the mind of its freight and curbing one's habits of linear thought, only by letting "noncausal, nontransitional, nonprocesslike thinking" back into the creative act, might one recapture the "free, liberated, unhinged sounds" of true music.

Pretty cagey for a serialist, this. And sure enough, John Cage and Wolpe were friends. But where Cage sought surprise and enigma in nature (and where the Boulezes and the Kreneks were then seeking it in the automatic writing of "total serialism"), Wolpe, with a confidence few managed to retain amid the spiritual fallout of the early atomic age, sought it within his own imagination. Wolpean liberation arose out of the play of contrasts—what Wolpe called "the unfolding and evolving of contrarieties." Form took shape through "the adjacency of opposites." The music Wolpe fashioned out of this volatile dialectic continues, against the odds, to make its way into the world.

First published in the *New York Times,* 22 May 1994. Copyright © 2008 The New York Times Company. Reprinted by permission.

On a Koch International CD (3-7112-2H1), performers associated with the Group for Contemporary Music offer the Sonata for Violin and Piano (1949), the Quartet for Oboe, Cello, Percussion and Piano (1955), and the *Trio in Two Parts* for flute, cello, and piano (1964), a work commissioned and first performed by the Group itself. The vehement sonata is given a suitably virtuosic performance by Jorja Fleezanis, leader of the Minnesota Orchestra, and the pianist Garrick Ohlsson, who studied with Irma Wolpe, the composer's second wife. The trio is performed fluently and a little coldly, the way the Group has often tended to perform. Played here by two members of its original cast, it gets what many would call an authentic reading. The quartet, in which the oboe part (written for Josef Marx, Wolpe's friend and champion) is radiantly played by Stephen Taylor, is the really treasurable item here.

On a Bridge release (BCD 9043), performers from Speculum Musicae offer the *Suite im Hexachord* for oboe and clarinet (1936) and the *Quintet with Voice* (1957), with its Webernesque variations finale. These are keenly shaped performances, and the disc is further graced by an elegant reading by Hilda Morley, Wolpe's widow, of her poem "Provence," on which the quintet's middle movement is based.

Fine as they are, though, these readings are inevitably overshadowed by the spectacular 15 March 1992 concert performance of the quasi-orchestral *Piece in Three Parts* for piano and sixteen players (1961) by the Chamber Music Society of Lincoln Center, with Peter Serkin in the concertante part and Oliver Knussen conducting. This was a major event in the life of Wolpe's music, and a performance at a level of accomplishment that simply did not exist when the piece was written.

One of the results of Wolpe's dialectical composing process was an extreme instability of rhythm and meter. A performance less than totally secure hangs on to the bars and transmits the rhythms in lurchy, explosive syncopations. That used to be the Wolpean norm, and it used to be thought the intention.

What Mr. Serkin, Mr. Knussen, and the society have achieved is much rarer and more difficult: the evaporation of all trace of the metrical notation—the cage of bar lines—and the emergence of a fluidly flexible "musical prose" with all the communicative directness of emotionally animated speech. One need not agree with Arnold Schoenberg (who coined the term) that musical prose represents a foreordained evolutionary advance to rejoice in its realization.

Cage liked to say that Wolpe's apartment, always full of devoted pupils, was "the true center of New York." But, he had to add, "it was an *unknown* center." At the time of his death in 1972, shortly before his seventieth birthday, Wolpe was a musician's musician, best known to those who attended Upper West Side new-music concerts.

Now, most unexpectedly and cheeringly, his music reaches a far wider public. There have been Wolpe festivals in Germany, the land of his birth, and in Canada, where Austin Clarkson, his indefatigable biographer and musical executor, lives and works. Important "mainstream" artists, notably pianists like Mr. Serkin and Mr. Ohlsson and oboists like Mr. Taylor and Heinz Holliger, have made Wolpe's music their cause. No other composer of Wolpe's generation, certainly no other serial composer, is so conspicuously on an upswing.

Why this surge of interest and enthusiasm at a time when modernism can otherwise seem so moribund? It may be because, unlike most other "serious" musicians of the cold war period but like his onetime pupil Morton Feldman (also on the rise of late), Wolpe managed to hold on to an avant-garde orientation.

Avant-garde and *modernist,* though often interchanged, are far from synonyms. Where "avant-garde," originally a military term, properly connotes a combative, countercultural position, "modernist" has long come to imply an entrenched (indeed, a tenured) high-cultural one. The avant-garde is an outsider faction; modernists are insiders. One faction challenges authority; the other wields it. One stands to gain, the other to lose. And so one is optimistic, the other pessimistic. Wolpe's optimism, by turns exuberant and serene, shines through the craggy surface of his work and wins it new friends. It energizes listeners.

But how does one maintain optimism in a century like this one? *It is good to know how not to know how much one is knowing.* Among the things Wolpe knew were racial and political persecution. A partisan of the political avant-garde (that is, a Communist) from about 1928, he would have had to flee Germany in 1933 even if he had not been born a Jew. In 1934, he went to Jerusalem to head the theory and composition faculty at the Palestine Conservatory, founded the year before by the violinist Emil Hauser. Yet Wolpe's continued, flamboyant commitment to avant-garde politics (a matter of flaunting red bandanas as well as preaching revolution—or so Hauser feared—to his pupils) cost him his job and helped precipitate his move to the United States in 1938.

In Europe and in Palestine, Wolpe placed his art directly in the service of his social ideals. He composed proletarian choruses and *Kampflieder* (socialist "battle songs"), and wrote "jazz" scores—the gangsta rap of its day—for Gustav von Wangenheim's theater of political satire. In America this side of Wolpe's activity was muted. Although he furnished music for Brecht productions as late as 1961, he concentrated increasingly on abstract genres and made a veritable specialty of noncommittal titles. (The oboe quartet recorded by Koch was at first called "Piece.") Political subtexts remained, but only tacitly.

One of his best-known pieces is a quartet, composed in 1950, for a typical Wangenheim ensemble of trumpet, sax, drums, and piano. The work still carried jazz resonances, but it was the bebop style—jazz's hermetic avant-garde—that now attracted Wolpe. Only after the composer's death was it revealed that the grim first movement memorialized Mao Zedong's Long March, and the ebullient finale celebrated the Chinese Communist victory. (On another occasion Wolpe maintained that the finale was inspired by Henri Cartier-Bresson's photo of children playing amid the rubble of the Spanish Civil War, a famous metaphor of optimism in the face of political catastrophe.)

In part this retreat into abstraction was a response—a fairly typical response—to the vicissitudes of the incipient cold war, when left-leaning artists came under suspicion in America. *It is good to know how not to know how much one is knowing*—or, at least, how not to let on. But there was more to it. Wolpe was disillusioned by the postwar political crackdown in the Soviet Union, too. The humiliation of Prokofieff horrified him. It confirmed and intensified his avant-gardism—his commitment to oppose all established power, which, he now saw, was by definition reactionary and intolerant of difference.

And so when he went back on a visit to his native Berlin in 1957, he found himself unable to comply with an invitation from the Wangenheims to play over his old *Kampflieder*. In the postwar context such music represented not protest but hegemony. Instead, feigning forgetfulness, he played them the old Esoteric LP of the saxophone quartet (the first recording ever made of his music), and was met with bewilderment.

Yet no matter how abstract, Wolpe's music remained unwaveringly expressionist. Franz Kline, Willem de Kooning, Philip Guston, Mark Rothko, and other abstract expressionist painters were among his friends, and he seems in retrospect far closer to them than to most of his musical contemporaries. Sometimes the apparent abstraction was a thin disguise. One of Wolpe's first postwar compositions was a little piano piece with an extravagant nineteen-word title that begins, "Displaced Spaces, Shocks, Negations." Not so hard to read through that to displaced persons, as war refugees were then called, and to the shocks they had received as their former lives were negated.

Even "Piece" (the oboe quartet) may not have been an altogether innocent title. Among Wolpe's later compositions this fragrant pastoral is the most expressive of inner peace. It was composed at Black Mountain College in North Carolina, the fabled avant-garde enclave, where Wolpe was director of music from 1952 to 1956. The time he spent in this nurturing environment coincided with the beginning of his third and most successful marriage, to Ms. Morley.

The quartet's first movement, "Early Morning Music," seems a sonic analogue to a Clemens Kalischer photo showing a beaming Wolpe greeting his wife, who is squinting in the bright morning light. The second movement ends magically, with a quiet eruption of ordinary consonant harmony in the piano and the cello, amiably set off by the bebop drummer's frisky susurrations. It beautifully illustrates a point Wolpe made in his California lecture about the way in which the constant juxtaposition of extremes can "render the state of averages rare and strangely fresh."

Such an obviously "marked" juxtaposition is uncommon in Wolpe. Yet the constant play of "adjacent opposites" always hints at an unenunciated message in his music, ineffable yet somehow plain. What lifts Wolpe's powerfully dramatized "enactments" (as he once actually called a piece) far above the inert displays of fetishized technique with which they usually shared the platform during his last period was an undiminished sense of moral fervor. From it arose the incomparable life-and-death urgency with which he manipulated his seemingly abstract but never dehumanized materials.

From this standpoint the overwhelming *Piece in Three Parts* is one of Wolpe's peaks, perhaps the summit. New insight into its expressive motivations is found in Austin Clarkson's edition of the score, published just last year. Mr. Clarkson reveals that a sudden upward sweep in the first movement, intensified by tremolos in the strings and winds and by tone clusters in the piano part, carries a label in the manuscript: "A Jewish phrase (like a musical scar) commemorating all the slaughtered Jews."

The relationship between the label and the music could be the ground for an endless and fruitless debate. It is obvious that without knowledge of the label the meaning of that particular phrase in isolation could not be guessed. It is just as obvious that mere knowledge of the label does not transform the whole piece into a Holocaust memorial. And yet the thought that prompted the label also prompted the music, and contributed to that special Wolpean ethic of tireless dialectical quest that never reaches synthesis but perseveres regardless. (The whole ensemble does come together on two chords in the finale that leave the listener drained and shaken. They are not, however, the last thing one hears: the music goes runny again, and ends on a desperately interrogative single note from the piano.)

Memories of atrocity and emotional scarring must also have conditioned the violent timpani part that commandeers the piece at strategic moments, leaving the listener at other moments an emotional hostage, dreading its return. The history of the twentieth century has left its harrowing, ineluctable trace on this music.

But the composer's ambivalence is palpable, and disquieting. He felt and acted upon two conflicting needs: on the one hand, to embody a reaction to the slaughter of the European Jews in his music and, on the other, to efface it from the finished product. The dilemma is familiar and intractable. The Holocaust is surefire box office and surefire politics. Has one a right, as an artist, to exploit it? (Did the Jews die to line your pockets or win you a Pulitzer or a Stalin Prize?) And yet has one a right, as a human being and a witness, to abandon such a theme?

Behind this ambivalence lies one even more profound. How did an artist with Wolpe's social conscience finally feel about a decision, however honestly arrived at, to insulate his artistic integrity within a music so abstract that its content would be a riddle, and so difficult that almost no one could play it? In its vehemence, Wolpe's late work could still be said to arise out of his old commitments, but it could no longer serve them. On the contrary, it was precisely the kind of music revolutionary politicians condemned and, when in power, suppressed.

The contradiction between the humanitarian passions that motivated such an art and the elite nature of its appeal could only be repressed. Wolpe's practically unique attempt to maintain an accommodation between social commitment and "disinterested" artistry was the most demanding dialectic of his career, the most stressful "adjacency of opposites." That unresolvable tension and the impossible dream of subsuming it—so characteristic of the twentieth century, its dashed hopes and its agonies—lie at the heart of Wolpe's music and contribute enormously to its irresistible yet discommoding power. *It is good to know how not to know how much one is knowing.*

6

A Survivor from the Teutonic Train Wreck

In the twentieth century, the symphony moved to the suburbs. Once the great vehicle of an acknowledged "central" classical tradition, whose dominance was built into the very structure of institutional music making (German maestros or their pupils at the helm of every symphony orchestra and every conservatory from San Francisco to St. Petersburg), it survived on the peripheries while the central tradition destroyed itself. There have been notable twentieth-century symphonic "schools" in the Soviet Union, the United States, England, and Scandinavia but not in Germany.

Fanatics of the Teutonic tradition have seen in this persistence a bootless defiance of history. (If we're going down, by golly, the only authentic thing to do is to go down with us.) The Wagnerian master narrative of music history, ensconced by now in every academic textbook, glorifies aggression and heroism, including heroic failure. But just as the Scandinavian welfare democracies have always quietly offered an unglamorous, easily despised counterexample to romanticists of the right and left, so the remarkably tenacious and productive Scandinavian symphonic tradition, though easily ignored as "regional," looks mighty healthy amid all the epic train wrecks now littering the modernist landscape.

Vagn Holmboe, who at eighty-four qualifies as the grand old man of Danish music and probably the greatest living traditional symphonist, has never been much of a presence on the international concert stage. Among record collectors, though, he has long been something of a cult figure, first sighted on the flip sides of early Nielsen LPs in the fifties and sixties. Even when little of his music was available, one could see from titles like Concerto No. 11 that he was prolific. Alienated avant-gardists never get up into numbers like that. Their union rules forbid it.

But Holmboe was obviously no "Vielschreiber," either, as Teutonic romanticists might be tempted to infer. He was no mere scribbler. He used a highly developed contemporary idiom that belied one's expectations of a "regionalist," and used it freshly. He had enormous contrapuntal energy, as one might expect from a pupil of Knud Jeppesen himself, the author of a dread counterpoint text that everybody used to struggle with. And he produced tight, tense musical arguments, based on the manipulation of terse melodic cells composers call motives, that demanded and rewarded close attention over lengthy spans.

It was music that stretched your listening abilities without mystifying. (Every baby composer quickly learns how easy it is to mystify; many never get beyond that narcissistic stage.) Where a lot of contemporary classical music, like a lot of pretentious university teaching, rendered one stupidly passive, Holmboe's, like the lectures of your best professors, challenged you to active intellectual engagement resulting in emotional exhilaration. One felt grateful, not resentful, for the effort expended. For all his evident seriousness, Holmboe seemed a generous spirit, pleased to please. No wonder, then, that there is real consumer demand for his music where he comes from, and that for the last thirty years he has been living off commissions.

The Welsh conductor Owain Arwel Hughes, leading the Aarhus Symphony, from Denmark's second city, has inaugurated a projected integral edition of Holmboe's dozen symphonies on the Swedish label Bis. The first installment includes excellent performances of four symphonies on two CDs. Renewed acquaintance with Holmboe and his work happily confirms the remembered impression.

The choral Fourth Symphony, subtitled "Sinfonia Sacra," written in 1941 and revised four years later, embodies a staunch response to the German wartime occupation in the form of a hymnlike Latin text by the composer. The last two movements are Stravinskian fantasias on liturgical words: a "Gloria in Excelsis" that echoes the "Gloria" chorus in Stravinsky's *Oedipus Rex,* and a final "Laudate Dominum" that deliberately transmutes the final movement of Stravinsky's *Symphony of Psalms,* which uses the same words, into a moving, Buxtehude-like chorale prelude.

The Fifth Symphony, composed in 1944, is also noticeably Stravinskian, but very creatively so. The Stravinsky scores it most resembles, the *Symphony in Three Movements* and the Concerto for Strings, were not yet written at the time. Like them, it would make a stunning Robbins or Balanchine (or Peter Martins?) ballet.

A disc containing the Sixth and Seventh Symphonies (Bis CD-573) is the one I'd recommend as an introduction to the composer. And I'd further recommend that the symphonies be listened to in reverse order. Both exhibit

Holmboe's virtuosic "metamorphosis" technique, as the composer has come to call it, at its most idiosyncratic and maturely realized.

In these works, traditionally "symphonic" in the purest, truest sense, the entire multimovement span is generated out of a single network of motives under perpetual transformation. Remotely placed variants no longer resemble one another directly but depend for their intelligibility on the listener's tracking a beautifully shaped and directed chain of intermediate relationships that in turn describes an overall progression of moods (in the Sixth toward epitome, in the Seventh toward repose). It is a technique that may derive conceptually from Scandinavian forebears like Sibelius or Nielsen, but it is worked out, with an abstract rigor that brings to mind the Schoenbergian concept of "basic shape" and the Schoenbergian technique of "developing variation," even though Holmboe's music—in which tonal centers are never abandoned and dissonance is never completely "emancipated"—has little in common stylistically with Schoenberg.

However captivating, though, the abstract design is ultimately accessory, as in Bartók or Shostakovich, to something bigger, something humanly pressing and direct. And yet that something achieves its bigness and its richness through the intensifying logic of the abstract design. Form and expressive content, in a word, are one. It is every symphonic composer's ideal, but very few achieve it so fully, so adultly.

In the Seventh Symphony (1950), the motivic argument takes place in smallish, climax-driven bites at fast tempos, with a refrainlike "intermedio" that periodically and helpfully reorients the listener. The Sixth Symphony (1947), the ultimate Holmboe experience, is a luxuriant half-hour's jungle growth of mutant motivic relations unfolding in two huge, brilliantly sustained (and brilliantly colored) spans. Such music not only demands but also actively induces keen awareness in the listener.

Once again, the analogy that comes to mind is academic discourse of a thrillingly high order. If you have never experienced or cannot imagine an academic thrill, this music may not be for you. But if you have ever left a lecture hall haunted and altered, this disc may offer a comparable cognitive adventure.

POSTSCRIPT, 2008

I called Vagn Holmboe "the greatest living traditional symphonist" just in time. He died, three months shy of his eighty-seventh birthday, on 1 September 1996, almost exactly two years after this appreciation appeared, with thirteen symphonies to his credit. There is no one living now to whom such an epithet could be meaningfully applied. With Holmboe, the Scandinavian symphonic school, the longest-surviving one, died out, and with it, the traditional ("numbered") symphony as a major genre.

7

Does Nature Call the Tune?

The University of Chicago Press has reissued one of the great books on contemporary music culture, Leonard B. Meyer's *Music, the Arts and Ideas.* Twenty-seven years after its first edition, it is still a book about contemporary music culture, not only because the author has updated it with a "postlude," but also because his notorious prognosis has in so many ways been borne out.

Twenty-seven years ago, academic serialists were claiming a unique historical legitimacy and creative authenticity that few dared challenge. Mr. Meyer, arguing from Gestalt psychology, information theory, and cybernetics—that is, from a position just as up to date and "scientistic" as theirs—contended that serial music was perceptually opaque even to its practitioners, that it would take an educational revolution for it to communicate meaningfully with listeners, and that since it offered so little pleasurable incentive, the revolution would be a long time coming, if ever. (Instead, he predicted, a multitude of styles would coexist in what he called "fluctuating stasis." Each would have its own coterie audience; none would dominate. If you seek confirmation within the newly eclectic "classical" world, look about you—but of course commercial music has come to dominate to an extent no one then foresaw.)

At the time, Mr. Meyer's targets actually found his attack flattering. They had no interest in what he called communication; they were devoted to "research," to fashioning arcane relationships that, like those in a cryptogram, could be formally deduced and demonstrated. (Who but an idiot expects a cryptogram to make sense when read aloud?) Their goal, as Milton Babbitt put it in a patronizing eulogy for Stravinsky, was "to have the history of music leave you ahead."

Since then, however, Mr. Meyer's theoretical surmises have been bolstered by solid empirical work in cognitive psychology and, especially, linguistics. His counterparts today, increasingly aware and respectful of the mind's hard-wiring, are less circumspect in their critiques of those who ignore rather than explore human nature. A Columbia composer, Fred Lerdahl, and an MIT linguist, Ray Jackendoff, have jointly offered a far bleaker diagnosis than Mr. Meyer's regarding most atonal music: where he said its opacity would be hard to overcome, they have not hesitated to pronounce the task humanly impossible.

Why? Consider the philosopher Walter J. Ong's comparison between computer "languages" and natural language. Computer languages, he writes, "do not grow out of the unconscious but directly out of consciousness." Their rules "are stated first and thereafter used," while "the 'rules' of grammar in natural human languages are used first and can be abstracted from usage and stated explicitly in words only with difficulty and never completely." Just so, on this analogy, serial music conveys little, because for all its vaunted complexity it is shallow, all surface, with no underlying, unconscious, and innate "deep structure."

But is music really a "natural human language"? The evidence mounts that in some ways it is. In 1974, Richard L. Crocker became the only musicologist ever to get his face on the front page of the *New York Times* by deciphering and performing a Sumerian song dated around 1400 B.C., by a wide margin the oldest tune on record. It turned out to be nothing much, actually, a great letdown to those expecting a sci-fi frisson. And that was precisely what was newsworthy. That the melody was so humdrum and familiar-sounding showed that what Mr. Crocker calls the "diatonic pitch set" was in people's heads three and a half millennia ago. And as we all know from experience, it's there still.

Of course, that age-old pitch set, though grounded in acoustic resonance, does not entirely conform to the physics of sound. Actual musical practice in all cultures departs significantly from what might be inferred on the basis of "nature" alone. That discrepancy used to be ascribed wholly to arbitrary convention. Now cognitive scientists are more willing to grant that there may be internal constraints on musical "hearing," supplementing external nature.

This, to many, not just to die-hard serialists, is unwelcome news. Indeed, if you strip the serialist position of its vainglory (admittedly no easy task), an attractive optimism about human adaptability remains. It is the same optimism that drives all utopian thinking. It underlies the trendy academic claim that those things between our legs are not biological organs but social constructions. Earlier it motivated the Soviet doctrine called Lysenkoism, after the Ukrainian botanist who claimed that acquired characteristics (acquired, say, under Socialism) could be inherited after all. Biological determinism is a brake on all that. It is pessimistic. And that is why it is never allowed to breed as "pure science" but is always dragged into the political arena for unmasking.

Unfortunately, those quickest to reject and denounce biological determinism are often determinists of another stripe, usually historical. When you are convinced that history has a purpose—your purpose—that must inevitably triumph, you can rationalize any means of helping the inevitable along. "I am the Party's servant," said Comrade Stalin, wiping his hands of blood and pinning a medal on Comrade Lysenko, "and the Party is the servant of history." Give me Mr. Meyer's gentle pessimism any day.

POSTSCRIPT, 2008

When you attack the claims of an interest group you can expect to be met by hysteria. This was one of the few *Times* pieces for which I actually (preemptively) suggested the headline, usually the province of editors. I insisted on its being cast in the form of a question, hoping to forestall the charge that I was asserting or advocating biological determinism. It was of course a forlorn hope. One irate correspondent accused me of "citing Darwin as an excuse to bury our heads (or ears in this case) and not to find new means of expression." Darwin? I never mentioned him. (And Darwin was no biological determinist.) Another letter faulted me for adding to the existing branches of music scholarship "a new category: prescriptive musicology." He may actually have meant "proscriptive," because he defined my position as arising out of "a need to define and restrict the compositional possibilities of the present and future." But is there no difference between a critic and a censor? No difference between raising a question and imposing a ban?

I was more concerned with evaluating the claims of the past than with forecasting the future. Those claims, too, were forecasts. The postman, to recall a typically optimistic prediction of Anton Webern's, is not yet whistling Webern's tunes a century later, and gives no sign of any such inclination. Perhaps it's time to ask why. The names I did cite—Meyer, Lerdahl and Jackendoff, Crocker—were early askers of that question. Answers, they implied, and I agree, may be available in cognitive psychology, which is much concerned of late with determining how much of the mind's information processing depends on conceptual hierarchies and stable assignment of functions, both of which twelve-tone music eschews, at least in the domain of pitch.

Of course I was accused of denying all esthetic value to the work of Schoenberg, Webern, and every other composer of twelve-tone music, and even of "danc[ing] on their graves." Yet one can (and I do) enjoy the music of these composers despite the cognitive opacity of their pitch organization. Both Schoenberg and Webern, in their different ways, compensated for the nonhierarchical organization of pitch relations by building ad hoc hierarchies into their products in the form of significantly recurring chords, rhythmic patterns, or melodic shapes, or by emphasizing symmetries whether melodic (in the form of pitch palindromes, especially in Webern) or harmonic (chords that have the same intervallic structure when inverted). But why should one have to compensate in this way? If Schoenberg and Webern achieved beauty and communicativeness in spite of their methods rather than because of them, the methods might possibly be worth a critical look. My correspondents' defensive elision of the difference between criticism and censorship is exactly what I had in mind when I wrote that dissenting scholarly hypotheses are liable to be "dragged into the political arena for unmasking."

And of course I was accused of beating dead horses. "Why are we still beating up on serialism?" one correspondent wanted to know. "The masters of serialism are either long dead or over sixty-five. The Caucasian male representatives of the school ceased to dominate the conservatory faculties and grant-giving committees ten or fifteen years ago. Serialism is now a dying small town in the tiny province of American music that still calls itself 'classical.'" The answer to that can best be given in the form of a letter that the *Times* selected for publication, by Jeff Nichols, a serial composer, then only thirty-seven years old and on the faculty of Harvard University:

> Surely Richard Taruskin does not mean to propose that "music is the universal language" just because there are ancient diatonic melodies. Traditional Japanese or Arabic music can sound as odd to the American on the street as Milton Babbitt, and diatonic scales, however apparently natural to us Westerners, have never been the sine qua non of music making in the world. Let's face it: music is universal the way food is universal. One culture's symbol of home and hearth is another's rotten cabbage.
>
> Does Mr. Taruskin really have scientific proof that atonality stinks? Of course not. He glibly invokes the recent work of cognitive psychologists, but that work is more concerned with how we recognize our mothers than how we recognize art. It will be a long time, if ever, before scientists claim authority on such issues as esthetic judgment. When he misappropriates their research to declare certain cultural artifacts unnatural, Mr. Taruskin, far from announcing to us the latest musical discoveries, is in fact reviving the most notorious attacks on modernism of the past.
>
> Mr. Taruskin's music history is equally suspect. He portrays atonality as the hermetic argot of a few "academic serialists" rather than an international style that has influenced all sorts of composers, from Bartók to Takemitsu to Zappa. Clearly, to acknowledge the breadth of the phenomenon would undermine Mr. Taruskin's argument. Psychologists are no more prepared to explain why thousands of composers have been writing gibberish for the last century than to validate his personal taste. The psychologists can relax. Despite his protestations of empiricism, it is Mr. Taruskin, not Babbitt, who is using theory to deny the realities of art.

That sort of invective, which merely shouts the question down, is its own indictment and a vindication of my premises. Fortunately, the *Times* also chose to print a letter from Steven J. Cahn, a music theorist and pianist on the faculty of the University of Cincinnati's College–Conservatory of Music, which engages courteously with the question, raising its own interesting and undogmatic questions in turn:

> As a musician who maintains a memorized repertory of tonal, atonal and serial music in his head, I offer the following rough analogies to characterize my experiences of tonal and atonal music.
>
> Resolution is the leading experience in tonal music, rather like the experience of resolution in a story. We don't feel we have experienced a story unless we know how it comes out. My experience of atonal music is less like reading a story than like reading an essay. Just as the initial themes of an essay grow more resonant in the mind through associations, shifts in perspective and intimations of limitless variation, so too do musical themes.
>
> Schoenberg's practice of recalling an opening motif at the end of a work produces not so much a sense of closure as a sensation of resonance. Both resolution, which depends heavily on syntax (chord grammar), and resonance, which does not, seem to me to be natural mental experiences unencumbered by the ideologies Mr. Taruskin critiques.
>
> The finest atonal and serial works are products of the mind and thus bear the stamp of the complex environment in which they were minted. They have engaged me as both a pianist and a listener in what I consider to be a natural way.

I might still object that, even though I invoked Walter Ong's distinction between computer languages and "natural language," I did not call any particular style of music natural or unnatural, nor did I claim anything more than that musical practices are "in some ways" based on natural phenomena and natural endowments. I would further object that calling something the "product of the mind" is not tantamount to calling it natural. The effects in Schoenberg to which Mr. Cahn calls attention correspond to what I have called his compensations for the lack of an intelligible pitch organization. But I do not dispute their capacity for giving pleasure or satisfaction.

8

Two Stabs at the Universe

After several attempts at conflation, I realized that these two pieces on Ives's inexhaustible "Universe" Symphony, one a record review and the other a concert promo, complemented each other like the realizations they described.

The first of them has had a considerable impact on the writing of music history—in the first instance, on my own conceptualization of the early twentieth century in the fourth volume of the *Oxford History of Western Music*. I cast successive chapters (nos. 50–52) as three variations on the theme of transcendentalism, each culminating in one of the "torsos" described in the essay (Scriabin, Ives, and Schoenberg, in that order). Later, I was pleased to find that Philip Lambert had taken my review seriously enough to expand upon it in a very serious article, "Ives's *Universe*," in a very serious book: *Ives Studies* (Cambridge: Cambridge University Press, 1997). What was gratifying was the implicit recognition that Ives ought to be released from the regionalist niche to which conventional music historiography has assigned him.

The same Cambridge volume contains an article by Larry Austin on his *Universe* realization, illustrated by sixteen photographic facsimiles of Ives's sketches.

AWAY WITH THE IVES MYTH: THE "UNIVERSE" IS HERE AT LAST

They said it couldn't be done, but Larry Austin, a composer best known for his "open-style" experiments in controlled improvisation and mixed media, has managed over a period of twenty years to produce a performing version

First published in the *New York Times*, 23 October 1994 and 2 June 1996. Copyright © 2008 The New York Times Company. Reprinted by permission.

of Charles Ives's legendary "Universe" Symphony. It has been recorded for all to hear by the assembled forces of the College–Conservatory of Music at the University of Cincinnati—the Cincinnati Philharmonia and the C.C.M. Percussion Ensemble, subdivided into eight "orchestras"—under the direction of Gerhard Samuel and four assisting conductors (Centaur CRC 2205; CD).

By now the Ives fans are out the door, racing to the record store. The rest of you, the ones still reading, stop. Go out and join them. Nothing I can write will give you an idea of the experience you are in for. All I can do is urge it upon you.

Still there? Why do you hesitate? Are you leery of completions and realizations? Were you burned by Barry Cooper's "Beethoven's Tenth"? By all those Mahler Tenths? By the suspiciously like-titled *Universe*, Aleksandr Nemtin's high-viscosity performing version of the "Prefatory Action" to Scriabin's world-destroying *Mysterium*?

Like these, Mr. Austin's work is a speculative composing-out—yes, an arrangement—of posthumous sketch material; and like the other composer-outers, Mr. Austin claims by dint of intuition and long hard work to have transcended the arranger's role and achieved metempsychosis—soul transfer—with the original composer. He wants his work, he tells us, "to be experienced and appreciated in performance as a 100 percent Ives composition."

No way. The "Universe" sketches have survived in what the pianist John Kirkpatrick, Ives's musical executor, called a "tragically fragmentary" state. What remains consists of little more than materials: verbal descriptions, plans, jottings of chords, scales, rhythms, occasional themelets, but little clue as to continuity. A typical surviving page is reproduced in Stuart Feder's fine psychological study of the composer, *My Father's Song*.

Mr. Feder suggests that the work was never meant to be completed, that its conceptual grandiosity (to the point, he maintains, of calculated unperformability) was a compensation for the composer's waning powers of fabrication. That may very well be: over the decade that followed the main body of work on the sketches, entered mainly between 1911 and 1915, Ives's creativity did gradually dry up. From 1921 until his death in 1954, a few months before his eightieth birthday, he wrote almost nothing, although he fiddled much (and controversially) with what he had done in his prime.

The last fiddling with the "Universe" sketches took place as late as 1951, but hardly with any serious thought of completion. On the contrary: some twenty years earlier, in what are now called his "Memos," Ives had already issued a despairing invitation to a posthumous collaborator to do exactly what Mr. Austin has done, and even left some instructions for the task. So this arranger, unlike his predecessors, can fairly claim to be acting in accordance with the composer's wishes—but an arranger he remains, and his work is best described exactly the way he described his own composition,

Phantasmagoria, of 1982: a "conjectural construction and fantasies on Ives's 'Universe' Symphony."

And what of that? Whoever started it or finished it, the work is what it is, and it is wonderful. It is Ives filtered through a sensibility obviously colored by the "spatialized" music of the 1950s avant-garde. The plethora of mallet percussion and the resolutely athematic texture bring to mind the Stockhausen of *Gruppen,* for three orchestras (or *Carré,* for four), and the Boulez of *Le Marteau sans maître.* This resemblance may disconcert some listeners, for as "realized" here, the work has none of the American regionalism one customarily or stereotypically associates with Ives—or rather, with the Ives myth.

But if it can help us overcome that myth, so much the better. The "Universe" Symphony may have little in common with any other American (let alone "Americanist") music, but it resonates uncannily with several contemporaneous (European) transcendental torsos and shows its composer to have been at least as finely attuned to the Zeitgeist—the core spirit of his time—as he was to the spirit of his then-provincial locality. Ives emerges here not as a tinkering or swaggering Gyro Gearloose of music, "anticipating" sundry modernist devices, but as a composer in the very thick of a contemporary musico-metaphysical crisis.

As described in the "Memos," the "Universe" Symphony was to be the Story of Everything, in three sections or movements played without pause or significant variation in tempo: "I. (Past) Formation of the waters and mountains. II. (Present) Earth, evolution in nature and humanity. III. (Future) Heaven, the rise of all to the spiritual."

This program puts the work directly in the line of European symphonic transcendentalism. That line began with the "Representation of Chaos" at the beginning of Haydn's oratorio *The Creation,* reached successive milestones with Beethoven's Ninth Symphony, Wagner's *Ring* cycle, and Mahler's *Song of the Earth* and achieved culmination in some of the most radical music of the early twentieth century.

All of these works strove to give through musical tones an intimation of the sublime—which is to say, the superhuman. All portrayed some aspect of the ascent to the spiritual that Ives specified in his program. In every case, the music evoked sensations of unfathomable or ungraspable space (what Freud would later call the "oceanic feeling"), often through the use of indefinite, long-held tones or spiraling figures at the threshold of audibility— just think of the beginning of the Ninth, or of the *Rheingold* Prelude. As the music historian Edward Lippman was among the first to note, the transporting effect thus achieved was the very nub of musical romanticism.

And that is just what happens at the beginning of the "Universe" Symphony. A faint, endless, unchanging chord in the low strings (Ives called it the "Chord of the Earth") forms the background to a fantastic accumulating montage of polyrhythmic percussion mantras, coordinated in Mr. Austin's performing version by the use of click tracks, representing the "Life Pulse."

All of this goes on for more than twenty minutes before anything else happens, and it is sheer metaphysical sorcery. After two or three minutes of it, I happened to glance at the time counter on my CD player and found that fourteen minutes had gone by. Ives and Austin have vastly magnified the effect of the Ninth's opening bars as described by Nietzsche: "The thinker feels himself floating above the earth in an astral dome, with the dream of immortality in his heart: all the stars seem to glimmer about him, and the earth seems to sink ever further downward." The Ninth at one end and the "Universe" Symphony at the other: together they enclose the transcendentalist epoch in music.

The second section of the "Universe" Symphony adds complex, static chords, sounding and resounding in the various suborchestras, to the running time river, and the third caps the work with an eight-orchestra tutti, set up by six seconds of throbbing silence, that for amplitude and loftiness surpasses any other musical experience of its kind. (And the recording does an astonishing job of capturing it.) These later sections of the "Universe" Symphony bring unexpectedly (and marvelously) to mind two works that were its exact contemporaries: Scriabin's *Mysterium* and Schoenberg's oratorio *Die Jakobsleiter* (Jacob's Ladder)

Like Ives's, which epitomized Emersonian transcendentalism, these works, too, were epitomes of mystical philosophies (in Scriabin's case theosophist, in Schoenberg's Swedenborgian). They, too, were portrayals of heaven and the Godhead, and inducers of out-of-body experience. They, too, were torsos, unfinished (and, arguably, unfinishable) by their composers. But they, too, have been speculatively "realized" (Schoenberg's by his pupil Winfried Zillig) and have been recorded, so that a listener may compare them. (*Die Jakobsleiter* is on a Sony Classical CD; the Scriabin-Nemtin *Universe* was released by Melodiya.) And what emerges from the comparison is that the prospect of representing the universe drew the same maximal response from all three composers. All three, acting without precedent or collusion, contrived textures and individual chords that comprised all twelve notes of the chromatic scale—and, in Ives's case, some quarter tones as well, as if to add microcosm to macrocosm.

It marked a musical limit; and to Schoenberg it gave the first intimation of twelve-tone composition, graphically illustrating the birth of modernism out of the spirit of romantic transcendentalism. These awesome torsos stunningly proclaim the spiritual impulse that induced the birth of atonality, an impulse later countered by academic rationalization.

This philosophy-driven saturation of musical space produced that musico-metaphysical crisis. Though hidden at the time, its consequences were decisive for the history of twentieth-century composition, and Ives was one of its protagonists. You can hear it happen in the quick, as it were, precisely 34 minutes 27 seconds into the long first track of the present CD. Do you need any further inducement?

The remaining tracks contain very spacious, engrossing performances of Ives's Orchestral Set No. 2 and the oft-recorded *Unanswered Question*. Each movement in the Orchestral Set, a kind of symphonic triptych, reaches for the same epiphanic effect as the "Universe" Symphony: murky beginnings gradually coalescing into revelatory declarations (with a poignant falloff at the very end). It is a shape Ives overused to the point of cliché, but at its best it has the force of prophecy.

After the newfound "Universe" Symphony, perhaps the most searing Ivesian epiphany is the one that takes place at the end of the third movement in the Set. Titled "From Hanover Square North, at the End of a Tragic Day, the Voice of the People Again Arose," it is an idealized representation of a transcendental moment Ives himself witnessed (he tells us) while waiting for his elevated commuter train on 7 May 1915, the day the *Lusitania* was sunk and the inevitability of world war became apparent.

At the prompting of a hurdy-gurdy playing on the street below, the passengers on the platform broke impromptu into the gospel hymn "The Sweet Bye and Bye." Its orchestral sublimation is gripping indeed, but next to the ineffable "Universe" Symphony it sounds, in its specificity . . . well, too effable. Or maybe it's the general stink nowadays surrounding nationalism that renders it somewhat paltry and parochial this time around, despite the wonderful performance, surely the best on records.

OUT OF HIBERNATION: IVES'S MYTHICAL BEAST

One fine October day in 1915, elated by the landscape of the Keene Valley in the Adirondacks, where he was visiting relatives, Charles Ives was seized with an artistic vision to set alongside Wagner's *Ring*. He called it the "Universe in Tones" or "Universe" Symphony. It would be "a striving," as he called it, trying frantically to capture his conception in words, "to present and to contemplate in tones rather than in music as such, that is—not exactly written in the general term or meaning as it is so understood—to paint the creation, the mysterious beginnings of all things, known through God to man, to trace with tonal imprints the vastness, the evolution of all life, in nature of humanity, from the great roots of life to the spiritual eternities from the great unknown to the great unknown."

Ever since the existence of this breathtaking if inscrutable plan was first made known—by the composer Henry Cowell and his wife, Sidney Robertson Cowell, in their Ives biography of 1955—the "Universe" Symphony has haunted the history of American music like a mythical beast. On Thursday at Alice Tully Hall, as the culmination of the Fifteenth American Festival of

Microtonal Music, Ives's unicorn will sing at last, in an hourlong performance by a seventy-piece orchestra that will have more flutists than violinists, and more percussionists than flutists, all under the direction of the composer Johnny Reinhard, the festival's director.

Why the long wait? It is, alas, a typical Ives story: the most typical, indeed quintessential, Ives story of them all.

In 1915, at the age of forty-one, Ives was in the visionary prime of his life, bursting with a fantastic creative energy that was not only finding expression in radical musical ideas but was revolutionizing the insurance business as well. (He is remembered in the insurance world as the father of estate planning, and his training manual, "The Amount to Carry," was still in use in the mid-1980s. By the time he retired, his firm, Ives & Myrick, is estimated to have sold half a billion dollars' worth of coverage.) Over the next decade or so, sketches for the "Universe" Symphony accumulated. But during that same period, Ives's health suffered serious reverses, and by the end of the 1920s, he was living as a recluse on East 74th Street in Manhattan, no longer composing.

In 1932, aged fifty-eight but altogether enfeebled, Ives dashed off a poignant memo in which he tried to summarize the progress he had made on his magnum opus. There would be three orchestras, the first consisting of nothing but percussion and representing "the pulse of the universe's life beat." The other two would divide the remaining instruments into high and low groups. And there would be three overlapping movements: The first ("Past") would depict the formation of the waters and mountains; the second ("Present") would represent "Earth, evolution in nature and humanity"; and the finale ("Future") would portray "Heaven, the rise of all to the spiritual." At the end of the memo, mixing pathos and bathos, Ives wrote, "I am just referring to the above because, in case I don't get to finishing this, somebody might like to try to work out the idea, and the sketch that I've already done would make more sense to anybody looking at it with this explanation."

Ives hung on into his eightieth year, an extinct creative volcano. By the time of his death in 1954, sporadic performances of his music—notably by the pianist John Kirkpatrick and the conductors Lou Harrison and Leonard Bernstein—had made his name a legend, but most of his works were left inaccessible to performers, in the form of unedited (and often barely legible) manuscripts. A dedicated team of Ives devotees, headed by Cowell and Kirkpatrick, set about sorting, listing, copying, editing, and publishing them. The project continues to this day, spearheaded by the Charles Ives Society, a consortium of scholars and music editors working in concert with the composer's estate and the publishing house of Peermusic.

Yet despite the composer's own urgent invitation to complete it, the "Universe" Symphony long rested undisturbed. Kirkpatrick, who made the first attempt to catalog Ives's musical legacy, judged that at least half of the sketches for the work were missing. The Cowells claimed that the piece was

an early, grandiose example of "conceptual art," never meant for performance at all. Ives's psychoanalytic biographer, Stuart Feder, thought that the
work was intentionally unfinishable, so that it could function for Ives as an
enduring vicarious link with his revered father, George, a bandmaster and
musical tinker, whose sterile musical imaginings it perpetuated. An earlier
performance version, by the composer Larry Austin (recorded on Centaur),
supplemented authentic sketch material with original interpolations and
speculative interpretations, some of them involving technologies (like electronic "click tracks" for coordinating complex rhythms) that were unavailable to Ives.

Mr. Reinhard, the work's most recent realizer, convinced that Ives had in
fact finished the piece and that the sketches were intact but out of order, resolved to assemble a performable version that added nothing to what Ives
had left behind. His success in this undertaking has been recognized by the
Charles Ives Society, which has formally declared that Mr. Reinhard may describe his version as "realized exclusively from Ives's 'Universe Symphony'
sketches."

Artistically, of course, such an assurance counts for little. It appeals not to
the artist but to the curator that lurks, for better or worse, within the soul of
every twentieth-century musician and music lover. In fact, even Mr. Reinhard's version has its speculative side. To say this, however, is far from an as-
persion. It is one of the things that give "realizations" their inevitable fascination, whether we are talking Beethoven via Barry Cooper (the "Tenth
Symphony"), Mahler via Deryck Cooke among others (also a "tenth") or the
various works by Henry Cowell, Edgard Varèse, or Harry Partch that Mr.
Reinhard has "realized" for his festivals in the past.

What all of Mr. Reinhard's realizations have in common is the "microtonal" aspect to which he has devoted his career. Microtones are often perhaps overnarrowly defined as intervals or pitch differences smaller than a
semitone, the smallest pitch discrimination that is regarded as meaningful
in most Western music theory. The most common way of splitting this musical atom is to divide it by two, producing "quarter tones." One of the earliest
experimenters with quarter tones, it so happens, was George Ives. According to his son, the elder Ives built various microtonal contraptions (one of
them a box of violin strings with weights attached) to overcome the limitations of arbitrary theory and "enjoy an original relation to the universe," as
Ralph Waldo Emerson, an Ivesian household god, once put it. For microtones, which we hear whenever we listen to "nonmusical" sounds, exist in unlimited unordered profusion in the untheorized world of nature. A music
that incorporated microtones would be, in the Ivesian view, a more natural
and "universal" music than one that limited itself to the stingy fare vouchsafed by official theory. Only such a music would give access to a truly transcendental experience, in Emersonian terms.

Ives's whole career was a quest for such a greening experience: "my father's song," as he put it in a poem he once set to music. His father's mechanical experiments provided him with a conceptual precedent, if not exactly a practical one. Ives's "universe in tones" would unfold through a chorus of transcendentally unified microtonal tunings: "some perfectly tuned correct scales, some well-tempered little scales, a scale of overtones with the divisions as near as determinable by acousticon, scales of smaller division than a semitone, scales of uneven division greater than a whole tone, scales with no octave, some of them with no octave for several octaves," as he put it, bewilderingly, in his word salad of 1932. And yet all of those scales would find their fundamental pitch in a single "fixed tone," the A at the lower end of the piano keyboard.

What was missing was any description of the technical means by which these state-of-nature scales would be produced. And so Mr. Reinhard has had to devise—yes, speculatively—the "overtone machines" and the adapted instruments that would supply the "perfectly tuned correct scales" whose notes fall in the cracks between the notes recognized by traditional unnatural music theory. His solution, besides retuning a harp according to Ives's specifications, was to adapt an electric guitar (the latter corresponding to Ives's "acousticon") to produce exactly measured intervals unavailable on ordinary instruments. These are most conspicuously displayed in the second section of the symphony. The third section, the one that depicts the transcendental ascent into the realm of spirit, features full orchestral chordal harmony in quarter tones.

The "acousticon" will be played at the concert by Jon Catler, with whom Mr. Reinhard has been collaborating since 1980, when both of them placed classified ads in different local papers to find microtonal playing partners and discovered each other. Mr. Reinhard, a bassoonist, had come out of the "quarter tone" tradition, originally through contact with pupils of the composer and recorder virtuoso Tui St. George Tucker. Mr. Catler had come out of the "just-intonation" tradition associated with Harry Partch (and with a history going back through the Renaissance to the Greeks). Where these traditions had been practiced in the twentieth century mainly by mutually suspicious purists, Mr. Reinhard and Mr. Catler take an ecumenical, eclectic (shall we call it postmodern?) view of microtonal possibilities, one that gladly takes in microtonal manifestations in all kinds of contemporary music including blues, sci-fi sound tracks, rock, and rap. And commercials, too, Mr. Reinhard points out with glee. "The old Oldsmobile car horn—da-dee-da-DEEE—had a 'neutral' third midway between major and minor, on top," he reminded a caller.

Indeed, that horn signal was the futuristic emblem of the General Motors pavilion at the New York World's Fair of 1939. In their Ivesian context, the microtones link the natural past with the spiritual, if not the commercial, future. To chalk up the coincidence as another coup for the Great Anticipator might seem trivial, but it symbolizes in its way a more significant anticipation. Ives's omnivorous "Universe," at least as mediated by Mr. Reinhard, foreshadows today's musical scene in all its polymorphous perversity, its rejection of stingy theorizing, and its reopening to universal possibility.

9

In Search of the "Good" Hindemith Legacy

"You know, I've written a lot of music," Paul Hindemith once remarked to the American composer Otto Luening. "Yes, you certainly have," Mr. Luening agreed. "And you know," Hindemith continued, "80 percent of it is bad." "Then why did you write it?" Mr. Luening asked, with Hindemithian tact. "Because without the 80 percent," came the reply, "there would never have been the 20 percent."

So what *is* that 20 percent, and where is it? one may well ask in this centenary year of Hindemith's birth. After all, the five-day Carnegie Hall choral workshop led by Robert Shaw beginning on Tuesday, devoted chiefly to Hindemith's "Requiem for Those We Love," will give the composer more attention than he receives in an average year in New York.

Is the "good" Hindemith to be found in the music he wrote during his young years as the enfant terrible of the early Weimar Republic? In the lurid expressionism of *Sancta Susanna,* an opera of sexual obsession in a nunnery? In the still-shocking (and newly timely?) *Murderer, the Hope of Womankind,* to a text by Oskar Kokoschka? In the neo-dada of *Neues vom Tage* (Extra! Extra!), a spoof of modern publicity, satirizing (forty years before Warhol) everybody's fifteen minutes of fame? In his "shimmies" and "bostons," up-to-the-minute equivalents of minuets and gigues, with their built-in obsolescence that challenged performers who went on playing minuets and gigues to justify their regressive habits?

Is it to be found in the music of the later Weimar years, when along with so many of his fellow artists Hindemith developed an exacting social conscience? In his furiously antiromantic "Kammermusiken" and "Spiel-

First published in the *New York Times,* 8 January 1995. Copyright © 2008 The New York Times Company. Reprinted by permission.

musiken," those bustling sonatas and concertos in which the viola-scraping Hindemith proclaimed the death of metaphysics? There was nothing more to music, he now implied, than the here-and-now activity of the performer. Away with the lie of immortality! Away with idealism! Even his performance directions became slogans: "Tonschönheit ist Nebensache," he asserted in the score of his magnificently ugly Sonata for Solo Viola: "Beauty of tone is secondary." Get out there, do your thing, get the circulation going. Then go home. Tomorrow play something else.

Or is it to be found in the even more radical, even more contingent category of *Gebrauchsmusik?* Literally, the word meant "music for use," but what it actually meant was music with a defined social function—or better, music with a *socializing* function. *Gebrauchsmusik* and everything it stood for was epitomized in Hindemith's *Plöner Musiktag* (Music Day at Plön) of 1932, in which an entire day at children's camp was organized around specially composed music. The closest precedent to this curious mega-cantata, if there is one, might be a medieval "office," or daily round of monastic services with music.

And that's about as far as you can get from the "absolute music" worshiped in the concert hall. *Gebrauchsmusik* was vehemently anti-esthetic art. It exemplified and tried to instill an anti-transcendent, anti-idealist ideal—an art restored to vital symbiosis with daily life, an art that teaches the virtues of collective, communal, and (to get back to music's ancient meaning) *harmonious* endeavor. To anyone steeped in the lonely, heroic romantic tradition, and that included most modernists, this was sheer subversion.

Or as the Hindemith who spoke to Mr. Luening fervently believed, was the saving 20 percent to be found in the music he was writing in the New World? That music argued passionately against all his earlier ideas; indeed, it often polemicized directly with his earlier music.

In his fascinatingly disingenuous book *A Composer's World,* based on lectures given at Harvard in 1949 and 1950 and published in 1951, Hindemith specifically disavowed *Gebrauchsmusik,* a meaningless term (as he now saw it) that he had unfortunately coined in a chance conversation with German choral directors and that the newspapers had picked up and (as newspapers will) blown all out of proportion. All music has use, he now insisted, including romantic concert music (it's used at concerts, right?), so to create a special category of useful music is silly.

The argument was doubly disingenuous, because in disavowing the term Hindemith also claimed credit for it, and that credit was not his due. The term *Gebrauchsmusik* (as Stephen Hinton, a music historian at Stanford, has demonstrated) was actually coined in the early twenties by the Prague music historian Paul Nettl, as a way of distinguishing dances you dance to from dances (like those in suites) you just listen to. The ideological spin had been given to it by musical followers of the German philosopher Martin Heidegger. They sought a music that could express what Heidegger called "Faktizität," primordial, unmediated knowledge and experience. The Heidegger connection was not important to Hindemith at the time, and not relevant to his use of the term, but it was very relevant indeed to his later rejection of it.

As to music's actually polemicizing with music, there is hardly a case in history to compare with Hindemith's postwar revision (published in 1948) of his Weimar masterpiece *Das Marienleben* (The Life of Mary), a 1923 song cycle on mystical texts by Rainer Maria Rilke. What had been a sublime expressionistic ecstasy was transformed into a calmly meditative, pellucid, and impersonal trio sonata for voice and two hands at the piano, producing among them a beautifully crafted, marvelously controlled web of tonal counterpoint. Beauty was back, and so was transcendence.

At the time, Hindemith explained the change on purely musical grounds. The new *Marienleben* was simply an improvement prompted by the composer's mastery of a mature and consummately responsible academic style he had worked out over years of practical composition teaching (first at the Berlin Hochschule für Musik, now at Yale). To channel that mastery not only into new composition but also into recomposition suggests a demonstrative purpose that goes beyond the craftsmanly into more primal matters. The source of that purpose is not hard to locate in the travails Hindemith suffered under the Nazi regime. For the Nazis put into unexpected and horrifying practice the utopian ideals of collective, communal, harmonious endeavor that had formerly claimed Hindemith's allegiance. Nor could you argue with them, because they had primordial, irrational immediacy of knowledge.

His rival and fellow émigré Ernst Krenek was mean-spirited to insinuate (in a book published in 1939) that there was "an unbroken line" leading from "Hindemith's concerto grosso style to the Hitler youth, of whom it is told that they give vent to their indomitable spirit of independence by secretly performing Hindemith's *Spielmusik*." But Hindemith's own esthetic about-face corroborates Krenek's diagnosis. Hindemith saw the connection, too, but it took him rather a long time.

(What estranged him from the Nazis, it is important if painful to admit, was their shortsighted rejection of him despite the entreaties of Wilhelm Furtwängler, Hitler's showcase conductor, not Hindemith's principled rejection of them. And what made it necessary for Hindemith to emigrate rather than, like Furtwängler, to compromise was the fact that his wife was Jewish, a circumstance beyond bargaining. Throughout his stay in the United States Hindemith acted out his resentment at having been unfairly barred from the musical life of Germany, the most musical of nations, in outrageously, now legendarily haughty behavior toward his American students and colleagues.)

Hindemith at first recoiled from the Nazi co-optation of his esthetic (if not his stylistic) agenda by recoiling from overt social commitment altogether— what the Nazis called "inner emigration." And yet the recoil produced its own sort of commitment, first symbolized (and sublimated) in the figure of

Mathis der Maler (the painter Matthias Grünewald), the title character of Hindemith's opera of 1934.

Mathis retreats, spiritually wounded, from the turbulent world of fifteenth-century politics—a world replete with class warfare and book burnings—into the timeless world of art. At the time of the opera's belated Zürich première, in 1938, the recently expatriated composer identified himself not only with Mathis, who "decides in his work to develop traditional art to its fullest extent," but also with J. S. Bach, "who two centuries later proves to be a traditionalist in the stream of musical development."

Spiritual alignment with Bach the traditionalist and transcendentalist colored Hindemith's entire late career. (Just think of his testament, the *Ludus Tonalis* of 1942. The first major work he wrote at Yale, it is a monumental series of preludes and fugues for piano like *The Well-Tempered Clavier* and a self-avowed translation of Bach's legacy into the language of the twentieth century.) His late Bachianism expressed Hindemith's embittered rejection of modernity, now, thanks to the Nazis and their triumphant mass production of death, a tainted ideal.

But there was enormous irony in Hindemith's new stance, for Bach—a different Bach—had been the idol of Hindemith the cheery *Gebrauchsmusiker* as well. Then it was Bach the community musician, a man who turned out well-made, socially useful goods to order, who provided the inspiration. Now it was Bach who "defeated the realm of substance and penetrated the unlimited region of thought," as Hindemith put it in a bicentennial lecture of 1950. The Bach of the left, you might say, and the Bach of the right. Whatever your mission, whatever your ethos, there is a Bach to guide you, to lend you authenticity.

Nowhere was Hindemith's late Bachianism more appropriately or convincingly evoked than in his *Requiem for Those We Love*, composed in 1946 on commission from Robert Shaw and the Collegiate Chorale. A setting of "When Lilacs Last in the Dooryard Bloom'd," Walt Whitman's elegy to Abraham Lincoln, it was widely read at the time as a similar offering to the memory of Franklin D. Roosevelt.

On the face of it, Whitman in midcareer and the late Hindemith seemed an odd couple: America's loftiest, most gorgeous poetic voice filtered through the taciturn music of Europe's most obdurately prosy composer. And it cannot be said that Hindemith captured any sort of Whitmanian spirit in his *Requiem* (the way Delius did, for one magnificent example, in his flushed and glowing, indecently neglected *Sea Drift*). When he tried, as in the regrettable offstage bugle sounding "Taps" against fussy, bustly, all too "Hindemithian" counterpoint, all he managed to achieve (as Howard Taubman remarked in the *Times* after the première) was corniness.

Bach provided a meeting place. One cannot listen long to Hindemith's *Requiem*, with its stately 12/8 meters and its English-horn obbligatos, without thinking of the Bach Passions, the *St. Matthew* in particular. (And why not? Both Lincoln and Roosevelt died around Easter time.) But once one has thought of them, and of their richly apposite field of associations—martyrdom, redemption, devotion—the correspondences come crowding in astonishing abundance and with astonishing specificity.

The oft-recurring ritornello in the *Requiem*'s central episode, the song of Whitman's wood thrush ("Sing on, you gray-brown bird!") has not only the 12/8 meter and the English-horn obbligato but also the figuration of "O Mensch, bewein" (Weep, O man), the chorale fantasia at the end of the first part of the *St. Matthew Passion*.

The finale, "Passing the visions, passing the night," has the heartrending purity of the flute timbre without bass accompaniment in the soprano's Passion aria "Aus Liebe will mein Heiland sterben" (My Saviour would die for love of me) and the palpitating dotted rhythm of the alto recitative 'Erbarm' es Gott!" (Have pity, God!). The passacaglia bass that speeds the "strong Deliveress" on her way in Hindemith's setting of Whitman's "Death Carol" has of course other Bachian resonances, multifarious ones.

They do not add up to a Whitmanesque catharsis, perhaps, but they affirm continuity of the fallen present, if not with a glorious future (that myth seemed dashed forever), at least with a remote, still honorable past. That was all the solace the smarting, sorrowing late Hindemith could tender. It was an honest, dignified message after a time of rampant lies, and in its gray-brown way it remains a moving one.

POSTSCRIPT, 2008

This piece received some useful musicological footnotes. In a posting to the American Musicological Society's Web list, David Neumeyer, a Hindemith specialist trained at the American source (Yale), then on the faculty of Indiana University (and now Leslie Waggener Professor in Fine Arts at the University of Texas at Austin), pointed out that the revision of *Das Marienleben* was actually begun (or at least announced) before the war, in a footnote to the first edition (1937) of *The Craft of Musical Composition*. Overreacting a bit to what he read as an accusation that Hindemith collaborated with the Nazi regime—my point was that they never gave him the opportunity—Neumeyer added:

> My complaint about Hindemith is not collaborationism . . . but failure of will, or what I'll call the "Swiss syndrome." From the time of his marriage in 1924, Switzerland was Hindemith's vacation site. When he emigrated in 1938, he was a very prominent public figure and could have used Switzerland as a base for vigorous criticism of the German government—but he didn't. Similarly, after the war, he was essentially offered control of West Germany's educational institutions, but he declined. Instead, he shuttled back and forth between New

Haven and Zürich till 1953, when he retired to Blonay (above Montreux). All this, alas, *is* consistent with the story of *Mathis,* who did not deny the struggle but still retired from it because he doubted his efficacy as a combatant.

Fair enough.

The other indispensable footnote was added by Kim H. Kowalke, professor of musicology at the Eastman School of Music and president of the Kurt Weill Foundation for Music, in an article in the *Journal of the American Musicological Society* ("For Those We Love: Hindemith, Whitman and 'An American Requiem,'" *JAMS* 50 [1997]: 133–74). Prof. Kowalke discovered that the subtitle "For Those We Love" was in fact the incipit of "Gaza," a hymn "For the Departed," which Hindemith found in the Episcopal *Hymnal* (1940), where it is described as a "traditional Jewish melody." Hindemith quotes it verbatim in the eighth section of the *Requiem* (an instrumental passage explicitly labeled "Hymn, 'For Those We Love'"), and derives the counterpoint that surrounds the allusion to "Taps" from it as well. It may not save the spot from corniness, but it does add a specifically post-Holocaust resonance.

10

Six Times Six
A Bach Suite Selection

Pablo Casals did for Bach's cello suites what Fyodor Chaliapin did for the role of Boris Godunov in Musorgsky's opera: revived them from the dead, made them a classic, created their performance practice, and—as interpretations of consummate authority inevitably will—ruined them for generations to come. No one coming after Chaliapin could evade his example. Alternatives were unthinkable; all one could do was emulate in vain hopes of surpassing. But efforts to surpass Chaliapin's histrionics fell ineluctably into parody, until eyes were opened to what had happened and tradition could be broken.

The Bach style Casals bequeathed to his progeny was the product of the cellist's deep belief in the music and the effort to sell it at a time when Bach was thought cold. So Casals's Bach was perforce red-hot. Everything else was sacrificed to expression. Preludes were maelstroms ending in tidal waves. Allemandes and sarabandes were passionate arias. Courantes were juggernauts. Gigues were kermesses. The *galanteries*—minuets, bourrées, gavottes—were Jovian scherzos. Dynamics, special effects aside, fluctuated between fortissimo and mezzo fortissimo. Multiple stops—four-note chords in particular—were grandly rhetorical: broken two-by-two with a flourish, the upper double stop held loud until the end, with a sforzando termination. "Good notes" (and also special dissonances) were agogically lengthened.

The most impressive sacrifice of all was tone. Where the early-twentieth-century string ideal was represented by Kreisler's easy elegance or Heifetz's scary brilliance (or, to confine matters to the cello, Feuermann's inconceivable polish), Casals played Bach with a deliberately scratchy, ugly, effortful tone. (If you doubt that it was deliberate, dig out his recordings, now virtually forgotten, of Popper, Sarasate, and other virtuoso fare of his day; he

Originally published in *Strings* 9, no. 4 (January–February 1995): 117–21.

could pull out the whole Feuermann shtick when he wished.) When speaking musical German, Casals could have authored Hindemith's notorious modernist slogan of the period: *Tonschönheit ist Nebensache,* "beauty of tone is secondary."

But Casals was no modernist—was he? He was a romantic—wasn't he? Yes and no to both. For there is really no contradiction, and the questions are wrong. Romantics (true romantics, that is, not Kreisler or Heifetz) and modernists actually have a lot in common. Both think beauty is secondary. To what? To truth, of course, which (to Keats) was beauty all along. And to Casals (no less than to Hindemith or Stravinsky or even Schoenberg in their neoclassical phase), Bach was the ultimate, universal source of truth, the fount and origin of Western musical values. Casals's Bachian ideal was an ethical ideal, founded not on a pleasure principle but on a reverent work ethic. It epitomized the secular religion of art, preached—and, increasingly, practiced   on a virtually monastic plane.

As we may need to be reminded by now, as Casals outlived his musical prime he entered a period of ethical iconhood in his own right, born of an ascetic political stance and solemnized through a redoubled dedication to Bach. The first Casals festival—convoked in 1950 in Prades in the French Pyrenees by his admirers at a time when Casals would not venture away from home to perform in countries that recognized the Franco regime—was a Bach bicentennial festival. When, eventually, Casals came out of exile to perform at the United Nations, he of course performed Bach.

That kind of moral force could scarcely be denied; so for cellists, the Bach style was the Casals style. If we are over thirty-five, we were surely trained in it. We probably studied the Suites from the "analytical edition" of Diran Alexanian, Casals's disciple, whose weird notations were meant to codify and propagate the Spanish master's insights. The edition came out in 1929, and Casals's testamentary recordings followed in 1936–39. Like no other recordings I know, they were treated as religious articles by their devotees.

Listening to them now (on a two-volume CD set, EMI CDH-7 61028 2 and 60129 2) is still a bit otherworldly; and it is still difficult to keep one's critical faculties engaged. I want to say that they require no excuses, however tastes (and ethics) may have changed since their day. The monster-difficult Prelude of the Sixth Suite is the technical equal of any that has appeared since (and unlike all the rest, it was recorded in real time!); and if the soulfully orated slow-motion Allemande that follows it is rendered musically inscrutable by the tempo and the phrasing, that only enhances its sublimity. And yet by now Casals's recordings are not only historic but historical as well. As in the case of Chaliapin, there was an ensuing decadence, and now there are clear alternatives.

The decadence consisted, as always, in a magnification of virtues to excess, and in the assumption of false converses (e.g., if virtuous playing tolerates an ugly tone, then an ugly tone is virtuous). It can be seen most dramatically in the work of Mstislav Rostropovich. The first time I heard him in recital, in a virtually empty Carnegie Hall in fall 1959, he played the Fifth Suite (with normal tuning, as everyone then did). It was the most controversial item on the program, because it did not conform to the high-effort, high-viscosity Casals manner. The tempos were dazzlingly brisk, the tone was gold and silk by turns, and it was thought altogether vulgar, the consequence of a Soviet artist's provincial isolation. While fully understanding and accepting (and even parroting) the hostility to it that my own cello teacher (an Alexanian pupil) expressed, I guiltily loved it, American churl that I was.

The only time I have ever felt I hated the Bach Suites came exactly thirty years later, when I switched on the television news and saw the same Rostropovich, now as old as Casals was when he made his Bach records, playing the Sarabande from the same Fifth Suite at the newly opened, soon-to-be-razed Berlin Wall. His jaw was jutting, his mouth was working furiously, his forehead was beaded. The tone was frightfully turgid, the tempo glacial. I had never heard such overplaying. It was an abject Casals wannabe that I now beheld—in every sense, musical and extramusical. For Rostropovich, too, was then a (well-remunerated) political exile, playing the role to the hilt. Bach and the Casals *maniera* were his props.

And that is one reason why—though Casals will always be revered, and justly—one now wants something new from Bach, a new approach to the Suites. To the extent that they fail to supply it, younger cellists than Rostropovich are not doing their duty by Bach, or even by Casals. As the incident at the Berlin Wall made urgently plain, Bach (like any loved cultural object) must be renewed to stay alive. And Casals is done no honor by being turned into a brake against that necessary project.

So with regrets, for they are formidable players, I must dismiss the recordings of Nathaniel Rosen (John Marks Records JMR 6 and 7) and Ralph Kirshbaum (Virgin Classics VCD 5 45086 2). They are not helpful now. The conventions to which they adhere have been exhausted of their meaning. One hears Rosen slam into the Prelude from the Fifth Suite (for all that he tunes the top string down, as written), or snarl his way through the Courante (the only real French courante in the lot), and winces. One hears Kirshbaum trilling for emphasis on final notes (yes, there is one such notation in the Fourth Suite, but that should show how rare is such a thing, and prompt the question why) or break the root-fifth-octave chords so that pieces end on loud-sustained dissonant fourths, and cringes. Virtually everything is too loud. One laughs, but mirthlessly, at the second Bourrée in the Fourth or the second Gavotte in the Sixth. What is meant to mince galumphs.

The alternative is Anner Bylsma, on his second go-round (Sony Vivarte S2K 48 047), now playing the Smithsonian Institution's unimaginably resonant and beautiful "Servais" Stradivari (in Suites 1–5), which almost succeeds in upstaging him. Every cellist should hear this set—not to imitate it (for that would only lead to a new decadence), but just to be assured that other ways are possible. Bylsma's reputation notwithstanding, this is not "early music" playing. Indeed, the early-music camp followers among previous reviewers have found the set especially problematic, because the playing is as subversive of their dogmas as it is of older ones.

But if it is not antiquarian playing, Bylsma's way with the Suites does show the benefit of his association with antiquarian performers. It is clear that he now envisions these pieces in a wholly different context from the one most cellists habitually assume for them. They are for him not remote ancestors and source of the rest of the cello rep but suites among suites. Bylsma knows the "broken style" as it is played by the lutenists whose forebears invented it, and so his preludes do not try to make melodies out of their arpeggios. He plays for resonance—bow in the air, dipping into the notes—and keeps his fingers down until they are needed elsewhere, so that harmonies can be built up and resound. No previous cellist on records has managed such a harmonic ambience in the Prelude to the Fourth Suite (E-flat Major), where there is such a dearth of open-string resonance.

Resonance is the thing the Casals manner has always killed. Now that the compensatory intensity has become suspect, one basks and revels in Bylsma's relaxed yet ringing tone production. It is aided, to be sure, by the stringing and the setup or internal adjustment. (Cellos that must play in or against modern orchestras have to be outfitted like panzers and tightened into a virtually muscle-bound condition.) But the difference is mainly in the bowing and the fingering; one achieves maximum resonance or maximum intensity, never both. That is one thing cellists can learn from Bylsma's recording without necessarily adopting his interpretive mannerisms.

In the Sixth Suite, of course, the hardware is a more decisive factor. In fact it is crucial. Now that Bylsma's sterling rendition on a five-string violoncello piccolo is available, there is little reason to listen to any performance on a standard instrument. The lack of the E string is simply too much of a handicap; it is not simply a matter of parlous intonation or, more trivially, of notes lost from chords, but, again, a matter of resonance and of ease of production. On a four-string cello one must (literally and figuratively) choke up. Practically the whole piece is played in higher positions, on all strings, and the tone is inevitably (to put it euphemistically) enriched.

I am neither adamant enough nor naive enough to think that conventional cellists will give up on the Sixth Suite just because its hardware demands are being met at last by some (well, by one). But in four-string renditions, the listener's response must shift from enjoyment of the thing performed to admiration, when merited, of the performer's ability to cope.

Yet that said, it must be added that Yo-Yo Ma (CBS M2K 37867) copes magnificently, indeed somewhat miraculously. Until reaching the Fourth

Suite (that is, the hard half of the set), I was decidedly unimpressed with Ma's performance. Touted by some as the world's greatest cellist, to me he sounded more like the world's greatest cello student. The performances sounded careful, correct, and (in the rushed courantes especially) immature. But when the going got tough . . . well, you know. Except for Bylsma, with his many advantages, I had never heard anyone play the Allemande from the Sixth Suite so coherently, or organize its wayward melody and harmony so effectively around the slow metrical pulse. And I'm sure I don't know how Ma managed to achieve such an effortlessly resonant sonority in the Sarabande (but I know it was not studio trickery, because I have heard him play the piece live). Though it is not the same, or (be it said) as treasurable as the sheer delight in the music that Bylsma affords, the admiration Ma evokes in the Sixth Suite is also an exuberating experience. If only the rest of his set were at anything like a comparable level of excellence.

Last, and surely least, Pieter Wispelwey (Channel Classics CCS 1090): a well-trained and, one readily grants, talented cellist (Bylsma was among his teachers)—but a callow youth. A change from the old decadence but an alarming foretaste of the new. It is valuable to have his Sixth Suite as proof (lest any sorehead be moved to belittle Bylsma) that hardware guarantees nothing. Wispelwey was not ready to record the piece, whether on a cello piccolo or any other sort of piccolo, and the fact that he went ahead and produced such an ungainly version of it is a specimen of the hardware arrogance that has been known to give "early music" a bad name.

Elsewhere, Wispelwey's work tends to be derivative of his teacher's, except where he strives after novel renditions. The trouble is that what he evidently regards as novelties often turn out to be bromides, like the routine bariolage he dully interpolates where the notation in the Prelude to the Second Suite lapses into half-note shorthand. (Here, too, Bylsma is original and convincing; the old believers confuse shorthand with climax.) Let Wispelwey redo the set in ten years' time, when both he and the style of playing he now espouses have had a chance to mature. I predict good results, and promise to report them.

POSTSCRIPT, 2008

He did, and they were, so I must (not that anyone minds admitting they were right). Wispelwey's remake (Channel Classics 12298) came only five years later, but what a difference! It matches the difference in the jacket photos, in fact: greater weight though far from heavy, a more focused outlook, more adult all around. And his virtuosity is not just showy now, but masterly. The test, as always, is the Sixth Suite, which this time emerges as a set of stately and graceful dances, not an agonizing bout on the potty. I sense that Wispelwey has replaced Ma as the most influential model for budding cellists in this repertoire, and that is altogether to the good.

11

A Beethoven Season?

So it's to be a Beethoven year. Carnegie Hall has announced a "Focus on Beethoven" for the coming season (as if Carnegie Hall had ever had another focus). Maurizio Pollini will play all thirty-two piano sonatas there beginning next month. Alfred Brendel will play all five piano concertos with the New York Philharmonic under Kurt Masur at Avery Fisher Hall in March. The Chamber Music Society of Lincoln Center will present a Beethoven festival at Alice Tully Hall in January. All these performances will surely be magnificent; but with all due respect to the performers, a focus on Beethoven is exactly what we do not need.

Who could have anything against Beethoven? Surely not I, though once I did feel I hated his music, or what we'd made of it. That was the evening of Christmas, 1989, when I turned on the television and beheld Leonard Bernstein leading a hurriedly hand-picked international orchestra in Berlin through a sloppy performance of the Ninth Symphony, in celebration of the sundering of the Berlin Wall. The old warhorse had been specially renovated for the occasion, with "Freiheit!" (Freedom!) replacing "Freude!" (Joy!) in the choral finale.

Despite that gesture, I could only wince and grieve at the way Bernstein and Beethoven—and all of classical music, or so it seemed—had been reduced to the level of ambulance chasers, intruders on a historic scene. What did it mean, playing Beethoven at that time and in that place? As if the East Germans did not also have their Beethovenfests. As if the high culture and all its icons had not been exploited by every dictatorship (and

First published in the *New York Times*, 10 September 1995. Copyright © 2008 The New York Times Company. Reprinted by permission.

every commercial interest), used as a bludgeon to beat down spontaneous (popular, counter-) culture and sell every consumer product.

The true musical emblems of that glorious moment were the guitar-strumming kids in jeans atop the wall playing a music that would have landed them in jail the day before. They were the ones who symbolized Freiheit. What did Beethoven symbolize? Just packaged greatness, I'm afraid, and all that that implies of smugness and dullness and ritualism. Just what the revolutions of '89 were revolting against.

And that is why classical music is failing, and in particular why intellectuals, as a class, and even the educated public, have been deserting it. The defection began in the sixties, when all at once it was popular music that engaged passionately—adequately or not, but often seriously and even challengingly—with scary, risky matters of public concern, while classical music engaged only frivolously (remember radical chic?) or escaped into technocratic utopias. By now, the people who used to form the audience for "serious" music are very many of them listening to something else.

The best evidence of that is the drastically reduced press coverage classical music now gets, and the correspondingly greater attention paid to pop in all the serious media. Some classical spokespeople, deploring this, seem to think it a symptom of some new preoccupation with entertainment in our culture. But no, the center of gravity in our culture has shifted; the pop critics are often the more serious ones, and very often the more interesting ones.

They are the ones who take the risks these days. If there is any real musical controversy to cover, like the recent one over rap lyrics, the pop critics are the ones who get to cover it. Classical critics, for the most part, just spend their time packaging and repackaging greatness. No wonder their space is diminishing.

So unless subversively performed or critiqued, the repertory that Beethoven begot has to a distressing extent turned into a dead weight, a stagnant pond, and continued preoccupation with its packaging and repackaging can only further marginalize classical music from current intellectual and human concerns. Why, then, if this is so, does preoccupation not only persist, but even seem to be increasing?

An answer comes to mind, based on my experiences as an exchange student in Russia back in the depths of what is now called the Brezhnevite stagnation, when packaging and repackaging a different sort of greatness reached a now thoroughly discredited peak. During my early weeks in Moscow, gawking at those palatial subway stations, I noticed that the marble or granite slab proclaiming their dedication to the memory of V. I. Lenin was always slightly off-color compared with the surrounding slabs, and finally asked why.

The reason was not surprising, even at first a little amusing. The subway had originally been named after Lazar M. Kaganovich, the old Moscow party boss, who had supervised its construction. When he was disgraced by Khrushchev in 1957, off came his name—and in that unsettled moment, the only safe substitute was the name of the great founder, by then a mythical being. It was something that happened countless times in the Soviet Union over the years, especially during de-Stalinization.

Stalin prizes became Lenin prizes. Villages called Stalino became Lenino. A line in a famous Soviet "fakesong," or phony folk song, about the Two Falcons went from "one was Lenin, the other Stalin" to "one was Lenin, the other, also Lenin." One of my Soviet friends, told me, giggling, that the Siberian city in which he was brought up had twenty-five Lenin Prospects (First Leninsky, Second Leninsky, etc.), most of which had once borne names no longer kosher.

I giggled, too, to hear about it; but by then it no longer seemed so funny. Long before it was christened, stagnation was palpable in the land of the Soviets. This society, founded on bright visions of the future, had become obsessed with the past, with its own creation myth. It had turned that myth into an ineffectual compensation for a disillusioning present. The endless invocations of Big Lenny proclaimed Soviet reality to be, all those Siberian streets notwithstanding, a present without prospects.

That, it seems to me, is one way to read the comparable move now being made within the classical music establishment. It is another case of refuge in the creation myth. Beethoven—that is, his ever-magnifying posthumous reputation—was the creator spirit of classical music as we know it. His example established the masterwork—the fixed and "timeless" musical text rather than the ephemeral performance—as the primary object in which "art" music trades. The whole difference between art and pop as musical categories depends on this distinction, one we so take for granted that we forget it has a history, but one that no pre-Beethoven composer would have understood, not even Mozart.

So it is to Beethoven (that is, to his commanding example) that we trace the ritualism of our smug, dull concert life; by celebrating and yet again repackaging the undeniably great and daring fountainhead of our undeniably narrow, pusillanimous performance rites, we ward off threats to our complacency. But anxiety lurks withal.

That anxiety arises from our repression of the Germanic, nationalistic roots of what we reflexively—and, if pressed, angrily—proclaim to be our "universal" musical values. "As Italy has its Naples, France its revolution, England its Navy, etc., so the Germans have their Beethoven symphonies," wrote Schumann in 1839, as both modern concert life and German nation building were getting under way. "With Beethoven," he continued, a German "imagines that he has reversed the fortunes of the battles that he lost to Napoleon."

In fact, with its music, the German nation turned the tables on those awful, artificially "Enlightened" French and accomplished on the cultural plane a more sweeping, more effective conquest than Napoleon ever dreamed of. As historians of German nationalism have observed, Beethoven provided the Germans with the supreme expression of their greatness as a people— and their superiority to the Latins and the Slavs.

In the twentieth century, perhaps needless to say, the German chauvinism at the heart of the Beethoven myth is no longer tolerable. And so the myth has been cleansed, made "transcendent" and "universal." Other countries are "national," the history books tell us. Other composers are "nationalists." They represent this or that. The German masters alone are universal individuals (myths license oxymorons) and represent us all. It is on this mythology that classical music has rested its claim, despite all the inescapable evidence to the contrary, that it alone among musics, and Beethoven's music preeminently, represents not this, not that, but all the transcendent, unnamable human universals.

A myth so hedged around with protective submyths is no longer a safe haven. Its security must be incessantly patrolled and defended. The results have been sanctimony and double standards. Desperate dependency on the father figure has made the repertory hopelessly anachronistic, and denial may forever preclude perestroika. But Big Lenny could not save the Soviets. Will Big Louie save the classics?

POSTSCRIPT, 2008

Some of my best friends winced at this one, although I am happy to say that most of the wincers eventually came around. As one of them warmed my heart quite recently by admitting, the piece "wasn't really against Beethoven after all, as much as against the context in which he was being canonized and recycled," and the sore points it raises are not indictments of Beethoven's putative transgressions but rather concern "the ethical issues that performance raises"—as well, I'll add, as interpretation.

There is still a need for this piece and more like it, as I hope at least some Beethoven lovers will agree. I drafted this postscript during the very week in October 2005 when a new popular biography of Beethoven appeared by Edmund Morris, the same author who fictionalized himself in a desperate measure to give some life to *Dutch,* his biography of Ronald Reagan. Its title: *Beethoven: The Universal Composer.* Still going. If classical music has an Energizer Bunny, here he is.

And there is an even greater need now for forums where dissident voices can be raised, since the *Times* is no longer hospitable to such contentiousness as Jim Oestreich was allowed, ten years ago, to solicit from me. The 2004–5 concert season witnessed another periodic bout of frantic Beethoven fever, but this time the *Times* heralded it with a puff by a cub reporter (or "news assistant," as the *Times* describes her), consisting of interviews with arts executives, publicists, and concertgoers, all chirping on cue. "With no birth or death commemoration of Beethoven in the offing," the cub kicked things off by asking, "why so much Beethoven now?"

> "What a great question," said the pianist Wu Han, who serves as co-artistic director of the [Lincoln Center] Chamber Music Society with her husband, David Finckel, the cellist of the Emerson String Quartet. "I think what every musician probably thinks: he is the center of gravity of all music. He really can speak the most profound thoughts and also the most earthy feelings, all in the same breath. That's why his music is so incredibly inspiring for all of us."
>
> Mr. Finckel interjected: "In times of need, on great occasions when people have looked for something in art of a suitable magnitude to dignify or commemorate an occasion, the music of Beethoven is turned to over and over again. I think it's a feeling of universality."[1]

And so it went. It was perfectly understandable that music marketers would spin retrenchment as adventure, but it was painful to see the *Times* playing along.

Universalism: that is the intellectual realm abutting utopianism and ethnocentrism. "There are universal values, and they happen to be mine," was Stanley Hoffman's delightful definition of the latter.[2] Like utopianism and ethnocentrism, universalism normalizes, excludes, and shouts down. If "universal" does not mean universally accepted, then it means nothing. Those who do not accept must therefore at least be marginalized, and if possible stigmatized. In American politics, the stigma is called "special interests." That is how rich white male lawmakers refer to those who are not rich, not white, or not male when their own special interests are exposed, and it would be mere comical hypocrisy were it not such a handy weapon for discrediting legislation on behalf of the civil or economic rights of minorities, of women, of labor, or of the indigent.

The stakes are lower in the arts, perhaps, but just as necessary to expose, if only because the tactic has turned so unfailingly counterproductive. The operative term in music used to be *classicism.* Here is how Paul Henry Lang, author of *Music in Western Civilization,* the most influential music history textbook of the mid-twentieth century, defined classicism half a century ago:

> By the end of the eighteenth century we no longer speak of German music, for this music became the musical language of the world, as in the two previous supreme syntheses the musical language of the Franco-Flemish and later of the Neapolitans became the language of the world [in sixteenth-century church music and eighteenth-century opera, respectively]. For in the symphonies of Haydn, as in the works of Mozart and of the other masters of the era, there speaks a musicianship that is universal, timeless, and valid under all circumstances. This music is not one solution or one aspect, nor is it a personal matter; it speaks to all peoples.[3]

This sort of thing doesn't wash so well anymore. Ruling out personal decision in favor of an obligatory consensus is a move that nowadays advertises its political character much more obviously than in Lang's day. Indeed, the contradiction in Lang's argument is apt to leap out at readers by now: if the Franco-Flemish and Neapolitan "syntheses" did not ultimately prove to be "universal, timeless, and valid under all circumstances," why should we expect the German one to do so? Nobody believes any longer that it does. To maintain it as a battle cry, like many who responded to my challenge in the *Times*, only means excluding greater and greater majorities from the ranks of those recognized as viable humans while the "universal" comes to represent an ever-shrinking, ever more laughably isolated coterie.

Readers wrote in to inform me that Beethoven was not German—or rather, not merely German—and that to refer to his nationality was demeaning. One such protester affected agreement about the "myth that only German music is 'universal,'" adding that "no one cherishes it except for a few who yearn for the Hapsburgs." And yet, he went on:

> It is not surprising that we never refer to a concert of "German music," as we might of Russian or English music. From the time of Haydn to that of Schoenberg at least, Germany and Austria have been at the center of classical music, and the English and Russians have been mostly peripheral, for the simple reason that the Germans wrote vastly *more* excellent music than did the others. This is easily demonstrable, I think: all you do is count.

Bruce Adolphe, a composer, wrote to the *Times* to feign commiseration with me. "Your bitter cynicism has deafened you to the true meaning of art," he mourned, and imparted another simple truth: "Music brings us past nationalism, past politics, past words to a universal mystery. This is why we need music, and why we will always need Beethoven."

Paul Griffiths, then writing for the *New Yorker,* greeted the new season at which I was scoffing by feigning admission that "with our greater knowledge of the diverse accomplishments of human societies, we're bound to see Beethoven's much vaunted universality as, to say the least, tempered by particular conditions of time and place." But anyone who wasn't reading Griffiths for the first time knew that a "nevertheless" was coming, and what followed it was a cunning update of Lang:

> The success with which Beethoven's music has communicated itself—even in cultures that, like those of modern Japan or Korea, have few points of correspondence with the culture of imperial Vienna—might suggest that his language is, if not a fact of musical nature, certainly something that can be learned, and that people want to learn.
>
> The other day, browsing through some compact disks that had come into the office, I happened to move straight from a recording of Cambodian court music (a circulating melody on an oboelike instrument, heard through

patterns of xylophones and percussion) to one of Robert Taub playing Beethoven's Opus 78 sonata. Nothing could have pointed up more swiftly what distinguishes Beethoven and, by extension, the Western tradition that his music helped form: in a word, transparency. You hear what's going on. Musical events are items in dialogues of response and courses of change. Thought is in motion. Though we might be reluctant to conclude that what we're hearing is Beethoven's thought, since the mercurial process that presents itself to us is so far from the laborious process by which we know Beethoven habitually made his pieces, still something here is speaking to us—and by its speech, creating the curved time through which that speech is possible, creating the high, erratic instability of development passages, the settled relaxation of reprises. Something is engendering and then operating within a world utterly unlike that of the evenly unfolding Cambodian music.

It remains possible that to a Cambodian the music of the court ensemble of Phnom Penh might be as lucid as Beethoven is (I like to think) to me. But we are at liberty to doubt this. For one thing, Beethoven's music has stimulated a library of explications, commentaries, and analyses for which there is no parallel in any non-Western, nonclassical musical form. For another, the richness and depth of relationships in Beethoven seems to be dependent on a device that has been taken much further in Western music than in any other: notation. And for a third, Beethoven could refer—again because of notation—to a tradition going back a century, to Bach and Handel, and could, by such references, refine and particularize his musical speech.[4]

A little farther down, Griffiths proposed that "to the extent that belief in the possibility of progress has become universal, so has Beethoven's music."

There was the nexus of utopianism and universalism plain, and the rest seems, in its self-congratulation, as if composed for no other purpose than to demonstrate Hoffman's version of ethnocentrism. The suggestion that the existence of a vast library of exegesis was evidence of transparency and lucidity might have been a witty sally, but Griffiths seemed to mean it. To tout Beethoven's century-long tradition in the face of the much longer tradition that lies behind all unwritten music (and especially court music like Cambodia's) is to vie with Beethoven in deafness. And to speak of lucidity except in relation to a particular receiving mind (while declaring one's liberty to doubt, in similarly absolutist terms, the lucidity of something else in relation to a purely hypothetical receiver)—well, what is that but to make oneself the measure of all things?

That sort of casual—yes, transparent—partiality is perhaps even more typically a sin of gender than of nation in today's Western world, and feminist critics have been conspicuously on Beethoven's case at least since Susan McClary heard a rapist's rage in the stormy first-movement recapitulation in the Ninth. McClary reconsidered the specificity of her charge when revising that notorious passage, originally published in the tiny *Minnesota Composers Forum Newsletter*, for reprinting in *Feminine Endings*, her very influential book of essays. The second time around she spoke, more broadly (and even admiringly), of the "juxtaposition of desire and unspeakable violence in this moment that creates its unparalleled fusion of murderous rage and yet a kind of pleasure in its fulfillment of formal demands."[5] That has not prevented angry men from wreaking ever more generalized vengeance on the original phrase for nearly two decades now, and using McClary as a touchstone of guilt by association to condemn all heretics. She and I have been often linked in infamy, sometimes by altogether admirable musicians like Robert Silverman, the Canadian pianist, who denies me the cover of anonymity he proffers my partner in crime: "One well-known scholar has accused Beethoven's music of representing rape, while Richard Taruskin wrote in the *New York Times* that the music establishment uses Beethoven as an icon to hold new musical ideas at bay, much as the Russian Communists transformed the revolutionary spirit of Marx and Lenin into one of the severest forms of reaction we have known in our lifetimes."[6]

Except for the implicit endorsement of Marx and Lenin, this is accurate enough, and Silverman is also discerning enough to notice that my complaints are directed not at Beethoven but at his exploiters. But whether or not one agrees with McClary's hearing of Beethoven, her response weighs heavily against the assumption of Beethoven's universality. Clearly, there exist some, perhaps a whole class of people, who do not identify with the messages they read in Beethoven's music. It is precisely here, of course, that the political agenda of those who claim to be "past politics" swings into action. Consider the peroration to the entry on Beethoven in a *Reader's Guide to Music* that I was asked to evaluate for a publisher in February 1996, at the height of the Beethoven season I had greeted five months earlier:

> That Beethoven's image will survive as the acme of Western art music is proved rather than disproved by late twentieth-century feminist attacks on his work. Adrienne Rich has complained of his "controlling power," and one critic notoriously compared the first-movement climax of the Ninth Symphony to the "murderous rage of a rapist incapable of attaining release." Such tendentiousness, while suggesting both that there is something unparalleled in that crescendo and that women cannot identify with climaxes, will nonetheless keep listeners focused on Beethoven's musical "meaning" as long as there survive orchestras to perform his music.

The inability of women to identify with him will not deter "listeners." Who are these listeners? Recall W. H. Auden's legendary blurt, which haunted his obituaries: "Why don't these women leave? Can't they see that people are talking?"

So that is why I sought the opportunity to deplore the myth of Beethoven's universality. There are two ironic footnotes to append. First: about the only friendly response this piece elicited (besides a nice letter to the *Times* from the veteran Chicago critic Robert C. Marsh) came from Germany. It appeared more than six years later in *Der Spiegel,* the German news magazine, at the end of a screed titled "Der göttliche Gassenhauer" (The Divine Alley Tune) by its culture editor Klaus Umbach, the author of two muckraking books about the music industry, one a biography of the Romanian-born conductor Sergiu Celibidache and the other an exposé called *Geldschein-Sonate* (Banknote Sonata). The banner gives the flavor: "Beethoven's Ninth Symphony, the traditional edifying New Year's hit, is to be ranked by UNESCO among the treasures of the 'World's Memory.' The piece, which many musicians revile as a 'hideous mess,' has served Hitler and Communists alike as hymn." Among the illustrations is a diptych of Hitler and Furtwängler over the caption, "Two Ninth Fans." The tirade begins with mockery of the yearly Japanese Ninth rites, surely the most obviously ritualized and sacralized use to which classical music is now put; it continues with derision at Deutsche Grammophon Gesellschaft's slick marketing of Bernstein's bestselling "Freiheit" Ninth, each CD accompanied by a little sliver of the Berlin Wall as a bonus; and it concludes with my remarks about the guitar-strumming kids in jeans atop the wall.

"Only they symbolized Freiheit," the German pundit slightly misquoted me as saying. "Beethoven, to the contrary, says the American observer, stands only for 'canned greatness' [*konservierte Grösse,* the closest he could come to 'packaged'], with all that that brings with it in self-satisfaction, dullness and ritual. Just what the revolutions of '89 condemned.' Just what the Ninth has long so darkly hinted."[7] Umbach's piece vastly outstripped my own in vulgarity—the author seems to be the continental equivalent of Norman Lebrecht—and targeted the Ninth for "unmasking" in a fashion I'd never countenance.[8] Still, it was nice to see that some Germans have become as fed up as I with the pretense of German universalism, and with the conviction that classical music is its chief embodiment.

But, second and finally: Prof. Thomas Christensen of the University of Chicago, who really was an observer at the scene that night in 1989 (rather than a TV onlooker like me), reports that among the tunes the guitars were strumming was . . . yes, you guessed it, the "Ode to Joy" theme from the Ninth. Yet consider: is this really a counterexample? Those playing the Ninth atop the wall had gleaned it from the oral tradition, not the literate one that vouchsafes, for Paul Griffiths, the superiority of Western art music over all others and underwrites its appeal to cultural social climbers. For the guitar-strumming crowd, as for countless others, the Ode to Joy is folk music; that is exactly what Herr Umbach meant when he called it *der göttliche Gassenhauer.* That status was its ticket out of the complacent, dull, and ritualized world the New York concert establishment was calling on Beethoven to sanctify yet again, and into the renewed possibility of spontaneous musical response to lived experience. That still did not make it universal. But it did make it newly meaningful.

NOTES

1. Kathryn Shattuck, "Still Immortal, Still Beloved, Still Heard Everywhere," *New York Times*, 30 January 2005.

2. "Us and Them," *New Republic*, 12 July 1993, 32.

3. "Music and History" (1952), in P. H. Lang, *Musicology and Performance*, ed. Alfred Mann and George Buelow (New Haven: Yale University Press, 1997), 38.

4. "Now Beethoven," *New Yorker*, 16 December 1995, 101–2.

5. Susan McClary, *Feminine Endings* (Minneapolis: University of Minnesota Press, 1991), 128.

6. Robert Silverman, "On Beethoven," www.robert-silverman.com/pages/beethoven.html.

7. Klaus Umbach, "Der göttliche Gassenhauer," *Spiegel*, 29 December 2001, 166.

8. See "Resisting the Ninth," in Richard Taruskin, *Text and Act* (New York: Oxford University Press, 1995), 235–62.

12

Dispelling the Contagious Wagnerian Mist

It had to happen. As surely as the irresistible force had to meet the immovable object, as surely as Frankenstein had to meet the Wolfman, Roger Norrington and his London Classical Players had to confront Richard Wagner, the fountainhead of everything against which Mr. Norrington and all of early music have been in constant zealous revolt. The resulting CD (EMI Classics 5 55479 2), which contains the *Rienzi* Overture, the Prelude to act 3 of *Lohengrin,* the Prelude and "Liebestod" from *Tristan und Isolde,* the *Meistersinger* Prelude, the *Siegfried Idyll,* and the *Parsifal* Prelude, is one of the most fascinating recordings of the year just past, and one of the most important. Which is not necessarily to imply that the performances it preserves are any good.

Wagner, the paragon of the "elastic beat" (as he called it himself), the bottomless Adagio, the vertiginous climacteric? Wagner, the hypnotist, the narcotizer, the theologian of lust, the snuffer of Enlightenment, the reactivator of pagan myths and striker (according to a Bavarian fan) of "the fundamental chord of German being"? The very least one could say about Wagner is that he was the un-Classical incarnate.

Till now, that is. Like his Beethoven and his Berlioz, his Weber and his Verdi, Mr. Norrington's Wagner turns out to have been a crypto-classicist all along. Like the others (and like everyone else Mr. Norrington's baton has touched), Wagner secretly liked his music to sound light, fleet, and steady. Did he not himself complain, in his treatise on conducting, that other conductors took his pieces too slowly? And for the past hundred years have they not been getting slower?

Like Mozart, or like Stravinsky, Wagner cast virtually all of his music in dance or march rhythms, Mr. Norrington contends, elaborately though the composer may have disguised them. (The *Tristan* Prelude? A slow waltz, of course, just like "Un di felice" from Verdi's *Traviata.*) The best performance, Mr. Norrington implies, will be the one that ferrets out that underlying pulse and makes it palpable.

These are all novel, interesting ideas. The question, as usual, is how much they have to do with what Wagner (or his audience) wanted then and how much they have to do with what Mr. Norrington (and we, his audience) may want now. It comes as no surprise that the second possibility is much more plausible, and much more readily supported, than the first.

That is an old story by now, and it is high time Mr. Norrington and other "historical" performers dropped the historical pretense. The "classical" Wagner Mr. Norrington purveys is a Wagner adapted to a certain brand of modern taste. The appeal to history and the composer's intentions is just a way of claiming privilege. Mr. Norrington himself turns out to be the best witness against his own historical claims. "Ever since I first heard the later operas," he declares, "I have been gripped by a desire to treat Wagner as if it were music and not some unique mystic substance that could only be perceived through a very slowly swirling mist." That desire preceded and guided whatever historical research Mr. Norrington has done, and it is a very modern desire—the quintessential modernist desire, in fact, as José Ortega y Gasset noted seventy years ago in his great essay "The Dehumanization of Art."

Ortega's somewhat scary title actually refers to nothing more than the modernist wish to strip away the illusion that art represents or embodies the attributes of human beings. Instead, Ortega insisted, we should prefer to see art for what it really is: pure artifice, the diverting product of consummate skill deployed for no other purpose than play. And play—delight in pattern, in finding solutions to self-imposed problems and arbitrary constraints, in doing things for the sake of the doing and making things for the sake of the making: play is the highest human calling. It is that precisely because it is the one farthest removed from biological necessities, and because it calls forth the purest exercise of reason, the faculty that sets humans apart from other life-forms. As Ortega famously put it, "Art must not proceed by psychic contagion, for psychic contagion is an unconscious phenomenon, and art ought to be full clarity, high noon of the intellect."

There has never been an artist more wholly identified with psychic contagion and all its dark perils than Wagner. Resistance to Wagner, which has always accompanied devotion to him (even within a single, divided mind, as many of us can testify), is founded on perception of that threat. These are the real stakes behind Mr. Norrington's opposition of music to Wagner's "mystic substance" and "swirling mist." His performances, far from a historical restoration, are the exact opposite: an exorcism. And therefore, as a cultural statement, they are at least a thousand times as significant as any historical restoration could be.

Nevertheless, Mr. Norrington cites Wagner's writings wherever he can in support of his approach, and in one case his efforts to hide his exorcism behind a screen of fidelity have ruined his rendition. That one case is the *Meistersinger* Prelude, the one composition for which we have Wagner's detailed description of his own performances. He conducted the opening section, marked "Sehr mässig bewegt" (Moving very moderately), in four broad beats to the bar, he tells us, and that broad four is to be regarded as the "Hauptzeitmass"—the main tempo—of the prelude. But he also tells us that he managed to bring in the whole piece in just over eight minutes. Always attracted by speediness, Mr. Norrington takes the eight-minute boast as a challenge and resolves the contradiction between the stipulated tempo and the stipulated duration by deliberately misreading Wagner's text. He applies the composer's description of the basic meter in its fastest modification, some ninety measures into the piece, to the opening theme with ludicrous results. The pompous march turns into a panting canter. The "vigorous quarter notes" Wagner describes go by too fast to be felt as beats. The often highly detailed rhythmic surface of the music becomes a finicky muddle, and the four horns, three trumpets, three trombones, and tuba in Wagner's orchestra (for all that they are mellow "period" models with narrow bores) sound like so many pachyderms in joyless lockstep.

It is altogether possible that Wagner did conduct the *Meistersinger* Prelude to his own satisfaction in eight minutes; but if so, he must have found a relationship among its various tempos that has so far eluded Mr. Norrington. The conductor's downfall, in his ill-considered race with the composer, was the sin of prideful pedantry—but how delicious! As lovers of *Die Meistersinger* will note with relish, it's Beckmesser's revenge.

Fortunately, Wagner did not specify the durations of the other pieces here, or describe his performances. Mr. Norrington, therefore, is free to rely on selectively marshaled "contemporary information and playing style," and on what he frankly calls his "instinct." Basically, this means following the old canard—how often must it be disproved?—that nineteenth-century musicians did not use vibrato. And it means applying a bit of proudly advertised string portamento (sliding pitch), which amounts, maybe, to one one-hundredth of what Wagner would have considered normal, and therefore unremarkable to the ear.

Such effects are flimsy selling ploys. Relying on instinct is much the better policy. But of course no one is born with Wagnerian instincts. When musicians speak of instinct, they mean prejudice. And when Mr. Norrington's anti-Wagnerian prejudices lead him into direct collision with the composer's presumable intentions, things get interesting. *Tristan*, the ultimate bearer of psychic contagion, is the inevitable touchstone.

Once again, Mr. Norrington's prejudices are demonstrably those of a modernist. His performance is fascinatingly of a piece with a curious little article by Ira Braus, a music theorist of similar modernist bent, that recently appeared, sporting a contentious question for a title: "Why Doesn't Anyone Play Bars 1–11 of *Tristan* in Tempo?" Answers would seem to come readily enough. How about because the score is marked "Slowly and languishingly" *(Langsam und schmachtend)?* Or because the whole thrust of Wagner's remarks on conducting had to do with achieving a sufficiently nuanced and flexible execution? Or because the interrupted cadences, and the silences between them, give tangible form to the "yearning, yearning, unquenchable, ever-regenerated longing—languishing, thirsting" of which the whole story of the opera, according to Wagner's famous program note, is a metaphor? Mr. Braus, however, sweeps all of that away. Unless the piece is played in strict tempo, he asserts, its structure is obscured. That structure is something wholly independent of all the contingencies that are usually—and irrelevantly—brought to bear on the act of performing it.

Mr. Braus's ideas about structure are peculiar (though familiar enough in the academy), and I would hardly expect Mr. Norrington to share them. But two aspects of Mr. Braus's discussion illuminate Mr. Norrington's project very effectively. One is its profoundly ahistorical, even antihistorical stance. As a structure, the prelude is absolutely autonomous: independent of its maker's intent, of the story it introduces, of all metaphor. All of that amounts to no more than the historical circumstances of its origin, long since left behind. For all Mr. Norrington's talk of historical practice, his performance, which comes close to realizing Mr. Braus's prescription, is similarly focused on the autonomous structure. That is the music, as he puts it, as opposed to the contingencies—the "swirling mist"—through which we are usually (but no longer!) forced to perceive it.

The other pertinent premise is the "factual" nature of the structure as both Mr. Braus and Mr. Norrington reveal it. Through rigorously "objective" formal analysis like Mr. Braus's—or "objective," minimally nuanced execution like Mr. Norrington's—the music is revealed in a fashion that is objectively verifiable by reference to the score, and therefore accessible to all. That kind of universality was the Enlightened ideal: Kant's *sensus communis* (common sense) in its original, most radical formulation. It is a democratic ideal and a socially uniting one. It requires no inspiration, no special gifts.

By contrast, the insights of romantic genius, the interpretations of a Maestro conductor, or the "readings" of a master critic deny the commonness, or "in-commonness," of sense. They foster social difference, distinction between the elect and the mass. Wagner was a great fetishizer of such value-laden divisions: between the inspired Walthers and the pedantic Beckmessers, between holy German art and Gallic artifice, between honest Gentile and rootless Jew. Mr. Norrington's attempt to "classicize" and rationalize him—in short, to render him accessible to common sense—all at once assumes the character of a trenchant social and political critique.

That critique takes place through what is surely the most metrically exact performance the Prelude and "Liebestod" have ever received. The first eleven bars, to apply the Braus test, are not entirely "in tempo," but all pauses and hesitations are coordinated precisely in terms of that "slow waltz" beat. You can hear it ticking away: one extra waltz measure between the first and second phrases, two between the third and fourth. There is, in short, nothing "irrational" about the pauses. We can all beat time along with the conductor, even during the silences. Thereafter, Mr. Norrington keeps things moving briskly in flagrant violation of Wagner's expressly marked ritenutos and rallentandos. So much for the composer's intentions. Mr. Norrington is after bigger game. And so much for poor Jane Eaglen, the soprano who, as Isolde, gets to express nothing but what is there on the page, accessible to all. No erotic rapture, no goose bumps, no psychic contagion, just a forced march to premature Transfiguration that in its speed and regularity greatly cheapens the music by calling unwanted attention to its glaring overreliance on melodic sequences.

It is all high noon of the intellect and sharp commentary—as un-Wagnerian as could be, but a blazing manifesto of the twentieth century's drastic rejection of swirling mists and Germanic inwardness. No Wagner lover will ever listen to Mr. Norrington's magnificent subversion for pleasure. The pleasure is for the Wagner hater who lurks within each of us, Wagner lovers included. The dread Teutonic forest beast is at last defanged. The Enlightenment strikes back. This disc belongs in every home.

13

How Talented Composers
Become Useless

The nice thing about an ism, someone once observed, is how quickly it becomes a wasm. Some musical wasms—academic-wasm, for example, and its dependent varieties of modern-wasm and serial-wasm—continue to linger on artificial life support, though, and continue to threaten the increasingly fragile classical ecosystem. A pair of new Albany CDs of music by Donald Martino, now the Walter Bigelow Rosen Professor of Music Emeritus at Harvard, have recently come my way like a gust of musty air. They prompt me to throw open a window on the miseducation of musicians in America.

One disc, consisting entirely of piano music, is especially dispiriting, precisely because the performances, by David Holtzman, are so superfluously good. The other contains two reissues of Nonesuch LPs (*Notturno,* Mr. Martino's best-known piece, recorded in 1974, and Triple Concerto for three clarinets and chamber ensemble, recorded in 1978). There is also a brilliant performance by Mr. Holtzman of *Pianississimo,* a virtuoso piano sonata composed in 1970 and hailed in its time by Andrew Porter as "a peak of 20th-century piano music." That such a critic could say such a thing of such a work is indeed a sign of times gone by, but there is still something that needs saying about this music.

Once, a long time ago, in a famous article that ever since has served as a bible of academic arrogance, Milton Babbitt tried to laugh the audience's claims on twentieth- century music right out of court. "Imagine a layman chancing upon a lecture on 'Pointwise Periodic Homeomorphisms,'" he wrote. "At the conclusion, he announces, 'I didn't like it.'"

Leaving the snobbery to one side, the analogy did make a philosophical point worth pondering. By comparing "serious" or "original" contemporary

music to mathematics (and appropriating concepts like seriousness and originality to one kind of music was where the arrogance lay), Mr. Babbitt was saying, in effect, that such music was to be valued and judged not for the pleasure it gave but for the truth it contained. Truth, in music as in math, lay in
accountability to basic principles of relatedness. In the case of math, these
were axioms and theorems: basic truth assumptions and the proofs they enabled. In the case of music, truth lay in the relationship of all its details to a
basic axiomatic premise called the twelve-tone row.

Again, Mr. Babbitt's implied contempt and his claims of exclusivity
apart, the point could be viewed as valid. Why not allow that there could
be the musical equivalent of an audience of math professors? It was a harmless enough concept in itself—although when the math professors went on
to claim funds and resources that would otherwise go to the maintenance
of the "lay" repertory, it was clear that the concept did not really exist "in
itself"; it inescapably impinged on social and economic concerns. Yet calling his work the equivalent of a math lecture did at least make the composer's intentions and expectations clear. You could take them or leave
them. Honestly asserted, they had a certain authenticity, and so did the
music.

But now imagine that one engaged Claire Bloom to read "Pointwise Periodic Homeomorphisms" with all the expressive resources of voice and gesture she would bring to the role of Ophelia or Desdemona. Her performance
would add nothing to the paper so far as the math professors were concerned. The "layman" would find something to admire in the beauty of her
rendition (as anyone listening to Mr. Holtzman's performances of Mr. Martino's compositions on these Albany CDs will surely admire his sterling qualities of touch, timing, and tone). And yet the lack of connection between the
content of the utterance and the manner of its delivery would be a constant
irritant both for the professors and for the layman. Both would find the performance somehow silly and gratuitous, though their reasons would vary, and
though they might both be reluctant to say so. The incongruity would be
equally manifest, moreover, whether Ms. Bloom read the paper in the semi-
nar room or on the Stratford stage.

That is the problem with Mr. Martino's piano music, which strives for conventional expressivity while trying to maintain all the privileged and prestigious truth claims of academic modernism. Because there is no structural
connection between the expressive gestures and the twelve-tone harmonic
language, the gestures are not supported by the musical content (the way
they are in Schumann, for example, whose music Mr. Martino professes to
admire and emulate). And while the persistent academic claim is that music
like Mr. Martino's is too complex and advanced for lay listeners to comprehend, in fact the expressive gestures, unsupported by the music's syntax or
semantics, are primitive and simplistic in the extreme.

Insofar as he seeks to be expressive, the composer is forced to do without language altogether. Where Schumann could make his most telling expressive points by means of subtle gradations of harmony, Mr. Martino can be expressive only in essentially inarticulate ways, the way one might communicate one's grossest needs and moods through grunts and body language. Huge contrasts in loudness and register, being the only means available, are constant. The combination of gross expressive gestures for the layman and arcane pitch relationships for the math professors is a perpetual contradiction. It fatally undermines the esthetic integrity of the music.

The only harmonic support the composer can give the expressive surface is the occasional (and by now, old and tired) device of finagling some intermittent consonant harmony out of his serial procedures. Composers who do this call it "tonal implication" or "tonal reference," but it is really nothing of the kind, because tonality is a syntax, not just a vocabulary. Invoking consonance is just another gross distinction, another primitive and largely meaningless gesture.

These may be harsh judgments, but they are necessary ones. Academic composers still maintain a smug front. In a sixtieth-birthday interview Mr. Martino was still blaming everyone but himself for the lack of headway his music had made, despite all his prizes and plum academic posts. He was still heaping Babbittian scorn on "laymen," lobbying, as he put it, for a "potty-trained audience" and contending that "what we need are concert hall bouncers." And, of course, he was still simultaneously bragging that audiences disliked *Notturno*, his Pulitzer Prize–winning sextet, and whining that his works were not more regularly performed before such audiences.

The reason it is still necessary to expose these hypocrisies, even after the vaunted "postmodern" demise of serialism, is that the old-fashioned modernist position still thrives in its old bastion, the academy. Composers like Mr. Martino are still miseducating their pupils just as he was miseducated himself, dooming them to uselessness. Critics and "theorists," many of them similarly miseducated, are still propagandizing for Pointwise Periodic Homeomorphisms in the concert hall, offering their blandishments as consolation for the loss of a musical language and decrying the attempts of younger composers to find a new one. Excellent performers like Mr. Holtzman, whose recordings of Stefan Wolpe show that his talents can be put to much better use, are still content to seek cozy academic approbation instead of seeking to establish a viable role for new music in the public sphere.

It is not reinforcement in their contempt of audiences, or protection from them, that young composers and performers need, but encouragement in the risky business of establishing a new symbiosis with them. Mr. Martino and his music set an entirely negative example. The only constructive purpose the circulation of these records could serve today would be a cautionary one.

POSTSCRIPT, 2008

Some faces launch a thousand ships; this piece launched a million words, from angry letters to wild postings to refereed journal articles to whole books. The book—*The Pleasure of Modernist Music,* edited by Arved Ashby (Rochester: University of Rochester Press, 2004)—takes as its epigraph my opening sentence (about isms and wasms, echoing a witticism encountered by happy chance in an ancient *Saturday Review* piece by Irving Kolodin) and, in its editor's words, seeks "a principled middle ground between two standard polemical positions about modernist music: the one attacking it as elitist, overly intellectual, and often incomprehensible; the other defending it as a music-evolutionary stage deemed 'necessary' but also beyond the reach of words."

The assumption, made explicit by William Bolcom in a contribution to the book that originated as a letter to the *Times,* was that the latter position had provoked the former, at least in academic critics like me. "Taruskin's screed," he wrote, "against what is now anything but a current musical style—so many years after its hegemony—must come from a long-pent-up anger at what was, in its time, an almost fascistic doctrine of historical inevitability adopted by some serialists." At least Bolcom conceded there was once such a hegemony (and backed the point up anecdotally). Others tried to deny it. But the infuriated response to my piece from strong adherents to the style Bolcom wrote off prematurely as passé, convinced as ever of its—and their—historical rights (a short alphabetical list of the better known: Ross Bauer, Martin Brody, Eric Chasalow, Bruce Hobson, Jeff Nichols, Joshua Rifkin, Walter Winslow, Charles Wuorinen, Rolv Yttrehus), belied Bolcom's main premise. His minor premise, that "the music of Donald Martino is proof that a strict twelve-tone composer can still make sensuous and passionate music," was beside the point, because I did not deny it. What I did claim was that such attempts at traditional expressivity within a twelve-tone syntax were likely to be—and Martino's definitely were—crude (and the *Times* obliged with a cartoon, no doubt as infuriating as the article, that showed a long-hair pianist *en frac* performing before an audience of club-wielding cavemen).

For the rest, Ashby's volume is the usual assortment of special pleading, double standards, and invective, leavened by a novel strain of duplicity. That strain was the sudden claim that academic serial music had never differed in its aims or claims from any other kind of music, and was, all of it, conventionally beautiful, and that anyone's refusal or inability to recognize it as such was a form of persecution. This form of defense—of which Fred Everett Maus, a leader in male-feminist and gay/lesbian criticism, has been the pioneer—turns modernist studies into a variety of identity politics, or "victimology" as it is informally known. "Non-tonal compositions are queers in the concert hall,"

Maus reminds us, and if we find fault with them . . . well, the implied threat is plain enough, and odious: a new way of maintaining hegemony, now that the older scientistic defense, as Maus acknowledges, has "backfired."[1]

But this desperate defense is just another abuse of analogy, and it, too, backfires. As I pointed out in the article itself, the claim that the music was closed to nonprofessionals and was only to be evaluated by its practitioners had integrity. Its assertive truth claims were credible; its defensive claim of beauty is not. It was only when its apologists began claiming for academic serialism qualities that lay audiences complained of missing that allegations of bad faith became common, and I was far from the first to advance them. Edward Harsh, reviewing Andrew Mead's *An Introduction to the Music of Milton Babbitt,* took somewhat sardonic account of the author's frequent vague references to "the strong emotional and expressive charge" of Babbitt's music, its "great sensuous beauty," and its "lasting emotional drama" by observing:

> This recourse to the language of common practice aesthetics demonstrates just how much the ground has shifted in recent years beneath the feet of the postwar avant-garde. Challenges to the tenets of modernist thinking (among them the ideology of inevitable, linear artistic progress) have increased of late, and it is these very tenets that in the past have elevated the work of "research and development" composers such as Babbitt. Perhaps the erosion of the ideological foundation that provided unquestioned justification for this body of work has inspired a perceived need in some quarters to reassociate the work of these composers with certain aspects of the "classical music" tradition.
>
> Whatever the motivation, such a rehabilitation is unlikely to succeed in Babbitt's case. His music stubbornly is what it is, resisting any attempt (even a sympathetic one like Mead's) to graft onto it aesthetic qualities that its advocates have long rejected. The composer himself has produced a substantial body of prose arguing for his music's new and radical system of values. All this cannot simply be swept under the rug now that company is coming.[2]

Another sort of methodological abuse (surely it was not just naïveté) was summoned up by Joseph Straus in his retort to me, "The Myth of Serial 'Tyranny' in the 1950s and 1960s,"[3] an article that sought to disprove the myth with a simple census of all composers working during the two designated decades. Out of 448 "active American composers" surveyed, the author identifies only 66 (approx. 13.5%) as "serial" and 118 (approx. 23.5%) as "atonal." The majority was "tonal," and the smallest group was "experimental." These relative proportions held fairly steady through a number of other statistical breakdowns: composers teaching at "doctorate-granting universities," publications, performances and recordings, prizes won, press coverage. All of which proves, according to Straus, that tonal music was dominant throughout the period of alleged serial hegemony.

But Straus's statistics were both meaningless and deviously manipulated, reminiscent of Soviet apologists who loved to pretend that their Communist Party, with only 10 million members, could never dominate a country of 200 million. It is precisely the example of Soviet totalitarianism that demonstrates the power of an organized minority. Nobody has ever alleged that serial music dominated the commercial performance, broadcasting, and recording of classical music, and so to include these figures in the survey was merely a distraction, a classic red herring. Meanwhile, to look for evidence of serialist hegemony in the prizes awarded or teaching jobs obtained in the 1950s or even the 1960s was another disingenuous ploy. In order to measure the influence of serialists in those domains, one must survey the decades in which such composers were found among the senior generations (that is, the ones deciding who got the prizes and the jobs), and those decades were the 1970s and 1980s, when powerful figures like Milton Babbitt at Princeton and the music theorist Allen Forte at Yale placed their trainees everywhere, and when serialists and atonalists were indeed the disproportionate beneficiaries of emoluments. (Recall 1986, when Babbitt, Wuorinen, and George Perle—the last not a twelve-tone composer but often taken for one on account of his role in explicating serial techniques—were all awarded MacArthur Fellowships.)

Straus himself offered some methodological disclaimers, mainly involving the incompleteness of his figures, given the cursory nature of his research. These should already have alerted the editors of the *Musical Quarterly* that the piece was unfit for publication. But the most damning admission was inadvertent, and came early. "Statistics cannot tell the whole story," Straus allowed.

> For example, they cannot measure prestige. Certainly serialism in this period commanded an intellectual interest out of proportion to its actual measurable presence on the musical scene. Its outsized prestige derived from a number of factors, including its scientific aura, its association with the most recent European developments, and its simple novelty.[4]

Leaving "simple novelty" aside as a simple gaffe, these are precisely the factors that sociologists study, and music historians are beginning to catch on. To make a serious attempt to answer the questions Straus has set himself, one would need to consider the political structure of American universities and the academic turf wars of the day (here Babbitt's "Who Cares If You Listen?" to which my article made its veiled reference, was especially relevant), patterns of patronage (including the rise of foundations and an analysis of their boards of advisers), and the rhetoric of the cold war as it affected musicians in America and Europe, to name only three particularly obvious areas Straus overlooks. To ignore institutions and mediation and look only at the stylistic orientation and activities of composers is to perpetuate the "poietic fallacy" that has so blinkered the historiography of twentieth-century music. Straus's innocence of sociology is further attested by his willingness to substitute ill-considered inference for the sort of oral history the subject demands:

> Serial composers tended to be younger and were widely viewed as being on the cutting edge of musical fashion. Composers who wanted to identify themselves with a youthful avant-garde may have felt pressure to write serial music. *But such pressure would have been generated internally, not institutionally.* The dominant, senior academic composers, the ones who largely controlled hiring and firing and who admitted and taught the majority of composition students, were largely tonal in orientation throughout the period.[5]

Anyone who studied composition in an American academic institution in the 1960s will recall how the old cowered in those days before the young. The stratum to be watching, in those days, if one wanted to measure the progress of serial composition in the academy, was that of the untenured faculty, not the stratum Straus so unperceptively persisted in calling "dominant." But there is no need to continue this bill of indictment. I find it hard to believe that Straus's article, the work of an established scholar, could have been genuinely so incompetent. Rather, it was a blast of last-ditch propaganda, aimed in the first instance at wringing apologies from miscreants like me, whose writings, in light of Straus's highly selective statistics, "appear as false as they are offensive."[6]

Moving down to the level of postings and letters, there is one such that demands attention because of the journalistic reportage that it elicited. I received a private communication from Reinhold Brinkmann, a German musicologist at Harvard (thus a colleague of Donald Martino), who registered an impassioned protest at what he regarded as a damaging personal attack, reminiscent of the Nazi broadsides at Schoenberg that he remembered from his youth. I replied to him that it would indeed have been a heinous thing were Martino in a vulnerable position, as Schoenberg had been, but that the career of a Harvard professor emeritus in America is no longer in any jeopardy from the likes of me, and his reputation with the general public, being close to nonexistent, was not likely to suffer either from my airing of issues that transcended personalities. I do choose my targets with some discretion.

There would be neither reason nor justification for publicly paraphrasing either Brinkmann's private letter or my private response to it, except that Paul Mitchinson, a Canadian journalist writing in *Lingua franca,* the short-lived academic gossip mag, had already paraphrased Brinkmann's side, playing up the Nazi connection in particular.[7] That makes it both permissible and, I think, necessary to protest an attempt to convict me by association. The Nazis had every right to criticize Schoenberg, as do we all. It is not for their criticism that we all revile them. The confusion of criticism with censorship or worse is one of the paramount vices that chill the free exchange of ideas. It is nothing more than a crybaby tactic, and those who invoke it when their ox is the one being gored often learn to their cost that it can just as easily cut the other way.

NOTES

1. Fred Everett Maus, "Sexual and Musical Categories," in *The Pleasure of Modernist Music*, ed. Arved Ashby (Rochester: University of Rochester Press, 2004), 159, 170.

2. Edward Harsh, review of Andrew Mead, *An Introduction to the Music of Milton Babbitt* (Princeton: Princeton University Press, 1994), *Music Library Association Notes* 52 (1995–96): 788–89.

3. Joseph Straus, "The Myth of Serial 'Tyranny' in the 1950s and 1960s," *Musical Quarterly* 83 (1999): 301–43.

4. Ibid., 303.

5. Ibid., 310; italics added to underscore the most counterfactual assertion.

6. Ibid., 334; Straus's paper received a strong retort in its own venue from Anne C. Shreffler, who pointed out in conclusion that "the 'rightness' of the path [of serial music in the academy] was supported by the political, ideological, and cultural status of this music, which functioned independently of the beliefs of any individual composer" ("The Myth of Empirical Historiography: A Response to Joseph N. Straus," *Musical Quarterly* 84 [2000]: 30–39, at 36).

7. Paul Mitchinson, "Settling Scores," *Lingua franca* (July–August 2001): 40.

14

Making a Stand against Sterility

"Why did they do it?" Czeslaw Milosz wants to know. "What were they thinking?" In *The Year of the Hunter,* his recently published diary, the Nobel
Prize–winning poet finds occasion to bewail "the hideous music of the second half of the nineteenth century," and wonders why composers ever
abandoned "that heavenly sculpting in sound as in Bach, Haydn, Mozart,
and not only in them; lesser composers, too, partook of that beautiful style."

Don't we know it! All you have to do is switch on your FM radio to hear
heavenly sculpting in sound, wall-to-wall, round-the-clock, by every lesser
contemporary of Bach, Haydn, and Mozart you'll ever want to half-hear.
And how like a writer, one is tempted to think, especially a great writer, to
assume that meaning—serious "content"—is the exclusive preserve of his
medium and that music is there to provide a pleasant tinkle to accompany
fine food and drink, or keep you company in your car (where Mr. Milosz did
his musical musing).

But musicians, alas, seem not to disagree. There appears to be a concerted
effort afoot to turn the hideous music of the second half of the nineteenth
century, as far as possible, into heavenly sculpting in sound. Everybody, it
seems, is cleaning up. Roger Norrington is cleaning up Wagner. Pierre
Boulez is cleaning up Mahler. John Eliot Gardiner is cleaning up Brahms.
And in every case the conductors or their spokesmen have insisted that only
now are we getting the music right.

Well, it isn't so. And Bach, Haydn, and Mozart weren't all that squeaky
clean either. Bach's cantatas and Mozart's operas contain some pretty harrowing (yes, hideous) stuff that you won't hear on FM, and nobody ever

First published in the *New York Times,* 2 February 1997. Copyright © 2008 The New York Times
Company. Reprinted by permission.

created a more consummate musical Chaos than Haydn's, in *The Creation*. The cleanup crew has been driven by modern thinking very similar to Mr. Milosz's, albeit a variety of modern thinking that passes itself off as "early music."

How refreshing, then, to find a group of excellent musicians—"early" musicians, yet—who are making a stand against militant sterility. On a new BMG Classics CD called *Transfiguration* (Deutsche Harmonia Mundi 05472 77374 2), the Smithsonian Chamber Players, a string orchestra expertly conducted by the cellist (and sometime violist da gamba) Kenneth Slowik, have tried, in the conductor's words, to revive "an entire school of playing rooted in the 19th century, one which gradually disappeared between the two World Wars." Mr. Slowik quotes Willem Mengelberg, the legendary conductor of the Amsterdam Concertgebouw Orchestra, who observed that "faithfulness to the notes is a recent invention"—one that Mengelberg himself had witnessed to his ineffable dismay. ("Why did they do it?" he must have wondered. "What were they thinking?") Mr. Slowik also quotes Mengelberg's mentor, Gustav Mahler, the object of so much recent dusting off, who held passionately that "what is most important in music is not to be found in the printed notes." It is to be found richly documented in recordings, though; and Mengelberg's recordings of Mahler are for Mr. Slowik what treatises, tutors, and archival records have been to more conventional researcher-performers.

As proud of his findings as any successful researcher, Mr. Slowik puts his evidence right up front. He supplements his own performance of the slow movement from Mahler's Fifth Symphony (the famous Adagietto for strings and harp) with an excerpt from Mengelberg's 1926 Concertgebouw recording, plus another by Bruno Walter and the Vienna Philharmonic dating from early 1938 (right before Walter was hounded out of Austria), to show how radically performance styles were changing in those decades, even among Mahlerian adepts. Compared with Mengelberg, Walter is practically Roger Norrington.

To remove all doubt that the emphatic and expressive performance style he wants to resurrect was born of the "literary" impulse that literary people so detest in music, Mr. Slowik also reprints a few lines of incontestably hideous doggerel that Mengelberg inscribed in his conducting score for the Adagietto. The verses accord with what is known about the piece (a love offering from Mahler to Alma Schindler, his wife-to-be) and fit its opening melody "note-for-syllable," as Mr. Slowik writes. Their appearance in Mengelberg's score might seem to imply that they were imparted to the conductor by the composer. You can't get more authentic than that. They begin, "Wie ich dich liebe / Du meine Sonne" (How I do love thee, O thou my sun). At the start of the second line ("Du mei- . . ."), where the melody makes its first leap, Mengelberg's violinists do what Mahler would have expected any trained musician to do: they slide—slowly!—from note to note, producing what is known as a *portamento,* a "carrying of the voice," for it is indeed a technique that string players had learned from singers, who when singing smoothly do it by necessity. Now, of course, it would make any violin teacher see red and most listeners cringe. Play like that at your audition and starve, so completely has today's instrumental music making repressed its time-honored connection with singing. Not even the Smithsonian players dare the sort of uncoordinated slide (everyone at a different speed) that the Concertgebouw fiddlers produced as a matter of expressive course. To us it sounds sloppy, not expressive.

And so I would not necessarily insist on a better imitation. If all that a modern performer can come up with is a copy of an old record, then we are only dealing (as Bernard Sherman, a sharp observer of the early-music scene, likes to say) with a sedate version of Elvis impersonation. Mr. Slowik's performance is his performance, not Mengelberg's. But Mengelberg's example—portamento, "hairpin" dynamics, elastic beat, and all—has spurred him and his players into a rendition far more shapely and eloquent, and more imbued with personal initiative, than our complacent cleaner-uppers have dreamt of in their note-bound philosophy.

The same qualities distinguish the exhilarating Smithsonian performance of Arnold Schoenberg's early tone poem, *Verklärte Nacht* (Transfigured Night), from which the album takes its name. Once again, Mr. Slowik bites the literary bullet. He is not content merely to reprint the Richard Dehmel poem that inspired the music. He has even asked Richard Hoffmann, Schoenberg's former California secretary, to read aloud, in a Vienna-accented voice that sounds uncannily like Schoenberg's own, the composer's late English-language program note that relates the music to the poem in graphic—and by squeamish modern standards, embarrassing—detail. (It was first published on the back of an ancient Schoenberg-supervised Capitol LP with the Hollywood Quartet and "friends.") Even Schoenberg, by 1949, admitted—shades of Czeslaw Milosz—that Dehmel's poem was one that "many a person today might call repulsive," and that, if so, one was justified in approaching his score as "pure music." I suspect that it was the subject matter (a legitimately pregnant but unfaithful wife confessing her "guilt" to her lover) to which the composer was alluding. Today it would more likely be the poem's misogyny (a sinful modern Eve forgiven and redeemed by a godlike magnanimous man) that offends. And yet only a performance as sensitive as Mr. Slowik's to all the minutely shifting narrative connections that Schoenberg's program note sets forth (despite his disclaimer) can make the most of the composer's musical rhetoric and forestall the boredom that a too evenly paced, "purely musical," performance of this thinnish composition all too easily invites.

There is one major disappointment on this disc, though, and that is the performance of Mahler's 1898 string-orchestra arrangement of Beethoven's Quartet in F minor (Op. 95, the "Serioso"). What could be the purpose of unearthing this curiosity if not to perform it the way Mahler would have performed it? And what could be the purpose of performing it that way if not to hint (as I believe) that a Mahlerian performance of Beethoven is far more truly Beethovenian than a Boulezian or Norringtonian performance? There is lots of evidence to support the idea, including the unanimous reports of ear-witnesses that Beethoven was in his day a radical innovator when it came to *tempo rubato,* the elastic beat now wrongly attributed to the "hideous" Wagnerian influence. There is also plenty of evidence in the score itself: big melodic leaps that are slurred and even marked "espressivo," suggesting that Beethoven was counting on the portamento delivery so essential to Mahler and so anathema today. But you will hear next to nothing of that in Mr. Slowik's performance. A couple of pusillanimous little slides apart, it is just a bloated "modern" reading, not one that takes seriously Mahler's contention in arranging the piece that "performance by four players would absolutely no longer suffice" to convey the expressive content of such great music. Only a performance in the style of Mahler's own Adagietto would convey its content as he envisioned it, and I, for one, would be terribly curious to hear such a reading.

Of course it is the time traveler in me that feels that curiosity at this point, not the musician. The musician might or might not be convinced by such a performance—we won't know till we've tried it—but neither time traveler nor musician will gain much from this one. It suffers from that pernicious academic vice of our time that will brook no "mere" artistic speculation, even in matters of art. Without records to offer corroboration (and Beethoven, sadly, never landed a recording contract), no necks get stuck out. Pity. But anyone who feels, as I do, that our modern musical cleanliness is a long way from godliness will find the Mahler and Schoenberg performances on this disc encouraging. I hope that some performers will hear them and be inspired to go farther than Mr. Slowik has dared along the path that he has valuably marked out.

15

A Sturdy Musical Bridge to the Twenty-first Century

As our century nears an end, it seems a good bet that Steve Reich will turn out to be the oldest twentieth-century composer in whom twenty-first-century musicians will find a kindred spirit. This proposition can now be tested conveniently with the help of Nonesuch Records, which has commemorated the composer's sixtieth birthday with a big box of new and reissued recordings containing just about every composition on which Mr. Reich's reputation is based (79451–2; ten CDs). That such an item strikes a major classical label as marketable suggests that perhaps classical music is not coming to the dead end so many have predicted but rather undergoing a systemic evolution. And it is particularly fitting to honor Mr. Reich's achievement with recordings, because recordings are what made that achievement, and that evolution, possible.

To composers imbued with a nineteenth-century worldview, artistic traditions are transmitted "vertically." Nineteenth-century music historiography is an epic narrative of texts arranged in single file. It assumes that artists are primarily concerned—whether to emulate or to rebel—with the texts of their immediate precursors. These assumptions have led to an obsession with lines of stylistic influence, with stylistic pedigree, ultimately (and destructively) with stylistic purity or, worse, progress. This is the altogether anachronistic view most classical composers still imbibe in college or conservatory.

Mr. Reich went to college, at Cornell, but majored in philosophy. To him the main medium of musical transmission was not texts but recordings, and his view of the music surrounding him, accordingly, was "horizontal." The epiphany that made him a composer, he has said, came at the relatively advanced age of fourteen, when he heard in close succession recordings of Stravinsky's *Rite of Spring*, Bach's "Brandenburg" Concerto No. 5, and bebop. Someone trained to look at music in terms of vertical traditions would not have sought a common denominator here, nor would such a person, at least in 1950, have thought jazz, a largely unwritten music, commensurable with the others. But the common denominator leapt from the records to Mr. Reich's happily unprejudiced ear.

Stravinsky's "Russian" style, Bach's style, and bebop are all driven and regulated by what music theorists call a "subtactile pulse": a strongly articulated, rock-steady rhythmic unit that lies beneath the level of the "felt beat," or *tactus*, the beat that conductors show or that we normally walk or waltz or exercise to. (When the drill sergeant tells the squad to march "double time," he is telling it to march at the rate of the subtactile pulse.) Most "Western" music of the Germanic "common practice" period is strongly tactile, with at best a weakly articulated subtactile component. But much music of the rest of the world—Asian or African music; earlier, later, or more easterly European music; and, of course, American popular music—is intricately coordinated at the subtactile level, allowing overwhelming cumulative processes, or fascinating asymmetrical patterning, or viscerally compelling lurches to take place at the tactile surface. (Think of the "Danse Sacrale" from *The Rite,* or the harpsichord "cadenza" in "Brandenburg" No. 5.) Later Mr. Reich found more musics (always, at first, through recordings) that exhibited this "rhythmic profile," as he calls it: West African drumming, Indonesian gamelan, medieval organum and hocket. These provided the models for the ubiquitous chug-chug-chug without which Reich would not be Reich, against which the gradually unfolding or playfully shifting surface processes of his music are measured and become intelligible. The best early demonstration of its magic is *Four Organs* (1970), the first Reich piece to win a large audience, in which the systematically expanding phrases on the surface would be as uninterestingly arcane as most contemporary classical music, instead of riveting and elating, but for the maracas that sound out the subtactile pulse.

Eventually Mr. Reich went to Ghana and to Berkeley, California (where Balinese gamelans flourished), to gain hands-on experience and body involvement with the styles that now fascinated him. A few earlyish pieces sound a bit like imitations of "oriental" musics in the manner of Cage's prepared-piano works or Colin McPhee. But Mr. Reich's most characteristic pieces fuse everything into a unique personal idiom that arises out of the glorious assumption of an ecumenical heritage stored electronically, in which sounding music from every time and place is instantly available as part of a notional Here and Now to which we all have equal eclectic access.

At more technical levels, too, Mr. Reich's breakthroughs would have been unthinkable without recording technology. The earliest pieces that are recognizably Reichian are his "phase" pieces of the mid-sixties. The technique was a serendipity discovered when Mr. Reich played two copies of a single tape loop through different tape recorders into the two channels in a set of headphones. (They contained the phrase "It's Gonna Rain," drawn from a gospel sermon.) One loop began gaining on the other in time. "The sensation I had in my head," Mr. Reich recalled, "was that the sound moved over to my left ear, moved down to my left shoulder, down my left arm, down my leg, out across the floor to the left, and finally began to reverberate and shake" and eventually "came back together in the center of my head."

Of greatest interest here—and, as things turned out, of historical significance—is that Mr. Reich was more concerned with the effect of the music (first of all on his own body) than with the technique of its fashioning. That implicit (in modernist terms, heretical) solidarity with the audience was characteristic of the early phase pieces, lending them a quasi-political—shall we call it "sixties"?—appeal that compensated for their sometimes thin musical content. In *It's Gonna Rain* (1965), Mr. Reich was willing to decide that the phase phenomenon itself was more interesting than anything he might do with it, so he simply allowed it to play itself out. In its provocative modesty it was a genuinely avant-garde, shock-the-bourgeois gesture, and it was amply repaid with abuse from the relevant bourgeoisie, the technocratic modernists lately ensconced in university music departments.

But the avant-garde Mr. Reich represented differed from previous ones, roundly refuting the conventional "theory of the avant-garde" put forth by modernist pundits like Renato Poggioli or Theodor W. Adorno. Like any avant-garde, it was the opposite of conservative or nostalgic. It sought no return to older styles. If it used consonant harmonies, it was only to focus the site of innovation elsewhere, not to reinstate traditional harmonic hierarchies. Unlike the "traditional" avant-garde, though, it was also the opposite of socially alienated. It sought connection; indeed, the status of African drumming and gamelan performance as models of harmonious social interaction was among their attractions for Mr. Reich. Like those musics, his was viscerally engaging and often produced euphoria in its hearers. It became popular with "nonclassical" audiences and commercially successful. And so, of course, the modern-music establishment denied its seriousness. A popular avant-garde might seem as much a contradiction as a tenured one.

An advance guard is avant-garde, however, only with respect to a status quo; and in that respect Mr. Reich has been a potent, and a very serious, force for change. He has remained not only a serious artist but also a restless one, whose continuing creative quest has led him toward solutions to a couple of esthetic problems that his "serious" contemporaries have notoriously failed to solve, or even acknowledge. One problem is that of addressing a whole person in music. We have had lots of new music, God knows, that reduces listeners to their cerebral cortex and, in opposition to that, lots (including most "minimalism") that reduces them to their autonomic nervous system. Mr. Reich, happily, along with Gyorgy Ligeti, Conlon Nancarrow, and only a few others, has seen the need to treat his listeners as fully conscious, fully sentient human beings.

After discovering the phase process he immediately began adapting it to traditional instrumental and vocal media, producing perhaps the earliest "live" music that deliberately aped recorded music. The complicated layered textures that have resulted from this adaptation can be arduous to execute with the required precision. Mr. Reich insisted on making the difficult "back transfer" where sticking to tape would have made things easy for all concerned, because the effort and the arduousness conspired to humanize the product and make it communicative. But no matter how complex the patterns or processes in Mr. Reich's music, they can be grasped by the naked ear and parsed by the rational mind, adding intellectual to physical involvement and banishing the sort of discouraged mental passivity so much new music induces. Musically sophisticated audiences—audiences who like "challenging" music—find much to their liking in the textures and harmonic subtleties of Mr. Reich's "Counterpoints" for "whole consorts" of homogeneous timbre, prerecorded instruments interacting antically with live soloists.

Yet Mr. Reich's sonic world is not just a multicultural playground. In the 1980s he began to expand his horizons, reengaging with texts, first in *Tehillim* (1981), a lilting, melodically inventive setting of Hebrew psalms for three pure-toned "early music" sopranos (usually in close "phaselike" canons) and orchestra. Then, in *The Desert Music* (1983), an ambitious cantata stretched out over a few earnestly exhorting fragments from poems by William Carlos Williams, Mr. Reich broadened his harmonic palette into intense chromatic terrain and equipped it to deal with sober, even somber matters. Finally, in *Different Trains* (1988), Mr. Reich went the full distance and earned his place among the great composers of the century. For here is where he solved the other problem. He has composed the only adequate musical response—one of the few adequate artistic responses in any medium—to the Holocaust.

With famous and flatulent self-importance, Adorno announced that after Auschwitz, poetry had become impossible. The kind of art Adorno upheld—pretentiously abstract, ostentatiously alienated and self-involved—surely did ring hollow after the art-loving Nazis, co-opting the masterpieces of the past, had unmasked the moral contingency of high "humanistic" esthetics. What was desperately needed, though, was a poetry that gave significant form to that contingency and disillusion. Most of what was put forth, from the heavy tomes of existentialist philosophy to the bloated cantatas of the socialist realists, ludicrously contradicted by its bombast the sensibility it sought to embody. Or else it sought with mendacious sentimentality to retrieve a message of uplift from the abyss.

Arnold Schoenberg's *Survivor from Warsaw* (1947), the most famous musical memorial to the Holocaust, falls easy prey to these pitfalls. Were the name of its composer not surrounded by a historiographical aureole, were its musical idiom not safeguarded by its inscrutability, its B-movie clichés— the Erich von Stroheim Nazi barking "Achtung," the kitsch-triumphalism of the climactic Jewish credo—would be painfully obvious, and no one would ever think to program such banality alongside Beethoven's Ninth as has become fashionable. That kind of post-Auschwitz poetry is indeed a confession of art's impotence.

Different Trains does it, well, differently. In a tradition going back through Janáček and Musorgsky to the music of the Greeks as the Renaissance Italians imagined it, Mr. Reich based the melodic content of the piece on the contour and rhythm of ordinary human speech. But in his case the speech consisted of fragments of oral history (recordings again!), looped into Reichian ostinatos, then resolved into musical phrases conforming to the normal tunings, scales, and rhythms of "Western music," imaginatively scored for string quartet. These speech melodies were set in counterpoint with the original speech samples, all of it measured against the constant Reichian chug.

Only this time the chug is given an "objective correlative" in the actual chug and clack of moving trains, evoked also by periodic whistles adjusted to the ever-modulating tonalities of the speech samples. In the first of three sections, the speech samples are voices from Mr. Reich's own past, recalling the transcontinental train rides of his childhood. In the second, train whistles give way to air-raid sirens, and the collage of speech melodies is drawn from archival tapes of Holocaust survivors recalling their childhood ride to Auschwitz. A third section synthesizes the two sets of recollections over the unremitting subtactile pulse.

There are no villains and no heroes. There is no role for a Ralph Fiennes or a Werner Klemperer to flatter your sense of moral superiority. And there is no bathetic glory to comfort you with a trumped-up Triumph of the Human Spirit. There is just the perception that while this happened here, that happened there, and a stony invitation to reflect. The only moment that could be said to point to a moral is the matter-of-fact statement by one of the speakers in the third section that "today, they're all gone." Remembering his voice from the first section, we know he was talking about the American transcontinental trains of the thirties. But we also remember the second section, so now he's talking about the Jewish children, too. It is a true synthesis, and it is also an exquisitely understated closure of the musical form. It brings an ache, and a shiver.

So successful a mapping of structure and meaning, so thorough an interpenetration of sonic material and conceptual metaphor, is the mark of a master composer. (The word, recall, means "putter-together.") More than that, it is the work of a mature human being, perhaps even more of a rarity in today's musical world. So perfectly realized is *Different Trains* that I was sorry to see Mr. Reich, in later works like *The Cave* (1993) and *City Life* (1994), turning the voice-sampling technique into a routine. And I was sorry to see the pithiness and indirection of *Different Trains* turn, in *The Cave,* into a rambling, somewhat hectoring sermon on Arab-Israeli relations. The work as presented here was adapted from the sound track to a reportedly dazzling video documentary. Perhaps it was not a good idea to issue it as an independent audio experience.

But as far as I am concerned, Mr. Reich can go permanently astray now and never lose the distinction of having given classical music back first its youth and finally its soul in the waning years of the twentieth century. It is something for which the musicians of the twenty-first century will remember him and be grateful. We can be grateful already.

16

Calling All Pundits
No More Predictions!

A millennium is looming. We are in for a lot of big thought and big talk. Resist! Big thought and big talk have made nothing but trouble for music. My millennial wish is that the twenty-first century will discard them and get over the obsession with centuries and millennia that gives people the itch to micromanage decades.

Pundits get lots of invitations these days to air big thoughts on the future of music. Reflecting, after receiving one, on why I found the idea so revolting, I remembered two predictions delivered in close succession during my student days. I offer them now in a spirit of caution.

The first appeared in 1963 in the journal *Perspectives of New Music,* then financed by the music-loving businessman Paul Fromm. Before his recoil in dismay, a couple of decades later, at the monstrosities of artistic bigotry his money had wrought, Mr. Fromm's patronage was one of the pillars supporting what was then called (with straight face, so far as I could tell) the "academic avant-garde." The author of the piece was Charles Wuorinen. "I must unequivocally state that pitch serialization is no longer an issue," he began. Only twelve-tone composers were henceforth to be regarded as composers— or at least (as Mr. Wuorinen would later put it) "serious composers of the mainstream." The truth having been revealed, innovation was over. In a spirit of frank totalitarianism, young composers were warned to seek no new paths but devote their careers strictly and obediently to "acting out the implications of the older generation's work."

Then came the jeremiads. "Within a generation or two there will be no orchestra music," for the orchestra, having failed to come to terms with those

implications, was no longer "a medium relevant to living music." The choic-
est bit was addressed to "singers and singing teachers," who "have ignored the
advance of music for so long that at present even a complete reversal of their
attitudes seems insufficient to save them from extinction." It's easy enough
to laugh now at these fantasies of infantile omnipotence, but the atmosphere
they exemplify—of verbal assault and hawkish bluster—was the air young
composers breathed in those days. The epitome was Milton Babbitt's famous
prediction that unless the universities stepped in and protected this most
narrow-minded of all composerly visions, "music will cease to evolve and, in
that important sense, will cease to live."

Big Talk. But of course it was the sheerest and silliest "vulgar Darwinism":
the view of evolution that sees it as having Us (whoever We may be) as its desired goal. Like its bloodier cousin, vulgar Marxism, it offered a marvelous
rationale for intolerance (and, when in power, aggression) toward Nean-
derthals, social democrats, tonalists, and other underevolved species whose
continued existence was only foiling Nature's plan. That was then. By now,
outside of a few reactionary music departments and journalistic diehards,
vulgar Darwinism has been repudiated everywhere, turning the old academic avant-garde into a congregation of crybabies, spouting paranoid speculations and conspiracy theories, railing at "society" for failing to support
their projects of self-indulgence and social contempt. Ralph Shapey, a Chicago veteran, contends that European conductors of American orchestras
deliberately program the worst local stuff to discredit "American serious
composers" like him. Donald Martino of Harvard now declares that *serial* is
just a term of journalistic abuse. Mr. Wuorinen likes to pretend nowadays
that "the word's meaning has always escaped me." The chorus of denial has
a familiar ring to anyone who has been listening lately to the likes of the East
German spymaster Markus Wolf or the Albanian widow Hoxha, relics of another discredited elite.

The other prediction was friendlier, more informal. It was made in 1965
by Gustave Reese, the grand old man of American musical scholarship, who
had just delivered an oration on the history of the tritone, if memory serves.
Reacting to its ambitious historical sweep, a member of the audience asked
Prof. Reese if he would care to offer any conjectures about the future. He
seemed ready—indeed, waiting—for the chance. He pointed out that periods of great complexity in music were often succeeded by periods of great
simplicity. The fiendishly polyrhythmic courtly chansons of the late fourteenth century were followed by Guillaume Du Fay's limpid hymns in
"fauxbourdon" (chordal) style. The contrapuntal intricacies of Bach's *Art of
Fugue* gave way to the folksy charm of Pergolesi's *Serva Padrona*. (Here the
chronology was off, but the point did not seem to suffer.) Was it not reasonable, then, to expect "a period of great consonance" in the wake of the academic avant-garde?

The gray-bearded musicologists beamed. Younger fry, educated by the Babbitts and the Wuorinens, could only shake their heads at the sad spectacle of the mighty Gustave in his dotage. But he was right! At a recent millennial punditfest, I had the pleasure of turning to Steve Reich and saying, "See? He predicted you."

But no, he didn't, not really. He was only applying another abstract model—the "pendulum" or "cyclic" model—without any evidence. As much as Mr. Wuorinen's, Prof. Reese's prediction was mere wish fulfillment. What they had most profoundly and deplorably in common was belief that the history of art is sealed off from the history of everything else, and follows its own deterministic "laws," which it is the historian's (or pseudohistorian's) task to discover. That composers should ever have accepted such a view of their history was a disaster. But that's what happens when you go to college and learn to think big.

POSTSCRIPT, 2008

This piece was based on an impromptu talk, delivered a few weeks earlier in Miller (formerly McMillin) Theater at the Columbia University music department's centennial observances. I had as an undergraduate read Wuorinen's screed with loathing and indignation, and as a graduate student heard Reese's talk with detached amusement, in the very building where I was now offering gray-bearded reminiscences.

Charles Wuorinen's "The Outlook for Young Composers" (*Perspectives of New Music* 1, no. 2 [spring 1963]: 54–61) is worth looking up as a marvelous period piece: a compendium of all the positions Wuorinen and the other members of his cohort now claim they never upheld. But uphold them they did, and do. Eight years later, in 1971, denied tenure by the music faculty for what Paul Henry Lang described as his "arrogance, ruthlessness, and contempt for anything outside his bailiwick," Wuorinen was railing that the university administration was acting out of "hostility to the present, and to those who advocate it in music."[1] In 1979 he put that contempt on display in the opening paragraph of a textbook: "While the tonal system, in an atrophied or vestigial form, is still used today in popular and commercial music, and even occasionally in the works of backward-looking serious composers, it is no longer employed by serious composers of the mainstream. It has been replaced or succeeded by the 12-tone system."[2] In 1982 he once again universalized what Lang had called his bailiwick, insisting to an interviewer that, the existence of other approaches notwithstanding, "there is one main way of doing things."[3]

In 1988, faced with what seemed the fait accompli of his marginalization, he was still threatening doom. "Pluralism has been carried much too far," he whined when another interviewer brought up the subject of newer trends that had displaced serialism from its once acknowledged position of dominance. "A dependence on marketing reveals the tendency to view art not for its intrinsic merit but as a tool for social engineering. The public is made the judge. That means we have a world in which the instant response of the untutored becomes the sole criterion for judgment." In fine, "the current tendency of transmuting art into entertainment will cause serious music to cease to exist." Asked how he would remedy the situation, he replied, "I would try to change the present relationship of the composer to the public from one in which the composer says, 'Please judge me,' to one in which I say, 'I have something to show you and offer my leadership.'"[4] That's right, he offered the "leadership principle."

I adduce these fairly ancient and fairly recent quotes to give a context to the pretense and the denials to which my little talk, and the squib I later extracted from it, referred. The one attributed to Wuorinen came from yet another interview, in which Mike Silverton, an unusually complaisant interlocutor, invited him to comment on my then-recent "How Talented Composers Become Useless" (chapter 13 in the present collection):

> In the course of such an article, Taruskin makes frequent use, as others have done, of a term—serialism. The word's meaning has always escaped me. I think for such writers, it's music that goes bloop-bleep or isn't in C major, or something like that. I'm not really sure. Even if one wanted to be charitable—oh, they mean some kind of 12-tone music maybe—that term too is almost without meaning.[5]

Most recently, Wuorinen tried to waffle the point again with a much sharper interviewer, Daniel Wakin of the *Times*. Asked whether the perception that he is "a serialist" was correct, Wuorinen attempted evasive action:

> An interesting question to ask someone about one or the other of us, "Oh, he's this way or that way," is "Which particular piece are you referring to?" You won't get an answer, I guarantee you. These categories have very little meaning. To call me a serial composer, I think, is—first of all, the term has to be defined, and no one ever bothers to do it. My work is centered not in a tonal or diatonic way but in a hierarchical way that it is not dissimilar from that of older music.

Confronted with his earlier, explicit, textbook assertions, Wuorinen tried first to laugh them off ("Never write a book") and then continued quibbling:

> Well, that's a categorical statement which cannot be—of course, it had more to it then, although to some extent it is obsolete now. But it depends on what you mean by the tonal system.[6]

The question, of course, is what Wuorinen meant by "the tonal system," which was never a system at all in the sense that the twelve-tone system was a system (or at least that is what Milton Babbitt and Charles Wuorinen always told students in the days of their ascendancy). I submit that his evasions and subterfuges are exactly comparable to those of the deposed totalitarians to whom I likened them in my piece, and it is high time to call the revisionist bluff.

NOTES

1. Charles Wuorinen, "Are the Arts Doomed on Campus?" *New York Times,* 8 August 1971, D11; Paul Henry Lang, "Music at Columbia Will Endure, Even Without Wuorinen," *New York Times,* 29 August 1971, D11.

2. Charles Wuorinen, *Simple Composition* (New York: Longman, 1979), 3.

3. Cole Gagne and Tracy Caras, *Soundpieces: Interviews with American Composers* (Metuchen, N.J.: Scarecrow Press, 1982), 394.

4. Joan Peyser, "Wuorinen's Bleak View of the Future," *New York Times,* 5 June 1988.

5. "Charles Wuorinen: The Winds," liner notes to New World Records 80517 (1996).

6. Daniel J. Wakin, "Schoenberg, Bach and Us," *New York Times,* 27 March 2005.

17

In *The Rake's Progress,* Love Conquers (Almost) All

On Thursday evening, the Metropolitan Opera will give its first performance of Igor Stravinsky's *Rake's Progress* since 1953, when the opera was brand new. It was conceived almost exactly fifty years ago, on 30 September 1947, when W. H. Auden met in New York with Ralph Hawkes of Boosey & Hawkes, Stravinsky's publisher, and agreed to furnish the libretto. What had up to then been only Stravinsky's vague wish, to write an opera in English on the theme of some Hogarth engravings that he had seen in Chicago, became a project on that day.

The poet, who had been recommended by Aldous Huxley, flew to California and together with Stravinsky worked out a draft scenario, completed on 18 November. The actual text, written in collaboration with Auden's friend Chester Kallman, went like the wind. Auden was able to mail the third and final act on 9 February 1948, less than twelve weeks after returning to New York. The much bigger task of writing the music took a lot longer. Stravinsky barely managed to complete the third act in time for the opera's scheduled première, at Venice's Teatro la Fenice, on 11 September 1951, just short of four years from its inception.

The effort, which Stravinsky found exhausting (and which, as it turned out, literally exhausted his "neoclassical" manner), has been amply rewarded. Very much against the predictions of the opera's early critics, the work has thrived. By now it is fair to say that *The Rake* has joined the tiny handful of operas produced since World War II that have achieved repertory status. Along with Prokofieff's *War and Peace,* Britten's *Peter Grimes,* and Poulenc's *Dialogues of the Carmelites, The Rake* is a staple the world over—even, lately, in Russia.

First published in the *New York Times,* 16 November 1997. Copyright © 2008 The New York Times Company. Reprinted by permission.

Why?

Stravinsky was the last composer from whom one had any right or reason, in 1947, to expect a successful opera. Possibly because his father had been a great opera singer, he professed a lifelong aversion to the genre. He made his early fame as a staff composer for Sergey Diaghilev's Ballets Russes, and vociferously supported Diaghilev's commercially motivated contention that opera was an outmoded art form, undeserving of survival in the twentieth century. Interviews with the young Stravinsky were never complete without an arch pronouncement like this one, from 1913: "I dislike opera. Music can be married to gesture or to words—not to both without bigamy. That is why the artistic basis of opera is wrong and why Wagner sounds at his best in the concert-room."

Fulminations against Wagner were still rife in lectures Stravinsky delivered at Harvard as late as 1940. Nor could a single one of the pieces Stravinsky had composed for the lyric stage as of 1947—*The Nightingale, Mavra, Renard, Oedipus Rex, Persephone*—be described as a true (or at least a conventional) opera. They were pageants, skits, collages, oratorios, melodramas, anything but. Besides, Stravinsky had always had funny ideas about setting words to music. He regarded prosody, the matching of verbal lengths and accents to musical ones, as an abstract element of design that could be freely manipulated by the composer. His settings of English and French, languages he spoke with considerable originality, are often dismissed by native speakers as stubbornly inept.

Robert Craft, the composer's longtime assistant, was originally hired in 1948 to read the *Rake* libretto so that Stravinsky could hear the "normal" stresses and know what he was manipulating. But at first even Mr. Craft thought the composer merely obstinate. "Saw new pages of 'Rake,'" he wrote to the harpsichordist Sylvia Marlowe in October 1949, "and the English is hideously mis-set, impossibly awkward. What can I do with that man."

But Stravinsky's mis-settings were knowing. You can see them evolving in his sketches on the basis of perfectly correct, Craft-assisted preliminary settings. They are fascinating to musicians, but they dependably defeat audiences, the way modernist music is supposed to do. Nobody really understands the *Rake* libretto as sung. Its verbal beauties are discoverable only on the printed page, or in supertitles. Even when the words are understood, the opera's plot line remains a problem, coy farrago that it is of Greek mythology, Arabian Nights, Augustan oratory, Victorian moralism, dime-store existentialism (the most obvious "period" flavor of all, by now) and opera-queenery. It is doubtful that anybody has ever taken much pleasure in witnessing the Rake's three wishes or their attendant temptations: the dowdy brothel scene, the tired anticapitalist parable of the stones-to-bread machine, or especially the episode with Baba the Turk, the bearded bride.

This last, a madcap gay inversion of the conventional "trouser role" (especially when played, as it sometimes used to be, by John Ferrante, a countertenor), was Auden and Kallman's catty little joke at the expense of the elderly, conventionally homophobic and decidedly unhip composer. Stravinsky's lawyer saw through it and advised him to pull out. Nowadays, post-Stonewall and postcloset, it's merely embarrassing, another hurdle for the opera to scale.

But the biggest hurdle, at the outset, was the opera's retrospective style, interpreted at the time of the first performance as a reactionary holdout against the march of time. Typical were the questions with which Pierre Souvtchinsky, Stravinsky's old friend, tormented Ned Rorem, then living in Paris and just back from the *Rake* première: "Don't you think that Boulez's is the only music today? That he is taking the only possible path?" They made Mr. Rorem's blood boil, but even he, a conservative youth, had thought Stravinsky's opera old hat and never wanted to hear it again. For nobody could hear music in those early cold-war days. People heard only styles. That even went for Auden and Kallman, who followed up on *The Rake* with *Delia,* another libretto for Stravinsky, couched in an even stiffer period style. It would, Auden said, have satirized "some of our bugaboos like 12-Toners, Sociologists, etc." Stravinsky never set it to music, partly because in the wake of *The Rake* and its disappointing early reception, he refashioned himself as a bugaboo (no, not a sociologist).

By now, with Stravinsky's 1951 style and Boulez's equally dead (and safely "historical"), the clamor of stylistic polemics has thankfully receded, allowing the opera's musical details to register. And here at last we come to the reason for its survival. It lives, like all living operas, in its musical details, particularly those mediated through the one character to whom Auden and Kallman, confirmed misogynists, attached no importance whatever. Anne Trulove, the Rake's spurned but ever-loving good angel, was, according to Auden, "one of those operatic sopranos who would be a terrible bore to have to sit next to at dinner, but to whom on stage all is forgiven." Kallman called her "a *very* good girl." Stravinsky, perhaps the most uxorious of all the great composers, saw her differently: not as a simpering annoyance or a see-through plot mechanism but, quite ingenuously, as an emanation from paradise. She stirred the deepest music in him and redeemed the opera as well as her errant beloved.

Stravinsky was preoccupied during the 1940s with a certain cold technical device: the mixture or juxtaposition of major and minor harmonies over a single root pitch, and particularly with wobbly oscillations or vacillations between major and minor versions of a single chord. The Symphony in Three Movements and the String Concerto of 1946 are obsessed with these oscillations, and so is *The Rake.* In the opera, though, the device takes on a warming human significance. The inflection of minor to major within a chord is the symbol there of the earthly paradise of love—what the Rake possesses without valuing it at the beginning, foolishly chucks for the sake of vain temptations, and only regains at the cost of his reason. The very first sung notes in the opera, Anne's "The woods [are green]," inflect minor to major and, in so doing, set the mood of idyllic pastoral that Tom, the Rake, will at first echo, then mock, and finally, tragically, parody.

In the third scene of act 1, Anne's solo, in which she resolves to pursue Tom and try to save him from himself, the moment of decision—"Love hears, Love knows, Love answers him across the silent miles, and goes"—is capped with a direct reference to the opening inflection, ecstatically expanded this time by an octave. Her momentary wavering, right before the fast fireworks begin, is overcome with a triumph of major over minor, expressed through a similar melodic inflection on the words "strengthen my resolve." Halfway through the opera, Tom will heartbreakingly reprise this phrase in the throes of his greatest delusion, when he trusts the infernal stones-to-bread machine to create an earthly paradise of plenty and enable him "to deserve dear Anne at last." Anne's offstage voice, intervening miraculously in the final act to rescue the Rake from destruction at the devil's hand, sounds a thrillingly complex array of emotionally charged inflections. And her last solo line in the moralizing epilogue ("Not every man is given an Anne to take the place of Duty") ends with the same pair of idyllically inflected notes that had started the opera on its way, now promising paradise regained. *The Rake's Progress* is one opera in which love really does conquer all.

Well, almost all. Anne doesn't win the Rake back from the devil quite in one piece. His mind is gone. Many commentators, beginning with Joseph Kerman in his still unsurpassed early appreciation of the opera, have complained at this. Madness, they contend, is an undramatic device, because it robs a character of volition, reducing him or her to what Kallman (recognizing the pitfall) called "passive sufferance" and precluding a truly tragic tone. Here the librettists were not to blame. Stravinsky, much taken with Hogarth's Bedlam scene, ended his first feeler to Auden by noting that "as the end of any work is of importance, I think that the hero's end in an asylum scratching a fiddle would make a meritorious conclusion to his stormy life—don't you think so?" From Auden's reply it is obvious that he didn't think so. He managed politely to scotch the fiddle-scratching but took the asylum ending as a command from the boss and tried to make the best of it, remarking in passing that "it is the librettist's job to satisfy the composer not the other way round."

The Rake's Progress, it is clear in retrospect, was a broth created by a committee of not terribly well matched chefs. It had every reason to fail, for it had (and has) "problems" galore, to which critics will never tire of calling attention. But in Anne it also has an unforgettable and truly operatic character— a character made unforgettable in and through the medium of music, through whom the workings of the musical material become the workings of the drama. That achievement, and that alone, justifies opera as a dramatic form. It has become a rarity in the twentieth century, but as long as it can happen at all, all opera is redeemed by it. It is just too wonderfully ironic that Stravinsky, the century's most ostentatious opera hater, should have been one of the blessed few who brought it off.

POSTSCRIPT, 2008

And to think I thought this was a harmless puff. It was nothing I said about the opera that offended, though; it was what I said about its creators. Somehow, we still want the artists we admire to be moral paragons, and if they aren't, then kill the messenger who says so.

Patricia Blake, a fine scholar of Russian literature, who considered herself a better-qualified judge of *The Rake* than I because she was personally acquainted both with Stravinsky (through the composer and culture czar Nicolas Nabokov, of whom she was the third of five wives) and Auden (with whom she collaborated on a translation of Andrey Voznesensky's *Antiworlds*), wrote in to denounce my references to Auden's misogyny and "opera-queenery" and Stravinsky's "conventional homophobia." I meant no serious moral indictment, or any general characterization, and I am sure that that much was plain to most readers. Perhaps I should have said "casual" rather than "conventional." In both cases it was the sort of untroubled and unreflective assumption that others can be lumped in groups to which one can feel generally and comfortably superior. It by no means precludes forming friendships with individual members of the groups to which one condescends, nor does it necessarily entail acquiescence in anyone's mistreatment. But before women and gays began protesting it and forcing it into people's consciousness, it was pervasive. So to write, as Ms. Blake did, that—

> It is absurd to label Stravinsky homophobic and Auden misogynist. This flies in the face of the testimony of the many women, including me, who have written about Auden's wonderful gift for friendship with us.

—is merely to commit a non sequitur.

It is all so easily documented. In Auden's case, the main place to look is Alan Ansen's Boswell-like compilation, *The Table Talk of W. H. Auden*, in which the gem already quoted in the postscript to chapter 11 can be found. Stravinsky's condescension to homosexuals is most notoriously expressed in his belittling comments about Benjamin Britten, whose popular success he envied. He referred to Britten in print, maliciously, as a "bachelor composer," and even permitted himself a reference to Britten and his partner, the tenor Peter Pears, as "Aunt Britten and Uncle Pears" in a letter that his assistant, Robert Craft (who enjoyed such catty allusions and often indulged in them himself), published after Stravinsky's death.[1]

According to Ms. Blake, my piece "isn't music criticism; it's a coy farrago of insinuations and other bits of mischief designed to belittle this magnificent opera as the work of authors at sexual cross-purposes." That is her opinion, and I quarrel with it. It does not belittle the opera to comment on its makers' foibles. If the opera has problems—and everyone, Ms. Blake included, agrees that it does—then it is the proper task of music criticism to try to explain them. Stravinsky's anti-Semitism, now universally acknowledged but which I was the first to bring to public consciousness as recently as 1988 (in chapter 31), is another case in point. On first meeting Stravinsky, Auden himself found it shocking. Just back from California, he told Ansen:

> Some of his anti-Semitic remarks were a little hard to take. Oh no, it wasn't anything extreme, but he kept saying, "Why do they call themselves Russians?" That sort of thing.[2]

That sort of thing may diminish the man, but it does not diminish his artistic achievement, except insofar as it is directly reflected in the work and becomes a legitimate issue in its reception. (For Stravinsky, that work is the *Cantata* of 1952; see chapter 41, below.)

Baba the Turk is pretty well universally recognized as the biggest problem besetting *The Rake*. Nobody knows what to make of "her," exactly. As David Schiff pointed out in a perceptive review exactly coeval with my own much shorter piece, "There has always been confusion about whether Baba is supposed to be a woman or a man," and even "after a decade or more of 'gender studies' and androgynous rock stars, one might assume that a bearded lady would no longer kill a show, but perhaps wrongly." "Homosexual composers," Schiff remarks (and it *is* remarkable),

> didn't seem to appreciate [Baba] any more than ostensibly straight critics did. Virgil Thomson praised the opera but predicted—correctly, as it has turned out—that Baba, "a character drawn from female impersonation," would not be easy to make convincing. Benjamin Britten, whose works are full of homosexual allusions, reportedly termed the opera "perverse."[3]

Hence the tendency to cast the role as a countertenor, an actual female impersonator. Robert T. Jones, a veteran critic, contributed an interesting perspective on John Ferrante's Baba to a discussion my piece provoked on the "Opera-L" Web list (17 November 1997):

> What's really impossible about Baba the Turk as written is that the big punch line and *coup de théâtre* comes at the end of Act Two when she removes her veil and reveals her beard. It HAS to be a shock and a sensation, and it never is that in the theater. A lot more than a beard is needed to live up to the situation. As I recall it, John Ferrante provided that visual punch: he was a big guy, built like a wrestler, and one side of him was female and the other was male. He looked

like a highly effeminate sumo wrestler, and his voice was a piercing soprano (well, maybe alto). This was absolutely the only Baba I've ever seen who was over the wall far enough to make the thing work. BTW, Stravinsky saw the famous Sarah Caldwell production featuring Ferrante, for he was in the audience the same night I saw *The Rake* (in Los Angeles, circa 1969), but he was already beginning to lose contact with the world, so I don't know what his reaction was.

And yet Schiff reports, after seeing "a Swedish movie of *The Rake's Progress* in which Baba was clearly a man, sung by a male alto with a short goatee," that "instead of solving the problem, the TV movie just showed that in our enlightened age a drag queen is less threatening than a woman with a beard—and proved that Baba makes no sense at all as a cross-dressed man." David Alexander Terry, a countertenor who wrote in to the *Times* with some interesting reminiscences of Stravinsky at Santa Fe, agreed that "a countertenor's singing Baba makes as little musical or dramatic sense as his singing Cherubino, Octavian or Oscar," famous trousers roles in Mozart's *The Marriage of Figaro*, Richard Strauss's *Der Rosenkavalier*, and Verdi's *Un Ballo in Maschera*, respectively. And I agree.

David Schiff solved the problem to his own satisfaction by speculating:

Whatever the personal sources of the character, . . . Baba was Auden's way of embodying his love for the genre of opera in all its glorious absurdity. Baba breathes the spirit of opera itself—for she is nothing less—into the dead bones of *The Rake*. She throws the whole tidy moral universe of *The Rake* into confusion by showing us how dull it has grown. Morality is fine, she seems to say, but could we have some entertainment, please? And not a moment too soon.

This is convincing, at least insofar as it concerns Auden's probable intention, and it is just what I meant by my allusion to "opera-queenery."[4] And yet even Schiff has to admit:

My own fondness for Baba perhaps shows that I remain an armchair opera lover. In the theater Baba remains one of the many enigmatic features of *The Rake's Progress* that make it seem more like a perverse waxworks opera than like the real thing. I can describe Baba as the spirit of opera, but few directors can sell Baba to the audience, as they can easily sell the character of Zerbinetta, in Strauss's *Ariadne auf Naxos*, who has a similar symbolic purpose.[5]

Thus, unless we admit that the opera audience has no say in defining "the spirit of opera" (and it would take a cast-iron modernist temper—Auden's or Stravinsky's, maybe, but not Schiff's and certainly not mine—to say that), then the problem remains unsolved, and probably insoluble.

It is too bad the *Times* editors cut Ms. Blake's letter where they did. From their perspective it was twice too long, and I guess the cut was inevitable, but the second half of it contained a valuable reminiscence, and a lovely reminder, both far more worthy of preservation in print than her passing vitriol. I take pleasure in appending it.

> The musical weight of Anne's role in the opera depends largely on who is singing it. I have attended many productions of *The Rake,* beginning with the first, in Venice in 1951. On that occasion Anne was sung by Elisabeth Schwarzkopf, whose already over-seasoned voice and grand opera persona scarcely suited that wisp of a country maiden. Anne's music sounded thinner and thinner as the formidable Schwarzkopf strained to push it to implausible lengths. Many sopranos later I found myself carried away by Anne's music for the first time when I heard Dawn Upshaw—that supremely intelligent interpreter of contemporary music—in last year's performance of *The Rake* with Seiji Ozawa and the Boston Symphony Orchestra. I am thrilled that she is singing it again at the Metropolitan Opera. Still, Kallman was right when he joked that Anne is "a very good girl." Too good. Though melodically lovely and vocally challenging, Anne's arias are, in essence, emotionally simplistic. For a bolt of all-conquering love one must turn elsewhere in *The Rake.*

> Though rarely at a loss for sexual explication, Mr. Taruskin has overlooked the real site of love in this drama: the whorehouse. He dismisses the episode in Mother Goose's establishment as a "dowdy brothel scene." On the contrary, it is a richly exuberant, bawdy scene, a choral celebration of Venus and Mars by the whores and roaring boys, while the rake-in-progress is readied for his initiation. Suddenly, at the sound of the word "love," Tom exclaims in a heartstopping aside, "Love, love! That precious word is like a fiery coal / It burns my lips, strikes terror to my soul."

> There follows Tom's aria, a cavatina so beautiful and so moving as to rival the greatest tenor love music in all opera. Whoever ventures to sing it, its musical and verbal meaning is wholly intelligible, capturing as it does the deepest sense of this great work of art. Tom begins:

>> Love, so frequently betrayed
>> For some plausible desire
>> Or the world's enchanted fire,
>> Still thy traitor in his sleep
>> Renews the vow he did not keep,
>> Weeping, weeping,
>> He kneels before thy wounded shade. . . .

Auden wrote it. Stravinsky was proud of it; he called the scene's final words "the most wonderful gift a librettist ever made to a composer." Like others in the audience, I weep every time I hear it.

NOTES

1. Igor Stravinsky and Robert Craft, *Themes and Episodes* (New York: Knopf, 1966), 101; Stravinsky to Nicolas Nabokov, 15 December 1949, in Robert Craft, ed., *Stravinsky: Selected Correspondence,* vol. 1 (New York: Knopf, 1982), 369 n. 93.

2. Alan Ansen, *The Table Talk of W. H. Auden,* ed. Nicholas Jenkins (London: Faber and Faber, 1991), 86 (entry of 21 November 1947).

3. David Schiff, "Redeeming the Rake," *Atlantic Monthly,* November 1997, 138.

4. This, too, was no slur, although Patricia Blake took it as one. See Mitchell Morris, "Reading as an Opera Queen," in *Musicology and Difference: Gender and Sexuality in Music Scholarship,* ed. Ruth Solie (Berkeley: University of California Press, 1993), 184–200.

5. Schiff, "Redeeming the Rake," 139.

18

Markevitch as Icarus

Tall, gauntly handsome, icily cultivated, the subject of many reverential memoirs and just as many backbiting or salacious rumors, Igor Markevitch was for more than five decades a spook of the first magnitude in the musical life of Europe and some of its North American artistic colonies like Cuba and French Canada. In the United States, however, he has been relatively little known, or known only as a conductor, a situation that may begin to change when the American Symphony Orchestra, directed by Leon Botstein, performs *Icare*, Markevitch's reputed masterpiece, on Wednesday evening at Avery Fisher Hall.

Like Prokofieff's *Prodigal Son*, a farewell offering to Sergey Diaghilev and the Ballets Russes before the composer's return to the U.S.S.R., Markevitch's Icarus ballet has been all too easily interpreted as a metaphor for its composer's fate. Intended as a memorial to Diaghilev, in 1932, it tells of the arrogant high-flying youth of Greek mythology who fell to earth and perished in consequence of his hubris. Along with Erich Wolfgang Korngold one of the twentieth century's most amazing composer prodigies, Markevitch burned himself out creatively by the age of thirty. For most of the next forty years, although he maintained an active career as a conductor, he never performed his own music, which mainly languished unpublished, and neither did anybody else.

Although his former pupils, many of whom have far outstripped him in fame and fortune, still swear by him as one of the great conductors of the century, Markevitch never held a major post. The best-known orchestra he ever directed was that of the Concerts Lamoureux in Paris, with which he made

First published in the *New York Times,* 10 May 1998. Copyright © 2008 The New York Times Company. Reprinted by permission.

recordings in the late 1950s that are highly prized by collectors. For the rest, he worked in Stockholm, Montreal, Havana, Madrid, and Monte Carlo, appeared frequently in England (where he made more legendary records), and held court for many summers at the Salzburg Mozarteum. A curmudgeonly stickler for textual fidelity, Markevitch retreated in his late years into the realm of maverick scholarship, leading to a vast study of Beethoven's symphonies published in German in 1983, shortly before his death, at seventy-one. His tell-all (but in fact, withhold-most) autobiography had come out in French a few years before. An earlier memoir about his wartime experiences in the Italian underground was written in English. This was a man of parts, a man of legend.

But behind the legend of the phantom conductor-ascetic lay the bigger legend of the wild wunderkind composer. Now that story can at last be told with musical illustrations, thanks to the yeoman work of the English conductor Christopher Lyndon-Gee, who has recorded Markevitch's complete orchestral music—eight works in all, dating from 1929 to 1937—with the Arnhem Philharmonic Orchestra, a Dutch ensemble, on three Marco Polo CDs (8.223653, 8.223666, 8.223724). On a companion disc (Largo LC 8943), Mr. Lyndon-Gee and other excellent musicians perform four chamber works, including a version of the Icarus ballet for a Bartókian ensemble of pianists and percussionists.

So, how high did Markevitch fly?

Born in Kiev in 1912 but raised abroad from his second year, he composed his first published piece, a stylish little suite for piano called *Noces* (Wedding) at thirteen. (It's on the Largo disc.) On the strength of it, he became a protégé of Alfred Cortot, who taught him piano and farmed him out to Nadia Boulanger for training in harmony and counterpoint. He quickly progressed to free composition, since (as Boulanger liked to say) he was born knowing all the rules. In 1928 he played part of a Stravinsky-saturated Sinfonietta for Diaghilev, who fell hard for him and immediately began touting the young man as his latest great discovery. In this case, Diaghilev's passion was requited only artistically. As with his other young men—Vaslav Nijinsky, whom he presented to Paris at nineteen, or Boris Kochno, who wrote the libretto for Stravinsky's *Mavra* at seventeen—the great impresario took over the young Markevitch's life. He "unveiled" the lad in a concert hurriedly held at Covent Garden in 1929, twelve days before Markevitch's birthday, so he could still be presented as a sixteen-year-old in a hastily composed Piano Concerto Diaghilev had commissioned from him. (It is the one piece that the publisher Boosey & Hawkes, when it belatedly signed Markevitch on as a composer in 1978, could not get him to reissue.)

A couple of days earlier, Diaghilev had published an open letter in the *Times* of London proclaiming that his "young countryman" would finally put an end to the gaudy "Paris orgies" of the past two decades: artistic orgies that

Diaghilev himself, of course, had perpetrated, but of which he now blaringly repented. It could even be said (and was said) that the great man laid down his life for his last boy toy. Against his doctor's orders, Diaghilev romanced Markevitch with a whirlwind tour of Germany, where they met with Hindemith, heard Mozart (under Richard Strauss) and Wagner *(Tristan und Isolde)*, and went to all the museums. Diaghilev returned to Venice exhausted, and died twelve days later. He left Markevitch a marked man, at seventeen already a figure of jealous controversy. The protagonists of the "Paris orgies," Stravinsky and Prokofieff, not pleased with what they had been reading, snubbed him.

Stravinsky settled scores with the young Markevitch, as he did with so many others, in his books of "Conversations" with Robert Craft. He tried (unsuccessfully) to prevent his own German publisher, Schott, from taking an interest in Markevitch's work, writing that the boy was not so much wunderkind as "altklug," a precocious flash-in-the-pan. He even sent his son Soulima, also a pianist and composer, to insult Markevitch at the première of a choral cantata in 1930. "It must be awful being another Igor," Soulima taunted. "It must be worse to be another Stravinsky," little Igor shot back. The anecdote comes courtesy of Prokofieff, who included it in a letter home along with uncomplimentary remarks of his own. But Prokofieff's put-down, however ill meant, gives insight into why Markevitch's composerly career ultimately fizzled. "He has definite abilities," Prokofieff allowed, "but the good moments drown in waves of Beckmesserisms."

The reference to Wagner's inept mastersinger, whose name is synonymous with clumsy pedantry, was Prokofieff's catty way of signaling that Markevitch suffered from German influences, mainly Hindemith's. Probably few listeners today would agree, even though one of the pieces now recorded, the Concerto Grosso of 1930, took Hindemith's Concerto for Orchestra as a model. The composer whose music Markevitch's most resembles is Arthur Honegger: not the Honegger of Les Six (though there's an echo of those composers in Markevitch's *Galop*, which would make ideal theme music for *The Simpsons*) but the biblical Honegger of *King David* and *Judith* and the muscular "polytonal" Honegger of the early symphonic poems *(Chant de Joie, Rugby, Pacific 231)*.

Even without benefit of Hindemith, though, Beckmesserisms there certainly were. Markevitch's great flair was for colorful orchestral textures, often polyrhythmic. In works like *Icare* and *Rebus* (his other ballet) and in two monumental suites—*Hymnes* (1933) and *Le Nouvel Age* (The New Age, 1937)—he often builds up magnificent sonic montages combining concurrent ostinatos with two, three, four, six, and nine beats to the bar. But then, usually, his imagination stalls, and he just sits on them, or alternates a couple or three, for pages at a time. Not only that, but the units so tiresomely reiterated are almost invariably a dull two or four bars in length.

Foursquareness also pervades the harmonic rhythm, the rate at which chords change. The *Cantique d'Amour,* of 1936, a lush jungle growth of virtually themeless orchestral tissue, is an obvious homage to the Scriabin of the "Poem of Ecstasy," and also, perhaps, to the Brasilianas of Villa-Lobos, then a frequent presence in Paris concert programs. Its sensuality quickly palls, however, as polyharmony succeeds hyperharmony (as Rimsky-Korsakov would have said) with clockwork predictability at every bar line. Call it the march of ecstasy or the poem of accuracy: either way, the effect is nugatory.

The deadness of his "larger rhythm" despite all the inventive tinycraft is Markevitch's most obvious liability today. When his work was new, there were esthetic handicaps as well. The music is resolutely modernistic yet old-fashioned at the same time, because what it tended to flaunt was yesterday's modernism, or even the day before's. This was something about which Diaghilev cautioned Markevitch at their first meeting. Suspecting that his young idol was worshiping the thoroughly outmoded Ravel, Diaghilev upbraided him. "Why get so excited about yesterday?" he asked. The sixteen-year-old drew himself up as best he could and retorted, "I'm not interested in yesterday or today but in what is forever." From that moment, Diaghilev was smitten.

But he was right. Markevitch remained always about a decade behind the avant-garde, and in avant-garde circles a decade or two is maximum lag. Stravinsky sensed Markevitch's fixation on his own *Rite of Spring* (of which the later Markevitch became an intrepid exponent on the podium) and chided him mercilessly in a letter of 1934 about his devotion to a work "from whose esthetic tendencies I have been moving further and further away in what I have been doing for more than 15 years." Stravinsky may have had in mind *Hymnes,* a set of four noisy paeans to contemporary life that kept alive (or on artificial life support) the neoprimitivist esthetic of *The Rite* long into the age of neoclassicism. They also reverberated with the "Symphony of Machines" rhetoric of the Italian futurists, already stale in George Antheil's *Ballet Mécanique,* by then a decade old. The second movement, the "Hymne au Travail" (Hymn to Work), even smacks of Alexander Mosolov's dowdy old *Iron Foundry,* the emblematic "constructivist" opus of the Soviet twenties, and it is no surprise to learn from the CD booklet that Sergey Eisenstein, the great director, tried to entice Markevitch to return to Soviet Russia at the height of Stalinism to collaborate on films. (Only his mother's objections—her "irrational fear" of Soviet Communism, as the booklet puts it with remarkable obtuseness—prevented Markevitch's acceptance.)

But even Stravinsky was impressed with the Icarus ballet, the one piece that deserved a future. (Markevitch gave symbolic assent to this judgment in 1943, when he revised and simplified the ballet, originally titled *L'Envol d'Icare,* or "The Flight of Icarus," as the symphonic poem *Icare,* the version Mr. Botstein will conduct. It was his last creative act; only arrangements—Bach,

Musorgsky, and Johann Strauss, of all unlikely trios—lay ahead.) The ballet was planned in collaboration with the dancer and choreographer Serge Lifar, the other significant young man of Diaghilev's last years. Lifar, who in his autobiography claimed credit for the idea and for commissioning the ballet as a memorial to Diaghilev, pulled out, calling Markevitch's music "antidanceable." (Since he also said that of Stravinsky's music, the remark only shows why as a choreographer Lifar was only Lifar.) Nevertheless, its rhythmic momentum is irresistibly corporeal; for once the ostinatos and the polyrhythms conspire to produce exaltation and, yes, "elevation."

Ultramodernistic touches abound: quarter-tone harmonies (removed in the revision, after they had caused the BBC to reject Markevitch's own early recording as unsuitable for broadcast due to poor intonation); toneless blowing into the brass instruments when the slain Icarus's wings are discovered, a marvelous symbol of deflation and mute grief; measured accelerandos and ritardandos, anticipating Elliott Carter by fifteen years, in the section where the singing birds (anticipating Messaien) teach little Icarus to fly. But they are un-self-consciously evocative, never mere stylistic effrontery. Finally, there is the strangely moving ritual dance, set to imitation gamelan music, to mourn the hero's death. This score has magic. The poetic justice of its influence on Stravinsky's *Orpheus* (1948) is satisfying.

Unfortunately, like the rest of the orchestral music recorded by Marco Polo, it receives a somewhat shaky, tentatively paced, and haphazardly balanced performance from Mr. Lyndon-Gee and his orchestra. It is possible that one reason I have been left relatively unimpressed by Markevitch's polyrhythms is that I have not heard them performed with the requisite independence of parts. Big triplets, in particular, are reduced to rhumba rhythms in a manner that anyone who has rehearsed such a passage will instantly recognize. It's a hard task for any orchestra and for the conductor who has to teach the players how to "group" and "subdivide" their count against the general beat. I wish Mr. Botstein luck.

POSTSCRIPT, 2008

The *Times* gave this a pleonastic headline—"Markevitch as Composer: An Icarus Who Flew Too High?"—not because they didn't know any better, but because the title I offered (reinstated here) did not fill the requisite space. The piece brought me a nice letter from Markevitch's much younger brother, the cellist Dmitry Markevitch, which included a memoir worth recording:

> I don't know if he was really "burned out at thirty," but one of his rare explanations for stopping to compose was that music around 1940 had arrived at a sort of dead-end, and he saw no future for it. He was, maybe, not completely off in his thinking. At my last visit to Nadia Boulanger, shortly before she died,

she, who was always very close to Igor, asked me if I understood why he had cut short his composing career because it was still for her an absolute riddle.

It also elicited some nasty backbiting—I can't tell whether it is directed at me or at Markevitch—from Robert Craft, Stravinsky's jealous widow, who took time out in his autobiography to set "my good friend Richard Taruskin" straight about a thing or two:

> Described as "tall, gauntly handsome, icily cultivated," and "for more than five decades a spook of the first magnitude in the music life of Europe," he was actually of medium height, puny, with a pinched, expressionless face, and was never more than a marginal figure whose sole claim to fame was that at age sixteen he became Diaghilev's catamite. In 1929 "Diaghilev romanced [him] with a whirlwind tour," the article goes on, then "returned to Venice exhausted, and died twelve days later." In truth Diaghilev, refusing insulin, had died of diabetes. Markevitch denied that he had had any sexual affair with him, but Stravinsky saw him enter Diaghilev's sleeping compartment on the same Paris-to-London night train in July 1929.[1]

NOTE

1. Robert Craft, *An Improbable Life* (Nashville: Vanderbilt University Press, 2002), 402–3.

19

Let's Rescue Poor Schumann
from His Rescuers

Don't look now, but Robert Schumann is being rescued again. This time the deliverers are John Eliot Gardiner and the Orchestre Revolutionnaire et Romantique, his period-instrument ensemble, performing the four numbered "canonical" symphonies, plus the early unfinished one in G minor (in somebody's eclectic conflation of its two extant sources); the original 1841 version of the Fourth; the Overture, Scherzo and Finale; and the *Konzertstück* in F for four horns and orchestra, all in a three-CD Archiv set (457 591-2).

It happens about as regularly as El Niño. Some conductor suddenly realizes that Schumann was not the hopeless bumbler we thought he was but was rather a good composer, actually. All we have to do is trust him. In the sixties it was Leonard Bernstein. "Mr. Bernstein has faith in the rightness of Schumann's own instrumentation," the jackets of the New York Philharmonic's recordings proclaimed. They gave listeners a chance—nay, "the unique opportunity"—to hear the music "just as Schumann left it, unburdened with the usual revisions designed to 'correct' the composer's reputed deficiencies as an orchestrator." In the fifties it was George Szell, who promoted his Cleveland Orchestra set with an essay in these very pages announcing that "Schumann's symphonies can be a thrilling experience to both performers and audiences if Schumann's case is stated clearly and convincingly through the proper style of interpretation." Szell acknowledged Schumann's "inability to establish proper balances," admonishing further that "this can and must be helped with all means known to any professional conductor who professes to be a cultured and style-conscious musician." Retouching, however, must be applied with "much soul-searching and discrimination."

First published in the *New York Times*, 17 May 1998. Copyright © 2008 The New York Times Company. Reprinted by permission.

Gustav Mahler (who had not yet been canonized but was about to be) took some ritual lumps. He had made "a most unfortunate mistake" by resorting to "wholesale reorchestration" of the symphonies, in perpetrating which he "adulterates the character of these works by wrapping them in a meretricious garb of sound completely alien to their nature and, in some instances, even goes so far as to change the music itself." Szell's own amendments covered "the whole range from subtle adjustment of dynamic marks to the radical surgery of reorchestrating whole stretches" (as distinct, somehow, from "wholesale reorchestration"), but this was not mentioned on the record jackets. Instead, in a move that anticipated by decades the claims of early-music maestros today, the emphasis was placed on hardware. "Listeners may note the unusually mellow trumpet sound," the sleeve note suggested. "Known as 'Austrian trumpets,' the instruments used here are of wide bore and have rotary valves."

Now come Mr. Gardiner and his band, elevating the rhetoric still higher. "The general view is that Schumann was a gifted amateur who could not orchestrate," the conductor has been telling interviewers. In the booklet, he writes about removing "the false patina of late-Romantic orchestral sonorities which is totally alien to Schumann's esthetic and ideals," maintaining that any problem conductors have had with Schumann within living memory "simply evaporates in an accomplished period performance." By reducing the orchestra to the size "for which Schumann had assiduously fashioned his symphonies," by restoring the right "bowing styles, phrasing and articulation, as well as the spatial deployment of the musicians (with violins and violas standing for symphonies, as was the custom then in Leipzig)," one dispels the "web of myth" and reveals Schumann as he really was, "an intuitively able and imaginative composer for the orchestra of his day."

Stuff and nonsense, every word. By now it is easy to see what performers are really seeking when they noisily side with the composer against critics real or imagined (including "practical critics," like Mahler) and presume to speak on his behalf. They are seeking authority (code name: "authenticity") and privilege. "Criticize me, and you're no friend of Schumann," is the threatening implication. *L'auteur, c'est moi.* This is an old ventriloquists' ploy, and now, of course, it is especially rife among early-musickers. "What do you think Bach would say if he were here?" the harpsichordist Davitt Moroney asked a student at a master class in Berkeley, California, not long ago, immediately casting himself as Edgar Bergen to old Sebastian's Charlie McCarthy. Hand on heart, I swear and depose that the first thing Mr. Moroney's Bach puppet wanted to know was, "What edition are you using?"

It's not always that risible, but the position is always false, and in the case of Schumann its mendacity goes right to the first assumption, that the composer needs defenders. Well over a century ago, in the first edition of the *Grove Dictionary of Music and Musicians*, the great German scholar Philipp

Spitta wrote that "Schumann's symphonies may without injustice be considered as the most important which have been written since Beethoven." Surely few today would disagree that they were the most important classical-style symphonies to appear between Beethoven's and Brahms's. Nor were Mahler's interventions the arbitrary vandalism that Szell and now Mr. Gardiner in his booklet have alleged. They did not amount to a whole new score, just retouchings and (in particular) textural thinnings that Mahler marked in his performance scores and had copied into the players' parts. They were never published, but the scores and parts have been available on rental from Universal Edition since Mahler's time, and have even been recorded (by Aldo Ceccato and the Bergen Philharmonic on two Bis CDs). Their lightening effect is actually quite similar to what Mr. Gardiner achieves with his period band.

So the "general view" Mr. Gardiner cites is his own little web of myth. If Schumann's reputation as a symphonist ever suffered an eclipse, it was during the period from the 1850s to the 1870s, when, under pressure from Liszt, Wagner, and the so-called New Germans, the symphony itself briefly suffered one. It was Brahms who rescued Schumann, not Bernstein or Szell, let alone the Orchestre Revolutionnaire et Romantique.

But revolutionary? Romantic? Prim and perky would be more like it. The tradition that feeds Mr. Gardiner's approach to Schumann is that of twentieth-century modernism and nothing earlier. If these were really "period" performances, they would be awash in tempo rubato, string portamento, and other practices of which Mr. Gardiner, as a twentieth-century musician, heartily disapproves. Not that his tempos are completely inflexible. He even lets his strings slide ever so gingerly through large slurred intervals (as in the introduction to the Overture, Scherzo, and Finale). But these are grudging, chary concessions to "performance practice," not the joyful recovery of forgotten lore that they might have been. And that is because the "false patina" Mr. Gardiner deplores was the historical reality. His attempt to scrub it away could not be more anachronistic.

This really should not bother anyone. Remaking the classics is the only way to keep them alive. The trouble is that the bright, fresh, delightfully clean and clear-textured if somewhat top-heavy sonority Mr. Gardiner elicits from his band is rarely matched by any comparable novelty in interpretation. Tempos, to begin with what is objectively testable, are almost always what we're used to, not what Schumann prescribed with his metronome. Again, there is nothing wrong with that. At least one of Schumann's metronome settings, for the finale of the Second Symphony, is generally conceded to be unplayable, and it is not attempted here. But falling back on the modern consensus hardly validates a claim to the composer's authority.

In the First Symphony, Mr. Gardiner's tempos are fully in accord with those listed two decades ago by Brian Schlotel, an English scholar, in a useful survey of midcentury recordings, including Szell's. As in most of the others, Mr. Gardiner's first movement is faster than Schumann's, his second movement slower, and the finale much faster. The speeds of the scherzo and the first trio in the third movement, unlike those Schumann notated but like most of the ones Mr. Schlotel calibrated, are in a simple proportional relationship: two beats of scherzo equal three of trio. The Boston conductor David Epstein, in his recent book, *Shaping Time,* claims that the pleasure we take in proportional tempos is "natural" and that music in repertory inevitably slips into such relationships over time, making them "traditional." That sort of tradition, Mr. Epstein suggests, is what keeps repertories alive. But the period-performance movement is founded, at least in theory, on resistance to socially mediated tradition, what Mr. Gardiner so sneeringly calls the "patina." (So is modernist music making, of course, beginning with Mahler's famous battle cry equating tradition with sloppiness.) Should he not practice what he preaches, or else stop preaching?

His performances differ noticeably from traditional ones only in the niceties of timbre and balance. And nice niceties they are. But are they enough? In the *Konzertstück* for four horns, they certainly are. The soloists' opening riff is hair-raising, almost worth the price of the album. Ditto the early version of the Fourth Symphony. The lightness of the orchestration contrasts all the more tellingly, in Mr. Gardiner's hands, with the dark, thickly laden version that we know, making the latter's sterner, even somewhat dingy coloration (the result of massive doubling of lines) seem less a miscalculation and more a deliberately struck, Beethovenian "D minor" attitude.

Mr. Gardiner's chief reason for preferring the earlier version is different, though, and symptomatic: the original audience found it baffling. To a modernist that reaction is a plus. To Schumann it was a reason to revise. The revision was successful in that it was well received. To Mr. Gardiner, however, Schumann's success smacked of compromise, "as though he was willfully expunging some of the more audacious features of the original, replacing them with something safer but, in the process, more commonplace." Yet anyone listening to the original version who knows the standard one will miss the thematic recalls in the finale, which occurred to Schumann only as he was revising. They are something added, not expunged, and they are the opposite of commonplace.

In the canonical symphonies, as opposed to the novelty items, there is as much loss as gain in Mr. Gardiner's performances; and what is lost, unfortunately, has a lot to do with why the symphonies are loved (that is, why they have become canonical and familiar). Arguing against foolproofing the scores, Mr. Schlotel put it this way: "The sense of striving for high ideals, which the symphonies communicate, is in a way echoed by the orchestra striving for effect in those passages that are difficult to bring off." In other words, there is an ethical dimension, endemic to the romantic concept of art, that is lost from the sleek sound-surface that modern performers—and period performers, paradoxically, most of all—have fetishized. The really crucial and compelling aspects of romantic music are precisely what is undreamt of in their philosophy.

The upshot, simply, is that Mr. Gardiner's "esthetic and ideals" are very different from Schumann's. And why not? He's entitled. And we are equally entitled to prefer his brisk Lipton-tea approach to the music if, like him, we are leery of anything stronger. His performances are full of charming details (my favorite: the articulation of the woodwind accents in the second theme from the opening movement of the First Symphony). And like many scrupulous period bands, the Orchestre Revolutionnaire et Romantique is much more alert to dynamics than are most standard orchestras today, which is also a pleasure. But to the odious claim of privilege he has alleged, Mr. Gardiner and his band are manifestly not entitled. Its dishonesty diminishes them. It taints their excellent musicianship with charlatanry. They really ought to give it up.

20

Early Music
Truly Old-Fashioned at Last?

If two new CDs by the English violinist Andrew Manze are any indication, early music may finally be shedding one of classical music's most venerable but useless assumptions: to wit, the funny notion abroad among classical-music reviewers that the best thing a performer can do is disappear.

Ian Bostridge, an English tenor, was warmly praised recently for what one critic, Paul Griffiths, somewhat infelicitously called his "self-elimination" during a performance of Schumann's *Dichterliebe,* of all things. Pianists and violinists who fail to duplicate Mr. Bostridge's feat during concerto appearances regularly take their lumps, in these pages and elsewhere, for distracting the audience's attention from "the music." Since the complaint is voiced just as frequently in reviews of recordings, the offending distractions must be not merely visual (up-thrown limbs, tossing manes, whatever), but aural, too. Yet what can it mean to say that the sounds of the performance distract from the music? Aren't those sounds the music?

Apparently not. "My God, what has sound got to do with music!" Charles Ives blustered in his *Essays before a Sonata.* Or, as Sir Thomas Beecham once opined, "The British public doesn't really care for music, but it simply adores the noise it makes." Contempt for crowd-pleasing virtuosos is often touted as a blow against romanticism, that all-purpose punching bag. But critics who distinguish between the sounds and the music share with Ives and Beecham the assumption that a piece of music—"great" music, anyway—is a fixed and sacrosanct "idea" rather than a bunch of noises that may vary greatly from performance to performance. That is idealism, and idealism is romanticism at its most extreme.

First published in the *New York Times,* 14 June 1998. Copyright © 2008 The New York Times Company. Reprinted by permission.

129

Romanticism's transition into its "late, late" phase called modernism (as the music theorist Leonard B. Meyer so delightfully puts it) can be gauged by noting the mounting hostility toward performers as the twentieth century reached its middle. For Arnold Schoenberg, whose career actually enacted the move from late romanticism to late-late, performance was at best a necessary evil, of value only to those lacking the skills required to derive the full experience of a musical composition from silent perusal of the score. Pierre Boulez, in his bomb-throwing youth, actually declared performances obsolete for contemporary music, since the only information of interest to intelligent musicians was the kind that notation conveyed to the eye, and the eye to the mind. Hearing added nothing. Even Brahms, more than half a century before the peak phase, voiced a kindred thought when he turned down an invitation to Mozart's *Don Giovanni* with the remark that if he sat at home with the score he'd hear a better performance.

Mozart would not have known what on earth Brahms was talking about. In his preromantic age, the score was not the sacred repository of the fragile idea that critics were sworn to defend against marauders. The score was simply what enabled a performance and furnished its springboard. The more one bunch of notes thus enabled varied from another, the better. The performer's contribution was cherished and eagerly awaited. To fail to astonish or surprise—in a word, to distract—the audience with one's novel take on the familiar would have been regarded as an insult. Performers who self-eliminated could expect to be flushed away.

Of no one was this truer than of Mozart himself. As we know from the deliberately incomplete notation of the scores, he left himself plenty of room for spontaneous display in his own concertos and expected the same of anybody else who played them. That is why it has always been so bizarre, even if inevitable, that early-music performers, though they specialize in preromantic repertory, have been especially prone to impose on themselves all the puritanical inhibitions with which romantic idealism has shackled the performance of classical music.

The result, we may as well admit, has been pious boredom. How could it be otherwise, when notations meant as springboards for fancy diving are treated as holy writ? You might as well stare at a diving board and call it the Olympics. What early music has been needing even more urgently than other branches of classical music has been a new infusion of old-fashioned— *truly* old-fashioned—performerly values: not self-elimination but self-asserting, crowd-pleasing exhibitionism and vulgarity, the kind for which Mozart was famous, and Handel, and Vivaldi.

For some time, the only promising figure on the horizon has been the pianist Robert Levin, happily more famous than notorious by now for his improvised cadenzas, florid embellishments, and other distractions from "the music" of Mozart's concertos. Now there is another: Mr. Manze, who in a pair of new Harmonia Mundi CDs of music by Vivaldi (*Concert for the Prince of Poland*, HMU 907230) and Giuseppe Tartini (*The Devil's Sonata and Other Works*, HMU 907213) combines formidable fiddling virtuosity with a truly baroque (that is, over-the-top) taste for the outlandish. What results from this cross-fertilization—especially in the astonishing Tartini disc, where Mr. Manze goes it alone, unaccompanied and under high magnification, for sixty-eight minutes of enthralling mischief—is one of the most encouraging defiances of late-late romantic taste I've heard in years.

The Vivaldi program reconstructs the evening of 21 March 1740, when Friedrich Christian, the German heir to the Polish throne (and, incidentally, the son of J. S. Bach's nominal patron) paid a visit to the Ospedale della Pieta, the Venetian foundling home for girls where Vivaldi spent many years as music master. Four of the composer's most colorfully scored orchestral works were played in the visitor's honor to frame a performance of a serenata, or choral ode, that has not survived. On the present disc these pieces— a sinfonia for strings, and concertos for lute and viola d'amore, for violin and "echo violins," and for a large band including early clarinets and mandolins—are dispatched neatly and (as usual) all too respectfully by the Academy of Ancient Music, the London-based ensemble founded by Christopher Hogwood. The spectacular items are the two titled concertos, both from Vivaldi's Opus 8 (which also contains the "Four Seasons"), that Mr. Manze performs in place of the missing serenata.

In "La Tempesta di Mare" (Storm at Sea), the turbulent outer movements are performed appropriately, to say the least. But the special moment comes in the Largo, where Mr. Manze deploys some weird timbres and articulations, and a gruesome cadenza inserted just where the harmony is at its purplest, to evoke, and possibly transmit, a case of seasickness. (Is it just my depraved imagination, or is he parodying for this purpose some of the mannerisms of Dutch-style "Baroque" fiddling, vintage 1970?) In "Il Piacere" (Something to Please), Mr. Manze disrupts the last movement with a stunning cadenza of *bariolage*, or wild string-crossing, inspired (as he admits) by Tartini but reminiscent of another German visitor's description of Vivaldi's own playing. At the end of an aria, the traveler reported, Vivaldi "added an improvisation that really frightened me, for I doubt anything like it was ever done before, or ever will be again: he came to within a hairbreadth of the bridge, leaving no room for the bow, and this on all four strings, with imitations and at an incredible speed." It only remains to add that Mr. Manze's frightening playing here, as everywhere, is perfectly in tune, as I'll bet Vivaldi's was not. Perfect intonation is something recordings have enforced.

But the Tartini devil-disc is the one every violinist should hear. The title piece, Tartini's most famous, is the one that (according to the composer's proto-Paganinian boast) came to him in a dream when he handed his violin to the Devil "to see if he might manage some pretty tunes; but imagine my astonishment when I heard a sonata so unusual and so beautiful, performed with such mastery and intelligence, on a level I had never before conceived was possible!" In addition, the disc contains two other sonatas, one an old-fashioned long-winded affair ending in an "aria" with five virtuoso variations, the other a Pastorale in a *scordatura,* or special tuning, that imitates bagpipes. Finally there is a selection from Tartini's treatise *L'Arte del arco* (The Art of the Bow), a colossal violinistic track meet consisting of dozens of variations on a gavotte by Arcangelo Corelli, the Baroque fiddler's patron saint.

As "music," none of this amounts to much. The sounds, however, as Mr. Manze emits them, are magic. And that is because Mr. Manze has recovered the preromantic, pre-idealistic esthetic that gives them life. Although Tartini published his pieces with figured bass, Mr. Manze plays them without accompaniment, the way Tartini said he preferred. This means that Mr. Manze, like Tartini before him, wreaks total havoc with the score as written, adding chords wholesale (some of them quite weird, like Vivaldi's), transposing by octaves ad lib, and indulging speculatively in all kinds of violinistic effects that were not only unwritten but unwritable at the time.

Without any prompting save informed imagination and native chutzpah, the violinist plays *sul tasto* (bowing over the fingerboard for ethereal effects) and *sul ponticello* (bowing close to the bridge for ghostly ones). He slides achingly whenever he feels like it, not only between widely spaced notes, but also between consecutive scale degrees. He plays open and stopped notes in unison, then bends the pitch of the latter to produce a grotesquely expressive wow. He doubles pitches at the third, adds swells and tremolos, interpolates pizzicatos and natural harmonics with abandon. With his bow he produces a range of colors and articulations never before heard on "Baroque" violin. In the Pastorale, he even tweaks up the fourth degree of the scale by a quarter tone or so, the way actual rustic bagpipes often do.

In short, he never lets you forget he's there, adding his skills and inspiration to those of the composer, as often as not upstaging him. And what emerges is a violinistic masterpiece, in which abstract composing and real-time performing have merged—or "remerged," since that is how it used to be—into a single act. It is the most convincing "period performance" I have ever heard, which of course is not to say that it is anything other than make-believe. But the chaste literalism that we're used to, and that has been stifling classical music, is also make-believe—and, for early music, the greater anachronism. Let's leave the self-eliminators to their appropriately sterile repertory (roughly middle Stravinsky to early Princeton) and stop policing the rest. Mr. Manze's version of historically informed performance can point the way toward a healthy desterilization. I wish him lots of competition.

21

Bartók and Stravinsky
Odd Couple Reunited?

"I never could share his lifelong gusto for his native folklore," said Igor Stravinsky of Bela Bartók in 1959. And what is more, "I couldn't help regretting it in the great musician." Stravinsky was seeking distance from a composer with whom, he felt, he was too often compared. On Wednesday and Friday evenings, the Hungarian pianist András Schiff, the Hungarian conductor Ivan Fischer, and the Budapest Festival Orchestra bring their countryman and the latter's unwilling Russian counterpart back together at Carnegie Hall, setting Bartók's three piano concertos in what the performers evidently consider their proper Stravinskian context.

It's about time. Stravinsky's declaration about Bartók wasn't made under oath, so it may not rise to the level of an impeachable offense. But like most of what the aging composer told his many interlocutors, it was a half-truth at best. By 1959, a dozen years into the cold war, Stravinsky was following the herd and trying to establish credentials as a twelve-tone composer. That meant seeking the "universal" (and politically safe) truth of numbers to validate his art rather than the particular (and politically risky) reality of nation.

A Russian living in America might have had especially strong reasons just then to repudiate his national heritage, but Stravinsky's reasons went farther back, to his years as a "white émigré" in Paris. In 1939, lecturing in French at Harvard University, the Parisian Stravinsky went out of his way to deride the "dancing collective farm" and the "symphony of Socialism." These were the musical emblems, popularized by Shostakovich, of the Red Russia Stravinsky abhorred, where an art "national in form and Socialist in content" (in Stalin's words) was official, enforceable cultural policy.

First published in the *New York Times*, 6 June 1999. Copyright © 2008 The New York Times Company. Reprinted by permission.

But Stravinsky originally made his name as a staff composer for Sergey Diaghilev's Ballets Russes, purveying music that positively dripped with native folklore. He continued to write in this vein until the early 1920s, when it became clear that the Bolsheviks were there to stay and he could never go home again. His extraordinary knack for blending folklore and modernism was an inspiration to many composers, Bartók most of all. A practicing "comparative musicologist" (as ethnomusicologists were known in those days) and a matchless connoisseur of not only Hungarian, but many kinds of folk music, Bartók was convinced of the authenticity of Stravinsky's folk sources. And that, he believed, was what gave Stravinsky's modernism its authenticity. In a lecture of 1943 (also, as it happened, given at Harvard), he asserted flat out that Stravinsky's Diaghilev ballets were based on "Russian peasant music" and that in the most modernistic of them, *The Rite of Spring*, the peasant influence was most pervasive of all. "Almost all the motives" in that ballet, Bartók said, "seem to be Russian peasant music motives or their excellent imitations." And what is more, it was precisely the most novel aspects of Stravinsky's music, its form and rhythm, that were most heavily indebted to folklore. "Even the origin of the rough-grained, brittle and jerky musical structure backed by ostinatos," Bartok marveled, "which is so completely different from any structural proceeding of the past, may be sought in the short-breathed Russian peasant motives."

Stravinsky fairly screamed denial until the day he died, but Bartók was right. We now know that at least a dozen themes in *The Rite* (besides the opening bassoon melody, the one acknowledged borrowing) came from published folk song anthologies, and we'll never know how many more may have come from oral tradition. So sure was Bartók of Stravinsky's fidelity to the folk that he actually thought he needed to defend the possibility that "among the thematic material of Stravinsky's there are some of his own invention." However Stravinsky might have winced, this was meant as highest praise.

Bartók did not live to witness or react to the cold war, but he suffered its consequences posthumously. His legacy, which drew its authenticity in his own eyes from its seamless Stravinskian blend of folklore and modernism, was ruthlessly partitioned, like Europe itself, into Eastern and Western zones. In his homeland, the works in which folklore was perceived to predominate were touted by the culture politicians as obligatory models, and the rest was anathematized or, in some cases, banned. The Western European avant-garde, meanwhile, made virtual fetishes of aggressively modernistic works like the Third and Fourth String Quartets, and accused the composer of the late but audience-friendly *Concerto for Orchestra* of "compromise." In the aftermath of World War II, that word—applied to Bartók by René Leibowitz, an early mentor of Pierre Boulez, in an infamous article of 1947—had a chilling ring. Never let it be said again that modern music evolved in lofty or innocent detachment from modern politics.

But it's yesterday's politics. It lives on in pockets of superannuated opinion like Washington think tanks and academic music departments, but if we don't want Bartók and Stravinsky to become yesterday's music, we need to put their work in new contexts, like the one Mr. Schiff and Mr. Fischer are proposing. Each of their programs will feature a Bartók concerto or two as centerpiece, flanked on one side by one of Stravinsky's later, ostensibly cosmopolitan works (Symphony in Three Movements on Wednesday, *Jeu de Cartes* on Friday) and on the other by a folkloric ballet *(Firebird* Suite and *Petrushka).* Stravinsky, you might say, will provide the antitheses, Bartók the synthesis.

It's a neat idea. And when *Petrushka* follows Bartók's Second Concerto, which practically quotes from it (and from *Firebird* as well), but in a decidedly "neoclassical" context, the idea is bound to hit home. All the labels we customarily apply in our efforts to sort out the politics (ei, styles) of modern music are arbitrary, simplistic, and in their origins invidious. Juxtapositions like the ones Mr. Schiff and Mr. Fischer will offer invite us to approach the crosscurrents of twentieth-century taste and idiom with less prejudice and a heightened awareness of the complex interaction of the personal and the political.

It is a pity, though, that Mr. Schiff is not going to perform Stravinsky's Concerto for Piano and Winds alongside Bartók's First Concerto, because that would have been the most ear-opening juxtaposition of all. The concertos were composed two years apart, Bartók's under the strong impression not only of Stravinsky's score but also of Stravinsky's performance of it as pianist in Budapest in March 1926. As the Bartók scholar David Schneider has recently demonstrated in fascinating detail, Bartók found Stravinsky's work at once irresistible and repellent. The tension this ambivalent reaction created in him was one of the most powerful stimulants he ever received. It roused him from a three-year creative block and led him to his maturest style.

Stravinsky's concerto was the bellwether of its uprooted composer's "objective" or "neoclassical" manner. It spoke (or tried to speak) neither Russian nor any other particular dialect but rather a musical Esperanto, its vocabulary laced with references to Bach, the perceived fountainhead of "universal" or "timeless" values. A letter from Bartók's wife to his mother about Stravinsky's performance expressed serious reservations about this project. "We very, very much enjoyed the evening," she wrote. "Truly one gets caught up in his miraculously beautiful-sounding machine music, music of pulsating rhythm." But it was a music in which "there is absolutely no room for feelings, in which you can find no part that causes tears to come to your eyes." In short, she wrote, "this music is not my homeland."

Bartók saw it as his task to reconcile that dynamic pulsation, in which he sensed the lingering reverberations of Stravinsky's earlier manner, with a sense of homeland that would restore the missing feelings and tears. The

First Concerto, the most direct emulation the pianist-composer Bartók could have offered the pianist-composer Stravinsky, was the outcome. The love-hate relationship with Stravinsky is manifest at all levels of the concerto's form and substance, from reflexive near-quotations on the surface to profound transformations in which Stravinsky's monumental abstract rhythmic gearshifts are morphed into what László Somfai, the leading Hungarian Bartók scholar, calls "Hungarian culmination points": sudden heavy infusions of national style at an abruptly broadened tempo. Hearing the two concertos side by side would have been electrifying.

And so it would have been to hear Bartók's *Concerto for Orchestra* alongside Stravinsky's Symphony in Three Movements. The Third Piano Concerto, composed in America just before Bartók's death, will be a serviceable stand-in. It, too, will make the point that the war years brought a new urgency of communication to the work of both composers, and a sense of social solidarity that mitigated their earlier commitment to modernism. But whereas the piano concerto makes the point serenely and perhaps a bit sentimentally, the *Concerto for Orchestra* retains a characteristic Bartókian ambivalence. That ambivalence is heard most clearly in the famous put-down of Shostakovich's Seventh Symphony that "interrupts" the concerto's fourth movement. When overdone (or when politically mandated), Bartók seems to imply, even urgent communication and sincere social commitment can turn destructive and lead art into blatancy and banality. The exiled Hungarian seems here to be echoing the exiled Russian's contempt for "symphonies of Socialism." But interestingly enough, the Symphony in Three Movements shows Stravinsky himself coming perilously close to writing a socialist realist score at the prompting of wartime emotion.

Much of it sounds like movie music. And indeed, much of it was. The second movement was written on spec for the 1943 film *The Song of Bernadette* (20th Century-Fox wasn't buying; the job went to Alfred Newman), and the third, by Stravinsky's own admission, was an imaginary newsreel sound track to accompany scenes of battle and victory. Stravinsky even recovered a sense of Russian patriotism in wartime Hollywood. A couple of scores from the mid-1940s secretly quote Russian folk tunes, and the scoring of the Symphony in Three Movements pays covert homage to Glinka. Its first movement features a piano obbligato. In the second, a solo harp holds forth. In the third, the two solo instruments play in tandem, producing a silvery tinkle in which any Russian opera lover will recognize the evocation of the minstrel's *gusli* (a Russian folk psaltery) in the Prologue to *Ruslan and Ludmila,* that great national epic of heroic deeds.

Stravinsky, as we know, lapsed quickly back into modernist respectability and social indifference. In the 1950s, he suffered a Schoenberg crisis as profound and transforming as Bartók's Stravinsky crisis had been in the 1920s. Few, though, would claim today that he weathered his crisis as successfully as

Bartók had done, or that his capitulation to historical determinism was less damaging a "compromise" than Bartók's reconciliation with the public. By now it is obvious that there were envy and repressed repentance in the barbs he hurled not only at Bartók, but at all and sundry in his late memoirs.

Bartók ended his career in a state of neglect and seeming weakness. In the Third Concerto's slow movement, written literally on his deathbed, he wistfully paraphrased Beethoven's *Heiliger Dankgesang*, the "Solemn Song of Thanksgiving" from the A minor String Quartet, which celebrated a recovery from illness that Bartók knew he would not duplicate. But I suspect that he will emerge, at Carnegie Hall this week, as the stronger, more compelling human presence. If he does, and if we are able to count his humanity as a musical plus, then the musical cold war is truly over.

22

Wagner's Antichrist Crashes
a Pagan Party

They probably didn't plan it that way, but San Francisco's leading classical-music organizations will come into an interesting collision this week. At the War Memorial Opera House, the San Francisco Opera will stir up pagan ecstasy with several complete cycles of Richard Wagner's *Ring of the Nibelung*, beginning on Wednesday. Meanwhile, beginning on Thursday across the street at Davies Symphony Hall, and in a couple of other spots around town (including a Roman Catholic church), Michael Tilson Thomas and the San Francisco Symphony will celebrate the life and times of Igor Stravinsky, who loved to bill himself as Wagner's Antichrist, and for whom the *Ring*, with its "miasmic vapors" and its labyrinth of leitmotives, amounted to nothing more than "a sort of vast musical city directory."

That last bit was a typical anti-Wagnerian wisecrack of a kind everybody makes, Wagnerians included. (Stravinsky attributed it to Debussy.) Everybody feels oppressed during a Wagner performance. That is part of its appeal. Having endured martyrdom, we are cleansed—or we are just irritated. "Before, music strove to delight people," groused another Russian, Chaikovsky, after sitting through a *Ring*. "Now they are tormented and exhausted." But even the irritated—no, especially the irritated—know that the experience they have suffered was art-transcending and religious (or at least religiose), and therefore threatening to all who would prefer to take their religion, or their art, straight.

A third Russian, Leo Tolstoy, was probably the all-time champion Wagner hater. Late in life, after he had given up literature in favor of full-time Christian moralizing, Tolstoy produced a tract called *What Is Art?* in which good

First published in the *New York Times*, 6 June 1999. Copyright © 2008 The New York Times Company. Reprinted by permission.

art was distinguished from bad solely on the basis of "message." The prime exhibit of "counterfeit art" was, of course, the *Ring*. It is subjected to more than a dozen pages of hilarious abuse, including a plot summary even funnier than Anna Russell's but almost unbearable to read because of the blood-red hatred that drips from every word. A sample: "Having finished this conversation, Siegfried seizes one of the pieces of what is meant to represent the broken sword, saws it up, puts it on what is meant to represent the forge, melts it, and then forges it and sings: 'Heiho! heiho! heiho! Ho! ho! Aha! oho! aha! Heiaho! heiaho! heiaho! Ho! ho! Hahei! hoho! hahei!' and Act I finishes."

Another sample, still about *Siegfried,* a little less funny because the dead-pan wavers, but more pointed: "The dragon is represented by two men: it is dressed in a green scale skin and waves a tail at one end while at the other it opens a kind of crocodile's jaw that is fastened on and from which flames appear. This dragon (who is meant to be dreadful and may seem so to 5-year-old children) utters some words in a terribly bass voice. This is all so stupid, so like what is done in a booth at a fair, that it is surprising that people over 7 years of age can witness it seriously; yet thousands of quasi-cultured people sit and attentively hear and see it, and are delighted."

And finally, the coup de grâce, a description not of a performance but of a rehearsal. After recounting a tirade administered to the cast by the exasperated conductor, Tolstoy muses: "I have seen one workman abuse another for not supporting the weight piled upon him when goods were being unloaded, or at haystacking, the village Elder scold a peasant for not making the rick right, and the man submitted in silence. And however unpleasant it was to witness the scene, the unpleasantness was lessened by the consciousness that the business in hand was necessary and important, and the fault for which the Elder scolded the laborer was one which might spoil a necessary undertaking. But what was being done here? For what, and for whom?" Tolstoy's was the anti-Wagnerianism of the truly religious, expressed at a time when Wagner was taken seriously as a religious thinker. It was a protest against the overvaluing of art. At the end of a century during which the overvaluing of art has come close to destroying it, one looks back and shudders.

Stravinsky's was the anti-Wagnerianism of the purely esthetic, expressed at a time when artists were in revolt against adulteration of their product, especially if adulteration came by way of social or humane concerns. The main thing Stravinsky held against Wagner was the "synthesis of the arts," his term for what Wagnerians (even when speaking other languages than German) call the *Gesamtkunstwerk,* or total work of art. It mixed music with such message-mongering media as the visual and (especially) the literary. "I do not merely condemn it for its lack of tradition, its nouveau riche smugness," Stravinsky told a Harvard audience in 1939. "What makes its case much worse is the fact that the application of its theories has inflicted a terrible blow upon music itself." The Wagnerian system, "far from having raised the level of musical culture, has never ceased to undermine it and finally to debase it." And the reason for the debasement was the fruitless denial of music's essential nature as "a purely sensual delight."

Against Wagner, Stravinsky offered Chabrier, Gounod, Delibes, Bizet, exactly the counterbid Chaikovsky had endorsed sixty years before, updated by a fresh pair of names: Andre Messager, a composer of operettas, and Henri Sauguet, the youngest composer in Sergey Diaghilev's stable. (Stravinsky probably didn't know that Messager had been famous in his youth as a Wagner conductor.) But don't expect any Messager or Sauguet festivals in San Francisco, or anywhere else, anytime soon. Wagner, on one side of the balance, easily outweighs everybody Stravinsky placed on the other side. But then so does Stravinsky himself. Was the composer of *The Rite of Spring* really a Gounod fan?

Probably not, really. But between the world wars, and especially during the anxious days of German rearmament when Stravinsky (then a French citizen) delivered his Harvard lectures, it seemed to him, as it did to many, terribly important to tout everything French over everything "Boche." From having been a surrogate Kaiser, the aggressively Germanic Wagner was already becoming a surrogate Hitler. And so he has remained for the many who can never rid their minds of all the horrific subtexts that have accrued to Wagner's works since they left his hands: not his fault, perhaps, but definitely our problem.

Stravinsky's anti-Wagner problem was different. (In anti-Semitism he could easily vie for honors with his bête noire, although nothing prevented either of them from having Jewish friends or attracting Jewish advocates like Maestro Thomas.) Like any composer's anti-Wagnerianism, Stravinsky's was not only political but also personal, and it crystallized a little—albeit very little—before World War I.

In his earliest days, as the son of an opera singer, Stravinsky actually wallowed in the very miasma he later deplored. New Year's (and new century's) greetings that an admiring critic sent Stravinsky *père* on 28 December 1900 ended with felicitations "to your lovely son, the Wagnerite musician," then an eighteen-year-old who had composed nothing. Stravinsky's period of study with Rimsky-Korsakov, contrary to legend, did nothing to lessen his Wagner worship. In winter and spring 1908, the last year of Rimsky's life, teacher and pupil attended a "Ring" cycle together. Rimsky's Boswell, a banker named Vasily Yastrebtsev, bumped into Stravinsky during the first intermission at *Siegfried*. In his diary he noted that "Igor Fyodorovich and I shared our delight in the first act of that opera, a work of genius." You know, "Ho! ho! Hahei! hoho! hahei!"

Virgil Thomson once tried to write off Stravinsky's "Russian" ballets as just the "Wagnerian theater symphony" updated, and as usual he was mean but right. The leitmotif-laden *Firebird* was as much a musical city directory as any Wagnerian spectacle, and *The Rite* was as much a pagan ecstasy. *Petrushka*, as an embodiment of Russian symbolism, was especially Wagnerian in its heritage, and it was lauded by its co-creator, Alexandre Benois, as the ultimate *Gesamtkunstwerk*, a total artwork that actually managed to beat the wizard of Bayreuth at his own game.

What finally turned Stravinsky against Wagner was another collision between them, eerily akin to the one about to take place in San Francisco. First, in May 1913, there was the riotous première of *The Rite of Spring* at the Théâtre des Champs-Elysées in Paris. Despite the myth that you will read in any music history textbook, Stravinsky experienced it as a depressing fiasco. The ballet was redeemed the next spring, when Pierre Monteux gave it a pair of concert performances that Stravinsky remembered for the rest of his life as the triumph of his career. But a scant five weeks later, on June 3, 1914, *Parsifal* had its Paris première in the same theater as *The Rite* the year before. It ran alongside the whole Diaghilev season of 1914 (which included the première of Stravinsky's *Nightingale*) and put it in the shade. Reviewers who had just hailed *The Rite* in concert now called it ephemeral, a trifle, next to Wagner's eternal genius. All the Russians, but particularly Stravinsky, were mortified. He swore revenge.

The main chance came two decades later, when he published his autobiography, *Chronicles of My Life*. One of the few richly detailed passages in that notoriously tight-lipped little book was a description of a (possibly apocryphal) visit to Bayreuth in summer 1912 to hear *Parsifal*. It joined Tolstoy's description of *Siegfried* in the annals of immortal Wagner-spite. A sample: "The very atmosphere of the theater, its design and its setting, seemed lugubrious. It was like a crematorium, and a very old-fashioned one at that, and one expected to see the gentleman in black who had been entrusted with the task of singing the praises of the departed. The order to devote oneself to contemplation was given by a blast of trumpets. I sat humble and motionless, but at the end of a quarter of an hour I could bear no more. My limbs were numb, and I had to change my position. Crack! Now I had done it! My chair had made a noise which drew down on me the furious scowls of a hundred pairs of eyes. Once more I withdrew into myself, but I could think of only one thing, and that was the end of the act, which would put an end to my martyrdom."

Like Tolstoy, Stravinsky reached for a chilling peroration. To mix art and religion "is to give proof of a complete lack of discernment, and certainly of bad taste," he railed. "But is it at all surprising that such confusion should arise at a time like the present, when the openly irreligious masses in their degradation of spiritual values and debasement of human thought necessarily lead us to utter brutalization?" William Bennett, Gary Bauer, eat your hearts out. Stravinsky said it all before, better than you.

Reconciliation with Wagner came after World War II, when it suddenly became important to Stravinsky to forge retrospective links with Wagner's self-styled heirs. He was responding to the panic he felt on returning to Europe and seeing that young composers, belatedly discovering the twelve-tone music of Schoenberg and the New Vienna School, now thought his music passé. Not only did he take up twelve-tone composition himself, Stravinsky also accepted, hook, line, and sinker, the historiographical myths that supported the Schoenbergian claim to musical supremacy. Typical of the newly suppliant Stravinsky were self-pitying pronouncements like this one, made shortly after his eightieth birthday: "I relate only from an angle to the German stem (Bach-Haydn-Mozart-Beethoven-Schubert-Brahms-Wagner-Mahler-Schoenberg)."

But look again at that list of composers. It is out of order. And Wagner is the telling anachronism. Only sixteen years younger than Schubert, he was old enough to be Brahms's father. Stravinsky's asserted mainstream was a fiction, constructed by historians (Schoenberg and Webern moonlighting among them) who replayed in forward motion a lineage that had been traced backward to justify atonal and twelve-tone music as the inevitable outcome of the "crisis of tonality" Wagner had supposedly set in motion. Putting Brahms ahead of Wagner got rid of a pesky bump in the road of progress.

According to Carl Dahlhaus, the most influential German music historian of recent times, "The assertion that Schoenberg's atonality represents a consequence of the chromaticism of *Tristan* has long been a commonplace (and remains difficult to challenge)." But it is not difficult at all to challenge—indeed, to refute. Wagner used the chromaticism of *Tristan und Isolde* to delay to the point of torture the harmonic resolution that would symbolize the slaking of sexual desire. That harmonic tension not only conveyed the dramatic situation with a force no other art could equal, but was the mainspring that controlled the syntax of what we now call "tonal" music. Did the delays caused by Wagner's chromaticism attenuate that harmonic tension? Don't be silly. They only magnified it, vastly so. Wagner's chromaticism gave tonality a new source of strength and expressivity. The consequences Schoenberg drew from Wagner's musical style were entirely idiosyncratic and ahistorical, inevitable only in eyes blinded by "dialectic." To say the very least, they had nothing to do with Wagner's creative aims, least of all in *Tristan*. So the Wagnerian "crisis of tonality" was not Wagnerian at all. It was read back into Wagner by Schoenberg's apologists, eventually including the intimidated Stravinsky.

Well, all that is behind us now. Perhaps everything is behind us now. How else to explain the ease with which, at century's end, we swallow down smorgasbords, like simultaneous Wagner and Stravinsky festivals, on which our ancestors would have gagged? That eclecticism of taste—the universal tolerance that finds nothing incompatible with anything—is now touted as a bounty of postmodernism. The rejection of "meta-narratives," postmodernists call it, meaning the rejection of universal truth claims. But do we therefore reject all truth claims? Could our failure to take sides, or even to see that sides might be taken, be masking an apathy that knoweth not its name?

Karol Berger, a Stanford musicologist, seems to hint as much when he reminds us of the comfy middle-class assumptions on which the latest cultural revolution rests. "The vision of a plurality of equally valid co-existing life forms may be compelling," he writes in his ambitious book, *A Theory of Art,* "only to those whose outlook is underpinned by one more meta-narrative, that of a continuous and rapid global growth of prosperity." And he suggests, wickedly, that "the postmodern vision remains plausible only so long as we imagine that the only dilemmas we shall ever face are on the order of 'Shall I get a cappuccino or a caffe latte, buy a Volvo or a BMW?'" Ouch. Those are Bay Area questions, all right.

Here's another: Has Mr. Berger identified the only terms on which one can now debate Stravinsky contra Wagner—as rival emblems of conspicuous culture consumption? When a San Francisco critic can tout the *Ring* as *Star Wars* for the wealthy (albeit conceding that Wagner's music is, after all, "considerably richer, bolder and more nuanced" than John Williams's), Tolstoy's frightening old question—What is being done here, and for whom?—comes roaring back to life.

23

A Surrealist Composer Comes to the Rescue of Modernism

"Nowadays you're eclectic or you're nothing," a graduate student at Princeton University said recently when I inquired about the reigning philosophy of composition at that old bastion of utopian purity. Talk about signs of the times! By that new-Princetonian token, Thomas Adès, the English composing phenom (still under thirty) is really something, and the records keep coming. The fourth and latest Adès disc from EMI Classics brings *Asyla,* the twenty-three-minute symphony-in-all-but-name that has just won its young composer Louisville University's Grawemeyer Award, the biggest plum the classical-music world now offers.

Is all the shouting merited? Yes indeed. If the attention being paid the twenty-eight-year-old Mr. Adès is another sign of the times in classical music, there is reason, at this time of millennial stock-taking and auguries of doom, for renewed hope. Mr. Adès has in effect extended to a satisfying end-of-century culmination the far side or other face of serious modern music, the alternative current that has always shadowed the severely abstract variety of modernism that hogged the headlines until it ran out of gas.

The title of the prize-winning piece, the plural of *asylum,* plays poetically (and yes, a little pedantically) on the word's ambiguity. Refuge? Madhouse? A little of both? It's a gentle tease and, like the music, sportively provocative. It may well have had its origins in "a beautiful statement about music," as the musicologist Joseph Kerman rightly calls it, from Emerson's *Journals.* (Mr. Kerman quotes it at the end of *Concerto Conversations,* a graceful set of ruminations just published by Harvard University Press.) "So is music an asylum," Emerson wrote. "It takes us out of the actual and whispers to us dim secrets that startle our wonder as to who we are, and for what, whence and whereto."

Wonder too much about such things and you might well end up in the madhouse (or at a rave), Mr. Adès seems to hint in his antic third movement. For the most part, though, *Asyla* is appropriately consoling and uncommonly heartfelt in a time of compulsive flimflam and simulacra. It had a big and gushy press on its première, last year, by Sir Simon Rattle and the City of Birmingham Symphony Orchestra, and the present recording (EMI Classics 5 56818 2; CD, with other Adès works conducted by the composer) is a composite of their live performances. They do it *con amore,* as one rarely hears contemporary orchestral music done. That sense of love and trust is what makes the recorded performance of *Asyla* seem a major event, not just a wunderkind's breakthrough into compositional adulthood.

Indeed, from the beginning and, according to some reports, right down to his gloomy recent "Message for the Millennium" at the New York Philharmonic, Mr. Adès's work has been unusual in its air of sincerity. For all its precocious technical sophistication and its omnivorous range of reference— fifteenth-century England to seventeenth-century France to contemporary Hungary; gamelans and ouds; Billie Holiday, Astor Piazzolla, the Chemical Brothers—it does not put everything "in quotes." It has urgency and fervor, and communicates directly. What has put *Powder Her Face,* Mr. Adès's first opera (also on EMI), in such demand worldwide as to be newsworthy, it seems to me, is not just the notorious fellatio aria. It is rather that having set up its main character, an aging nymphomaniac duchess, as a figure of cruel and predictable fun, it turns around and honors her, and the audience as well, with unsentimental and affecting sympathy at the lonely end.

So for all his spectacular eclecticism, don't call Mr. Adès a postmodernist just yet. For one thing, his spoiled-brat behavior, so much commented on in the press, shows that he is still playing the part our culture has written for a modernist artist. But more positively, as long as there are strong controlling hands like his at the stylistic mixing board, there will be enough life left in modernism, taking that word now to mean the late-romantic projection of a strong creative personality, to last well into the coming century. Also symptomatic is the way Andrew Porter, a self-described "hoary critic" who has made it a mission to search out and destroy postmodernism wherever it shows its face, has cast himself as Mr. Adès's happy hyper, in informative if somewhat frantic program notes for all the composer's CDs so far.

He has good reason. In Mr. Adès late modernism has a winner at last, a respectably hard-core talent to whom audiences, trusting their noses, have responded with enthusiasm, as (despite Mr. Porter's decades of devoted ministration) they have not responded to Sir Harrison Birtwistle or Brian Ferneyhough, and never will. Mr. Adès can be promoted without recourse to the imperial haberdasher's manual.

For the origins of Mr. Adès's eclecticism, and a validation of his modernist credentials, consider a passage from a new biography of Richard Strauss by Bryan Gilliam, the leading American authority on the composer, published by Cambridge University Press. "Taking a step well beyond the old-fashioned, decadent, fin-de-siècle *Salome*," Mr. Gilliam writes, "Strauss realized that the musical language for the new century should be one that intentionally lacks stylistic uniformity, a language that reflects a modernist preoccupation with the dilemma of history, one that arguably foreshadows the dissolution of the ideology of style in the late 20th century." The immediate result was *Der Rosenkavalier*, an opera from which, as it happens, Mr. Adès quotes delectably in *Powder Her Face*.

Mr. Gilliam's sentence is a beautifully calculated slap in the face of conventional historiography, which has always regarded *Salome* (together with its immediate successor, *Elektra*) as Strauss's modernist peak, and therefore his high-water mark as a creative figure, and *Der Rosenkavalier* as the beginning of the stylistic backslide that eventually condemned Strauss to historical irrelevance. Mr. Gilliam's proposed revision would locate the origins of an authentic modernism in the very eclecticism that is now billed, and sometimes written off, as postmodern.

Mr. Gilliam's "dilemma of history" might more pointedly be called the problem of an accumulated repertory: a past that has remained an eternally present and intimidating challenge to its successors. One solution—Strauss's, as Mr. Gilliam describes it—was to accept that eternally present past as a mine. Another, Schoenberg's, was to try at all costs to outdistance it with labored innovation. That quixotic effort demanded the sacrifice of any hope of robust communication with a nonprofessional public. The short-range compensation was the tiresome bromide that cast public rejection as a badge of honor. The long-range consequences were drastic: "the futile chase," as the *New Yorker* critic Alex Ross puts it, "after progressively more arcane and irrelevant musics 'of the future.'"

That is the sad side of the story, the one the textbooks have been telling. Its lingering exponents are history's castaways, ungracefully aging and resentful. The other, happier side of the story has achieved its first full-scale telling in *Untwisting the Serpent*, a book by Daniel Albright, a professor of comparative literature, published by the University of Chicago Press. This marvelous study, the first survey of the arts to regard the twentieth century as a completed whole, proposes a more radically revised canon. It finds authentic modernism not in utopian purification rituals but in polymorphously perverse joinings and copulations.

Among its treasures is the first adequate account of musical surrealism. The cast of main characters, ranged against the traditional modernist Mighty Handful (the Vienna Trinity and its graying latter-day saints), includes such often marginalized figures as Weill, Britten, Satie and Les Six, Ravel, Martinů,

Virgil Thomson, George Antheil, even the Sunday composer Ezra Pound. The hero of the tale, the explicitly designated anti-Schoenberg, is Francis Poulenc, whom Mr. Albright's narrative will greatly (and, I hope, permanently) magnify.

"Poulenc was original," writes Mr. Albright, "not in the way that his music sounds but in the way that his music means." Rather than Schoenberg's vaunted harmonic dissonance, Poulenc offered "semantic dissonance." Mr. Adès is lucky enough to be original both in the way that his music sounds and in the way that it means, and he works hard at his individuality (another reason not to call him a postmodernist). But that he is a committed and already masterly musical surrealist is evident within minutes, no matter which piece of his you choose to listen to.

His polymorphous perversity is only the beginning. More telling by far is the way he contrives his music so that it seems, contradicting what is thought to be the essential nature of the medium, to inhabit not time but space. It is "painterly" rather than "narrative" music. It achieves its special atmosphere, and projects its special meanings, through improbable sonic collages and mobiles: outlandish juxtapositions of evocative sound-objects that hover, shimmering, or dreamily revolve, in a seemingly motionless sonic emulsion.

I know of no other music quite like it in these defining respects, but many paintings, by Dalí, de Chirico, Magritte. Mr. Adès himself seems to "see" his music rather than hear it: he describes the wispy final movement of his early Chamber Symphony as "a serene overview of the preceding music, as if from a great height." Indeed, great heights—and depths—of pitch are among the elements Mr. Adès musters to produce his uncanny effects of "spatial form," to cite the term coined by the literary critic Joseph Frank more than half a century ago. The top notes of the piano and the bottom notes of the tuba or contrabassoon, rarities in anybody else's music, are among Mr. Adès's most characteristic sonorities, and he often deploys them in tandem. The counterpoint of extreme registers immediately (and literally) arrests the ear with the impression of a vast expanse within which musical events taking place in more normal registers—often very ordinary events, like common chords or particles of diatonic melody—seem objects bizarrely suspended and, in consequence, made newly strange. The orchestration, full of pointillistic percussion and cunning resonance devices, adds a shiny edge or murky penumbra to the sound, transforming timbres and locating them in sonic space with often amazing precision.

Perhaps even more striking is the quality of Mr. Adès's rhythm. At the textural extremes one is likely to hear the kind of stretched-out tones that have long conjured up infinite expanse in picturesque orchestral music. But the music is not deprived of impulse and beat. Fast ostinatos, often of a tricky, ear-beguiling complexity, coexist at varying speeds in contrasting colors and registers, evoking not linear distance but gyres and vortexes: sound in motion but not going anywhere. Most telling of all is the technique—reminiscent of medieval "mensuration canons" and in all likelihood learned by Mr. Adès in music history class, God bless him—of putting slow melodies in counterpoints that move at different speeds and with beats of differing length. When such lines are contrived so that their beats coincide neither with the bar lines nor with each other, the music becomes effectively meterless, sometimes for long stretches. The unfolding counterpoint is regulated by the conductor's signals, but the signals have no correlate in actual sound. There is movement aplenty but no momentum.

So if Poulenc was the anti-Schoenberg, then Mr. Adès is the anti-Beethoven. But of course it is only the Beethoven of the dynamic middle period—the most influential of the Beethovens—that Mr. Adès is "against." Like the late Beethoven string quartets and piano sonatas, Mr. Adès's music opens up a magical domain for the ear's mind to explore at what seems its leisure. "An image," Ezra Pound wrote in a passage memorably glossed by Joseph Frank, "is that which presents an intellectual and emotional complex in an instant of time." Pound meant "as if in an instant," of course, since he was writing about poetry, a temporal art like music. Mr. Adès's music, like that of the contemplative, even quiescent late Beethoven, is full of transporting Poundian "images."

Let the rapt second movement of *Asyla* exemplify it all. The main tune is a long descent by alternating close and wide intervals, first played by the bass oboe, or heckelphone, an instrument that otherwise turns up only rarely, in monster scores by Strauss or Delius. It is a typically recondite Adès color. Maestro Rattle has told an interviewer that the slow music in *Asyla* reminds him of *Parsifal;* the heckelphone tune reminds me of the oboe d'amore and oboe da caccia parts in Bach's cantatas and Passions. In either case, the music recalled is transfigured by the rare timbre into a mythical beast; and, imitated by myriad accompanying lines floating and overlapping in registers from superhigh to superlow, it seems to beget a whole surrealist bestiary.

The sweltering, droopy descent thus initiated is accompanied by a harmonic mudslide in which an upright piano tuned a quarter-tone flat smoothens the perpetual lowering of the pitch with queasy notes "in the cracks." I swear that this study in bottomless sinking and lassitude had already reminded me of Dalí's *Persistence of Memory* (yes, the wilting watches and recognizable if unidentifiable carcass) before I put two and two together and verified the agreeable surmise that the composer's mother was in fact Dawn Adès, the author of important books on Dalí, Duchamp, and the dada and surrealist movements.

What to make of this all-too-suggestive family connection is anybody's guess. But it does invite one to imagine that growing up surrounded by the captivating if academically disreputable imagery of dream realism during abstract expressionism's waning days might have given a gifted young composer the confidence to resist what was still a powerful and entirely comparable conformist pressure during his tutelary years. Mr. Adès was thus able to buck sterile utopia while avoiding the opposing pitfall of ironic pastiche. What raises his music so far above today's average is his phenomenal success at toe-ing the line—the finest line there is—between the arcane and the banal. The music never loses touch with its base in the common listening experience of real audiences, so that it is genuinely evocative. At the same time it is quirkily inventive and constantly surprising in the small: enough so to confound short-range predictions and elude obviousness of reference even when models (often Stravinsky) are nameable. And that makes it genuinely novel.

Better yet, the music makes more than a vivid first impression. Subtly fash-ioned and highly detailed, it haunts the memory and invites rehearings that often yield new and intriguing finds, like the recurrence of the main theme from the first movement of *Asyla,* inverted, in the last. This sort of thing, too, is an experience one often has with surrealist paintings. As youngsters we all loved to revisit Tchelitchew's *Hide and Seek* at the Museum of Modern Art be-fore the dour utopians consigned it to the basement. Mr. Adès has kept a child's capacity for serious fun. His music does what José Ortega y Gasset thought all modern art should do, "instill youthfulness into an ancient world." With conventional modernism gone geriatric, a thing of nostalgic or downright acrimonious eightieth and ninetieth birthdays, Mr. Adès's youth-fulness (not just his youth) is balm.

Even rarer, and best of all, he never—well, hardly ever—overloads. His music is not simple, but its complexity is rich and "earned." The ear (all right, my ear), so often fatigued and insulted in the music of recent decades by senseless self-indulgent complication, accepts and explores Mr. Adès's intricacies with joy. They recall the wonderful opening of "The Bulgarian Poetess," one of John Updike's *Bech* stories. "Your poems. Are they difficult?" Bech asks, patronizing. "They are difficult—to write," the poetess replies, confounding him.

On the eve of the millennium, I'll drink to that scale of values. Here's a health to you, Mr. A.

POSTSCRIPT, 2008

The response to this piece was an especially crisp illustration of the old rule: those who like it write to you, those who hate it write to the *Times.* I had lovely personal communications from musicians I admire, most gratifyingly from John Carewe, the great conducting teacher. The *Times* mailbox filled up with spite and vituperation from disgruntled lobbyists.

It was a funny assortment. From Jay Hoffman, who identified himself as "president of a communications firm specializing in music promotions," came a complaint that in praising Adès I neglected "such exciting young Americans as Michael Daugherty, Lowell Liebermann, Aaron Jay Kernis and, lest we forget, Europeans like the 28-year-old German Matthias Pinscher, Norway's Rolf Wallin and Finland's Magnus Lindberg"—no doubt a list of his clients. He also insisted that Adès's eclecticism was as nothing compared with Elliott Carter's. It only underscored my point about the revenge of the geriatrics.

From the composer Martin Brody, the Catherine Mills Davis Professor of Music at Wellesley College, came a plea: "When do we stop squabbling about the winners and losers of modern music and confront its truly challenging legacy: the thrilling, if sometimes bewildering, profusion of approaches to musical creation and reception that it gave us?" This would have come with better grace from someone who, before the tide turned, had not been so intransigent a campaigner against stylistic diversity.

To me, the most amusing response came from John Halle, a younger composer on the faculty of Yale University. It is genuinely witty. "Mr. Taruskin," he wrote,

> makes note of the failure of the high-modernist composers Brian Ferneyhough and Harrison Birtwistle to survive the "tender ministrations" of the critical establishment, most notably those of Andrew Porter. These are not isolated cases. An important aspect of the history of musical modernism is that of the public's stubborn refusal to buy into critical hype for what have been perceived, rightly it now appears, as sterile academic exercises. Mr. Taruskin assures us that this time it's different, evidently because it is he who is doing the huffing and puffing. Those with longer memories might be somewhat skeptical of Mr. Taruskin's credibility in this regard. Have audiences flocked to the music of John Thow, Olly Wilson or Vagn Holmboe, to mention three recipients of Mr. Taruskin's lavish praise? Have audiences wised up to the bankruptcy of the music of John Harbison, a composer severely censured by Mr. Taruskin in the past? As an admirer of Mr. Adès's recent work, I hope this young composer will survive the critical kisses of death that are being so passionately bestowed on him by critics with an egregious history of misleading audiences about contemporary music.

What Mr. Halle omitted from his tirade was that not only I but also Olly Wilson and the late John Thow had been among his teachers at Berkeley. We had all previously endured tirades aplenty from this most exceptionally angry young man. And this is where the matter stops being amusing. The degree of resentment that persists among academic composers, and that comes rushing forth to meet any and all critical assessments, whether positive (as in my review of Adès) or negative (as in my review of Martino), is the most disheartening evidence of their miseducation and their cultural irrelevance, and the frustration that it has bred.

A letter from a Princeton alum provided more sad evidence of miseducation. "Well, O.K.," wrote David Claman,

> I, too, find some modernist rhetoric extreme, but that could be said of any artistic movement. I try to see music in its historical context, even when that music

is bolstered by idealistic aesthetics—not exactly a rarity in the history of music. For example, I find the romantic program to Berlioz's *Symphonie Fantastique* laughable, but not the symphony. I recognize the program as a product of its time, as something that had meaning for Berlioz and that clearly informed the composition of a great piece of music. I take modernist aesthetics in a similar vein, aware that some wonderful music grew from it.

He had been trained, in other words, to listen to all music, even the *Symphonie fantastique,* as nothing but notes (and, despite his claim, entirely out of historical context), and that puts him, like so many others, in danger of writing music that consists of nothing but notes—and then complaining when audiences find his offerings unsatisfying.

And of course there were the critics who wanted Adès to stumble, as they would anyone who achieved success without their permission. Ivan Hewett of the London *Daily Telegraph* saved my review for more than four years so that he could summon it up for the peroration of a remarkably mean-spirited assault in the days leading up to the première of Adès's second opera, *The Tempest,* in February 2004. Noting that "every few decades the British musical world discovers a bright new star"—Walton, then Britten, then Knussen, now Adès—Hewett did his best to dampen the light, just, it seemed, for the hell of it, the way all the jowl-waggers went after Britten in the fifties. After paraphrasing my description of *Asyla*—"a succession of vivid images, where time appears frozen; in between are uncanny passages where the images melt, and what was tight and focused bends and skitters out into extremes: high piccolos, growling tubas, glistening string harmonics"—he delivers the coup de grâce:

> The American musicologist Richard Taruskin gives a surrealist interpretation to this melting quality, likening it to the famous Dali watch. The comparison with Dali is more revealing than Taruskin intended, as it points to a facile cleverness and an emotional chilliness that for me can sometimes be the aftertaste of Adès's undeniable brilliance and magic.[1]

Shades of the fifties again! Just what the Darmstadters were saying about Britten, just what the Clement Greenbergs were saying about Dalí. Poor Hewett simply didn't know how prissy and old-fashioned he was sounding.

What a relief it was to turn from all this ranting to a letter from Annette Shandler Levitt, a professor of literature, who queried the notion of surrealist music:

> As someone who has taught and written on surrealism for 25 years, I am not convinced that music, per se, can even be surreal: lacking representational elements, music cannot create the disjunction that is a requisite of surrealism. There must first be a realism before there can be a surrealism. Indeed, Mr. Taruskin, using language like "collage" and "juxtaposition," needs the objective correlatives of visual art in order to make his argument. And the music of

Poulenc and Les Six, which he cites and which functions within surrealism, does so in the service of words and images—as in Apollinaire's opera-theater *The Breasts of Tiresias* and Cocteau's ballet-theater *The Wedding on the Eiffel Tower.*

These are interesting points, but they proceed from an erroneous premise. It is only from a very blinkered modernist perspective, the very one that hobbles musicians like Mr. Claman, that music is without "representational elements." Music can imitate nature onomatopoetically, as in Vivaldi's *Four Seasons,* or metaphorically, as in Debussy's *Nuages.* It carries generic associations—where would Beethoven's Ninth be without its religious, martial, and pastoral tropes?—and it can also allude to other music. It can not only point outside of itself, as in these examples, but also inward, as when a thematic development or recapitulation represents the components of a musical form (which can be completed or distorted), or when operatic "reminiscence motives" provide wordless links between dramatic moments. Indeed, the device of "polytonality," particularly associated with Poulenc and the other members of Les Six (especially Darius Milhaud), can be viewed as a surrealist technique. Surrealism achieves many of its effects by juxtaposing items of ordinary experience in extraordinary ways. A similar effect is achieved when "ordinary" C major and "ordinary" D major are combined into an extraordinary, unheard-of texture. It is a big subject, worthy of a book. I've tried to make a start on it in chapter 56 of my *Oxford History of Western Music.*

NOTE

1. Ivan Hewett, "He's Brilliant, But Can He Deliver?" *Daily Telegraph,* 2 February 2004.

24

Corraling a Herd of
Musical Mavericks

The ironies were thick on the ground. "A.T.&T. is the main corporate sponsor of American Mavericks" was the sign that hit your eye as you entered Davies Symphony Hall last month. Then you picked up your program and read an essay by Alan Rich, "No Brands, No Labels, No Boundaries," which did little but tack a brand label on the favored elite and reinforce an implicit boundary that enraged advocates of the unfavored many. Their postings clogged classical cyberspace in the weeks leading up to the San Francisco Symphony's American Mavericks festival and all through it. Everybody, it seemed, wanted in to the vaunted pack of loners, the in-group of outsiders, the icons of iconoclasm.

Michael Tilson Thomas, the orchestra's music director and the gate-keeper of this Studio 54 of the excluded, worked hard to invest the theme with coherence. He carefully explained in a newspaper interview shortly before the festivities commenced that Elliott Carter, while a "significant figure" and "to be admired," was no American Maverick because he was "Eurocentric" and "brainy." So was this to be a replay of Philip Rahv's creaky old attempt to classify American writers as redskins and palefaces, Walt Whitmans and Henry Jameses, with no middle ground? Even John Adams, in a pre-concert interview, invoked this stale bisection, old before he was born, to justify his inclusion among the mavericks. But Mr. Adams (tailed that evening by a PBS camera crew), while a significant figure and to be admired, is by now the very model of mainstream success, having earned his place in the sun by taming the excesses of minimalism, once a maverick style, and reconciling it with traditional audience expectations.

And who should turn up in the first program anyway? Milton Babbitt, the very icon of tenured palefacery. Nor, despite Mr. Thomas's anti-intellectual reassurances, did it turn out to be the Un-Carter Festival. Ursula Oppens, here to apply her elbows to Henry Cowell's Piano Concerto (pure-blooded redskin Schlockmaninoff, this), sneaked four recent Carter pieces into a pre-concert feature. Pale they did seem. But in the company he kept that night (Cage, Cowell, David Del Tredici, Varèse), Mr. Carter was definitely the odd man out. In short, a maverick.

Well, enough of loophole-poking. For a couple of weeks it was the Bay Area's parlor game of choice, but now we're tired of it. There is more to be said—seriously—about the theme and about themes generally; but first some words of thanks are in order. Never in my concertgoing experience had I encountered such a catholic barrage of not-to-be-missed programming: Charles Ives, Morton Feldman, Terry Riley, Carl Ruggles, Ruth Crawford Seeger, Lukas Foss, Meredith Monk, Duke Ellington, George Antheil, Lou Harrison, Steve Reich, Earle Brown, Steven Mackey, Frank Zappa, Conlon Nancarrow, and Aaron Copland, to run down the remaining roster of Mr. Thomas's choices in order of first appearance. The performances had their ups and downs, but even the downs were mostly good enough, while the ups were amazing. And big summer audiences (40 percent Symphony subscribers and 27 percent first-time attendees, according to the marketing department) lapped it all up. The evening of June 9 will stay forever in my memory for its sheer generosity. After Ruggles's *Sun-Treader,* Crawford Seeger's Andante for string orchestra, Mr. Foss's *Time Cycle,* and three choruses from Ms. Monk's *Atlas,* Ives's Fourth Symphony was still to come. And after all that, hundreds of spectators stayed for Mr. Thomas's postconcert discussion with Mr. Foss, Mr. Harrison, and Ms. Monk.

Nor was the conductor's energetic largess his only, or even his most conspicuous, virtue. His energy flagged noticeably, if understandably, during the last week, which was largely given over to an, alas, equivocal showcase for his Miami-based training orchestra, the New World Symphony. With its fatigued maestro at the helm it gave a dullish concert, ending with a downright disengaged reading of Ives's Second Symphony that failed to solve, or even seriously address, the work's notorious balance problems. But everywhere else the maestro shone. His technique and his musical scrupulousness are simply beyond praise; in difficult music he is all business, giving beats and cues of impeccable clarity. And like Leonard Bernstein, with whom he is so often (and by now, I believe, justly) compared, he has the gift of vivid shape. The two-siren wail at the climax of Varèse's *Amériques* was so expertly judged, and the rest of the performance so admirably paced around it, that it became more than a moment of deafening exuberance (though it was that, too). It fixed the whole piece, in all its abounding detail, in a firm, indelible gestalt.

Only once did the maestro seem to put himself before the music, when he turned Terry Riley's venerable *In C* into a public-relations stunt. Audience members were invited to bring along their instruments and participate in the performance. The predictable clambake was made worse when Mr. Thomas, in an effort to keep everyone amused (or keep himself at the center of things), usurped control over the proceedings, now hushing the parquet to allow the sounds from the balcony through, now running around the hall like Jerry Springer with a stick, to encourage (and comically overconduct) the riffings of individual audience members. Could he really have so misunderstood Mr. Riley's intentions? Or respected them so little? A good time was had by all; but the composer, forewarned, had stayed away. In the end the paying customers were cheated. Had they heard a real performance of the piece, its magical impersonal shimmer might have taken hold, and the improbable victory of the "minimalist revolution"—an avant-garde of harmonious simplicity, neither redskinned nor palefaced, not yet conventionalized for mainstream consumption—might have been illuminated.

But if an occasional overreach, or a bit of pandering in the press, is the price of the remarkable trust Mr. Thomas has built up with his audience (and his management), I'm ready to forgive and forget. His freedom to indulge his passionate predilections must be the envy of his peers, and it has redounded enormously to the benefit of the Bay Area's musical life. Put all the kvetching that follows in the perspective of the overriding debt of gratitude one owes for being given so much to think and yammer about.

The opportunity to think and kvetch is of course the great value—and the great danger—of thematic programming. Mr. Thomas acknowledged what he saw as the danger on opening night, when he confessed himself (or affected) to be "taken aback" at the intensity with which the Mavericks idea—just a marketing ploy, after all—was being debated, implying that we might do better if we just sat back and listened.

Sorry, Maestro. No can do. Welcome to the world of discourse (or buzz, if you're not an academic). Nobody just sits back and listens. Culture is baggage, and music cannot reach our ears except through a field of interpretation. The difference between a thematic program or festival and an "ordinary" concert is that an explicit field of interpretation is being proposed, and we can no more ignore it than we can follow the friendly alchemist's surefire recipe for turning lead into gold. (Ready? Just melt it down and stir for three hours without thinking of the word *rhinoceros*.)

This time the theme proposed was fraught with volatile issues concerning American identity and the place of the arts in an egalitarian society. The danger is not that thinking about such things distracts our ears from pure sensuous or "esthetic" engagement. Only Kant could ever be that "disinterested," and only on a good day. No, the danger is that once the thinking starts, it cannot be contained. It leads where it will, if we're mentally alive, and not always to the intended celebration.

Take that wonderful 9 June program. The opening was breathtaking. The timpanist, bestriding the top of an implied pyramid on a riser at the orchestra's rear, whacked out his barbaric yawp at the beginning of Ruggles's *Sun-Treader* with marvelously simulated abandon. Mr. Thomas pulled off his patented trick: never had the piece emerged with such expressive force but at the same time such lucidity of structure. And never, for all its redskinned, bear-skinned Americanism, had its line of descent from the majestic opening of Brahms's First Symphony been more robustly proclaimed. The trouble was, that very clarity of structure bred unease by the time the piece was over. It is a sort of rondo, I realized, organized around three insistent returns of that opening tattoo. But by the fourth time around, that insistence, reinforced by the spectacular placement of the drummer, had become annoying. "Oh, take it in the woods with Robert Bly," came unbidden to my mind's lips. And, yes, it even crossed my mind that Brahms might belong there, too. It's rather late in the day to be proclaiming one's Americanness, or one's musicality, with defiant displays of machismo. Never had Ruggles seemed so dated. Ditto Ives. Ditto Varèse.

The program notes were eloquent about the problems Crawford Seeger had to endure in her day because of the American modern-music world's misogyny, and about the impact of Babbittry (George this time, not Milton) on her style. Her Andante, gentle by comparison with *Sun-Treader* (as, in all fairness, is some of Ruggles), strongly resembles Samuel Barber's nearly contemporaneous Adagio for Strings. Both works are arrangements of slow movements from string quartets, and both follow a trajectory (at once formal and expressive) from a darkly plaintive low register to a plangent high. The difference is that Crawford Seeger's piece was pervasively "dissonated" (to take a word from the vocabulary of Charles Seeger, her husband and mentor) in obedience to the norms of maverick manliness, while Barber, a male composer with a solid conservatory education and good connections, was confident enough to withstand the pressure. With Toscanini on his side, he didn't need maverick credentials; academic credentials would do.

But with the institutional victory of academic modernism after World War II, the shoe went on the other foot. Now it is Barber who stands in the cold, stigmatized as weak, derivative, unoriginal, unadventurous, safe (all euphemisms, of course, for "sissy"). Mr. Thomas's show may not have been an un-Carter festival, but it certainly was an un-Barber festival. It would be rash to assume that Crawford Seeger tailored her style to macho expectations unwillingly. (I remember my mother walking on air after a truck driver leaned out of his cab and shouted, "Lady, you drive just like a man.") But the shortness of her career and the paucity of her output raise questions about the stresses she faced. Pushed to one extreme, she bounced (as radical conformists will) all the way to the other, forsaking classical composition for folk-song arranging. Meredith Monk's music, which avoids extremes and finds a place somewhere between classical intricacy and imagined folklore, answered Crawford Seeger's across the decades, hopefully suggesting that now there is room for a feminine perspective in "serious" music—or, even better, that gender perspectives may no longer be all-ruling.

But what about Ruggles? Was he not warped as well by those gender stresses? His works, too, were lamentably few, as were Varèse's. Since the publication of Ives's *Memos* in the 1970s, we've known for a documented fact about the toll that male anxiety took on the maverick of all mavericks. The artificiality with which a lot of "ultramodern" American music was spiked up—sometimes, as in Ives's well-known case, retroactively, when performances loomed—may not have been just a response to an "inevitable" historical process. It may also have been a response to a noxious psychological pressure, one that such music, when uncritically celebrated, might continue to exert on its listeners.

Mr. Thomas put the best face on it. At the postconcert symposium he offered the suggestion that what makes Ives and Ruggles and Crawford Seeger so "wondrous" (his favorite word) is that for them dissonance was not ugly but "affirmative." Yes, perhaps, but just what did it affirm? A passage in Leta E. Miller and Fredric Lieberman's excellent new biography of the latter-day maverick Lou Harrison sheds some chilling light on the question. Mr. Harrison began his career as a votary of Ives and Ruggles; but, as we heard in the late works of his that were played at the festival, he made a conscious detour, amounting to a repudiation, from the path of "affirmative dissonance." His biographers associate that swerve with "a luncheon at Pennsylvania Station in New York at which Ruggles blurted out antiblack and anti-Semitic slurs at the top of his lungs" to Mr. Harrison's acute discomfiture. I for one am not prepared to assume that all the blurting at the top of his lungs that fills Ruggles's *Sun-Treader* is unrelated to the animus that appalled his friends, or that his magnificent artistic creations have played no part in its propagation.

Mr. Thomas himself furnished a case in point, when he took an especially blustery and embarrassing leaf from Ives's *Memos* to lend at least some negative coherence to his festival theme. "What the mavericks did not do," he asserted in the program book, "was make nice little pieces to fit comfortably into the nice little holes of traditional concert life." Doesn't he know that "nice" was Ives's code word for effeminate, and that it carried overtones of both misogyny and homophobia? Didn't he feel any hesitation before seconding Ives's and Ruggles's antiquated rhetoric of fear and loathing, one that would in all likelihood have applied to Mr. Thomas himself as it would to any Jewish or gay musician?

Placing Mr. Harrison alongside his erstwhile mentors, like pitting Ms. Monk against Crawford Seeger, tacitly put the maverick generations in dialogue.

That dialogue was most pointed on the touchy subject of technology. The official Mavericks line, as put out in San Francisco, hailed it with unbridled, naive optimism. Technology was the otherwise improbable Milton Babbitt's ticket of admission to maverickhood: he was represented by *Philomel,* a virtuoso aria for soprano (sung by Lauren Flanigan—into her music stand, alas) with a taped accompaniment produced in 1964 on the room-filling RCA Mark II Synthesizer, the techiest medium of its day, with a price tag of $175,000 to prove it. Techmania reached its zenith on Antheil night, which featured the San Francisco première of the original 1924 version of *Ballet mécanique* with sixteen roaring pianolas and a whole kitchen of percussion. It was considered unperformable until last year, when Paul D. Lehrman, then on the faculty of the University of Massachusetts, coded its every note on a computer disk that could be hooked up via MIDI technology to a phalanx of Yamaha Disklaviers. The results were spectacularly loud, all right, and impressively rigorous, but they also exposed the spectacularly uninventive, vapid contents of the score on which all that care had been lavished.

Antheil would no doubt have claimed in rebuttal that although the performance was powerful enough to overheat and disable two of the Disklaviers, it still did not fulfill his intentions, since, as Mr. Lehrman admitted, even with today's technology Antheil's prescribed tempos remain out of reach. The "charm of impossibilities," as Messiaen used to call it, still works its cheap magic. But as any composer (well, any honest composer) will tell you, to be difficult is the easiest thing in the world, and to be impossible takes no more than insouciance. The devoted to-do over Antheil's hoary charlatanry (though it brought us out in droves to hear it) was depressing to behold.

It was consistent, however, with the negative reception accorded the one Mavericks offering that challenged the decrepit futurist esthetic. That was "Hindenburg," the first act of *Three Tales,* a documentary video opera in progress by Steve Reich and Beryl Korot, which delivered an unsubtle but effective sermon on technology gone wrong. The audience hated it. The postconcert discussion was a roast: no bad thing in itself, in fact a refreshing contrast to the perfunctory standing ovations most concerts nowadays elicit. But it was mostly beside the point, as were the fulminations in the *San Francisco Chronicle* a couple of days later concerning the wordless third scene, a fantasy on the Nibelung motif from Wagner's *Ring* that accompanied scenes of zeppelin construction.

Mr. Reich was accused of drawing a "causal link" between Wagner and the Third Reich. He did no such thing. The subjugation of the Nibelungs was not Wagner's doing, after all, but that of Alberich, the Jew capitalist in Wagner's intended allegory. Mr. Reich's point was complicated and ironic, and it was clear that he had touched a nerve. In so doing, he earned the only reception that matched the vaunted maverick legend of uncomprehending rejection. (But of course the ironies do not end there. They never end. Shaking a stick at scientific hubris is not exactly the freshest thing artists can do at the end of the twentieth century, especially if their critique of high technology is mediated by state-of-the-art amplification and video equipment.)

That one brush with controversy made the concluding Copland program seem a bit tame and safe, especially to those of us who had been tantalized by advance publicity promising a rare performance of *The Lonesome Train* by Earl Robinson alongside Copland. Trouble in obtaining performance material was officially cited as the reason for the cancellation, as well as the unavailability, I was told by the orchestra's publicist, of a "name actor" for the narrator's part. But when one recalled that the corny old cantata manages to put a paraphrase of the concluding line of the *Communist Manifesto* in Abraham Lincoln's mouth, it was hard to shake the suspicion that it had been dropped for other reasons.

Too bad if it was. Like it or not, Popular Front Communists (a category that included Copland) were genuine political mavericks in America, and the very best thing this festival could have accomplished would have been to get some neoconservative critics yelling. As it was, we had a brilliantly guided museum tour, but we heard little evidence, Mr. Reich apart, that any real maverick spirit survives in classical music today.

POSTSCRIPT, 2008

The crybabies and professional victims came out in force to greet this latest imaginary insult, and this time they included some from whom I would have expected better. Kyle Gann, normally a seer-througher, led the pack, grousing on the American Music Center's NewMusicBox Web site that

> when a major American new-music event happens, such as John Cage's death or the American Mavericks festival, then some critic like Ed Rothstein or Richard Taruskin, writing an obituary or review, suddenly looks at these American composers and accuses them of fraud: Why, they're not mavericks at all, they're influenced by lots of people and ideas, they all support each other. And the critics are right—except that those composers never claimed to be lonely individualists.

Who was he talking about? Whom had I accused of fraud? I did twit the orchestra management and Maestro Thomas for their marketing hype—a sharp young musicologist, Nadya Zimmerman, compared their ploys with the Sprite slogan, "Image is nothing, taste is everything" (the image of spurning image)—but how did that translate into an insult to the composers? Such thin skins do tell a tale of insecurity and immature self-importance, as does the lumping impulse ("some critic like R. or T."—it's us against them).

As usual, reference to stereotypes and prejudices was taken as endorsement. Judith Tick, whose excellent biography of Ruth Crawford Seeger sheds enormous light on the question of what it meant to be a woman composer in an atmosphere of aggressive machismo, nevertheless thought it necessary to defend her against my "linking her use of dissonance so strongly to masculinity":

> It is true that many critics in her time called Crawford Seeger's music "virile" and made her the exception to their stereotype of the sentimentalizing "woman composer," but that was their perspective, not hers. Influenced in the 1920s by Eastern mysticism, theosophy, and the writings of Emerson, Thoreau and Whitman, Crawford Seeger treated dissonance as a spiritual concept, writing about it as a metaphor for transcendentalism rather than gender.

That is a fair point, but composers do not single-handedly make their reputations or control the discourse about their work, nor are they (in my experience) as indifferent to that discourse as idealizing historians like to believe. But Prof. Tick's response was the considered reaction of a scholar. Others, particularly self-professed male feminists, found my review, in the words of Fred Everett Maus, "distressing in some ways," because it

> seemed to promote the equation of dissonance with masculinism/anti-feminism in an especially flat, simplistic way. I can't accept that particular way of linking feminism and anti-modernism (with, for instance, its interpretation of Ruth Crawford as somehow self-alienated and "masculine" because of the dissonance of her music).

But that particular stereotype was so rife in Crawford Seeger's day that it strains credulity to think she could have insulated herself from it. Whether true or false, the old story retailed by Henry and Sidney Cowell in their biography of Charles Ives—that Ives stood up at a concert to rebuke a man who was protesting a piece by Ruggles with the words, "Stop being such a goddamned sissy! Can't you stand up to such fine strong music and use your ears like a man?"—encapsulates the discourse and corroborates Lou Harrison's memory of Ruggles himself. And, as I was careful to note, the "self-alienation" of which Maus speaks was felt as keenly by men in the musical profession (Ives and Ruggles above all) as it was by women. All were reacting to the genteel view that classical music was women's work, and all who felt oppressed by it, male and female alike, used their dissonances to combat it. To acknowledge that situation is not to promote it; indeed, it is the necessary first step toward obviating it.

25

Can We Give Poor Orff
a Pass at Last?

Leon Botstein and the American Symphony Orchestra are teasing us again about music and politics. In recent concerts they have given us politically excruciating but musically attractive cantatas by Franz Schmidt, who toadied to Hitler, and Sergey Prokofieff, who groveled to Stalin. As a follow-up, one might expect a program of musically excruciating but politically attractive works. But no, we don't need the American Symphony for that. Such pieces are all over the map, what with Joseph Schwantner's banalities in praise of the Rev. Dr. Martin Luther King Jr. *(New Morning for the World)*, John Harbison's in furtherance of Middle East peace *(Four Psalms)*, Ellen Taaffe Zwilich's in defense of the environment (Symphony No. 4: "The Gardens"), or Philip Glass's on behalf of every piety in sight (Symphony No. 5: "Requiem, Bardo, Nirmanakaya"), just to name a few.

Instead, the same formula, with its implied torture to our collective conscience, will be ridden again, pitting politics everybody loves to hate against music many hate to love but find vexingly irresistible. Under the title "After *Carmina Burana:* A Historical Perspective," the orchestra is sponsoring a day-long symposium next Sunday at LaGuardia High School near Lincoln Center, and a concert on 16 May at Avery Fisher Hall, devoted to Carl Orff's *Catulli Carmina* (1943) and his rarely heard *Trionfo di Afrodite* (1951).

Together with *Carmina Burana* (1936), which, as it happens, Zdenek Macal and the New Jersey Symphony will perform beginning on 16 May at the New Jersey Performing Arts Center in Newark, these two cantatas—or, as originally intended, choral ballets—make up a trilogy called *Trionfi*, first performed at La Scala in Milan in 1953. Widely regarded as a magnified (or inflated) and popularized (or dumbed-down) sequel to (or knockoff of) *Les Noces,* Stravinsky's choral ballet of 1923, *Trionfi* stands as a monument to . . . what? The triumph of artistic independence (and prescient accessibility) in an age of musical hermeticism and conformism mandated by the cold war? The persistence of instinctive affirmation of life in an age of thermonuclear threat and existential disillusion? The survival of Nazi-inspired artistic barbarism under cover of classical simplicity?

The possibilities don't end there, although these three have had vocal exponents, and they will probably get a heated airing at the symposium. But why, exactly, has the Nazi taint stuck so doggedly to Orff, who (unlike Herbert von Karajan or Elisabeth Schwarzkopf) never belonged to the Nazi Party? Is it because two-thirds of his trilogy was very successfully performed under Nazi auspices? If being loved by the Nazis were enough to damn, we would have to take leave not only of Orff, and not only of Wagner, but also of Bach, Beethoven, and Brahms. Is it because Orff's cantatas are the only musical fruits of the Third Reich (apart, perhaps, from the later, less popular operas of Richard Strauss) to survive in active repertory today? Then why do we tolerate all that Soviet music? Or is it merely because the Nazis offer an "objective" pretext for dismissal to those who subjectively disapprove of Orff's music for other reasons: reasons having to do, could it be, with prudery?

Unlike Prokofieff and Shostakovich, Orff never wrote music in actual praise of his Leader or explicitly touting a totalitarian party line. Prokofieff's *Zdravitsa* or *Toast to Stalin,* performed by the American Symphony in December, is fairly well known. Shostakovich's film score for *The Fall of Berlin* ends with a resounding paean to the dictator. (It will take a heap of ingenuity to find hidden dissidence in that one.) Both Russians also wrote plenty of Communist mass songs to order. Orff's controversial cantatas, by contrast, set medieval German poetry (in Latin and Bavarian dialect) and classical texts by Catullus, Sappho, and Euripides in the original languages, along with additional Latin lyrics by the composer himself, a trained "humanist."

The worst Orff can be accused of is opportunism. He accepted a 1938 commission from the mayor of Frankfurt to compose incidental music for *A Midsummer Night's Dream* to replace Mendelssohn's racially banned score. But even here, an extenuating case can be argued. Shakespeare's play had long attracted Orff. He had composed music for it as early as 1917, and he added more in 1927, before there was any Nazi government to curry favor with. Shabbier than anything he did under the Nazis was his behavior immediately after the war. An obvious beneficiary of the regime, one of only twelve composers to receive a full military exemption from Goebbels's propaganda ministry, Orff regaled his denazification interrogators with half-truths and outright lies to get himself classified Gray-Acceptable (that is, professionally employable) by the Allied military government.

The *Midsummer* score, he assured them, was not composed under orders (true only insofar as a commission can be distinguished from an order). "He swears that it was not written to try to replace Mendelssohn's music," reads the official report filed by the American officer in charge of political screenings, "and he admits that he chose an unfortunate moment in history to write it." Orff also maintained that "he never had any connection with prominent Nazis." The truth of such a statement depends, of course, on definitions: of "prominent" as well as "Nazi."

But these prevarications pale before the whopper Orff put over on his personal hearing officer: Capt. Newell Jenkins, a musician who had studied with Orff before the war and who later became familiar to New York audiences as the director of Clarion Concerts, a pioneering early-music organization. Orff convinced Jenkins that he had been a cofounder of the White Rose resistance movement and that he had fled for his life into the Bavarian Alps when the "other" founder, the musicologist Kurt Huber, was exposed, arrested, and executed in 1943. Orff and Huber were well acquainted: they had collaborated on an anthology of Bavarian folk songs. As Huber's widow has testified, when Huber was arrested Orff was terrified at the prospect of guilt by association. But his claim to that very "guilt" in retrospect has been exploded by the historian Michael H. Kater in his recent book, *Composers of the Nazi Era.*

Not every recent commentator has been as scrupulous as Mr. Kater. Alberto Fassone, author of the Orff article in the second edition of *The New Grove Dictionary* (sure to become the standard source of information on the composer for inquiring English-speaking minds), colludes with the composer's exculpating equivocations. Orff told his screeners that "his music was not appreciated by the Nazis and that he never got a favorable review by a Nazi music critic." Mr. Fassone elaborates: "The fact that *Carmina Burana* had been torn to shreds by Herbert Gerigk, the influential critic of the *Völkischer Beobachter,* who referred to the 'incomprehensibility of the language' colored by a 'jazzy atmosphere,' caused many of Germany's opera intendants to fear staging the work after its premiere."

Case dismissed? Not so fast. Gerigk's paper was the main Nazi Party organ, to be sure, and the critic was a protégé of Alfred Rosenberg, the Nazi ideologist. But another reviewer, Horst Büttner, a protégé of Joseph Goebbels, waxed ecstatic after the 1937 première about "the radiant, strength-filled life-joy" Orff's settings of bawdy medieval ballads expressed through their "folk-like structure." And that opinion won out. By 1940, even the *Völkischer Beobachter* was on board, hailing *Carmina Burana* as "the kind of clear, stormy and yet always disciplined music that our time requires."

Phrases like "strength-filled life-joy," and the emphasis on stormy discipline, do begin to smack of Nazi slogans. Through them we can leave the composer's person behind and go back to the music, which is all that matters now. To saddle the music with the composer's personal shortcomings would merely be to practice another kind of guilt by association; and in any case, Orff is dead. His works are what live and continue to affect our lives. Even if we admit that *Carmina Burana* was the original "Springtime for Hitler," with its theme of vernal lust and its tunes redolent (according to a German acquaintance of mine) of the songs sung in the thirties by Nazi youth clubs, can't we take Hitler away now and just leave innocent springtime—or, at least, innocent music?

Sorry, no. The innocence of music is for many an article of faith, if often an expedient one. The German conductor Christian Thielemann, recently embroiled in discussions over whether he really called Daniel Barenboim's dispute with the Staatsoper in Berlin "the Jewish mess," sought refuge in the notion. "What has C sharp minor got to do with fascism?" he asked a British interviewer. But that is like asking what the letter *F* has to do with fascism. It all depends on what letters follow it—that is, on the context. Sing the "Horst Wessel Lied" in C sharp minor—all right, that tune is in the major, but just suppose—and the key can have a lot to do with fascism.

But there are more sophisticated ways of asking the question. The American musicologist Kim Kowalke notes that Orff first employed his primitivistic idiom, the one now associated with his "Nazi" pieces, in songs predating the Nazi regime, to words by the eventual Hitler refugee Franz Werfel and by the eventual Communist poet laureate Bertolt Brecht. Armed with this information, Mr. Kowalke seeks to challenge a position that many, this writer included, have taken: "If the musical idiom of *Carmina Burana* derives from settings of Brecht's poetry, can it *inherently* inscribe, as Brecht would argue in general and Richard Taruskin would assert in particular, a 'celebration of Nazi youth culture'?"

Yet surely Mr. Kowalke knows that his italicized word loads the dice. There is no inherent difference, perhaps, between music that accompanies leftist propaganda and music that accompanies rightist propaganda. But one may argue nevertheless that Orff's music is well—nay, obviously—suited to accompany propaganda. What makes its suitability so obvious, one may argue further, are indeed its inherent qualities. And such music, one may conclude, can have undesirable effects on listeners, similar to those of propaganda.

The first point—that Orff's music is "obviously" suited to accompany propaganda—is corroborated by its ubiquitous employment for such purposes even today. Not all propaganda is political, after all; and most people who recognize Orff's music today do so because of its exploitation in commercials for chocolate, beer, and juvenile action heroes (not to mention Michael Jackson's "Dangerous" tour). Alex Ross has argued in the *New York Times* that the co-optation of *Carmina Burana* for sales propaganda "is proof that it contains no diabolical message, indeed that it contains no message whatsoever."

But change the word *contains* to *channels* and Orff is back on the hook. His music can channel any diabolical message that text or context may suggest, and no music does it better. How does it accomplish this sinister task? That's what Orff learned from Stravinsky, master of the pounding rhythm and the endless ostinato. Repeat anything often enough, Dr. Goebbels said (quoting Stalin), and it becomes the truth. Stravinsky himself has been accused of the dehumanizing effect we now attribute to mass propaganda, most notoriously by Theodor W. Adorno in his 1948 book, *Philosophy of New Music*. But Stravinsky's early music, though admittedly "written with an ax" (as the composer put it to his fellow Russian exile Vladimir Ussachevsky), is subtlety itself compared with the work of his German imitator.

And yes, *imitator* is definitely the word. *Carmina Burana* abounds in out-and-out plagiarisms from *Les Noces*. The choral yawp ("niet-niet-niet-niet-niet!") at the end of "Circa mea pectora" (No. 18 of the 25 tiny numbers that make up Orff's 55-minute score) exactly reproduces the choral writing at the climax of Stravinsky's third tableau. Another little choral mantra ("trillirivos-trillirivos-trillirivos") in Orff's No. 20 ("Veni, veni, venias") echoes the acclamations to the patron saints halfway through the second tableau of Stravinsky's ballet. And these are only the most blatant cases.

In *Catulli Carmina*, Orff aped the distinctive four-piano-plus-percussion scoring of *Les Noces*, upping the percussion ante from 6 players on 16 instruments to 12 on 23. Surrounding a central episode in which the story of Catullus's doomed love for Lesbia is danced to an accompaniment of a cappella choruses, the piano-cum-percussion clangor accompanies torrid bust- and crotch-groping lyrics by the composer: real "pornophony," to recall the epithet the *New York Sun* lavished on Shostakovich's *The Lady Macbeth of the Mtsensk District* in 1935. (In the noble tradition of Krafft-Ebing, at least half of Orff's Latin verses are left untranslated on record jackets I've seen.)

Finally, in *Trionfo di Afrodite* Orff copied the actual scenario of *Les Noces*, a ritualized wedding ceremony, although the music now harks back to Stravinsky's more decorous mythological period with echoes of *Oedipus Rex* and *Perséphone*, along with an unexpected fantasy in the middle on the Shrovetide music from *Petrushka*. Even the most seemingly original music in *Trionfo*, Orff's imaginary equivalent of the lascivious Greek "chromatic genus" (to which he sets the bride's and groom's lines), turns out to be a Stravinsky surrogate, derived from the "octatonic" scale of alternating half and whole steps that Stravinsky inherited from his teacher, Rimsky-Korsakov, who got it from Liszt.

Even if one agrees with Adorno's strictures about Stravinsky, though, one must also allow that the degree of barbarization represented by Orff's leering rewrite so far exceeds Stravinsky's as to amount to a difference in kind. When *Les Noces* is actually performed as a ballet, especially in Bronislava Nijinska's original choreography, the visible characters behave with what a contemporary folklorist called the "profound gravity" and "cool, inevitable intention" of ritual. They march off to the wedding bed in a robotic lockstep, symbolizing the grip of remorseless, immemorial tradition that ensures the immortality of the race even as it diminishes individual freedom of choice.

By contrast, the penultimate scene in *Trionfo di Afrodite,* to a text by Sappho, may be the most graphic musical description of the sex act ever put on paper. Every sigh, moan, and squeal is precisely notated, so that despite the ostensibly recondite text in a dead language, even the dullest member of the audience will get the titillating point. (At least Orff was an equal-opportunity orgiast: his bride wails and whimpers as much as his groom, whereas in *Les Noces* the bride, silent at the end, is just the groom's "nocturnal amusement.")

Stravinsky's repetitions are offset by rhythmic irregularities so that they elude easy memorization and remain surprising even after many hearings. As a result, the overall mood of *Les Noces* and *The Rite of Spring,* his loudest pseudoaboriginal scores, is grim, even terrifying. Orff's rhythms are uniformly foursquare, his melodies catchy, his moods ingratiating. His music provides what the Australian musicologist Margaret King recently called "an instant tape loop for the mind," something that, grasped fully and immediately, reverberates in the head the way propaganda is supposed to do. As Mr. Ross put it, even after half a century or more, Orff's music remains "as adept as ever at rousing primitive, unreflective enthusiasm."

Is that a reason to love it or to hate it? Everybody likes to indulge the herd instinct now and then, as Thomas Mann so chillingly reminded us in *Mario and the Magician.* It is just because we like it that we ought perhaps to resist it. Could the Nazi Holocaust have been carried off without expertly rousing primitive, unreflective enthusiasm in millions? Was Orff's neopaganism unrelated to the ideology that reigned in his homeland when he wrote his most famous scores?

In 1937, the year in which *Carmina Burana* enjoyed its smashing success, the National Socialists were engaged in a furious propaganda battle with the churches of Germany, countering the Christian message of compassion with neopagan worship of holy hatred. And what could better support the Nazi claim that the Germans, precisely in their Aryan neopaganism, were the true heirs of Greco-Roman ("Western") culture than Orff's animalistic settings of Greek and Latin poets?

Did Orff intend precisely this? Was he a Nazi? These questions are ultimately immaterial. They allow the deflection of any criticism of his work into irrelevant questions of rights: Orff's right to compose his music, our right to perform and listen to it. Without questioning either, one may still regard his music as toxic, whether it does its animalizing work at Nazi rallies, in school auditoriums, at rock concerts, in films, in the sound tracks that accompany commercials, or in Avery Fisher Hall.

POSTSCRIPT, 2008

I fought them tooth and nail, but the *Times* editors insisted on running this piece with a title—"Orff's Musical and Moral Failings"—that prejudged the case and ensured a distorted response. Need I even mention that the article was denounced for its "political correctness" by those obsessed with the red-herring issue of rights, just as I predicted in the last paragraph? Or that a feuilletonist in a German newspaper (make that a Munich newspaper) sought to dismiss the whole question, straining for nonchalance, as a big *Klischee?*[1] The prize for non sequitur went to John Rockwell, in a promo for another *Carmina Burana* performance a couple of years later. After summarizing my facts and arguments, he announced (on the authority of Michael Kater) that Orff was one-eighth Jewish and pronounced what the Vatican calls a *nihil obstat:* "So enjoy yourselves guilt-free, you singers and audience members at tonight's *Carmina Burana* at Lincoln Center. It is perfectly legitimate to like this music."[2]

Go right ahead; don't let me stand in your way. But why is a nice American writer like John Rockwell applying Nazi standards (*Achteljude,* yet!) to assess Jewishness? And not even correctly: having one Jewish great-grandparent did not condemn one in "Naziland," so by what logic does it now serve to denazify? And lest it be argued that the Nazi definition is Israel's as well—it all depends on which great-grandparent. If it's the mother's mother's mother, come right in; but did Mr. Kater, or Mr. Rockwell, check?

NOTES

1. Andrian Kreye, "Ewig gestrig," *Süddeutscher Zeitung,* 15 May 2001. (The banner: "Was Deutschland genau ist, wissen die amerikanischen Medien nicht, aber eines steht fest: Es ist Naziland.")

2. "Going Beyond 'Carmina Burana,' and Beyond Orff's Stigma," *New York Times,* 3 December 2003.

26

The Danger of Music and
the Case for Control

And on top of everything else, the Taliban hate music, too. In an interview in October with Nicholas Wroe, a columnist for the British newspaper the *Guardian,* John Baily, an ethnomusicologist on the faculty of Goldsmiths College, London, gave the details. After taking power in 1996, the Islamic fundamentalists who ruled most of Afghanistan undertook search-and-destroy missions in which musical instruments and cassette players were seized and burned in public pyres. Wooden poles were festooned with great ribbons of confiscated audio- and videotape as a reminder of the ban, imposed in keeping with a maxim attributed to the prophet Muhammad warning "those who listen to music and songs in this world" that "on the Day of Judgment molten lead will be poured into their ears." Musicians caught in the act were beaten with their instruments and imprisoned for as many as forty days. The interdiction on professional music making closed off yet another avenue to women's participation in public life. The only sounds on the Taliban-dominated radio that Western ears would recognize as musical were those of ritual chanting (something quite distinct from "music," both conceptually and linguistically, in Islamic thought as in many of the world's cultures).

So what else is new? Utopians, puritans, and totalitarians have always sought to regulate music if not forbid it outright. Ayatollah Ruhollah Khomeini, probably the Taliban's immediate model, banned it from Iranian radio and television in 1979, because its effects, he said, were like those of opium, "stupefying persons listening to it and making their brains inactive and frivolous." But our own "Western" tradition is just as full of suspicion toward music, much of it religious. In the fourth century, St. Augustine confessed that as a result of his sensuous enjoyment of the melodies he heard in church, "I have become a problem unto myself." In the twelfth, John of Salisbury complained that the spectacular music sung in the Paris Cathedral of Notre Dame could "more easily occasion titillation between the legs than a sense of devotion in the brain." Protestant reformers in England and Switzerland seized and burned books containing "popish ditties" with Talibanish zeal. Somewhat later, the Orthodox patriarch of Moscow ordered bonfires of musical instruments, thought to be avatars of paganism.

Religious distrust of music often arises out of distrust of its conduits, especially when female. St. John Chrysostom, the great father of the Greek Orthodox Church, complained that when marriages were solemnized, "dancing, and cymbals and flutes, and shameful words and songs from the lips of painted girls" were introduced, and with them "all the Devil's great heap of garbage." Near the beginning of my career as a college music teacher, a young Hasidic man in fringes and gabardines approached me on the first day of class to inform me that he was willing to take my course but that he would sit near the door, and I was to warn him whenever I would play a record that contained the sound of a woman's voice so that he could slip into the hall and avoid it. (Don't do me any favors, I replied.)

Secular thinkers have been no less leery of music. In a famous passage from Plato's *Republic,* Socrates advocates banning most of the musical modes or scales, "because more than anything else rhythm and harmony find their way to the inmost soul and take strongest hold upon it, bringing with them and imparting grace, if one is rightly trained, and otherwise the contrary." If Plato were writing today (or less euphemistically), he might have put body in place of soul. For surely it is the all but irresistible kinesthetic response that music evokes that makes it such a potent influence on behavior, thence on morals and belief.

That is what sets music off from literature and painting, and attracts the special attention of censors despite its relative abstractness, which might seem to exempt it from the need for political policing. Tolstoy compared its effects to those of hypnosis, linking right up with Ayatollah Khomeini's strictures. And it can only be a similar discomfort about music's affinity with our grosser animal nature that led so many musical modernists to put so much squeamish distance between their cerebral art and viscerally engaging popular culture. In any case, Plato's mingled awe and suspicion of music's uncanny power over our minds and bodies have echoed through the ages wherever governments have tried to harness music to uphold the public order (or at least keep music from disrupting it).

They found the greatest resonance in those twentieth-century totalitarian states that tried to turn the arts into a delivery system for political propaganda. Here is how one of Plato's heirs, Joseph Goebbels, retorted to the conductor Wilhelm Furtwängler's plea for moderation in implementing Nazi arts policies: "Art, in an absolute sense, as liberal democracy knows it, has no right to exist. Any attempt to further such an art could, in the end, cause a people to lose its inner relationship to art and the artist to isolate himself from the moving forces of his time, shut in the airless chambers of 'art for art's sake.' Art must be good but, beyond that, conscious of its responsibility, competent, close to the people and combative in spirit." The same kind of pronouncements and policy directives emanated from the Soviets, nominally the Nazis' enemies. Awful memories of the 1948 show trials convened by Andrei Zhdanov, Stalin's de facto cultural commissar, at which the leading Soviet composers (among them Prokofieff and Shostakovich) were humiliated for their "formalist" misdeeds, feed the current mania for vindicating the same composers, absurdly, as dissidents.

The similarity of Nazi and Soviet views on the arts is only one reason political classifications nowadays tend to group the old far right and far left together, in opposition to the "liberal democracy" that appeared, until 11 September, to have beaten all of its opponents into submission. That is probably why the Taliban's ban on musical performances, while in no way an unusual historical event (and not even really news), has suddenly drawn so much comment. It symbolizes the survival of impulses we might naively have thought discredited for good and all—as dead, in their way, as smallpox, with whose revival we are also unexpectedly threatened in these unsettled times.

Anything that conjures up both Nazis and Soviets, and now the Taliban, can have few friends in contemporary Western society. As Mayor Rudolph Giuliani found out before he became our hero, hardly anything a politician can do will elicit a more dependable outcry across the political spectrum than a move in the direction of arts censorship, even if it threatens no direct intervention in the affairs of artists but only the withholding of municipal largess from institutions (like the Brooklyn Museum of Art) that support them. There is near-unanimity in the West today that when it comes to the arts, laissez-faire (coupled, perhaps illogically, with handouts) is the way to go.

But who takes art more seriously? Those who want it left alone or those who want to regulate it? Moreover, the laissez-faire position entails some serious denials. Some say that art is inherently uplifting (if it is really art). Others say that art is inherently transgressive (if it is really art). The words in parentheses, designed to discourage counterexamples and make refutation impossible, merely empty the statements of real meaning. Does such a defense really show a commitment to the value of art or merely an unwillingness to think about it?

And what about public opinion, which sometimes demands abstentions from the performance or exhibition of artworks? Is that just another censorship tribunal? The musical test case par excellence has always been the taboo on Wagner performances in Israel. Breaching it makes headlines, as the conductor Daniel Barenboim knows very well. He did it last summer to a great din of public protest and righteous indignation. But those who defended Mr. Barenboim's provocation often failed to distinguish between voluntary abstinence out of consideration for people's feelings and a mandated imposition on people's rights. It was only a social contract that Mr. Barenboim defied, but he seemed to want credit for defying a ban. His act implied that the feelings of Holocaust survivors had been coddled long enough and that continuing to honor them was both an intolerable infringement on his career and an insult to artistic greatness. To agree with him, one had to stretch the definition of censorship way beyond that associated with Nazis, Soviets, and Islamic fundamentalists, into moral terrain usually associated with forbearance or discretion or mutual respect.

Now the issue has been joined again, even more pointedly and painfully, in the aftermath of the 11 September terrorist attacks. Announcing that it preferred "to err on the side of being sensitive," the management of the Boston Symphony Orchestra recently canceled its scheduled performances of choruses from *The Death of Klinghoffer,* the notoriously controversial opera—masterminded by the director Peter Sellars, with a libretto by the poet Alice Goodman and a score by John Adams—that reenacts and comments on the murder of an American Jew by Palestinian terrorists aboard the cruise ship *Achille Lauro* in fall 1985.

For thus showing forbearance and discretion, the Boston Symphony has taken some pies in the face. In an exceptionally vulgar rant that appeared in the *San Francisco Chronicle,* the arts columnist David Wiegand, enraged at what he perceived as a slight to Mr. Adams (a Bay Area luminary), wrote, "There is something deeply wrong when a nation galvanizes its forces, its men and women, its determination and its resolve, to preserve the right of the yahoos at the Boston Symphony Orchestra to decide to spare its listeners something that might challenge them or make them think."

What nation had done that? And why shouldn't people be spared reminders of recent personal pain when they attend a concert? A month earlier, Mark Swed, chief music critic for the *Los Angeles Times,* had expressed a similar opinion, only slightly more decorously, when he boasted that, "preferring answers and understanding to comfort," he had listened to the Nonesuch recording of *Klinghoffer* the day after the World Trade Center had collapsed. But whence this quaintly macho impulse to despise comfort? Women's work? And whence the idea of seeking answers and understanding in an opera peopled by wholly fictional terrorists and semifictionalized victims rather than in more relevant sources of information?

Anthony Tommasini, in the *New York Times,* endorsed Mr. Adams's contention that his opera offers "the sad solace of truth." What truth? *The Death of Klinghoffer* trades in the tritest undergraduate fantasies. If the events of 11 September could not jar some artists and critics out of their habit of romantically idealizing criminals, then nothing will. But isn't it time for artists and critics to grow up with the rest of us, now that the unthinkable has occurred?

If terrorism—specifically, the commission or advocacy of deliberate acts of deadly violence directed randomly at the innocent—is to be defeated, world public opinion must turn decisively against it. The only way to achieve that is to focus resolutely on the acts rather than their claimed (or conjectured) motivations, and to characterize all such acts, whatever their motivation, as crimes. This means no longer romanticizing terrorists as Robin Hoods and no longer idealizing their deeds as rough poetic justice. If we indulge such notions when we happen to agree or sympathize with the aims, then we have forfeited the moral ground from which any such acts can be convincingly condemned.

Does *The Death of Klinghoffer* romanticize the perpetrators of deadly violence toward the innocent? Its creators tacitly acknowledged that it did, when they revised the opera for American consumption after its European premières in Brussels and Lyon. In its original version, the opening "Chorus of Exiled Palestinians" was followed not by a balancing "Chorus of Exiled Jews" but by a scene, now dropped from the score, that showed the Klinghoffers' suburban neighbors gossiping merrily about their impending cruise ("The dollar's up. Good news for the Klinghoffers") to an accompaniment of hackneyed pop-style music. That contrast set the vastly unequal terms on which the conflict of Palestinians and Jews would be perceived throughout the opera. The portrayal of suffering Palestinians in the musical language of myth and ritual was immediately juxtaposed with a musically trivial portrayal of contented, materialistic American Jews, straight from a sitcom. The paired characterizations could not help linking up with lines sung later by "Rambo," one of the fictional terrorists, who (right before the murder) wrathfully dismisses Leon Klinghoffer's protest at his treatment with the accusation that "wherever poor men are gathered you can find Jews getting fat."

Is it unfair to discuss a version of the opera that has been withdrawn from publication and remains unrecorded? It would have been, except that Mr. Adams, throwing his own pie at the Boston Symphony in an interview published recently on the Andante.com Web site, saw fit to point out that the opera "has never seemed particularly shocking to audiences in Europe." He was playing the shame game, trying to make the Boston cancellation look provincial. But when one takes into account that the version European audiences saw in 1991 catered to so many of their favorite prejudices—anti-American, anti-Semitic, anti-bourgeois—the shame would seem rather to go the other way.

Nor have these prejudices been erased from the opera in its revised form. The libretto commits many notorious breaches of evenhandedness, but the greatest one is to be found in Mr. Adams's music. In his interview, the composer repeats the oft-drawn comparison between the operatic Leon Klinghoffer and the "sacrificial victim" who is "at the heart of the Bach Passions."

But his music, precisely insofar as it relies on Bach's example, undermines the facile analogy. In the *St. Matthew Passion,* Bach accompanies the words of Jesus with an aureole of violins and violas that sets him off as numinous, the way a halo would do in a painting. There is a comparable effect in *Klinghoffer:* long, quiet, drawn-out tones in the highest violin register (occasionally spelled by electronic synthesizers or high oboe tones). They recall not only the Bachian aureole but also effects of limitless expanse in time or space, familiar from many romantic scores. (An example is the beginning of Borodin's *In the Steppes of Central Asia.*) These numinous, "timeless" tones accompany virtually all the utterances of the choral Palestinians or the terrorists, beginning with the opening chorus.

They underscore the words spoken by the fictitious terrorist Molqui: "We are not criminals and we are not vandals, but men of ideals." Together with an exotically "Oriental" obbligato bassoon, they accompany the fictitious terrorist Mamoud's endearing reverie about his favorite love songs. They add resonance to the fictitious terrorist Omar's impassioned yearnings for a martyr's afterlife; and they also appear when the ship's captain tries to mediate between the terrorists and the victims. They do not accompany the victims, except in the allegorical "Aria of the Falling Body," sung by the slain Klinghoffer's remains as they are tossed overboard by the terrorists. Only after death does the familiar American middle-class Jew join the glamorously exotic Palestinians in mythic timelessness. Only as his body falls lifeless is his music exalted to a comparably romanticized spiritual dimension.

Why should we want to hear this music now? Is it an edifying challenge, as Mr. Wiegand and Mr. Tommasini contend? Does it give us answers that we should prefer, with Mr. Swed, to comfort? Or does it express a reprehensible contempt for the real-life victims of its imagined "men of ideals," all too easily transferable to the victims who perished on 11 September? In a fine recent essay, the literary critic and queer theorist Jonathan Dollimore writes that "to take art seriously—to recognize its potential—must be to recognize that there might be reasonable grounds for wanting to control it." Where should control come from? Unless we are willing to trust the Taliban, it has to come from within.

What is called for is self-control. That is what the Boston Symphony laudably exercised; and I hope that musicians who play to Israeli audiences will resume exercising it. There is no need to shove Wagner in the faces of Holocaust survivors in Israel and no need to torment people stunned by previously unimaginable horrors with offensive "challenges" like *The Death of Klinghoffer.* Censorship is always deplorable, but the exercise of forbearance can be noble. Not to be able to distinguish the noble from the deplorable is morally obtuse. In the wake of 11 September, we might want, finally, to get beyond sentimental complacency about art. Art is not blameless. Art can inflict harm. The Taliban know that. It's about time we learned.

POSTSCRIPT, 2008

"He used the word 'control'!" John Adams raged to a sympathetic reporter for the *Guardian,* reprising for the umpteenth time the crybaby role for which I had rebuked him in the first place, denouncing me for resorting to "an interesting Goebbels term that comes from the worst kind of regimes in western and eastern history."[1] But you have just read the offending article, and you have seen that the word appears in it three times: in the headline, which was written by the editors; in a quotation, not from Goebbels but from Jonathan Dollimore, a queer theorist, acknowledging the dilemma that it is, perplexingly, totalitarians who really take art seriously in today's world; and in the final paragraphs, where it is at last revealed that it is self-control that I was advocating, something that John Adams would seem to have in very short supply.

The misrepresentation was typical. Earlier, Adams had told an interviewer for the program book of the London Sinfonietta that I had "argue[d] that *Klinghoffer* is so virulent and so twisted a work of art that it should be banned forever."[2] But as you have just read, my actual question was, "Why should we want to hear this music now?" that is, in the immediate aftermath of 9/11. I did and do maintain that in its original form, with the comic second scene included, the opera had catered to anti-Semitic, anti-American, and anti-bourgeois prejudices among Europeans—and even without that scene, as Adams reports, "in Europe it's actually, much to my amazement, my most produced piece, more than *Nixon in China,* more than any other piece of mine."[3] What could be less amazing? But countless journalists by now have joined the composer in misquoting my sentence as if it referred not to European prejudices but to the opera's immanently anti-Semitic, anti-American, and anti-bourgeois properties. The record holder for misrepresentation may be Anthony Holden, the royal biographer and poker authority, already distinguished in musical circles for his conspiracy theorizing on the subject of Chaikovsky's "suicide." Also writing in the *Guardian,* Holden refers to me, a New York native, as the "eminent, if erratic, Russian-born, American-based musicologist Richard Taruskin," who accused Adams of anti-Semitism and "further charged him with anti-Americanism."[4]

In short, the degree to which this article has been distorted by its paraphrasers is unprecedented in my experience. The distortions, along with other dishonorable tactics, began with an interview John Adams gave yet another *Guardian* reporter, Martin Kettle, that was published, as "The Witch-Hunt," less than a week after my article's appearance. "Not long ago our attorney general, John Ashcroft, said that anyone who questioned his policies on civil rights after September 11 was aiding terrorists; what Taruskin said was the aesthetic version of that," Adams whined. "If there is an aesthetic viewpoint that does not agree with his, it should not be heard. I find that very disturbing indeed." Toward the end of the interview he circled back to my "attack," this time speaking perhaps a bit more frankly than he intended:

> "In this country, there is almost no option for the other side, no space for the presentation of the Palestinian point of view in a work of art," Adams says. "Susan Sontag said recently that she found the mood unprecedented in more than 40 years, and I agree. I see all these people driving their SUVs through the town with their American flags flying from them, and it's really quite something, I can tell you."

And here is how Martin Kettle chimed in to conclude:

> Adams is a famously positive person, but there are signs that the pressure is beginning to get to him. He is about to stop work on a commission—the first time he has done so for years. But he is working on another opera, with Goodman once more his librettist.
>
> "After 10 years of thinking, I have found another subject," he says. "It has to do with the cold war in the US and the enormous moral ambiguities of the creation of the hydrogen bomb. It's set in the time of McCarthy and of James Dean."
>
> It might be best not to tell John Ashcroft and Richard Taruskin about that just yet.[5]

As long as they brought it up, it might be best not to tell, within Mr. Kettle's or Mr. Adams's earshot, the reason Alice Goodman pulled out of (or was dropped from) the project that eventually became *Dr. Atomic,* the third Sellars-Adams opera, an oratorio-like affair first performed in San Francisco on October 1, 2005, with an anthology of source readings assembled by Sellars standing in place of a libretto. According to an interview in the *BBC Music Magazine,* it was because Ms. Goodman's portrayal of J. Robert Oppenheimer and Edward Teller turned out to be, in her own words, "incredibly anti-Semitic."[6] And yet, when asked for a comment on my critique, the best Ms. Goodman could do was reach for the nearest bromide, charging me, stereotypically and pleonastically, with "pathological Jewish self-hatred."[7] That came with a weird ring from someone who had actually repented of Judaism. (Ms. Goodman is now a curate in the Church of England.)

All these responses to my piece betokened hysteria, a hysteria that reached an early peak in a statement Adams was coaxed into making to yet another British reporter, who had challenged him to answer my "allegations":

> Taruskin has two modes of writing: his formal musicological work and his "pop" pieces for the *New York Times.* In the latter he has made a specialty of character assassination. This makes good copy. It's sort of like watching those tacky "true crime" shows on television: there must always be a body count at the end, whether the target is Prokofiev, Shostakovich scholars, or anyone else he decides to humiliate. The operative mode for reading his pieces is schadenfreude. Like

any true passive-aggressive, he delights in besmirching not only a person's artistic credibility but also in calling into doubt one's whole moral character. I don't think anyone has taken Taruskin's attack on me seriously. I don't think Taruskin himself takes it seriously. It was a rant, a "riff," an ugly personal attack and an appeal to the worst kind of neo-conservatism in this country. Its musical "analysis" of my opera wouldn't have stood the test of any of his own PhD candidates. And his logic was astonishing. Those who read the article to the end were treated with the absurd conclusion that while the Taliban might be wrong in banning music, the Boston Symphony was to be commended by [sic] canceling *Klinghoffer*. One was censorship, the other admirable 'self-control.'[8]

A rant indeed, and an ugly personal attack. Mr. Adams's hysteria has only increased with time, understandably enough given the way my article has been dogging him. Hardly any interviewer fails to bring it up. When the German newsmagazine *Der Spiegel* did an Adams feature, my picture was there alongside the composer's, and the headline reflected the German reporter's typically distorted version of my charges,[9] as did a previous feature in the French newspaper *Le Monde*, ostensibly devoted to covering Adams's 9/11 memorial piece, *On the Transmigration of Souls*.[10] Naturally, I take all the hysteria as so much backhanded confirmation.

Take the latest *Guardian* reporter, Tom Service, who accepted Adams's allegation that I had called for an interdiction on *Klinghoffer*. (Other Europeans have gone even further: according to Bernd Feuchtner, director of the Heidelberg Opera, "since the Taruskin debates *The Death of Klinghoffer* has been banned in America.")[11] Like so many complacent Gentiles, Mr. Service took it upon himself to instruct jumpy Jews like me on matters of ethnic prejudice. "To call the piece anti-semitic is nonsense," he rumbled. "Anybody who has seen Penny Woolcock's film of it, or Scottish Opera's production at this year's Edinburgh festival, will know that the work is important because it dares to depict both terrorists and hostages as human beings." I have not seen the Scottish production, but I did see the Woolcock film; and, like the published (revised, post-Brooklyn) version of the opera itself, it reflects changes obviously made in response to the very criticisms the opera's defenders claim to be unwarranted.

One of the grossest of the opera's asymmetries—noted at its first American performance by Edward Rothstein of the *New York Times* but few others[12]—was the fact that its Palestinians were balanced not by Israelis but by American Jewish tourists, Jews who obviously had no claim at all to the contested land. This Penny Woolcock sought to remedy by accompanying the "Chorus of the Exiled Jews" with footage showing the arrival of a European Jewish refugee, identifiable by the tattooed number on his arm, not in the United States but in Israel, and then showing the same Holocaust-surviving Jew, accompanied by his Israeli spouse, among the passengers on the *Achille Lauro*. The Israelis thus newly imported into the opera never get to sing, because Goodman and Adams had given them nothing to sing, but their mute presence was somehow supposed to counterbalance the weight of the Palestinian characters. All it did, of course, was to shine a spotlight on the original imbalance.

But why should so enormous a brouhaha have been set off by the BSO cancellation? And why the persistent mischaracterization, as a "covert form of censorship,"[13] of an action that was neither covert nor censorship? Michelle Dulak, writing in the San Francisco Classical Voice Web site, put her finger on the essential hypocrisy of Adams's complaints and those entered on his behalf:

> American composers must often envy their fellows in countries less free. There is so much less scope for bravado here; so much less to protest. We are reduced to inveighing against an orchestra's change of program. And even that we don't do particularly well. In an interview on the Web site Andante.com, John Adams said: "Classical music consumers are being typecast as the most timid and emotionally fragile of all audiences. I think this is an insult to a very sophisticated group of people, and I can't believe that the kind of person who regularly attends concerts in Boston wouldn't be enraged to think that someone had made an executive decision to protect the fragility of their emotions."
>
> Ah yes, those fragile emotions, and those sophisticated Bostonians. But the same interview confirms that London performances of Adams's *Short Ride in a Fast Machine* have been cancelled twice, once just after Princess Diana's death in a car crash some years ago, and once just after 9/11. Adams says, in the Andante.com interview, that he approved the cancellations of *Short Ride,* but that "[he doesn't] think the BSO's decision to cancel [the *Klinghoffer* choruses] was made in the same spirit." Surely it's unfair to tweak the BSO for "protecting" its audience from the content of a piece, if it's okay for other orchestras to "protect" their listeners even from the title of another. Who are these shrinking violets who can't get past a piece's title?

I would rather it were not so, but the explanation for the double standard seems to lie in the political fashionableness of the Palestinian cause, especially among the tattered remnants of the British left, and the eagerness with which Peter Sellars and John Adams have been exploiting it. The leftover left has magnified in its impotence the power worship and the cult of violence that had always been the hard left's fatal weakness in the eyes of liberals, and, as Geoffrey Wheatcroft observes, that aura of spurious heroism has descended from General-Secretary Stalin and Chairman Mao (who received his meed of tribute in *Nixon in China*) down to "almost any gang of killers."[14] Anti-Semitism in particular is always in search of respectable covers, and *The Death of Klinghoffer* has been providing one. An example, flagrant enough to be beyond alibis, was an article by Tom Sutcliffe in which he called my article "without a doubt one of the most disreputable pieces of pseudo-academic flummery published in recent years" and claimed that I had called for a general ban on the opera for questioning "whether some forms of terrorism may not be a necessary and inevitable response to aspects of historic injustice (and not only in the Israel-Palestine context)."[15] The other context, the implication was clear enough, was 9/11 itself, which put Sutcliffe's column in the company of the infamous exercise in schadenfreude that the *London Review of Books* commissioned from its stable of regular authors and ran in its issue of 4 October 2001. Adams himself has made a few incautiously revealing comments, telling yet another British reporter, for example, "Taking *Klinghoffer* to Brooklyn, the white-hot epicentre of Jewish culture in the US, was probably a daft thing to do."[16] What kind of person is it who imagines a monolith of Jews (or of "Jewish culture") acting in concert?

And yet the most foolish commentary on the *Klinghoffer* affair, I regret to say, came not from a party to the issue, or even from a journalist, but from an academic onlooker. In "*Klinghoffer* in Brooklyn Heights: Opera, Anti-Semitism, and the Politics of Representation," Robert Fink seeks to answer a naive question I never posed—"Is *The Death of Klinghoffer* anti-Semitic?"—by mounting an elaborately clever rebuttal, motivated by the author's conviction that the opera "deserves to take its place alongside the *Oresteia* and the *St. Matthew Passion*."[17] It begins by condescending to American Jews of my generation for their (our) hypersensitivity and the social insecurity that must have bred it ("the not-so-secret fear of the highly assimilated"),[18] proceeds through an attempted refutation of my musical evidence,[19] and ends with the surprising counterclaim that the opera is in fact "philo-Semitic."

Even before considering the claim, the premise must be dismissed, since it seeks to adjudicate the issue by examining "intention" (according to the old poietic fallacy) rather than reception. As in the case of nationalism, where a scholarly consensus has by now realized that works of art are to be regarded as historically nationalist (or not) by virtue of the way they are perceived, whatever the maker's intention, the approach Fink has chosen to adopt is tantamount to looking the wrong way through a telescope, and ultimately (and inevitably) ends up in a futile contestation over rights. "It will be necessary," he writes, "to demobilize *The Death of Klinghoffer* from the war on terror, and relocate it back to Brooklyn Heights in the long, hot summer of 1991," if we are to determine whether it "is" anti-Semitic.[20] You might as well argue on that basis that Weber's *Der Freischütz* is not nationalistic, since the factors that have made it an emblem of German nationalism (beginning with its première at the reopening of the "National Theater" in Berlin) postdated Weber's work on it. Fink's is simply not a historian's argument, despite its being advanced by someone who calls himself a music historian.

But even on its own poietic terms the argument is silly, because it depends on the assertion that sentiments expressed by characters—in this case, the

Rumor family, the friends portrayed, ironically enough, in the scene that had been removed as a concession to Jewish sensibilities—were to be taken at face value as the sentiments of the opera's creators. "Adams's choice to cut this scene from the recording and published score after the debacle [of the opera's reception] in Brooklyn was doubly unfortunate," Fink writes: "not only did it imply a guilty conscience (as Taruskin realized in 2001); it has had the effect of sequestering valuable evidence of the creator's complex intent."[21] That intent, not at all complex as it turns out, is revealed when Alma Rumor, the mother in the family, refers to Leon Klinghoffer as "a decent man."[22] Case closed.

This is the sort of arbitrary and opportunistic reading one is accustomed to correcting in the work of one's undergraduates, not in the work of academic colleagues. "Can one imagine a more bald collective statement of authorial intent?" Fink wants to know. All one can say to that is, "Right you are if you think you are," and possibly point out that if the statement had indeed been so bald, surely Adams, or Sellars, or especially Goodman might have pointed to it in their own defense. (More commonly the opera's defenders have cited Marilyn Klinghoffer's final soliloquy—her "wrenching final aria," to quote one—as the bearer of the opera's true "resonance,"[23] although Jewish listeners just as commonly see the episode as a caricature of a "yenta.") But they were artists enough to know that such a recourse would have been fatuous. If one allows Fink his conceit, then one would have to allow a similar argument to those (not I) who would with equal naïveté locate that bald collective statement in "Rambo"'s notorious line, "wherever poor men are gathered you can find Jews getting fat."

"This opera does not romanticize terror," Fink concludes.

It tries for something much more difficult, so difficult that its failure has been splattered for decades over the pages of the American press. *The Death of Klinghoffer* attempts to counterpoise to terror's deadly glamour the life-affirming virtues of the ordinary, of the decent man, of *small things.*[24]

Would that, small or great, things were ever that simple.

NOTES

1. "This Was the Start of a New Epoch in Human History," *Guardian,* 29 September 2005.

2. "Making Musical History," at www.londonsinfonietta.org.uk/interact/ask_adams.html.

3. "Eloquent Voice Can Shock, Too," *Sydney Morning Herald,* 19 August 2005.

4. "Troubled Waters," *Guardian,* 28 August 2005.

5. Martin Kettle, "The Witch-Hunt," *Guardian,* 15 December 2001.

6. Robert Thicknesse, "If I Had Words . . . ," *BBC Music Magazine* 13, no. 9 (May 2005): 43.

7. Rupert Christiansen, "Breaking Taboos (Portrait of Alice Goodman)," *Opera,* May 2003; rpt. in Thomas May, *The John Adams Reader* (Pompton Plains, N.J.: Amadeus Press, 2006), 256.

8. Anna Picard, "John Adams: 'It Was a Rant, a Riff and an Ugly Personal Attack,'" *Independent,* 13 January 2002. Ms. Picard was among those who read my article as "branding *Klinghoffer* 'anti-American, anti-bourgeois, and anti-Semitic'"; these were the "allegations" to which Adams was invited to respond.

9. Klaus Umbach, "Rassismus in der Oper?" *Spiegel,* September 2005, 152–55.

10. Renaud Machart, "Johns *[sic]* Adams, compositeur du réel," *Le Monde,* 20 September 2002.

11. "Seit der Taruskin-Debatte war 'The Death of Klinghoffer' in Amerika blockiert." www.feuchtner.de/projekte/pr_Klinghoffer_Debatte.html.

12. "Seeking Symmetry between Palestinians and Jews," *New York Times,* 7 September 1991.

13. Christiansen, "Breaking Taboos," 255.

14. Geoffrey Wheatcroft, "Left within the Pages," *Times Literary Supplement,* 28 July 2006, 7.

15. "The Gospel according to Sellars: A Life in Full," *Independent,* 25 May 2003.

16. Andrew Clark, "Substance Rather than Style," *Financial Times,* 11 January 2002.

17. Robert Fink, "*Klinghoffer* in Brooklyn Heights: Opera, Anti-Semitism, and the Politics of Representation," *Cambridge Opera Journal* 17 (2005): 175.

18. Ibid., 182.

19. Fink adduces two passages in which, he claims, Leon Klinghoffer's words are surrounded by the same high, sustained violins-cum-synthesizer tones as those that create the romantic "aureole" around the Palestinians, but a mere glance at his examples (178–80) exposes the sophistry of the claim: the sustained tones accompanying Klinghoffer are all an octave or more below the aureole's register.

20. Fink, "*Klinghoffer* in Brooklyn Heights," 175.

21. Ibid., 203.

22. Ibid., 205.

23. Ingram Marshall, "Music's Dangers: A Tragic Drama" (letter to the editor), *New York Times,* 23 December 2001.

24. Fink, "*Klinghoffer* in Brooklyn Heights," 206.

27

Ezra Pound

A Slim Sound Claim to Musical Immortality

According to an old and highly unreliable story, Pablo Picasso gave a few poems he had written to Gertrude Stein for comment. In the middle of the night, he was roused violently from sleep. It was Miss Stein, shaking him furiously and shouting: "Pablo! Pablo! Get up and paint!" There are times when—listening to *Ego Scriptor Cantilenae: The Music of Ezra Pound,* a comprehensive sampling of the poet's little-known musical output—one wants to shout: "Pound! Pound! Write a poem!" More often, though, one listens quite fascinated. Much of it is strangely compelling, if eccentric, stuff.

The career of no other artist, perhaps, so nakedly exposes the fineness of the line dividing crackpot from genius. Pound's crackpot theories of social, racial, and economic justice famously landed him in a mental hospital (the only alternative to prison) after World War II. He loved playing the fool, describing his esthetic theories, the authentic fruit of his genius, in a semiliterate patois familiar to anyone who has read his letters or scanned the titles of his essays (gathered, for example, in a volume called *Guide to Kulchur*). And those theories drove him to compose music despite a confessed inability—vouched for by his fellow poets William Carlos Williams and W. B. Yeats, among others—to carry a tune.

His best music clothed poetry: never his own, but that of the ancient models on whom he based his revolutionary methods. Pound sought the means to "Make It New" (as the title of his testamentary work of theory would have it) by studying the very old. His main "teachers" included classical Greeks and Latins, but especially the early European vernacular poets in the Romance languages: eleventh- and twelfth-century troubadours like Arnaut

First published in the *New York Times,* 23 July 2003. Copyright © 2008 The New York Times Company. Reprinted by permission.

Daniel and Gaucelm Faidit, who wrote in Provençal; thirteenth-century French *trouvères* like Guillaume le Vinier; and their fourteenth- and fifteenth-century heirs like Dante, Cavalcanti, and Villon. From them he drew the convictions with which he challenged the romantic (or realist) assumption that emotion and form had become virtual opposites. The inevitable results, Pound insisted, had been amateurism and incompetence and a misguided directness of expression that only hindered the cause of poetry.

Pound's musical experiments were a by-product of his studies in poetic versification. "The grand bogies for young men who want really to learn strophe writing"—that is, composition in strict forms—"are Catullus and Villon," he wrote. "I personally have been reduced to setting them to music, as I cannot translate them." The reason form was so important was that in it lay the "music" of all poetry, whether actually set to music or not, and in the music lay the magic (or as Pound put it, "'the sublime' in the old sense"). "Don't ask me to explain it," Pound has Cavalcanti imaginarily exclaim about one of the poems Pound chose to set. "You've not got to understand it, you've got to learn the damn thing." The poetry is in the sound aura, not the semantics. And for the same reason, Pound insisted that poetry was not "literature" but a performance art. "The idea that music and poetry can be separated," he wrote, "is an idea current in ages of degradation and decadence when both arts are in the hands of lazy imbeciles." Move over, Mr. Wagner, your successor (in theory, anyway) has arrived.

Pound's musicking, like Wagner's, mainly took the form of idiosyncratic operas. The first, after Villon, was finished in 1923 and performed both in public and over the radio during Pound's lifetime. Two others, after Cavalcanti and Catullus, were planned and partly realized. But calling them operas was as idiosyncratic as everything else about them. They are medleys of poems tenuously connected by action, or by mere narration, based on events in the lives of the poets.

As Margaret Fisher points out in her notes for the new CD (produced by the San Francisco company Other Minds, www.otherminds.org), Pound surely got the idea from the song books, or *chansonniers,* in which the troubadour melodies are inscribed. The collected works of each poet are accompanied there by his *vida,* or much-embroidered life story. The situation that motivates *Le Testament de François Villon* of 1923, Pound's magnum opus, is the poem in which the great poet-highwayman—penniless, under sentence of death, taking refuge on the lam in the courtyard of a brothel—sardonically wills his poems to various friends and relations, who then appear to sing them.

As preface to the medley, Pound set "Dictes Moy" (Tell Me), the most famous lyric of Villon (yes, "Where are the snows of yesteryear?"), and it can serve here as a prototype. The tune is a fairly creditable (if anachronistic) imitation of a troubadour melody, worked out on a bassoon. It was a genre

Pound knew well enough both from studying actual *chansonniers* and from making singing translations of troubadour verse for a publication by his friend the pianist William Morse Rummel, who equipped the tunes with ornate and conventional accompaniments that turned them into parlor art songs. (A tune by Guillaume le Vinier from this collection, shorn of both its accompaniment and its translation, found its way into the Villon opera, surrounded by Pound's imitations, from which it hardly seems to differ in any significant way.) Pound's own musical project was a revolt against the kind of genteel arrangement he had helped Rummel produce. Instead, he left his tune unharmonized, merely doubling it with instruments according to theories then rife, now discredited, about troubadour practices.

But Pound was after far more than historical verisimilitude; and here the crackpot took over. The accompanying instruments were deployed almost at random, changing colors phrase by phrase, or even in midphrase, and sometimes departing unpredictably from the solo line to make rather senseless harmonics. This much sounds like the kind of dubious decoration university collegiums and early-music groups used to apply ad lib. In fact the whole production (replete, when performed in full, with a plummy-voiced actor to recite the connective tissue) sounds like something the Hell Pro Musica might have put on, directed by the shade of Arnold Dolmetsch, a Pound friend and adviser.

At once more serious and zanier were the rhythms in which Pound cast his pseudomedieval sung lines. The troubadour originals used a notation that showed only pitch, not rhythm. That left Pound free to follow his own dogmatic theories, meticulously setting the poem not as a strophic song (the way the troubadours themselves had, as Pound knew perfectly well) but as a fanatically worked-out, through-composed replica of his own spoken performance, notated with impossibly finicky meter sequences (7/16, 25/32, 9/8, 1/4) that his composer friend George Antheil helped him capture on paper. This gave his score a forbidding modern-music look that long kept it from being performed—a modernist triumph. It was only after Pound was persuaded to simplify the notation that anyone attempted it. But of course the aim of the whole painstakingly artificial enterprise was to achieve an exact simulacrum of an effortless, "natural" spoken delivery. If Thomas Edison was right that genius is 2 percent inspiration and 98 percent perspiration, the line dividing Pound the perspiring genius from Pound the contented crackpot looks blurrier than ever.

And yet, performed by singers who are knowing enough to know the effect at which the quixotic rhythms were aiming, Pound's settings can be somehow superb. Much as I tried to follow the translation of "Dictes Moy" that came with the CD, my eye kept straying back to the old French original, which I understood far from perfectly but which nevertheless spoke to me through Pound with uncanny force. That went for all the other poems in the

Villon "opera" as well: the eighty-year-old whore Hëaulmiere's frantic lament over her withered charms (the opera's mad scene, if you will, or as Pound called it, "the fireworks"); the poet's mother's appeal to the Virgin Mary for salvation (set exquisitely by Debussy, infernally by Pound in a manner that conveys a believer's fear); the drunkards' prayer ("Père Noé," performed by a raucous chorus with amazing turn-on-a-dime precision); and finally, "Frères Humains," the bone-freezing plea, in weird Martian-medieval barbershop harmony, of a line of hanged corpses, Villon among them, for fellow feeling. No doubt about it: as George Szell once said of Glenn Gould, that nut was a genius.

Le Testament de Villon was recorded complete, in 1971, by a cast from the touring and educational wing of the San Francisco Opera under Robert Hughes, a Bay Area composer and conductor who has devoted himself in a major way to unearthing and promoting Pound's musical legacy and who is the driving force behind the CD as well. That older recording was issued in 1972 by Fantasy Records, and I wish the performance it preserved had been reissued in its entirety. The set of Villon excerpts included here, four drawn from the Fantasy recording and two from more recent stagings, do not come near to re-creating its effect. Hëaulmiere's aria, in particular, suffers by comparison. The performance on the CD comes from a live recording at the York Festival in England in 1992. The singer, Anna Myatt, gives a messy, screechy rendition in miserable French. It may have been exciting to witness, but it sounds better suited to agitprop theater—say, Eisler or Brecht—than to the kind of dignified if harrowing enterprise Pound was trying to foster. Dorothy Barnhouse's version in the complete recording had fireworks to spare but also precision. It's worth seeking out.

The rest of the CD offers seven items from *Cavalcanti*, Pound's second opera, and the one number—an epithalamium or appeal to Hymen, the wedding god, reconstructed by Ms. Fisher from a sketch—that remains from the third, *Collis o Heliconii* (You Who Abide on Mount Helicon), after Catullus. They are interesting to hear, and well performed under Mr. Hughes (mostly from their belated premières, in 1983 and 2001), but far less affecting than the Villon opera. Pound's inspiration was running thin. The music was becoming more derivative, even commonplace—to the point, in one song, of inadvertently cribbing "Joy to the World," the sort of hackneyed bric-a-brac that clutters everybody's musical memory, crackpot and genius alike.

Then there is a raft of unaccompanied items for violin, some of them collected into a suite called *Fiddle Music,* which Pound composed, mostly in the 1920s, for the American expatriate violinist Olga Rudge, his devoted companion. (Rudge was also one of the movers, along with Pound, of the Italian Vivaldi revival.) Sounding at times like the violin part from Stravinsky's *Histoire du Soldat,* at other times like ersatz medieval dances and at most times

like nothing in particular, it is negligible stuff. Including it is a fine testimonial to the devotion of Mr. Hughes, who searched for it high and low, and to
that of Charles Amirkhanian, the equally indefatigable director of Other
Minds. It is played with heartfelt reverence by Nathan Rubin, a beloved Bay
Area musician. But if including it was the reason the rest of *Le Testament de
Villon* got squeezed out, it was a crime. The Villon opera, and it alone, constitutes Ezra Pound's slim sound claim to musical immortality.

28

Underneath the Dissonance Beat
a Brahmsian Heart

"An American Original," the New York Philharmonic calls its current commemoration of Charles Ives on the fiftieth anniversary of his death, and probably few would dispute that designation. But it is misleadingly—and tellingly—incomplete.

The Philharmonic's association with Ives dates from 1951, when Leonard Bernstein led the première of the Second Symphony, composed between 1897 and 1909. The time lag was typical for Ives, who withdrew from the musical profession in 1902, after the première of his very respectable cantata *The Celestial Country* at the Central Presbyterian Church in New York, where he had been working as organist and choirmaster. He traded this fairly high prestige job for a lowlier one as an actuary with the Mutual Insurance Company. By 1906 he and a partner, Julian Myrick, were in business for themselves, and soon Ives & Myrick became the most successful insurance company in America.

Not another note by Ives would be heard in public for more than twenty years, a period that enclosed practically his whole composing career, which ended around 1921, when Ives was forty-seven, although he lived to seventy-nine. For the next thirty years, Ives averaged one important performance per decade: two movements of the Fourth Symphony under Eugene Goossens in 1927; the "Concord" Sonata by the pianist John Kirkpatrick in 1939; and the Third Symphony (which earned the long-retired insurance man a Pulitzer Prize) under Lou Harrison in 1947. Ives became a fashionable composer a decade after his death, thanks in large measure to Bernstein's efforts.

Ives's sacrifice of one career and his success in the other made him a potent but ambiguous symbol. From one point of view he "chose integrity over compromise," as the composer David Schiff once put it. Freedom from the need to please an audience, in this romanticized version, enabled Ives to create the startlingly original works that the Philharmonic is now venerating. But from a less romantic standpoint, Mr. Schiff continued, Ives "chose to become a millionaire rather than an artist."

That choice reflected typically American social pressures, according to the historian Frank Rossiter, whose eye-opening *Charles Ives and His America* (1975) laid the foundations for today's Ives scholarship. They had to do with gender roles. In Rossiter's blunt assessment, the dominant American view during what historians now call the Progressive Era (or, less approvingly, the "gilded age") was that "classical music was for sissies and women." It was no place for an American man of Ives's family background. True, Ives's worshiped father, George, was a musician: the youngest Union bandleader during the Civil War, in fact. But as both Rossiter and the psychoanalyst Stuart Feder have pointed out (Mr. Feder in a full-scale psychobiography, *Charles Ives: My Father's Song*, of 1992), George Ives had been the black sheep of a family distinguished in business and the professions, and was regarded by his relatives as a ne'er-do-well. Mr. Feder contends that Ives was caught in a double bind that made the prospect of musical success as frightening as failure, since success "would declare Charlie once and for all superior to George," implicating the son in the family's judgment of the father.

These interpretations jibe convincingly with the now-famous music Ives wrote after renouncing a musical career. Its outlandish style, full of dissonance and echoes of disreputable genres, was surely constructed in part to counteract the image of the sissy musician. (And the margins in some of Ives's manuscripts abound in painfully misogynistic and homophobic "humor.") Such a style was also calculated to alienate the musical establishment, thus guaranteeing an automatic failure that kept George's reputation safe from his more gifted son. Yet the same style guaranteed eventual success after European composers had made heavy dissonance and certain kinds of ironic disreputability highly reputable. Once a modernist canon had developed, Ives was readily assimilated into it.

These terms of reception were set by the most famous review Ives ever received: Lawrence Gilman's ecstatic write-up in the *New York Herald Tribune* of the "Concord" Sonata première in 1939, which turned Ives overnight into a still unplayed but awe-inspiring living legend. Gilman began by proclaiming the sonata "exceptionally great music—it is, indeed, the greatest music composed by an American, and the most deeply and essentially American in impulse and implication." He ended by noting that "before he was 25," Ives "had begun those audacious experiments in the organization of sound" that in the critic's considered opinion made "the typical utterances of Schoenberg sound like Haydn sonatas." Then, downright jingoistically, Gilman reminded his readers that "when Ives was evolving this incredible ultramodernism of the American 90's, Schoenberg, then in his early 20's, had not yet ventured even upon the adolescent Wagnerism of his *Verklärte Nacht;* and the youthful Stravinsky was playing marbles in Oranienbaum."

Thus was Ives effectively plugged into a powerful discourse that valued artists chiefly in proportion to their technical and formal innovations. It was not necessarily the best vantage point from which to view Ives (or, some might argue, any artist). But the long-frustrated composer bought into it for a while, and it turned the Ives boom into a bubble that might easily be pricked. If Ives was merely the Great Anticipator (as a skeptical joke of the boom years had it), his reputation was flimsy and vulnerable. The inevitable debunking started with Elliott Carter, who had known Ives as a boy and recalled his "jacking up the level of dissonance" in his scores long after he had ostensibly finished them to enhance his newfound credentials. It continued, even more damagingly, with an article by the musicologist Maynard Solomon that purported to catch the composer falsifying the dates on his manuscripts for the sake of patent-office priority.

The patent-office view continues to be the Philharmonic's view. The orchestra is surrounding Ives with works by his "ultramodern" friends Henry Cowell and Carl Ruggles, along with some friendly Americana by composers of later generations (Copland, Cage, John Adams) who have claimed Ives as a forebear. But Ives is also, predictably, being put into the company of Debussy, Ravel, Stravinsky, and especially (in two programs) Edgard Varèse, composers Ives cordially despised. "Varase—Go to Hell!" was Ives's unsent answer, uncovered by Rossiter, to a request for a meeting.

Meanwhile, equally predictably, nowhere in the Philharmonic programs is any music by the composers whom Ives revered and to whom he felt himself most directly comparable: "César Franck, Brahms, d'Indy or even Elgar," as he listed them in *Essays before a Sonata,* a book that accompanied the piece that elicited Gilman's legend-making praise. A continuing taste for such composers (Brahms excepted) after World War I was as dated as a taste for Rossini in Wagner's heyday. It shows Ives to have been, dissonance notwithstanding, no modernist at all but a nostalgist, with all that the word implies in cultural and social conservatism. When he sent Varèse to hell, it was really the modern urban and industrial world—the world Varèse celebrated in his futuristic scores—that Ives cursed. The world he loved and imaginatively inhabited was the world of the American "agrarian myth" (in the historian Richard Hofstadter's phrase), a neoprimitivist fable proclaiming the moral superiority of the unspoiled, abundant country over the polluted, corrupt, and disgusting modern city. That was what Ives's most famous works—the symphonies, the "Concord" Sonata, *Three Places in New England*—all celebrated.

Debussy, Ravel, and Stravinsky were depraved sensualists by Ivesian standards. What his preferred composers possessed, what Ives sought to emulate, was the opposite of sensuality: doughty Victorian virtues of "wholesomeness, manliness, humility and deep spiritual, possibly religious feeling," as he put it in the *Essays*. He considered these indispensables to be "missing and not made up for" in the work of the European modernists or even in Wagner, whose "manner and eloquence" Ives found vacant and, as exaggerated by post-Wagnerians like Strauss and Debussy, downright "slimy."

Ives's choice of words is significant. *Manner* was for him almost a dirty word. What mattered was *substance,* music's spiritual message. Connoisseurs of Victorian thought will recognize the once-familiar principles of Matthew Arnold, the critic who sought moral uplift—"Sweetness and Light"—in art and found in it "a secular religious force capable of formulating principles of individual and social value." Ives had imbibed his Arnold at Yale from William Lyon Phelps, the faculty member (next to Horatio Parker, his music professor) to whom he was closest. Phelps specialized in the poetry of Robert Browning, to whom Ives dedicated an overture and whose verses he set in quantity.

Some of Ives's mature thoughts about music owe a lot to Phelps's example. Phelps collected his thoughts on the subject—many adapted straight from Browning—in *Music,* a little volume published in 1930. An aphorism there comes very close to what Ives valued in music: "When we hear the Ninth Symphony, we are listening to the voice of God." And that is surely why Ives's special favorite composer was Franck, whose Symphony in D minor was as haunted by Beethoven's Ninth (and his late quartets) as Ives's "Concord" Sonata was by Beethoven's Fifth. Love of Franck followed in part from Ives's background as an organist: he kept a reproduction of Jeanne Rongier's famous portrait of Franck seated at the organ tacked to the door of his music studio. In its "aspiring" quality and its emphasis on the "moral obligations of the artist," the Franck symphony had already strongly influenced the "Boston school" of Yankee composers, which included Edward Burlingame Hill of Harvard (author of the quoted phrases) and George Whitefield Chadwick of the New England Conservatory, along with Ives's Professor Parker at Yale. It was also a favorite text for exegesis by early "music appreciation" writers, who furnished Arnoldian interpretations of the classics for the edification of concertgoers and record buyers.

Compare two sermons. The first is by Charles O'Connell, an American organist and conductor who studied in Paris with Charles-Marie Widor, Franck's disciple and successor at the Paris Conservatory, before becoming an executive at the Victor Talking Machine Company. In *The Victor Book of the Symphony,* a text geared to the marketing needs of Victor's classical division as of 1935, O'Connell described the most "mystic" moment in the Franck symphony: a transformation in the second movement of the opening theme of the first, which Franck had borrowed from Beethoven's last quartet. "There are flights toward that light as the movement progresses," O'Connell wrote, "flights of swift muted notes, like the beatings of thousands of invisible wings, coursing the misty upper airs in clouds of vibrant color and life. Incredibly we find that even this will-o'-the-wisp figure is remotely derived from the eternal question of the first movement—notwithstanding its soaring hopefulness. The meaning seems clear: out of eternal questioning, someday comes an answer; out of living, life."

The second sermon is by Charles Ives, describing the four-note motif (yes, da-da-da-DAA) from Beethoven's Fifth, on which he had based the melodic and spiritual "substance" of the "Concord" Sonata: "There is an 'oracle' at the beginning of the Fifth Symphony—in those four notes lies one of Beethoven's greatest messages. We would place its translation above the relentlessness of fate knocking at the door, above the greater human message of destiny and strive to bring it towards the spiritual message of Emerson's revelations— even to the 'common heart' of Concord—the Soul of humanity knocking at the door of the Divine mysteries, radiant in the faith that it will be opened— and the human become the Divine!"

These pronouncements are so obviously cut from the same cloth that it can seem a wonder that Ives and Franck are not habitually linked. But of course the twentieth century taught us all to pay more attention to manner than to substance. I am far from suggesting that Ives was just another Franck, Brahms, or Elgar. But even less was he another Debussy, Stravinsky, or Varèse. We might learn something new about him, and perhaps get closer to him, if the next time there is an Ives festival we placed a little less emphasis on his familiar—indeed, hackneyed—image as an "American" and an "original" and risked a greater emphasis on the dowdy, corny "substance" he shared with the composers who actually mattered to him. Placing him for a change in the company that he preferred rather than the company that we prefer (though without remembering why) might add some depth to our understanding of why Ives matters to us now.

29

Enter Boris Goudenow,
Just 295 Years Late

An early-music festival might not seem the likeliest place to witness a world première. But that is what the audience at the Cutler Majestic Theater will do this week when, after a 295-year delay, the Boston Early Music Festival presents the first fully staged production of the opera *Boris Goudenow, or The Throne Attained through Cunning, or Honor Joined Happily with Affection,* by the German Baroque composer Johann Mattheson. The four-performance run begins on Tuesday evening and ends next Sunday afternoon. From there the production will go to the Tanglewood Festival in Lenox, Massachusetts, this month, and to Moscow and St. Petersburg in September.

Any questions?

Yes, the title character is the same notorious fellow you may remember from Musorgsky's famous masterpiece of realism, *Boris Godunov,* composed a century and a half later. Even in the early eighteenth century, Boris's name was being mispronounced by non-Russians: Mattheson set the first name with the accent on the first syllable (oh, you didn't know that was wrong?), and you don't even want to hear what he did to the surname. But by 1710 Boris Godunov, the ill-fated caretaker tsar who reigned for five years at the turn of the seventeenth century before being overthrown by a pretender in league with the Poles, was already a legendary figure.

The events of Russia's Time of Troubles, the stormy period between the extinction of the first Russian royal dynasty in 1598 and the election of the last in 1612, were grist for fictional and dramatic treatments even before they had played themselves out. Lope de Vega, the great Spanish playwright, began writing *El Gran Duque de Moscovia y Emperador Perseguido* in 1607.

First published in the *New York Times,* 12 June 2005. Copyright © 2008 The New York Times Company. Reprinted by permission.

A hundred years later there were plays and "histories" about Boris and his nemesis, the False Dmitry, in English and German as well. Mattheson's chief source for the story seems to have been *Stories and Report of the Grand Duchy of Muschow* by the Swedish traveler Petrus Petrejus, which was published in Leipzig in 1620, when Sweden and Russia were bitter enemies. You can imagine how events in "Muschow" were portrayed there. But Mattheson, who wrote his own libretto, took little from actual history, and what little he took he (or Petrejus) often got wrong.

Mattheson's title character is not a usurper, merely a good politician on the Machiavellian model. ("He who wants to reign happily," an aria reminds us, "must practice deceit.") There is no talk of the rampant suspicions that fueled Musorgsky's opera, namely, that Boris had cleared his way to the throne by ordering the murder of the rightful heir, the boy prince Dmitry, Ivan the Terrible's youngest child. Dmitry is mentioned just once, when Boris's weary predecessor Theodorus (that is, Tsar Feodor I, who never appears in Musorgsky's work) says he would like to join his poor son in heaven. (The real Feodor, also a son of Ivan the Terrible, would have said his brother.) There are no Pretender, no crazy scenes, no death of Boris. Mattheson ends the story just where Musorgsky's begins, in fact, with Boris's coronation.

So the only point where the two plots coincide is in the middle of Mattheson's second act. After letting us know in another aria that "Upward! Upward! shall be my constant motto," the crafty Boris withdraws from the crowd of squabbling claimants to the throne after Theodorus's death, announcing that in the face of such bereavement, he would prefer to end his days in the peace and solitude of a monastery. He is visited there, as in Musorgsky's first scene, by a crowd of suppliants who finally succeed in, um, persuading him to accept the crown.

Thus the first of the opera's subtitles, the one about cunning, which appears in the autograph score. But no opera is judged, finally, on its fidelity to history or any other external source. That is where the second subtitle comes in, the one about love and honor, which stood at the head of the now-lost autograph libretto. It could have been pinned on practically any opera composed at that time and in that place.

Mattheson wrote six of his seven dramatic works for the famous "Goose-market" opera house in Hamburg, where he worked from 1696 to 1711. He was the local boy wonder. In 1699, at seventeen, he produced his first stage work, *The Pleiades,* and (according to his own not overly modest report) "sang the main role, directed the entire production and put the audience in a pleasurable state of amazement." When not singing, he officiated at the harpsichord. The house where Mattheson learned his trade had opened in 1678, and it was the first public opera theater outside Venice. It had to be in Hamburg. Like Venice, Hamburg was a free city with a thriving port, and as

Mattheson himself observed, "where the best banks are found, so, too, are found the best opera houses." The early commercial theaters were what turned opera from an edifying court spectacle into the grosser, extravagant shows of today, where singers rule, no matter how many high-minded critics protest, and where production values routinely outrank dramatic ones.

So Mattheson's *Boris* is a kaleidoscopic entertainment that catered to its audience's presumed attention span with a multitude of tiny numbers (more than seventy!) for a varied cast of ten soloists and a prominent chorus; with serious and comic scenes intermixed à la Shakespeare in defiance of courtly neoclassical principle; and with dancing bodies vying for notice with singing ones. Stylistically, like many operas by Hamburgers, it is a sandwich of French bread and Italian fillers. Like a Versailles court extravaganza by Lully, it begins with a pompous overture and ends with a stage- and eye-filling chaconne. Along the way, many of the arias, especially amorous ones, are sung in Italian—although just as many, and all the dialogues, are sung in German—simply because, as Mattheson wrote, "the Italian language suits music very well."

And there are lots of amorous arias, because—like any other opera of its time—Mattheson's *Boris Goudenow* is in essence a story of multiple lovers gone astray but happily united at the end. To give all the singers the necessary motivation, they are cast in various he-loves / she-loves combinations that owe little to history (or even to drama, as we normally use the word) and everything to the requirements of the contemporary musical stage. Of the main characters, only Boris himself and the dying Theodorus are not involved in some love intrigue. Of the remainder, only two characters—Irina, Boris's sister, and Axinia, his daughter—are identifiable historical personages. The rest, an assortment of claimants, usurpers, foreign invaders, and the women who love them, are made-up characters whose charmingly garbled names alone—Gavust (Gustav?), Josennah (Johannes?), Fedro (Feodor?)—are in Petrejus. The remaining character, Bogda (Bogdan?), is the cynical comic servant without whom no Venetian or Hamburg libretto was complete. His ambition, while those around him scheme for power or at least for sex, is to get a hearty dinner and sleep till noon. When Boris finally sorts out everyone's love life and banishes the evil Josennah, he rewards Bogda with a nice, soft bed.

Hardly a masterpiece of realism this, but it was indeed a fine example of its innocently diverting type. So why was it never staged? Mattheson, writing thirty years later, recalled that he had held it back owing to "certain circumstances." (To quote Ring Lardner, "'Shut up,' he explained.") We are left to conjecture, so let's not. But among the reasons this lavish farrago is being so eagerly restored today is the fact that for some fifty years, Mattheson's whole unpublished legacy was missing and presumed lost in the maelstrom of World War II. The Hamburg Municipal Library, where the composer had deposited his scores, was destroyed, along with most of its contents, in an Allied firebombing in 1943. Not until the 1990s was it revealed that the collection's rare books and manuscripts had been sent for wartime safekeeping to a castle near Dresden, where they were claimed as booty by the Red Army. They were dispersed to various libraries in the Soviet Union. Mattheson's scores turned up in Yerevan, the capital of Armenia, and were repatriated in 1998.

Yet *Boris Goudenow* had not been wholly forgotten. Between 1938 and 1941, the German musicologist Helmuth Christian Wolff copied several of its numbers for a dissertation on the Hamburg Opera, published in 1957. On the basis of his work, a recording of excerpts from Mattheson's unperformed opera was released about forty years ago, providing collectors with aural evidence that it was indeed a musically attractive if dramatically trivial work. That impression is amply confirmed by the full score, graciously supplied by the festival.

Mattheson was capable of genuine tours de force, like an aria for four characters who muse about the fate of the Russian crown in the form of a (potentially) perpetual canon. It is possible to overrate such effects. Despite what the Boston revivers claim in their publicity package, this was no precocious anticipation of Mozart's great ensembles. All the characters sing the same words, and they do not simultaneously express contrasting views of the action. But the music of *Boris Goudenow* does show a lively young talent full of promise and eager to show off. Those who know Mattheson mainly from his own catty recollection of his famous brawl with George Frideric Handel (then still Georg Friedrich Händel) in the Hamburg pit over who would preside that evening at the harpsichord will find him a worthy rival to that more famous composer, at least when Mattheson was twenty-three and Handel nineteen.

Mattheson did not get to compete with Handel for very long, even though he outlived him by five years. His composing and performing career was frustrated by deafness by the time he reached his mid-forties. Thereafter he devoted all his energies to the unparalleled series of more than two dozen musical treatises covering every conceivable subject from keyboard playing to harmony to emotional expression to orchestration to ornamentation to esthetics to history to criticism to collective biography to plain old gossip (especially about Handel). Published between 1713 and 1761, these books, pamphlets, and journals were Mattheson's true monument, earning him immortality among historians as the preeminent musical encyclopedist of the High Baroque. Audiences in Boston will have a renewed opportunity, unavailable since he retired from the musical stage, to compare his preaching with his practice.

30

The First Modernist

Debussy Letters, ed. François Lesure and Roger Nichols, trans. Roger Nichols (Cambridge, Mass.: Harvard University Press, 1987; 355 pp.)

Although he lived less than eighteen of his fifty-six years after 1900, Claude Debussy is by common consent the first twentieth-century composer, the man with whom modern music begins. With the exception of his somewhat younger friend and comrade Erik Satie (who possessed nothing approaching his range), the rest of what a demographer would call Debussy's age cohort consisted of "post-Wagnerians" at the last, or next to last, outpost of romanticism (Strauss, Mahler), regional epigones of the symphonic tradition (Nielsen, Sibelius, Glazunov), post-Lisztian piano craftsmen at the "national" peripheries (Albéniz, MacDowell, Granados), and Franco-Italian *veristi* (Puccini, Leoncavallo, Mascagni, Charpentier). These others stand at the end of historiographical chapters. Debussy alone managed, at a time when the dominant musical mood was one of exhaustion, to turn over a new leaf. His achievement remains extraordinary and enigmatic, and the opportunity to inspect the man at closer range, through his letters, is more than welcome.

This selection comprises roughly a quarter of Debussy's surviving correspondence. Prior to the appearance in 1980 of the original French edition, his published letters were scattered among a dozen or so small assemblages, each limited to one or two epistolary partners, some of them in back issues of rather obscure French periodicals. Access was cumbersome. François Lesure, head of the music division of the Bibliothèque Nationale, who has already put us in his debt for a comprehensive collection of Debussy's critical prose, has made a very judicious selection.

I found practically all the Debussy letters I remembered to look for. The one excluded favorite: to Stravinsky, 19 August 1913, with wry thanks for the

First published in the *New Republic,* 28 December 1987.

dedication of *Le Roi des étoiles* (in Russian, *Zvezdolikiy*), including the observation, "It's probably the very 'harmony of the eternal spheres' of which Plato
speaks (but don't ask me on what page!)," and the—alas, accurate—
prediction that the cantata would receive more performances on Sirius or
Aldebaran than on "our more modest planet." Roger Nichols, who has been
a ranking English-speaking Debussyan since his biography of the composer,
has augmented Lesure's text with an additional fifty-six letters—including a
handful, mainly from American archives, that had never appeared before—
and translated the whole, enlarging somewhat on Lesure's annotations.

He has done a superb job. Debussy's epistolary style, like his music, is
ironic, nuanced, allusive, ambiguous. Everything means more than it says.
Like the characters in *Pelléas et Mélisande*—whom, in his later correspondence,
he actually fell into the habit of quoting—Debussy intones his little sentences
deadpan, depending on a vast reservoir of subtext to complete the meaning.
Nichols is amazingly resourceful. Only occasionally is he forced to explain Debussy's wordplay and allusion in the footnotes. Elsewhere he finds marvelously
apt English counterparts for Debussy's elusive locutions, and his words flow
with ease, a faithful reflection of a great letter writer's thought and style.

So let us take up the promised inspection. It is timely. Now that modernism is decisively on the wane, historians have been setting in packs on
the carcass. The letters of music's Ur-modernist should help take its measure. Indeed, answers to Harry Levin's old question, "What Was Modernism?" come almost too quickly—and disquietingly. Observing its first
stirrings prompts dreary comparison with the death throes we see around
us. Rarely has modernism seemed more moribund than it does in the light
of this book.

Debussy's attitudes defined themselves, first of all, by what they opposed.
Like all self-professed avant-gardists in music, from Schumann on down, he
fastidiously despised the bourgeois public and the artists who catered to it.
The book really catches fire with letter No. 25, written in February 1893 to
André Poniatowski, a rich aristocrat and entrepreneur who amused himself
by patronizing advanced artists in all media (besides Debussy, they included
Mallarmé and Degas). "There's also a new star on the musical horizon called
Gustave Charpentier," fumed the as-yet-unrecognized Debussy,

> destined, it seems to me, to achieve glory, riches, and complete freedom from
> aesthetic considerations. . . . He's a man of the people: to the extent, it seems,
> of writing an opera to be called *Marie* [it would eventually be called *Louise*] and
> set in Montmartre. The work which has just endeared him to the populace is
> called *La Vie du Poète.* The faded romanticism of the title tells us something
> about it but what you cannot possibly imagine is the work's total absence of
> taste—what you might call "the triumph of the Brasserie." It smells of tobacco
> and there are whiskers all over it. Just to give you one brief example, the final
> movement of the symphony represents the Moulin Rouge where the poet

(surprise, surprise!) has reached his ultimate degradation, complete with a prostitute who utters orgasmic moans.

Poor music, when I see people like that dragging you in the mud!

But of course, the people *were* the mud. Although, as Lesure astutely points out in his introduction, "no other composer has ever been so committed to finding ways of revitalizing music from outside the musical world," Debussy's world beyond was the world of art and the world of nature, not the world of men. One finds representations aplenty in his instrumental music of the sea, of the wind, of gardens in the rain and balconies in the moonlight, but precious few of people, unless viewed en masse and from afar (*Fêtes*), or unless mythical (fauns, sirens), artificial (Golliwog, alias "le petit Nigar"), or already embodied in art ("Danseuses de Delphes"). His landscapes are uninhabited (even if they bear traces of former habitation, as in "Des Pas sur la neige"). His, in sum, was not an art of empathy. In the same letter to Ponia towski, he wrote that music is "not even the expression of feeling, it's the feeling itself." (Stravinsky, trying to echo this exquisite distillation of formalist sentiment forty years later, fumbled badly.) Least of all was Debussy's art introspective or "sincere."

Zealous commitment to high culture at its most rarefied—attended inevitably by fear at the prospect of its contamination at the hands of the mob, always hungry for sensation—led Debussy into an affected purism. "Music really ought to have been a hermetical science," he writes at one point, "enshrined in texts so hard and laborious to decipher as to discourage the herd of people who treat it as casually as they do a handkerchief! I'd go further and, instead of spreading music among the populace, I propose the foundation of a 'Society of Musical Esotericism.'"

As early as the 1880s, his correspondence is full of "decadent" enthusiasm for old ciphers and texts: Bach, it goes without saying, especially as decoded by that precious aesthete Pierre Louÿs, Debussy's closest friend at the time, at his harmonium. ("Nobody else plays me Bach with those delightful imaginative touches with which you alone know how to adorn such antiquities.") But he also embraced "les maîtres primitifs," as one called them then, meaning, by and large, the composers of the Counter-Reformation. To an early supporter he wrote back, during his unhappy Rome Prize sojourn at the Villa Medici:

I must tell you about my only outing this month. I went to hear two masses, one by Palestrina, the other by Orlando de Lassus, in a church called the [Santa Maria dell'] Anima. . . . I liked [the Anima] very much; it's very simple and pure in style, quite different from so many of the others, which are dominated by a riot of sculptures, paintings, and mosaics—all rather too theatrical for my taste. . . . The Anima is certainly the right place to hear that kind of music, the only church music I regard as legitimate. That of Gounod & Co. strikes me as the product of hysterical mysticism—it's like a sinister practical joke. The two

above-named gentlemen are true masters, especially Orlando, who is more decorative, more human than Palestrina. I'm truly amazed at the effects they can
get simply from a vast knowledge of counterpoint. I expect you think of counterpoint as the most forbidding article in the whole of music. But in their hands
it becomes something wonderful, adding an extraordinary depth to the meaning of the words. And every now and then the melodic lines unroll and expand,
reminding you of the illuminations in ancient missals. And these are the only
occasions when my real musical self has given a slight stir.

This fin-de-siècle antiquarianism did not impede the search for the new.
Debussy was seduced by Orlando into an emulation not of the latter's counterpoint but rather of his purity, his decorativeness, his freedom from the-
atricality and hysteria. Counterpoint as such was a thing of the academy, from
which (after he'd been through the mill with honors) Debussy retained a
horror of technical routine that lasted and grew to his dying day. Not even
Bach was spared toward the end. In the last year of his life Debussy accepted
a commission from his publisher, Durand, to edit the six sonatas for violin
and the three for viola da gamba with harpsichord. "Never correct J. S. Bach's
accompanied violin sonatas on a rainy Sunday!" he wrote back to Durand.

> I've just finished revising [them] and I can feel the rain within me. . . . If he'd
> had a friend—a publisher, perhaps—who could have told him to take a day off
> every week, perhaps, then we'd have been spared several hundreds of pages in
> which you have to walk between rows of mercilessly regulated and joyless bars,
> each one with its rascally little "subject" and "countersubject."

In fact he was full of contempt for the materials of his art. They were to be
transcended, not "mastered." He set no store by métier. Facility nauseated
him, his own above all; and that is what kept him from being prolific. The
letters dating from the early phases of work on *Pelléas* (1894–95) are especially full of struggle against the crudity of the *matière sonore* and raillery at the
limits that training placed on fantasy:

> I've spent days trying to capture that 'nothing' that Mélisande is made of.

> [Arkel] comes from beyond the grave and has that objective, prophetic gen-
> tleness of those who are soon to die—all of which has to be expressed with doh,
> ray, me, fah, sol, lah, te, doh!!! What a profession!

> Impossible to count how often since Gluck people have died to the chord of the
> sixth, and now, from Manon to Isolde, they do it to the diminished seventh! And
> as for that idiotic thing called a perfect triad, it's only a habit, like going to a café!

Ditto harmonic relations: tonic and dominant had become "empty shadows
of use only to stupid children." Fifteen years later, his main accomplishment
behind him, his mind withal unchanged, Debussy could still work himself
into a lather at

the many who don't hear music for itself but for what, to their ears, it brings with it of traditions laboriously learned; and they can't change these without running the risk of no longer understanding anything. . . . It's the sort of blind, idiotic superstition which goes on for centuries and spreads itself over everything that's submitted to human judgment.

As for the seat of superstition, "the Conservatoire remains the same gloomy, dirty place we remember, where the dust of unhealthy traditions still sticks to the fingers."

Sentiments like these come easy to the outsider. Adolescents and charlatans, as well as geniuses, profess them daily. What made them hard and heroic was that Debussy was an insider, or could have been. Instead he willingly alienated himself from the seats of musical power, preferring to operate on the margins of Parisian musical life. Long after he had settled with his second wife into a respectable family life in a suburban house with garden, wearing three-piece suits even on the beach, he remained resolutely bohemian in his art, preferring, as ever, the company of poets and painters to that of his fellow musicians—which is what has led to so many misleading attempts to pigeon-hole him as an impressionist or a symbolist. Unlike the established composers of his time and place, Debussy could not bear to write in standardized rhetorical forms. There are no symphonies or concertos in his catalog (until the war years, no sonatas either). His opera, written against every tradition of the genre, exhausted him; like his string quartet, it remains a single, unrepeated essay. "Artists themselves have a struggle not simply to create new stereotypes in place of the old," he warned himself. That is why, alone among his generation, he resisted Wagner, or tried to. Hailed everywhere as a musical messiah who opened the door to the future, Wagner, for Debussy, had only closed the door on the past, irrevocably. He too had to be exorcised. "I was premature in crying 'success' over [an early sketch for] *Pelléas et Mélisande*," he confided to Ernest Chausson. "After a sleepless night (the bringer of truth) I had to admit it wouldn't do at all. It was like the duet by M. So-and-so, or nobody in particular, and worst of all the ghost of old Klingsor, alias R. Wagner, kept appearing in the corner of a bar, so I've torn the whole thing up."

The combination of attitudes and aptitudes that Debussy's letters enable us to trace, which together define his position as first among musical modernists, was a rare compound of highly volatile elements: hermetic elitism, aristocratic detachment, recherché aestheticism, disgust at rhetoric, belief in masterpieces and in individual greatness, scorn for métier (justified by secure possession of same), contempt for authority, abhorrence of routine, rejection of expression but not of sensuous appeal, faith in an ultimate simplicity, insistence above all on scrupulous exactitude of realization and the uniqueness of the individual creative act. "The emotional satisfaction one gets from putting the right chord in the right place can't be equaled in any of the other arts," he wrote exultantly in 1915, after a year of blocked inactivity. "Forgive me. I sound as if I've just discovered music. But in all humility, that's rather what I feel like." In all honesty, that's exactly what he did.

The Debussy compound has long since broken down. Nothing like it exists in the world of music today, and hasn't, to be precise, since the death of Edgar Varèse (a protégé of Debussy) in 1965. Present claimants to the mantle of high modernism, who have enshrined Debussy in their pantheon (and thereby asserted proprietary rights to his legacy), share with him only his elitism. In every other way they are antipodal to him, for his paramount article of faith was opposition to the academy. Those who call themselves his heirs today *are* the academy. They are supported by powerful institutions both private (the great American universities) and public (Pierre Boulez's IRCAM), and they are every bit as authoritarian as the institutions from which Debussy held himself defensively aloof.

Where Debussy contended with his mighty forebears out of principle, his heirs have embraced a willing epigonism. One of their number, Charles Wuorinen, speaking a quarter century ago on behalf of his generation of young university composers, prefaced a sternly prescriptive enumeration of the tenets of what we continue with a straight face to call the "academic avant-garde" by noting that "it is probably safe to say that the major 20th-century revolutions in musical thought are behind us." Wuorinen then continued: "So many aspects of the musical achievements of the first half of the century are as yet undigested that the present generation of young composers must concern itself more with consolidation and synthesis, with acting out the implications of the older generation's work, than with innovation." It is hard to believe that the author of those words was twenty-five years old, not sixty-five.

But so he and his cohort have been doing, with all that the phrase "consolidation and synthesis" implies about veneration of authority, obsession with métier, exaltation of professional routine, reactionary resistance to innovation. What Debussy would have thought of their pyrotechnics, in which neither communication nor sensuous decorativeness subsists, and in which the specific realization of a hard-won simplicity is sacrificed to generalized theorizing of a facile complexity, can be inferred easily enough from his attitude toward the academic *routiniers* he knew. Were he to surface today, he would surely be cried down by the Wuorinens and the Boulezes as some kind of "postmodernist."

But into that camp he fits no better, for he insisted on an absolute demarcation between popular culture and high culture, between art and nonart; he would have recoiled from postmodernist relativism and stylistic promiscuity as from something cynical and polluted. His was an art that sought to address the cerebral cortex *and* the autonomic nervous system. There is precious little music being written today that does not seem to deny the existence of the one or the other. Reading the intimate, if taciturn, confessions of music's first modernist has deepened in me the uneasy sense that since Stravinsky's death we have been living in an age dominated by Glazunovs and Leoncavallos— precisely what, minus Debussy, Debussy's age would have been; precisely what, minus a few unpredictable and exceptional figures, all ages are.

Nor is that the end of gloomy reflection to which this fascinating book gives rise. The improbable Debussyan compound held together only so long as one particular ingredient, all but ubiquitous in the art of the late nine- teenth century, was somehow miraculously withheld from it. Listing his hates in 1895, Debussy included, alongside the expected "crowds and universal suf- frage," something that Nichols translates as "nationalistic phrases." (It is *les phrases tricolores* in the original.) World War I changed all that. Debussy began waving the tricolor everywhere. His wonted artistic intransigence took on a new and sinister tint. "The longer I live," he wrote in 1912, as the alliances and ententes were hardening, "the more I find we're wrong to forget our past and listen to foreign voices which don't perhaps sing as well in tune as our own!"

After the war began, he preached to the composer of *Le Sacre du printemps* (as converted a soul as anyone ever preached to)—in a letter inadvertently mangled by Nichols, who leaves out the italicized phrase:

> My dear Stravinsky, you are a great artist! *Try your best to be a great Russian artist! [Soyez de toutes vos forces, un grand artiste russe!]* It's a fine thing to belong to one's country, to be attached to the earth like the humblest of peasants! And when the foreigner sets foot on it, all the talk of the internationalists has a bitter taste.

Behind Stravinsky's back, to Robert Godet, Debussy revealed what prompted this gratuitous pep talk: "One asks oneself at the moment whose arms music might be falling into. The young Russian school is extending hers but, as I see it, they've become as un-Russian as can be. Stravinsky himself is leaning dangerously toward Schoenberg." The dark side of all this is fully bared when we read that the opera *Ariane et Barbe-bleu* "is a masterpiece, but it's not a masterpiece of French music." What can this be if not a reference to the fact that Paul Dukas, its composer, was a Jew?

It is in this light that we have to understand Debussy's last works, the three "sonatas" (out of a projected set of six) through which he sought a *reprise de contact* with "la musique classique française." To be *classique* was a way of being *tricolore*. One thinks with a shudder of Debussy's probable response, had he lived, to the *rappel à l'ordre* issued between the wars, to which his *grand artiste russe* proved so susceptible, this forming the subtext of his—of everybody's—"neoclassicism." Ezra Pound may have traveled farther than any other artist to the beat of this drum, but he had plenty of company at the start of the march; and it is evident that Claude Debussy, *musicien français,* would have been of that number.

31

The Dark Side of the Moon

Harvey Sachs, *Music in Fascist Italy* (New York: W. W. Norton, 1987; 271 pp.)

"There must be a Caesar . . . for there to be a Virgil," said Luigi Pirandello, voicing the opportunism that brought so many more Italian artists and intellectuals to Mussolini's side than conviction alone could have mustered. This is not a book about Virgils, though, but about a host of squabbling tootlers and fiddlers falling over one another in their efforts to curry the imperial favor. And it is about another, the Anti-Caesar, who curried not, but became a god.

Harvey Sachs, best known for his biography of Toscanini, frankly informs us at the outset that his book grew out of his previous research. Having "examined many documents that concerned the evolution of [Toscanini's] resistance to fascism," he found himself wondering about the conductor's contemporaries and countrymen. "Did they not understand what was happening? Did any of them protest, and if so with what consequences?" The culminating chapter is a close look at the circumstances attending a famous slap the Maestro received from a young hooligan in the name of the Duce. It was delivered on May 13, 1931, outside Bologna's Teatro Communale, after Toscanini refused to begin a concert that evening with "Giovinezza," the fascist hymn.

These are vulgar premises, and they have led Sachs to a skewed and ruinously simplified perspective. The whole phenomenon of music under fascism is prejudged in the light of Toscanini's anti-fascism, which is itself subjected to no analysis, but is thoughtlessly equated (or so it seems) with the author's own unexamined allegiances. It is not just solemn, it is also a little obtuse to be resurrecting tired Arendtisms only to pin them on the likes of Beniamino Gigli (who sang for Hitler and Göring, and claimed to be unaware of their "political activities"). An unfortunate casualty of all this banality-of-evil banality is any sense at all of fascism's early appeal, to which

Originally published in the *New Republic*, 5 September 1988; original title restored.

even Toscanini briefly succumbed. In any case, it is not fascism as an ideology with which this book is concerned, only fascism as a brutish, somewhat ridiculous form of government and a tediously encumbered way of life.

The first chapter sets the tone, with lengthy extracts from a pamphlet called *Mussolini musicista* (Mussolini the Musician) by one Raffaelo de Rensis, a minor groveler on the make. (My favorite bit is his oafish tribute to the Duce's violin playing, despite the fact that he had "not yet been allowed the great honor" of hearing it.) We are introduced to the cast of an opera buffa: sundry louts and blackguards surrounding the Duce, the opera stars who shared their beds, the clownish sycophants who administered the fascist musical establishment (a trio of forgotten composers: Adriano Lualdi, Giuseppe Mulè, Alceo Toni). By the end of the chapter, however, it's clear that not only isn't this book going to tell us anything about fascism, it isn't even going to tell us much about music in fascist Italy, since it remains fixated throughout on externals: collective anecdotal biography on the one hand and the labyrinthine corporate system of the Italian state on the other.

Of the two, the latter emphasis is decidedly the more valuable. Sachs's hefty, quite formidably researched section on "Institutions" is far and away the most substantial and original section of his book. Yet even here, the detail is stultifying, the story (though skillfully narrated) less than gripping. One reason for this the author himself points out. As he has chosen to describe it:

> Study of Italian music under fascism reveals a picture of workaday infighting and intrigue in abundance, much grotesque opportunism, occasional examples of naïve good faith in the government, and very little real political opposition. Through it all, there flowed an endless torrent of fluctuating government directives on musical education, the management of opera houses, the formation of innumerable musicians' unions, corporations, councils, and committees, and the organization of festivals, congresses, competitions, and musical showcases— all brainchildren of various party Excellencies or of musical personalities who had ingratiated themselves with the fascists.

More attention to the musical works and performances all of this activity promoted and disseminated might have relieved the ennui.

.   .   .

Perhaps the larger problem is that Italian fascism was not worse. The history of the arts under Stalin is a juicy tale of ideological repressions and thought control. Under Hitler . . . well, no need to go into that here. Mussolini's Italy, until the Ethiopian adventure anyway, behaved more like one of those cozy authoritarian regimes neoconservatives like Jeane Kirkpatrick used to tout in the waning days of the cold war, keeping the trains on schedule, and offering cooperative artists a bottomless feeding trough. It is precisely for this reason that even in the opinion of a man who did not cooperate—Massimo

Mila, a critic and historian who served some time in the 1930s for antifascist activity, and who was interviewed for this book—fascism ultimately failed to have any significant influence on Italy's musical life: "You have only to look at the fact that the fascists gave a little bit of support to everybody."

Not even modernists were shut out. To be sure, Sgri. Lualdi, Mulè, and Toni were as philistine as their counterparts anywhere; they authored blustery, well-publicized manifestos against "atonal and polytonal honking" and "so-called objective music," and they intrigued clumsily against their betters. But only one man's opinion counted in Italy, and the Duce liked to keep artistically abreast. He supported Casella, Malipiero, even the young Dallapiccola. He was proud to have Italy play host to international festivals of contemporary music at which every modern master was *persona grata.* Schoenberg, atonal honker par excellence, toured Italy with *Pierrot lunaire* in 1924, and his music continued to be performed there under prestigious auspices until 1938 (five years after the composer had been forced out of Germany)—that is, until Italy finally passed racial laws of its own. Alban Berg's concert aria *Der Wein* had its Italian première at the Venice Biennale in 1934. (The composer, in attendance, was loudly fêted.) *Wozzeck* was given at the Rome opera, believe it or not, as late as 1942.

Also performed during that wartime season was *The Miraculous Mandarin,* a ballet by Bartók, easily the most outspoken antifascist among modernists. (By then Bartók had been a voluntary exile from Europe for two years.) These examples of artistic tolerance, moreover, were more than matched by the racial tolerance that the fascist government quite demonstratively exhibited, in distinction to Germany, until 1938. Refugees from Hitler like Bruno Walter and Otto Klemperer regularly performed under Mussolini; and Ernest Bloch's *Sacred Service,* a setting of the Reform Jewish liturgy, actually had its world première over Radio Turin in 1934.

In such an environment, should we be surprised to find "very little real political opposition"? Do we have a reasonable right to demand more in retrospect? How appropriate, one has to ask, are the prosecutorial questions ("Did they not understand? Did they not protest?") that Sachs insists on pressing so hard? Sitting in easy judgment, he commits painful moral solecisms of his own:

> Had the behavior of [composer Ildebrando] Pizzetti and his colleagues really resulted from a true, heartfelt conviction that fascism was the miraculous system its leaders claimed it to be, it would be easier to accept. Then it could be said they were blind, deluded, mad—perhaps even evil. But Pizzetti and most of his colleagues were guilty of nothing so grand. Their self-seeking was small, gray, banal, and workaday: a mildly evil semi-delusion.

What a boomerang! And what could be more fascist, ultimately, than to prefer a grand crime to a petty one?

·   ·   ·

Musical matters, to the extent that they arise in Sachs's book, are handled gauchely. An author better informed about the nature of fascism and the history of music would not have found cause to wonder that an Italian composer could be (as so many were) an ardent fascist *and* a musical modernist. For Sachs, this is "trying to be simultaneously an orthodox follower of two religions." It was nothing of the sort. Sachs must see a contradiction here because he has been brought up to approve of modernism and to disapprove of fascism (and he may be drawing facile parallels with other totalitarian states). Yet his own data show how fashionable modernism was in fascist Italy, which liked to bill itself as the only true twentieth-century state. And more disquietingly, they show how attractive the policies of the fascist state were to modernists.

Even Luigi Dallapiccola, "the principal pioneer of dodecaphony in Italy" (according to the *New Grove Dictionary*), who also possesses a high moral distinction for having written a number of wartime pieces that strike a note of political protest (such as the choral *Canti di prigiona*), was a faithful follower of the Duce, even a fervent one, until the racial campaign threatened his Jewish wife. One of Sachs's more striking revelations, imparted by the composer Goffredo Petrassi in another interview with the author, is that Dallapiccola had prefaced a major work composed in 1935, the year of Ethiopia, with the motto "Paradise in the shadow of the sword."

So, the story of musical institutions in fascist Italy and the behavior of the eminently human beings who had to make their careers within them turns out to be rather lacking in drama. The Bologna slap is about as violent as things get. Sachs rightly calls his account "depressing rather than enraging." I would go further. For yet another problem conspires to limit its effectiveness, perhaps the most troublesome of all.

It is simply this: while Italy in the twentieth century is obviously a good place to observe fascism, Italy in the twentieth century is rather a poor place to observe music. With the death of Puccini in 1924 (in an archer mood I might have said, with the death of Verdi in 1901), the nation that had once enjoyed a virtual musical hegemony—so great, indeed, that it is still reflected in the technical vocabulary of the art—became a musical backwater. And the Italians knew it. Such musical flag-waving as Sachs reports was distinctly wistful (not exactly the quintessential fascist sentiment), full of references to "the art of music, of which we were once the glorious teachers for the entire world," and "the history of music (which is mainly *our* history)." Precisely so: Italian music was history. The fact is, Sachs's dramatis personae include not a single composer one still cares about except Dallapiccola (and possibly Petrassi), who became internationally prominent only after the war.

Once again the contrast with Germany and Russia is pertinent. The stories of Schoenberg's tribulations at the hands of the Nazis (or of Webern's deluded enthusiasm for them) and Shostakovich's repeated collisions with

Soviet power will retain their human interest and their value as cautionary tales as long as these composers and their works remain our lives' companions. And only as long as that. Stories of Malipiero's, Pizzetti's, Giordano's, or Casella's relationships with the regime, or with one another, have no such value, for these men have lost any relationship with us.

One could even say that the history of music in fascist Italy was the least interesting and important phase of the relationship between twentieth-century music and fascism. As John C. G. Waterhouse pointed out in the *Musical Times,* Sachs missed out on the one major repression he could have described: the banning, after its first Italian performance, in March 1934, of Gian Francesco Malipiero's opera *La favola del figlio cambiato,* to a libretto by Pirandello. The episode is reminiscent of the way, two years later, Shostakovich's opera *The Lady Macbeth of the Mtsensk District* was persecuted by the Soviets. There is a circumstantial parallel insofar as prudery, so endemic to totalitarian regimes, figured in both incidents. (In the case of *La favola,* it was the libretto that offended, not the music.) But Malipiero's difficulties did not come during a general reign of terror. He was not made out a scapegoat and a general example of degeneracy. The suppression of his work was not a calculated assertion of state control. His others works were not affected. And beyond such political considerations, moreover, is the fact that Shostakovich's work was the second opera of an unquestionable genius of the genre, and its terrifying suppression, since it spelled the end of his operatic career, was more than an episode in the history of Stalinism; it was a tragedy for world art. Malipiero's opera was the fruit of a notably garrulous and uneven talent in decline, and its history is without any such wider resonance. Only one musical Italian who matters to us now was at the peak of his career during the fascist double-decade, and he was not a composer.

.   .   .   .

And so we come at last to Harvey Sachs's musical and moral paragon. There is hardly a touchier topic in music right now than Toscanini. One enters such an arena with apprehension, mindful that any refusal to go along with the great conductor's hagiographers will be decried as a general smear or imputed to a frivolous debunking bent. (Sachs's savage review of Joseph Horowitz's *Understanding Toscanini* in these very pages is already evidence of the danger.) But what can I do? I find the story of Toscanini's resistance to Mussolini not an inspiring saga of political courage in the face of despotism but a rather less edifying spectacle of two *Duci* engaged in a protracted battle of wills.

Since Sachs insists on measuring every other Italian musician against Toscanini's example and finding them all wanting, that example had better be examined pretty closely. It doesn't stand up to scrutiny. When Mussolini came to power, Toscanini, who was sixteen years the Duce's senior—and who had supported him in his earlier socialist and republican phase (and also supported such harbingers of the new order as Gabriele D'Annunzio's seizure of the port city of Fiume)—had arrived at a position of dominance in Italian music every bit as complete as Mussolini's in Italian politics. He had a world following that effectively shielded him from reprisals, no matter whose. In his domain he was a law unto himself, and a despot of despots. He could dictate artistic terms to anyone—even to Puccini, who referred to him, not altogether approvingly, as *il Dio*, "the God." He tyrannized the musicians under him in a way that has become legend.

Whatever Toscanini's abstract commitment to democracy, it did not affect the way he lived and dealt with people. On the very eve of the famous slap he unwittingly revealed his double standard, when (according to an interview he later gave) he told the orchestra of the Teatro Comunale, "Gentlemen, be democrats in life but aristocrats in art." His homes, his sartorial habits, his demeanor—his "life," in short—were nevertheless those of a seigneur, not a man of the people. (Seignorial, too, were his fees; in *Philharmonic: A History of New York's Orchestra,* Howard Shanet effectively exploded the myth of Toscanini's indifference to emolument by showing what astronomical payments he exacted at a time when the depression was forcing—or enabling—the orchestra management to cut back musicians' wages.)

Toscanini's run-ins with Mussolini had mainly to do with the latter's attempts to infringe on the conductor's prerogatives at La Scala, where Toscanini was ensconced by 1922 as a veritable potentate. It was from the beginning a matter of symbolic trifles, like playing the "Giovinezza" before the performances, or displaying the Duce's portrait in the foyer. And the real sticking point, it seems, was not what Mussolini had come to stand for in actual political terms but rather the idea that the God would have to render unto the Caesar. Sachs gives no evidence that Toscanini was regarded in Italy as a political resister. He actually declined his one documented opportunity to give public voice to a principled political resistance, when he would not sign Benedetto Croce's antifascist manifesto of 1925.

Sachs's extenuating speculations ("He may have felt he did not have the right to endanger La Scala's economic survival by making his political beliefs public") are hardly consistent with the picture he otherwise draws of the Maestro. The only recorded threat the La Scala directors ever received from Mussolini on Toscanini's account (reported in Sachs's earlier book but not here) was actually pretty feeble. "If they could not control Toscanini," the directors were warned, "they would either have to get rid of him or never expect to see Mussolini in the theater." It would be fairer to admit that Toscanini's image as defender of democracy was formed mainly in America, during the war, when he allowed himself to be portrayed—inaccurately—as an exile, and when "fascist" and "Nazi" had become synonymous. Whatever reputation he could claim as martyr was a gift from young Leo Longanesi, the Bologna slapper.

Meanwhile, Toscanini's revolutionary transformation of orchestral performance—he virtually created the modern standard of clean, efficient, uncomplicated (in a word, streamlined) execution—chimed excellently with fascist ideals of polity. He contributed more than anyone else toward turning the art of musical performance into an "art of being ruled" (to borrow a phrase from Wyndham Lewis). Mussolini saw this clearly, and so should we. In 1931 he sent round what Sachs calls a "secret circular" to Italian diplomats abroad on the need for projecting a new image of Italy. "It is high time that the world . . . got to know a different type of Italian from that of yesterday— the eternal tenor and mandolinist." He condemned "Caruso and the like" as symbols of "the old Italy" and wished to replace such symbols with a new paradigm—"symphony orchestras, whose performances also give an idea of collective group discipline." Now that's really understanding Toscanini.

. . .

The double standards that mar this book show how little we have come to terms with the phenomenon of fascism with respect to the arts. The Ezra Pound affair, not to mention more recent revelations about Martin Heidegger and Paul de Man, may have forced the literary world to struggle with the problem, but the musical world has remained complacent. Sachs is stern enough when dealing with the Mascagnis and the Pizzettis; but when a great composer like Stravinsky proclaims to all the world (and right before an audience with the Duce in 1930)—

> I don't believe that anyone venerates Mussolini more than I. To me, he is the *one man who counts* nowadays in the whole world. I have traveled a great deal: I know many exalted personages, and my artist's mind does not shrink from political and social issues. Well, after having seen so many events and so many more or less representative men, I have an overpowering urge to render homage to your Duce. His is the savior of Italy and–let us hope—of Europe.

—he must be immediately excused as "bamboozled" (Sachs's term) by the attention he was being paid, written off as an unsuspecting dupe, musicians being of course congenitally "apolitical."

Yet Stravinsky's eyes were open (and, of course, attention was paid him everywhere). He was far from the only twentieth-century artist to show his contempt of liberalism and democracy. (As Robert Craft, his longtime assistant, has put it, he felt "comfortable with oligarchies and autocracies"); and he did not flinch from far uglier forms of interwar totalitarianism than Mussolini's. Shortly after Hitler took power, Stravinsky was writing to his publisher, "I am surprised to have received no proposals from Germany for next season, since my negative attitude toward communism and Judaism—not to put it in stronger terms—is a matter of common knowledge." (His anti-Semitism was deeply ingrained; when Carl van Vechten, in a book published in 1915, idly speculated that Stravinsky might be Jewish, he received a furious protest from the composer and a demand for public retraction.)

Stravinsky performed not only in Italy but also in Germany, right up to the beginning of the war. His recording of the ballet *Jeu de cartes* with the Berlin Philharmonic was made in 1938, long after the orchestra was *judenrein*. His only response to the Nazi persecutions was to ask (in another letter to his publisher): "Is it politically wise vis-à-vis Germany to identify myself with Jews like Klemperer and Walter, who are being exiled?" Had it not been for the providential invitation from Harvard to occupy the Norton chair of poetry for the academic year 1939–40 (which made an American of him in the nick of time), Stravinsky might very well have ended, like his pianist son Soulima (who spent the war years in Paris), under a collaborationist cloud.

For unlike most of the Italian musicians whom Sachs ambiguously condemns, Stravinsky was, between the wars, a fascist by conviction. (America changed him, to be sure, as witness a remark recorded by Nicolas Nabokov in 1947: "As far as I am concerned they can have their Marshals and Fuehrers. Leave me Mr. Truman and I'm quite satisfied.") Many things fed into it. There was hatred of the Bolsheviks, of course, who had disinherited him from his considerable property in Russia. (It is not widely known, but Stravinsky was a member of the untitled nobility, and many of his relatives had been landed gentry.) Any enemy of Lenin or "Braunstein" (i.e., Trotsky) Stravinsky had to count a friend. (Hence, too, his morbid distress at being labeled an artistic "revolutionary.") There was a deep dread of paralyzing disorder that predisposed him toward a heavily asserted authoritarianism. Perhaps most compelling for an "advanced" artist-for-art's-sake who saw himself participating in a (or "the") great tradition (here, of course, Eliot comes to mind along with Stravinsky), there was fear for the survival of high culture in an age of rampant proletariats.

If Bolshevism meant the use of violence to overthrow existing orders, fascism could mean the use of violence to preserve them. The protection of intransigent state power—seen as threatening the other, naturally, never oneself—was one of fascism's main promises to those obsessed with maintaining a status quo of one sort or another. Of course it was "esthetic" fascism—fascism as a vision, not a clanking state bureaucracy; and a fascism without consequences—that attracted the likes of Eliot and Stravinsky. That is why the interaction of art and fascism can be most interestingly observed where the fascists were *not* in power. For as an ideal, acting on first-class artistic imaginations (something in short supply among Mussolini's *musicisti*), fascism was intimately bound up with some of the most significant tendencies in twentieth-century art.

.   .   .

First among them was neoclassicism. "If you asked a man of a certain set whether he preferred the classics to the romantics," wrote the prescient

T. E. Hulme, "you could deduce from that what his politics were." Elsewhere Hulme wrote, "It was romanticism that made the revolution; they [who] hate the revolution . . . hate romanticism." And hence the concerted effort, made by artists "of a certain set" in all media, to recapture what Hulme called "the dry hardness which you get in the classics" in the aftermath of the Great War. With Stravinsky this effort can be seen most vividly in those prickly piano pieces of the middle 1920s—the *Concerto* (with wind orchestra), the *Serenade en la,* and particularly the *Sonate* (first performed by the composer in 1925 in Venice's Teatro La Fenice at a contemporary music festival organized "sotto il patronato di S. E. Benito Mussolini")—which the unsympathetic Prokofieff compared to the music of "a pock-marked Bach."

At this period Stravinsky was loudly proclaiming himself an "anti-modernist," the word *modernism* having become for him a code for that specifically postromantic legacy of revolution and chaos exemplified in politics by the Bolsheviks, and in music by the expressionistic atonal works of Schoenberg. "MODERNISTS HAVE RUINED MODERN MUSIC," screamed the headline on an interview Stravinsky gave *Musical America* in the year of the *Sonate.* Six years later, his amanuensis Arthur Lourié would proclaim him "the dictator of the reaction against the anarchy into which modernism degenerated." This would have done perfectly well as a description of the Duce himself, and the echo was doubtless intended. Stravinsky, it is clear, identified with Mussolini in the most literal sense of the word, and in ways that were of fundamental significance for his art.

What is even more remarkable, however, is something Stravinsky found out only decades later (and which many, including Sachs, have never realized): Schoenberg joined in the postwar reaction, too. What many continue to view as the most radical step he or any twentieth-century musician ever took—the establishment of the twelve-tone method of composition—was in reality a response to the same call to order that motivated Stravinsky. It was accompanied by a return (perhaps even more explicit than Stravinsky's) to "dry, hard," abstract formal procedures along eighteenth-century lines.

Although it was not accompanied by outspokenly fascistic oaths or pronouncements, Schoenberg's neoclassical conversion exhibited similar traits of authoritarian intransigence, fealty to a rigid social hierarchy, and (something Stravinsky could not espouse) the aggressive propagation of a national hegemony. Schoenberg made common cause with the blue blood against the masses, and sought its protection. His letter of acceptance to Prince Max Egon von Fürstenberg, who had invited Schoenberg to conduct one of his earliest twelve-tone compositions at the prince's prestigious Donaueschingen festival in 1924, gives fulsome evidence of this rapport:

> The splendid enterprise in Donaueschingen . . . is reminiscent of the fairest, alas bygone, days of art when a prince stood as a protector before an artist,

showing the rabble that art, a matter for princes, is beyond the judgment of common people. And only the authority of such personages, in that it permits the artist to participate in the distinctive position bestowed by a higher power, is able to demonstrate this demarcation in a sensuously tangible manner to all those who are merely educated, who have merely worked their way up, and to make manifest the difference between those who have become what they are and those who were born what they are.

Schoenberg's personality was as absolutist and despotic as any dictator's. In a recent interview, one of his Viennese disciples, Paul Pisk, responded to a question about the internal decision-making process of a concert series with which Schoenberg was involved immediately after the war (the Society for Private Musical Performances) by recalling that there was no such process. Schoenberg's were the only opinions the group entertained. His personal relationships could be repellently exploitative (see the recently published volume of Schoenberg's correspondence with Alban Berg, one of the most unpleasant books of its kind). As for hegemony, many will recall the extraordinary way Schoenberg chose to announce the formulation of the twelve-tone method to his pupil and assistant Joseph Rufer: "I have made a discovery thanks to which the supremacy of German music is ensured for the next hundred years."

Of course the whole house of cards collapsed when this adamant German nationalist found himself branded an undesirable outsider by the country to whose supremacy he was devoted. (His immediate response was to reconvert from Protestantism to the Judaism from which he had originally been converted and, later, to offer his services—as dictator, of course—to the Zionist cause.) But Schoenberg's traumatic exile did not affect Webern's thinking in the least; and though they banned his music along with his teacher's, Webern welcomed the Nazis to Vienna with joy. (A heartbreaking interview with the violinist Louis Krasner in a recent issue of *Fanfare* magazine tells the whole story.)

Even more quixotic was Heinrich Schenker, the great Austrian music theorist, who was frankly antagonistic toward modern music and hence more literally devoted than any of the modernists to the defense and preservation of the Germanic classical tradition. Like Schoenberg before his exile, Schenker was at once a Jew and a fanatical German supremacist. He died in 1935, before the Anschluss, and therefore never had to experience Webern's tragic disillusionment. But even taking all of that into account, the rabid identification with Hitler he revealed in a letter he sent one of his pupils in May 1933 verges on the unbelievable:

> The historical achievement of Hitler, the extermination of Marxism, will be celebrated by posterity (including the French, the English and all the exploiters of crimes against Germany) no less gratefully than the great deeds of

the greatest Germans. If only a man were born to music, who would finally ex-
terminate the musical Marxists: for this it would be necessary for the masses
to become better acquainted with this inherently elusive art—but this is, and
must remain, a contradiction in terms. "Art" and the masses have never belonged together: so where would one ever find the quantity of musical "brown-
shirts" necessary to chase away the musical Marxists? I have already provided
the weapons; but the music, the true German music of the greats, is in no way
understood by the masses who are supposed to bear the weapons.

For a Jew to think such thoughts was obviously "blind, deluded, mad," and
to write them "perhaps even evil." It was a madness and an evil to which many
more succumbed than we are prepared to remember, and it touched on
questions of real artistic substance that most of us still prefer to bracket off
from "life" and thereby hope to neutralize. The moral issues at stake go far
beyond the safe and spurious ones Harvey Sachs has chosen to raise in his
complacent book. They are with us still, nor are they confined to the persistent bureaucratic and political meddling in the affairs of Italian opera
houses, where Sachs sees the enduring legacy of fascism. The legacy of fascism is an inseparable if still largely unacknowledged facet of the lofty legacy
of modernism. Confrontations with this unpalatable truth will have to take
place if ever health is to be restored to our fragmented, acrimonious, and unhappy musical culture—particularly what is left of the "high culture" that has
of late so blatantly advertised its inauthenticity by turning "authenticity" into
such a contentious issue. But that is another chapter, another imbroglio.

POSTSCRIPT, 2008

I objected strongly, albeit fruitlessly, to the vulgar title—"The Dark Side of
Modern Music: The Sins of Toscanini, Stravinsky, Schoenberg"—that the editors of the New Republic placed atop this review when they published it. (In
a feat of inadvertent clairvoyance, Steven J. Cahn mistakenly restored the
original title in a footnote to "The Artist as Modern Prophet: A Study of Historical Consciousness and Its Expression in Schoenberg's 'Vorgefühl,' op. 22,
no. 4," his contribution to Schoenberg and Words: The Modernist Years, edited
by Charlotte M. Cross [New York: Garland, 2000].) But after all I had it coming. I did calculate the language and tone of the piece to produce a shock,
and I have to admit that the sensationalism the editors enhanced with their
title was not without its counterpart in the text.

I say this not with satisfaction, exactly, but not in apology either. My intent,
while somewhat belligerent, was not mischievous; and I have attempted more
fully nuanced and responsibly contextualized treatments of the politics of interwar modernism in several later publications, including the Stravinsky
chapters of Defining Russia Musically (Princeton: Princeton University Press,
1997) and the review essays published here as chapters 39 and 41. But if,

thanks to those efforts and to work by other scholars, including Charles Joseph and Joan Evans, the matters I raised toward the end of the present essay have become common knowledge, the present essay was in fact their first public airing, at least with regard to Stravinsky, and it proved explosive. Repercussions were heard afar, even (inevitably) in Germany. The Munich newspaper *Süddeutsche Zeitung* ran a full-page spread in its Sunday supplement the next month under the headline "War Strawinsky ein Faschist?" and it was echoed in other German papers. It was as close to a scandal as I have skirted, and not everyone has forgiven me even yet. As recently as spring 2004 Leo Treitler took some gratuitous swipes in the *Kurt Weill Newsletter* (vol. 22, no. 1, pp. 20–21) at my by then sixteen-year-old feuilleton, in a review of a book to which I had not contributed—*Music and Nazism: Art under Tyranny, 1933–45*, edited by Michael H. Kater and Albrecht Riethmüller (Laaber-Verlag, 2003)— just to scold me for having started a nefarious ball rolling. (Treitler, though, should have known better than to attribute the title to me, even if in his view it "hints at the broader, more inclusive polemic against musical modernism" that he fancies I have been "conduct[ing] over many years.")

Why did I do it? A composer friend had passed along to me a little anthology of extracts from Stravinsky's unpublished correspondence that Robert Craft had prepared for the lawyers representing the Stravinsky children, to alert them to the danger of making Stravinsky's archive public and to help make the case that parts of it should remain closed even after its sale to the Paul Sacher Foundation (or, as was then still a possibility, to the New York Public Library, where I had done some of my own Stravinsky research during the period of its temporary custodianship). My friend told me to do with it what I thought fitting, which for several years meant doing nothing. It was only the disgust I felt at the complacency and the double standards informing Harvey Sachs's wretched book that convinced me that it might do some good (albeit not necessarily to Stravinsky's reputation) to make public some small part of what I had learned.

The first response came from John Rockwell in the *New York Times*, who somewhat lazily cannibalized my piece for a column of his own ("Music View: Reactionary Musical Modernists," 11 September 1988) and megaphoned its resonance. I was a little miffed at the appropriation (though I received due credit), but an admission Mr. Rockwell made in the course of his précis reassured me that I had done the right thing in spreading the unlovely news. "I used to wonder," he wrote, "how could highly politicized neo-conservative critics like Hilton Kramer and Samuel Lipman idolize modernism? Surely, I assumed, modernism had a built-in revolutionary component." That was precisely the naïveté I was trying to bring to light, above all so as to show that the "highly politicized" reception of modernism continued, and that it continued covertly to accomplish regressive political and social-policy objectives.

Nor was it only self-professed right-wingers like Kramer and Lipman who were capitalizing on naive assumptions about art and artists. The basest exploitation I've encountered of such woolly thinking (unless it was actually an example of it) was an attempt by the music critic Paul Griffiths, in the same newspaper, to insinuate a moral equivalency between rejecting Schoenberg and embracing Hitler. "What makes Pfitzner more provoking than Stenhammar or MacDowell," Griffiths wrote, reviewing a performance of their music ("Gifted but Obtuse: Pfitzner's Odd Lot," 25 July 1997), "is not the music alone, but the interpenetration of music and life, for he had the deficiency of luck, character or judgment to go wholeheartedly for the wrong side, and not just once but twice. He became a vituperative opponent of Schoenberg and Berg. And then he lent his name, his music and his actions to the Nazi cause."

As long as there are critics and historians who will conjure up fascism in an effort to smear artistic "conservatives," there will be reason enough to call attention to its embrace by more than a few "radicals." But the next question Mr. Rockwell raised embodied the reasons for my initial hesitation. It was a question I had deliberately refrained from raising in my review of Sachs:

> Should any of this dampen our enthusiasm for the music of Stravinsky or Schoenberg or Webern? Those for whom political and moral correctness is inseparable from art, and who consider themselves staunch defenders of democracy and the Jewish tradition, and who have heretofore loved Stravinsky's music but were unaware of his beliefs, may have a problem.

They shouldn't, any more than those offended by Musorgsky's caricature of Diaspora Jews in *Pictures at an Exhibition* need avoid performances of *Boris Godunov* or those offended by Wagner's anti-Semitic tract *Das Judenthum in der Musik* need resist the beauties of *Tristan und Isolde*. Fortunately, Mr. Rockwell concluded his column on a more grown-up note, judging that "the real lesson here is that human lives and values are more complex than any ready equation of art and politics and morality, and that it is dangerous to assume that someone who espouses a doctrine you admire (like modernism) abhors a doctrine you dislike (like Fascism)."

What I did not mention in the Sachs review is that Stravinsky (in America, as it happens, not in Europe) did set a couple of anti-Semitic texts to music, and these settings raise more legitimate, and much more difficult, issues. (Chapter 41, first presented as the Proms Inaugural Lecture in London in 1996, is an attempt to address them.) The dangerous assumption to which Mr. Rockwell referred at the end of his article shows its true dangerousness when it causes people to perform intellectual back-flips in denial, claiming that the texts are not really anti-Semitic, or that setting them in the context of high art somehow sanitizes them, or that Stravinsky's stature as an artist renders nonartistic evaluations of his work impertinent or altogether inadmissible.

That was the tenor of most of the mail the present article generated. A letter from a distinguished composer to the *New Republic* finally proved too lengthy to fit into the letters column (probably because the arts were a low priority there) but contained a couple of points I really did wish I'd had the opportunity to answer. "Nowhere in his article," read one of them, "is there the faintest suggestion that an artist can have any motivation whatever in his choice of technical means and artistic styles other than a political one, or one that can at least be politically evaluated." But can't anything be politically evaluated? If not, then on whose say-so shall political evaluation be ruled out? If the point was intended as a defense of liberty, it was a strange defense indeed. Like many ostensible defenses of liberty it was merely a defense of *my* liberty (not yours).

The other point that struck me as interesting was a defense of Schoenberg's remark about German musical supremacy. To compare it with German political nationalism was "shocking behavior for a musical historian," my critic maintained. "There was much speculation," he continued,

> in the years immediately following the First World War, on the likelihood that the great Austro-German tradition, to which we still owe the major part of our standard orchestral repertory, was coming to an end. Why should we be surprised that a post-bellum Austro-German composer would hope that that tradition had not "had its day."

But what surprises me is the ease with which notions of supremacy and survival can be elided. Forgive me, but that equation does have a Nazi ring.

Harvey Sachs also wrote an unprintably long letter to the editors of the *New Republic,* chiefly in defense of Toscanini. Since he incorporated it later into one of his books—*Reflections on Toscanini* (New York: Grove Weidenfeld, 1991), 95–99—I will allow it to pass without comment here, except to apologize for a mistranscription from his text that is corrected in the present version of my own.

Finally, there was the long and unpleasant exchange with Robert Craft that disrupted, and ultimately ended, the cordial relations for which I have in several places expressed to him my sincerest gratitude. Craft published a response to Rockwell's response to my review in the *New York Review of Books* under the title "Jews and Geniuses" (16 February 1989), in which he correctly identified the weaknesses and the superficiality of Rockwell's hasty squib but then went on to deride "scholarship" like mine, "based entirely on the almighty document," excused Stravinsky for his typical "Russian anti-Semitism, imbibed with mother's milk," and quibbled as to whether Stravinsky's 1938 recording with the Berlin Philharmonic really amounted to a public performance in Hitler's Germany. He proceeded to list Stravinsky's Jewish friends (Samuel Dushkin, Roland Manuel, Ingolf Dahl, etc.), as if that cliché defense were not a standing joke, and compounded the grim humor by including a couple of figures—the *Achteljude* Alexandre Benois and the ardent Catholic convert Arthur Lourié—who were Jewish only according to the Nazi racial definition.

I felt I had to reply for the sake of scholarly honor (in defense, as it were, of the documents), although I now regret having done so. In an exchange with Craft published in the issue of 15 June 1989, I insisted that anti-Semitism is a matter for which the individual must bear responsibility, and supported that insistence in the case of Stravinsky by citing the case of Rimsky-Korsakov, a virtual surrogate father to the younger composer, who was (in the manner of many liberal aristocrats like Vladimir Nabokov) contemptuous of the bigotry that so many Russians imbibed with mother's milk and so could have offered Stravinsky a salutary example. Rimsky, as I put it there, demonstrated his tolerance for Jews "in a proverbial way: he encouraged his daughter to marry one." The Jew in question, Maximilian Steinberg (another composition pupil of Rimsky's), was Stravinsky's chief rival for Rimsky's quasi-paternal affection, and had bested him. "No amount of success," I added,

> could ever assuage the envy a musical scion of the Polish nobility felt toward this upstart Vilna Jew who had displaced him in Rimsky-Korsakov's esteem and in his ménage. More than half a century after Rimsky's death—and sixteen years after Steinberg's own—that envy was still consuming him when Stravinsky wrote of his old rival (in *Expositions and Developments*) as "one of these ephemeral, prize-winning, front-page types, in whose eyes conceit for ever burns, like an electric light in daytime." These feelings lay behind Stravinsky's modernist revolt and his anti-Semitism alike, fanned them both, and linked them.

I wrote this in a spirit of *tout comprendre, c'est tout pardonner,* but my correspondent refused to understand. "The notion," he wrote, "that the composer of *Le Sacre du printemps* felt deep and lasting envy for the composer of *Midas* [a ballet by Steinberg that Diaghilev produced, with no success, in 1914] is risible." I refuse to believe that Robert Craft is really so obtuse as to leave it there. But that is what always happens when polemics grow shrill. Nobody comes off looking good. Mr. Craft's gambit in rebuttal—"Richard Taruskin, the meticulous scholar I first met eight years ago and through correspondence came to know and like, has lately turned into a sloppy, thersitical journalist, more judgmental than Dr. Johnson"—stung me with its meed of truth. Not that I regarded myself as sloppy (however fallible) or thought the allusion to Homer's Thersites (the mocker from the sidelines in *The Iliad*) justified, but I did feel discomfort at having sat in judgment on Stravinsky the man, when all that mattered (or should have) was the music. Yet whenever devotion to music seems to require that a blind eye be turned toward things that matter even more than music, I continue to rebel. And so, like St. Augustine in the presence of music, "I have become a problem to myself"—and perhaps to you.

32

Of Kings and Divas

Idoménée, by André Campra; William Christie with Les Arts Florissants (Harmonia Mundi 901396.98, 3 CDs)

Médée, by Marc-Antoine Charpentier; William Christie with Les Arts Florissants (Harmonia Mundi 901139.41, 3 CDs)

Jephté, by Michel Pignolet de Montéclair; William Christie with Les Arts Florissants (Harmonia Mundi 901424.25, 2 CDs)

Atys, by Jean-Baptiste Lully; William Christie with Les Arts Florissants (Harmonia Mundi 901257.59, 3 CDs)

Castor et Pollux, by Jean-Philippe Rameau; William Christie with Les Arts Florissants (Harmonia Mundi 901435.37, 3 CDs)

Les Indes galantes, by Jean-Philippe Rameau; William Christie with Les Arts Florissants (Harmonia Mundi 901367.69, 3 CDs)

Tous les matins du monde, a film by Alain Corneau (October); sound track with music by Marin Marais, Saint-Colombe, François Couperin, Jean-Baptiste Lully, et al. (Travelling K 4640)

"The more an artwork succeeds as politics," the composer Ned Rorem has declared, "the more it fails as art." With less panache and many more words, Representative Henry Hyde agrees: "Good art is evocative rather than provocative," he has written, meaning that it is "neither art at the service of some political program nor art as an ideological instrument, but art as one means by which man gains a glimpse of the transcendent dimension of the human experience." Brute interventions of American politics in the affairs of art have brought frightened artists and canting politicians together in denial. There is, or should be, no relationship between art and politics, they both assure us.

Yet both have abjured politics only to serve it. Hyde wished to justify censorship, in the form of the Helms Amendment that hobbled the National Endowment for the Arts, and Rorem wished to counter censorship. Their arguments were interchangeable, though their purposes were opposed—which

Originally published in the *New Republic,* 13 December 1993.

shows that their arguments are not really arguments at all. Asked what his assertion could possibly mean, Rorem elaborated:

> Politics means propaganda, and propaganda means indoctrination, or the attempt to alter another's thinking. Propaganda is direct, while art is reflective; a speech by a leader, evil or benign, is surely more effective at inciting change (from lethargy to patriotism) than even the greatest—or indeed, the crassest—art.
>
> Art, insofar as it is art, does not change us; rather it shows us what we did not know we knew, intensifying our already held convictions. Music that does impel action tends to be not even music per se, but a hypnotic beat inciting us to battle. (Could I compose a piece that would make us march away from battle, I would devote my career to that and to hell with art!)

This clarifies nothing. It merely multiplies the arbitrary premises and the empty distinctions. Adding the precaution "insofar as it is art" to the definition of art as inherently nonpolitical only perfects the tautology, and passes some powerful ammunition to Senator Helms. Besides, the conceit that art cannot change us is contradicted by Rorem's own life: the experience of art changed him into an artist. Only by somebody's fiat (and let's hope he's out of office) can art and politics ever be so categorically dichotomized, because neither art nor politics is a single category. There are all kinds of art (even of "good" art), and there are all kinds of politics.

The politics that Rorem wishes to separate from art is affirmational or celebratory politics, the kind that totalitarian states require of their artist-citizens. The demand that artists assent to somebody else's politics deprives their art of the autonomy that artists in the postromantic tradition prize above all else. And it is oppositional politics that Hyde would exclude from the definition of art. It is not "some" political program that troubles him, but the "provocative" one, the one that threatens "family values" and is associated with such bêtes noires of the NEA as Robert Mapplethorpe and Andre Serrano. It is not "an" ideological instrument that Hyde fears, but "the" ideological instrument, the leftist one, signaled on his side of the aisle by the very use of the word *ideological*. (His own politics, naturally, "transcend" ideology.)

Would Congressman Hyde condemn Aaron Copland's *A Lincoln Portrait*, an artwork glorifying a fellow Illinoisan? He may even have performed the speaker's part himself, as so many politicians have done. Copland's piece is "evocative" of all the best American traditions, of values transcending the mere politics of the moment. Shall I remind the congressman that it was composed in 1942 in the spirit of the Popular Front, and in direct formal emulation of Soviet agitprop cantatas? (Rorem would need no reminder; as a card-carrying modernist he disapproves of affirmational art in principle, beginning with Beethoven's Ninth Symphony, for him "the first piece of junk in the grand style.") Hyde's Republican forebears had not forgotten its origins, or its composer's past political associations, when they banned *A Lincoln Portrait* from President Eisenhower's inaugural exercises in 1953. But its comely politics of affirmation has survived the leftist taint, and it has been performed by now not only by Charlton Heston and Alan Simpson but even by the Baroness Thatcher herself.

So it is never merely a question of politics. It is a question of which politics: the politics of power or the politics of contention. Art can serve either one. Nor does the artist always have final say in the matter, for only under despotism (and not always then) is the meaning of a work of art a wholly vested meaning. In an open, mobile polity, art and its possible meanings, like all things public, are subject to endless appropriation and negotiation. To insist on seeking the political meaning of artworks solely in their makers' explicit designs is naive or, more often, a dodge.

Doubtless Ned Rorem and Henry Hyde would each, for their differing reasons, have objected just as vociferously as did Samuel Lipman, publisher of the *New Criterion*, to a remark made at a recent panel discussion by the producer Christopher Hunt. The topic was "Opera as a Vehicle for Social Commentary or Activism in Today's Society," and (as quoted by Lipman) Hunt said, "All art is political: art either seeks change or is a propagandist for the status quo." Lipman found this laughable and pernicious. Indeed, the formulation is crude. Yet in rebutting it, in arguing at length against the notion of art as politics, Lipman let slip a Hydeish aside that placed him where we knew he was all along, and exquisitely confirmed Hunt's point. "It seems to me," he said, "that the preponderance of great art has in fact reinforced and passed on, rather than challenged and destroyed, the prevailing values of society." Such a statement, offered as evidence of art's nonpolitical nature, is a masterpiece of incoherence. But it is typical of the level of the debate.

.   .   .

Until the age of Beethoven—or more accurately, the age of Kant, who invented the "transcendent dimension" that Hyde extols—the idea of political art made nobody squeamish. High art was produced for, and served the interests of, social and political elites; that was what made it "high." When, during the Renaissance, artists came to be employed in large numbers to serve the interests of secular authorities, political art in a form approaching the modern idea of it came into being. The political art par excellence was opera, and so it has remained.

Opera was invented at the end of the sixteenth century by a group of Florentine noblemen. All the earliest *favole in musica,* or musical tales, were fashioned to adorn northern Italian court festivities, flattering the assemblages of "renowned heroes, blood royal of kings" who were privileged to hear them, potentates "of whom Fame tells glorious deeds though falling short of truth," as La Musica herself puts it in the prologue to Monteverdi's *Orfeo,* first performed during the carnival season of 1607 to fête Francesco Gonzaga, prince of Mantua. The words were written by the prince's secretary, Alessandro Striggio.

The neoclassical impulse that gave birth to opera, usually described (following the conventions of romantic historiography) in "poietic" terms—in terms, that is, of the artist-maker's expressive aspirations—had also an "esthesic" side, reflecting the expectations of the audience. The revived musical drama reflected, and was meant to reflect, the glory and the grandeur of antiquity on the princes who were its patrons. In a still unsurpassed essay titled "The Sociology of Baroque Music" written in 1947, Manfred Bukofzer, the tragically short-lived Panofsky of musicology, characterized early opera as the quintessential temporal expression of the twin triumphs of absolutism and mercantilism, an expression that brought to its pinnacle the exploitation of the arts "as a means of representing power." It was precisely this exploitation that, in Bukofzer's view, brought about the stylistic metamorphosis from "Renaissance" to "Baroque."

Bukofzer was as unflinching as any contemporary New Historicist about the social costs of this magnificent artistic efflorescence:

> Display of splendor was one of the main social functions of music for the Counter-Reformation and the baroque courts, made possible only through money; and the more money spent, the more powerful was the representation. Consistent with the mercantile ideas of wealth the sumptuousness in the arts became actually an end in itself. . . . However, viewed from the social angle the shining lights of the flowering arts cast the blackest shadows. Hand in hand with the brilliant development of court and church music went the Inquisition and the ruthless exploitation of the lower classes by means of oppressive taxes.

With the spread of opera from the opulent courts of Italy to the petty courts of northern Europe, the costs became ever more exorbitant and the bankrolling methods ever more drastic. "The Duke of Brunswick, for one, relied not only on the most ingenious forms of direct and indirect taxation but resorted even to the slave trade," Bukofzer reports. "He financed his operatic amusements by selling his subjects as soldiers so that his flourishing opera depended literally on the blood of the lower classes."

The court spectacles thus bought and thus paid for apotheosized political power in at least three ways. The first and most spectacular was the fusion of all the arts in the common enterprise of princely aggrandizement. The monster assemblages of singers and instrumentalists (the former neoclassically deployed in dancing choruses, the latter massed in the first true orchestras) were matched, and even exceeded, by the luxuriously elaborate stage sets and theatrical machinery. Second, the plots, involving mythological or ancient historical heroes caught up in stereotyped conflicts of love and honor, were self-evident allegories of the sponsoring rulers, who were addressed directly in the obligatory prologues that linked the story of the opera to the events of their reign.

Third, and possibly most revealing, severe limits were set on the virtuosity of soloists lest, by indecorously representing their own power, they upstage the personages portrayed, or worse, the personages allegorically magnified. The ban on virtuosity reflected an aristocratic prejudice as old as Aristotle. It found its most influential Renaissance expression in Castiglione's *Book of the Courtier* (1528), in which noble amateurs are enjoined to affect "a certain negligence" in singing (it was called *sprezzatura*), lest they compromise their standing as "free men" by an infusion of servile professionalism.

But virtuosity found a home in commercial opera, which came into being—inevitably, it now seems—in Venice, Europe's great meeting place and merchant center, when the Teatro S. Cassiano opened its doors to the public in the carnival season of 1637. "There and then," in the words of Ellen Rosand, the early Venetian opera's leading historian, "opera as we know it assumed its definitive identity—as a mixed theatrical spectacle available to a socially diversified and paying audience: a public art." Where the court opera now seems a fossil—ceremonially exhumed and exhibited to sober praise from time to time, but undeniably dead—the early commercial opera bequeathed to us the conventions by which opera has lived, in glory and in infamy, into our own time. As Rosand observes, modern operagoers can still recognize in seventeenth-century Venetian works "the roots of favorite scenes: Cherubino's song, Tatiana's letter, Lucia's mad scene, Ulrica's invocation, even Tristan and Iseult's love duet."

Not by accident, Rosand names four puissant females, one fairly neutered masculine partner, and a delectable cross-dresser. Ever since opera opened its doors to a public that had to be lured, it has been a prima donna circus with a lively transsexual sideshow. Uncanny, nature-defying vocalism easily compensated for the courtly accoutrements—the sumptuous sets, the intricate choruses and ballets, the rich orchestras—that the early commercial opera theaters could not afford. Never mind the lofty union of the arts. What Fyodor Chaliapin later called "educated screaming" is the only bait that public opera has ever really needed, and its attraction has never waned.

The greatest screamers of all, and the most completely "educated" (that is, cultivated) ones, were the male prima donnas known as castratos, opera's first international stars, whose astounding sonority and preternaturally florid style confirmed opera in its abiding aura of the eerie. Although castratos originated not in the theater but in the churches of sixteenth-century Italy, where females could not perform but a full range of singers was desired, and where (as John Roselli puts it in the *New Grove Dictionary of Opera*) "choirboys were no sooner trained than lost," the burgeoning commercial opera stage with its exhibitionism and its heroics gave these unearthly singers their true arena. In an age that valued symbolic artifice, these magnificent singing objects—artists made, not born—were "naturally" the gods, the generals, the athletes, and the lovers. Eighteenth-century "serious opera" is unthinkable (and unrevivable) without them.

By the eighteenth century, however, the serious—the noble and the heroic—was only one of the available operatic styles. As Rosand points out, commercial opera was from the first a bastard genre, in which crowd-pleasing comic characters and burlesque scenes or interludes compromised lofty classical or historical themes in violation of traditional dramatic rules, before being segregated (by snobbish dramatic purists) into discrete categories. Here was the other great difference between court opera and commercial opera: the latter, at first under cover of comedy, introduced oppositional politics into the genre. The commercial (later the comic) opera was a hotbed of "carnivalism," that is, of authority stood on its head.

It was already a license to display operatic divas, veritable warbling courtesans, to the public gaze, and a notorious Jesuit critic lost no time in rising to the bait, denouncing the theaters of the "mercenarii musici" as voluptuous and corrupting in contrast to the edifying spectacles mounted "ne' palazzi de' principi grandi." But the most significant licenses were as much political as moral, and marked the public opera indelibly. Opera became a world where satyrs romped and Eros reigned, where servant girls chastised their masters, where philandering counts were humiliated, and where, later and more earnestly, rabbles were roused and revolutions abetted. In post-Napoleonic Europe, especially after 1830, when Auber's *La Muette de Portici* sparked the riot that led to Belgian independence, opera was for the best of reasons the most stringently watchdogged and censored of all forms of art.

Examples of opera's disruptive and destabilizing vectors can be drawn from virtually all stages of its history. In the beginning, Monteverdi's two most famous operas, sole survivors in the twentieth-century repertory of the court and market genres of seventeenth-century Italy, epitomized the two extremes. *L'Orfeo*, his first opera, with its splendid orchestra, its revised mythology (no rioting Bacchantes at the end, just serene apotheosis), its focus on natural male vocal ranges, and (in Orpheus's appeal to Charon) its pointed clash between virtuosity and eloquence, was the quintessential princely spectacle. It contains no real love music. Orpheus sings on and on about his love for Eurydice, but he does not express it directly through music—that is, to her. (Indeed, as the feminist critic Susan McClary has finally pointed out, Eurydice is hardly a character in the opera at all.)

L'Incoronazione di Poppea, Monteverdi's last opera, written for Venice in 1642, has two superbly developed prima donna roles (the more virtuosic of them the fork-tongued, string-pulling title character), two parts for shrill castrato singers (the higher of them the feminized, manipulated Emperor Nero), and a quartet of lowborn comic characters—one of them, a ghastly crone often played in drag, now the very emblem of the type—who spoof the passions and the gestures of their betters. The culminating number (not by Monteverdi, it is now agreed, but what of that?) is an arching, bristlingly sensual lust duet for two sopranos, impossible to savor today at full outlandish strength (for Nero is generally sung now, transposed, by a "natural" man). This duet symbolizes and formally celebrates, in the guise of a *ciaccona,* a slow dance over a mesmerizing ground bass, a craving that has subverted all moral and political codes. Where *Orfeo,* the court pageant, celebrates established order and authority and the cool moderation its hero tragically violates, *Poppea,* the carnival show, brings it all down: passion wins out over reason, woman over man, guile over truth, impulse over wisdom, license over law, artifice (in persuasion, in the singing of it, in the voice itself) over nature.

Consider also a later example. *Guillaume Tell,* Rossini's last opera, produced in 1829, was generally sung during its composer's ample remaining lifetime, which was the time of the post-Metternich reaction, to an imposed alternate libretto that replaced Schiller's dangerous freedom-loving protagonist with Andreas Hofer, leader of the loyal Tyrolean resistance to Napoleon. Despite his devotion to the Austrian crown, however, even this character was considered a ticklish prospect in Russia, and the events depicted too recent; and so a second ersatz, *Charles the Bold,* which transferred the action back to the seemingly innocuous fifteenth century, had to be concocted by an official of the Russian Imperial Theaters. It was then translated for the use of the tsar's personally subsidized Italian opera troupe, who presented it as *Carlo il Temerario.*

Still, despite all precautions, as many a wry memoir attests, Rossini's opera—and the Italian opera generally, brought to Russia as a representation of the tsar's power and as an instrument of his diplomacy—became a rallying point for antitsarist politics. "Ovations were especially strong when they gave some slight pretext for hints of what then passed for a liberal drift," wrote one old theater hand. The great tenor Tamberlik "would be forced to repeat the phrase '*Cercar la liberta!*' in *Guillaume Tell* three and even five times." As long as the radical students of the 1850s and 1860s could congregate in the passages and the uppermost gallery of St. Petersburg's old Bolshoi Theater and, standing in what Prince Peter Kropotkin, the famous anarchist, called "a Turkish bath atmosphere," roar their approval of Tamberlik's high C-sharp, they could enjoy a sense of solidarity that was denied them in any other sphere of Russian public life. Nowhere but at the state-supported Italian opera, in short, did Russian radicals enjoy the right of assembly.

Thus opera has always, and in superbly overdetermined fashion, succeeded as politics. Only since the onset of "transcendent" neoromantic apathy toward the world and its predicaments, moreover, has opera begun to fail as art. In every way that counts, opera as we know it (or used to know it) is the carnivalized spectacle that was born in Venice in 1637, not the uplifting performance that was born in Florence in 1600. Every one of opera's periodic neoclassical "reforms," from the Metastasian to the Gluckian to the Wagnerian, has been an effort to recover prelapsarian, precommercial, pre-Venetian values, which meant recovering a politics of affirmation under the protection of a court, "Holy Roman," French, or Bavarian. To the extent that these reforms have "succeeded," it has been because they have been successfully co-opted and subverted by the singers and the audiences whom the reformers despised.

Yet as the Italian scholar Lorenzo Bianconi, among others, has forcefully complained, it is the court opera that has been privileged in the historiography of the genre (and, I would add, in snob criticism as well). In consequence, opera's defining attributes have been made to look like deviations. (Even Rosand, within the seventeenth century, as it were, speaks of "decadence" and "perversion of original values" and associates the fall from grace with the rise of the prima donna.) That is why opera's repertory, that is, what is actually performed and applauded, has always overlapped so little with its canon, that is, what is ritually praised and professionally studied.

The "canonical" viewpoint on opera, an amalgam of neo-Wagnerianism and New Criticism, is most adamantly asserted (or, perhaps one ought to say by now, defended) in Joseph Kerman's classic *Opera as Drama*, now half a century old but still very much alive in a new edition. Its purview resolutely excludes performers and the public, except to disparage them. There is no room in Kerman's idealized conception of opera for anything more than the composer and the text. It is thus a wholly literary, or rather literaturized, conception of the form. The dramatic values that it endorses are imported from literary prototypes.

So, of course, were those of the court opera, and Kerman is as intransigent an upholder of moralizing, plain-sung court opera aesthetics—and as much a deplorer of the subversive, sexy, antiliterary politics of voice—as Wagner, Gluck, or even old Giulio Caccini, the inventor of recitative. The early loss of properly dramatic value in opera coincides, for Kerman, with the early rise of commercial opera, and, with it, of anticlassicizing performance values as determinants not only of success but of creative procedure as well. It is worth noting, in the light of Kerman's New Critical bias, that even the earliest court operas were always published, as souvenirs, in fully edited, idealized texts that resembled books. Commercial operas, by contrast, were not published until comparatively recent times but existed during their runs and revivals in a ceaseless maelstrom of negotiation and revision, never attaining the status of finished texts.

What such a fluid situation violates, of course, is the ideal of "poietics," of sovereign artistic control. Kerman solemnizes his tiny canon of exemplary operas—three by Mozart and one each by Monteverdi, Verdi, Wagner, Debussy, Berg, and Stravinsky—with a quote from (who else?) T. S. Eliot: "It is

a function of all art to give us some perception of an order in life, by imposing an order upon it." But this is a political program—specifically, it is the
time-honored program of aristocratic affirmational politics. By appropriating it, Kerman reassures us that whatever the mischances on the surface of a
Wozzeck, whatever the injustices on the surface of a *Figaro*, there is a force in
the world that makes everything harmonious and whole: *Io la Musica son*, in
the words Monteverdi's muse sang to the courtiers of Mantua in 1607, before
opera went astray, "Music am I, who with sweet melody know how to calm
every troubled heart." The Prospero who can summon forth this goddess and
wield her healing force is the composing mastermind (Kerman's very word)
who commands the show. In a postabsolutist world, a world that has renounced the absolute political power that art used to affirm, the politics of
affirmation now worships the artist—in proportion, of course, to the absoluteness (the "transcendence") of his achievement.

But not all art does what an Eliot or a Rorem or a Hyde says art does, unless that is how you choose, in exclusionary tautology, to define art. Not
much opera does it, as Kerman is the first to agree. (With such a working
definition, it is no wonder that his book is slim.) A different, far more generous critical perspective on opera now seems gradually to be gaining the
upper hand, just as, with Bianconi and some others, a new historiography
of the genre is taking shape. It rejects the utopian *promesse du bonheur*, the
promise of a perfect poietic wholeness, and centers on esthesis, on performance and reception as the locus of operatic value. Three recent books—
Unsung Voices by Carolyn Abbate, *The Angel's Cry* by Michel Poizat, and *The
Queen's Throat* by Wayne Koestenbaum—collectively sum it up. Voice, cry,
throat: that is where opera lives. The best we can expect from the art, say these
authors (a musicologist, a psychoanalyst, and a poet), and it is more than
enough, are moments of extravagant (and, yes, often regressive) bliss to
comfort us in a world of forlorn desire. The bringer of this *jouissance* is not
the mastermind but the vibrant body, immediate minister to our ills, that
stands literally or metaphorically before us with throat aquiver, radiating
uncanny din.

Diva worship is certainly nothing new, and a lot of frankly anti-intellectual
fan-mag palaver makes similar claims. What is new is the seriousness with
which the diva's (or "voice-object's") cause is now advanced—important to
note because Kerman had staked exclusive rights to "the serious position" on
opera—and the way in which the new strain of sophisticated opera critics has
opened up formerly unrespectable and even unmentionable aspects of the
genre. The breach between the New and the newer criticism of opera, however, is just the latest battleground in the war that has been going on since
the first century of operatic history. Ever since 1637 the two political
strains—authoritarian and anarchic, affirmational and oppositional—have
unpeacefully coexisted in opera, conditioning everything about it: its forms,

its styles, its meanings (or its attempts to circumvent meaning), its performance practices, its followings, its critical traditions. The same political tension lies behind every one of the press skirmishes and *querrelles* that dot operatic history, and it informs the intermission disputes of today. Nothing else attests so well to opera's cultural importance, and nothing else so well explains the durability of this oldest of living musical art forms in the West.

.   .   .

The fiercest *querrelles* of all took place in France, the giant among seventeenth-century European autocracies, where opera had to succeed as politics before it had any chance of succeeding as art. Like their English counterparts, who also possessed a glorious tradition of spoken theater (as the Italians did not), the aristocrats of seventeenth-century France saw only a child's babble in *dramma per musica*. To their minds, the art of music and the art of drama simply would not mix. "Would you know what an Opera is?" wrote Saint-Evremond, an exiled French courtier and a famous wit, to the Duke of Buckingham. "I'll tell you that it is an odd medley of poetry and music, wherein the poet and musician, equally confined one by the other, take a world of pains to compose a wretched performance."

Music in the theater, for the thinking French as for the thinking English, was at best an elegant bauble, more likely a nuisance. High tragedians spurned it. Corneille would admit music only into a *pièce à machines*, a play that already adulterated the seriousness of the drama for the sake of spectacle in the form of flying machines on which gods descended or winged chariots took off. And even then, he wrote in 1650 in the preface to *Andromède*, "I have been very careful to have nothing sung that is essential to the understanding of the play, since words that are sung are usually understood poorly by the audience." But then artists and critics who value understanding have always been hostile to what Samuel Johnson liked to call "an exotick and irrational Entertainment." Music has never been reason's ally.

The irrational, though, has its rational uses, and nobody knew that better than Jules Mazarin, the seventeenth century's most artful politician. It was Cardinal Mazarin, né Giulio Mazzarini, the Italian-born de facto regent of France, who took the first steps, in the earliest years of the boy-king Louis XIV's reign, to establish opera in his adopted country. By recruiting the services of Luigi Rossi, the leading composer of Rome, whose *Orfeo* of 1647 was the first opera expressly composed for the French court, Mazarin secured for himself a prestige that rivaled that of his own mentor, Cardinal Antonio Barberini, who had been Rossi's patron. The Italian spectacles, full of everything *merveilleux*, bedizened the French court more gloriously than any rationalistic drama could do, for "the purpose of such spectacles," wrote the moralist La Bruyère, a latter-day convert, "is to hold the mind, the eye and the ear equally enthralled."

And there was something else as well. Rossi, in his turn, recruited for his performances a troupe of Roman singers and instrumentalists, a little colony of Italians in the French capital who were personally loyal to Mazarin, and who, in the time-honored fashion of traveling virtuosi, could serve him as secret agents and spies in his diplomatic maneuvers with the papal court. All of this was a lesson to Mazarin's apprentice, the king, who thus received instruction, as the historian Madeleine Laurain-Portemer has put it, in "the political importance of *le mécénat*." The foundations were laid for what the French still call their *grand siècle*, and opera was destined to be its grandest manifestation.

Yet it was a very special sort of opera that would reign in France, one tailored to accommodate national prejudices, court traditions, and royal prerogatives. As the French court was the exemplary aristocratic establishment, so the French national opera was the courtiest court opera that ever was— and hence the one most committed to the politics of affirmation. Like every other aspect of French administrative culture, it was wholly centralized. Its primary purpose was to furnish "propaganda for the state and for the divine right of the king," as Neal Zaslaw has written, and only secondarily to provide "entertainment for the nobility and bourgeoisie." Indeed, no operatic spectacle could be shown to the French public that had not been prescreened, and approved, at court. At the same time, French opera aimed far higher than the "musical tale" of the Italians, which was essentially a pastoral play. The French form aspired to the status of a full-fledged *tragédie en musique*, later *tragédie lyrique*, which meant that the values of the spoken drama, France's greatest cultural treasure, were as far as possible to be preserved in spite of the music.

To reconcile the claims of court pageantry with those of dramatic gravity was no mean trick. Only a very special genius could bring it off. At the time of Luigi Rossi's momentous sojourn in France, another far less distinguished Italian musician—an apprentice, really—was already living there: Giovanni Battista Lulli, a Florentine boy who had been brought over in 1646, at the age of thirteen, to serve as *garçon de chambre* to Madame de Montpensier, a Parisian lady who wanted to practice her Italian. She also supported his training in courtly dancing and violin playing. When his patroness, a Frondist, was exiled in 1652, Lulli secured release from her employ and found work as a dancer and a mime at the royal court, where he danced alongside, and made friends with, the teenaged king. Upon the death of his violin teacher the next year, Lulli assumed his position as court composer of instrumental music.His rise to supreme power was steady and unstoppable, for Lulli was a veritable musical Mazarin, an Italian-born French political manipulator of genius. With the founding in 1669 of the Académie Royale de Musique, Louis XIV's opera establishment (which the king shortly deeded over to his by then naturalized friend who, like Mazarin, had Frenchified his name), Jean-Baptiste

Lully became himself a musical Sun King, the absolute autocrat of French music, which he re-created in his own image. He died in 1687 (with his boots on, as it were, following a mishap with a time-beating cane), having produced thirteen *tragédies lyriques*. The pattern that he set with them became the standard to which any composer aspiring to a court performance had to conform. Two generations of French musicians thus became Lully's dynastic heirs. His works would dominate the repertory for half a century after his death, in response not to market forces or to public demand but by royal decree, giving Lully a vicarious reign comparable in length of years to his patron's, and extending through most of the reign of the next king, Louis XV. His style did not merely define an art form; it defined a national identity. *La musique,* he might have said, *c'est moi.*

The ultimate "representation of power," the Lullian *tragédie lyrique* was from first to last a sumptuously outfitted—but, in another sense, quite thinly clad—metaphor for the grandeur and the authority of the court that it adorned. The monumental mythological or heroic-historical plots, some at first chosen by the king himself, celebrated the implacable universal order and the supremacy of divine or divinely appointed rulers. Themes of sacrifice and self-sacrifice—Alcestis, Idomeneus, even the biblical Jephthe—predominated.

A metaphor from first to last. First, following a marchlike overture whose stilted rhythms became a universal code for pomp, there had to be a panegyric prologue of a full act's duration. Here mythological beings were summoned to extol the French king's magnificent person and his deeds of war and peace with choral pageantry and with suites of dances modeled on the actual *ballet de cour,* an elaborate ritual, in which the king himself took part, that symbolized the social hierarchy. At times the mythological characters could be joshed a little, as in Jean-Philippe Rameau's *Castor et Pollux,* where Louis XV's successful prosecution of the War of Polish Succession is symbolized textually by an amorous concord of Venus and Mars and musically by a delightfully incongruous love duet of flute and trumpet that only Rameau, a master of the grotesque, could have brought off; or as in Michel Pignolet de Montéclair's *Jephté,* where Roman deities scurry out of the way of the Holy Scripture. Such levity was tolerable in a prologue, for it only enhanced the exaltation of the king above his mythological admirers.

Throughout the spectacle that followed, dancing, ceremonial movement accompanied by the grandest and most disciplined orchestra in Europe, would furnish a lavish symbolic counterpoint to the words, at times enlarging on the dramatic action, at times contrasting with it, as when Jupiter, in the second act of *Castor et Pollux,* orders up a lengthy Arcadian divertissement just to show his errant son what he will have to give up if he goes through with his planned self-sacrifice. Everything reached culmination in a monumental *chaconne* or *passacaille,* a stately choral dance over a ground bass that could go on for literally hundreds of measures, enlisting all the dramatis personae for the purpose of announcing an explicit moral. "C'est la valeur qui fait les Dieux / Et la beauté fait les Déesses!" is the one enunciated in *Castor et Pollux*. And the metaphorical significance of the final dance is spelled out with special clarity in that opera. "C'est la fête de l'univers!" Jupiter declares, and his words are taken up as a refrain by the ensemble, representing all the planets and the stars in the sky in an orgy of temporal panegyric.

The contemporary relevance of the allegory, proclaimed at the first and affirmed at the last, was what really counted in a *tragédie lyrique*. To drive it home the players wore "modern dress," adapted from contemporary court regalia, just as the dances they danced were the sarabands, the gavottes, and the passepieds of the contemporary ballroom. The theatrical pageant was not merely reminiscent of a social dance; it *was* a social dance enacted by professional proxies. The whole drama was conceived as a sublimated court ritual. Royal and noble spectators were looking not for transcendence but for validation. They did not value the kind of verisimilitude that makes the imaginary seem real. They wanted just the opposite: to see the real—that is, themselves—projected into the fabulous and the archetypal.

Along with this peerless feast of symbolic movement and rich sonority went an unparalleled courtly intolerance of virtuoso singing, abjured not only for the usual negative reasons—uppity singers symbolized a polity in disarray—but for more positive reasons having to do with the theatrical traditions of France. Here verisimilitude of a very particular sort—fidelity to articulate language, which is the first thing that goes in florid, legato, "operatic" singing—suddenly loomed very large. The lead performers in French court opera remained nominally *acteurs,* and the voice of the castrato went unheard in the land even when (in Lully's *Atys*) the plot actually hinged on castration. (But of course the castrato voice was anything but self-referential; the one thing it never symbolized was eunuchhood.)

Rarely were French singing actors called upon to contend with the full orchestra. Their interminable scenes and confrontations were played against a bare figured bass in a stately, richly nuanced recitative whose supple rhythms in mixed meters caught the lofty cadence of French theatrical declamation. Lully, for whom French was a second language, was said to have modeled this style directly on the closely observed delivery—the contours, the tempos, the rhythms, and the inflections—of La Champmeslé, Racine's handpicked tragedienne. There were no roulades and no cadenzas, but there were an infinity of "graces": tiny conventional embellishments—shakes, slides, swells—that worked in harness with the bass harmony to punctuate the lines and to enhance their rhetorical projection. And there were all kinds of subtly graded transitions in and out of minuscule, simply structured "airs," set in plain couplets to dance rhythms, that animated the prosody while placing minimum barriers in the way of understanding.

This, in its way, was the perfect opera for opera haters: an eyeful of spectacle, one ear full of opulent instrumental timbre, the other ear full of high rhetorical declamation. Vocal melody was far from the first ingredient or the most potent one, and the singers were held forcibly in check. Vocal virtuosity was admitted only in a decorative capacity on a par with orchestral color and stage machinery—never as a metaphor of emotion run amok!—and had to emanate from the lips of anonymous coryphées: members of the populace, shades, athletes, planets. The dazzling general impression took absolute precedence over the particular participants. The concert of myriad forces in perfect harness under the aegis of a mastermind was the real message, whatever the story. While even Saint-Evremond had to admit that "no man can perform better than Lully upon an ill-conceived subject," he turned it into a barb: "I don't question but that in operas at the Palace-Royal, Lully is 100 times more thought of than Theseus or Cadmus," his heroes. But that was all right, since the king was even more thought of than Lully.

When the style of Lully—Mr. Music, "Monsieur Ut-mi-ut-sol," as the encyclopedist Diderot called him—was finally challenged in the 1730s (and not without a major press war), it was only by an intensified version of itself created by Jean-Philippe Rameau ("Monsieur Utremifasollasiututut"): richer in harmony, more sumptuous in sonority, more laden in texture, more heroic in rhythm and rhetoric, more impressively masterminded than ever. When Andre Campra said of the sixty-year-old Rameau's maiden opera that it contained enough music for ten operas, he did not mean it as a compliment. That same opera, *Hippolyte et Aricie,* was the very first musical work to which the adjective *baroque* was attached, and it was no compliment either. (The career of *baroque,* originally a pejorative denoting irregular shape and connoting unnaturalness, as a neutral period label for music does not extend even as far back as the beginning of the twentieth century; the French still avoid it, preferring to call their ancien régime repertoire *la musique classique française.*)

Rameau's prodigality of invention was taken as a hubris, a representation of personal power and therefore a lèse-majesté, offensive not only to the memory of the great founder, whose works were the first true "classics" in the history of music, sacramentally perpetuated in repertory, but also to what the founder's style had memorialized. Indeed, if one turns from Lully's dulcet *Atys* of 1676—Louis XIV's favorite, famous for its erotic *sommeil,* or dream symphony—to Rameau's pungent, even violent *Castor et Pollux* of 1737, one can experience a bit of a shock. Until, that is, one reckons that the span of time separating these two works is greater than the span that separates Bach's B-minor Mass from Beethoven's *Eroica* Symphony, or Verdi's *Il Trovatore* from Stravinsky's *The Rite of Spring;* and the shock of the new gives way to amazement at the hold of tradition, a hold that testifies first of all to the potency of administrative centralism and absolute political authority.

The real challenge came fifteen years later, with the "War of the Buffoons," in which the French court opera at last confronted the Italian commercial opera head-on, and received, according to Jean-Jacques Rousseau, "a blow from which it never recovered." Rousseau was a dilettante composer, and he had an interest in seeing the grand machinery of the official French style, with which he could never hope to cope, replaced by the sketchy "natural" spontaneity of the Italians. (He rode the coattails of the Italians in Paris to some popular success with his own little rustic *intermède* called *Le Devin du village*, or *The Village Soothsayer*.) But Rousseau was much more than a musician, and his intense interest in the affair suggests that much more than music was at stake. Historians now agree that what seems a ludicrously inflated press scuffle about opera was in fact a coded episode, and an important one, in the ongoing battle between absolutism and enlightenment. As always, the Italian commercial opera—epitomized this time in Pergolesi's farce *La serva padrona,* in which a plucky maidservant cows and dominates her master, subverting the social hierarchy it was the business of the French opera to affirm—exemplified and stimulated the politics of opposition.

.   .   .

I've chosen *Atys* and *Castor et Pollux* to exemplify the idiom of the old regime at its Lullian and Ramellian poles, because we can actually hear these two operas side by side, along with most of the other operas discussed above, thanks to William Christie, an amazing American musician residing in Paris, and thanks to Les Arts Florissants, his ensemble. Over the past ten years, Christie and his musicians have been resurrecting a corpus of French court operas, in theaters and in recordings. Their performances are as nearly perfect as can be imagined.

But no, one cannot imagine these performances until one has heard them, so different are they from any previous attempt to perform these exacting works within living earshot, and so much more convincing. The Arts Florissants style is altogether foreign to what anybody would recognize today as normal operatic technique, which has been formed, since the seventeenth century, on the repertory toward which the French opera was adversarial. To persuade today's audiences of the viability of this repertory, the French aristocratic manner had to be invented afresh. The integrity and the cogency with which Christie and his troupe have accomplished the reconstruction is something of a miracle, perhaps the finest achievement that the early-music movement can claim. These performers, like most in their field, also make the higher, obviously unwarrantable claim of restoration. As far as I am concerned, they are entitled to it. They are in fact the only early-music performers today to whom I would willingly grant the freedom of the term. But I grant it only on condition that all its meanings be comprehended.

Because it is so literary, so bound by written and unwritten conventions, and therefore so specialized, the French manner has always been the "difficult" Baroque style, the one in which it is hardest to achieve fluency. This was as true then as it is now. Handel's eighteenth-century biographer, Mainwaring, relates how Arcangelo Corelli, the great Italian violinist, politely handed some music back to the "dear Saxon" because it was "in the French style, which I do not understand." No music depends more utterly for its successful performance on the possession of *école*.

The only place on earth where one can acquire this schooling now is in William Christie's class at the Paris Conservatoire, he being the first American ever hired by that snooty institution. Just like Lully himself, another favored immigrant, Christie has been officially charged with teaching the French to be French. But where did Christie learn how? Right from the sources, early-music practitioners like to say, and in the case of the French court opera there may even be some truth in the claim. Precisely because it was a centralized, bureaucratic institution, Lully's Académie generated a huge quantity of prosaic documentation in the form of payment records, personnel lists, and production books. When Les Arts Florissants do Lully, their orchestra and chorus have precisely the size and the makeup of Lully's orchestra; when they do Rameau, the cyclopean band is Rameau's, precisely.

But how did musicians actually play for Lully and Rameau? And how can we be sure that that is how they are playing for us? Once again the documentation is exceptional. Lully's band remained so famous after its mâitre's death that a Savoyard violinist composer named Georg Muffat, who apprenticed in Paris and who worked in his maturity for the episcopal court of Passau, one of those ambitious mini-Versailleses that dotted the Germanic landscape, saw fit in 1698 to peddle a little guide for string players that promised to reveal all the secrets of "the French Manner According to the Late Monsieur Lully's Method."

Most of these secrets have to do with maintaining uniformity of bowing and sharp articulation of meter. (Others have to do with tuning low to avoid shrillness and strain, with altering the ostensibly even rhythms of the notated music to avoid "the sluggish, the crude and the dull," and with the proper execution of graces.) A string player following Muffat's rules will find his bow far more often in the air, and the notes far less connected (legato), than one who follows the path of least resistance—and this conforms exactly to the difference between the French way and the ordinary "operatic" way of delivering a texted line. The one emphasizes consonants, the other vowels. The one emphasizes the words, the other the feeling-tone. The one favors Apollonian understanding, the other emotional afflatus.

It would be an understatement to say that Christie has absorbed all this information and rejoices in it. But while early-music revivalists like to emphasize their dependence on hard evidence—it lends authority, after all, to what they do—that does not explain their best accomplishments. Quite the contrary, it sells them short. All that hard evidence can do is furnish a base. To hew closely to that base, as many do in the name of "authenticity," is to turn minimum requirements into limits. Christie, by dint not only of his gifts but also of long experience and tough self-criticism, has broken through to a level of internalized discipline that comes across as "naturalness" and "freedom" within tight constraints. He has left the sources far behind.

But not even that explains Christie's magnificent results. There is also the matter (which he has rightly stressed) of language and diction, and its relationship not only to the rhythm of the music but also to its dynamic inflection in conjunction with harmony—and not only to the vocal music but to the instrumental music as well. Christie's mastery of this dimension of the performance, still bound up fast with French musical self-identity, has been greatly abetted by the use of French-speaking casts (with some impressive American exceptions, such as the tenor Howard Crook and the soprano Ann Monoyios, who took the lead roles in Christie's performances of *Atys* at the Brooklyn Academy of Music last year). And Christie ensures the courtly predominance of the verbal and the literary through an exacting rehearsal technique that begins (as he has described it) with spoken mastery of the libretto. A decidedly actorish and unsingerly kind of vocal nuance enlivens the recitatives in a Christie performance. This is what really sets his work apart, and, one willingly imagines, marries it to its historical model.

Still, in this musicological age one must assume that others are equally conversant with the historical record; and there have been enough earlier attempts to revive French court operas with native casts and native conductors to indicate that the real secret of *l'école* Christie must lie somewhere else. It is, in fact, the Lully secret, but not everyone can be a Lully. Not every gifted musician, in other words, is so luckily situated and so blessed with nerve as to become an absolute despot. Christie, combining the roles of teacher and employer, has a great and self-renewing reservoir of fresh talent at his disposal, and he does not hesitate to exploit it in ruthless pursuit of his vision down to the smallest detail. "A great many of my soloists began as my pupils and this is integral to what we do," he has told an interviewer. "I believe that one thing that very quickly destroys French music is a lack of homogeneity. When everyone has his or her own idea of what French vocal style should be—that is fatal." Even more frankly, he allows that if his singers have worked out a homogeneous approach, "this is because the need for a sense of homogeneity has been drummed into them."

Spoken like Lully himself—or like his king. This is the old, practically defunct conception of maestrohood. It was memorably described by the English lawyer Roger North, a contemporary of Lully, who in the late seventeenth century was already lamenting its decline; a musical entertainment, he wrote,

> ought to proceed as a drama, firework or indeed every public delight, by judicious steps, one setting off another, and the whole in a series connected and concluding in a perfect acme, and then ceasing all at once—all which cannot be done but by an absolute dictator, who may coerce and punish the republican mob of music masters.

Christie is such an imperious one. Even audiences (to judge by the reports of their public spokesmen, the newspaper reviewers) feel the pressure of his glare. The really conspicuous difference between his exquisitely refined Apollonian shows and other operatic performances at a comparable level of achievement is a political difference: for all the singing planets and the dancing constellations, there are no stars on Christie's stage. Which is just the way it used to be at the Palais Royal, where the only star (as Saint-Evremond so airily attested) was the *batteur de mesure* in the pit, who jealously guarded his prerogatives and eventually paid for them with his life.

The closely integrated, noncompetitive sense of ensemble that results from this control has been described as "democratic"—just the sort of cruel, unintended joke that used to be embodied in the official name of Honecker's Germany. But the pretense of democracy is not Christie's. He openly avows the political source of his artistic success. And even if one gets it as wrong as the reviewer I have quoted, one cannot affirm the artistic success without affirming the politics that underwrites it. It is still a politics of sacrifice.

Does that matter? When we applaud the perfection of execution that can be achieved only by the suppression of human individuality, are we applauding only the results or also the suppression? When we are swayed by a vision like Christie's, is it only an artistic vision—a "transcendent" vision, as some of us like to say—that sways us, or is it a vision of the world? When faced with a beautiful art that affirms an ugly politics, can we vote for the art and reject the politics? Are these distinctions, finally, tenable at all?

These questions used to be easier to answer; but the ones whose easy answers set the tone—Eliot, Pound, Stravinsky—have turned out to be painfully complicated figures with whom we can no longer easily come to terms. And so the nettling questions persist. For in the works of French Baroque opera, no less than in the works of Eliot, Pound, and Stravinsky, what is ugly about the politics in large part determined the nature of the art.

Because it must affirm an elaborate established order, the art of the ancien régime can never allow signification—the strict filtering of all sensory impressions through an elaborate, established code of meaning—to give way to a more primal, less mediated response that might prove socially disruptive. (Remember the anarchists in the balcony of the St. Petersburg opera.)

For this reason, such an art can brook no prima donnas of any sex. It can allow no voice to be heard that is capable not only of playing a god but also of being a god or (what is more usual) a goddess, a diva.

And that is why the tone of fastidious anti-diva criticism, from Saint-Evremond through Joseph Kerman and on into the discourse of "early music" and "authenticity," so often swells up beyond primness into a tone of shrill desperation. Such criticism always means far more than it says, precisely because the issues it raises are at bottom inescapably, if tacitly, political. Opera criticism, and even opera history, will always be about lots more than opera, because opera is about lots more than music. Conventional snob criticism and conventional academic historiography, which have dependably promoted courtly values over commercial ones, and which have always exalted the notated score over the sounding medium, are all about control. They are sacrificial politics by other means.

So while one cannot fail to respond with delight to any one of Christie's tasteful evocations of a vanished absolutist world, something there is that does not love the vogue they have achieved. There is about it a certain *je ne sais quoi* that is very much not to taste. Could it be, perhaps, a *soupçon* of *revanchiste* nostalgia? Risibly belated, perhaps, but there it is. The audience for early music, like the audience for new music, tends to be a self-congratulating coterie, and musical antiquarians do tend to be Tories. I find it difficult to shake off the smug animadversions about the French Revolution that the musicologist Hugh Macdonald, for example, saw fit to work into a lecture on Beethoven's Ninth during the revolutionary bicentennial year, even as the daily headlines detailing the collapse of totalitarianism in Europe might have furnished a more appropriate focus for his remarks. "The French Revolution didn't have much to do with fraternity at all," he gibed; "Beethoven in his deluded way went on thinking it did." The self-mythologizing operatic legacy of the ancien régime and the project of its revival (lavishly subsidized by the nationalistic and self-mythologizing if nominally Socialist nouveau régime of François Mitterrand) seem quite haughty enough without the gratuitous digs that William Christie habitually aims at the mass public, which is unaware (to quote one of his sallies) "that Pluto is not just the name of a funny Walt Disney dog."

Christie, who in his adopted country is a bit of a political figure in his own (far) right and a notorious crony of the powerful, does a lot of gloating. Some of it verges on the pharisaical. During a visit to New York in 1992 that coincided with the peak of tension arising out of the vicissitudes of the NEA, he blustered to a reporter that residence in a cultured nation like France has spared him all such hassle. But surely he realized even as he spoke that projects such as his, artistically unassailable and at the same time unthreatening to established power, are just the ones that the NEA feels safest in sponsoring; and surely he understands that the whole reason for controversy about the NEA was precisely the exposure, and the turning into overt policy, of the abiding interest that our government shares with all other governments in furthering projects that embody, just like Christie's, a politics of affirmation.

.   .   .

So the War of the Buffoons is not over. The music of the seventeenth and eighteenth centuries is still a site of political contention. And to confirm this, you do not have to seek out Les Arts Florissants or develop a taste for its recondite repertoire. You have only to go to the movies, where a film by Alain Corneau titled *Tous les matins du monde* (after the novel by Pascal Quignard, on which the author based the screenplay) has become the improbable object of a growing cult. In this country the film has not had the wild commercial success that it enjoyed in France, where it was seen by millions, ran away with the Oscars (that is, Césars), and produced a sound track spin-off (distributed here by Harmonia Mundi USA, which is also William Christie's record company) that had a Michael Jacksonish sale. But its appeal in America, even so, has been spectacular, considering its subject (the lives and loves of viola da gamba players) and considering that it takes music—the genuine historical article, "historically" (and beautifully) performed by well-known early-music specialists—so seriously.

The "early music" movement has been happily baffled by this success, which seems to represent a breakthrough in public recognition for an altogether esoteric branch of classical music (and this at a time when classical music generally is perceived to be undergoing terminal marginalization). Continuous screenings of the film were joyously incorporated into the program of this year's Boston Early Music Festival, and the early-music press has been in ecstasy. And yet the reviewer for the *Times Literary Supplement,* Julie Anne Sadie, herself a gambist, while relishing the ostensible triumph of her cause, admits that it "gives pause" to think "that all this should catch the public imagination."

There is less of paradox here than meets the eye, I think. *Tous les matins du monde* is not really about seventeenth-century music at all. While expertly camouflaged by period and local color—a camouflage that unusually extends in very welcome fashion to the sound track as well as the lovely sets, costumes, and paysages—the notions and the values in which the film trades are not merely anachronistic, they are positively antithetical to those of the period in which it is set. Far from a celebration of the esthetic embodied in the work of Christie and the other authentic revivalists of the period, the film is a pointed reaction or defense against it. *Tous les matins du monde* is not a very good guide to the world of seventeenth-century French music, but it is an excellent guide, perhaps the best of guides, to some popular musical attitudes of the present day.

The plot is based on the relationship between Marin Marais (1656–1728), probably the greatest of the French gambists at the peak of his instrument's prestige (he is played as a youth by Guillaume Depardieu and as a man by Depardieu's famous father, Gérard), and Marais's teacher, Jean de Sainte-Colombe (d. ca. 1701), played by Pierre Marielle. About Marais, a great public figure who published a wealth of music for his instrument and wrote a famous opera, historians know a great deal. (This knowledge is mostly ignored in the screenplay.) About Sainte-Colombe, practically nothing is known. His surviving works, none of them published until 1973, consist of a single manuscript of rather sketchy viol duets, once in the famous library of the pianist Alfred Cortot, and a couple of solo pieces found in a manuscript now at Durham cathedral in England (together with a *tombeau* in his memory by his gambist son, absent in the movie, where Sainte-Colombe is given only daughters).

Nature may abhor a vacuum, but nothing better suits a historical fictioneer. From a few scattered facts and anecdotes culled from dedications, newspaper items, the duet manuscript, and particularly from the gossipy biography of Marais in Titon du Tillet's *Parnasse françois* of 1732, one gathers that Sainte-Colombe was an outstanding virtuoso who reformed the playing technique of his instrument but remained unattached to the royal court. Why? Evidently because he was a *sieur*, a noble amateur, and did not need to work for a living. On the empty slate of his biography, however, Quignard has inscribed a more useful answer. The "Sainte-Colombe" of the novel and the movie is a mythical being constructed in calculated opposition to all the institutions that ruled the world in which the historical Sieur de Sainte-Colombe lived: he is a rustic, a recluse, a Jansenist, an ascetic, a figure of inarticulate, tortured passions who despises court life, all diplomacy, all savoir faire. Jansenism apart, this is merely the stock romantic formula for artistic genius. The model for this hero is no seventeenth-century figure; it is Beethoven (or Byron or Berlioz or Alfred de Musset) as popularly, or mythically, conceived. In back of it all, of course, lies Frenhofer, the archetypal mad genius in Balzac's story, "The Unknown Masterpiece," another "seventeenth-century" avatar of romantic idealism.

Quignard's Sainte-Colombe spends all his time alone with his viol in a tree house that he ordered built for his solitude after the insupportable loss of his wife. (We know about the tree house from Titon du Tillet; the wife—that is, her untimely demise—is the novelist's invention.) But he is not quite alone there. By playing a tombeau in her memory ("Les pleurs," adapted from one of the duets by the Catalonian gambist Jordi Savall, the movie's music director), he finds that he can conjure up her shade and have her silent company. It is a lovely conceit, especially since it is centered lovingly around such a touching, dolorous, sensuous—and in its mellifluous legato, probably anachronistic—performance by Savall. Still, it advances a conception of music—as personal effusion, as transport from the here and now, as private retreat, as "transcendent"—that is the product of our pop-romantic time, not

Sainte-Colombe's, and it fosters a mystique of art and its lonely makers ("creating for themselves alone . . .") that has ineluctable political implications.

That mystique forms the very basis of the movie's engrossing exploration of the relationship between Sainte-Colombe and Marais, and provides the basis for what drama there is in this contemplative film. Marais is caught between his teacher's idealism and the worldly success to which his teacher's instruction gives him access—another trite staple of film biography but redeemed again by the way the marvelously performed music is allowed to do so much of the actors' talking for them. Ultimately, and inevitably, Marais is thrown out. "You don't play badly," Sainte-Colombe roars, "but you don't have *la musique!*" Now that strikes a chord! How many of us have been similarly tortured by our teachers with mystifying dressings-down (even if they no longer dare hurl our instruments against the wall), and then wondered agonizingly for years what this "music" that we didn't have might be? (There has even been an anthropological study, and an illuminating one, of "music" as a postromantic discourse of power negotiation in the world of the contemporary conservatory: *Music, Talent and Performance* by Henry Kingsbury.) At the end of the movie, the same hallucinogenic property of "Les pleurs" enables a posthumous reconciliation.

The dilemma of divided loyalty is symbolized in the person of Sainte-Colombe's elder daughter, Madeleine (played by Anne Brochet), who betrays her father by continuing to pass on his secrets to Marais, who leads Marais under the tree house in order that he may become his former teacher's secret sharer and who finally takes him as her lover. In the later sequences her health declines (as atonement, perhaps, but also as a reproach) as his career ascends. There is a final confrontation in which she, on the verge of death, cruelly criticizes his performance of a piece that he had dedicated to her, thus finally assuming her father's voice.

By this time Marais has become Lully's successor at Versailles, and his rare appearances chez Sainte-Colombe in plumed hat and rouged face contrast jarringly with the dark surroundings. Another time-honored, or shopworn, romantic metaphor is being prepared. He is summoned to Madeleine's dismal deathbed from a rehearsal at the Sun King's palace (of a trivial piece of Lully's, naturally, the "Marche pour la Cérémonie des Turcs" from *Le Bourgeois gentil' homme,* performed with regimental spit and polish by Savall's ensemble, Le Concert des Nations). After her death Marais, too, becomes guiltily obsessed with "Les pleurs" and begins paying nocturnal visits of penitence on solitary horseback from the court's chandeliered brilliance to the mute, sylvan gloom of the Sainte-Colombe estate, where he stakes out the tree house in hopes that the aging master, twice bereaved, will break his melancholy silence and play so that he, Marais, might discover *la musique* at last. Sainte-Colombe is thus formally identified as the truth-bearing medium of Night, "the land where sunlight casts no beams; the sacred realm from which my mother sent me forth," in the words of Wagner's Tristan. It is the realm to which the true artist's soul craves return from the "brillant soleil" tawdrily worshiped at court (to cite a famous number from Rameau's *Les Indes galantes,* recorded with aplomb by William Christie).

These secret visits go on for three years, we are told, until Marais finally confronts Sainte-Colombe and demands one final lesson. At last "Les pleurs" is heard complete, the way Sainte-Colombe wrote it, as a duet for two viols, performed in almost total darkness. It is an unforgettably fraught scene of atonement and male bonding; and the way that the music is integrated into the cinematic vision does honor to both arts.

That it has nothing to do with the role of music, or of musical thought, in the seventeenth century would be an unworthy cavil, were it not for all the claims to the contrary. (The historical Sainte-Colombe's "Les pleurs," while harmonically rich and poetically recitative-like, is in fact just one section extracted from a "concert a deux violes esgales" that places it not in a context of intense personal pathos but in a typically "baroque" descriptive and mythological sequence that includes carillon effects, an "Apel de Charon," and even a gavotte titled "Joye des Elizées," Elysian Revels.) That is of no artistic account. The scene is powerful, as is the film, because it has everything to do with our contemporary assumptions about "musicality," about "genius," about expressive purpose. No film that I have seen affirms these assumptions as earnestly or as effectively, albeit behind an anachronistic, antiquarian screen.

And of course the film has a lot to say, implicitly, about politics—about today's politics. Here, of course, is where the anachronisms loom largest. They are actively abetted by Harmonia Mundi in its marketing strategy. Its "Teaching Guide" to *Tous les matins,* meant to encourage its use in schools, lists the following leading questions among suggested "Discussion Points":

· Sainte-Colombe asks Marais, "Can your heart not feel? Music," he says, "is not for pleasing kings' ears or for dancers. I will take you on for your grief, not your skill." How might the conflict that Sainte-Colombe refers to be a concern to all artists?

· Patronage of the arts reached a pinnacle under Louis XIV. What sort of complications might a relationship between a patron and an artist cause?

· "I like sunlight in my hand, not gold," says Sainte-Colombe, responding to an invitation to become a court musician. In what way might employment compromise an artist's devotion to his or her art?

Thus American schoolchildren are to receive their basic training in oppositional politics, as decreed by a thrice-familiar pop-romantic or pop-modernist discourse that diagnoses artistic temperament as an asocial or narcissistic character trait.

It is a bad lesson as well as a banal one, for it universalizes and inculcates attitudes that have led the "serious" arts into their twentieth-century cul-de-sac. (And it is a hypocritical lesson, too, when it comes from the commercial sector as part of a sales pitch.) Such notions originated precisely in reaction to the decline of noble patronage, and had never existed before worldly conditions called them forth. Lully may well have been as grandiose a sociopath as ever emerged from the ranks of musicians and as superb a genius, but his concept of art was based on service. If he was opposed, it was only by those who wished to supplant him in his opportunity to serve.

Le Sieur de Sainte-Colombe might have been one of them, though we probably will never know. Quignard's and Corneau's "Sainte-Colombe," like so many modern artists, has purchased his freedom from conflicts, complications, and compromise at the price of irrelevance and impotence. A man of mysteriously independent means, he can afford it, just as he can afford to toss Marais a purse to replace the instrument that he has destroyed in a fit of highfalutin pique. That is the most insidious lesson of all. The wealthy are not the ones to be preaching virtuous privation. And politically savvy members of Congress, musicians, filmmakers, and promoters are not the ones to be preaching about the political innocence of art.

33

The Golden Age of Kitsch

Das Wunder der Heliane, by Erich Wolfgang Korngold; RSO Berlin conducted by John Mauceri (Decca/London 436 636-2, 3 CDs)

Jonny spielt auf, by Ernst Krenek; Leipzig Orchestra conducted by Lothar Zagrosek (Decca/London 436 631-2, 2 CDs)

First complete recordings of two famous yet unknown operas, both dating from 1927, have been issued by Decca/London amid huge fanfare, to inaugurate a projected series of releases devoted to the music of German composers who for reasons of race, taste, or politics fell out of favor with the Nazi regime. One is *Jonny spielt auf* (Johnny Goes to Town), the fabled "jazz opera" by Ernst Krenek, which was first performed in Leipzig on February 10. The other, vastly dissimilar, is *Das Wunder der Heliane* (Heliane's Miracle), the most ambitious of Erich Wolfgang Korngold's five operas (and the only one from which resonances from "light music" were resolutely, if not altogether successfully, excluded), which was presented for the first time in Hamburg on October 10, exactly eight months later, near the start of the next season. The Decca/London series takes its name, *Entartete Musik,* or Degenerate Music, from the name of an exhibition that was organized in Düsseldorf in May 1938, echoing the infamous show of paintings held the previous year in Munich under the rubric *Entartete Kunst,* or Degenerate Art. The Nazi concept of artistic degeneracy was incoherent and opportunistic, and so is Decca/London's marketing strategy. It took very little to run afoul of the Nazis then, and it costs very little to deplore them now. Their opposition, especially when it was passively incurred, conferred no distinction, unless their approval is thought to confer distinction on the likes of Beethoven or Wagner. There are no lessons to be learned from studying the Nazi index of banned musical works, which, like the Nazi canon, contained masterpieces, ephemerae, kitsch, and trash, covering a wide stylistic and ideological range.

The record company's implied invitation to join in a chorus of ritual exe-

Originally published in the *New Republic,* 21 March 1994.

cration against the least risky of all the great Satans is, at best, an invitation to complacency. Worse, it smears issues of real moment—the social responsibility of artists, or the social value of high art—with a tar brush, and blunts criticism of the works that it presents. Like a documentary that I saw recently glorifying the history of rock 'n' roll, in which the only dissenting sound bites came from spokesmen for the White Citizens Council, the promotional campaign implies a threat: like it or be lumped. There are less trivializing reasons to welcome these records.

The incoherence of the degeneracy concept, whether viewed from the side of the Nazis or from the side of the angels, can lead to unintended comedy. In its press package, Decca/London circulates to reviewers a documentary videotape that includes a film sequence of Hitler opening a government-sponsored museum for official German art. I'm sure that the idea was to accompany the footage with the portentous strains of something like Siegfried's *Trauermarsch* from *Götterdämmerung*, the standard Nazi pomp-and-circumstance item; but instead the sound track editor came up with another Wagnerian *Trauermarsch,* the one that opens the Fifth Symphony by the archdegenerate Mahler, classified by one Nazi race-critic as "the fanatic archetype of the Eastern Jewish Rabbi" and denounced by another for "wishing to achieve by force a bond with the spirit of German music that is forever denied him by blood." Never mind. Mahler's music fits the scene to perfection, for it is replete with all the "ferocity of Siegfried's funeral music—breathtaking in its violence as well as its grandeur" that for Paul Lawrence Rose, an essentialist from the other camp, stamps Wagner's music as intrinsically anti-Semitic. *That* simple things never were.

The Nazis derived their concept of degeneracy in part from the theories of the nineteenth-century psychiatrist Cesare Lombroso, who sought through science to account for criminal proclivities and thereby (the chilling part) to predict them, by identifying the "born criminal" or *l'uomo delinquente,* as a distinct anthropological "type" with measurable physical and mental "stigmata." (Lombroso checked particularly for imperfections in the shape of the outer ear.) Such "stigmata," Lombroso asserted, were the product of a morbid genetic atavism brought about by inbreeding (the Nazis added miscegenation), or by what we now call substance abuse.

The application of these theories to art and literature was first made by Lombroso's disciple, the Hungarian physician Max Nordau, in a two-volume blockbuster baldly titled *Entartung,* which appeared in 1892–93 and went through many printings. (The anonymous English translation, *Degeneration,* had reached its fifth edition by 1895, and it is appearing again this season from the University of Nebraska Press.) Nordau drew abundant sensational connections—or more precisely, asserted lots of facile analogies—between genetic mental or physiological decay as described by Lombroso and fin-de-siècle "decadence" in the arts, which amounted, from Nordau's hawkishly middle-class perspective, to "contempt for traditional views of custom and morality." Nordau maintained that the eroticized mysticism of the pre-Raphaelites and the symbolists, the egomania of the Parnassians and the Aesthetes (with special attention to Wilde and Nietzsche), the gruesome naturalism of Zola and his epigones, all had the same pathological basis.

That this was pseudoscience in the service of philistinism is confirmed by the nature of the "evidence" that Nordau adduced, entirely speculative and tautological:

> There might be a sure means of proving that the application of the term "degenerates" to the originators of all the fin de siècle movements in art and literature is not arbitrary, that it is no baseless conceit, but a fact; and that would be a careful physical examination of the persons concerned, and an inquiry into their pedigree. In almost all cases, relatives would be met with who were undoubtedly degenerate, and one or more stigmata discovered which would indisputably establish the diagnosis of "Degeneration."

Most circular of all is the proof of mental degeneracy in authors and artists:

> Science has found, together with these physical stigmata, others of a mental order, which betoken degeneracy quite as clearly as the former; . . . so that it is not necessary to measure the cranium of an author, or to see the lobe of a painter's ear, in order to recognize the fact that he belongs to the class of degenerates. . . . Quite a number of different designations have been found for these persons. . . . Lombroso speaks of "mattoids" (from matto, the Italian for insane), and "graphomaniacs,"under which he classifies those semi insane persons who feel a strong impulse to write.

Contemplating Nordau's 566 pages of drivel, one feels he might well have measured a few craniums at home. But what is ultimately redeeming, even endearing, is the kicker, the supreme irony: Max Nordau (né Südfeld) was not only a Jew, he was an early Zionist leader; mattoid number one, for him, was Richard Wagner; and among the chief symptoms of moral insanity (that is, decadence) in his diagnosis were anti-Semitism and what he called "Teutonomaniacal Chauvinism." "The Bayreuth festival theater," he wrote, "the *Bayreuther Blätter*, the Parisian *Revue Wagnérienne*, are lasting monuments by which posterity will be able to measure the whole breadth and depth of the degeneration and hysteria of the age." Needless to say, many copies of Dr. Nordau's *Entartung* must have fed Dr. Goebbels's bonfires even as the book's theses were being oh-so-selectively appropriated to fuel the latter's propaganda mill.

So just this once let's forget the Nazis. They had nothing to do with Krenek's opera or Korngold's opera. They didn't even ban them. They didn't have to ban them, for both works had fallen out of the repertory by 1933. True, the Reichsmusikkammer, the official administrative body for music that was first figureheaded by Richard Strauss, retained a special nostalgic horror of *Jonny spielt auf.* It made the blackface title character into the apelike saxophone-tooting emblem of the *Entartete Musik* exhibition, and it indexed the Austrian Catholic composer (along with other specially favored Gentiles such as Alexander Glazunov, Maurice Ravel, Erik Satie, and Camille Saint-Saëns) as an honorary Jew. (In Krenek's case, the classification was *jüdisch versippt,* or Jewish by marriage.)

It is also true that *Das Wunder der Heliane* has a nude scene; but so does Reichsmusikkammerpräsident Strauss's *Salome,* the most brazenly pornographic of operas, in which an arch-fin-de-siècle text by the archdegenerate Oscar Wilde is garishly set off in leering, lily-gilding harmonic and orchestral colors. *Salome* played steadily to good Aryan audiences throughout the Hitler years. Yes, Strauss's opera ends as if in deference to the Hays Code, visiting retribution upon the royal stripper, while Korngold's royal stripper achieves a blasphemous apotheosis. But the reason for *Salome'*s survival was simply the venerable name of its composer—"international celebrity, German, late romanticist, advocate for copyright protection and senior citizen," in the words of Pamela Potter, America's best-informed historian of the Nazi musical establishment. (It was his interest in lengthening the term of copyright for composers that induced Strauss to accept a bureaucratic post.) Strauss's collaboration, like that of Wilhelm Furtwängler, offered the Nazis the most potent insurance they could buy against the charge of barbarism. Which is why, for the Nazis, the first question about a work of art was never, What does it say? It was, Who is speaking, friend or foe?

Thus the Slav-blooded, naturalized Parisian Igor Stravinsky, because he was assumed to be a foe, became an exhibit in the Düsseldorf show. The mortified composer, through his German publisher, B. Schotts Söhne, protested to the German Bureau of Foreign Affairs at his inclusion, explicitly disavowing "Jewish cultural Bolshevism" and objecting in particular that the insulting caption under his portrait in Düsseldorf read, "Whoever invented the story that Stravinsky is descended from Russian noble stock?" As he had previously taken the precaution of submitting an affidavit to his publisher, in lieu of the Reichsmusikkammer's official questionnaire establishing Aryan heredity (and as the publisher had placed an item in the papers quoting Richard Strauss on Stravinsky's enthusiasm for Hitler's ideas), he was able to receive the satisfaction of a declaration from the German government affirming its "benevolent neutrality" toward him, and his career suffered no further setbacks in the Third Reich until the war. In 1938 he came to the German capital and recorded his ballet *Jeu de cartes* with the *ganz judenrein* Berlin Philharmonic Orchestra.

And it was because he was a national of an Axis ally that Béla Bartók, like the composers of Mussolini's Italy, was assumed to be a friend of the Reich and was therefore left out of the exhibition of *Entartete Musik.* The Hungarian composer, who had refused his publisher's request to fill out what he called "the questionnaire about grandfathers," attached the e-word to himself in protest at his exemption, and tried to prevent the performance of his music in Germany and Italy. Early in 1939 he wrote to an official of the Deutscher Rundfunk about his own First Piano Concerto that he was "astonished that such 'degenerate' music should be selected for—of all things—a radio broadcast."

As to the latest appropriation of the *Entartete* cachet, I mean Decca/London's, how does it apply to Hindemith's opera *Die Harmonie der Welt*, a musical biography of the astronomer Johannes Kepler that was not even written until the Nazis were more than a decade gone (and which had its all-too-peaceful première in Munich)? Hindemith's opera is slated for inclusion in the Decca/London series. But what can it mean to call this severe, cerebral work degenerate? Who ever called it that? No, the Nazis are just a perverse window dressing here. Their negative imprimatur, the record company thinks, will move its merchandise. Now *that* is degenerate.

.   .   .

What makes these first releases fascinating is not what they have to say about the Nazis but what they have to say about the artistic atmosphere of the Weimar Republic, which had a thriving operatic economy—the last truly thriving, that is, consumption-driven, economy in the history of opera. Composers wrote for a market. Their work was in demand. They strove not for eventual immortality but for immediate success. Producers could recoup their investment in new works and sometimes exceed it, so they sought out new works. Premières were more noteworthy than revivals, and commanded the interest of the press.

Was this a degenerative ecology? Did it lead to exploitative "populist" formulas, or to weak imitation? No, it was synergistic; it led to experimentalism and to emulation, with the aim of surpassing previous standards of novelty and distinction. The most lasting fruit of this efflorescence was Berg's *Wozzeck*, which now enjoys the aura of a modernist classic, entailing the myth of its countercultural status, its difficulty of comprehension (much abetted by an esoteric literature that has grown up around it since the 1950s), and its victory over suppression. (Anyone who remembers its belated première at the Metropolitan Opera in 1958 will remember the way its underground status was touted.) What is missing from this account is the story of *Wozzeck*'s early market success. Between its première in Berlin in 1925 and the advent of the National Socialist regime eight years later, this very demanding opera had seventeen productions in Germany, including some productions at small provincial houses, and ten abroad. No opera produced anywhere since 1933 can match that record of quick, widespread public success.

But during the Weimar years several operas exceeded it. Hindemith's *Cardillac* (1926) had sixteen productions during its first season alone; Weill's *Der Zar lässt sich photographieren* (The Tsar Allows Himself to Be Photographed,

1928), recently revived in Santa Fe, had twenty-one; the forgotten *Maschinist Hopkins* (1929), by the forgotten Max Brand, scored twenty. The champion as of its day was *Jonny spielt auf,* which racked up forty-five productions and 421 performances during the 1927–28 season, and carried another opera of Krenek's, a flimsy "burleske Operette" called *Schwergewicht: oder die Ehre der Nation* (The Heavyweight: or, The Nation's Pride), to impressive statistics on its coattails. Even *Jonny* was beaten, though, by a flashy Czech import: Jaromir Weinberger's *Schwanda, der Dudelsackpfeifer* (Schwanda the Bagpiper, 1927), from which a "Polka and Fugue" was once a pops-and-proms specialty; it reached 600 performances in Germany within two years, and had another 200 or so before dropping into Lethe after four seasons.

Sudden eclipse was part of the bargain. An opera had its place in the sun if it managed to earn one, and then it moved out of the way. Ephemerality was not just the price of a booming operatic economy, it was also the proof; it implied a constant interest in the new. It was not because *Schwanda* lost the stage after its allotted span that its composer committed suicide in Florida in 1967, or because his three subsequent operas (including a *Lide z Pokerflatu,* after Bret Harte's story, following the vogue for all things American) failed to duplicate his early success. It was because Weinberger, in nearly three decades of Hitler-induced exile, could find no outlet or opportunity for his chief calling. The nurturing operatic ecology that sustained Weinberger, and Berg, and Weill, and Krenek, and Hindemith had come to an end, not only in Germany, but everywhere. And the Nazis were not the culprits.

What had happened? Most obviously and proximately, the depression, which closed many theaters beginning in 1931, and forced impresarios to flee from the copyrighted contemporary repertoire into the public domain. But whereas the spoken theater eventually regained and surpassed its previous artistic and economic levels, contemporary operatic culture was effectively killed. So what killed it?

Talkies. Which were really singies, even without songs. The movies did not only preempt the operatic audience. At a profound level, the movies became the operas of the mid- to late twentieth century, leaving the actual opera houses with a closed-off museum repertoire and a specialized audience of aficionados, rather than a general entertainment public hungry for sensation. With the advent of the sound film, opera found its preeminence as a union of the arts compromised and its standing as the grandest of all spectacles usurped. The kinds of subjects that had been its chief preserves—myth and epic, historical costume drama, romantic melodrama, fast-paced farce—suited the new medium even better. Actors and actresses on film were literally, not just metaphorically, larger than life. The mythic aura of the diva attached itself irrecoverably to them.

Cinematic transport to distant times and climes was instantaneous. Evocative atmosphere, exotic or realistic, could be more potently conjured up on film than on the best-equipped operatic stage, and the narrative techniques of the movies were unprecedentedly flexible and compelling. Film, in short, could keep the promise of romanticism, and preserve its flame more effectively than opera, which had been the romantic art par excellence. At the inward, expressionist extreme, Schoenberg saw in movies the potential for "the utmost unreality" and the unmediated visualization of music "not as dream" (as in opera), and not through sign or symbol, "but as chords, the play of colors, forms." At the opposite extreme, movies could far more adequately represent the effervescence of modern urban life.

To the extent that music gave opera a reason for being by enhancing scale, magnifying characters, providing imaginative transport, and framing possibilities that went beyond those of the spoken theater, it found itself trumped in turn. (Now, with opera in extremis, there is a perverse, somewhat forlorn impulse to borrow back its former glory from the movies. William Bolcom's *McTeague* is a replay of Erich von Stroheim's silent classic *Greed,* and it was produced by the Chicago Lyric Opera under the direction of Robert Altman; another movie director, Herbert Ross, has been hired by the Los Angeles Opera to stage *La Bohème,* already a Metropolitan Opera specialty in a version by Franco Zeffirelli; and Ezra Laderman's *Marilyn* and Dominick Argento's *Dream of Valentino* have been presented this season at the New York City Opera and the Washington Opera, respectively.)

But what of music as a delineator or inducer of mood, as emotional expression, as sheer sensuous presence? Here, at least, opera would always reign supreme, or so you would have thought. But it turns out that the movie sound track can be remarkably like an operatic score in its function, if not necessarily in its sonorous means. Both have the effect of surrounding an action in a metaphorical, sonic ambience that represents and objectifies feeling. Cinematic characters, like operatic ones, do not hear, as characters, the sounds that attend their behavior. They live in the sounds and through them. When music is actually performed in the course of the action, which happens in almost every opera and every film, a fascinating and endlessly variable tension is set up in both media between two levels of musically represented reality. (Carolyn Abbate, who has done the most to explore this code and the way that audiences learn to read it, calls the heard melodies the "phenomenal music" of opera or film and, borrowing from Plato by way of Kant, calls the unheard melodies the "noumenal music," for they represent what is within the world of the artwork a more essential reality.)

It is by no means stretching a point, therefore, to say that movies are the operas of the twentieth century. The creative energy that used to be invested in the opera business now goes into the movie industry; and the blockbuster emotional experiences that operas used to deliver are now far more dependably administered by the big screen. All that opera can uniquely claim (and it is, of course, a big thing) is the charismatic dramatic singer. But the charismatic opera singers of today, and they are notoriously few, exercise their numinous powers almost exclusively in the museum repertory, not in the contemporary one. Contemporary composers of operas do not even call upon their services—unless, like John Corigliano in *The Ghosts of Versailles,* they are trading in pastiche, which is another way of acknowledging the eclipse of opera as a contemporary art.

The transmutation of opera into film is neatly—well, a bit too neatly— epitomized by the career of the Viennese composer Erich Wolfgang Korngold, who wrote *Das Wunder der Heliane,* and once tied with Schoenberg in a local newspaper poll as the greatest living composer. When his flourishing, Mozarteanly precocious career as a composer for the German musical stage was disrupted in 1938 by the Anschluss, Korngold (who had already followed the director Max Reinhardt to Hollywood to arrange Mendelssohn's music for Reinhardt's film of *A Midsummer Night's Dream*) accepted a contract as a staff composer at Warner Brothers. Between 1935 and 1946 he furnished original scores for nineteen films and won two Oscars. After *Die Kathrin* (an operetta, but with continuous music, that was already in progress when he went to America), he never wrote another opera.

Except that he was writing opera all along. Korngold never had to adapt his style in any way to the exigencies of the new medium; it was perfectly suited. The style of Viennese opera that Korngold inherited and extended became the Hollywood style of the thirties and forties, as established not only by Korngold but also by such other Central European immigrants as Max Steiner, another Viennese prodigy, nine years Korngold's senior, who was in Hollywood as early as 1929. It was Steiner who pioneered the techniques of "underscoring," or putting continuous, leitmotif-laden "noumenal" music behind the dialogue, and this enabled the mutation of opera into cinema. (Korngold and Steiner were inevitably cast as rivals, but friendly ones. The anecdotes are legion: "How is it, Korngold, that for the last ten years my music has been getting better and yours has been getting worse?" "That's simple, Steiner, you've been stealing from me and I've been stealing from you.")

Perhaps the finest operatic scene that Korngold ever wrought was the love scene from *Anthony Adverse* (1936), his third original score and one of the two scores that earned him an Academy Award. The opulently swooping, restlessly modulating music could be spliced right into *Das Wunder der Heliane.* The Tristanesque "Night" sequence from *Another Dawn,* Korngold's second Hollywood feature, accompanied the ardent confessions of Kay Francis and Errol Flynn with a solo violin and a cello quartet to stand in for the lovers' voices. It later furnished the thematic basis for the first movement of Korngold's violin concerto, written for Heifetz in 1945, a haunting work that could easily have borne the subtitle of the violinist-composer Louis Spohr's once-popular Eighth Concerto: "in modo de scena cantante," alias *Gesangszene*. It, too, was a sublimated operatic scene, nostalgically evoking the vanished world that Korngold once inhabited, and that he had helped to transform.

.   .   .

But wait. Isn't there another difference, a bigger one? Opera, however popular, remains an art, while movies, or at least Hollywood movies, are a massproduced and mass-reproduced medium and amount only to kitsch. Or so we are often told. I am not so sure.

The operatic world from which Korngold and Krenek emerged, like the wider world of art in the period following the Great War, was a bitterly divided world. The division was not simply between stylistic radicalism and conservatism, or between a liberating iconoclasm and a hidebound tradition, though that is how a stubbornly Whiggish historiography continues to represent it. Nor was it primarily a division between a senile romanticism and a new classicism, as so many artists of the time liked to say. It was, rather, a difference in the way that art was viewed in relation to the world.

The heart of the matter, as it pertains to music, was grasped with great lucidity by the early Soviet critic Boris Asafyev, writing at a time when the new Russia, not yet fully transformed from a radical social experiment into a totalitarian prison, was still at the forefront of artistic innovation, and when NEP-period Soviet opera houses were very much abreast of developments in the West, if not actually ahead of them. It is startling now to recollect that *Wozzeck* had its third production in Leningrad, in advance of all German stages but Berlin, and that *Jonny spielt auf* was staged both in Leningrad and in Moscow during the season of 1928–29. (Both operas stimulated the work of the young Shostakovich.) "There is a growing contrast in contemporary music," Asafyev wrote in 1924,

> between works built on the principle of maximum concentration, economy and conciseness, and those which dispose their materials in breadth and employ the largest possible number of performers. . . . In the first case, the music asserts the dynamics of life; in the second it is ruled by an emotional hypnosis and a sterile hedonism. . . . [The new art] is nearer to the life of public actuality than to that of philosophical seclusion. . . . Its style is essentially dynamic, for it is rooted in the sensations of contemporary life and culture and not merely in personal sentiments and emotions.

Jonny spielt auf and *Das Wunder der Heliane* represent the contradiction described by Asafyev at its polar extremes, which were extremes not yet reached when he wrote. Though they are being marketed now under a crude common rubric, they embodied antithetical values. On the surface, at least, they represent (in Asafyev's terms) a sort of before and after: fat round *Heliane*, swooning, slow-moving, full of puffy, sublimated waltzes, versus lean mean *Jonny*, speedy, angular, alert, twitching with new-world rhythms. Korngold's father, a powerful Viennese critic and a disciple of Bruckner, made strenuous and counterproductive efforts to suppress Krenek's opera, efforts that were only partly attributable to nepotism. In fortuitous (and, in the light of things to come, excruciatingly ironic) alliance with the Nazi press, the Jewish critic sought to uphold the sanctity of *die heil'ge deutsche Kunst* (to quote Wagner's Hans Sachs), "holy German art," values that the elder Korngold associated with a particular musical ethos and his temporary allies associated with a particular mythology of race.

Since Wagner's time, the German art of music had brought to a pitch of perfection the most consummately developed technique ever devised for representing the idealized experience of subjective feeling in tones. Philosophers and psychologists who have reflected upon the methods, highly manipulative in several meanings of the word, by which composers in the German tradition achieved this representation, have tended to fall under its spell. They have attributed universality to a local, highly specialized idiom. They have cast it in essential terms, as the culminating realization of music's intrinsic or "absolute" properties. (Recall Susanne K. Langer's formulation that music and emotion are "isomorphic," or the more pragmatic version, by the American psychologist Carroll C. Pratt, that "music sounds the way moods feel.") What is analogized by music that may be described in these terms is the waxing and waning—the onsets, the peaks, the subsidence—that characterize the experience of many kinds of feeling, conspicuously including sexual arousal. A music that traffics in the emotive effects created by fluctuating tension will place a high premium on process and flux. Its unfolding is marked, therefore, by a constant modification in whatever is most obviously variable—chiefly tempo, loudness, and implied harmonic direction.

The last is strictly the province of the composer; and it is fair to say that the main technical preoccupation of composers and musical theorists, in the century that led up to the post-Wagnerian period, was the staking out and the rationalization of a vastly enlarged field (or "sea," as Wagner liked to call it) of harmonic relationships, enabling the control of an increasingly versatile and protean range of "modulation," that is, directed harmonic change. The other variables, speed and loudness, can be specified by the composer (and were so specified, increasingly), but they can also be modified ad libitum in the act of performance. And so there arose an "emotional" performance practice as well, which could be applied not just to the Germanic music of subjective emotion, but (appropriately or not) to any sort of music. Whenever and wherever the Germanic emotive style was taken as an essential musical truth, its "Wagnerian" performance practice was universalized as well. (Try Wilhelm Furtwängler's or Willem Mengelberg's performances of Bach or Mozart.)

Again it was a matter of perpetual "becoming," of constant and gradu-ated change: tempo rubato (the constant adjustment of speed) and shaded dynamics (the constant adjustment of loudness), which were coordinated with the new "freedom" of finely calculated harmonic shift. Myriad con-ventions arose whereby impressions of mounting pressure and relaxing pressure, ranging in intensity from the infinitesimal to the cataclysmic, were reinforced in all three dimensions. Articulation, or the absence of it, also played a part, making emotional representation-by-analogy a four-dimen-sional affair. It was in the post-Wagnerian period that portamento, sliding gradually from pitch to pitch in imitation of operatic singing, became a fixture of string playing; and so did the constant use of vibrato, a throb produced by minute and subtly variable frequency or amplitude modulations. Virtuosos on all instruments sought the maximum connection between notes known as legato, and virtuoso orchestrators experimented with contin-uous orchestral pitch (which was much facilitated by the harp, whose swooping glissando technique could make every change of pitch sound like a porta-mento).

With all of these effects in simultaneous operation, no music ever pro-duced stronger climaxes. Nor could any other music stave off climax or clo-sure so long and so effectively. For, as *Tristan und Isolde* taught several gener-ations of composers, the most potent maneuver of all was the feint. Wagner's harmonic feints are his most famous legacy, but his dynamic feints were no less masterly. The crescendo leading to the climax of the love duet in the sec-ond act of *Tristan,* and to its recapitulation in Isolde's final transfiguration, or *Liebestod,* is just as potent an augur of culmination as the progressively con-centrated (finally, explosively, released) harmonic tension; and it is broken tellingly by a sudden lessening of volume, so as to build again with still more power.

With such an efficacious strategy of forecasting events and delaying them, of arousing expectations and frustrating them, music could actually produce affect, not merely portray it. The perpetual waxing and waning of Wagner-ian and post-Wagnerian music, its endless process of becoming, thus had a way of emotionally engulfing listeners, taking control of their sentient lives for the duration—and becoming, for all practical purposes, noumenal music, the music of ultimate (well, virtual) reality. It was what Schopenhauer, who believed in it, called the direct embodiment of Will, and what Asafyev, who did not believe in it, called "emotional hypnosis."

The act of submitting to such music turns one temporarily into a solipsist. Succumbing to its hypnosis was valued as religious experience, as erotic ex-perience, as narcotic experience, in any combination or all at once. Music that could produce such experiences and such states of consciousness was thought by its devotees to be the most sanctifying and exalting art in the world. Which is precisely why such music was, for Max Nordau, but not for the Nazis, the ultimate *Entartete Kunst.*

.   .   .

There was no hypnotist in music more expert than Erich Wolfgang Korngold. He commanded the resources that Wagner had pioneered with a routined virtuosity even greater than Wagner's and with a higher gloss, owing to advances both in orchestral technology and in orchestrational know-how, where Strauss had led the way. Korngold's use of the harp, and of brass harmonics, transformed the orchestra into a virtual continuous-tone instrument. The Straussian celesta, the earlier composer's sauce piquante, mutates in Korngold's orchestra into an indefatigably churning section of keyboard and mallet instruments—xylophone, glockenspiel, harmonium, piano, organ, and even the infrequent *glockenklavier,* a set of tubular chimes attached to a keyboard—that oozes endless aromatic goo.

There is hardly a measure in *Das Wunder der Heliane,* as the conductor John Mauceri reports, that is without tempo or dynamic modification. Korngold's sea of harmony is aslosh with intoxicants—progressions by whole tones, by minor thirds, by encircling appoggiaturas, by "extra" semitones—that were not standard in Wagner's day but had become standard in Strauss and Debussy and, perhaps above all, in Delius (in *A Mass of Life* and *Sea Drift,* and in the operas *A Village Romeo and Juliet* and *Fennimore and Gerda,* all works first performed in Germany before the composer won acceptance in his native England).

Listeners to *Das Wunder der Heliane* are sensually surfeited and emotionally buffeted to a degree that not even Strauss or Scriabin ever attempted. It was a style so fraught with excess and extremity as to require a subject matter of corresponding magnitude. Nothing less than eschatological mystery would do, which is what the librettist Hans Müller, adapting a "Mysterienspiel" by Hans Kaltneker, tried to supply. The action takes place, like a typical expressionist drama, in an unspecified time and space. Except for Heliane, the characters have no names, just generic labels. The stage directions virtually harp on transcendence: "There is no trace of realism," the remark for act 1 reads; "the characters are timeless both in their garments and their movements." The instruction for act 3 insists that a crowd onstage mill about, come and go, rear up and crouch down, but "never in realistic poses." No social actuality is to impinge on metaphysics here. We are going to gaze on Good and Evil plain.

A messianic Stranger, imprisoned for insurrection by an evil Ruler, awaits execution. Heliane, the Ruler's wife, secretly comes to the Stranger's cell to comfort him. He demands to caress her hair, then to fondle her feet, finally to gaze upon her naked body. She complies with every request. The Ruler, an Alberich-like figure who has traded love for power, returns to strike a bargain with the Stranger: if the Stranger will teach the Ruler, who has never known the virginal Heliane's love, how to conquer her sexually, he will be spared. On discovering the naked Heliane in the Stranger's cell, the Ruler convenes a court to condemn her. Heliane insists on the purity of her mission of mercy. The Stranger asks the court for a moment alone with Heliane, during which he kills himself in a love ecstasy. The Ruler forces the Chief Judge to agree to a trial of Heliane's purity: if she can restore the Stranger to life, she will be spared. Heliane, despite self-doubt and an attempted confession of sin, succeeds in her task before the assembled populace, who are thus inspired to depose the Ruler, but not before he strikes his wife dead. The Stranger now resurrects Heliane in turn, and the two, having thus consummated through mutual arousal and erection a holier and purer matrimony than any earthly sacrament can bless, are admitted to eternal life together.

Could there be any purer kitsch? This operatic consecration of comfy family values, by means of an ersatz religiosity accompanied by the crassest voyeurism, seems as if written expressly to illustrate the central point in the Austrian novelist Hermann Broch's "Notes on the Problem of Kitsch":

> The new age—i.e., the age of the middle classes—wants monogamy, but at the same time wants to enjoy all the pleasures of libertinage, in an even more concentrated form if possible. They are thus not content to raise the monogamous sexual act to the stars; the stars, and everything else that is eternal, are obliged to come down to earth to concern themselves with men's sexual lives and enable them to reach the highest pitch of pleasure.

No doubt about it: Korngold was the master of musical sacroporn. Here it is the music, as in all opera deserving of the name, that makes the essential point, and draws the crucial connection between the pseudoreligious and the pseudoerotic, most powerfully in the swaying waltz that reaches its most full-blown statement in "Ich ging zu ihm" (I went to him), Heliane's act 2 aria of self-justification before the court, in which she recounts in lingering detail the eight-minute nude scene that the audience has already witnessed. It was coyly staged with lighting effects, according to the memoirs of Lotte Lehmann, who created the role in Vienna.

This connection between religiosity and eroticism, of course, was a hoary artistic cliché. Where the religiosity and the eroticism have been frank, they have conspired to produce masterpieces of art; but Heliane is of another order, less a Bernini saint than a Kim Basinger madonna. She is the domesticated descendant of a long line of Wagnerian heroines and antiheroines, a composite of Elisabeth, the pure bride in *Tannhäuser*, and Kundry in *Parsifal*, whose "Dienen, dienen" (To serve! To serve!) is parodied directly when

Heliane, immediately before the clothes come off, exclaims ecstatically "Ich bin! Ich diene!" while harp glissandos and celesta appoggiaturas proliferate in the pit like kudzu.

Nordau, it happens, was rather droll (and even prescient in a feminist way) on the subject of Wagner's women and the obsessional trope of the mystical erotic. For Wagner and his followers, who lived in an age of burgeoning women's rights and independence, the Eternal Feminine manifested herself as "a terrible force of nature," to which man could only offer resistance with the aid of

> a pure and unselfish virgin, who forms the antithesis to the sphinx with soft woman's body and lion's paws. In conformity with the psychological law of contrast, Wagner invents as a counterpart to the terrible woman of his inmost perception an angelic woman, who is all love, all devotion, all celestial mildness; a woman who asks for nothing and gives all; a woman soothing, caressing and healing, in whom the half-conscious idea is struggling for form, viz., that safety lies in purity, continence or in the possession of a wife having no sort of individuality, no desire and no rights, and hence incapable of proving dangerous to the man.

Kundry had combined the two sides of woman in one, or had struggled to advance from sphinx to saintly minister; but unlike Heliane, the kitsch-Kundry, she does not get the man because she is not virginal and cannot volunteer herself as the wife of the bourgeois paterfamilias's dreams, who combines the roles of "Dirn' und Engel," whore and angel (as Heliane is actually labeled at her trial).

Korngold's opera, with its myriad references to the works of his predecessors, furthers the bourgeois trivialization of once-noble themes that is so often noted and condemned in Strauss (as in *Die Frau ohne Schatten,* another drama of trial and redemption with a largely anonymous cast of characters, which with its angelic choir of unborn children amounts to a pro-life *Magic Flute*). The opera that it most insistently recalls in music, by virtue of its ceaseless celesta chatter, is *Der Rosenkavalier;* and the final duet for Heliane and the Stranger, with its bright, diatonic (read: folklike, naive) recapitulation of formerly sinister chromatic motifs, puts one inescapably in mind of the final duet of Octavian and Sophie.

That set piece, and the ending of Strauss's opera generally, has taken many lumps for what is alleged to be its pandering sentimentality. *Heliane* is its best defense. The *Rosenkavalier* duet, after all, starts out as a trio, in which the Marschallin's self-controlled resignation sets the optimistic calf-love of the young protagonists in perspective. Hers, not theirs, is the epiphany that brings the music of the opera to its radiant climax; the duet proper is just a coda. Her acceptance of a reality that they are in no position to grasp exposes the callowness of their bliss; the triumph of two hearts beating solipsistically as one is not accepted as ultimate truth. There is an aristocratic reserve—or better, an aristocratic reservation—about this ending that cools sentiment just below the sticky point.

Das Wunder der Heliane, by contrast, ends with unending, unreserved affirmations of eschatological truth and pious purity. The word *Ewigkeit,* or eternity, gets rehearsed in act 3 just as obsessively as the word *nackt,* or naked, had been milked in the act 2 trial scene. But the apotheosis of chaste, uxorial devotion is set against a lush orgiastic orchestra that, still harping (literally) on *nackt,* contradicts every word, turning it into papa's masturbatory fantasy, and not even a good one.

Because its prurient core is caked in shame, Korngold's sacroporn fails to produce the "spasm upon spasm of physical delight" that the composer Ethel Smyth was able to draw from the wanton celesta chords in *Der Rosenkavalier;* it produces only discomfiture at its vapid sanctimony. The proper name for the resplendent, oneiric terrain where the kitsch-Kundry reigns is Tinseltown. How right Korngold was, finally, to adjust his sights to the less pretentious level of the Hollywood dream factory, which (as Jeremy Tambling points out in his engaging *Opera, Ideology and Film*) also sanctions "a domesticated, home-consumption view of love as faintly mystical, in its nonrational association with music." In Hollywood kitsch depreciates to schmaltz, which is less of a lie, because it makes no exalted claim to truth. In Hollywood Korngold could pull out all the stops and have it understood, and respected, as an honest, small deed.

.   .   .

The devolution of high romanticism to the celluloid bargain basement, and the consequent death of grand opera as an art form of contemporary relevance, marked a victory for the "new sobriety" or the "new matter-of-factness" (or however one may prefer to translate *neue Sachlichkeit*) that came urgently to the fore in Germany and its artistic colonies between the wars. "Contemporary life," Asafyev wrote, "with its concentration of experience, its capricious rhythms, its cinematographic quality, its madly fast pace—the quality of this life has weaned us away from slow and leisurely contemplation." No more hypnosis; no more dreams; and most important of all, no more solipsism. An authentic modern music, Asafyev insisted, would have to be "nearer to the street than to the salon, nearer to the life of public actuality than to that of philosophical seclusion."

Jonny spielt auf echoes this wake-up call, literally and earsplittingly, with four onstage alarm bells that suddenly go off before the final scene. These, plus a siren, a roaring locomotive, and the sounds of mechanically reproduced music emanating from record players and radios, are the grating artifacts of the "life of public actuality" that impinge upon, and overwhelm, the cushioned philosophical seclusion in which the post-Wagnerians had hidden away their senses. Where Korngold had divested his opera of actuality, insisting on an action disembodied in time and space and a music that bodied forth the eternal noumenon of spirit (though constantly veering, like Strauss's, into cosmic waltz-time), Krenek insisted on the actual, the specific, the temporal, and the phenomenal. He insisted so forcefully that his opera was immediately taken as the prototype of a new genre, christened *Zeitoper,* or "now-opera," to which operas by composers such as Weill, Hindemith, the American expatriate George Antheil, and others were assimilated.

"Now-opera" was not simply a matter of contemporary action, of reference to current events and American pop-genres (shimmies, tangos, blues, *Neger-Spiritualen*) and pop-timbres (sax, banjo), though these were the grounds for *Jonny*'s immediate audience appeal and its subsequent (misleading) reputation as a "jazz opera." Its main novelty was irony: the clash between the ephemeral content and the "classical" form. And this implied another, more fundamental clash: in place of the music of timeless inner feeling, its unabating fluidity of tempo dissolving chronometric reality, there was now to be a music that proceeded just as unabatingly through busy ostinatos at what Krenek at one point labeled "schnelles Grammophon-Tempo," emphasizing uniformity of physical and physiological motion and banishing psychology. It was a music of corporeal elation and spiritual nihilism, a tonic for the tired and the disillusioned, for people who felt betrayed by the lie of transcendence. It was, in short, the music not of America but of "Americanism." And so the now-opera was not really *sachlich* after all but still *märchenhaft,* embodying not a new reality but a new fairy tale, a new allegory and, yes, a new kitsch.

In *Jonny spielt auf,* the first now-opera, the allegory is overt and sledgehammer-subtle. The protagonist is not the title character—a Negro bandleader vaguely modeled, it seems, on Sam Wooding, whose *Chocolate Kiddies Revue* swept Germany in 1925–26—but Max, a Central European composer of traditional transcendental bent (vaguely modeled, it seems, on Ernst Krenek), whose favorite hangout is the Alpine glacier on which the curtain rises for act 1. In the first scene Max meets his *ewig-weibliche,* an operatic diva named Anita who sports a Pucciniesque leitmotif and plays the banjo and tries to lead him not ever upward but down into the maw of commercial success. She goes to Paris and triumphs in Max's opera, but he will not follow her. There she meets Jonny, the hotel bandleader, and Daniello, a slick, matinee-idol "classical" virtuoso, whose violin, following the ancient fairy-tale formula, is the enchanted source of élan vital.

Both try to seduce her. Daniello, with his magic tool, succeeds; while he and Anita are in bed together, however, Jonny (with the help of a chambermaid whom he has seduced) steals Daniello's instrument. The complicated chain of events thus set in motion—in which the violin passes from Anita back to Jonny, then to Max, then back to Jonny—ends with Daniello's death under the wheels of a train that will shortly carry Max and Anita on the first leg of a journey to America, and with Jonny, in triumphant possession of the violin, striking up his theme song and leading a stage full of rejuvenated Europeans in an ecstatic "American" dance.

The most attractive aspect of the opera is the efficiency with which the stylistically eclectic score links all the plot's components, achieving an allegorical conjunction between the abundant phenomenal music and the noumenal. A tiny leitmotif, just a descent through the interval of a fourth to a downbeat, pervades everything. (Anyone who has heard Ravel's "jazz"-tinged *L'Enfant et les sortilèges* of 1925 will recall this very distinctive idea as the "Maman!" motif. Did Krenek?) Scored impressively as a kind of brass chorale, it opens the opera. It is the thematic kernel of "Du Lumpenkerl" (You lout!), Jonny's main "jazz" number, a "Blues" (meaning here just a song with a "blue note") that became a genuine "Schlager," a hit-tune recorded by actual jazz bands many times over as a single. Its climactic chorus "Leb' wohl, mein Schatz" (Bye-bye, baby) returns to crown both act finales, and crowns them blazingly indeed.

More surprisingly, and tellingly, the same descending fourth is the motif by which the glacier (singing as an offstage female chorus; it is the best scene in the opera, and so much for *Sachlichkeit*) answers Max's entreaties to receive him (*Wer ruft?* "Who calls?") and sends him back (*Zu-rück!*) into life and action. The motif is thus the musically distilled essence of the same life force that inhabits the violin and that animates and allegorizes the su perficial Americanisms. The last reprise of all is surprisingly quiet: a series of lulling, reassuring reiterations, by Jonny, on Daniello's necromantic violin, of the motif in its simplest, primal terms, played out decrescendo over a throbbing blues accompaniment. It makes a haunting, indeed a hypnotic, envoi.

One can only marvel at the professional élan with which the twenty-six-year-old composer-cum-librettist went about his business, and at the shapely formal integration that he managed to forge out of such heterogeneous contents, with the music, on the "microstructural" plane, playing the essential fusing role, pointing up the hidden correspondences between the plot's levels and between inner and outer levels of consciousness. If only the music were as interesting as it is skillful. But alas, throughout his long career, Krenek proved to be an amiable mimic of prototypes from Schubert to Boulez and an ingenious contriver, but a drab inventor.

In the instance of *Jonny*, the mimicry is off as well, because the composer knew so little whereof he aped. (John L. Stewart, Krenek's biographer, acknowledges that "when he conceived his libretto, Krenek had never met a Negro or an American.") Jonny, in a passage that must have especially delighted the Nazis, spies Anita in the Paris hotel and leers, "Oh, by Jove, *die weisse Frau ist schön!*" The "neger-amerikanische" music in this opera is just about as convincing as the purported black American patois.

But this hardly mattered to the audience. What they wanted to see, and what Krenek set out to provide, was a jolly, down-to-earth version of Korngold's messianic Stranger: a hope-inspiring Pied Piper, or better, as Krenek later put it, a "latter-day Papageno," a Mr. Natural, as alluringly Other as possible. The condescension implicit in the illicit and alluring and ostensibly liberating stereotype was not directed at blacks alone but more generally at Americans. But Jonny's indispensable Otherness is what finally undoes the now-opera premise. As Stewart concedes, the now-element, that is, the dance music, "was surprising only in that it was used in an opera. Considered strictly as music, it was singularly bland."

Opera, in other words, has a sort of Heisenberg problem. The *alltäglich,* the *zeitlich,* and the *sachlich,* the everyday, the ephemeral, and the phenomenal—the new prescription that would make art safe for Weimarish democracy—could function convincingly within the world of opera only as an exotic import. By its very presence, it was exceptional, numinous, and threatening. So now-opera was still opera. It could only be a special case, a subgenre; and it could not escape the fate of the genre as a whole.

But what really disturbs in *Jonny spielt auf* is what so often disturbs in "Weimar" art, especially the kind that pretended to a new objectivity. Amoral, antireflective, primitively spontaneous and "biological," glorifying mass culture, this art prefigures fascism. Why are we expected to cheer Jonny when he steals Daniello's violin? Is it because the metaphorical torch has gone from an exhausted Europe to America, the hope of the world? No, torches are passed, not swiped. It is the simple audacity of the deed that justifies it, and that condemns its victim.

When the glacier sends Max back down into the world, it is to act, not to think. Only when he is provoked into decisive, lawless action, fighting his way free of the police who had arrested him for possession of Daniello's violin and hopping recklessly on Anita's boat train for America, does Max finally win her. As their train makes its triumphant exit, the final tableau is that of a stage full of dancing puppets, like the one in Mann's "Mario and the Magician," in mindless thrall to a charismatic leader. Some wide-awakeness. Some liberation.

The freedom celebrated at the end of *Jonny spielt auf* is only the freedom to seek new masters, to submit to a new hypnosis. The difference between Krenek's hypnosis and Korngold's is that it is no longer the unseen charlatan, the Oz-like composer-operator of the Wagnerian tradition, who seeks to exercise control; it is a visible character onstage. And the control that he exercises is physiological, not spiritual. Korngold manipulates subjectivity directly; Krenek, denying subjectivity, works through Jonny on the autonomic nervous system. One can hardly listen to the last scene of *Jonny,* even on records, without twitching in loutish kinesthetic response to the breakneck reprise of "Du

Lumpenkerl." (It is realized to rowdy perfection in the recording, at a truly improbable *Grammophon-Tempo*.) One hates oneself in the morning.

.   .   .

The tendency has been to forgive both of these works their cynicism, to accept *Jonny spielt auf* as a "mildly naughty" period romp (Stewart) and *Das Wunder der Heliane* as a "two-and-a-half-hour drench," to quote the English composer Robin Holloway, at which "one smiles in acquiescent pleasure." The indulgence, it seems pretty clear, is purchased courtesy of the Nazis. Take away their seal of disapproval, and we are left not with easily dismissed "degeneracy" but with decadence, which is more real, more disquieting, and much harder to get a grip on.

This was the downside of the thriving consumer culture that, in our day, with opera a walking corpse, seems at first so enviable. But this was a culture of frisson and titillation posing as a culture of liberation and uplift. However it may tickle our sense of irony to contemplate it, and even if we choose to excuse its practitioners on grounds of naïveté or sincere bad taste, it entailed a lack of moral purpose that rendered the "serious" arts defenseless against totalitarian rhetoric, and passively complicit in its triumph. It has often enough been said that the demise of the Weimar Republic was as much a suicide as a murder. These valuable recordings of trashy operas provide excellent documentation in support of such a judgment.

And if that is not jeremiad enough, it is worth adding a few words about the newly revived *Zeitoper* concept in which some have seen the possibility of opera's salvation in our time. *Nixon in China* and *The Death of Klinghoffer*, operas masterminded by the director Peter Sellars and executed by the librettist Alice Goodman and the composer John Adams, seem to go the Weimar now-operas one better in "actuality" by using real figures from recent history and the news as characters.

The events portrayed are, to say the least, conducive to political and moral debate; and the more we can get used to thinking about high art—and classical music in particular—in such terms, the better. Except for the little estheticist and formalist detour of the past seventy years or so, the traditional way of thinking about art and talking about art, except among those whose business it is to make it, has always emphasized the political and the moral. There is no reason why artists' shoptalk should remain the dominant mode of art criticism. To return human concerns to center stage, as the Sellars-Goodman-Adams operas appear to do, can only do serious art good. For the less irrelevant such art may again begin to seem to ordinary human values and needs, the less we may be inclined to condone its marginalization in our culture.

But what these operas have really done is idealize and transcendentalize the actual, on the estheticist assumption that that is what high art is supposed to do. The result is a moral evasion, particularly acute in *Klinghoffer*, where a crime is involved, where the complacent nonjudgmental affectation only reinforces the sense that "high" artists no longer possess the means or the disposition to respond adequately to human dilemmas, and where, worse yet, the forms of old sacred genres (in this instance, the Bach Passions) are appropriated to cloak moral blankness and opportunism in a simulated religiosity. *Klinghoffer* and *Heliane* are kitsch cousins.

The worst of it was the critical response, at any rate a large part of it, which ratified the false premise that opera, as high art, should be above matters of mere life and death. "As the authors' approach to this sensitive subject is classical," the reviewer for the *San Francisco Chronicle* wrote, unbelievably, of *Klinghoffer,* "no 'sides' are taken." Bach, the ostensible model, who knew not from "classical," took sides, all right. Or should we prefer a "classical" Passion, in which Christ and his betrayers are treated "evenhandedly"? If such moral indifference is an accurate measure of what the "classical" has now become, then the "classical" deserves its fate. Its death, like the death of Weimar, may ultimately be judged a suicide.

34

No Ear for Music
The Scary Purity of John Cage

David Revill, *The Roaring Silence* (New York: Arcade, 1992; 375 pp.)

Richard Kostelanetz, ed., *Conversing with Cage* (New York: Limelight, 1988; 300 pp.)

Pierre Boulez and John Cage, *Correspondance et documents,* edited by Jean-Jacques Nattiez (Winterthur: Amadeus, 1990; 234 pp.); trans. Robert Samuels, *The Boulez-Cage Correspondence* (Cambridge: Cambridge University Press, 1993; 168 pp.)

John Cage, *The Complete Quartets;* Arditti Quartet (Mode 17 & 27, 2 CDs)

John Cage, *The Perilous Night; Four Walls;* Margaret Leng Tan (New Albion 37)

John Cage, *Lecture on Nothing; Works for Cello;* Frances-Marie Uitti (Etcetera 2016)

Lenny Bruce had a routine in which he sent audiences into paroxysms by classifying any artifact of contemporary culture to which they referred him as Jewish or goyish. The high point, on the recording that I heard, came when someone shouted, I think, "instant scrambled eggs," and Bruce went, "ooh . . . scary goyish." There is no better way of understanding what John Cage has meant to us, why he was so notorious and then so famous, and why his name will long remain an emblem. For half a century he stalked the world of music as its scariest goy.

This had nothing to do with religion, or with the ethnic complexion of modern America. It wasn't even a question of Us and Them. What made the classification funny was that all the mundane items classified belonged to Us. The classification showed up the contradictions in the shared culture, and in its values. What was "Jewish" confirmed our cherished notions of ourselves; what was "goyish" disconfirmed them. But confirmation and disconfirmation alike begot a shock of recognition, as did Cage. It was always vexingly clear that this disconfirming presence was not only in the music world, but oh, so tellingly and chillingly of it.

People often wrote him off as a jester, with his homemade instruments ("prepared" pianos jangling with inserted household objects, pots-'n'-pans

First published in the *New Republic*, 15 March 1993.

percussion orchestras), his anarchic happenings and "musicircuses," his pieces for radios (or for nothing at all), his music-generating games of chance (latterly high-tech, computerized), his New Agey orientalism, his inscrutable droning lectures ("magnificently boring," his new biographer says). But no, you don't get mad at jesters, or at mere eccentrics, and everybody got mad at Cage. As the critic Peter Yates once put it, Cage's name was always "popping up like the Devil in Punch and Judy" in the grimmer music journals, "to be batted down each time by verbal bludgeon or flung brick." (Lukas Foss invited Cage actually to play the Devil in a performance in 1966 of Stravinsky's *Histoire du soldat,* and Cage recalled, "Everybody thought I was well cast.") When Cage masterminded a complete nineteen-hour performance of *Vexations,* a homely little chorale for piano by Erik Satie (Cage's anti-Beethovenizing hero and another reputed jester) that carried the direction "play 840 times," many were not amused. "While the avant-garde played on, couldn't they hear Satie's chuckling?" one critic wrote. "The old master of *blague* continues to victimize his squarish disciples."

That critic was even righter than he knew. Though late in life he grinned a lot and (besieged by interviewers) became a fount of self-protecting whimsy, Cage was fabulously humorless and literalistic, every bit as ascetic as his most truculent critics, the elite modernists of academe. He was just as esoteric, just as contemptuous of the crowd, just as determined to have no purpose that could be called good or useful. Norman O. Brown saw right through Cage's defenses—the studied naïveté, the Holy Foolery—when he called Cage the quintessential Apollonian. Yes, indeed: never was a musician more cerebral or less sensuous, and, for all his lifelong involvement with dancers, never one less attuned to physical impulse. (Nothing, except perhaps lovely harmony, so repelled Cage in any music as a beat.)

No one was ever less a master of *blague.* The slightest sense of irony would have made the fanatical intensity with which he carried out his mission impossible. What for years kept Cage from going through with *4'33"* (pronounced "four thirty-three"), his so-called silent piece, was his fear that "it would appear as if I were making a joke." One might even say that no one ever had less appreciation for Satie's obvious qualities than his most fervent American disciple; but misunderstanding of this sort, as we know perfectly well without any help from Harold Bloom, is precisely what drives the history of art. Virgil Thomson imitated Satie and was barren. John Cage completely misread him and became charismatically fecund.Thus, on one of the many Cage CDs on the Wergo label one can hear an affecting performance of Satie's magnum opus, the Platonic "symphonic drama" *Socrate,* followed by *Cheap Imitation,* Cage's chance determined recomposition of the piece. All the music's humanity, all its communicative warmth, is systematically, anhedonically squeezed out. On a Hat Hut disc, following Cage's suggestion that its individual parts may be extracted for performance ad libitum, Eberhard

Blum has overdubbed the three very sparse flute lines from *Atlas Eclipticalis,* the huge orchestral work that became famous when the New York Philharmonic rebelled against it in 1964. It is sixty minutes of virtual sensory deprivation, a discipline that, inflicted on an audience of nonadepts, can seem an act of puritanical aggression. Whoever started the rumor that this composer was Mr. Fun?

It was a defensive myth created and circulated by academic modernists in order to marginalize the one who always managed to seem so effortlessly farther-out-than-thou. That apparent effortlessness was what enraged people and made them vengeful. Where uptowners like Milton Babbitt sweated anxiously over complicated "precompositional" serial schemes, Cage just sat in his loft tossing coins. In a celestially snooty review of Cage's book *Silence,* John Hollander tried to exorcise the baleful presence by proposing that Cage's activity finally lacked "a certain kind of hard work" identified with perfectionism, "that peculiar labor of art itself, the incredible agony of the real artist in his struggles with lethargy and with misplaced zeal, with despair and with the temptations of his recent successes, to get better."

But one of the things you learn from David Revill's useful if somewhat reverential biography is how hard Cage worked, how doggedly he pursued his clearly envisaged goals. His schemes were just as complicated, just as exacting, just as pitiless, as any serialist's. Chance operations were anything but labor saving. To put together the *Williams Mix,* Cage's first tape piece, he and Earle Brown chained themselves to the splicing table for five months, twelve hours a day. His works went through false starts and rejected drafts as often as any other composer's. His methods guaranteed no tautological success, and he suffered a fair measure of agony.

By Hollander's definition, then, Cage was a "real artist." What he was not was legit. What he lacked, almost totally, were traditional conservatory skills, even baby ear-training. "The whole pitch aspect of music eludes me," he cheerfully told an interviewer. (You might as well say, "The whole lexical aspect of literature eludes me," or "The whole color aspect of painting eludes me.") Any success that such a musician might enjoy would devalue legitimacy. Which is scary, especially to those who traded on ever more exigent and exclusionary standards of legitimation.

Where the activities of conventional modernists had to flaunt their difficulty, Cage's were of another order. They were so mindless at times as to seem *infra dig* not only to clubby professionals, but even to the average onlooker. "There are people who say, 'If music's that easy to write, I could do it,'" Cage wrote. "Of course they could, but they don't." His art required heroic powers of renunciation, and what you had to renounce were the very things ("education and theory," as Cage once put it) that normally gained you prestige. While working on his monumentally serious piano cycle *Music of Changes* (1951), the first opus in which his compositional choices were entirely determined by operations adapted from the ancient Chinese divination manual known as the "Book of Changes" *(I Ching)*, Cage apologized for writing a skimpy letter to Pierre Boulez, then a close friend: "You must realize that I spend a great deal of time tossing coins, and the emptiness of head that that induces begins to penetrate the rest of my time as well."

The very elegance of the phrasing shows how much personality and cultivated intellect Cage had to be willing to renounce. But renunciation is shaming, and scary, and had to be denied; and so the myth of the jester was born. "I like fun," Hollander sneered, but "I shall resist the impulse to have as much fun being a critic as Mr. Cage has being a composer." Mr. Cage was not having fun. His motives did not differ from those of the composers that Hollander admired. His product in those days resembled theirs far more than they could afford to admit. All that differed were the means—and how! That means could matter so much more than motives and ends says a lot about modernism.

Music of Changes was written in emulation of Boulez's Second Piano Sonata, which had left Cage "trembling in the face of great complexity" when the composer played it for him in 1949. The work it most resembles, however, is Boulez's *Structures* for two pianos, written in 1952 under the reciprocal influence of Cage. What both composers accomplished with these works was the replacement of spontaneous compositional choices—choices that, in Cage's oft-incanted phrase, represented "memory, tastes, likes and dislikes"—with transcendent and impersonal procedures. It was a common goal in the early atomic age, when selves seemed frangible and insignificant. The difference between Boulez and Cage was only superficially a conflict between order and anarchy. It was, rather, a conflict between disciplines, both eminently authoritarian, both bent on stamping out the artist's puny person so that something "realer," less vulnerable, might emerge.

Cage's "chance operations," very rigorous and very tedious, were just as effective a path to transcendence as Boulez's or Babbitt's mathematical algorithms. Where Boulez, in the words of the Canadian scholar Roger Savage, "handed the work's structure over to the serial operations which control it," Cage ceremoniously handed the structure of his work over to Dame Fortune. The difference was that serial operations established multifarious arbitrary relationships among the events that took place in the score, while chance operations generated atomistic sequences in which every event was generated independently of every other. Cage's methods explicitly destroyed relationships ("weeded them out," he crowed) because attention to the fashioning of relationships, being egoistic, defeated impersonalism and also, Cage thought, the reality of music.

"Composers," he wrote, "are spoken of as having ears for music which generally means that nothing presented to their ears can be heard by them." Boulez's product, being full of relationships, could be analyzed in traditional ways: its events could be reduced to principles; it could be conceptualized in "levels." All of which not only made the institutional wheels go round, but gave reassuring evidence of "an ear for music"—a controlling intelligence, a respectable moral accountability. But as Cage implied with his mischievous characterization of the "musical ear," the coherence of the serial structure could only be demonstrated conceptually—that is, on paper—to professionals. As increasing numbers of musicians are now willing to concede, there is no possibility of perceptual corroboration; and musical psychologists are beginning to suspect that the mind's structure may actually preclude the cognitive processing—the "understanding"—of nonhierarchical pitch and rhythmic information. Thus Cage's open renunciation of the discriminating, theory-laden "musical ear" in favor of the literal, physical, uncritically accepting biological ear was especially scary to postwar serialists, because it tainted their ostentatious rationalism with a hint of fraud, producing not just musical dissonance but cognitive dissonance, too.

The fact is, *Structures* and *Music of Changes,* while quite different in texture (Cage's piece is characteristically much sparser), impress the naked ear as equally desultory complexities, and induce an equally passive reception. In a blind test it would be difficult to guess which was the product of "total organization" and which the product of "random selection." The disquiet that this situation produced among the European (and, later, the American) serialists gave rise to casuistic denial and a mania for scholastic analysis that (as Cage deftly implied) all too easily replaced the sounding music as the primary focus of interest.

Cage's scary presence split the avant-garde into anxious "sentimental poets," the kind (as Schiller put it) "whose soul suffers no impression without at once turning to contemplate its own play," and "naïve" ones, with Cage their king, who celebrate "the object itself," not "what the reflective understanding of the poet has made." While his antagonists did their dervish dance of negation, Cage could afford to grin. Self-schooled in "a spirit of acceptance, rather than a spirit of control," he gladly acknowledged the incomprehensibility of his results—and of theirs as well. Catching at the ancient aura of the sublime and so being truer than his opponents to the impulse that brought forth Schoenbergian atonality, Cage maintained "that the division is between understanding and experiencing, and many people think that art has to do with understanding, but it doesn't."

In other ways, too, radically though his means may have differed, Cage's ends meshed with those of his ostensible adversaries. He and Babbitt are often viewed (and surely viewed themselves) as antipodean figures, but they jointly embodied what may be called the "research" model (as opposed to the "communication" model) of composerly behavior, so characteristic of midcentury modernism. Both were wholly fixated on their own activity, on the game of making. Both were obsessed with formulating the rules of the game, with finding ever more efficient methods of production. And both were wholly unconcerned with reception.

"Who Cares If You Listen?" was the title (given by editors, but not inaccurately) of a famous article by Babbitt, published in 1958. Cage, according to Revill, rejected communication as a goal out of bitter personal experience. *The Perilous Night* (1943–44), a six-movement suite for prepared piano (superbly recorded by Margaret Leng Tan on the New Albion label) that Revill describes as "a lost, sad and rather desperate piece"—and that Cage himself has described in painful autobiographical terms we can now (partly thanks to Revill) link up with his traumatic sexual reorientation and divorce in 1945—was frivolously dismissed by a critic as sounding like "a woodpecker in a church belfry." The wounded composer talked about this experience for the rest of his life. Thenceforth "I could not accept the academic idea that the purpose of music was communication," he once observed. Another time, more strongly, he said that, after the *Perilous Night* fiasco, "I determined to give up composition unless I could find a better reason for doing it than communication." The bruise that Cage received from an insouciant philistine turned him inward, and equipped him with the resentment and the aggression that a modernist giant needs.

What better reasons did he find? The one that he loved to adduce for interviewers was spiritualistic and Eastern, picked up in the forties from an Indian friend, Gita Sarabhai, who said that the purpose of music was to "sober and quiet the mind, thus making it susceptible to divine influences." (Pressed, he produced a less "churchy" version: "The function of music is to change the mind so that it does become open to experience, which inevitably is interesting.") Ultimate purposes, however, do not produce a program of action. For managing his career from day to day and work to work, Cage enthusiastically embraced the model—inherited, he always said, from his inventor father—of experimental science. Art justified itself in the making. Experiments could succeed or fail, but "sometimes they could tell you what to do next."

What made John Cage such a scary goy, then, was the way he reflected back at the orthodox—more consistently, more nonchalantly, more "honestly"—their own follies of extremism. And they hated him for it. But since the follies of modernism were the follies of the mainstream magnified, mainstream musicians also found in Cage a discomforting reflection.

And then, suddenly, they didn't. By the time the enfant terrible qualified for Medicare, he had been transformed into a grand old man (well, a sweet old guy) at whom no one ever got angry, at whom everyone grinned back, on whom everyone showered praise and thanks. Pockets of resistance lingered among the militant bourgeois, who disapproved of his lifestyle (he was a scary gay, too), and feared the destabilizing implications of his work for the "canon," and kept up a tired game of gotcha with this "liberator" who actually believed in rules (forgetting what was being liberated, and from whom), and pronounced his latter-day acceptance and prestige (in Edward Roth-stein's words) to be "symptoms of our era's poverty." But they were symptoms of something else. Somewhere between the early sixties and the late seventies, Cage and all his squabbling brethren had lost their teeth. He was no longer a threat. And that, if anything, defined the transition from the modern to the postmodern.

It is not that the world caught up to Cage. He was, rather, left behind; or kicked upstairs. (Babbitt, too, went suddenly from pariah to elder statesman, and Boulez became caught up in institutional power politics and has not produced an important work since *Répons* in 1981.) Revill senses this, and his conclusion is shrewd, if a little wistful:

> Cage has lived through a time when the "avant-garde" meant what it said. As the twentieth century nears its end, there is no avant-garde of which to speak: the term has come to refer to a midcentury movement, and not to each successive advance on received artistic wisdom. Indeed, arguably times from the eighties have been recuperative rather than revolutionary.

The word *recuperative* carries a bit of stigma; and Revill hints farther down the page at "a certain lack of integrity and engagement among artists." He is understandably nostalgic. A heroic time is past. But what has happened in music since the seventies cannot be dismissed as "retro," though some of it has been that. One may justifiably view the newly serious trend toward softening the boundaries between genres and roles, and toward abolishing the hierarchy of existing categories, as regenerative, whatever one may think of what has so far been brought forth. And though Cage liked to promote himself as the champion of the excluded, he upheld many traditional categories and boundaries as zealously and as rigidly as any midcentury elitist.

As his lifelong vendetta against Beethoven endlessly affirmed, Beethoven never stopped being for Cage the one to beat. Beethoven was the gatekeeper of the tradition that Cage shared with Schoenberg his teacher and with Babbitt his adversary—but perhaps no longer with us. By now Cage's values can look almost academic: anti-jazz, anti-pop (except briefly in the sixties, when rock seemed "revolutionary"), anti-improvisational (until, near the end, he figured out a way of dehumanizing improvisation). "Composing's one thing, performing's another, listening's a third," he wrote in an essay unbendingly (and oxymoronically) titled "Experimental Music: Doctrine." "What can they have to do with one another?" Composing unperformable or unlistenable works was the inevitable outcome of such an attitude, but such an outcome entailed no loss of value. In its way it was the supreme insulator, guaranteeing a sterile authenticity.

So let's hear no more about Cage the first postmodernist, or (pace the *New York Times*'s egregious obituary) about Cage the first minimalist. He was anything but. All that Cage had to say of the work of Riley, Reich, or Glass (ungratefully enough, for they worshiped him) was, "I can't use it." To him, they were backsliders. Like Schoenberg, Cage was a self-appointed Hegelian protagonist on whom History made demands. He referred to his work as "what I was obliged to do." Hence, "I'm practically Germanic in my insistence on doing what is necessary." And what is necessary? "Now, obviously, the things that it is necessary to do are not the things that have been done, but the ones that have not yet been done," which was another way of saying that he was as "devoted" as any modernist "to the principle of originality." That is maximalism, not minimalism. "Anything goes," Cage did write, sure enough, just as his enemies accused him of doing. "However, not everything is attempted. . . . There is endless work to be done."

.   .   .

The superstitious category "genius" was made for the likes of Cage. Like Schoenberg (or perhaps despite Schoenberg), Cage was a primitive. And as Schoenberg said, "Talent learns from others; genius learns from itself." The mark of the genius, on the late, late romantic terms of high modernism, was the faculty of self-validation, which gave one the magical capacity to validate others. "He has immense authority," the art dealer Leo Castelli said of Cage. "He is, after all, a guru; and just the fact that he was there with his fantastic assurance was important to us all." The painter Robert Rauschenberg said that it was Cage's example that "gave me license to do anything." Morton Feldman claimed that Cage gave not just him but everybody "permission." "Permission granted," Cage liked to say in that enigmatically clarifying way of his, "but not to do whatever you want."

But who gave Cage permission? Not Schoenberg, that's for sure. Schoenberg was uniformly sarcastic and dismissive toward his American pupils, and Cage (legends to the contrary notwithstanding) was no exception. Schoenberg had given himself permission to remake the world by first putting himself through the traditional mill to the point where he had become the miller in chief. Cage built his own mill and never asked permission. The mill produced flour. Scary.

His really extraordinary endowment was for turning crippling limitations into special aptitudes. As Revill writes gracefully, "His ideas and practices have gradually been made adequate to, and have clarified, his inclinations." Not that he didn't have his own gurus. He fairly trumpeted them, in fact: "I didn't study music with just anybody: I studied with Schoenberg. I didn't study Zen with just anybody: I studied with Suzuki. I've always gone, insofar as I could, to the president of the company." But they did not create him. On the contrary, he created them ex post facto, from his own cloth, in the authentic tradition of modernist mythmaking.

Michael Hicks, a composer and scholar at Brigham Young University who has done the kind of skeptical research on Cage that the more devoted Revill has not attempted, has effectively demolished the legend of a special relationship between Schoenberg and Cage, or any special transmission from the one to the other. Cage never took private lessons from this master; he just audited some courses at USC and UCLA. He had one very discouraging interview with Schoenberg, which he romanticized in memoirs and interviews into a kind of initiation, Schoenberg agreeing to teach him gratis in return for an oath of lifelong dedication to music. Hicks has shown that free instruction from Schoenberg was more the rule than the exception (for those actually studying with him, as Cage was not), and quotes a letter from a very dissatisfied Cage that contradicts his later professions of filial adoration. Repudiating the very idea of calling himself "a Schoenberg pupil," Cage complained, "Tthat designation is so cheap now that I am not interested in it; it is being bandied about by all those whose ears are vacant passageways for his words."

Schoenberg emerges from Cage's accounts as a kind of Zen master. ("If I followed the rules too strictly he would say, 'Why don't you take a little more liberty?' and then when I would break the rules, he'd say, 'Why do you break the rules?'") But the teacher who did the most for Cage, though no guru, was Henry Cowell. It was Cowell, not Schoenberg, who provided Cage with pertinent precedents: an interest in Asian music, an untraditional approach to the piano, a penchant for percussion. (Cowell was also Cage's first impresario, first publisher, and first publicist.) The British scholar David Nicholls has tried, in characteristic mother-country fashion, to fix Cage in the context of Cowell's essentially regionalist tradition, but the effort is finally unconvincing. As Cage well recognized, Cowell's experimentation was an aspect of an overriding eclecticism that was wholly foreign to Cage. His was a vision of purity. No amount of source study or documentation can account for the astonishing lecture, "The Future of Music: Credo," that Cage delivered in Seattle in 1937. What astonishes is not so much the twenty-five-year-old nobody's singleness of vision or his prescience but what Castelli called his "fantastic assurance."

Cage did his best to link his work retrospectively to Schoenberg's—giving himself, as it were, Schoenberg's permission. If Schoenberg had "emancipated the dissonance" (that is, erased the distinction between consonance and dissonance in his own work, and legislated the erasure for the work of everyone else), then Cage would complete the job and emancipate noise. This, he claimed, was the foundation of his interest in percussion music, which saw him through his first important creative period (1939–43). What he really accomplished, though, was not merely the replacement of one type of sound with another on the surface of the music, but something much more fundamental. Cage's earliest percussion music (like most of the music he would write forever after, even $4'33''$) is already based on abstract durational

schemes—"empty containers," as he called them, to be filled with sounds—
that replaced the abstract harmonic schemes of the classical tradition.

It was a way of circumventing "the whole pitch aspect." Duration, Cage
would argue, was the fundamental musical element, since all sounds—and silence, too—had it in common. And therefore, he could aver, he was the only
composer who was dealing with music on its most fundamental level. (It was
a claim that Elliott Carter, ignoring the scary goy, would revive in the late forties; Cage dismissed Carter as merely "adding a new wing to the academy.")
Cage contrived more imaginary precedents for his activity in the work of Webern and, of course, Satie. They, too, became totemic ancestors, two more
self-created gurus through which he could give himself permission. In
Webern's sparseness of texture (which he did emulate for a while), Cage
heard a rejection "of sound as discourse in favor of sound as sound itself."
(Webern, a fastidious serialist, would have scoffed.) "In Satie," Cage further
asserted, "the structures have to do with time, not pitch." In Paris he thought
he found evidence: some notebooks in which Satie had written lists of numbers similar in appearance to the proportional matrices that Cage worked
out for his percussion pieces. He never could get anyone else to agree with
him about those numbers (Milhaud told him they were shopping lists), but
they gave him the green light.

Only in *Cheap Imitation,* which dates from 1969, does Satie finally sound
the way Cage heard him. *Cheap Imitation,* like at least half of Cage's output,
was meant to accompany the dance. His four-decade career as Merce Cun-
ningham's music director was his primary creative outlet. And it was a Seattle dancer named Syvilla Fort, who performed in a space too small to accommodate an ensemble, who mothered the invention in 1940 of the
one-man percussion orchestra, a.k.a. the prepared piano, and gave Cage the
medium that saw him through his second creative phase (1942–48).

The body of work that he created for this instrument is the one most likely
to be recognized as a permanent contribution to the literature of music.
Cage can be ranked alongside Ravel and Prokofieff as a major twentieth-
century keyboard composer—though, again, anything but legit. Many of his
keyboard compositions can be mastered by amateurs, and most of them are
disarmingly "communicative." The magnum opus of the period, the cycle of
Sonatas and Interludes of 1946–48, aspires beyond communication to the
monumental representation of the nine "permanent emotions" of Hindu
philosophy, but it remains Cage's most accessible large-scale composition. It
is his one conspicuous concession to then-fashionable neoclassicism, otherwise his great bête noire.

The sonatas are cast, like Scarlatti's, in regular two-part forms with repeats,
and proceed through infectious dance rhythms and ostinatos. The last
sonata, the one toward which the whole cycle inclines, is a gorgeously static
delineation of tranquillity, the emotion that balances the rest, and presages

Cage's involvement with the quietism of Zen. Revill is at his best (though, as ever, vague where Cage was vague) in reporting this phase, about whose importance he is commendably skeptical. He shows that the extreme philosophical realism of Zen, its ideology of indiscriminate passive acceptance, and its rejection of subjectivity were already present in Cage's thinking by the time he, the ageless auditor, began dropping in on Daisetz Suzuki's classes at Columbia sometime in the late forties.

And all of this was contradicted in some way, even where Cage meant consciously to embody it. Accepting he may have been of nature's offerings, but he remained bitterly and bombastically rejecting of the (musical) works of (most) men. He may, as instructed, have denigrated conceptual thinking in favor of taking things as he found them, but practically to the end he remained faithful to his predetermined, idealistically rationalized durational "containers." In sum, Revill suggests, for Cage, as for many casual enthusiasts, Zen was more a personal therapy than a philosophy. It brought relief to his perilous night—his period of anguished sexual readjustment—and it enabled him to embark with renewed self-confidence on his long-presaged art of noncommunication. It provided him with a handy rhetoric for advertising his new manner. But it did not give him permission.

The fifties and early sixties were Cage's heroic age—the era of the *Music of Changes*, the *Williams Mix*, the *Imaginary Landscape No. 4* (in which the percussion ensembles of yore were replaced by radios playing whatever happened to be on), the *Cartridge Music* (in which a teeming universe of "microaudial" sound was electronically explored as if in inverse answer to the exploration of space), the *Atlas Eclipticalis* (another space age extravaganza, arcanely derived from sidereal maps), and, of course, *4'33"*. It was the age of his notoriety and his guruhood.

It culminated in the grandiose *HPSCHD* (computerese for "harpsichord"), a flamboyant mixed-media performance created in collaboration with the computer engineer and composer Lejaren Hiller. Its first performance, at the University of Illinois on May 16, 1969, lasted four and a half hours, and enlisted seven keyboard players, fifty-two tape recorders, fifty-two film projectors, and sixty-four slide projectors. ("The following Sunday," Revill adds, pleasingly, "Apollo Ten was launched.") From the chary composer of Nothing, Cage had become the voracious composer of Everything.

HPSCHD was a response not only to baroque science but also to sixties carnivalism, which caught Cage in its tide and, it seems, washed him out to sea. In the seventies and into the eighties he turned Dionysiac. He became a gourmandizing collagist (as in the famous Cage-supervised Deutsche Grammophon LP that piled *Atlas Eclipticalis* on top of *Cartridge Music* on top of the *Winter Music* for piano). He became a perpetrator of happenings, a sentimental Maoist, a nostalgic futurist, a scribbler of gibberish poetry. Worst of all, he became derivative for the first and only time, "writing through" texts by Joyce and Thoreau by turning their work mechanically into arcane acrostics and performing them amid a welter of sonic "ready-mades" (as Marcel Duchamp, Cage's last guru, would have called them) in three- or four-ring "musicircuses," which culminated in a series of parasitic assemblages of cultural debris whose portmanteau title, *Europera,* tells all. It is the single arguably "postmodern" facet of Cage's career, but it is glaringly the weakest, postmodern only in the most banal sense of the term.

In his last decades Cage mellowed interestingly. He turned back to fully determined (though still chance-composed) compositions in a fairly conventional notation, including some impressive virtuoso studies for instrumentalist friends (*Études Australes* for the pianist Grete Sultan, *Freeman Etudes* for the violinist Paul Zukofsky) and a long series of abstract solos and ensembles, the titles of which are derived from the number of performers, from one to 103. His last finished composition, which was first performed in July 1992, a month before his death at seventy-nine, was *Four*[6] (the sixth work for four), for two vocalists (one of them at the première the remarkably youthful Cage himself), a pianist, and a percussionist. At the première the pianist was Leonard Stein, an old Schoenberg hand from California, whose participation brought things touchingly full circle.

The second half of Cage's career was no match for the first, and Revill does not flinch from saying so (attributing the decline not to imaginative fatigue but to the distractions of fame). Still, there were some late gems. Two were for string quartet: *Music for Four* (1987) and *Four* (1989), both of them restrained, elegiac studies in sustained tones reminiscent of, and perhaps a tribute to, Cage's old friend Morton Feldman. When performed as plainly and devotedly as the Arditti Quartet performs them they are sublime lullabies, gloriously realizing not only the quietism of Zen as Cage professed it, but the qualities of "naïve poetry" as described by Schiller: "tranquillity, purity and joy."

.   .   .

It seems right to end this survey of Cage's output on a German romantic note. There is ultimately nothing exotic about him. His ties to the traditional esthetic of the West that he claimed and strove to break were never broken. He is well, if latently, understood. Far more than he (or we) ever acknowledged in his lifetime, far more than he (or we) may even have known, Cage not only subscribed to the fundamental values—no, I'll be brave, to the singular bedrock tenet—of Western art, he brought it to its purest, scariest peak. In an address that he gave in 1954, called "45' for a Speaker," Cage tried to encapsulate in two sentences his somewhat adulterated understanding of Zen (adulterated, that is, with a phrase borrowed from the Indian scholar Ananda Coomaraswamy): "The highest purpose is to have no purpose at all. This puts one in accord with nature in her manner of operation."

These were the catch phrases that he would intone and inscribe, in hundreds of permutations, for the rest of his life. Revill does an excellent job relating the notion of "purposeful purposelessness" to Cage's work, which depended equally on knowing with certainty what to do and on having no expectation of the result.

But the phrase is just a variation (or, to put it musically, an inversion) of the "purposeless purposefulness" *(Zweckmässigkeit ohne Zweck)* by which Kant defined the brand-new concept of "the esthetic" more than two centuries ago. The esthetic, in the classical Kantian definition, was a quality of beauty wholly transcending utility. Esthetic objects existed—that is, were made— entirely for their own sake, requiring both disinterestedness and zealous application on the part of the maker, and a corresponding act of disinterested, self-abnegating contemplation on the part of the apprehender. Autonomous works of art occupied a special hallowed sphere, for which special places were set aside (museums and concert halls, "temples of art"), and where special modes of reverent behavior were observed, or, when necessary, imposed.

Music, inherently abstract to a degree owing to its lack of an obvious natural model, quickly became the romantic art of choice, the most sacred of the autonomous arts. Not only for that reason, but because it was a performing art in which a middleman stood between maker and apprehender, music developed the most ritualized and the most hierarchical social practice, one that Cage was far from alone in crying down: "The composer was the genius, the conductor ordered everyone around and the performers were slaves." (And the listener? An innocent bystander.)

The composer's status was enhanced and the performer's demeaned precisely because the new concept of the autonomous artwork sharply differentiated their roles for the first time, and assigned them vastly unequal value. The composer created the perdurable esthetic object. The performer was just an ephemeral mediator. Musical works that were too closely allied with egoistical performance values, or that too obviously catered to the needs or the whims of an audience, or even that too grossly represented the personality of the composer, were regarded as sullied because they had a *Zweck,* a purpose that compromised their autonomy. The only truly artistic purpose was that of transcending purpose.

The art that most fully met this prescription was "absolute music." And how does that differ from what Cage called "Zen"? Only in its degree of rigor. The work of the midcentury avant-garde vastly magnified and purified the romantic notion of esthetic autonomy, and among the midcentury avant-garde it was Cage, in his compositions of the early fifties, who reached the most astounding, self-subverting purism of all. In that way he reexposed in maximal terms the problematic and the contradictory aspects of the idea of absolute music. How does an art form that is inherently temporal achieve transcendent objectification? What is the ontological status of the autonomous musical work? How does the work relate to its performances? To its written score? (The question was posed most teasingly by the Polish philosopher Roman Ingarden when he asked, "Where is Chopin's B-minor Sonata?") We have seen that the essential structure, the essential "workhood," of a formalistic opus such as, say, Boulez's *Structures* can have rather little to do with its aural experience. Cage's highly determinate containers were even more arcane, because they had even less to do with the often wholly indeterminate sounds that filled them. Cage's awareness of these problems and his sometimes playful, sometimes deadly, engagement with them are memorably set out in his seductively Gertrude-Steinish "Lecture on Nothing" of 1959, one of the essential Cage experiences, whose subject is largely the filling in of its own preplanned durational matrix ("Here we are now at the beginning of the thirteenth unit of the fourth large part of this talk . . ."). It is an easy introduction to Cage's maximalized romanticism, since the sounds that fill the container are familiar words in grammatical sentences.

In the *Imaginary Landscape No. 4* for twenty-four players on twelve radios plus conductor, the concept of "the work" is more abstract and difficult. The piece has an elaborate score in fairly conventional musical notation, but there is no way of "reading" it, since the score has no determinate relationship to the sounds that will occur in performance. The intricately contrapuntal "structure" can only be realized haphazardly in performance, because what is prescribed is not a set of sounds but a set of actions. (This in itself is far from unprecedented; ancient "tablatures" for keyboard and lute did likewise.) The players are directed to turn the knobs on the radios to specified frequencies (where there may or may not be a broadcast) and amplitudes (often just this side, or even that side, of the threshold of perception). The conductor executes all kinds of tempo changes that relate only to the "work," not to the aural experience; his elaborately choreographed actions, eliciting no discernible result, pointedly signal the abstractness and the autonomy of the work-concept. Any whiff of spoof—there is always nervous laughter at performances—is definitely an illusion. (When Virgil Thomson told Cage he didn't think a piece like that ought to be performed before a paying audience, Revill tells us, Cage took extreme umbrage, and it caused a permanent rift in their relationship.) Needless to say, there is no recording.

Strangely enough, *4′33″* has been recorded several times, icon that it has become—but an icon of what? Even Cage, who loved it best of all his children and, according to Revill, treated it "reverentially," called it his "silent piece." That is a misnomer. It is, rather, a piece for a silent performer, who enters a performing space, signals the beginnings and the ends of three movements whose timings and internal "structural" subdivisions have been predetermined by chance operations, but makes no intentional sound. (Usually the signal is given by most carefully and noiselessly closing and raising the keyboard lid on a piano.) The piece consists of whatever sounds occur within a listener's earshot during these articulated spans.

This would seem to be the very antithesis of an autonomous work of art, since the sounds are wholly contingent, outside the composer's control. (Cage often maintained that his aim in composing it was to erase the boundary between art and life.) But sounds are not the only thing that a composer controls, and sounds are not the only thing that constitutes a musical work. Under the social regimen of esthetic autonomy, the composer controls not just sounds but people, and a work is defined not just by its contents but also by the behavior that it actuates. As the philosopher Lydia Goehr, Cage's shrewdest exegete, has observed:

> It is because of [Cage's] specifications that people gather together, usually in a concert hall, to listen to the sounds of the hall for the allotted time period. In ironic gesture, it is Cage who specifies that a pianist should sit at a piano to go through the motions of performance. The performer is applauded and the composer granted recognition for the "work." Whatever changes have come about in our material understanding of musical sound, the formal constraints of the work-concept have ironically been maintained.

And she comments tactfully, in the form of a question, "Did Cage come to the compositional decisions that he did out of recognition that people will only listen to the sounds around them if they are forced to do so under traditional, formal constraints?"

It is a profound political point. A work that is touted as a liberation from esthetics in fact brings an alert philosopher to a fuller awareness of all the constraints that the category of "the esthetic" imposes. Sounds that were noise on one side of an arbitrary framing gesture are suddenly music, a "work of art," on the other side; the esthetic comes into being by sheer fiat, at the drop of a piano lid. The audience is invited—no, commanded—to listen to ambient or natural sounds with the same attitude of reverent contemplation they would assume if they were listening to Beethoven's Ninth.

This is an attitude that is born not of nature but of Beethoven. By the act of triggering it, art is not brought down to earth; "life" is brought up for the duration into the empyrean. $4'33''$ is thus the ultimate esthetic aggrandizement, an act of transcendental empyrialism. There is nothing ironic about it, and nothing, so far as I can see, of Zen. (And $4'33''$ has a published, copyrighted score. The space on its pages, measured from left to right, corresponds to the elapsing time. Most of the pages have vertical lines drawn on them, denoting the chance-calculated time articulations on which the duration of the piece depends. One of the pages, bypassed by these markers, remains blank. If copyrighting a blank page is not modernist chutzpah, I don't know what is.)

So Cage's radical conceptions were as much intensifications of traditional practices, including traditional power relations, as departures from them. His dealings with performers were especially symptomatic; here is where, if you're looking, you can find a contradiction worthy of rebuke. More than once Cage went beyond mere audience hostility and got into confrontational situations with players. Orchestral musicians in particular have taken his works as affronts. Cage and his supporters have made much of the philistin- ism of the players' resistance, not without some justification in the case of the members of the New York Philharmonic who stamped on the contact mi- crophones they were asked to attach to their instruments for performances of *Atlas Eclipticalis*. (The penurious composer was forced to replace them out of pocket.)

But Cage himself has acknowledged that the social practices that have grown up around the sacralized work object have tended to dehumanize per- formers, especially those who play under conductors. The only way that such musicians are able to retain a sense of personal dignity is by believing de- voutly in the esthetic of "communication" or "self-expression" (expanded to encompass a notion of collective self-expression), and this is the notion the midcentury avant-garde has worked most militantly to discredit.

Works based on a principle of nonintention present musicians with a set of especially arbitrary, hence especially demeaning, commands. They are intol- erably deprived of their usual illusions of creative collaboration. The contact mikes, feeding each player's sound into a mixer that, operating on the usual chance principles, added an extra dimension of unpredictability to the pro- ceedings, were a special outrage. As Earle Brown explained to Revill, "Even if you were making your choices with diligence, you might be turned off. Maybe you were heard, maybe you weren't." The composer, though ostensibly aiming at ego effacement (and ostensibly opposed, as Cage put it, to "the conventional musical situation of a composer telling others what to do"), became more than ever the peremptory genius, the players more than ever the slaves.

Even soloists devoted to Cage have recognized the paradoxical reinforce- ment that his work has given to the old hierarchical dispensation. By the use of chance operations, Cage says, he is able to shift his "responsibility from making choices to asking questions." When the work is finished he can have the pleasure of discovering it along with the audience. The only one who cannot share the pleasure is the performer, to whom the buck is passed, who cannot evade the choices, who must supply laborious answers to the com- poser's diverting questions. The pianist Margaret Leng Tan, perhaps the leading exponent of Cage's music today, complained to Revill of being cut out of the fun. Her freedom in performing "chance music" is not enhanced but diminished: "By the time you've worked out all this material, can you really give a spontaneous performance? It's a discovery for him [Cage] if he's hearing it for the first time, but it's not a discovery for me." Once again the composer's authority over the performer (and over the listener, who is reduced to a passive auditor) is paradoxically magnified. The grandiosity of genius is affirmed.

.   .   .

When the job description "artist" stops requiring chutzpah, postmodernism begins. At that point far-outness stops being impressive and becomes quaint. The disinterestedness of the artist and the transcendence of the artifact, maximalized under modernism, have long since metamorphosed into indifference and irrelevance. Cage's esthetic, now that all is said and done, promoted not the integration of art and life but rather a hypertrophied estheticism that transgressed the normal boundaries of art and invaded life. Carrying his esthetic credo, acceptance of all things, beyond those boundaries, Cage often said that there was not too much pain in the world, that there was just the right amount. That was estheticized politics at its most unappetizing. It was the residue of yet another outmoded romantic stereotype, the artist as public oracle, that began, as usual, with Beethoven, reached an unsavory peak in Wagner (or, from the critical perspective, in Adorno), ran to seed with Stockhausen, and now, let us hope, has run its course.

The honors that John Cage reaped in his final decades, and the celebrity status that he achieved, betokened the eclipse of his relevance as an artist. His work and his persona now have a musty period flavor. It is a critical commonplace to laud his influence over other composers (and not only composers), since that is the primary measure of modernist achievement. The *New Grove Dictionary of American Music* claims flatly that Cage "has had a greater impact on world music than any other American composer of the twentieth century." Yet as one looks around at today's music world, it is hard to find evidence of that.

True, a great many composers around the world (Lutosławski perhaps most successfully) have dabbled with "indeterminate" notation, but only as an effect, an occasional blur. Particularly in Eastern Europe, where everything was a symbol, Cage was a symbol for a while. (I knew that perestroika had got out of hand when I saw his face grinning at me from the pages of *Sovetskaya muzïka*, the organ of the now-defunct Union of Soviet Composers.) There are some excellent Hungarian recordings of his work (including a 4'33" with Zoltán Kocsis dropping the lid). In Germany, where everything musical is taken much too seriously, Cage remains a cult figure. They know *E-Musik* (*ernste Musik*, "serious music") when they hear it. Few composers have ever carried less taint of the opposite category, mere *Unterhaltung* (entertainment), than Cage. In 1992 the grandest birthday-cum-memorial festival of his music took place in Frankfurt.

Predictably, some critics have berated the American musical establishment for allowing itself to be out-Caged by Europe, but I find that pleasing. "Once in Amsterdam," Cage recalled, "a Dutch musician said to me, 'It must be very difficult for you in America to write music, for you are so far away from the centers of tradition.' I had to say, 'It must be very difficult for you in Europe to write music, for you are so close to the centers of tradition.'" He is now viewed by Europeans, and properly, as central to their tradition. America is moving on. We are giving up the totalizing dream and are becoming engaged in a newer, truer integration of art and life. Cage, as Boulez once said of Schoenberg, is dead.

Some of his work may live on. My hunch is that we will shed the lofty metaphysical Cage and incorporate the earlier dynamic and fleshly Cage—the Cage of the percussion pieces and the prepared piano—into the fringes of the repertory, insofar as their unusual media will allow. There has been a surge of interest in this music in recent years, partly, no doubt, because of the way it seems to forecast recent trends like "minimalism" and "fusion."

In any case, that music has all been documented in excellent recordings (most extensively by the Germans, naturally) and deserves its place in our cultural museum. My very favorite Cage piece, the *String Quartet in Four Parts* (1950), a thing of wondrous hockets and ecstatic stillness, composed right before chance took over, is in the Arditti set on Mode, which, together with Tan's piano recordings, is the best Cage to be had on records. (The hockets were even more beguiling, though, and the stillness yet more rapt, on the old New Music Quartet recording, issued by Columbia when the music was new.) Two historical items should be mentioned. The Smithsonian Institution has reissued the thirty-year-old Folkways album called *Indeterminacy*, with Cage inimitably droning through a series of marvelous one-minute anecdotes while his faithful accomplice David Tudor strums away at the random *Fontana Mix* in the background. And George Avakian is mooting the reissue of his recording of the landmark "Twenty-five-Year Retrospective Concert," held in New York's Town Hall on 15 May 1958 before an audience overwhelmingly composed of painters and gallery owners. Musicians then were not paying attention.

David Revill's biography is the first of its kind, and obviously it fills a need, even if it contributes little new information and concentrates (perhaps taking its likely audience of artists and dancers and philosophers—the traditional Cage audience—into account) on Cage's career and *mentalité*, steering pretty well clear of the music. Much of what it does contain can be gleaned from the horse's mouth in Richard Kostelanetz's indispensable mélange of interviews, *Conversing with Cage*. Revill arranges all this raw material in chronological order, and furnishes an almost complete list of works (about two hundred). His book is becomingly written, at times piquantly perceptive, and not entirely uncritical. (He does not hesitate to call Cage's late social philosophizing "fatuous.") An embarrassing number of names are misspelled, however, and the book is culpably unreliable on factual background, characterizing Satie's *Socrate*, for example, as a "programmatic orchestral piece" and calling Cowell's *Banshee* "the first known composition to use the sounds of the piano strings directly strummed and plucked" (it had at least two predecessors among Cowell's works).

Revill's book will be quickly superseded as fundamental research on Cage gains steam. Spadework by Michael Hicks and by Robert Stevenson gives a foretaste. The first scholarly book on the composer, by James Pritchett, has been accepted for publication by Cambridge University Press. [It was issued, as *The Music of John Cage*, later in 1993.] And more biographies are in the works, by Europeans and American alike, as well as a catalogue raisonné of sources and other impedimenta. Yes, our scary goy will get the full treatment. And why not? He was a master. Of the old school.

35

Sacred Entertainments

Ever since the cultural watershed of the 1960s, predictions of the imminent demise of classical music, especially in America, have been rife. Its audience, undermined by the precipitate decline in public music education and decimated by defections to pop (respectable for aspiring intellectuals from the moment rock became British), was assumed to be aging, indeed dying off. Whether as a symptom of this process or as one of its causes, media coverage for classical music steadily and drastically diminished over the 1970s and 1980s (coinciding with the rise of serious pop coverage), as did the number of radio stations that offered it.

In the 1970s, classical music accounted for 20 percent of record sales in Japan, its most avid market, 10 percent in Western Europe, and 5 percent in North America. As the medium of commercial recording switched in the mid-1980s from LP to CD, and the American market share for classical record sales stabilized at approximately 3 percent (about the same as jazz, increasingly regarded and described as "America's classical music"), its status was relegated to that of a niche product, serving a tiny, closed-off clientele whose needs could be met with reissues rather than costly new recordings of standard repertory. Major symphony orchestras, especially in the United States, found themselves without recording contracts, with serious consequences for the incomes of their personnel. Major labels began concentrating on "crossover" projects, in which the most popular classical performers collaborated with artists from other walks of musical life in an effort to achieve sales that might transcend the limits of the classical niche. The huge fees such artists commanded virtually squeezed others out of the recording

Originally published in *Cambridge Opera Journal* 15 (2003): 109–26. Copyright Cambridge University Press, reprinted with permission.

budget altogether. Classical music seemed irrevocably destined to become the culture industry's basket case.

The implications for composers seemed particularly grave, since this period of attrition had no offect on the numbers trained within the protected walls of the academy, which as always offered insulation, albeit temporary, from the vagaries of the market. The result was a vast overpopulation of composers, whose numbers swelled even as their outlets contracted. Their activity came ironically to resemble the sort of self-publication and self-promotion that was known in the declining Soviet Union (where it was a response to political rather than economic pressure) as samizdat. Their work met no measurable consumer demand and found little source of subsidy. Its main purpose became the securing of academic employment and promotion—another sort of niche—that enabled its creators to train the next generation of socially unsupported and unwanted composers, and so on in meaningless perpetuity.

In the late 1980s and 1990s, however, that pattern began unexpectedly to change, permitting the emergence of a composing elite—tiny, perhaps, but larger than ever before—whose work was suddenly in demand, sought out by traditional performance organizations for performance at major venues, and who could in some cases live comfortably off their commissions and performance royalties without seeking academic employment. New York's Metropolitan Opera, for example, which had not presented a single première since the 1960s, commissioned four operas during this period, of which three achieved production. First, in 1991, came *The Ghosts of Versailles,* an opera by John Corigliano based on *La Mère coupable* (The Guilty Mother), the one remaining member of Beaumarchais's Figaro trilogy that had not already been turned into an operatic classic. The next year, on Columbus Day, the Met presented *The Voyage* by Philip Glass, which commemorated the 500th anniversary of the great explorer's arrival in the New World. Finally, there was John Harbison's *The Great Gatsby,* first performed on New Year's Day, 2000, a period costume drama based on F. Scott Fitzgerald's jazz age novel.   The Harbison work had been jointly commissioned by the Met and the Chicago Lyric Opera, thus ensuring that it would have a life beyond its première production, and also giving the composer a chance to revise the opera on the basis of its reception, as was traditional in opera's heyday but discouraged in the later twentieth century both by economic conditions and by the ideology of modernism. The Met and the Chicago Lyric also issued a tandem commission to William Bolcom for an opera based on Arthur Miller's play *A View from the Bridge,* premièred in Chicago in 1999 and considerably revised for its New York production in 2002. Nor were these houses alone: the San Francisco Opera commissioned several works in the 1990s, including André Previn's *A Streetcar Named Desire,* after Tennessee Williams's play, and Jake Heggie's *Dead Man Walking,* based on the memoir of Death

Row prisoners by Sister Helen Prejean that had been already turned into a major Hollywood movie. Just how bankable a commodity the Met thought new opera might now become is indicated by the generous terms of its commissions—especially the one to Glass, who received $325,000. (Expenditures on the production approached $2 million.)

In part this seeming rebirth was a result of the changes wrought by "postmodernism" in the relative prestige of composing styles. Harbison had been trained as a serialist, and of course Glass was one of the founders, in the 1960s, of hard-core minimalism. Both had abandoned their earlier avant-garde positions and were now meeting in the vast moderate middle ground called "neoromanticism." And yet there had always been relatively "accessible" composers available for commissioning, including some specialists in vocal or theatrical genres like Ned Rorem or Hugo Weisgall, who had gone untapped by the major houses all during the 1970s and 1980s. It seemed that the new interest in opera had to do with new sources of money to support it. It was tied, that is, to the interests of new patrons.

The new interest in supporting classical composition in traditional "audience" genres affected the concert hall as well as the opera house. The most spectacular case, perhaps, was that of Corigliano's First Symphony (1989), first performed in 1990 by the Chicago Symphony Orchestra, and later, internationally, by almost one hundred others. Along with its lavish orchestration (including parts for virtuoso piano and cello soloists), its rhetorical intensity, and its at times poignant use of collage, the symphony's topicality contributed to its success. A memorial to victims of the AIDS epidemic, each of its four movements was dedicated to the memory of a deceased friend, and gave public expression to the composer's "feelings of loss, anger, and frustration," in alternation with "the bittersweet nostalgia of remembering."

So if the composer John Adams's "impression," voiced to an interviewer in November 2000, was a true one—namely, "that in terms of commissions there's never been a more bullish period in American history" than the 1990s—it is testimony to a new consensus among composers and their patrons that contemporary classical music can and should have the sort of topical relevance more usually found in popular culture, and that works relevant to the topical concerns of the contemporary cultural elite are the ones that will be (and should be) rewarded.[1]

.   .   .

Adams was in a good position to know, having been among the most conspicuous beneficiaries of this dispensation. One of the moments that defined its emergence, in fact, took place in 1990, when the San Francisco Opera rescinded a commission it had given to Hugo Weisgall for an opera on the "timeless" biblical story of Esther in favor of Adams's *The Death of Klinghoffer*, a topical opera based on the killing by Palestinian terrorists of an American

Jew on board the Italian cruise ship *Achille Lauro* in 1985. *Klinghoffer* was the second opera Adams had composed in collaboration with the poet Alice Goodman and the director Peter Sellars. The first, *Nixon in China* (1987), was the work that originally stimulated the new wave of operatic commissions. Largely on the strength of Sellars's reputation as an operatic enfant terrible (known for topical updatings of familiar operas such as a *Don Giovanni* set in the New York slums and a *Marriage of Figaro* set in a gaudy luxury apartment house often assumed to be Trump Tower), and on the assumption that it would satirize one of America's most controversial political figures, the opera had been jointly commissioned by four houses: the Houston Grand Opera, the Brooklyn Academy of Music, the John F. Kennedy Center for the Performing Arts in Washington, D.C., and the Netherlands Opera (or rather, by their corporate sponsors). Its four premières took place between November 1987 and June 1988.

The work confounded expectations by being cast not as a farce but as a heroic opera that turned the title character, as well as the Chinese leaders Mao Zedong and Zhou Enlai, into mythical representatives of their countries—naively idealistic young America and ancient, visionary China. Adams's music, like that of Glass's *Voyage*, was set in what could be called a "postminimalist" style, in which the freely grouped and regrouped rapid pulses and arpeggios of minimalism, and interesting textures obtained by pitting different pulse patterns in counterpoint, were reconciled with a fairly conventional harmonic idiom, naturalistic vocal declamation, a neat number-opera format replete with entertaining choral and dance sequences, and frequent references to various styles of popular music. Adams gave his fairly standard orchestra a late-twentieth-century, somewhat Steve-Reichian sonic edge by replacing the bassoons with a quartet of saxophones, and by adding a pair of pianos and a keyboard sampler to the percussion section.

Nixon in China thus differed from most twentieth-century operas by reinvoking music's power of enchantment, surrounding figures from recent history with a "transcendent" aura that turned them into detemporalized, godlike figures. In particular, this characteristic set Adams's opera off from the topical operas, or *Zeitopern*, of the 1920s and 1930s, like Paul Hindemith's cynical *Neues vom Tage* or Ernst Krenek's jazzy *Jonny spielt auf*. Where in the disillusioned aftermath of World War I audiences enjoyed an operatic genre that debunked the myth of timeless art, in the super-affluent, triumphant post–cold war decade audiences sought through art the monumentalization of their own historical experience.

The operatic mythologizing of Richard M. Nixon's signal diplomatic coup displeased a minority who objected to the way it helped turn memory away from the domestic scandal that ended his presidency. It disturbed others for the callow way it cast the bloody Chinese Communist dictatorship, fresh from the excesses of the Cultural Revolution, in an uncritical, heroic light. But the critical consensus that formed over the remaining years of the twentieth century seemed to favor the esthetic eclipse of "mere" history or politics. The critic Alex Ross, writing in the *New Yorker,* went so far as to predict that "a century from now audiences will still be fascinated by this opera, and that some listeners will have to double-check the plot summary in order to remember who Richard Nixon was." Its value, like that of all great art, Ross implied, was independent of its relationship to external reality, and that value was its capacity to create spiritual archetypes.

And yet that very evaluation, that very assignment of values, was the product of an external reality. At a time of gross materialism and commercialism widely compared in America to the "Gilded Age" at the end of the previous century, classical music (Wagner then; Adams now) was being marketed for its powers of "uplift" to a guiltily affluent audience ("robber barons" then; "yuppies" now) eager to depict itself as humane. Peter Sellars, the mastermind behind both Adams-Goodman operas, made the claim quite forthrightly. "I think in this age of television and Hollywood film, if classical music is going to stick around, there'd better be a very good reason," he told an interviewer. Then, shifting bizarrely but characteristically into the language of commerce, he added, "We have to offer something that is not available otherwise. I think it is spiritual content, which is what's missing from the commercial culture that surrounds us."

This time, the subject under discussion was not an opera but a new collaboration by Sellars and Adams, and a more overtly religiose one: a topically slanted nativity oratorio called *El Niño,* commissioned by another international consortium—Théâtre du Châtelet (Paris), the San Francisco Symphony, Lincoln Center for the Performing Arts (New York), the Barbican Centre (London), and the British Broadcasting Corporation—and performed according to the terms of the commission in Paris, San Francisco, Berlin, New York, and London between December 2000 and December 2001. *El Niño* was one of a number of works of flamboyant "spiritual content" commissioned and performed under prestigious auspices to solemnize the new millennium. Another, Philip Glass's Fifth Symphony, was (like several of Mahler's symphonies, or the finale of Beethoven's Ninth) an oratorio in all but name, scored for five vocal soloists, mixed chorus, children's choir, and orchestra. Its subtitle, "Requiem, Bardo, Nirmanakaya," pits the Latin title of the service for the dead (representing the world's past) against the Tibetan word for "in between" (as in the Tibetan Book of the Dead—*Bardo Thodol*—which describes the soul's journey after death) and the Sanskrit Mahayana Buddhist term for rebirth or bodily transformation (representing mankind's hoped-for future). The text draws on "a broad spectrum of many of the world's great 'wisdom' traditions," as the composer put it in a program note, translated from Greek, Hebrew, Arabic, Persian, Sanskrit, Bengali, Chinese, Japanese, Tibetan, Hawaiian, Zuñi, Mayan, Bantu, and Bulu scriptures. The symphony was commissioned by the ASCII Corporation,, a computer software company, for performance at the Salzburger Festspiele, Europe's most exclusive summer music festival.

Another example was the cycle of four Passions—Matthew, Mark, Luke, and John—that the German choral conductor Helmut Rilling, with the support of the city of Stuttgart and the publisher Hänssler Musikverlag, commissioned from a quartet of composers, one German (Wolfgang Rihm, who did Luke) and three with conspicuously "multicultural" backgrounds, for première performances in Rilling's home city, to be followed by world tours. Mark went to Osvaldo Golijov, an Argentinian-born Jew residing in the United States, who assembled a lavish collage of Latin American, Afro-Cuban, and Jewish cantorial idioms and stole the show. Matthew was assigned to Tan Dun, a Chinese composer trained at the Beijing Conservatory and Columbia University, who had demonstrated his suitability for the Passions project with a work titled *Symphony 1997 (Heaven Earth Mankind)* for orchestra, children's chorus, an ensemble of Chinese temple bells, and a solo cello part written for Yo-Yo Ma, the Paris-born American cellist of Chinese descent who had been making a specialty of "crossover" undertakings involving repertoires as diverse as jazz, Appalachian folklore, and the classical music of Central Asia. John was assigned to Sofia Gubaidulina, a post-Soviet composer of actual Central Asian ("Tatar," or Mongolian) descent but living in Germany, whose predilection for religious subject matter had been considered a mark of political dissidence in the waning years of Soviet authority. The very fact that two of the composers chosen for the Passion project were not Christian—Golijov, for one, cheerfully admitting that it was only after receiving the commission that he looked into the New Testament for the first time—suggests that the impulse behind it was something other than religious in the customary or doctrinal sense of the word.

The Adams-Sellars oratorio was also of distinctly "multicultural" content. Its texts were drawn from the New Testament, the Apocrypha, the Wakefield Mystery Plays, and a Latin hymn by the now-ubiquitous Hildegard von Bingen, supplemented by modern poems by several Latin Americans, including the seventeenth-century Sister Juana Inés de la Cruz, the nineteenth-century Rubén Darío, the twentieth-century Gabriela Mistral, and, most prominently, Rosario Castellanos, who combined an artistic career with a diplomatic one, serving at the time of her death in 1974 as the Mexican ambassador to Israel. One of the oratorio's most striking moments was the juxtaposition, near the end, of the terse biblical account of the Slaughter of the Innocents (Herod's massacre of all the children in Bethlehem to ensure that the infant Jesus would not survive) with "Memorial de Tlatelolco" (Memorandum on Tlatelolco), a long poem by Castellanos sung by the soprano soloist with choral support, that furiously protests the violent police repression of a student demonstration that took place on 2 October 1968 at

Tlatelolco Square in Mexico City, which more than four hundred years earlier had been the site of the last bloody confrontation between the Aztecs and the Spanish conquistadors led by Hernando Cortés.

The poem bears witness to a crime that went unreported at the time by the government-controlled Mexican press. Its inclusion in the oratorio text draws explicit parallels between religious observance, acts of political conscience or resistance, and the role of artists as keepers of public memory and conscience. (Golijov, too, made much of the fact that his *St. Mark Passion* celebrated the grassroots efforts of Latin American "people's priests" rather than the "out of touch" doctrines of the hierarchical Catholic Church.) Adams's setting of Castellanos's poem reaches, within the limits of the composer's openly declared commitment to an ingratiating idiom, a pitch of intensity reminiscent of expressionism in its use of wide intervals to distort the lyric line.

His oratorio's final number balances the vehemence of the "Memorial de Tlatelolco" by juxtaposing an Apocryphal account of the Infant Jesus's first miracle, in which he commanded a palm tree to bend down so that his mother could gather its dates, with a consoling poem by Castellanos that pays respects to an Israeli palm tree for inspiring a moment of peaceful reflection amid the turbulence of the contemporary Middle East. Here Adams underscores the message of solace and chastened optimism by, as it were, resurrecting the Innocents in a children's chorus that gets to sing the oratorio's last word—"Poesía" (Poetry)—accompanied by a pair of Spanish guitars. *El Niño* provides the best evidence yet that at the beginning of the third millennium spiritual or sacred entertainments have become the most marketable and profitable genre the literate (or "art") tradition of music can boast at a time when its end, for reasons both economic and technological, has become foreseeable.

·   ·   ·

The sacred as marketable, as profitable: it seems a paradoxical notion, even a blasphemous one, but there are plenty of precedents. Nearly three hundred years ago, Handel's oratorios made similarly opportunistic—and similarly successful—use of sacred subject matter to exploit the market. And just as we now resolve the paradox in Handel's case by reading through the sacred metaphor to what most scholars take to be the Handelian oratorio's "real" (i.e., nationalistic) appeal, it may not be too early to attempt a similar diagnosis of the multicultural religiosity that found such widespread musical expression at the end of the twentieth century.

Historians agree that Handel's oratorios achieved their amazing success not only by dint of their musical caliber but also by flattering their elite English audience—a mixture of nobility and high bourgeoisie (comprising "the first Quality of the Nation," according to a review of *Israel in Egypt* on its 1739 première)—with comparisons to the biblical Hebrews, God's chosen people.[2] The audience that patronizes the work of the successful sliver at the top of today's seething heap of struggling classical composers is a new social elite, the one recently identified by the social critic David Brooks in an amusing but penetrating analysis published in 2000 under the title *Bobos in Paradise.*

Brooks's Bobos, short for "bourgeois bohemians," are the highly educated nouveaux riches of the Information Age, who live comfortably and fashionably but retain a sentimental attachment to the "sixties" concerns of their youth, and who are most effectively flattered by art that reflects their ethical self-image. "The people who thrive in this period are the ones who can turn ideas and emotions into products," Brooks writes. And that, among other things, is what composers do. The cherished Bobo self-image is one of personal authenticity, constructed not in terms of a wholly original worldview but in terms of eclecticism—an individual selection from among the unlimited choices on the global cultural and spiritual menu. The greatest challenge the new establishment faces, according to Brooks, is "how to navigate the shoals between their affluence and their self-respect; how to reconcile their success with their spirituality, their élite status with their egalitarian ideals."[3] Their task, in constructing their identity, is to reconcile values that had been traditionally at odds: bourgeois values of ambition, social stability, and material comfort, on the one hand, and, on the other, bohemian values that identified with the victims of the bourgeois order: the poor, the criminal, the ethnic and racial outcast. The essential dilemma is that of reconciling the need for spirituality with the even more pressing need for personal autonomy and unlimited choice, since "real" religion imposes obligations and demands sacrifices.

It is not too difficult to see how the spiritualized classical music of the turn-of-millennium (prefigured in the 1960s and 1970s by the "Kaddish" Symphony and *Mass* by Leonard Bernstein, the original Bobo) has catered to these needs and predicaments. Audiences looking for purifying experiences are easily beguiled by symbols of innocence, hence the ubiquitous children's choirs in the works described above. Not that that was anything new: children's voices have long been exploited as an insurance policy by traders in romantic nostalgia. Mahler's Second, Third, and Fourth Symphonies all feature real or metaphorical child performers, as did the work of Soviet composers at times of particularly intense political pressure. The success of "Holy Minimalists" like Arvo Pärt, Henryk Górecki, and John Tavener in the 1980s was more specifically related to the coming Bobo phenomenon. It already bespoke the desire for a way to return "esthetically" or "appreciatively" to a world of "spiritual wholeness" without assuming the burdens of an actual religious commitment.

The added attraction of multiculturalism—eclecticism writ large—in the works of the 1990s completes the parallel with the Bobo mentality, which places the highest premium on "personal" pastiche. A Princeton University study of contemporary religious practices, cited by Brooks, turned up an extreme but characteristic example: a twenty-six-year-old disabilities counselor, the daughter of a Methodist minister, who described herself to her interviewer as a "Methodist Taoist Native American Quaker Russian Orthodox Buddhist Jew."[4] Philip Glass's Fifth Symphony was made for her, indeed of her.

The Adams-Sellars *El Niño* tapped into another time-honored trope of innocent authenticity, especially as it was performed during its initial run, with dancers interpreting the content of the words alongside the singers, and with a simultaneous film by Sellars adding yet another level of commentary. The film paralleled the unfolding story of the Nativity with footage showing the unaffected lives of anonymous members of Los Angeles's Hispanic community: an attractive Chicano couple stood in for Joseph and Mary, their baby for Jesus, some rookie cops for the shepherds, some local fortune tellers for the Magi, and so on. Audience members and critics alike exclaimed on the beauty of the film, of the nameless actors, and of their uncomplicated but fulfilling emotional lives.[5]

One of the most scathing passages in Brooks's study is devoted to precisely this sort of updating of hoary neoprimitivist ideas. The immediate subject is travel:

> The Bobo, as always, is looking for stillness, for a place where people set down roots and repeat the simple rituals. In other words, Bobo travelers are generally looking to get away from their affluent, ascending selves into a spiritually superior world, a world that hasn't been influenced much by the global meritocracy. . . . Therefore, Bobos are suckers for darkly garbed peasants, aged farmers, hardy fishermen, remote craftsmen, weather-beaten pensioners, heavyset regional cooks—anybody who is likely to have never possessed or heard of frequent flier miles. So the Bobos flock to or read about the various folk locales where such "simple" people live in abundance—the hills of Provence, Tuscany, Greece, or the hamlets of the Andes or Nepal. These are places where the natives don't have credit card debts and relatively few people wear Michael Jordan T-shirts. Lives therefore seem connected to ancient patterns and age-old wisdom. Next to us, these natives seem serene. They are poorer people whose lives seem richer than our own.[6]

But as Adams and Sellars showed, you don't have to travel so far to ogle "indigenous peoples" or "noble savages." Any urban ghetto can supply them in quantity. Nor is it clear that displaying an estheticized, romanticized fantasy image of the poor for the edification or titillation of the sinful affluent really furthers egalitarian ideals. Will imagining the poor as leading lives richer than one's own inspire social action on their behalf? Will it inspire a true reconciliation between material comfort and social conscience? Or will it allow the comfortable to congratulate themselves on their benevolence and silence the nagging voice within?

Is the new spirituality, then, just another screen behind which high art engages in its traditional business of reinforcing social division by creating elite occasions? The old questions that bedeviled modernism have not gone away with the advent of postmodernity—which is yet another reason, perhaps, to doubt whether postmodernism is anything more than the latest modernist phase. Or are such moralizing concerns of dubious benefit to art or to artists, whose task of creating beauty is a constant imperative, transcending the politics (or the "political correctness") of the moment? The debate goes on.

.   .   .

A new wrinkle, or a new counterpoint, was added to the implicit debate in September 2002 with the American première—nineteen years after its first European performances, and a round decade since the composer's death—of Olivier Messiaen's only opera, *Saint François d'Assise.* It took place—inevitably?—in San Francisco, not only the saint's namesake city (a fact much touted in the attendant publicity, along with the fact that the score weighed twenty-five pounds) but also the city that has figured most prominently, with four mentions, in the discussion so far. The San Francisco Bay area—encompassing Silicon Valley, Marin County, Berkeley, and so on—is surely the Bobo capital of the world. *Saint François* was a hot ticket despite sky-high prices, and it was greeted by those who remained to the end with an ovation.

But unlike *El Niño,* or The Passion According to Golijov, this was no panderfest. At both performances I attended, including the first one, far from everyone made it to the end. At a Berkeley symposium cosponsored by the San Francisco Opera, the conductor, Donald Runnicles, grumbled like a good modernist at the audience's disrespect for the great composer, but disrespect had nothing to do with it. Messiaen's opera, like the Bach Passions, is the real spiritual article. Its religion is rigorously doctrinal: paralleling Bach's orthodox Lutheranism (which can be disquieting, especially to Jews, if properly reflected on), it offers pure Catholicism without the slightest multicultural palliative, a model of spirituality based not on consoling self-congratulation but on suffering. And at four hours' running time (over five with its two intermissions) it is demanding to the point of exhaustion, as an opera celebrating asceticism perhaps ought to be.

In eight static scenes, it portrays the stages of the saint's spiritual ascent. In the first, he counsels a wavering brother friar that perfect joy can be attained only by accepting the suffering of Christ as one's own. In the second, he praises God's creation and asks to be allowed to overcome his aversion to lepers, the one barrier to his attainment of universal brotherly love. In the third, egged on by a guardian angel, he cures the wished-for leper with his kiss. In the fourth, the angel, respectfully waiting for Francis to finish his prayers before revealing himself, exposes the hypocrisy of the abbot in charge of the monastery where Francis is secluded. In the fifth, the angel grants Francis a foretaste, through music, of heavenly bliss. In the sixth, Francis preaches his famous sermon to the birds. In the seventh, he solicits and receives Christ's stigmata. In the last, he dies and, ministered to by the angel and the leper, is reborn to new life.

Most people who approach this operatic leviathan via recordings find it an oppressive bore. In the house it was numinous, thanks in part to Hans Dieter Schaal's marvelously adaptable and multiply symbolic unit set, and the striking costume Andrea Schmidt-Futterer came up with for the Angel, the opera's one supernatural character: an electric-blue body suit (sprouting a single, quasi-symbolic wing) that contrasted tellingly with the drab apparel of the human characters. Laura Aikin, making her local debut as the Angel (referred to throughout as "he," but cast for a lyric soprano), sang with unforgettable radiance. The rest of the cast—particularly Willard White, who finished the horrendously demanding title role in undimmed vocal shape, and Chris Merritt in the shrieky part of the Leper—acquitted themselves with missionary zeal and a sense of appropriately steadfast devotion. Runnicles and the orchestra made the twenty-five-pound score sound buoyant. But mainly, coming together with the rest of the audience in a special place to experience it enhanced the sense of religious communion on which the opera depends, and which cannot be achieved in everyday surroundings. Now dazzled, now sedated, we received a new reminder of what serious music can accomplish when it takes its task (and its audience) seriously.

Like most works by Messiaen, *Saint François* perpetually skirts the fringe of kitsch, and one watches the composer, working to his own libretto, negotiate these spiritually mandated shoals with the fascination that a netless tightrope walker commands. In the fifth scene, which many listeners found the most affecting, he challenges himself to compose the "music of the invisible," the divine music of the spheres that, according to one of the legends on which the libretto draws, the Angel bowed for St. Francis on a viol. In Nicolas Brieger's production, the Angel plucks the giant strings of a Wagnerian world-harp. Messiaen's music consists of a wayward atonal melody produced by a trio of ondes martenot—an ancient electronic instrument that was invented seventy-five years ago, and that Messiaen's works have singlehandedly maintained in a sort of Nosferatu half-life—directing their unearthly sounds to speakers placed all around the hall, while a C major triad rustles faintly in the orchestra. After hearing it and being set atingle by its uncanny otherness, one could almost agree with St. Francis that if it had gone on a moment longer, "because of its unbearable sweetness my soul might have left my body."

But imagine the risk! The merest hint at this point of friendly banality, the "new spirituality's" stock-in-trade, would have pulled the whole opera down into a vortex of bathos. Messiaen, supremely sophisticated in technique yet naively direct in expression as only a believer could be, works throughout the opera—indeed worked throughout his career—at the ticklish borderline of cliché. But *Saint François* offers kitsch no lusty Bobo's embrace. For Messiaen, platitudes were a hazard to be borne, not a mine to be exploited. The shallow obviousness of his libretto; the doggedly simple, maniacally static and didactic way he harps on a small fund of musically unprepossessing themes (about half of them included as examples within a short program-book essay); his seeming ignorance—or perhaps his studied neglect—of any semblance of ordinary stagecraft; the virtual banishment from the texture of counterpoint and thematic development (the usual guarantors of "purely musical" interest), all bring to mind Pascal's dictum that the virtue of adherence to religious discipline is that it *vous fera croire et vous abêtira* (will make you believe, and make you stupid). But the fact that, despite its many near approaches to it, Messiaen's opera manages after all to avoid kitsch while retaining its naïveté is perhaps its most impressive feat—and at the present cultural moment, dominated by a profusion of extremely artful spiritual kitsch, an enormously provocative one.

The Austrian novelist Hermann Broch memorably defined kitsch as the artistically endorsed demand that the stars, "and everything else that is eternal," come down to earth for the sake of human temporal gratification.[7] Broch had sexual gratification first in mind, but placing the politics of the moment *sub specie aeternitatis,* especially the voyeuristic multicultural politics of Bobo art, seems no less flagrant an example of Brochian kitsch. Messiaen did not always escape the trap Broch identified. His grandiose, ten-movement *Turangalîla-symphonie,* commissioned by Serge Koussevitzky and first performed in Boston under Leonard Bernstein in 1949, is one of the great monuments of sacroporn in its attempt to marry Christian mysticism to the Kama Sutra with side-by-side movements bearing titles like "Joie du sang des étoiles" and "Jardin du sommeil d'amour."

The Indian element was musically represented by palindromic (or, as Messiaen put it, "nonretrogradable") rhythms, often in beat patterns that are organized around prime numbers, hence quite foreign to the uncomplicated duple or triple meters of traditional European art music. It was not multiculturalism or "ordinary" orientalism that sent Messiaen in search of the exotic music of the East—he first encountered an Indian prime-number pattern (seventeen beats) in the course of a desultory browse through a standard French reference source, Lavignac's *Encyclopédie de la musique et Dictionnaire du Conservatoire*—but rather the need for a musical representation of otherness that could stand in for the utter otherness of the divine. The same quest led to his lifelong fascination with the superhuman sonority of the ondes martenot: Messiaen began writing for it in 1937, when he was twenty-nine, and stayed with it to the end of his life in 1992, when he was eighty-three. In *Turangalîla,* it provided the climactic voice of ecstasy, alternately moaning low and belting out diatonic love songs from the *au-delà,* accompanied by the "added-sixth" harmonies of a celestial piano bar.

But if *Turangalîla* was Messiaen's eternally kiddable *chef d' oeuvre* of ingenuous excess, his quest for the uncanny otherness of the eternal (precisely the quality that distinguishes Catholic or Orthodox theology from Protestant) was earnest, lifelong, and crowned with some amazing successes, of which *Saint François* may have been the ultimate, and not just in terms of size. There is something genuinely scary about Messiaen at full strength. The leitmotif that heralds the Angel in *Saint François,* for example, is a bloodcurdling electronic screech, and when the Angel knocks lightly on the monastery door, all hell breaks loose in the orchestra. The same hellish—er, heavenly— pounding, redolent of Stravinsky's *Rite of Spring* but reaching a far more lacerating pitch of dissonance, returns in the penultimate scene to symbolize the imprinting of the stigmata on St, Francis's flesh. You feel his pain, which is the pain of the crucified Lamb of God. The light that receives the saint's soul at the end of the opera burns mortal eyes with its wattage; you've got to look away. No cute children's choirs here. No sexy Latin rhythm. Messiaen's spirituality was anything but warm and fuzzy, his style often the opposite of ingratiating, and that is what finally saves his work from kitsch. Of all the music of the twentieth century, his was the most genuinely (and essentially) theological, with all that the word implies in opposition to the debased secular humanism that drives John Adams's or Osvaldo Golijov's socially regressive visions of the commercial sublime.

.   .   .

"Let us have a *true* music," Messiaen wrote, italicizing the word himself; "that is to say, spiritual, a music which may be an act of faith; a music which may touch upon all subjects without ceasing to touch upon God; an original music, in short, whose language may open a few doors, take down some as yet distant stars."[8] For all their religious euphoria, these words come from the preface to Messiaen's *Technique de mon langage musical* (Technique of My Musical Language, 1944), one of the most systematic expositions any composer has ever given to the mechanisms of his art. And past the preface, the treatise is true to its title. It resolutely ignores all meaning and treats "language" alone—or as Messiaen put it, "technique and not sentiment," abstracted and broken down in extraordinarily schoolmasterly fashion into its rhythmic, melodic, and harmonic dimensions.[9] Any seeming paradox or contradiction is dispelled as soon as one considers the nature of the truth that Messiaen designed his art to convey. It is neither a personal credo nor an occult conceit but rather (as he put it) "the theological truths of the Catholic faith," as dog-matically set forth in scripture.[10]

Messiaen was an extreme rarity among leading twentieth-century com-posers (indeed, among composers since the advent of romanticism) in being a working church musician. For more than forty years, beginning in 1930, he served as regular Sunday organist at the Église de la Sainte-Trinité, one of the largest churches in Paris. Messiaen wrote many of his most important works for La Trinité's huge Cavaillé-Coll organ, and was without question the most important organist-composer of the twentieth century, as César Franck, who also served as organist for many years at a Parisian church, and who also wrote a highly spiritualized brand of modern music, had been (with Bruck-ner) in the nineteenth. As a further parallel, both Messiaen and Franck were famous and much sought-after teachers of composition, whose pupils and disciples formed an elite group of advanced composers who universalized their master's teaching and made it an important "mainstream" influence.

But Franck, whose career ended shortly before the great wave of mod-ernism broke, was never drawn to such radically novel means as Messiaen proposed, nor did he ever systematize his practices so thoroughly into a teachable method. It was the latter that made Messiaen such a potent force in the technique of contemporary music even among those who held his es-thetic principles at arm's length. He managed to transform theological dogma into musical dogma, and that is why Messiaen always objected to being called a mystic. Rather than a mystic he was a scholastic, in the me-dieval sense of the term. Like St. Thomas Aquinas, he sought to embody the mysteries of faith in a rational and transmissible discourse. No wonder his self-analysis was so "schoolmasterly," and so influential. What were means for him easily became ends for many.

Messiaen's treatise very rigorously analyzes his innovative techniques into their rhythmic and melodic/harmonic domains; and the remarkable thing about it is how much the pitch and durational aspects of his novel "language" had in common. The chief innovation with respect to pitch was the use of what Messiaen called "modes of limited transposition," and the chief dura-tional innovation was the preference we have already observed for what he called "nonretrogradable rhythms." Both of these impressively named de-vices depend on a single quality: invariance achieved by means of symmetry. Scales that reproduce themselves on transposition and rhythms that repro-duce themselves in reverse are both devices that arrest the sort of progres-sion on which musical "development" (i.e., the sonorous illusion of directed motion) depends. Nonprogressive structures are necessarry to any music that wants to represent or symbolize the atemporal (i.e., the eternal) within an inexorably temporal medium.

Only the name that Messiaen gave his modes of limited transposition was new. The concept had been familiar as such for almost a century, ever since

Franz Liszt had made his first systematic experiments with symmetrical cycles of major and minor thirds, and scales—ascending or descending by whole steps, or by alternating whole steps and half steps—derived from them. Messiaen had in good scholastic fashion carried the process of systematization, begun by Liszt and already developed to a single-minded peak by Scriabin (another composer interested, like Messiaen, in eschatological revelation), to the point of theoretical exhaustion. Where Liszt and Scriabin had employed two modes of limited transposition, Messiaen increased their number to eight—the mathematical limit.

Messiaen used his principle of nonretrogradable rhythm to organize long spans in which not only the number of beats per measure but also the length of the beats themselves were unpredictably variable, hence uncanny. The variable lengths come about by the interpolation, in every other bar, of an "added value" that arbitrarily lengthens one of the musical pulses that undergirds the rhythmic surface. The rhythms so arbitrarily dislocated are then patterned by working outward from a midpoint. Messiaen called the midpoint the "free value" or the "central common value." Functionally speaking, of course, it was an axis of symmetry.

Putting the two axes of symmetry together, the harmonic axis represented by the modes of limited transposition and the temporal axis represented by the nonretrogradable rhythms, allowed the coordination of the vertical (spatial) and horizontal (temporal) dimensions in dual representation of invariance = constancy = immutability = eternity. That is the time-transcending truth that religion reveals through music, its handmaiden, in Messiaen's esthetic universe. And that, Messiaen explicitly informs the reader, was the source of his mysterious hold on the listener. "Let us think now of the hearer of our modal and rhythmic music," he writes.

> He will not have time at the concert to inspect the nontranspositions and the nonretrogradations, and, at that moment, these questions will not interest him further; to be charmed will he his only desire. And that is precisely what will happen; in spite of himself he will submit to the strange charm of impossibilities: a certain effect of tonal ubiquity, in the nontransposition, a certain unity of movement (where beginning and end are confused because identical) in the nonretogradation, all things which will lead him progressively to that sort of theological rainbow which the musical language, of which we seek edification and theory, attempts to be.[11]

In language that almost seems borrowed from the Russian mystical symbolists who inspired Scriabin, but that Messiaen would no doubt have ascribed to St. Francis himself, he wrote that one of his primary aims in composing as he did is "l'atrophie du moi"—the atrophy, or wasting away, of the "I," the petty self. It will not be difficult to discover in his musical methods (to quote the English composer Wilfrid Mellers, one of Messiaen's most sympathetic critics) the means toward the "complete reversal of the will-domination of post-Renaissance Europe." One aspect of this reversal was simply and literally the revival of pre-Renaissance practices, contemporaneous with the medieval saints, long since considered obsolete by musicians caught up in the flux of history.

Many of the rhythmic techniques Messiaen described in his self-analyzing treatise of 1944—canons by augmentation, by diminution, by "the addition of the dot"—were common features of the so-called Ars Nova of the fourteenth and fifteenth centuries, as was the idea of organizing musical structures around what Messiaen called "rhythmic pedals," durational plans that could be mentally conceptualized but that could not be followed perceptually (that is, sensorily) during performance. Messiaen, who claimed to have been ignorant of it at the time, had in effect revived the concept of the "isorhythmic motet," and for the same purpose the original medieval practice had served: to represent (and in some small measure make available to human cognition) the divine eternal harmony of the cosmos, a harmony that expressed itself precisely in the coordinated movement of heavenly bodies in seemingly independent orbits.

Rhythmic pedals (*talea* in Latin; *tala* in Sanskrit) were the chief medieval means for representing cosmic harmony. And at the same time they provided a genuine meeting point between time-honored European (in fact, French) and Indian musical practices. But Messiaen also revived the other aspect of medieval isorhythm, namely, the abstractly conceived melodic ostinato or *color*—hidden sequences of pitches that are repeated at the bedrock of the texture. But they are not really hidden; they are merely too lengthy—that is, too great—for immediate detection. Like the truths of astronomy and many other scientific truths (as well, needless to say, as religious truths), the presence of a *color* is the sort of fact that reflective intellect reveals sooner than the senses. Putting such a thing into an artwork is an implicit warning against assuming that true knowledge can be gained empirically. The highest truths, Messiaen's music implies, are revealed truths. Theology was truth. Anything beyond that, Messiaen implied along with countless theologians, was mere human history.

.   .   .

And yet while the truths may be transcendent, the means of representation (the work, after all, of mortals) are inevitably historical, the product of the fleeting moment. Messiaen's music does not sound like a medieval motet. His ear, and the ears he addressed, had been otherwise conditioned. His "musical language" confronted and accommodated the musical styles of its time in an openly omnivorous and opportunistic spirit, even as it sought to extend them in the spirit of modernism. And that is why his work has been so useful as a model to many composers who not only failed to share his religious commitments, but were hopelessly caught up in "patent-office modernism," something Messiaen outwardly decried as the rat race of historicism, and yet something in which he was willy-nilly a participant, and a very successful one at that.

The high point of his modernist prestige came at the century's midpoint, when he was invited to lecture at the Darmstadt *Ferienkurse,* established in 1946 (by a German critic named Wolfgang Steinecke, but with the financial backing of the American army of occupation) to reacquaint the musicians of formerly fascist Europe with the work of the formerly suppressed avant-garde. A short piano piece called *Mode de valeurs et d'intensités* (translatable as "abstractly ordered durations and dynamics"), which Messiaen had composed in 1949 to see how far he could take the arcanely "scholastic" organizing principles of his technical treatise, was seized upon by Pierre Boulez (his pupil since 1942) and Karlheinz Stockhausen (who became his pupil as a result of it) as the harbinger of the impersonally scientific, "totally organized" music, based on a vast extension of Schoenbergian serial principles, that they regarded as the only viable musical language for a devastated Europe's "zero hour." They exalted Messiaen as the patriarch of the avant-garde.

But Messiaen, never a serialist, had no use for this secular distinction. However abstracted, he regarded his technique as being, *au fond,* a representational one, even if it represented things that could only be speculatively known. Indeed, shortly after composing *Mode de valeurs,* Messiaen made a sudden turn away from abstraction and toward naturalism of a sort, when he became obsessed with birdsong, drawn literally from life as far as the transcriber's acuity of ear (and the tuning of existing instruments) allowed, as the new foundation of his art.

This was no about-face. Not only theological tradition, but many of the world's ancient folk traditions as well, regarded birds as messengers from the *au-delà.* Divine inspiration had long been rendered in Christian iconography by showing the applicable prophet or saint (including St. Gregory the Great, legendarily the composer of the Catholic Church chant that bears his name) receiving it directly from the Holy Ghost in the form of a dove—and this belief survives incognito in our expression "a little bird told me." Schumann's prophet-bird, Wagner's forest-bird, Stravinsky's Firebird (and his teacher Rimsky-Korsakov's avian messengers in *The Tale of Invisible City of Kitezh*) sustained in romantic musical tradition the pagan (or Hindu) counterparts, possibly the paleo-Indo-European prototypes, of the Christian dove. Again, Messiaen took an existing mode of representation and scholastically systematized it, making bird-listening expeditions, beginning in 1952, throughout France, and later wherever his travels took him—including an express trip to New Caledonia in the South Pacific to transcribe in situ the especially exotic song of the rare gerygone that became one of the Angel's uncanny calling cards in *Saint François.*

The first work of Messiaen's to incorporate actual birdsong was *Le Merle noir* (1951) for flute and piano. The next was *Réveil des oiseaux*, a huge composition for piano and orchestra, first performed in Donaueschingen on 11 October 1953. This première was perhaps the greatest fiasco of Messiaen's career. Instead of pursuing the increasingly strict and arcane methods of *Mode de valeurs*, he was offering an audience of committed avant-gardists an obviously representational, and (what was worse) obviously joyous and "affirmative" tone poem that maintained demonstrative ties to all kinds of pre-zero-hour traditions. Shaken by the bad reviews, his publisher threatened unilaterally to rescind its mutual exclusivity agreement with the composer (proving, among other things, that the avant-garde is just as much a market category, and "disinterested" modernism just as marketable a commodity, as any other).

Messiaen, as if to demonstrate that his kingdom was not of this world, continued undaunted to write birdsong pieces, and Boulez, to his credit, used his own prestige to rescue that of his teacher, commissioning a chamber counterpart to *Réveil des oiseaux* called *Oiseaux exotiques* for performance at his own concert series, La Domaine musicale, in 1956. The birdsong line reached its pinnacle in the monumental cycle of piano pieces known, straightforwardly enough, as *Catalogue d'oiseaux* (1959). But not even this two-hour total immersion could work the songs of birds out of Messiaen's system. Once something had found a place in his musical theology, nothing could dislodge it. Everything that Messiaen described in his treatise of 1944 remained current in his style to the end; the birds merely joined the existing style and took up permanent residence within it.

This in its way was another expression of timeless truth. Messiaen's stylistic consistency, despite its heterogeneous sources, was the very opposite of eclectic. Rather, his steadfast adherence to his path despite all adversity (to put it in terms of one of the large themes in *Saint François*) is another expression of dogmatic faith. In a young people's book on comparative religion I recall riffling as a teenager, representatives of various denominations responded to a questionnaire that asked, among other things, whether they considered theirs to be the only true faith. Everyone waffled but the Catholic, who answered (as best I can reconstruct it), "Of course; if we thought someone else possessed the true faith, we'd follow him." That was Messiaen.

.   .   .

Messiaen's rigorously religious outlook in a relentlessly secular world made him an eccentric figure and a paradoxical one. Although he was certainly a towering figure in the history of twentieth-century music, he was not of it. In a peculiar way the twentieth century did not exist for him. When we look back on it we can hardly see it except in terms of gulags, holocausts, actual and threatened mass destruction, and spiritual emptiness, now capitally exemplified by what passes for spirituality in art. Messiaen, whose life spanned practically the entire century, got from one end of it to the other without expressing anything but joy: a joy that could appear monumentally excessive—and monumentally unobservant—to anyone not attuned to the composer's beatific disposition. "I have had the good fortune to be a Catholic," Messiaen wrote, adding, "I was born a believer." But that seeming unobservance, that eternally cloudless sky, could look, to one less fortunately born, like indifference, even an insult, to human suffering.

Those who hold Messiaen's Catholic affirmations against him can point to his early exploitation by Marshal Pétain's collaborationist regime, which issued Messiaen's early "symphonic meditation" *Les Offrandes oubliées* as part of a set of records sent around the world (or at least to the few countries whose governments recognized Vichy's legitimacy) to demonstrate the "nonpolitical" cultural achievements of the French as participants in the New Europe. "Unchaste" was the critic Andrew Porter's deliciously prim and Protestant reaction to the Himalayan ecstasies of *Saint François*.[12] Even those less inclined toward moral censure often find it hard to understand an esthetic that celebrates renunciation of the material and mortification of the flesh with such opulent—even voluptuous (not to mention expensive)—forces as Messiaen mustered up for *Saint François:* a chorus of 150 voices in as many as a dozen parts, and an orchestra that overflows the pit (and that the San Francisco Opera was constrained by its budget somewhat to curtail in the string department), notated on as many as seventy staves for the overwhelming concert of birdsong in scene 6, and supplemented not only by the trio of ondes martenot but also by a jangling gamelan of mallet percussion (xylophone, xylorimba, marimba, vibraphone, glockenspiel) that acts as a sort of amen corner, applauding every step of the title character's spiritual quest and going quite berserk with affirmational glissandos at the end.

But how else give a secular audience a convincing taste of the perfect joy of divinity: the joy that St. Francis describes in the opera's first scene as the goal of terrestrial existence, toward which every subsequent scene depicts another arduous step? That joy exists quite apart from anyone's experience of it. Among mortals only a saint can ever know it, but anyone can—must—try to imagine it, for to the believer it is the true—and only—existential reality: what we know on earth—gulags, stalags, Vichys, holocausts, and all—is mere Maya, "appearance." Messiaen's art was dedicated from the beginning to affirming the right of artists—and the duty of believers—not to pay attention to appearance but to keep their eyes fixed with constancy on the eternal prize.

Among the sufferings his art ignored were his own. The work that first made him famous was the *Quatuor pour la fin du temps* (1940). It was composed at a prisoner-of-war camp in Görlitz, Germany, where Messiaen was detained as one of thousands of military hostages to Pétain's craven armistice. Its scoring for violin, clarinet, cello, and piano was determined by the presence of virtuosos of those instruments (including Messiaen himself as pianist) among the composer's fellow inmates. Its title is often misconstrued to refer to their longing for the end of the "time" they were serving. Many commentators (and, of course, the record companies) have touted the work's connection with the war. In a recent study, the musicologist Leslie Sprout has shown how the work "has come to represent the plight not only of the captive French soldiers, but also of all victims of Nazi persecution, including those of the Holocaust."[13]

But of course Messiaen had the Apocalypse in mind, not his own predicament, and represented it with one of the early masterpieces of the time-arresting musical "language" he would describe a few years later in his treatise. Indeed, he told many interviewers that the opportunity to devote his mind to composing a work dedicated to a timeless theme amid the degrading conditions of temporal detention made him the one free man in the stalag. And when one compares his quartet, with its extremes of slowness and speed, its mesmerizingly sustained harmonies and its rhythmically elusive ecstatic dances (the kind angels do on the head of a pin), with the kind of art that does seek to memorialize twentieth-century human suffering on a scale to match its enormity, one can only be grateful that Messiaen's religious convictions precluded any such attempt.

For with only the rarest exceptions (like Steve Reich's *Different Trains,* an improbable masterpiece of modesty and indirection), Holocaust memorializing furnished the twentieth century with its greatest infusion of ephemeral, egoistic kitsch. Messiaen's *Quatuor* has survived that heap of artistic corpses, just as the oppressively lengthy and theologically alienating *Saint François* will surely survive the wave of *Niños* and multicultural *Passions* that glut our concert halls today. Robber barons and Bobos, and those who cater to them, come and go. The Kingdom of Heaven, the object of mankind's most consoling and necessary imagining, and the original subject and stimulus of artistic representation, endureth—even unto the twenty-first century, thanks to Messiaen, and to Pamela Rosenberg, the San Francisco Opera's visionary general director who plunged the company dangerously into the red for the sake of his opera, and ensured the termination of her tenure. Classical music may still be doomed by inexorable social and economic change. (In the long run, J. M. Keynes reminded us, we are all dead.) But if so, let it die as it lived, affording glimpses of other worlds and other minds, rather than in a desperate grab for the life raft of shabby topical hypocrisy.

NOTES

1. "In the Center of American Music" (interview with Frank J. Oteri conducted on 21 November 2000), *New Music Box,* no. 21 (vol. 2, no. 9): www.newmusicbox.org/first-person/jano1/5.html.

2. For the review, in the *London Daily Post* (18 April 1739), see Otto Erich Deutsch, *Handel: A Documentary Biography* (New York: W. W. Norton, 1955), 481; the most extensive interpretation of Handel's oratorios in the light of contemporary politics is Ruth Smith, *Handel's Oratorios and Eighteenth-Century Thought* (Cambridge: Cambridge University Press, 1995).

3. David Brooks, *Bobos in Paradise: The New Upper Class and How They Got There* (New York: Simon and Schuster, 2000), 40.

4. Ibid., 242.

5. See, for example, Bernard Holland, "With Ears and Eyes in Fierce Competition, the Eyes Have It," *New York Times,* 15 January 2001, B1.

6. Brooks, *Bobos in Paradise,* 206–7.

7. Hermann Broch, "Notes on the Problem of Kitsch," in *Kitsch: The World of Bad Taste,* ed. Gillo Dorfles (New York: Universe Books, 1969), 58.

8. Quoted from Olivier Messiaen, *The Technique of My Musical Language,* trans. John Satterfield (Paris: Durand, 1956), 8.

9. Ibid., 7–8.

10. Ibid., 13.

11. Messiaen, *The Technique of My Musical Language,* 21.

12. Andrew Porter, "Surfeit," *New Yorker,* 5 May 1986; rpt. in Andrew Porter, *Musical Events: A Chronicle, 1983–86* (New York: Summit Books, 1989), 480.

13. Leslie Sprout, "Messiaen's *Quatuor pour la fin du temps:* Modernism, Representation and a Soldier's Wartime Tale," in *Program and Abstracts of Papers Read at the Joint Meetings of the American Musicological Society and the Society for Music Theory, October 31–November 3, 2002* (n.p.: American Musicological Society, 2002), 149.

36

The Poietic Fallacy

Allen Shawn, *Arnold Schoenberg's Journey* (New York: Farrar, Straus & Giroux, 2002; paperback rpt. Cambridge, Mass.: Harvard University Press, 2004; 340 pp.)

During his lifetime, and even—astonishingly—in the half century since his death, the music of Arnold Schoenberg has been influential and controversial out of all proportion to the frequency with which it has ever been performed or otherwise disseminated. His name has been a battle cry, a punching bag, an article of faith, a term of abuse, a finger in the dike, and a symbol for anything and everything: progress, degeneracy, elitism, integrity, disintegration, regeneration, sublimity, ridiculousness. According to some, he is the reason serious music is dying. According to others, he is the only reason it has even lived this long. Nobody in the history of music has been a more dependable whipping boy; but neither has anyone been a trustier stick to beat with.

The din surrounding the name of this composer, in short, has always threatened to drown his music out. Allen Shawn, a composer on the faculty of Bennington College, wants to rescue the music from the din. In the introduction to his new book, a modest and friendly attempt to help willing music lovers discover a source of pleasure in Schoenberg, he writes that "one of the convictions" that motivated its writing was "that, from the very beginning, there were features in Schoenberg's work, personality, and perhaps even social position that led to his being explained and defended rather than listened to, that the works of Schoenberg have not had a fair chance to be experienced apart from the ideology that surrounds them."

As one who has spent years investigating, criticizing, and participating in the discourse surrounding music, I had better confess at the outset that while I applaud any effort to get people to listen to Schoenberg's music (or any classical music, come to that), and while I appreciate as well as anyone the already

First published in *Musical Times* 145, no. 1886 (Spring 2004): 7–34. © 2004 The Musical Times Publications, Ltd.

much-quoted quip that comes at the end of Shawn's introduction ("Perhaps Schoenberg's work deserves a more superficial treatment than it has hitherto received"), the way Shawn has formulated his purpose made me a little uneasy. And unease increased as I read on: "Schoenberg's voice as an artist, the voice that speaks to us through the work, has not been heard in a natural way without interference." Is there a "natural" way to listen to music, or to experience any cultural artifact? Whose way is the natural way? What does Shawn mean when he says, about Schoenberg's twelve-tone pieces, "It is only when one listens to these works as music that one appreciates what he accomplished"?

Let me further confess that as a professional musician with decades of composing, performing, teaching, and listening experience, I have no idea what that thrice-familiar tautology—"to listen to music as music"—means; and when I try to deduce what Shawn means by it from the substance and context of his argument, I am made uneasiest of all. What, after all, is "interference"? Shawn seems to think it consists in "words about" or "ideas about" the thing rather than "the thing itself." But if his understanding of Schoenberg has ripened over the years so that he now wants to share it with us, it can only be because he has had some benefit of interference. And what he offers us now is more interference.

In short, Shawn's book cannot dispel the din; all any book can do is add to it. To claim otherwise is to claim a privilege. The author writes with grace and sounds like a good guy (and a very effective teacher). And yet my faith that his discourse will be helpful suffered another little jolt before I finished the introduction, when he made his first attempt to deal with, or defuse, the issue of "difficulty," which surrounds Schoenberg as it does so much modernist art. "I in no way mean to play down the difficulties, depths, or conundrums inherent in this body of work," he writes.

> But I would suggest that Schoenberg's music is no more "difficult" than the work of other early-twentieth-century modernists such as Kandinsky, Eliot, Kafka, or Joyce, for whom even the general public has a feeling of affection, of receptivity, of the kind of trust that one accords great art in which there is much that one simply doesn't grasp at first or perhaps even ever.

I don't suppose that the author of *Arnold Schoenberg's Journey* remembers Lionel Trilling's great essay "On the Teaching of Modern Literature" (first published in 1961 in *Partisan Review* and most recently reprinted in *The Moral Obligation to Be Intelligent,* edited by Leon Wieseltier [New York: Farrar, Straus & Giroux, 2000]), that once-famous bout of hand-wringing over that very affection, receptivity, and trust, and the complacency for which they stand. But surely he knows about the difficulty—not the "difficulty," about which he writes so contentedly—that people have been having of late with Eliot? And surely he realizes that the "difficulty" of modernist art was as much a social stance as an esthetic one?

But no, it is clear that he does not, or that he thinks all that is just part of the interference. Those of us who have absorbed Trilling's lesson that in our role as teachers we should be adding to—or, as we now say, problematizing—the difficulty of the art that we teach, as a way of engaging with the issues and (emphatically) as a way of engaging with the artworks, may indeed wonder at this point about Shawn's advocacy of "natural" listening. Or do we think, as he seems to, that music is—by "nature"—exempt from "issues"?

.   .   .

Among the epigraphs adorning Shawn's book is an extract from the well-known letter of thanks that Schoenberg sent the distinguished American composer Roger Sessions in 1944, after Sessions had published a seventieth-birthday tribute titled "Schoenberg in the United States": "And finally I want to mention what I consider the greatest value for a possible appreciation of my music: that you say, one must listen to it in the same manner as to every other kind of music, forget the theories, the twelve-tone method, the dissonances, etc., and, I would add, if possible the author." For the record, here are Sessions's exact words: "It is not essential or even possible for the listener to apprehend [the twelve-tone row] in all its various transformations. He must listen to Schoenberg's music in exactly the same spirit as he listens to any music whatever, and bring to it the same kind of response. If he is fortunate he will from the first discover moments of profound and intense beauty which will tempt him further." This is Shawn's premise, too. His whole book, though far more charmingly written, is in effect a gloss on this passage from Sessions.

The trouble is, Sessions was a composer, not a listener—and a composer who, though never nearly as much in the public eye, faced a dilemma similar to Schoenberg's. In his obituary for Sessions in the *New York Times* in 1985, Donal Henahan quoted a fellow composer who had remarked that "everybody loves Roger Sessions except the public," and added, glumly but accurately, that Sessions's "works gained little acceptance during his lifetime beyond professional and academic circles." Can such a composer, however well intentioned, serve as a guide to nonprofessional listeners, however willing?

My question may seem ill intentioned, but assume for the moment that I write not in a spirit of contention but in an effort—an honest (and earnest) historian's effort—to understand a situation that everybody acknowledges, and that Shawn's book seeks honestly and earnestly to redress: the evident divergence in interests between those who have created much of the concert music of the twentieth century and those who have had to listen to it.

That divergence of interests is apparent from the very first sentence of Sessions's article: "In any survey of Schoenberg's work one fact must be emphasized above all: that no younger composer writes quite the same music as he would have written had Schoenberg's music not existed." That certainly is (or was) a fact—and a familiar one, constantly rehearsed in appreciations of Schoenberg. But to give it primary emphasis is to place primary value on an esthetically neutral aspect of the composer's work, one that is of no direct consequence to listeners (still less to their pleasure).

The gambit embarrassed Sessions a bit when he republished his article twenty-eight years later. He added a cautionary footnote about "an all too prevalent tendency . . . to confuse questions belonging to the realm of historical development . . . with those of inherent artistic value." Still, when it came to supplying a positive definition of inherent artistic value to complement the merely negative observation that it was not to be sought in technical methods as such, Sessions again emphatically ignored the listener:

> One can not too often insist that in music it is the composer's inner world of tone and rhythm which matters, and that whatever technical means he chooses in order to give it structure and coherence are subject to no a priori judgment whatever. The essential is that structure and coherence be present; and the demand which art makes on its creator is simply that his technique be sufficiently mastered to become an obedient and flexible instrument in his hands. . . . Once more—the significance of music springs solely from the composer's imagination and not from ideas about technique. The latter are merely tools which he forges for himself, for his own purposes. They gain what validity they possess from the results, in music, to which they make their imponderable contribution.

The all-important results are described entirely in terms of the making of the art object, not its effect. The significance of music inheres in its structure and coherence. These are the fruits of the composer's imagination, affording those moments of profound and intense beauty that the listener will discover "if he is fortunate." The composer's task and the value of the composer's product are again unrelated, except fortuitously, to the listener's pleasure.

This is the way most artists and critics have been talking about art for a very long time. In fact it is often one of the principal ways in which art is defined, especially by composers, or at least distinguished from its poorer cousins. A recent obituary for Ralph Shapey, an American composer far better known for his curmudgeonly attitudes than for his music, gave this as his credo: "I believe in something called art. Everyone has a right to it, but they have to go to it. It does not come to them." But who was Shapey paraphrasing? None other than the figure Allen Shawn wishes to popularize, who encased the definition in its most memorable nutshell: "If it is art it is not for everybody; if it is for everybody it is not art."

This is not—or not only—mere elitism. Schoenberg was a terrific phrasemaker, and he also claimed that it was not given to Beethoven, Bruckner, or Mahler to write tenth symphonies because they would have revealed more of the ultimate truth than it was given to man to know. There may be more important things than pleasure, just as there may be more important things than beauty; and to define art as a realm of occult or forbidden knowledge, from which the uninitiated may need protection, is an old romantic habit. (Schoenberg's *Harmonielehre*—the title just means "Harmony Textbook"—brims with philosophical and theological asides.)

But though there are many roads to it, the basic position at the root of the "divergence of interests" that bedevils modern art remains the same. I have come to call it the poietic fallacy: the conviction that what matters most (or more strongly yet, that all that matters) in a work of art is the making of it, the maker's input. The poietic fallacy is what has given rise to the situation that Shawn has made it a mission to counter, in which art criticism has been reduced to artists' shoptalk.

Just to explain the term: The word *poietic* comes from the field of semiotics, from which a now somewhat old-fashioned tripartite model of analysis, first proposed by the French linguist Jean Molino, was long fashionable in musicology. Communications have senders and receivers. An analysis that is concerned with the sending of the message, hence with its devising, is a poietic analysis (from the Greek *poiein*, "to make," but distinguished by the unusual spelling from *poetic* to avoid confusion with more ordinary usages). An analysis that is concerned with the receiving is an esthesic analysis (from the Greek *aisthesis*, "perception," similarly distinguished from *esthetic*).

There was also in Molino's original formulation a *niveau neutre,* a neutral level, that analyzed the structure of the message itself; it has been pretty much discarded once it was realized that analysis itself was an esthesic function. But the philosophy of art that is still sufficiently powerful in musical circles to warrant attempts such as Shawn's to challenge it is not so subtle as to realize that. It resolutely places esthesic concerns off limits as degrading. (That the cold war gave the poietic fallacy a boost in the West in the name of creative freedom should be obvious; some artists and critics—Elliott Carter among the former, Paul Griffiths among the latter—still speak of the "tyranny of the audience" and the tyranny of totalitarian regimes in the same breath.)

To return briefly to Sessions: the notion that the listener's pleasure is not, and must not be, the composer's primary objective is more than hinted when Sessions explains why, despite the infrequency of his performances in his adopted country, Schoenberg is nevertheless a significant and salutary presence in the United States:

> The enthusiasm of many of the most gifted among young musicians [for Schoenberg's American-published scores] as well as the gradually deepening interest of their elders is one of the striking phenomena of a period in which the prevailing trend seems superficially to be all in the direction of a not entirely genuine "mass appeal," facile and standardized effect, and a kind of hasty shabbiness of conception and workmanship.

No doubt Sessions had Shostakovich uppermost in mind in 1944; probably his old friend Copland, too. Nowadays one can read the same invective practically word for word when the defenders of Pierre Boulez or Elliott Carter (or Schoenberg) take off after Steve Reich or John Corigliano or Ellen Taaffe Zwilich.

I am somewhat reluctant to adduce one more quotation from Sessions's article, because it will raise such an invidious resonance in today's intellectual and ethical climate. But I must, and so I will, for even if I repressed it here the theme it broaches will force its way back into the discussion later. "In the last analysis," Sessions wrote, his birthday tribute to Schoenberg was "an act of gratitude to one who has, so much more than any other individual, been one of the masculine forces that have shaped the music of our time." That sentiment, too, is one of the props, as well as one of the ramifications, of the poietic fallacy, along with the ones already noted: the measurement of an artist's value in terms of influence on other artists, the concomitant overrating of technical innovation, the delimitation of the purview of criticism to matters of structure and craft, and the derogation of other critical approaches as vulgarian. Schoenberg, and discourse about Schoenberg, has always been among the chief bulwarks of the poietic fallacy in music.

. . .

Can this man, or his music, be successfully popularized? Ought they to be? Has Allen Shawn succeeded in doing so? On the face of it, he opposes the poietic fallacy. He constantly emphasizes listener response as a measure of Schoenberg's value, and constantly implies that that response should not be mediated by "theories," Schoenberg's or anyone else's. "I had one group of students lie down on the floor with their eyes closed while listening to 'Farben' [Colors] from the Five Pieces for Orchestra," he reports. "The response to the work, unencumbered by proselytizing or prejudice, has belied the prevalent notion that Schoenberg's music is repellent or remote or that it represents a 'wrong turn' taken by a master composer. The response, on the contrary, suggests that Schoenberg's art—in and of itself—moves people and speaks to them."

Shawn ought to read up a bit about speech acts and "illocution" if he thinks that proselytizing and prejudice played no role in the response that he elicited. If I tell you to lie down on the floor with your eyes closed, I am telling you to expect a restful experience; and then if I follow through with Schoenberg's most restful piece (the one he later subtitled "Morning by a Lake"—I trust Professor Shawn did not tell his students that), have I not prejudiced your view of Schoenberg just as much as I would have done had I played you the movement from the Five Pieces called "Peripeteia" while grinding broken glass into your forearm?

But at least Shawn shows some concern about response, with the "esthesic" side of the ledger. He even comes close to asserting esthesics as a guiding principle when he assures us, near the end of the book, that "the underlying structure of a work, which is often of an astonishing complexity and the re-sult of considerable contrivance, is not its ultimate meaning." Rather, "the meaning is in the experience you have when you listen to the work." Quite often, and winningly, Shawn reports his own responses. He tells us that he once injured his foot jockeying for a better seat at a screening of the film ver-sion of Schoenberg's opera *Moses und Aron*: "The sensation of watching this se-vere and illuminating version of the opera while being in intense—if strangely remote—pain has stayed with me. Somehow feelings of sacrifice, the sense that there is a cost to things, intimations that understanding and beauty do not come easily, have adhered, not inappropriately, to my feelings about this work."

I suppress the easy impulse to mock this story by turning it into a pre-scription ("if you want to enjoy Schoenberg, don't forget to bring a whip to the concert") or pointing out its likeness, in its glorification of submission, to the "slave mentality" derided more than a hundred years ago by Nietzsche. My problem, rather, is that Shawn again seems to underestimate, or strate-gically ignore, the performative aspect of such reports, especially when they are couched in terms not of "I" but "we." About *Erwartung*, Schoenberg's ex-pressionist "monodrama" of psychological torment, hysteria, and (possibly) psychosis, he writes: "Like the protagonist, we often feel lost, but we also pe-riodically find ourselves in very distinct places. Nevertheless, we are contin-uously captivated, even entranced. We have the dreamlike sensation of hav-ing been 'here' before, since the intimate, psychic states evoked here—the terror, the confusion, the aloneness—instantly remind us of our own."

Well, if you say so. And I don't necessarily say nay. But telling the reader that she is captivated and entranced is a way of captivating and entrancing. Though subtle, it is nevertheless a coercive rhetoric, a hard sell. Sometimes, indeed, the listener is actually ordered to ignore his immediate reaction. Near the end of *Erwartung*, we are told, "the disjointed shards of thought in the text are set to tiny scraps of song, but these nevertheless cohere and con-nect and carry the listener forward." At its most subtle, the technique relies on rhetorical questions, like this one about the second "Little Piano Piece" from Schoenberg's op. 19: "Why does the opening G–B third sound so per-fect after the chromaticisms of piece no. 1?" Do you see yonder cloud that's almost in shape of a camel?

This is all fine pedagogy and I cherish its purpose, just as I am delighted to see Shawn humanizing a composer so often portrayed as some kind of dis-embodied historical force or impossibly exigent authority. He shows us fam-ily photographs full of cute or chubby little Schoenbergs. We learn that their father made them peanut butter and jelly sandwiches in the morning and cut them up in fanciful animal shapes. We learn that Schoenberg loved to play games (tennis with Gershwin, for instance). He designed playing cards, painted at an exhibitable level, and threw himself passionately into Zionist

activity in response to Hitler (even vowing at one point to sacrifice his artistic career to the cause of Jewish survival). Shawn seems to think that if he can
get us to like the man we will like the music as well.

To an extent, of course, he is right. Many of Schoenberg's most "painful"
works—such as *Erwartung,* which may be the blindest leap into the musical
unknown that he (or any other composer) ever took—make their first appeal
on a visceral, humane level. At the time he wrote this piece, Schoenberg was
reeling from a marital crisis, and felt that the artist's highest and perhaps only
true calling was to give truly adequate expression to "inner experiences," psychological realities inaccessible to reasoned language or conventional
modes of representation. Why, after all, should the inner experiences of a
woman discovering her lover's bloody corpse be anything but bloodcurdling? Why shouldn't a musical representation of such experiences be horrendously dissonant and ugly? Artists in the realist tradition had been por-
traying ugly things in an ugly way for decades. Not to be ugly was to be
dishonest—no artist at all. All that Schoenberg did, in a sense, was take it further, make it "realer," more true to life, more honest—hence more genuinely
artistic. Shawn devotes a chapter to Schoenberg's assertion that he became
a radical reluctantly, under the sway of an "inner compulsion," a human need
with which he invites his readers to identify. "Indeed," Shawn writes, "he implies that entering this new musical domain has required courage and an
overcoming of resistance on his own part." If its motivation was human and
authentic, and morally commendable, so must be the music.

But the authenticity of the impulse costs little to concede. Schoenberg's
foes were as ready to recognize it as his friends. (When your opponent pays
tribute to your sincerity you know that he is not taking you seriously.) A hostile reviewer of the first performance of the Five Pieces for Orchestra, a work
that rivals the tormented idiom of *Erwartung* but without a text or program
to give the painful sounds a specific reference, ended his notice on a note of
commiseration: "We must be content with the composer's own assertion that
he has depicted his own experiences, for which he has our heartfelt sympathy." A mean joke, yes; but it is not unrelated to Shawn's claim that the music
gives an unprecedentedly true representation not only of Schoenberg's feelings but of ours as well. In his music as well as his paintings, Shawn tells us,
"Schoenberg uses his own face to depict and confront our common humanity." He steers perilously close to what Theodor Adorno called the "jargon of
authenticity" when he endorses Paul Rosenfeld's claim that Schoenberg's
career represents "the development of a man according to the law of life
which compels us, if we would live and grow, to become ever more fully and
nakedly what we essentially are."

To say that all of this is not "interference" or proselytizing is just plain silly,
and to that pretense I must righteously object, especially when the ground
of the argument shifts, as it so often does, from the esthesic to the poietic.

Like Roger Sessions, Allen Shawn is after all an academically trained composer; and although his tone and his demeanor are worlds away from Sessions's frosty detachment, he listens and thinks like any other member of the guild. And that means that beneath the surface of his argument the poietic fallacy remains in place.

Shawn's very last plea on Schoenberg's behalf fairly duplicates Sessions's first claim as quoted above. "As we close this book," the author writes,

> let us imagine the last century without Schoenberg: without the String Trio, *A Survivor from Warsaw*, the Violin Concerto, the Variations for Orchestra, *Moses und Aron, Pierrot Lunaire*, the Five Pieces for Orchestra, *Erwartung*, the opus 11 Piano Pieces, the *Book of the Hanging Gardens*, the *Gurre-Lieder, Verklärte Nacht* . . . without film music as it has been, or Carter or Boulez as they have been, or Stravinsky's works after 1951, or Webern or Berg as they were. Doing this one begins to see in this difficult life something indispensable. Without Schoenberg, the music of an astonishing number of other composers would have been much the poorer and the time in which we live would have lacked one of its most eloquent and characteristic musical voices. Without him, our era would have made a different sound.

.   .   .

So it's influence—still an esthetically neutral category, no matter how historically significant—that counts, after all. And alas, all the other esthetically irrelevant planks in the poieticist platform figure just as prominently in Shawn's apologia as they did in Sessions's. There is abundant overrating of innovation. The Chamber Symphony op. 9 is praised as "forward-looking." Schoenberg's songs to texts by Richard Dehmel "pointed a way forward." Even his little cabaret songs, composed at the age of twenty-six, are touted for having "anticipated by 25 years the sophisticated music theater style of Weill and Eisler."

The gigantic cantata *Gurrelieder* gets a particularly hard progressivist sell. "Here we are at the pivot of the century and arguably at one of the most fateful turning points in the thousand-year evolution of Western music," Shawn writes of its harmonious ending. "We now know that Schoenberg and much of twentieth-century music was progressing in exactly the opposite direction of this sequence of musical events: away from the tonal center and into a new way of hearing tones." This sort of thing was too much even for Stravinsky, master of modernist posturing though he was: in conversation with Robert Craft he ridiculed the critical standpoint that "evaluates solely in terms of where a thing comes from and where it is going."

Finally, from Shawn: "The *Gurre-Lieder* was one final, almost orgiastically beautiful evening-length work, for staggeringly large forces, on mythic subject matter. For a long time after it, anyone composing such a piece would seem to belong to a bygone age." Compare Boulez's most notorious utterance: "Since the Viennese discoveries, any musician who has not experienced—I do not say understood, but truly experienced—the necessity of the dodecaphonic language is USELESS. For his entire work brings him up short of the needs of his time." These apothegms are, all of them, the stuff of professional politics. They have nothing to do with listeners, except insofar as they may be intimidated.

And there is far more "immanent criticism" in Shawn's discussion, the sort of criticism that delimits its purview to matters of structure and craft, than the author lets on. There had to be. If the greatness of *Erwartung* is merely its hysteria, or that of *Moses und Aron* merely its moral severity, then we may as well regard them the way old Agesilaus of Sparta, in Plutarch's hoary anecdote, regarded the actor who could perfectly imitate the nightingale. Invited to hear him, the king declined, saying he had heard the nightingale itself. Why go to *Erwartung* to hear a crazy lady, when all you have to do is open up a window on Broadway?

There has to be some talk, in short, about what Susanne Langer called "significant form." There has to be some accounting of the way music communicates experience through its particular medium.

But Shawn (and he is hardly alone in this) often settles for something easier. He shows us instead how well composed the music is, according to a definition of good composing to which academically trained composers are indoctrinated but which means little to listeners. The proof of this is that the demonstration is almost always illustrated visually—that is, by musical examples, of which this book is surprisingly and inappropriately full, unless its intended audience is confined after all to the musically literate, by now a tiny coterie. (There are other ways; a number of authors of serious books on music for "generally educated" audiences have lately been experimenting with minutely correlated CDs.)

The sentence quoted earlier, for instance, about the "perfect" sounding G–B third is actually not quite as rhetorical a question as I made it out to be. It is followed by a sort of answer. Why does the G–B third sound so perfect? "At least in part because the same sound in the same register is contained in [bars 8–12] in piece no. 1. It is also contained in the very first gesture of that piece as well."

This is a familiar sort of casuistry. Shawn has ferreted the precedents he cites out of larger contexts in which the "G–B third" is not always aurally salient. At the beginning of piece no. 1, the "first gesture" as Shawn calls it, the B is a sustained note, against which the G is set in counterpoint as the third in a very quick group of four, none of which gets to register as a distinct harmony with the B. It is the kind of relationship that music theory students are taught to render visually by drawing what they often laughingly call "amoebas"—oddly shaped closed curves—around the pitches being grouped. The oddness of the shapes corresponds to the remoteness and the arbitrariness of the relationships that are being corralled and promoted as "structural" for the purpose of demonstrating the harmonic (or "motivic") unity of the composition. A whole analytic theory called pitch-class set analysis has grown up around this amoebic practice, the paradoxical purpose of which is to show that the early-twentieth-century music that elicited riots when first performed is really very well behaved and orderly.

Forgive the descent into shoptalk; but Shawn uses the amoeba method again and again to convince us of the quality and the power of the music he describes. About the constituent numbers in *Pierrot Lunaire,* he asserts that "to some extent, all the pieces in this set emerge" from the first seven notes in the first piece (which sounds very potent, considering the significance of the number seven in this collection of what Schoenberg called "thrice seven" little speech-songs). But the nine music examples that follow are far too approximate to justify the claim, and in every case they are arbitrarily "segmented" (to use the amoeba-drawer's term) out of larger contexts from which they are not aurally set off. Shawn even uses the method on Schoenberg's cabaret songs, to show why they are better than any others and really belong in the concert hall.

When it comes to analyzing twelve-tone music, the claim (and the "segmentation") may be less arbitrary: but only because the claim has become tautological. The twelve-tone method was invented precisely to produce the sort of maximalized motivic consistency and saturated texture that analysts look for. Clearly Schoenberg was motivated by the ideal that Shawn invokes to tout his work. But that does not make it any more pertinent or available to the listener's experience. And promoting it into a primary musical value is the ultimate poietic fallacy, the one that led modern music into the cul-de-sac where absurdly overcomposed monstrosities by Elliott Carter or Milton Babbitt have been reverently praised by critics and turned into obligatory models for emulation by teachers of composition.

So what are these seemingly misguided values pertinent to? That is a question very much worth investigating historically, for there is simply no point in maintaining the pretense that Schoenberg's music is music like any other music. More than any other body of music that I know, it represented a crux in the history of ideas. That does indeed make it (and him) supremely important. But that history has been largely forgotten, and (as Santayana might have warned us) its repercussions linger even into our shiny new postmodern millennium. We must do a better job of comprehending the sources of Schoenberg's "inner compulsion"—and of the poietic fallacy, too—if we want to escape from them, or even accept them in full, free consciousness.

·   ·   ·

In the last of his many assurances that music, even Schoenberg's music, can be fully appreciated in an intellectual and cultural vacuum, Shawn writes: "Until the twentieth century the purpose of music was probably only discussed, when it was, by philosophers and clerics, and the methods used to create it were in the background of the minds of its hearers. There was a minimum of conceptual or analytical self-consciousness to the act of listening. Music made the eardrums vibrate and entered the mind, and the psyche/body/spirit responded according to its mysterious laws."

Like most nostalgic pronouncements, this one is unbelievably off-base. Conceptual and analytical self-consciousness among artists and art lovers and speculation about artistic ends and means are as old as romanticism. It was Friedrich Schiller's very definition of a "sentimental poet." And its musical history goes much farther back, at least to the humanistic ferment that midwifed the birth of opera at the end of the sixteenth century, and even before that to the late Middle Ages, when a great composer was usually (as was said of John Dunstable in one of his epitaphs) "an astrologian, a mathematician, a musitian and what not."

In the nineteenth century, particularly, precious little innocent listening went on, since the newly public sphere of music now made room for two new professions—critics and historians—that bathed all listening in buzz (or "discourse," if you are an academic). Shawn's ideal of "uninterfered-with" listening is simply inadequate to deal with the music produced under these conditions. Compared, say, with Schoenberg's idea of listening, it is woefully impoverished. At the very least it is a poor prescription.

To find the source of the Schoenbergian crux we do not have to go back to John Dunstable. The middle of the nineteenth century will do for a starting point; and the seminal figure is neither a philosopher nor a cleric but a pianist, a critic, and a music historian named Franz Brendel, a man whose name has been forgotten but whose ideas bore copious and lasting fruit.

Brendel's great achievement was to write his century's most widely disseminated "universal" and "scientific" history of music: *Geschichte der Musik in Italien, Deutschland und Frankreich von den ersten christlichen Zeiten bis auf die Gegenwart* (History of Music in Italy, Germany, and France from the Earliest Christian Times to the Present). First published in 1852, it had gone through nine editions by 1906. The words put in quotation marks in this paragraph's first sentence constitute the book's inheritance from the Enlightenment. It aspired to say everything that was important, and to say it in a way that put all facts into an overriding system that gave them meaning. The reasons for putting the words in quotation marks constitute the book's inheritance from romanticism. The limitation, despite the claim of universality, to the richest and most powerful countries of Western Europe are already evidence of the author's commitment to a view of history cast in terms of the progressive realization of an essential European spirit of which those countries were collectively the protagonist. The science that gave Brendel's work system was Hegel's "dialectic." Brendel's was its first systematic application to the history of music.

What set the Hegelian dialectic apart from other interpretations of the great chain of being (such as Darwin's theory of biological evolution, which was almost immediately misinterpreted, to Darwin's disgust, in light of the dialectic) is that it purported to show not merely that things change, or under what conditions they change, but also the purpose of change. The stipulation that change has purpose turned random process into law. The basic law of history, as Hegel postulated it in the *Lectures on the Philosophy of History*, was this: "The history of the world is none other than the progress of the consciousness of Freedom." That is the first sentence of the book, and the axiom from which the entire subsequent argument and demonstration is drawn. According to it, all meaningfully or significantly "historical" change—all change, in other words, that is worthy of representation in the dialectic—has contributed to progress in the realization of human freedom, which Hegel called the progress of the "world soul." If it has not contributed to this progress, change has not been, in Hegelian terms, "historical."

As the first self-consciously Hegelian historian of music, Brendel cast his narrative in terms of successive emancipations, both of musicians and of the art itself. Before the sixteenth century, everything was primitive, mere "prehistory," because in Brendel's ears (and here he did not differ from his contemporaries) such music did not intelligibly express the ideas or the feelings of individual creators. All musicians were slaves to the mechanical rules of counterpoint, as people generally were enslaved by the dogmas of the medieval Church.

The first great composer, in Brendel's reckoning, was Palestrina, who, reflecting the romantic interpretation of the Renaissance, broke through to true spiritual expressivity. What he expressed, however, was not yet a personal sensibility but rather the collectively held beliefs of his religious community. His art was "sublime" rather than "beautiful," because it continued to address a higher-than-human plane. It still fulfilled prescribed ecclesiastical functions, but its euphony and its expressive power showed the way toward artistic autonomy.

The phase of "beauty" was reached, in Brendel's scheme, when the spiritual, freed from its ecclesiastical bonds, could be expressed in fully human (that is, secular) terms. The rise of opera bore witness to it. And the next stage—the fully fledged "esthetic"—came with the emancipation of music from words in the instrumental masterpieces of the German classical masters. Their music, now able to realize its own essential spirit, able at last to evolve spontaneously and autonomously (that is, according to its own laws), was effectively a metaphor for the advancement of humanity toward ultimate self-realization. The very autonomy of the new instrumental music (implying freedom from all "extramusical" association or constraint), made it a political symbol—thus reenmeshing it in extramusical ideas (a small example of the dialectic at work).

The value of music could be measured best, on the Hegelian view, in terms of the degree to which it embodied its own epoch's evolutionary synthesis and pointed the way to the next. Composers were valuable to the degree that their actions advanced the tendencies inherent in the musical materials toward further autonomous evolution. Unsurprisingly, the most advanced composers, and hence the most valuable ones, were Germans: in Brendel's view, they were Bach and Handel (the latter viewed bizarrely as a church musician), who were the last and most consummate representatives of the sublime epoch, and Gluck, Haydn, and Mozart, who brought to its first full fruition the epoch of the esthetic. Beethoven's popular image as music's emancipator supreme received a resounding confirmation.

But the most provocative chapter of Brendel's history was the last, because of the way the author maintained his account of progressive emancipation beyond Beethoven, into what was then the present. This was at the time a very unconventional and risky move, since it threatened the status of Mozart, Haydn, and Beethoven as "classics"—that is, as having set a timeless (and therefore unimprovable) standard. For a German historian, nothing short of the nation's honor was at stake in this historical "fact." Denying it was unthinkable. Brendel got around the problem in two ways. First, he posited that every age (or stage) had its perfect representatives. Hence Bach was not invalidated by Mozart, nor Mozart by Beethoven, and so Beethoven would never be invalidated either. Second, Brendel obediently gave the chapter concerning the present the title *Verfall*, "Decline," in keeping with what was by then an art historian's inescapable obligation.

And yet the chapter's contents roundly belied its title. The music of the man Brendel singled out as the greatest composer then living (let his identification wait) carried on the torch, advancing both the progressive consciousness of freedom and the progressive attainment of esthetic unity. This was the purpose that informed the history of music, and ever since Brendel formulated it there has been abroad the idea that the primary obligation of musicians is not to their audience but to that purpose—namely, the furthering of the "evolutionary" progress of the art toward autonomy and unity, for the sake of which any sacrifice is justified, including (or even especially) the sacrifice of the audience. Ever since the middle of the nineteenth century, the idea that one is morally obliged to serve the impersonal aims of history and the need for art to evolve has been one of the most powerful motivating forces, and one of the most exigent criteria of value, among composers and critics. As recently as 1993, Paul Griffiths, writing in the *New Yorker*, sought to discredit a new work (Ellen Taaffe Zwilich's Second Symphony) that had enjoyed audience acclaim by declaring that it did not "add anything to the universe of musical possibility."

Brendel's own way of putting it was to say that "the essence of today's art" can no longer be realized in "the old naturalistic way"—that is, instinctively or intuitively by musicians out to please their patrons or their listeners—but only with "the intervention of theory and criticism," and by "art's pre-supposing theory and criticism within itself." The age of creative innocence was over; self-conscious theory, based on a high consciousness of purpose and of history, was the only true path to the future. Moreover, that consciousness of purpose, being the road to self-realization, made the future graspable in the present. The path of destiny was marked out to those in the know. The others did not matter. The self-conscious few, history's self-appointed "advance guard," now saw themselves (following Shelley's famous definition of his own calling) as "the unacknowledged legislators of the world."

These contentions marked the beginnings of the modern—or "modernist"—age of music, which has also been the age of revolutionary politics. Both in art and in politics, it has been the age in which (to quote Richard Kostelanetz, a contemporary American theorist of the avant-garde) "an innovative minority makes the leaps that will be adopted by the many"—or that, according to the theory, ought by rights to be adopted. The invidious comparison implicit in this idea—or rather the elitism, to give it its contemporary nom de guerre—has understandably given rise to angry backlashes and counter-revolutions. Since the middle of the nineteenth century, the world of "classical music" has been a world riven with political factions and contentious publicity.

The poietic fallacy is the direct outgrowth of this Hegelianization of music history, especially in its vulgar Darwinized variant that saw each synthesis as invalidating all previous stages, at least insofar as the rights and duties of composers were concerned. Musicians and critics after Brendel did indeed conceptualize musical history in terms resembling Rudolf Zallinger's much-parodied depiction of the "Ascent of Man" from the lower simians to the sapient homos of today. Bernard Shaw, hoping to stir things up in a piece commissioned to honor Mozart's death centenary in 1891, wrote that Wagner, whom he called "The Liberator," was "greater than Beethoven by as much as Mozart was greater than Haydn." Having written that, Shaw immediately added, "And now I hope I have saved my reputation by saying something at which everybody will exclaim, 'Bless me! what nonsense!' Nevertheless, it is true." There is the poietic fallacy in action. (Mark Twain's immortal jape, "Wagner's music is better than it sounds," was already the perfect spoof of it.)

Here is an even better example, partly because it is older, and because it was entirely serious. Writing in 1859 in the journal *Neue Zeitschrift für Musik*, the radically romantic forum founded by Robert Schumann, the Russian critic and composer Alexander Serov massacred a biography of Mozart written in French by his countryman Alexander Ulybyshev, which upheld the era of Mozart as a "classical" golden age. In two dogmatic assertions—or "laws," as he made bold to call them—Serov summed up the neo-Hegelian position with breathtaking succinctness:

1. *Wenn eine Theorie nicht mit der Praxis eines Weltgenies stimmt, da wird sie nie bestehen, denn die Kunst lebt ihr Leben nicht in Büchern, sondern im Kunstwerk.*

[If theory (that is, classroom "music theory") does not accord with the practice of a world-genius, then it must always give way, for art lives its life not in books but in artworks.]

2. *Das Criterium des musikalischen Gesetzes liegt nicht in den Ohren des Consumenten, es liegt in der Kunstidee des Producenten.* [The basis of musical law lies not in the ear of the consumer but in the artistic inspiration (literally, the "art-idea") of the producer.]

Add economics to the preserves on which art theorizers were now prepared to poach in support of the new value system that equated innovation with liberation and that took as its objective the freeing of the artwork and its producers from dependence on social norms defined by consumers. Boring or annoying their contemporaries was not only considered by neo-Hegelians a fair price to pay; it was often taken in itself to be a mark of progress. ("Before, music strove to delight people," Serov's countryman Chaikovsky grumbled after the first Bayreuth *Ring,* "now they are tormented and exhausted.") But this was serious politics. The Hegelian notion of the *Weltgenie,* the "world-genius"—on the one hand, free to abrogate the laws of ordinary mortals and, on the other, charged with the making of new and ever more binding laws—was nothing if not a site of political power.

.   .   .

The role of the world-genius was precisely the role that Schoenberg claimed to have inherited, in endless pronouncements and anecdotes. "I knew I had to develop my ideas for the sake of progress in music," he wrote in later life, "whether I liked it or not." (That you did not like it he took for granted.) He loved to recall the answer that he gave an officer who asked him, when he reported for duty in World War I, whether he was *the* Arnold Schoenberg: "Somebody had to be, nobody else volunteered, so I answered the call." And of course there was the chilling way he announced to his pupil and assistant Josef Rufer that he had come up with the twelve-tone method: "Today I have made a discovery that will ensure the supremacy of German music for the next hundred years." But the surest sign of all that Schoenberg saw himself as the protagonist of the latest evolutionary stage was the way he cast his own development as a dialectical synthesis.

Up to Schoenberg, dialectical history was the exclusive method or propaganda tool of one side in the great debate to which Alexander Serov so zealously contributed, pitting the believers in unbounded progress—the "Zukunftists," or futurists, as their opponents called them, after the title of Wagner's tract *Das Kunstwerk der Zukunft* (The Artwork of the Future)—against the "classicists" who saw the period leading up to Beethoven as an unsurpassable (but, given sufficient talent and luck, maintainable) golden age. The editor and publisher of Schumann's journal at the time Serov contributed to it was none other than Franz Brendel, not only a critic and not only a historian but also a very active intervener in history, a musical politician who played hard at the game of kingmaking.

In 1859, the same year as Serov's contribution, the indefatigable editor organized at Weimar, Goethe's hometown, and in Leipzig, the journal's birthplace, a great convocation of musicians from all parts of Germany, out of which emerged an organization called the Allgemeiner deutscher Musikverein, or the All-German Musical Society, for the purpose of agitation and propaganda on behalf of the musical tendency to which Brendel had devoted the culminating chapter of his book seven years earlier. In his widely publicized keynote address, Brendel christened that faction the Neudeutsche Schule, or New German School (a term that, he vainly hoped, would replace "Zukunftist" once and for all). The guest of honor at the convocation, the honorary president of the society, and the figurehead of the New German School was the same man whose music Brendel had held aloft in his History as the beacon of "progress to a new consciousness" of music's historical obligation. He was Franz Liszt.

Sure enough, the Holy Roman Empire was neither holy nor Roman. The New German School had a Hungarian, albeit one living in Weimar, for a figurehead. (Brendel's other envisioned figurehead was Hector Berlioz, a Frenchman.) For this Brendel had a ready Hegelian explanation. Just as the "world-genius" fulfilled a "world spirit," anyone who took music further along the liberatory dialectical line established by Beethoven realized a German spirit regardless of his birthplace. As of 1859, Liszt's symphonic poems were the most advanced embodiments (as Berlioz's programmatic and dramatic symphonies had earlier been) of Brendel's cardinal principle that in truly significant or "historical" art, "content must create its own form." Soon afterward the Wagnerian music drama assumed this role and status, and became the New German rallying point.

And the rallying point of the opposition? Brahms, of course, who as a young kapellmeister had rashly signed a letter of protest at Brendel's inaugural address, and who in the period of his eminence had a public advocate in Eduard Hanslick (author of *Vom musikalisch-Schönen,* or *On the Musically Beautiful,* with its caustic plea for timeless, "purely musical" values) to play the Franz Brendel role on his behalf.

Schoenberg's affinity for the New German line is obvious, not only musically, but also in its nationalistic and political overtones. The big step that others called the leap into "atonality," a term that he deplored for its negativity, Schoenberg called the "emancipation of dissonance," a term that owes its seductive political vibes to the liberatory rhetoric of the dialectic. Obviously it was not dissonance itself that had been emancipated; it was the composer, the protagonist of the audience-mocking poietic fallacy. That is, the composer was liberated from the constraints of "voice leading rules" whereby dissonance was subordinated to consonance in traditional harmony and counterpoint.

But why was this necessary? Just because constraints existed? That is the usual vulgar Hegelian answer, but it is quite incorrect. The emancipation of dissonance was the result of a surprising synthesis between the New German ideology and its Brahmsian, "purely musical" antithesis. But even that is not quite right, because "purely musical" value was, at least for Schoenberg if not for Brahms, a metaphorical value with roots in the so-called extramusical world, the world of ideas.

The reference to "roots" is a clue to the metaphor. Here is another clue: after devising the tone row that would serve as the basis for the third movement of his Woodwind Quintet, op. 26, one of the milestones in the development of his twelve-tone technique, Schoenberg wrote in his sketchbook, "I think Goethe would be very pleased with me." Goethe, who in addition to his artistic pursuits was trained in—and contributed to—botany, optics, and other scientific disciplines, was the apostle of organicism, one of the main branches (and once a metaphor gets going, it's hard to stop it) of romantic art theory. Schoenberg was one of his most conscientious and enthusiastic heirs.

Goethe's science was a highly Platonized sort of science, devoted to the "discovery" (that is, the assertion) of archetypes. It may actually have been Plato who inspired Goethe's scientific inquiries, with his remark in *Phaedrus* that an artistic composition "should be like a living being, with a body of its own, as it were, and neither headless nor feetless, with a middle and with members adapted to each other and to the whole." This location of formal harmony in a theory of functional differentiation and mutual adaptation found corroboration in Goethe's elaboration of the *Urpflanze,* the archetypal plant. After making countless drawings of actual plants, Goethe tried (in his *Versuch die Metamorphose der Pflanzen zu erklären,* or *Attempt to Explain the Metamorphosis of Plants*) to abstract or to synthesize the functional principles of plant life in a master drawing that could be proposed as a primeval or universal model to which actual phenomena had to conform in order successfully, or validly, to exemplify planthood. It proposed the hidden organic unity that underlay the blooming, buzzing diversity of nature.

The Goethean *Urpflanze* lies behind all the many attempts by Schoenberg and his adepts (including Allen Shawn, as in his analysis of *Pierrot Lunaire*) to demonstrate the quality of a musical composition by relating its surface complexity to a simple and functionally unifying motif—or, to go further into specifically Schoenbergian territory, to a *Grundgestalt,* or basic shape. Not even the most expert commentators on Schoenberg (and here I am thinking of Severine Neff, the co-translator and coeditor of his most extended theoretical treatment of the subject) can give a concise and consistent definition of this most fundamental Schoenbergian concept, in part because

Schoenberg never gave one; but we do know that it was a conscious adaptation of Goethe's terminology for the components of the *Urpflanze* (especially "der innere Kern," the inner nucleus).

Schoenberg was sure that the permeation of a composition in all its dimensions by a unifying kernel was an objective measure of its value—a properly poietic criterion rather than an esthesic one. Of all the composers in the German tradition, Brahms had been the supreme master of the "basic shape." For many self-styled progressives, it was the reason for regarding Brahms as academic. For Schoenberg, as the title of one of his most famous essays proclaims, it made Brahms himself a "progressive"—far more of one, indeed, than Wagner.

Schoenberg showed his inheritance from Wagner and the other New Germans in works such as *Gurrelieder,* the mega-oratorio that so obviously contended with Wagner on the mythic site of *The Ring* (but in a "decadent" erotic manner reminiscent of *Tristan und Isolde*), and in *Verklärte Nacht* (Transfigured Night), a programmatic tone poem scored for a string sextet, in which Schoenberg conspicuously brought the principle of "content-determined form" into the quintessentially classical domain of chamber music. His inheritance from Brahms could be seen on what Schoenberg liked to call the "subcutaneous" level—the level of microstructure and microtexture—where he sought, through what he called the principle of "developing variation," to exceed both the outer diversity and the inner unity that earlier composers had attained and achieve the perfection, at a much more basic musical level, of content-determined form.

What had set limits on earlier accomplishment? Those very rules that subordinated dissonance to consonance. Under traditional constraints, not every melodic idea can also function as a harmonic idea. Under the regime of "emancipated dissonance," it can. Emancipating the dissonance made it possible to integrate the musical texture beyond all previous imagining. It also became the site of greatest tension between esthesic and poietic criteria. Harmonic syntax, in particular, became incomprehensible to most listeners (including composers, when listening). To reorient one's thinking so that harmony could be conceptualized as verticalized melody (or melody as horizontalized harmony) opened a notional trapdoor that avoided the problem. Never resolved, and perhaps never to be resolved, is the question that gives rise to all the battles: the extent to which esthesic perception can be validly sacrificed to (or subsumed within) poietic conception. ("But can you *hear* it?")

These questions became all the more urgent as the "freely atonal" music that Schoenberg composed from about 1908 to 1917 gave way to the "serialized" music that he wrote after inventing the twelve-tone technique around 1921. (The period in between was fallow, giving a nicely articulated shape to Schoenberg's career.) The beauty of a twelve-tone row, from the poietic standpoint, was that by furnishing a sort of quarry from which all the musical events in a composition—melodic, harmonic, contrapuntal, textural—would be hewn, it served as a sort of automatic *Grundgestalt,* absolutely ensuring the sort of demonstrable organic unity on which Goethean—that is, Schoenbergian—notions of artistic quality depended. It was not for nothing that Schoenberg imagined Goethe patting his head after coming up with a row (which was part of the precompositional or sketching process) rather than a piece. The row was the promise of perfected organicism. And yet the organicism of twelve-tone music, regarded by the composer as a given and often not particularly foregrounded at the sounding surface, can for that reason be even more esoteric to listeners than that of free atonal music, where the motivic saturation tended to be more actively demonstrated in traditional "thematic" terms.

.   .   .

Schoenberg was very much aware of these esthetic issues and took them seriously. He was well aware of the price that his creative decisions exacted. Sometimes he slyly mocked the emancipation of dissonance. A wonderful case in point is "Der Mondfleck" (The Moon-Spot), no. 18 in *Pierrot Lunaire,* the cycle for speaking voice and chamber quintet. Here is the text, translated into English from the text that Schoenberg set, namely, Otto Erich Hartleben's German translation of Albert Giraud's French original. Like all the poems in the cycle, it is cast as a rondel, with an ironic (here italicized) refrain:

> *A snowy fleck of shining moonlight*
> *on the back side of his smart new frock coat,*
> so sets forth Pierrot one balmy evening,
> in pursuit of fortune and adventure.

> Sudden—something's wrong with his appearance,
> he looks round and round and then he finds it—
> *a snowy fleck of shining moonlight*
> *on the back side of his smart new frock coat.*

> Hang it! thinks he: a speck of plaster!
> Wipes and wipes, but it won't vanish!
> On he goes, his pleasure poisoned,
> Rubs and rubs till almost morning at
> *a snowy fleck of shining moonlight.*

Schoenberg's setting is an analyst's delight: a strict canon at the octave between the violin and the cello, a freer canon (or perhaps a sort of fugue) at the twelfth between the clarinet and the piccolo, and in the piano part a harmonized version of the clarinet-piccolo canon, in doubled note-values (that is, at half the tempo), with the parts inverted, and with a third voice entering in the middle of the texture an octave below the first entry of the subject, so that the orthodox tonal relations of a fugue are seemingly maintained. Not only that, but in the middle of the tenth bar the string and wind parts reverse direction, producing a perfect melodic and rhythmic palindrome, while the piano continues to develop its fugue.

It is enough to boggle the mind, and it has elicited a lot of awestruck hyperbole, such as Charles Rosen's announcement that "Der Mondfleck" "is one of the most elaborately worked out canons since the end of the fifteenth century." Allen Shawn calls it "the apex of complexity and virtuosity," and compares its effect to vertigo: "it can only be compared to some primal and animal experience, such as suddenly finding oneself outside under a vast black sky filled with stars or unexpectedly looking over the edge of a cliff."

But how elaborately "worked out" is a canon or a fugue that is written in a style that recognizes no distinction between consonance and dissonance, so that harmonically speaking, literally anything goes? The essence of counterpoint has always been its "dissonance treatment." That, and that alone, is where skill is required and displayed. What makes Bach's *Musical Offering* or *The Art of Fugue* such astonishing tours de force is not just the complexity of the texture, but the fact that that complexity is achieved within such exacting harmonic constraints. Take away the constraints, and you have rendered the tour de force entirely pointless.

But of course Schoenberg knew this perfectly well—much better than his humorless admirers. Look again at the text: it is all about frenzied but pointless activity. That is a perfect description of an elaborate contrapuntal texture with emancipated dissonance. Or to put it the other way around, an elaborate contrapuntal texture with emancipated dissonance is a perfect metaphor for the urgent but ineffectual efforts that Pierrot is making. So from a bogus masterpiece of counterpoint, "Der Mondfleck" suddenly becomes a genuine masterpiece of self-mocking irony. Schoenberg once cracked to a pupil, "Now that I've emancipated dissonance, anybody can be a composer."

But although he could laugh at it, which is perhaps the most endearing and humanizing of his traits, Schoenberg regarded the emancipation of dissonance as something of the utmost necessity and gravity. In fact, it was holy. Its relationship to Goethe's *Urpflanze* does not explain its motivation fully. Breathtakingly overdetermined, it owed just as much in Schoenberg's thinking to the occult spiritual ideas that obsessed him at least up to the time of World War I, forming the basis for his brief but intense association with the Russian expatriate painter Wassily Kandinsky.

Alongside Schoenberg's fascination with "inner [that is, psychic] occurrences" was an equally strong interest in spiritual transcendence and the possibilities of representing it in art. From a rationalist perspective, the two impulses—psychological realism and occult revelation—can seem to be in contradiction, and both can séem to contradict the organicist basis of Schoenberg's very calculated musical technique. From a more accommodating perspective that regards psychic phenomena as emanations from a spiritual source, they can be viewed as complementary. It is when we adopt this complementary perspective that Schoenberg's musical innovations (or rather, his motivations toward them) form a coherent pattern.

In a letter to Kandinsky in 1912, Schoenberg proclaimed "a *unity of musical space demanding an absolute and unitary perception*" (the italics are his own) to be his creative ideal. He associated this aim with a book that both he and Kandinsky worshiped at the time, Honoré de Balzac's philosophical novel *Séraphîta* (1835), "perhaps the most glorious work in existence," as the composer gushed to the artist. The long central chapter in *Séraphîta* is an exposition (fanciful rather than wholly accurate) of the teachings of the occult philosopher Emanuel Swedenborg, as related to Wilfrid, a man of thirty, and Minna, a girl of seventeen, by an androgynous ethereal being with whom both are in love and who in the last chapter ascends to an angelic state. The two lovers, who are left to share the love they bore for the angel, are privileged to witness the assumption and are vouchsafed a vision of heaven:

> Wilfrid and Minna now understood some of the mysterious words of the being who on earth had appeared to them under the form which was intelligible to each—Séraphîtus to one, Séraphîta to the other—seeing that here all was homogeneous. Light gave birth to melody, and melody to light; colors were both light and melody; motion was number endowed by the Word; in short, everything was at once sonorous, diaphanous, and mobile; so that, everything existing in everything else, extension knew no limits, and the angels could traverse it everywhere to the utmost depths of the infinite.

Many details in Balzac's heavenly depiction found echo in Schoenberg's musical theorizing. Where in Balzac's heaven "colors were both light and melody," Schoenberg's *Harmonielehre* contained a famous speculation on the possibility of composing "tone-color melodies" that would add another dimension of integration to his utopian musical universe, with timbre playing a role normally assigned to pitch. (The closest he came to realizing it was in the third of the Five Pieces for Orchestra, Shawn's lie-on-the-floor-and-close-your-eyes piece, where very slowly changing harmonies shimmer with dovetailed instrumental voicings that cause the timbres of sustained tones to shift subtly before one's ears.)

But it was not just a vision that Schoenberg wanted to transmit. He also wanted to convey an experience: Wilfrid and Minna's experience in ascending to Séraphîta's abode, where "everything existed in everything else." That is why he much preferred the term *pantonality* to *atonality* as a description of the "rootless" music that followed from the emancipation of dissonance. He viewed pantonality very much the way Balzac had presented

Séraphîtus/Séraphîta. Surmounting the major/minor dichotomy, voiding all distinctions between particular keys, was for him an achievement comparable to embodying androgyny or double gender. Pantonal music, like Balzac's angel, was a perfected being. To his pupil Anton Webern he confided that pantonality, like androgyny, "has given rise to a higher race!"

Such a music embodied a spiritual worldview, a universal existential revelation. And it was this in addition to being a music of primal unconscious emotional expression and a music of unprecedented organic integrity. Once again we face the fact that the most important thing that the emancipation of dissonance vouchsafed was not the expression of catastrophic emotions, though that was a spectacular by-product, but the achievement of a fully integrated musical space, in which the "horizontal" and the "vertical" dimensions were made equivalent and everything musical could exist in everything else. Only by emancipating the dissonance, Schoenberg argued, could musical practice become fully adequate to the musical imagination. "Every musical configuration," he wrote,

> every movement of tones has to be comprehended primarily as a mutual relation of sounds, of oscillatory vibrations, appearing at different places and times. To the imaginative and creative faculty, relations in the material sphere are as independent from directions or planes as material objects are, in their sphere, to our perceptive faculties. Just as our mind always recognizes, for instance, a knife, a bottle, or a watch, regardless of its position, and can reproduce it in the imagination in every possible position, even so a musical creator's mind can operate subconsciously with a row of tones, regardless of their direction, regardless of the way in which a mirror might show the mutual relations, which remain a given quality.

Here we have another reason why the old "tonal" constraints had to go: they impeded these "mutual relations." As long as they were in force, a harmonic progression would no longer mean the same thing (whether "syntactically" or "semantically") if it were played in reverse, or if all or some of its intervals were inverted.

Consider a G-major triad followed by a C-major triad. In the context of the key of C major, this progression can mean "the end," as Beethoven thunderously insisted in the last coda to his Fifth Symphony. If reversed, however, it can mean anything but that. And if inverted, so that the G-major triad becomes a C-minor triad, and the C-major triad an F-minor triad, it would all of a sudden (in the same tonal context) lose its syntactical significance altogether and pick up instead a terrific freight of emotion. These trivial examples suffice to show that in "tonal" music, musical space is neither reversible nor invertible without fundamental change of meaning (and it is precisely such distinctions, many are beginning to readmit, that make musical meaning esthesically available at all).

But thanks to the emancipation of dissonance, the horizontal and the vertical do indeed become interchangeable, and retrogressions or inversions are functionally (or rather functionlessly) equivalent. Musical space has been unified, or equalized in every dimension, so that musical objects and ideas (that is, basic shapes and their motivic derivatives) can now be "reproduced," just as the mind can imagine them, "in every possible position, regardless of their direction." The "basic operations" of the twelve-tone technique—inversion, retrogression, retrograde inversion—can now be seen in their true spiritual light as vouchsafing to mortal man a glimpse of Swedenborgian heaven. Indeed, Schoenberg revealed in a letter to Nicolas Slonimsky that it was in the course of planning a symphony based on a grandiose unrealized project for an opera or oratorio on the subject of *Séraphîta* that in 1914 the first glimmer of the twelve-tone technique occurred to him.

·   ·   ·

At several points in his book Allen Shawn falls back on organicist metaphors ("in his tonal phase he carried the basic seeds of each work in his mind just as he would later carry his twelve-tone row forms, allowing relationships and combinations to germinate in his unconscious"), these being second nature to academically trained composers in Schoenberg's wake. At one point he even mentions *Séraphîta* but only, rather strangely, in connection with being short of stature (a characteristic, we learn, that Balzac's Wilfrid shared with Arnold Schoenberg and Allen Shawn). Nowhere does he show any real awareness of the roles that organicism and spiritualism played in the Schoenbergian evolution that he defends, preferring to base his advocacy on traits with which today's listeners are more likely to sympathize.

There is nothing new—and nothing necessarily disreputable—about rethinking a historical figure in contemporary terms. "Deproblematizing" problematical figures, however, comes at a price. Reducing Schoenberg to an administrator of emotional shocks and a stimulator of esthetic reverie runs the risk of reducing his significance (and that of his music), eliminating what is most interesting about him, and most worthy of attention.

What is most interesting and most worthy of attention is also at times the most unpleasant, and I am not at all persuaded that Schoenberg's cause is best served by averting our eyes or ears from the unpleasantness. Shawn exposes the sanitizing nature of his project most when he attempts, at the end of his discussion of the opera *Die glückliche Hand*, to explain "why this and so many other works by Schoenberg repelled a good part of its audience":

> We need first to remind ourselves that music itself has a unique power to disturb, that the wellsprings of its power to delight are also the source of its power to appall. The evanescent character of its substance, the mystery of its internal laws to nonmusicians, the potentially disturbing metaphorical nature of sound production—which mimics speech, breathing, the beating of our hearts—and

the incomprehensibility of the connection between the physical principles involved and the emotions aroused, all make for a situation in which the listener feels vulnerable and seeks familiarity and what he or she takes to be signposts of order.

This paragraph, and indeed the whole discussion of *Die glückliche Hand*, strikes me as a colossal evasion—one prefigured in Shawn's discussion of *Verklärte Nacht*, Schoenberg's most popular composition (perhaps his only popular composition). The Richard Dehmel poem on which Schoenberg based it deals with what the composer, in a program note he wrote near the end of his life to accompany the first LP recording of the piece, called "a staggeringly difficult human problem." An unhappily married woman confesses to her lover that she is carrying her unloved husband's child. She fears that this will prevent their blissful if illicit union; but at the poem's (and the music's) turning point, "the voice of a man speaks," as Schoenberg put it, "a man whose generosity is as sublime as his love," and who promises to love her child as his own. That is what "transfigures" the night; the music, formerly agitated and dissonant, dissolves in radiant, consonant warmth.

The poem, Schoenberg admitted in 1950, was one that "many a person today might call repulsive." He probably had in mind its bizarrely inverted (or perverted) theme of guilt over a legitimate but "inauthentic" pregnancy. Today it would more likely be the poem's misogyny (an immanently sinful modern Eve forgiven and redeemed by a godlike magnanimous man) that offends. In any event, Schoenberg claimed that his music performed a redemptive function similar to the man's. "Because it does not illustrate any action or drama, but was restricted to portray nature and to express human emotions," he wrote, "it seems that, due to this attitude, my composition has gained qualities which can also satisfy even if one does not know what it illustrates; or in other words, it offers the possibility to be appreciated as 'pure' music. Thus, perhaps, it can make you forget the poem."

This was one of Schoenberg's worst ideas, but like all of his ideas it has been hugely influential. He even wrote an odd essay called "On the Relationship with the Text," in which he recalled once realizing with a shock that he didn't have any idea what the words of some of his favorite Schubert songs were about. But then, having satisfied his curiosity, he concluded that he hadn't been missing anything: "On the contrary, it appeared that, without knowing the poem, I had grasped the content, the real content, perhaps even more profoundly than if I had clung to the surface of the mere thoughts expressed in words." Predictably enough, he related this discovery to the *Urpflanze*, finding in it further proof that "the work of art is like every other complete organism. It is so homogeneous in its composition that in every little detail it reveals its truest, inmost essence."

One may doubt this. (Would Schoenberg have allowed that just by knowing the poem one could grasp "the truest, inmost essence" of a song? It is, by his own claim, just as organic a part of the whole.) And one may deplore the consequences of the idea as well. Take *Die glückliche Hand,* which I do indeed find appalling, and not for any of the reasons that Shawn allows. Its text, by Schoenberg, so bellows its misogyny as almost to seem intended as an illustration of Otto Weininger's twisted treatise, *Sex and Character,* which carried essentialized notions of destructive female hysteria and creative male rationality (the types represented in the two halves of *Verklärte Nacht*) to their furthest extreme. Women, Weininger wrote, were "logically insane"; their often-admired "intuition" he attributed to "a lack of definiteness in their thinking capacity," which "gives the widest scope to vague associations." Only submission to an anchoring man can curb their destructive force by symbolically killing them. The most obvious musical offshoot from Weininger was Hindemith's early opera, *Mörder, Hoffnung der Frauen* (Murderer, Hope of Women), to a text by Oskar Kokoschka, the title of which marked out the road—the only road—to female redemption.

Schoenberg actually referred to Weininger in his *Harmonielehre* as a deep thinker, without making any specific reference to his crackpot ideas. But as David Schiff pointed out in a thought-provoking article in the *New York Times* on Schoenberg and sex, Schoenberg's two expressionistic operas furnish, between them, another representation of Weininger's dichotomy of gender, and a lurid one.

Though often represented (by Shawn, among many others) as a meditation on the universal human condition, the musical content of *Erwartung,* effortlessly composed in a matter of weeks in late summer 1909, is (in Schiff's words) "appropriately feminine in the Weiningerian sense: tingling and spasmodic, sensual, without structure or direction." In *Die glückliche Hand,* costively composed over a three-year period, 1910 to 1913, Schoenberg set out to fashion the masculine counterpart, the epitome of the strong silent type (called, simply, The Man in the libretto), shabbily betrayed by his Woman, who runs off with her effete, decadent (that is, feminized, possibly Judaized) friend the Gentleman (both silent, mimed roles) and draws The Man, in futile pursuit, from his natural medium, the realm of unfettered ideas. She insults him, even hurls boulders at him. At the very beginning we see The Man suffering in a more metaphorical way from her grip, beset by a catlike fantastic monster that has sunk its teeth into his neck to paralyze him.

The Man is infinitely and instinctively creative: without the benefit of training, he fashions an exquisite diadem at a single magnificent stroke. He speaks in lurchy, barely articulate ejaculations, set to curiously clunky music that in its effort to avoid fluid femininity slips at times into rather conventional patterns like imitative counterpoint and ostinatos. Schoenberg's effort to fashion a representation of the eternal male, with his superior mental and ethical equipage, has to be counted a failure if for no other reason than, compared with the fantastically imaginative (if suspiciously "intuitive") music of *Erwartung*, it sounds like a stylistic backslide. And its bathos is unendurable. If the work were better known, the line that Schoenberg wrote to accompany The Man's forging of the diadem would be a classic of unintended humor among English-speaking (well, Yinglish-speaking) connoisseurs: *So schafft man Schmuck,* "That's how you create jewels." Serves him right.

Can one attend to this self-pitying farrago with a straight face? Shawn writes with unironic reverence about its "breathtaking newness" and 'visionary' character" and its "peaks of intense complexity and dissonance," admires its "unflinching" idealism, and enthusiastically describes Schoenberg's detailed lighting scenario, the opera's most obviously innovative aspect. He again lavishes praise on the "disturbing" qualities of the music—"the density of thinking of a Bach, Beethoven, or Mozart was being revived and the listener was at the mercy of music as demanding and therefore threatening as the work of those masters, but now employing hitherto transitional, marginal, or outlawed combinations of rhythms and tones"—but never once confronts the disturbing aspects of the text. Instead there are some murky lucubrations on the essential Jewishness of Schoenberg's music (to "help account for the hostility and incomprehension engendered by his work") that would have surprised me less in a sixty-year-old publication from Joseph Goebbels's Reichsmusikkammer. And even here, let it be noted, Shawn is willing to speak only about style, not meaning.

.   .   .

I am tempted to say that only a composer could be this blind. But not only composers have their eyes wide shut. That most musicians and music lovers are inclined, or feel constrained, to turn a blind eye on the morally or politically dubious aspects of serious music—and thus imply that the only legitimate object of praise or censure in art is the quality of its making—represents the ultimate triumph of the poietic fallacy, and the best measure of the counterproductive mischief that it can make.

Looking at Schoenberg through the prism of the poietic fallacy makes it possible, even at this incredibly late date, to contend (and even believe) that the only thing militating against the widespread acceptance of his art is its novelty. On the contrary: its greatest obstacle is the exceedingly old-fashioned, even outmoded, esthetic—compounded of historical determinism, organicism, occultism, solipsism—that so obviously informs it, along with a host of hoary elitist and sexist clichés, and a megadose of the jargon of authenticity.

Schoenberg's advocates, especially the college teachers among them, love to point to their students' responses ("unprejudiced," they always claim, but no such claim by a figure of authority can be believed) as evidence of

Schoenberg's perennial contemporaneity. Shawn claims that "Schoenberg particularly moves, excites, and amazes young listeners," while Susan McClary, a professor at UCLA, reports (according to Marc Swed, music critic of the *Los Angeles Times*) that "among her students, the idealistic fans at the radical edges of pop music"—she specifically mentions kids in Nine Inch Nails T-shirts—"are most readily drawn to his uncompromising music and revolutionary spirit as soon as they are exposed to it."

I have seen that reaction, too. But just as often I have seen my students wrinkle their noses and say "ick" when forced to listen to *Verklärte Nacht,* and I owe my sensitivity to the sexist message being purveyed under cover of universalism in Schoenberg's expressionist works in considerable measure to my students—and not only to the women among them. That rebellious adolescents feel a kinship with Schoenbergian heroics, in any event, does not seem to me to be the most persuasive case one could be making on his behalf. That sort of appreciation testifies reliably to a shopworn romanticism.

Rather than the ones that smell like teen spirit, the Schoenberg works that seem to me destined to survive (or maybe just the ones I would like to see survive) are the ones in which he showed his ironic, playfully inventive side: *Pierrot Lunaire,* first of all, and (from the early period) the First String Quartet and the Chamber Symphony; but also a number of the early twelve-tone works like the Suite for Piano, op. 25, or the Septet-Suite, op. 29 (the piece that knocked Stravinsky's socks off and sent him down the serial road). Some of the late "American" works—the Fourth Quartet, the String Trio—produce such euphoria in the analyzing mind as to carry over into aural experience forever after; but I am not at all certain, Shawn's strenuous assurances notwithstanding, that the aural joy would come about without the earlier mental exertions. For me, though, they are definitely keepers.

The unbearably self-important operas, even *Moses und Aron,* belong one and all in the rapidly growing museum of rotten twentieth-century ideas. There they can be inspected, and even admired for their "fierce integrity" and their "transcendent mastery," without all the baggage of Heritage and Obligation that oppresses listeners today, thanks to well-meaning but misguided advocates, even Allen Shawn. And let the kitsch component be recognized as such, especially the pretentious Variations for orchestra op. 31, with its screaming references to the musical cipher B-A-C-H proclaiming Germanic hegemony, and the abominably banal *Survivor from Warsaw,* with its Erich von Stroheim Nazi and its trumped up Triumph of the Human Spirit.

Above all, let us drop the pretense that the history of Schoenberg's stylistic evolution represented *in nuce* that of the whole twentieth century, recently voiced by Anthony Tommasini in the *New York Times,* when he described the ending of the *Gurrelieder* as "a nostalgic but unavoidable farewell to the tonal era, one last embrace before the door is shut." The embrace was real enough, but of course the door was never shut. All that was shut were the minds of musicians still in thrall to the nineteenth-century musical politics of the New German School, of which Schoenberg was the twentieth century's outstanding representative.

When all of that is done; when Schoenberg is placed in proper perspective as one of the twentieth century's most powerful musical minds, but also one of its most eccentric; and when the poietic fallacy at last gives way to a view of "serious" music that takes adequate account of its function as a communicative medium, then such music (Schoenberg's, to be sure, but far more important, our own contemporary concert music) may once again—perhaps, eventually—become one of the arts that matter.

POSTSCRIPT, 2008

It was not exactly news when a male reader wrote in to the *Musical Times* from Germany to assure us all that, whatever Taruskin might think, Schoenberg was neither a misogynist nor a German chauvinist, or that someone would assume I was blaming Schoenberg for the poietic fallacy, and try to set me straight.[1] Great men will always have their retainers. A more interesting case was that of Joseph Auner, author of a documentary biography of Schoenberg (*A Schoenberg Reader: Documents of a Life* [New Haven: Yale University Press, 2003]), who set out to refute my thesis but only illustrated it. "While there is no doubt," he writes,

> that a "divergence of interests" has separated audiences and composers over the last century, the notion that this is due to the poietic fallacy is questionable, if the evidence from the broader musical culture and popular culture in general is any measure. Any attempt to determine what sort of information is pertinent for listeners needs to confront the striking *convergence* of interests between artists and audiences over the past century. Rather than the obsession of a few modernist apologists, what might be called the "poietic imperative" has become the dominant way of making and receiving art.[2]

Exactly. Is there any way to stop?

NOTES

1. Timothy Bond, "Speaking up for Schoenberg" (letter to the editor), *Musical Times* 145, no. 1889 (Winter 2004): 2–4; Michael Graubart, "Fallacies and Confusions," *Musical Times* 145, no. 1888 (Autumn 2004): 19–24.

2. Joseph Auner, "Composing on Stage: Schoenberg and the Creative Process as Public Performance," *19th-Century Music* 29 (2005): 69.

37

The Musical Mystique
Defending Classical Music against Its Devotees

Julian Johnson, *Who Needs Classical Music? Cultural Choice and Musical Value* (Oxford: Oxford University Press, 2002; 140 pp.)

Joshua Fineberg, *Classical Music, Why Bother? Hearing the World of Contemporary Culture through a Composer's Ears* (New York: Routledge, 2006; xvii, 162 pp.)

Lawrence Kramer, *Why Classical Music Still Matters* (Berkeley: University of California Press, 2007; viii, 242 pp.)

Last January, Gene Weingarten, a *Washington Post* columnist, persuaded the violinist Joshua Bell to join him in an experiment. Bell was to dress in jeans, a T-shirt, and a baseball cap, position himself at the head of the escalator in the L'Enfant Plaza subway station at the height of the morning rush hour, open his violin case, take out his $3.5 million Stradivarius, launch into Bach's D-minor Chaconne for solo violin, and see what happened.

Nothing much happened. People hurrying to work hurried by. Half a dozen or so, mainly those working in the station or early for appointments, listened for a little while and put some money in the open case. One passerby, a former violinist, knew the playing was superb and dropped a five. Another recognized the performer and dropped a twenty.

But of course it was no experiment. All concerned knew perfectly well that people at rush hour are preoccupied with other things than arts and leisure, and would not break their stride. But the fulfillment of the self-fulfilling prophecy gave Weingarten the pretext he sought, in an article titled "Pearls before Breakfast," to cluck and tut, to quote Kant and Tocqueville, and to carry on as if now we knew what really happened at Abu Ghraib.

Bloggers took up the refrain. Notice, wrote one, that "all the children wanted to stop and listen. They knew. But their parents kept them moving on. Sadly it reminds me of an occasion when children wanted to stop and listen to Christ but his disciples didn't let them." Saddest for me was that the Web list of the American Musicological Society, my professional organization, added its meed of clucking and cackling. Scholars are supposed to be skeptical of spin

First published in the *New Republic*, 22 October 2007.

and pose, but here we were piling on. My hat goes off to one Ben.H, a Netizen who saw through it all. "Perhaps the Post could do a whole series of articles about philistines ignoring Joshua Bell's sublime music-making in different locations," he suggested:

1. Outside a burning building (not one fireman stopped to listen!)
2. At a car crash site (one paramedic actually pushed him aside!)
3. During a graduation exam (shushed by the invigilators!)
4. At a school play (thrown out by angry parents!)
5. On an airport runway (passing jet liners seemed oblivious!)

In one respect, though, the caper was instructive. It offered answers to those who wonder why classical music now finds itself friendless in its moment of self-perceived crisis, a long moment that has given rise in recent years to a whole literature of elegy and jeremiad. These three books, by self-appointed counsels for the defense, constitute one of its subgenres. Others have argued the case for the prosecution. Their books include *Who Killed Classical Music? Maestros, Managers, and Corporate Politics,* by Norman Lebrecht, a sloppy but entertaining British muckraker; *Classical Music in America: A History of Its Rise and Fall,* by Joseph Horowitz, the latest version of a book that Horowitz has written several times by now, beginning with *Understanding Toscanini* in 1987; and *Mozart in the Jungle: Sex Drugs and Classical Music,* by Blair Tindall, a journalist and recovering oboist, which despite a pandering title actually contains the smartest and most constructive take on the situation.

What makes the classical music crisis suddenly newsworthy is itself a question worth asking. When has the place of classical music in modern society ever been secure? Reviewing Lawrence Kramer's offering in the *New York Times,* Edward Rothstein shrewdly observed that it might have appeared decades ago, but then it would have had a title more like "Why Contemporary Composers Don't Matter" or "Why Audiences Are Stuck in the Past." This is a weatherbeaten complaint, and one that no longer seems worth debating. To quote Pieter van der Merwe, a South African music historian, "For the general public, 'classical music' belongs mainly to the eighteenth and nineteenth centuries, carries on with rapidly diminishing vigor into the first few decades of the twentieth, and has ceased to exist by 1950." The difference is that the irrelevance to concert audiences of contemporary music now seems to be merely a special case of a problem facing the classical field as a whole. Doubts have widened, and Rothstein admits that he has come to share them: "Though I once tended to whine about its problems with cranky optimism, now even a stunning performance seems like a spray of flowers at a funeral."

If a supporter as staunch as Rothstein, who served as the classical music maven for this magazine before briefly assuming the post of chief classical critic for the *Times*, can fall away, you surely see why I speak of friendlessness. Classical music has itself—among others—to blame for the quandary it now faces, and I see the reason epitomized in the *Washington Post*'s disgusting "experiment" with Bell the busker. The discourse that supported its old prestige has lost its credibility. As with rising gorge I consumed the books I had agreed to review, the question that throbbed and pounded in my head was whether it was still possible to defend my beloved repertoire without recourse to pious tommyrot, double standards, false dichotomies, smug nostalgia, utopian delusions, social snobbery, tautology, hypocrisy, trivialization, pretense, innuendo, reactionary invective, or imperial haberdashery.

On the evidence before me, the answer is no. The discourse supporting classical music so reeks of historical blindness and sanctimonious self-regard as to render the object of its ministrations practically indefensible. Belief in its indispensability, or in its cultural superiority, is by now unrecoverable, and those who mount such arguments on its behalf morally indict themselves. Which is not to say that classical music, or any music, is morally reprehensible. Only people, not music, can be that. What is reprehensible is to see its cause as right against some wrong. What is destroying the credibility of classical music is an unacknowledged or misperceived collision of rights. The only defense classical music needs, and the only one that has any hope of succeeding, is the defense of classical music (in the words of T. W. Adorno, a premier offender) against its devotees.

.   .   .

It would take a book—Joseph Horowitz's book, for example, or Lawrence Levine's widely cited *Highbrow/Lowbrow*—to account for the cultural clout that classical music managed to acquire in such unlikely terrain as postbellum America; although maybe it is not such a riddle after all that the traditionally "high" musical genres should have amassed unassailable cultural capital in the "gilded" age of intensely concentrated wealth and increasing social stratification. Nor is it easy to describe the terms of its prestige in the period of its American ascendancy. It does have one rough and readily observable measure, though: the cultural prestige of an art medium can be calculated according to the extent to which there is perceived social advantage in claiming (or feigning) appreciation of it.

By that standard one can demonstrate that the high plateau of public esteem that classical music reached in America in the 1880s (the decade that saw the founding of the Boston Symphony and the Metropolitan Opera) lasted through the depression (when the Works Progress Administration was called in to rescue it) and the Good War, and into the Eisenhower decade, and that its decline thereafter was precipitous. In fall 1956, when Eisenhower was running for reelection, RCA Victor issued a long-playing disc called *The President's Favorite Music,* consisting of a selection of items from the firm's backlist, a cover illustration that is evidently an official White House portrait of the grinning occupant seated at his desk with the First Lady by his side, and a back cover containing a sort of benediction, signed with a facsimile of the president's handwriting, celebrating the role of musicians and of music in his life and in the life of the nation. The musical selections include some that had plausible connections with Eisenhower, such as Dmitry Tiomkin's title theme for *High Noon,* as well as inspirational numbers like Marian Anderson singing "He's Got the Whole World in His Hands" and Leopold Stokowski's arrangement of Bach's "Sheep May Safely Graze" (a paean, in case you've forgotten, not to the deity but to wise political leadership). But the bulk of the offering consists of three orchestral overtures: Beethoven's *Coriolan* (originally written to accompany a German tragedy, as the producers of the album had surely forgotten, about unwise political leadership), Mendelssohn's *Fingal's Cave,* and Strauss's *Fledermaus.* I have no idea how much actual input President Eisenhower had in the planning of this record, but it doesn't matter. What matters is that identification with classical music was considered, by him or his handlers as much as by the record folks, to be a significant enhancer of his image.

Even better proof that classical music consumption was seen as a political asset came during the next election season. In 1960, *Time* magazine reported on the musical tastes of the major-party candidates for president and vice president, as ascertained by Paul Hume, music critic of the *Washington Post* (whose main claim to fame was a contretemps with President Truman over his review of First Daughter Margaret's recital debut). John F. Kennedy responded to Hume's inquiry through his wife, who sent a letter listing Debussy's *Afternoon of a Faun,* Ravel's *La Valse,* the overture to Berlioz's *Benvenuto Cellini,* Musorgsky's *Boris Godunov,* and the Polovetsian Dances from Borodin's *Prince Igor.* (I'm pretty sure that this Franco-Russian repertoire reflected the future First Lady's taste. While a junior at George Washington University studying in Paris, Jacqueline Bouvier had won a *Vogue* magazine essay contest on "People I Wish I Had Known" with an entry on Oscar Wilde, Charles Baudelaire, and—most germane—Serge de Diaghilev; when Stravinsky heard about this list from President Kennedy at a White House dinner, he concluded that she had been researching pederasty.)

Richard Nixon confessed to *Time* that his sentimental favorites were *Oklahoma!* ("because it was the first show that he and Pat saw after moving to Washington") and Mexican folk songs ("because they reminded him of his honeymoon south of the border"), but he still complied with Hume's request for a classical choice and cited Chaikovsky's *Swan Lake.* Lyndon Johnson put himself down as "an indiscriminate admirer of Strauss waltzes." Henry Cabot Lodge, the true patrician in the company, named Mozart's Clarinet Quintet, K. 581 (he gave the Köchel number), alongside Handel's *Messiah* and (the noblesse oblige concession) recordings by the Dukes of Dixieland. (His wife added Bach's Suite No. 3 for Unaccompanied Cello, but only if "performed by Pablo Casals.")

And now? I learn from Joshua Fineberg's *Classical Music, Why Bother?* that George Herbert Walker Bush, every bit as much of a patrician as Henry Cabot Lodge, "was known to prefer the Beach Boys to the Philharmonic and saw no need to pretend a love for high culture." From Richard H. Solomon's *Chinese Political Negotiating Behavior, 1967–1984,* I learn that when Gerald R. Ford visited the People's Republic of China in 1975, his hosts made discreet inquiries as to what music he would like to be entertained with. It turned out to be the University of Michigan football song, "Hail to the Victors." (They goofed and played Michigan State's fight song instead.) When it was Vice President Walter Mondale's turn to visit in 1979, "the Chinese delighted their guest by playing his favorite songs from 'The Sound of Music' but left him most impressed with the degree of manipulation they were prepared to resort to in order to make a positive impression."

Fineberg takes a sour Spenglerian view of this devolution, and with startling fatuousness he blames it on a late-blooming "misreading" of dada's (yes, Cage's and Duchamp's) "attacks on the artistic status quo." But what actually happened was more like a *trahison des clercs,* a defection of intellectuals to pop culture that was a by-product of the social and cultural unrest of the 1960s. The first symptoms in music took the form of regal welcomes to the Beatles from conspicuously placed mandarins. First there was William Mann, chief music reviewer (which in those days, it went without saying, meant classical music reviewer) for the *Times of London,* and his surprise nomination of John Lennon and Paul McCartney as the outstanding new composers of 1963.

Then, far more decisively, came Ned Rorem, a well-known if not yet celebrated American composer with a recognized specialty in art songs, seething with resentment against an academic establishment, then dominated by twelve-tone composers, that despised him. Rorem contributed an essay called "The Music of the Beatles" to the four-year-old but already august *New York Review of Books.* It appeared early in the fateful year 1968, and began with a remarkable salvo: "I never go to classical concerts anymore, and I don't know anyone who does." Along the way there were yummy stinkbombs like this: "There *are* still people who exclaim: 'What's a nice musician like you putting us on about The Beatles for?' They are the same ones who at this late date take theater more seriously than movies and go to symphony concerts because pop insults their intelligence, unaware that the situation is now precisely reversed." (Between Mann and Rorem the boys from Liverpool were inducted into formal academic criticism via Richard Poirier's "Learning from the Beatles" in *Partisan Review,* replete with the mandatory dissertation prologue proclaiming that everyone who has written about this subject before the author is a dunce.)

Mann compared the Beatles to Mahler, Rorem to Poulenc (and Poirier—
yep—to T. S. Eliot). That sort of hype looks quaint now, because soon
enough there were highly educated critics aplenty who could write expertly
about rock and other popular genres, and about their histories, without having to validate them with comparisons to canonical greats. This new breed
of critic emerged first in "alternative" newspapers and samizdat fanzines, of
which *Crawdaddy!*, originally a mimeographed sheet with a print run of five
hundred, was the first. In an early essay from *Crawdaddy!* called "The Aesthetics of Rock," later widely anthologized and expanded into a book, Richard Meltzer (then a philosophy major at SUNY Stony Brook) gave the flavor
of this new pop criticism. The essay ranged from James Joyce to Hegel's *Phenomenology of Spirit* to Lennon and McCartney to Andy Warhol to Bob Dylan,
winding up with W. V. Quine. The idea that someone who read Hegel and
Quine would seek musical fulfillment in McCartney rather than Webern was
new, and very threatening to established authorities like Milton Babbitt, who
complained, in an interview published in 1979, "We receive brilliant, privileged freshmen at Princeton, who in their first year of college are likely to
take a philosophy of science course with [logical positivist] Carl Hempel, and
then return to their dormitories to play the same records that the least literate members of our society embrace as the only relevant music." Pierre
Bourdieu, were you listening? This came very close to enunciating as an explicit program the tacit view of art as a producer of social distinction that the
Joshua Bell "experiment" reinforced.

Babbitt's complaint came much too late to matter. Since the "British in-
vasion," nearly half a century ago, it has been socially acceptable, even fashionable, for intellectuals to pay attention primarily to commercial music, and
they often seem oblivious to the very existence of other genres. Of no other
art medium is this true. Intellectuals in America distinguish between commercial and "literary" fiction, between commercial and "fine" art, between
mass-market and "art" cinema. But the distinction in music is no longer
drawn, except by professionals. Nowadays most educated persons maintain
a lifelong fealty to the popular groups they embraced as adolescents, and
generation gaps between parents and children now manifest themselves musically in contests between rock styles.

Of course professionals can be just as oblivious, and they look funnier,
since they are blind not to a blip but to the main picture. I had a grim laugh
when I read an interview in the *New York Times* this past July with George Benjamin, a forty-seven-year-old British composer, in town for the American
première of a chamber opera he had written. He was pulling the usual long
face about the fact that music "is not valued in contemporary society." He
challenged the reporter interviewing him to "name a single politician who
shows interest in the music of our time." This was only days after the *Times*
had published an interview with John Edwards in which the candidate spoke

enthusiastically about U2, Bruce Springsteen, and Dave Matthews. Poppy Bush, as we've seen, is into the Beach Boys. Bill Clinton, the most musically savvy of our recent presidents, claimed no identification with the classics. He and Hillary even named their daughter after a Joni Mitchell song. But while his musical attitudes might not console George Benjamin, they do attest to an authentic involvement with the music of our time, and I for one rate our sax-toting president's participatory investment in music higher than anyone's passive consumption of the classics, to say nothing of the previously expected feigning of cultivated taste. Such authenticity is a positive change in our culture, connected to the generally enhanced level of seriousness with which America has been taking its professed social egalitarianism since the 1960s. Can classical music fit into that?

·   ·   ·

One would not think so, to judge by all the cutting back now going on. The big news this summer is the elimination or downgrading of classical music reviewing in the nation's newspapers and general interest magazines. The *Chicago Sun-Times* and the *Minneapolis Star-Tribune* eliminated their classical critics by buying them out and retiring their positions. The biggest story concerned *New York* magazine's Peter G. Davis, a veteran critic who once worked for the *Times* and is widely esteemed as a connoisseur of opera and singing. He was replaced, against his will, by Justin Davidson (formerly of *Newsday*), who will cover architecture as well as music. But although it made headlines this year, this development has long been in progress. The beat of this magazine's masthead music critic has gone over from classical to pop. The *Atlantic* once had a classical record column and for a while regularly printed excellent essays on classical music by the composer David Schiff, but now it spurns the topic. *The Nation* used to let Edward Said play at classical reviewing but now covers only pop and jazz with regularity.

Nor are print media the only, or even the most important, venue to suffer spectacular cutbacks. Classical radio stations have dropped like flies. New York has been a one-classical-station town since 1993, the San Francisco Bay Area since 1994. The Metropolitan Opera lost its national broadcast sponsor in 1987 as a result of the collapse of oil prices, and its broadcasts are now funded catch-as-catch-can. The Bay Area, home of the second most prestigious opera company in America, no longer receives them because no local sponsor finds them profitable, and the one remaining classical station, being a default monopoly, can afford to flout its opera-loving listeners. The collapse of big-ticket classical recording is also an old story (though hardy indie labels like Naxos, with low overheads, are still bucking the trend). Tower Records is gone, and classical CD sales mostly take place online. Most orchestras are now without major-label contracts. Some of them, like the San Francisco

Symphony, have gone into samizdat. Classical music is now generally regarded not as a common cultural heritage (except, perhaps, at funerals) but as an upscale niche product.

But the present collapse looks more dramatic than it really is, if that is any consolation. It follows a period of enthusiastic but unsustainable growth that coincided, ironically enough, precisely with the inauspicious changes in consumption patterns just surveyed—a testimony to the triumph of romanticism over realism in our musical culture. (This is the story that Tindall's book tells especially vividly, because its author is an angry victim of the bubble's burst.) It was only since the 1960s, the very decade when the prestige of classical music began losing ground, that most orchestras instituted year-round seasons. Professional arts education also ballooned in that decade: among the institutions founded at the time were the California Institute of the Arts and the North Carolina School of the Arts; the latter was the first state-supported school of its kind. Lincoln Center, dedicated by President Eisenhower in 1959, opened its first doors, to Philharmonic Hall (now Avery Fisher Hall), in 1962. Spurred by the cold war (which turned Van Cliburn's 1958 victory at the first Chaikovsky Competition in Moscow into a geopolitical triumph) and Lyndon Johnson's Great Society agenda, the federal government took up the task of arts funding—not as a bailout, as in the depression, but in the expectation that increased supply would increase demand. Johnson's National Council on the Arts (1964) led directly to the establishment the next year of the National Endowment for the Arts. The high-water mark for federal arts funding was reached under Nixon ("the NEA's messiah," in Tindall's words), who ratcheted its budget up to $40 million in 1971. By then, the New York State Council on the Arts, founded under the aegis of Governor Nelson Rockefeller, a seasoned arts patron, had been in business for a decade.

Especially in New York, then, the period roughly from the founding of Lincoln Center to Black Monday in 1987 was a golden age for art producers. Major organizations used public subsidies to supplement private donations and vastly improve the working conditions of their employees. Tiny groups, including several in which I then participated as a performing musician, proliferated. And I haven't even mentioned the corporate foundations, which also mushroomed both in number and in lavishness of largesse. The Ford Foundation, the biggest one pre-Gates, had been founded in 1936 to "strengthen democratic values, reduce poverty and injustice, promote international cooperation and advance human achievement." It took up the cause of the arts, including classical music, in the late 1950s. The Rockefeller Foundation, a much older organization, got on the arts bandwagon in connection with Lincoln Center. In the 1980s, the big name was Citicorp. During this period, as Tindall comments, "most performing arts groups were subsidized by unearned donated income, as well as tax incentives, and therefore did not always have to link revenue to the quantity, quality, or type of product they offered."

As long as this gravy train lasted, the attrition of the audience could be overlooked. The result of living for three decades in a fool's paradise was a vast overpopulation of classical musicians as many more were trained, and briefly employed, than a market economy could bear. The cutbacks that seemed to imply the sudden cruel rejection of classical music were really more in the nature of a market correction, reflecting the present scarcity of patronage and a long-deferred confrontation with the changed realities of demand.

·   ·   ·

There are two ways of dealing with the new pressure on classical music to go out and earn its living. One is accommodation, which can entail painful losses and have its excesses (the "dumbing-down" that everybody except management deplores). Blair Tindall's main grievance is the inadequate education she received at the North Carolina School of the Arts, which left her unskilled for other work. Her accommodation consisted of retraining as a journalist. Orchestras have accommodated by modifying their programming in a fashion that favors the Itzies and Pinkies and little divas. Composers have accommodated by adopting more "accessible" styles. Love it or hate it, such accommodation is a normal part of the evolutionary history of any art.

The other way is to hole up in such sanctuary as still exists and hurl imprecations and exhortations. That is the path of resistance to change and defense of the status quo, and it is the path chosen by the authors of the books here under review. The status quo in question, by now a veritable mummy, is the German romanticism that still reigns in many academic precincts, for the academy is the one area of musical life that can still effectively insulate its transient denizens (students) and luckier permanent residents (faculty) from the vagaries of the market. Inevitably, all three authors are professors. In its strongest, most "uncompromising" form the heritage of German romanticism is the ideology of modernism, and it is again no surprise to learn that two of the authors are composers who write in academically protected styles. (The third, Kramer, is also a dabbler in composition, but that is not his main profession.) Despite their obvious self-interest, they claim to be offering disinterested commentary and propounding universal values.

These values are now a little more than two centuries old, deriving from a discourse that originated with Moses Mendelssohn and Immanuel Kant in the late eighteenth century, made its first beachhead on musical terrain via E. T. A. Hoffmann in the first decade of the nineteenth century, reached an apogee with Schopenhauer, and had Adorno, who died in 1969, as its last authentic apostle. Although it began as an ethnocentric creed and continues to have German epigones, its chief bastion is now the Anglophone academy. (When I vented a rather vehement anti-Adornian position, somewhat along the lines of what will follow here, before a German audience in Berlin last year and encountered surprisingly little resistance, I asked one of my hosts about it and was told, "Oh my dear, Adorno is your problem now.") The main tenet of the creed is defense of the autonomy of the human subject as manifested in art that is created out of a purely esthetic, hence disinterested, impulse. Such art is without utilitarian purpose (although, as Kant famously insisted, it is "purposive"), but it serves as the symbolic embodiment of human freedom and the vehicle of transcendent metaphysical experience.

This is the most asocial definition of artistic value ever promulgated. Artists, responsible to themselves alone, provide a model of human self-realization. All social demands on the artist—whether made by state, by church, or by paying public—and all social or commercial mediation are inimical to the authenticity of the creative product.

Belief in the transcendent human value of creative labor has always invested German romantic esthetics with the trappings of a secular or humanistic religion. In the twentieth century, such a theory of art could be seen as a bulwark against totalitarianism. Adorno held it up as a counterforce, as well, to the instrumentalizing and rationalizing tendencies of "administered" capitalist society, which turn human subjects into objects of economic exploitation. Since he was trained in music, he held up classical music in its least "compromised" form (epitomized in the staunchly esoteric work of Arnold Schoenberg) as the chief example of "truth-bearing" art, as opposed to the dehumanizing popular music churned out by the culture industry for mass dissemination.

Skeptics of this viewpoint, while often appreciating the loftiness of its aspirations, have pointed to the ease with which high ideals can shade into complacency, autonomy into irrelevance, and disinterestedness into indifference. My admittedly tendentious diction ("serve," "vehicle") signals my own skepticism as to the genuineness of its disinterestedness. This skepticism is not mine alone. Many have noted the relationship between this highly individualistic and self-celebrating concept of art and the social emancipation (or perhaps more accurately, the social abandonment) of artists with the demise of reliable aristocratic patronage, and suspected it of seeking a compensatory advantage. "Materialist" historians have long investigated the relationship between its high-minded claims and actual marketing strategies.

Particularly as it pertains to music, the doctrine of esthetic autonomy was preeminently a congeries of German ideas about German art that consoled and inspired the Germans at a particular point in German history. Even in the nineteenth century, it never won much credence in France or Italy or Russia (though Britain was susceptible). Now that the whole twentieth century has run its course, and German music has run aground, the claim of universality is threadbare, recalling Stanley Hoffman's sublime definition of ethnocentrism, offered in these pages some years ago: "There are universal values, and they happen to be mine." The doctrines that Julian Johnson's, Joshua Fineberg's, and Lawrence Kramer's books continue to advance retain so little credibility that one has to ask what sort of reader they mean to persuade.

.   .   .

Who Needs Classical Music? the worst of them, is a painful thing to read. Julian Johnson declares himself an Adorno epigone, but the declaration is superfluous. Anyone who knows Adorno even by reputation will recognize this truculent book as the Cliff Notes version. But the dour Frankfurter, the most histrionically pessimistic of all cultural critics, is not the only presence in these pages. He functions here as the bad cop, yanked into an unlikely partnership with Matthew Arnold, the prophet of sweetness and light, but also the original herald of elitism ("the best that has been thought and said"). Johnson ladles out the Adornian brimstone and the Arnoldian bubble bath in indiscriminate gobbets, desperate as he is to recover for himself and the rest of his deposed cohort the unquestioned cultural authority and the unlimited official patronage that once were theirs. But the result, a sort of *Beyond the Fringe* parody of a parish sermon in some Anglican backwater, will convince no one but the choir. To have such a voice advocating one's own cause is mortifying.

The primary assertion, made on the first page of Johnson's introduction and reiterated endlessly thereafter, is that classical music is uniquely distinguished by "its claim to function *as art,* as opposed to entertainment." The whole book is an elaboration of this categorical, invidious, didactically italicized, and altogether untenable distinction, the purpose of which is to cancel the claims of consumers on the prerogatives of producers.

John Cage once observed that he was fortunate in that his work was also his entertainment. That was his explanation for his lifelong commitment to the practice of a particularly abstruse brand of art making that afforded little or no pecuniary return: he took pleasure in it, or (to quote my desk dictionary) found in it "an agreeable occupation for the mind." That pleasure, that agreeable mental pursuit that (if one is persistent and lucky) can repay the pursuer with a great intensity of delight, was certainly my own conduit into what has become my vocation. Wasn't it Johnson's? Isn't it everybody's? Can there be any other motivation for engagement with art? Before romanticism raised the stakes, the purpose of art was always described as that of "pleasing." All pretenses notwithstanding, other purposes, and especially Johnson's, remain secondary.

The reason for denigrating pleasure and claiming some other "higher" purpose for art (or, alternatively, denying that it has any purpose at all) had in the first place to do, perhaps, with the bad conscience that Kant's principle of disinterestedness imposed. But the notoriously tin-eared Kant did not deny pleasure, least of all to music, which he designated "the highest among those arts that are valued for their pleasantness." Granted, he intended no compliment, for he meant thereby to deny music a place among the arts that are valued "by the culture they supply to the mind." One can understand an impulse to try to reclaim for music the status thus denied it by downgrading its sensuous appeal and relegating that aspect to the low category of entertainment.

But pleasure does not have to be defined sensuously, and there are all kinds of pleasures: guilty pleasures, altruistic pleasures, animal pleasures, spiritual pleasures, perverse pleasures, the pleasure of a good meal, of a good cry, of worthy accomplishment, of self-improvement, of self-possession, of exclusion, of ascendancy, of dominion, of revenge. And, of course, there is also the pleasure known in Kant's native tongue as *Schadenfreude*. I reject the claims of those who affect to pursue the arts for reasons other than pleasure or satisfaction. The question, rather, is pleasure of what kind?

Johnson asserts high claims indeed. He contends that his commitment to classical music is an ethical choice. His exhortation to the prospective cultural consumer is akin to Betty Friedan's old combination of promise and threat—that if women "do not put forth, finally, that effort [and Johnson is forever reminding us how difficult and demanding classical music is] to become all that they have it in them to become, they will forfeit their own humanity." The difference is that Betty Friedan was talking about social and economic justice and Julian Johnson is only talking about some kind of music. That ethical pretense nevertheless gives him the pretext to open the floodgates to a deluge of supplementary invidious distinctions, chiefly at the expense of what (in German, inevitably) is known as "entertainment music" (*Unterhaltungsmusik*, or *U-Musik*), or what in English we call popular music. Of our authors, Johnson is the one least content to sing Arnoldian praises of his chosen genre. Like Adorno, he feels compelled to heap torrents of frantic abuse on the Big Other. These passages are shameful, in the first instance, because—again like Adorno—he shows himself to be exceedingly ill informed about the object of his derision. What is driving him? No doubt there is pleasure in it, but there is more.

Let us observe his invective at full tilt. The middle of the book contains the main elaboration of the art-versus-entertainment polemic. Here is its dizzy zenith, which I quote at some length, only slightly condensed, so that you may fairly judge its tenor. Contemporary popular culture, Johnson contends, is

> obsessed by packaging, image, and design. The surface is everything. . . . Even in music, visuals are everything: hence the ubiquity not only of the music video but the marketing of the star. And when it comes to the music itself, the surface sheen is everything; the music is literally one-dimensional—it has one sound,

one timbre, one kind of material. It rejects polyphony and discursive forms. It is as if the art of costume design were replaced by admiring pieces of cloth. . . .

What might seem harmless in relation to cultural practices, fashion, cars, or even music, is clearly invidious in relation to people. The ideal of humanity on which we have based our greatest religious, ethical, philosophical, and political thinking is not defined by our outward, material surface but by our capacity to exceed the limits of our material existence. Great art expresses this ideal in every work. In rejecting it to embrace the ideal of a blank and depthless surface embodied in contemporary culture, we reject that ideal of humanity and instead embrace a simulacrum—a synthetic and hollow substitute. Human potential is not well expressed by the fashionable, the glossy, or the chic, and yet we allow ourselves to be dominated by a culture defined almost exclusively in these terms. In doing so, we collude in our own reduction to objects.

The emphasis on the surface of things is essentially inhumane. It is pornographic because it fetishizes the materiality of human existence and denies the spiritual personality that vivifies it from within. Perhaps my use of the term "pornographic" seems inappropriate and sensationalist in relation to music. But the central category of pornography is perhaps not sex but the process by which the humane is reduced to the status of things. Pornography is reification employed in the sexual arena and displays all of its hallmarks: the reproducibility and interchangeability of all commodities, the reduction to an object, the importance of packaging, the reduction to pure surface, the simulacrum of desire, the formulaic sameness of posture, the domination of nature. But the sexual arena does not have a monopoly on the debasement of the humane. While society publicly deplores the objectification of the humane in pornography, it is busy colluding with it elsewhere through advertising, commodity fetishism, and music.

This harangue, from the musical equivalent of the religious right, is not something to be rebutted or otherwise "falsified" but to be gazed upon by those with a capacity for wonder. It commits virtually every one of the sins I enumerated above, from the false dichotomization of the material and spiritual (as if classical music did not have a material presence), to the double standard whereby the reification of classical music in the form of recordings and other manufactured goods is overlooked, to smug nostalgia for an uncommodified golden age, to the utopian delusion that such a paradise might be regained, to the hypocritical stance of moral superiority in the face of the author's obviously mendacious (unless stunningly ignorant) reduction of the other (as having only "one sound, one timbre, one kind of material"). The social snobbery borders on racism (we have minds; they have bodies) and the browbeating is blatant (assent or be lumped with Them). A page or so later, losing all self-control, Johnson tears into a description of people who don't seem to need classical music, in thrall to "prerational immediacy," lost in "libidinal energy," athirst "for the luxury of blind, adolescent emotions." What could be more "invidious in relation to people"?

But what renders this rant especially awful to anyone who knows the history of music and its discourses is its resonance with the most bigoted of all texts about music, Wagner's *Das Judenthum in der Musik,* or *Jewry in Music,* which appeared in 1850. The morally charged dichotomization of surface and depth is a romantic trope that—as the musicologist Holly Watkins has shown—goes back at least as far as the writings of Hoffmann. Between Hoffmann and Wagner, however, the metaphor of depth had been claimed by German writers as a national trait; and just as nationalism underwent its general transformation from a modernizing and liberalizing discourse into a belligerent and regressive one in the later nineteenth century, so the notion of spiritual depth had been turned into a weapon of national and racial aggrandizement in Wagner's hands. "In listening to either our naïve or our consciously artistic musical doings," wrote Wagner (in William Ashton Ellis's nineteenth-century translation),

> were the Jew to try to probe their heart and living sinews, he would find here really not one whit of likeness to *his* musical nature; and the utter strangeness of this phenomenon must scare him back so far, that he could never pluck up nerve again to mingle in our art-creating. Yet his whole position in our midst never tempts the Jew to so intimate a glimpse into our essence: wherefore, either intentionally (provided he recognizes this position of his towards us) or instinctively (if he is incapable of understanding us at all), he merely listens to the barest surface of our art, but not to its life-bestowing inner organism; and through this apathetic listening alone, can he trace external similarities with the only thing intelligible to his power of view, peculiar to this special nature.

More specific, and with an even more chilling echo of Johnson's language, is Wagner's characterization of Felix Mendelssohn, whose example

> has shown us that a Jew may have the amplest store of specific talents, may own the finest and most varied culture, the highest and the tenderest sense of honor—yet without all these pre-eminences helping him, were it but one single time, to call forth in us that deep, heart-searching effect which we await from Art because we know her capable thereof, because we have felt it many a time and oft, so soon as once a hero of our art has, so to say, but opened his mouth to speak to us. To professional critics, who haply have reached a like consciousness with ourselves hereon, it may be left to prove by specimens of Mendelssohn's art-products our statement of this indubitably certain thing; by way of illustrating our general impression, let us here be content with the fact that, in hearing a tone-piece of this composer's, we have only been able to feel engrossed where nothing beyond our more or less amusement-craving Phantasy was roused through the presentment, stringing-together and entanglement of the most elegant, the smoothest and most polished figures—as in the kaleidoscope's changeful play of form and color—but never where those figures were meant to take the shape of deep and stalwart feelings of the human heart.

Wagner's rhetoric, lacking the Arnoldian or possibly Leavisite strain on which Johnson draws, is less morally fraught than Johnson's, more purely racist. Does that let Johnson off the hook? Doubtless he would claim as much, but other esthetic moralists have been less sure. George Steiner, who surely defers to no man in what he himself has called "the worship—the word is hardly exaggerated—of the classic," finds himself at the tormented twilight of his life baffled by the example of the culture-loving Germans of the mid-twentieth century, Wagner's heirs, "who sang Schubert in the evening and tortured in the morning." He has confessed himself "haunted more and more by the question, 'Why did the humanities not humanize?' I don't have an answer." But that is because the question is wrong. It is all too obvious by now that teaching people that their love of Schubert makes them better people teaches them nothing but vainglory, and inspires attitudes that are the very opposite of humane. Julian Johnson's tract suppurates with attitudes like these. To cast esthetic preferences as moral or ethical choices at the dawn of the twenty-first century is an obscenity. Both the book itself and its reception (as recorded on Amazon.com) expose the sort of pleasure it promotes: that of solidarity in sanctimony. To all who have read it with enjoyment I urgently prescribe a reading of *Father Sergius,* Leo Tolstoy's parable of moral exhibitionism and its comeuppance. I will pray for the redemption of their souls.

.   .   .

You will not find anything comparably disgraceful in Joshua Fineberg's book, but his exhortations will prove no less futile. Fineberg is no moral grandstander. His vices are self-pity and false humility. Where *Who Needs Classical Music?* apes Adorno, the author of *Classical Music, Why Bother?* plays Uriah Heep. It may be a better way to capture the reader's benevolence, but it is a sham. Lost in the German romantic miasma, Fineberg still trades in universals and absolutes, and his strategy, like Johnson's, is to flatter his readers' elitist impulses.

So a few words about elitism before proceeding. All our authors argue strenuously that there is no necessary conflict between democratic or egalitarian ideals and striving for the best. Who would disagree? If that were all that elitism implied, there would be no debate. Contention swirls not around the question of whether there is such a thing as quality but around the question of how—and, especially, by whom—it is to be defined. When Johnson writes, "To argue that classical music, like art more generally, makes a claim to types of functions and meanings distinct from those of popular culture is to risk the charge of elitism," he is flagrantly disingenuous. "Distinct from" is a transparent euphemism for "higher (and better) than," and Johnson's recourse to euphemism betrays his guilty consciousness that his argument carries politically unacceptable baggage. He is arguing for privilege, not equality, and that

is why his index predictably contains seven entries under "political correctness," the discredited euphemism through which privileged people have
gone on the offensive in defense of their privileges.

Johnson borrows from Adorno the notion that what proponents of popular culture call democracy is instead the "pseudo-democracy of commercial
culture," which pretends to offer consumers free choice but in fact dehu-
manizes them by omnipotently and venally manipulating their desires.
People who consume popular music are not exercising taste, on this view, for
they have no taste to exercise. Rather, they robotically gobble up whatever the
culture industry doles out. Those who would ascribe autonomous cultural
agency to hoi polloi "might at least pause to wonder why today's hits, apparently deeply significant to millions, become objects of derision in a matter
of years," writes Johnson. Really? The Beatles? Elvis? Sinatra? And do the
touted geniuses of classical music always achieve timelessness? Read Bernard
Shaw on Hermann Goetz some time. Or Constant Lambert on Bernard van
Dieren. Or reread, in a decade or two, Julian Johnson on Jonathan Harvey
or Alex Ross on John Adams. The idea that in popular culture production
equals consumption was already a canard when first handed down from
Adorno's delphic armchair. (Think of all those rockers driving taxis who by
his logic should be millionaires.) That his followers still parrot him only
shows how utterly ideology trumps observation in the world of "critical theory," of all academic stances the least critical by far.

"For me personally," writes Joshua Fineberg, "the problem is not elites
based on merit, but elites of birth, gender, race, or class." Again, who would
(dare to) disagree? But until one has offered a definition of merit, the statement is empty; indeed, it is a Trojan horse. Fineberg knows better than to
load it with moralizing slogans, although he does not scruple to pour scorn
on those who "spout" the virtues of diversity. Instead he seeks his universals
and absolutes within the world of art itself. He preaches the faith forthrightly,
on its actual romantic merits, and with due reckoning of the price that it exacts in enlightenment. Just as religious belief demands the voluntary relin-
quishing of rational skepticism, he writes,

> a true belief in art is also predicated on an underlying conceptual framework
> that depends just as absolutely on a belief in abstract criteria of worth. This no-
> tion, which is profoundly out of fashion today, has formed the underpinning of
> artistic endeavor in the West for a very long time. Adherents of this idea believe
> that even if societal fashions or institutional structures are opposed to a partic-
> ular artist or work, some essential greatness (or lack thereof) will ultimately de-
> termine the worth of the art object if given the chance. And even if the work is
> never recognized, it is still of equal (albeit latent) value. In other words, a Rem-
> brandt hanging in the woods would still be great even if no one had the good
> fortune to see it.

You have to grant a certain respect to Fineberg's up-front promulgation of mystique. He does not try to argue the case for his objective criteria, although he does make some attempt to define them. He merely invites the reader, in what he calls "the artistic or aesthetic version of Pascal's wager," to consent to them. Pascal's wager, you will recall, is the proposition that believing in God, or at least acting as if you did and behaving yourself accordingly, is a good bet. If it turns out there is no God and no afterlife, then all you have lost is a bit of ephemeral terrestrial amusement. If it turns out that He does exist, you gain eternal bliss. So put aside your modern mind, dear reader, and follow the ancient path of righteousness.

Of course, Pascal was weighing something slightly more momentous than choosing a musical menu. And nobody need ask about the source of authority for religious dogma. But where shall the prospective musical novice turn? Turn to me, says Fineberg. I know what's good for you.

> Art is not about giving people what they want. It's about giving them something *they don't know they want*. It's about submitting to someone else's vision; forcing your aesthetic sense to assimilate the output of someone else's. . . . [A]ll art demands a surrendering of your vision in submission to the artist's or at least the museum or concert curator's.

Submit! Our youngest author, bizarrely enough, assumes the most patently paternalistic posture, regurgitating the immortal words of Lord Reith of Stonehaven, the first director general of the BBC: "We know precisely what the public wants, and by Heaven they're not going to get it!" You see why I thought of Uriah Heep. Behind the 'umble exterior is an iron will and an ego of positively Rushmorean proportions. Fineberg reminds his readers that the onus is theirs, not the artist's, when it comes to "deciphering his or her meaning," for "religious individuals do not achieve a worshipful state by being God" but "by contemplating God's actions (or the actions we attribute to a God)."

Unlike Johnson's, then, Fineberg's cards are on the table. What are his objective and abstract criteria of musical worth? Merely what any university or conservatory composition teacher will tell you they are. Their measure is the artist's degree of craft-plus-originality. Since craft can only be judged by practitioners, the appeal of an art-work to an audience can never serve as a valid measure of its value, except in reverse:

> The level of skill required to make most art of whatever type requires intense and (from society's viewpoint) expensive training. It seems clear that this training cannot be made freely available to all comers without posing a burden that society would never be willing to bear. Moreover, an art like contemporary classical music is doubly burdensome. Composers don't produce wealth as they become more successful; they consume it. Bigger, more prominent events lose even more money (and require more subsidies) than small student concerts. The success of a composer can be measured by taking the

inverse of the composer's market value: The more negative the market value, the more important the composer.

So kindly leave war to the generals, and pay up. But music is far too important to be left to the composers. Their interests and aims, when insulated from public judgment, are apt to be trivial, amounting to contests over academic turf and flare-ups of professional rivalry. The risible second half of Fineberg's book is a perfect illustration—risible, because after a hundred-page sermon on disinterestedness we get a sales pitch. The product he's flogging is "spectralism," a fairly recent French trend based on computer-assisted spectrographic analyses of instrumental timbres. And we also get a sectarian polemic against Julian Johnson's faction, the Vienna-derived twelve-tone school, now celebrating eighty years in the desert. My universal values, Fineberg assures us, can lick their universal values, and my technique is more advanced.

Will this sort of thing really persuade nonprofessional readers to bother about classical music? Obviously not, but the book is not really meant for them. Like Johnson's, it is sooner meant to comfort the author's own cohort—it has already called forth a hardy little amen corner in the blogosphere—and perhaps lull the dean into keeping the old curriculum in place.

.   .   .

With Lawrence Kramer we come at last to a writer who really addresses the readers whom he claims to address. He too writes from within the German romantic tradition, but he has the sense explicitly to reject Johnsonian-Adornian moralism (although, he admits, "part of me is in sympathy with it") and Finebergian mystification, along with all "condescending and authoritarian" attitudes. His approach picks up directly from E. T. A. Hoffmann, the fount of the tradition, perhaps as a way of skirting the pitfalls to which later proponents of classical music have so readily fallen prey. Indeed, Kramer quite resembles Hoffmann. Both are literary men—Kramer's scholarly training was in English and comparative literature—and both write about instrumental music in a way that turns it into a kind of wordless literature.

That was seen in Hoffmann's day as an elevation of music (*and* of literature). This strain of criticism reached an early peak—its pinnacle, I would say—in the writings of Robert Schumann. The trouble with the approach in hands other than Schumann's is that it readily descends into reductive verbal (usually narrative) paraphrase—into "readings"—which can then replace the music as the focus of interest and topic of discussion. Although Kramer's readings of music can make for entertaining and sometimes absorbing reading—and let it be said straightaway that he gives as much pleasure to the reader as his counterparts give pain—I am unpersuaded that they will win any souls to the cause. They are simply too secondary to the musical experience. As Hector Berlioz, another musico-literary paragon of early romanticism, once observed, music can give an idea of love, but love can give no idea of music. Explaining, no matter how appealingly, what music is "about" will not give anyone an idea of why people who listen to music find it so compelling. That is why I feel sure that Kramer's book will, like the others, mainly be read by those already convinced of its premise.

Although he invokes a famous screed by Virgil Thomson against the "music appreciation racket," Kramer's method is actually quite similar to that of appreciation lecturers (though handicapped by the absence of sounding examples). Those worthies are always pressing listeners to listen for "the theme," since tracing its course through an extended composition, supposedly, will instill the ability to perceive its form. For Kramer this is just "formalism," almost as great a sin for hermeneuts as it was for Stalinists. But his first and most substantial chapter, "The Fate of Melody and the Dream of Return," really amounts to the same thing, only now the theme being traced is "read" as the subject persona of a quasi-literary narrative. The formal routines that in the hands of music appreciators are scorned as sterile all at once become stirring life trajectories, symbolizing and catalyzing the listener's own emotional epiphanies (*Erlebnisse,* in the German original) in a manner very effectively described half a century ago in Susanne K. Langer's *Feeling and Form.* But this was no new insight even in Langer's day. It is a bedrock tenet of romanticism, and again goes straight back to Hoffmann. Its rise has been traced in a fascinating book by the cultural historian James H. Johnson, *Listening in Paris,* which shows how the kind of absorbed, attentive listening all proponents of classical music advocate, and the subjective identification with its progress that Kramer promotes, caught on in the mid-nineteenth century.

I bring up Langer and Johnson not to dispute a claim of originality that Kramer never makes but rather to emphasize that the musical properties and listening habits that Kramer wants to associate with classical music in general have a narrowly circumscribed history and range of application. Their starting point has been located by Karol Berger in *Bach's Cycle, Mozart's Arrow: An Essay on the Origins of Musical Modernity,* a recent and highly stimulating book. The model that Kramer proposes for classical music—that of forward-progressing narrative (the time arrow, in Berger's language)—is only one of a number of ways in which classical music is organized. It is the one best suited to music appreciation lectures, since it is the one in which it makes the best sense to trace the vicissitudes (a.k.a. the "development") of a theme— though Kramer's account misses the even more crucial role of goal-directed (or "functional") harmony in propelling the arrow, perhaps because he thought it too technical.

The thematic-development model, though it does turn a lot of nineteenth-century compositions into absorbing and thrilling emotional "journeys," lost its prominence in the twentieth century and characterizes very little recent classical music. The "minimalists," who now turn out the music of greatest proven audience appeal, have frankly eschewed it. Thus Kramer's view of his subject seems in its own, less objectionable way just as nostalgic as Julian Johnson's or Joshua Fineberg's. It entails a kind of music and—more to the point—a kind of listener that is receding into the past, and it is unlikely to help solve classical music's most pressing problem, which is the problem of audience renewal.

I am uneasy, moreover, about encouraging listeners to decode formal archetypes, as when Kramer uses Beethoven's symphonic trajectories to show how music can become the bearer of deep-seated cultural myths. Such stratagems descend ineluctably into abuse. Look what's happened to poor Shostakovich, whose symphonies and quartets, perhaps the twentieth century's paramount examples of music as *Bildungsroman,* have been turned into political footballs by interpreters who have no ear for music. Or to poor Chaikovsky, whose symphonies are now routinely read as evidence of his homosexual guilt and in support of ludicrous legends about his alleged suicide. If homophiles or homophobes can get their various kicks from a Chaikovsky symphony, or Communists or anti-Communists from Shostakovich, that's fine with me: I do not care why they listen as long as they go on listening. But when they tell me that they know what a piece objectively means, and that their certainty makes them better listeners than I, then I know that they have stopped listening. The paraphrase is all they hear.

What draws listeners to music—not just classical music, but any music—is what cannot be paraphrased: the stuff that sets your voice a-humming, your toes a-tapping, your mind's ear ringing, your ear's mind reeling. And that is not the kind of response that anyone's books can instill. It is picked up, like language, from exposure and reproduction, which eventually lead to internalization. Kramer leads prospective listeners astray when he counsels them, in a chapter about performing music, that the "most vital role for performance" in relation to the fixed score "is precisely to suggest verbal and imagistic connections with the world, the very thing that the traditional culture of classical music, in the twentieth century at any rate, tried to get us to regard as forbidden." If the value of music lies in the words and the pictures that it prompts, then why not cut out the middleman and go straight for the words and the pictures? Like a wise man of Chelm, a listener taking Kramer's advice will go to the market for a goose and come home with a bucket of water.

Nor is Kramer's account entirely devoid of vainglory and invidiousness. Nobody's defense of classical music, it seems, can do without these. He traces his own involvement with classical music "from the day that I first accidentally heard a Beethoven overture (someone bought the record by mistake) rocking through the chilly, lifeless suburban 'family room' of my early teens."

Ah, sensitive youth! And in a chapter on song, Kramer makes his only—inevitably, ignorant and prejudiced—comparisons between the classical and the popular, asserting that, because of its emancipated accompaniment, art song can convey complexity of feeling—irony, ambivalence, self-reflection—whereas popular song can offer no more than a good tune and an uncomplicated emotional payoff. Balderdash. Indeed, in another chapter Kramer himself takes note of Cole Porter's "wavering balance of irony and sentiment" (and I won't even mention the Beatles' "A Day in the Life" or "She's Leaving Home"). He will answer, no doubt, that Porter and McCartney had learned some tricks from classical music. No doubt they had, but that commerce has always been a two-way street.

Ultimately, Kramer betrays classical music by viewing it, along with Johnson and Fineberg, through an Eliotic scrim. Just as T. S. Eliot proclaimed that "it is a function of all art to give us some perception of an order in life, by imposing an order upon it," so all three authors see the key asset of classical music as that of providing repose and balance, control and restraint, amid the frightful hurly-burly of modern life. This leaves a lot out—where's *The Rite of Spring*? where's the *Grosse Fuge*?—and it colludes with the regressive, reductive tendencies that all three authors deplore, which threaten to turn classical music into an escapist pursuit or link it with high-end consumer goods. Our solitary Bay Area classical station has an ad in which, to the strains of Beethoven's *Pastoral* Symphony (one of Kramer's prime exhibits), the announcer soothingly intones, "On the homeward commute, when it's just you and the radio, reach for the good stuff, reach for KDFC." KDFC's emblematic offering is a daily hour called "The Island of Sanity."

But though I kvetch, I cannot deny that these contentments are among classical music's appeals, and no one has the right to declare them illegitimate. Indeed, I condemn attempts to hide classical music's association with creature comforts or its class affinities, because hypocrisy is the one thing a preacher's reputation cannot survive. That is why one of Julian Johnson's worst moves is to rail against Pierre Bourdieu's contention that classical music's "claim to difference is derived *entirely*" from its function "as a tool of class distinction." The overemphatic italics give him away. He knows that Bourdieu never made such a claim. And he also knows that the claim Bourdieu did make—that class distinction is among the factors that have propagated high culture in our society, particularly since (and owing to) the decline of hereditary aristocracy—is irrefutable. Johnson is reduced to arguing on the level of a marital spat: when one spouse says, "But what about x?" the other is sure to retort, "All you ever think about is x!"

·   ·   ·

Here Kramer manages to save the day. The best parts of his book, which I hope he will gather up and publish as a single essay so that they can be read without having to read the rest, are the ones in which he writes about the use of classical music in the movies. I prescribe them to Johnson and Fineberg, because they suggest the myriad positive ways in which classical music has operated—and will go on operating—in our culture. They transcend the silly opposition of the classical and the popular, because they show the ways in which the classical functions *within* the popular. And they evade the pitfalls of hermeneutics because here Kramer offers not readings of music but readings of readings. To ask "what does it mean?" is death for music; but to ask "what has it meant?" can be illuminating. The one imposes arbitrary limits; the other welcomes all comers to share in the pleasure of engagement and response.

One of these passages juxtaposes a number of films "that depend on performances of classical music to defeat joylessness, intolerance, hypocrisy, and worse." The best known is the venerable tearjerker *Brief Encounter,* in which Rachmaninoff's Second Piano Concerto, derided by many as outmoded, bloated, and sentimental, becomes—through these very attributes—a reliquary of thwarted love and dashed hopes as cathartically relived by an "ordinary," emotionally repressed Englishwoman, who missed her one extraordinary chance in life. Jazz or pop music could not have embodied transcendence of ordinary modern life in this context, Kramer implies, to which I'd add that something grander—say, Isolde's "Liebestod"—would have so exceeded its scale as to perpetrate a bathos. Other examples include a weird old Cary Grant comedy, *People Will Talk,* in which a euphoric amateur performance of Brahms's *Academic Festival Overture* (conducted by Grant, playing a med school professor and music buff) crowns a plot that combines redemption through love with the defeat of a McCarthyish academic intrigue; and *Impromptu,* my favorite composer biopic, whose lovely antiphilistine message Kramer smartly encapsulates by observing that, of all the artists, would-be artists, and anti-artists depicted in the movie, "only [George] Sand and Chopin understand that art enhances life only indirectly, by suggestion, never by program or pronouncement." (Take that, Johnson and Fineberg.)

But Kramer's chef d'oeuvre is the inspired juxtaposition of two recent films, *The Pianist* and *Master and Commander,* which employ the same classical composition in their sound tracks, the Prelude to Bach's first suite for unaccompanied cello. (As a lagniappe near the end of the book, he throws in yet another performance of the same morsel, Yo-Yo Ma's guest appearance on *The West Wing* in 2000.) The various handlings of the piece and its relevance to the action and mood of the two films and the television episode are vastly different, yet equally apt, and that in itself is already a superb point scored against attempts (including Kramer's own) to decode simple messages from complex musical designs. In the one context Kramer sees the piece as figuring fecundity and proliferation; in the other he reads withdrawal, maternal caring, and the fragility of life; while in the third, the Prelude, cast as it were against type, acts as a poisonous little madeleine on a character's memory, and ultimately as a bearer of truth. These descriptions all ring true, even if (like any verbalization) they limit the illimitable—and isn't that the point, at last?

Not that this overflow of uncontainable signification is classical music's unique attribute or achievement. Kramer goes out of his way to remind the reader that "classical music shares this potential with more vernacular types." But what Kramer does succeed in showing is that classical music contributes a particular register of discourse that other genres do not duplicate. The classic register—I borrow the term from a fine forthcoming book by Michael Long called *Beautiful Monsters: Imagining the Classic in Musical Media*—is typically an elevated, exalted, aspiring one. That makes it an easy butt of ridicule. Think of Margaret Dumont, Groucho Marx's "plus-sized muse" (as Long describes her)—but also recall that by the end of *A Night at the Opera*, Miss Dumont is no longer being satirized, and opera has worked its unmocked magic. Higher is not automatically better; but opponents of snobbish pretension would be foolish to lose sight of the reality of the high-low gamut. The proof of its reality is the way it reproduces itself within all discourses: now we have "classic jazz" and "classic rock," and I'll bet somebody somewhere is touting classic kitsch. We all draw on its full range, or as much of it as we can, and its narrowing would be a loss to everyone.

With that in mind, consider Kramer's cleverly titled final chapter, "Persephone's Fiddle," which is largely devoted to—guess what?—a violinist Kramer once heard busking unaccompanied Bach in the subway. Unlike Joshua Bell at L'Enfant Plaza, this fiddler drew a rapt crowd:

> It was early fall, the start of a new academic semester, and the performer on the platform—Times Square, my usual spot—looked like a music student trying to pick up some extra cash for books or scores. She was young, in her early twenties, blonde, attractive, and well dressed, which may help explain the unusual amount of attention she was getting from a crowd that in normal circumstances doesn't give a busker a second glance.
> Or maybe it was the music. . . .

Kramer goes on to speculate about what it was in Bach that so captivated fifteen or twenty listeners in that noisy atmosphere and moved them at the end to "a moment of complete silence followed by a smattering of applause." My question, rather, is whether you noticed the difference between the scene Kramer describes and the one Gene Weingarten engineered for Joshua Bell. It couldn't be simpler, or more crucial.

Bell was playing at the entrance to the station, where trains cannot be seen and everyone is hurrying to catch one. Kramer's little Persephone was playing down on the platform, where riders are apt to be at (enforced) leisure. Little Persephone knew that she needed an appropriate location to get across her message ("Isn't this beautiful?" or "Can I have some money?" or whatever you like). The *Post* reporter chose the least appropriate location possible. One of them was trying to make money; the other was trying to make a point. Bach served them both equally well.

As a team of Texas researchers have recently announced, there are exactly 237 known reasons why people have sex. There are at least as many reasons why they listen to classical music, of which to sit in solemn silence on a dull dark dock is only one. There will always be social reasons as well as purely esthetic ones, and thank God for that. There will always be people who make money from it—and why not?—as well as those who starve for love of it. Classical music is not dying; it is changing. (My favorite example right now is Gabriel Prokofiev, British-born grandson of the Russian composer, who studied electronic music in school, has headed a successful disco-punk band, and is now writing string quartets.) Change can be opposed and slowed, but it cannot be stopped. All three of our authors seem reluctant to acknowledge that ineluctable fact. But change is not always loss, and realizing this should not threaten but console.

Altered demographics and evolving social attitudes will work their inevitable effects. New or advancing media will continue to transform what they convey. We may not like the changes, any more than speakers of Latin may have liked the transformation of their language into French or Romanian. That, too, must have looked to some like corruption, degeneration, and death. Others learned to reap its rewards. Maybe it takes a historian to realize that mediation, the hydra-headed monster at which the sub-Adornos tilt, has been around as long as music has been, and its function is adaptive—which is to say, destructive and preservative in equal measure. Autonomous art, the recent product of a chance concatenation of circumstances, will last only as long as circumstances continue to permit. But its origin, whatever it was, and its end, whatever it will be, are points on a continuum.

Don't take it from me. There is a great moment in an early episode of *The Sopranos*, everybody's favorite example right now of popular culture transmuted into art, in which a Hasid, taking a beating from a team of enforcers with Tony Soprano at their head, is putting up unexpected resistance. He reminds his tormentors of Masada, where tough Jews held out against the Romans. "The Romans," he snorts. "Where are they now?" "You're lookin' at 'em, asshole!" says Tony. Do not expect nuance from a mob boss; but if you agree that the line is funny, you have recognized its kernel of truth. Toynbee could not have put it better.

38

Revising Revision

Kevin Korsyn, "Towards a New Poetics of Musical Influence," *Music Analysis* 10 (1991): 3–72.

Joseph N. Straus, *Remaking the Past: Musical Modernism and the Influence of the Tonal Tradition* (Cambridge, Mass.: Harvard University Press, 1990; ix, 207 pp.)

. . .

> the strongest and the fiercest Spirit
> That fought in Heav'n; now fiercer by despair.
> —MILTON, *Paradise Lost*, 2.44–45

> More than ever, contemporary poets insist that they are telling the truth in their work, and more than ever they tell continuous lies, particularly about their relations to one another, and most consistently about their relations to their precursors.
> —HAROLD BLOOM, *A Map of Misreading*

What has made Harold Bloom's agonistic theory of poetic influence so popular? It is not a pretty thing. At its core is bleakness—a view of human nature founded on jealousy, territoriality, resentment, and of human relations founded on corrosive rivalry, contention, strife. "Revisionism," the forcible recasting of what is received, is his announced subject, "and revisionism, in personal life, in society and its institutions, in religion, and in the arts and sciences and all the academic disciplines, is a fierce process, however that process conceals itself in the codes of civilization."[1] Bloom is in the company of Machiavelli, of Nietzsche, of Freud, indeed of all who have seen human beings chiefly as obstacles to other human beings.

Bloom agrees with other recent critics that literature is self-referential. Texts are "intertextual"; they refer not to the world at large but to other texts. "There are *no* texts," he goes so far as to assert (for the moment sounding very much like a deconstructionist), "but only relationships *between* texts."[2] Yet where deconstructionists see intertextuality as unbounded and indeterminate, and give themselves up with gusto to the hermeneutic of infinite regress, Bloom's intertextual criticism "has succeeded in returning poetry to history,"[3] if not a history with which music historians will necessarily care to identify. For Bloom, a poem is nothing more or less than a

Originally published in the *Journal of the American Musicological Society (JAMS)* 46 (1993): 114–38. Copyright © 1993 by the American Musicological Society.

deadly locking of horns, one particular human being's struggle with "strong" precursors, the ones who inspire feelings of inadequacy, of guilt, of "belatedness."

The history of literature—meaning the fallen literature of our sorry post-Enlightened, quasi-Alexandrian "late, late Romantic" age (as Leonard B. Meyer has called it)[4]—is for Bloom a history of appalling fathers, who have said everything, and sulking sons, obsessed at once with history and with themselves. Once again Freud is invoked, this time in the guise of family romancer. Poets—"strong" poets—begin as Oedipus and end as Laius. Success as a poet is achieved by parricide. The weapon of deliverance is contrary paraphrase: "To live, the poet must *misinterpret* the father, by the crucial act of misprision, which is the re-writing of the father."[5] The meaning of any poem is thus determined by its family ties: in the case of a strong poet, the meaning lies in the poem's distorting, opportunistic, perverse relationship—what Bloom has so famously christened "misreading"—to previous poems.

The whole theory, in short, is a celebration of strength—a strength revealed not in forbearance or magnanimity but (as Bloom says Nietzsche says) *only in fighting*. "Poetic strength," Bloom alleges, "comes only from a triumphant wrestling with the greatest of the dead, and from an even more triumphant solipsism." He has constructed, like Nabokov if for vastly different reasons, a "willful little pantheon" (as John Updike called Nabokov's),[6] Bloom's peopled only by those who have rapaciously ingested the threatening ghosts of their predecessors and metabolized them. "How is it / I extract strength from the beef I eat?" asks Whitman, one of Bloom's strong poets, in a solipsistic untitled verse from *Leaves of Grass* that happened to be set (as "Walt Whitman") by Charles Ives, himself no stranger to the anxiety of influence, as he acknowledged time and again by vehement denial. It is precisely the question to which Bloom's theory provides an impressively fine-tuned if repellent answer.

Thus the misreading strong, and only they, may defeat their belatedness and keep the history of poetry going. Like any elite, such artists are of course "infrequent." (Bloom recognizes only two consistently strong poets in English in the twentieth century, Wallace Stevens and Thomas Hardy.) Even "great poets," he maintains, "may fail of continuous strength," though if they are great they cannot fail continually (strength being the only measure of greatness). "And major innovators," he contends, "may never touch strength at all"—for Bloom could not care less about style or compositional technique or *their* histories.[7]

This last proviso will set many a musicologist's teeth on edge, for musicology has from the beginning been concerned primarily with style, with compositional technique, and with something it calls structure, none of which play any significant role in Bloom's theory. Strong composers have been defined musicologically as the protagonists of technical innovation—"*change and novelty,*" in Leo Treitler's oft-quoted words, being "the principal subjects of [music] history"[8]—and their works have been parsed and evaluated on the basis of formal and technical aspects that are taken musicologically to be their content. What academic music critics look for—what they find—is stylistic and formal integrity; what is most admired is a tandem of complexity and coherence. Bloom is primarily concerned with modes of meaning habitually ignored by norm-seeking musicology, if not banished altogether as "extramusical." In his antiformalism he quotes Emerson, an alter ego: "For it is not meters, but a meter-making argument that makes a poem,"[9] to which he adds, in his own voice, "To say that a poem is about itself is killing."[10] He revels in complexity, but it is a complexity that transcends and specifically denies the integrity of texts.

The model of influence musicologists have generally assumed is quite at variance with Bloom's. Theoretical formulation has been rare, but we have tended to uphold the model Bloom has tried to efface, of which the locus classicus is a celebrated essay, "Tradition and the Individual Talent," by T. S. Eliot—the "abominable Eliot" Bloom so furiously despises. It is a decorous model, centering not on uncontrollable belligerent contest but on voluntary benign submission, described by Eliot as the poet's "surrender of himself . . . to something which is more valuable."[11] Some*thing*, not someone—all have made the same willing sacrifice, and when one great artist influences another, it is a handing on of that higher, wholly impersonal thing known as tradition. Not that everything handed on is tradition: tradition to Eliot is what a musicologist (wittingly or not aping Tovey, for whom it was two words) will call "the mainstream."[12] Follow something else and you are not traditional but derivative.

Thus the slight squeamishness that often attaches to musicological attributions of personal influence, and also, perhaps, the paucity of theorizing on the subject. It is thought to be something of secondary account where important composers are concerned, not worthy of much attention—gossip, really. "It is by no means always clear what purpose the mention of a given influence is intended to serve," John Platoff (a rare theorizer) has recently cautioned, "or how it relates to any larger argument."[13] For Harold Bloom there is no larger argument, except to open the same argument out onto a more general revisionary terrain. We musicologists tend to instruct our young carefully in "what conditions must be fulfilled to demonstrate the existence of an influence,"[14] and these tend to be the same conditions—similarity and access—that govern the adjudication of plagiarism. Bloom does not require the first condition[15] (indeed he despises it as "weak") and disavows all interest in the second (mere "source study").[16]

Besides, musicologists habitually mix the notion of influence with that of model. Platoff submits Daniel Heartz's citation of Gluck's *Alceste* as a model for act 3 of *Idomeneo* (supported, though with less specificity, by previous writers, including Dent, Schrade, and Jahn) as an instance of influence. But of course a model is something freely chosen, or at least wittingly embraced, and (though there are well-known exceptions) usually something admired.[17] The emulation is deliberate if not actually grateful. The relationship, while often competitive, is not primarily adversarial.[18] Influence, especially in Bloom's formulation, arises out of just the opposite conditions. An influence is unwanted and inescapable.[19] What influences an artist is not what he loves but what he fears; his engagement with his ancestors is a compulsion born of an envious antagonism so strong that it is unconscious or masked as the love it may once have been. Its result is as often an absence as a presence. Artists are thus in no position to know, much less to acknowledge, who or what has influenced them.

The nature of Bloom's theory makes unconsciousness of influence an implicit certainty, virtually a requirement. As he describes it, an artist's creative personality is something feral: remorseless, aggressive, wholly selfish—all id, one is tempted to observe. So like the id it is encased in more acceptable modes of awareness that "conceal" the artist's true attitudes and appetites "in the codes of civilization" through repression, sublimation, the whole panoply of Freudian defensive mechanisms. An artist's own testimony, it follows, is the least reliable indicator of his real creative forebears, the ones whose work he has perversely reinscribed, except insofar as disavowal, betokening anxiety, may arouse suspicion ("for poets rightly idealize their activity; and all poets, weak and strong, agree in denying any share in the anxiety of influence").[20] The critic's task is to penetrate the defenses and bring the repressed, anxious-making relationship to light by divining and analyzing the artist's "misreadings." In the psychoanalyst's office such treatment could be called therapeutic, but out in the open with public reputations at stake it has to be called adversarial (and it has been denounced as such). The critic refuses to collude with the artist's ego; he wants to smoke out the id.

Charles Rosen, another rare author who has theorized about musical influence, exemplifies what may be the common assumption among musicologists—that composer and critic are allies, equally committed to and cooperating in elucidation. Detecting a similarity between the beginnings of Brahms's E-flat-Minor Scherzo for piano, op. 4, and Chopin's Scherzo in B-flat Minor (and another between the two trios), Rosen infers a process: "Having steeped himself in Chopin's style in order to absorb a now canonic conception of the virtuoso piano scherzo, Brahms displays the thematic reference at the opening in order to signal the presence of imitation." Chopin, on this view, was a model, not an influence, and Brahms, "a master of allusion," flaunted him like a trophy. Rosen even interprets Brahms's famous squelch about echoes of Beethoven's Ninth in his First Symphony ("Any ass can see that") as evidence that he "generally intended his references to be heard." Thus for Rosen it was "surprising" to discover that "Brahms claimed to have known no Chopin when writing the E-flat-Minor Scherzo."[21] Yet for Bloom, the claim is no surprise: it is the telltale, indispensable symptom of true influence, "the giving that famishes the taker."[22] More surprising is how Rosen reported the story of Brahms's denial, which came by way of William Mason's memoirs: he tucked it away in a footnote, and never thought to reconsider his premises in its light.

·   ·   ·

If you leave out any [pieces] at all [from op. 76] I should prefer it to be the A major, for although its middle movement is charming, it is too reminiscent of Chopin, and the beginning is too insignificant for Brahms—if you will excuse my saying so!
—CLARA SCHUMANN TO BRAHMS, 7 November 1878

What, then, is the appeal of this prickly theory? Why has it now begun to penetrate the discourse of musicology? For one general—not very appealing—thing, it is distinctly intimidating. Bloom claims to have seen through a veil (the "codes of civilization") to an underlying reality. By so radically opposing the mitigating codes, which everyone recognizes as codes, to the fierce reality that he asserts, he makes things difficult for opponents. To resist a Realpolitik is to court accusations of (at best) "noble idealization" or (at worst) complicity in a cover-up.[23] And to decry a cult of strength is to look weak.

Methodologically, Bloom's theory is as well insulated as the Freudian theory from which it borrows so heavily. If similarity is evidence of influence, but dissimilarity can be evidence of a stronger influence; if a poet's direct allusion, not to mention his open assent or avowal, can be evidence of his susceptibility, but the absence of an allusion and his denial can be evidence of a stronger susceptibility—then just what can disprove the theory? Nothing can: as a theory it is breezily "verificationist," and if it pretended to scientific status it would be laughed right out of court. But it is not science. It is connoisseurship, "a purely personal activity," Bloom has told an interviewer, having "exactly the same status as lyric poetry or narrative writing."[24] Everything depends on the quality of the performance, on its persuasiveness and its heuristic benefit. "Whether the theory is correct or not may be irrelevant to its usefulness for practical criticism, which I think can be demonstrated," he says—though he cannot resist adding that he takes resistance to his argument as its confirmation.[25]

Bloom's own encyclopedic performances are grandly virtuosic and impressive. Yet even more strategic for the theory's prestige and its spread has been the celebrated "map of misprision," first sketched out in *The Anxiety of Influence* and given fullest form in the more lucid, less lyrical sequel, *A Map of Misreading*, from which I have taken most of the quotations adduced above.[26] This handy tabular summary of complex deductions from the author's fundamental idea has been widely appropriated—against what Bloom has declared to be his wishes—as a tool to guide application, turning theory into method. It provides a set of flamboyantly esoteric terms or categories (the so-called revisionary ratios) by which to test and measure the exact relationship between a poem and the poems it anxiously misreads. The ratios are six in number, arranged in three dialectical pairs according to a model derived from another esoteric source, the exegetical tradition of Jewish gnosticism known as Kabbalah. Each ratio is provided with a counterpart in classical rhetoric (the familiar "tropes," or figures of speech) and in psychoanalytic theory (the psychic defenses, mechanisms of anxiety), and each is directly allied with a category of poetic imagery. Thus multiple points of hermeneutic access to any poem are vouchsafed, and multiple means of precise comparison suggested, in keeping with the overriding idea that criticism does not interpret single texts but interrelates them. The map, in short, is a tour de force of erudite synthesis. It is hard not to be seduced by its elegance, by its impassioned terminology, and of course by the lure (notwithstanding Bloom's disclaimers) of so eminently applicable an instrument: hence its contagion.[27]

As to what it specifically offers students of music, one can quote the author of what is up to now the most thorough application of the map of misprision to musical texts. "My appropriation of Bloom," writes Kevin Korsyn,

> does fulfil . . . many needs: it integrates musicology [i.e., music history], theory and criticism, giving us a method of critical evaluation that is both historical and analytical; it accommodates the paradoxes of influence showing originality and tradition, continuity and change in dialectical relation. Even if one rejects the idea of an organic work (as deconstruction advocates), it provides a model for analyzing compositions as relational events rather than as closed and static entities.[28]

What is promised is nothing less than a way out of the formalist impasse that so many have deplored, the stranglehold of what Korsyn calls "modes of music analysis [that] repress the imagination, fleeing from art towards an illusory objectivity" (14). He wants to explore not only "structure" but meaning as well, yet he resists methods that merely assimilate musical meaning to literary paraphrase ("imposing meanings external to music," as he puts it on p. 67). All of this he purports to accomplish by mapping out a new conceptual space for analysis, substituting for formalist methods a "new rhetorical poetics" based on an intertextual paradigm. The focus of study becomes the revisionary relationship between works and their precursors rather than the autonomy of individual compositions. While the methods of traditional analysis are by no means rejected—Korsyn invokes Schoenberg, Schenker, and Tovey, among many others—they are significantly "misread."

The focus on revision will restore historical perspective, the very thing most current analysis ignores or else misappropriates.[29] Musical meaning (or expressive content) is to be construed in terms of the revisionary strategies, on Bloom's analogy with the classical tropes and in line with his dictum, quoted by Korsyn, that "the meaning of a poem can only be a poem, but another poem, a poem not itself" (13). Works may be evaluated in terms of the relative strength of their misreadings, thus furnishing the promised critical dimension.

The crucial justifying task is to supply musical figures or gestures that may substitute for Bloom's verbal tropes as analogues to the six revisionary ratios. (This Korsyn calls his own "strong misreading" of Bloom.) Korsyn evolves these analogues in the course of a model analysis comparing Brahms's Romanze, op. 118, no. 5, with its alleged "central precursor-text," Chopin's Berceuse, op. 57. The Brahms/Chopin nexus was practically foreordained, not only by Brahms's well-established reputation as a revised anthology of his predecessors,[30] but also because his anxious relationship to Chopin had been unwittingly suggested (via Mason) by Rosen, whose article furnished Korsyn with his starting point. By choosing (or, as Bloom would put it, being chosen by) the feared Chopin's Berceuse as precursor to his Romanze—and choosing a title that connotes the genre of quest narrative—Brahms makes the piece a representation of his own quest for authentic selfhood, a dialectic, Korsyn says, that can be accomplished in music "only if it is mediated through the anxiety of influence, that is, only if the music of other composers is used in one's own piece to represent threats to the self" (67).

After briefly surveying the surface similarities that prompt the linking of the two pieces (which Korsyn, with Rosen and others, accepts as allusions, meant to be heard), Korsyn proceeds to the more interesting differences, in which Brahms asserts his authentic self by repressing Chopin and in which his piece asserts its uniqueness by misreading the Berceuse. Here is where the six revisionary ratios—the strong misreadings, the moves to overmaster—come into play.

1. The way Brahms saturates his variations theme with an incidental motive from Chopin's, and, further, extracts his method of linking variations from the same motive, is assimilated to the revisionary ratio Bloom called tessera (literally, "shard"), coordinated in the map of misprision with the trope of synecdoche (part for whole or whole for part). Brahms in effect fully executes what Chopin only casually implies, showing on two levels (motive as extracted from theme, theme as extracted from the variations

set) how the part can serve to represent the whole. (Korsyn, at once mis-reading Bloom and Schenker, relates this rhetorical trope to the motivic replications between levels in a Schenkerian graph and, less speculatively, to Christoph Bernhard's writings on "figures," which were among Schenker's central precursor-texts.)

2. The way Brahms frames his D-major middle section (where the overt allusions to Chopin are found) with sections in F major, thus subverting the tonal stability of the precursor, is assimilated to clinamen (literally, "swerve"), Bloom's ratio associated with irony (and with Freud's reaction-formation). In the context that Brahms creates for it, Chopin's very limited diatonic scope "says 'tonal stability' but means 'tonal instability'" (35), since the two keys have no established functional relationship. Brahms's swerve from the precursor calls invidious attention, as well, to its consistency, recasting Chopin's simplicity as limited vision. Brahms reflects, through his belated maturity, on the impossibility of recapturing the bliss of infantile undivided consciousness that the Berceuse naively symbolizes (in characterizing which Korsyn refers to several recent theories of musical temporality in relation to states of consciousness). The allusion to the Berceuse thus becomes simultaneously an invocation and a negation of its idea. Brahms has in effect killed the precursor, because having heard his antithetical misreading, we ourselves (according to Korsyn) lose the innocence of our response to Chopin.

3. The way Brahms ends his Chopin-saturated middle section, with a liquidation rather than a closure, is assimilated to kenosis (emptying-out), associated with metonymy, which puts an attribute in place of a thing. Here, all that is left of Chopin is some trills. Kenosis is also coordinated with the psychic defense of undoing, or regression; and Brahms here undoes the transition that had introduced the middle section, regressing to a reprise of the opening.

4. The way Brahms condenses the reprise, yet intensifies his veiled appropriation of a motive from Chopin through a quickened melodic sequence in triple octaves, is assimilated to daemonization, associated with the trope of hyperbole, exaggeration (here, the quickening intensification immediately preceding the long-delayed full closure), and the defense of repression (here, the condensation, which "forgets" its former self, and particularly the modulatory moves that had led to the overt allusion). In his discussion, Korsyn curiously ignores Bloom's complementary association of daemonization with litotes, the trope of understatement, which might also apply to this very quiet and reticent ending in which the Chopin motive, but for the hyperbolic sequence, is returned to the inner voices.

5. The ambiguous nature of Brahms's intertextual relationship to precursors (nobody having ever really figured out, for example, whether "any ass can see that" meant proud acknowledgment or apprehensive irritation,

identification or estrangement) is assimilated to askesis (self-curtailment), associated with metaphor and with sublimation. Korsyn sees this ambiguity as a recognition of separation from the precursor and as the predominant revisionary ratio in the Romanze, covering the whole piece. "Chopin" here stands metaphorically for the "otherness" of the past, which Brahms felt more keenly and dialectically than his less historically reflective, less self-conscious contemporaries.

6. The way Brahms's coda expires with a last whispered and radically concentrated recollection of the Chopin-saturated middle, alluding primarily to its cadential gesture, is assimilated to apophrades (return of the dead), associated with the trope of transumption (or metalepsis), meaning discontinuity, a leaping-over of middle terms. Transumption also implies an upward revision, and here the close of the middle section is promoted to close the whole piece, taking on a formerly missing stability. The associated defense is projection/introjection, a fantasy of the future or a casting-off of the past. Korsyn, prompted by the asymmetry of the reprise and what he perceives as unrealized registral implications, opts here for futurity, to which Brahms has entitled himself by virtue of his successful combat with the precursor and his mature refusal of the latter's regressive enchantment.

Thus the strong misreading: the meaning and the value of Brahms's Romanze are found in its re-visioning of a work by Chopin. The Brahms that is truly Brahms is the Brahms that is not Chopin. His presence can only be located in the other's absence; it has no independent essence. His strength is his power of exclusion. Along the way, a piece by Reger (*Träume am Kamin*, op. 143, no. 12) is adduced and unsurprisingly dismissed as a weak misreading of the same precursor-work. Reger does not successfully exclude Chopin, and to the extent that he departs he only weakens. There is no Reger that is truly Reger.

The foil does clarify the argument, but writing Reger off as a poor man's Brahms is nothing new. And that signals what seems to me the weakness in Korsyn's application, at this stage of his work: unlike Bloom (whose work on influence arose out of his earlier romantic revivalism, itself a militantly revisionist program), Korsyn evinces no revisionary impulse. His "new poetics" mainly reconfirms conventional judgments. The reconfirmation, meant to justify the new methodology, obviates the need for it. Further, like many analysts with a point to prove, Korsyn is inclined to ignore salient aspects of the pieces he treats while in pursuit of the arcana he regards as more pertinent to his agenda. (Never once does he mention, for example, the persistent, never fully resolved harmonic tritone D/G-sharp that occurs every fourth bar in Brahms's middle section; to be sure, the G-sharp does proceed to A, but to regard it as wholly normal on that account seems at least half-blind.)

Even more unlike Bloom, but very much like an old-reading musicologist,

Korsyn seeks the "compelling logic and unity" in the pieces he analyzes (21), even describing the essential compositional "problem" in the Berceuse as the endowing of a set of variations with these apparently obligatory values. (The "problem" could just as well have been posited from the opposite perspective, as that of securing maximum fantasy and diversity in a piece constrained by an ostinato.) The analyst, perhaps truer than he imagines to the traditions of his métier, has not rejected the comforting autonomy paradigm in favor of the risky "relational event." Though he clearly understands what intertextual references are for Bloom, for Korsyn they are (if I may inject a new trope, that of oxymoron) essentially attributes.

Compared with Bloom's example, moreover, most of Korsyn's applications of the revisionary ratios, while ingenious and elegantly formulated, are somewhat predictably vague and "gestural." As usually happens when music and language are compared on language's terms, the music makes an ineffectual, indeed deficient impression. Possibly out of his very eagerness to persuade, Korsyn holds back from the kind of assertive specificity that can antagonize through presumption. "I recognize the dangers of imaginative wildness," he assures the reader, "and will avoid them" (14). So, he evidently thinks, one has to talk to musicologists; but had Bloom done similarly, he would have gained neither his notoriety nor his disciples.

As a programmatic exemplification of a method, finally, the study suffers from overkill. The need to apply all six ratios for the sake of demonstration makes the author (in his own words) "an extremist in an exercise" (47) and freights the poor Romanze, after all a rather slight composition, with an extravagant load of import. The implication that the ratios may always be applied as desired might seem to signal the premature onset of a familiar dogmatism. Read more sympathetically, Korsyn's application underscores the artificiality of the method, the exposure of which is only honest—far more honest, indeed, than the usual analytical claim that meaning and structure are immanent properties awaiting discovery. If meaning inheres in the relationship between the parts of a text, and in the relationship between texts, it also inheres in the relationship between the text and the critical performer. It is not discovered but made; analysis *is* artifice.

Maybe it is premature to speak here of a "new poetics," but Korsyn claims no more than an "initial swerve" toward a new paradigm. At the least, he presents a responsible exposition of Bloom and a painstaking attempt to apply Bloom's ratios. Any musicologist reading Korsyn's essay will come away with an accurate picture of the theory and some idea of its possibilities. Many will be impressed with Korsyn's demonstrations, especially those of the tessera and the clinamen, which effectively integrate standard analytical procedures into the Bloomian operation, giving assurance that the new poetics may accommodate what to a musical professional will seem a competent engagement with musical particulars and yet subsume that engagement within a project more humane than what we have been used to.

.   .   .

My music, produced on German soil, without foreign influences, is a living example of an art able most effectively to oppose Latin and Slav hopes of hegemony.
—ARNOLD SCHOENBERG, "National Music" (1931)

Yes, I too like to admire great men, but only those whose works I do not understand.
—GEORG CHRISTOPH LICHTENBERG, quoted in Bloom, *The Anxiety of Influence*

If with his intensive dissection of a single revisionary relationship Kevin Korsyn has produced the most thorough application of Harold Bloom's theory of poetic influence to music, the most comprehensive musicological project to invoke Bloom up to now is Joseph Straus's *Remaking the Past,* which epitomizes and extends with many examples a thesis the author has been developing in lectures and articles for about a decade. Although Straus would classify himself a music theorist and although the book's argument unfolds through a series of analyses, what he has produced is actually a work of revisionist history, addressing an important historiographical crux: the problem of neoclassicism in the musical culture of the twentieth century.

Neoclassicism a problem? But yes, in many senses of the word. Its origins are obscure, its definition elusive, its purposes unclear, its implications—to many, and for many reasons—monstrous. Above all it has posed a problem to those who wish to see a clear evolutionary line in the music of our century, for it seems so profoundly antithetical to the music that preceded it—not only the music of late romanticism, but also (and especially) the radical New Music of the early twentieth century. The neoclassical tendency has seemed a "right deviation" (Adorno spoke of a "retrogression into the traditional"),[31] intolerable to a historiography that celebrates innovation. Historians simply have not known what to do with it.

While few historians today subscribe to overtly teleological or deterministic models, smacking as they do of pre- or post-Enlightened totalitarianism, loose conventional parlance continues tacitly to endorse such notions, if with a face-saving simulacrum of irony. "Progress" may be out, but *progressive* is still a viable term, and it still connotes value. It still saves reputations. We have had "Brahms the Progressive" since its publication in 1947 (it was written in 1933), and now we have "Bach the Progressive," "Britten the Progressive," and even "Dufay the Progressive." *Conservative* remains a pejorative that must be countered if the figure to whom it is applied is seen as having value.[32]

The central evolutionary problem is compounded by one of asserted legitimacy. Unlike tonality, atonality (the kind that survived) has one father. This has given rise to a cult of personality, has intensified polarization, and has lent the historiography of twentieth-century music a characteristically postromantic Caesaristic mode that has long been under siege but will not capitulate until those who have cast themselves as the victorious father's dynastic heirs have relinquished their power bases. Hence music history— once its narrative has reached the Napoleonic age, the age of the musical Caesars—has held fast to collective biography. The cast of characters is still divided into sheep and goats, strong and weak, rebels and conformists, and its central myth still hopelessly confuses all these categories by attempting to marry the Permanent Revolution to the Great Tradition.

Neoclassicism has been accommodated to this narrative in ways we have recently begun to see more clearly, thanks to their thematization by minoritarian and feminist culture critics. It has been constructed as an other, concomitantly reduced and totalized, and variously marginalized from the mainstream as a pusillanimous nostalgia, a reaction-formation, a temporary war-scare.

The problems with this view have long been obvious. The essential neo-classicizing impulse preceded the Great War—which only makes it the more inexplicable and inexcusable to linearists. The putative regression may be alternatively represented as a "normal" (that is, evolutionary) outgrowth of a different continuous principle—a counter mainstream—on the "other" side of a great dialectical divide.[33] In any case, the deviation lasted far too long to be written off as a fad or a scare. Worst of all, it had its own Caesar or anti-Caesar at the helm, who, following his deathbed conversion, is now safely canonized and installed in an honorary niche on the right side of the track, his legacy now read as embodying a teleology all its own.

Straus revises neoclassicism by adopting Bloom's notion of the strong misreader. If it can be shown by means of this theory that composers who all at once began resorting to forms long since outdated and harmonies long since outgrown were doing so in a spirit not of nostalgia or Eliotic submission but of contention, then the regressive deviation would disappear. If, following the famous second paragraph of *The Anxiety of Influence*, "poetic [and musical] history . . . is held to be indistinguishable from poetic influence, since strong poets [and composers] make that history by misreading one another, so as to clear imaginative space for themselves" (5), then a properly linear narrative can be salvaged. All is one again, and the strong are all together again, swimming with the tide.

Beyond the opportunistic appropriation of this one Bloomian notion, though, Straus's argument has only the most paradoxical relationship to the theory it purports to invoke. Is Straus then a strong misreader in his turn? So he might wish to argue, and so he has been read;[34] but having examined both the theory and a scrupulous musical application in some detail, we are positioned to dismiss that plea. A strong misreader irrepressibly represses the old to produce the new. Straus co-opts the new theory of influence to retell very old tales. Bloom is simply irrelevant to Straus's methods and purposes, the

main purpose being the neutralization—indeed the dematerialization—of
the "right deviation" so that its claims against the master narrative can be
canceled.

Bloom's irrelevance is apparent even in the preliminary paraphrase of his
ideas, which Straus attempts to reduce to four propositions. This is the third:

> The struggle between new poems and their precursors takes the form of mis-
> reading. Later poets willfully misinterpret their predecessors in a process anal-
> ogous to repression in Freudian psychoanalytic theory.[35]

Repression, though, is no more an act of will than the other psychic
defenses. They are, all of them, necessary and unconscious maneuvers of
self-preservation. And if one understands this much, one will understand
that the revisionary ratios are similarly involuntary. That is exactly why
Bloom calls them misreadings. The artist does not apply them. His anxiety
causes them. (Hence the poets' invariable denial that there is such a thing
as anxiety of influence—or even influence—let alone that they misread
their predecessors.) This insight was not Bloom's alone. It can also be
found in Cocteau's familiar dictum that an original artist has only to copy
something in order to demonstrate his originality. It goes back further yet,
to such of Bloom's acknowledged misread forebears as Nietzsche and
Emerson.

With respect to the notion of a text as a relational event, Straus paraphrases as follows: "For Bloom, the meaning of a poem resides in its relations
with other texts and, ultimately, with the entire world of literary language"
(13). But Bloom's whole project is explicitly directed against those who
would generalize influence in this way. He says that poems are words "that
refer to other words, . . . and so on, into the densely overpopulated world of
literary language."[36] His aim is to trace particular lines of influence within
that world; "Criticism," rings the last sentence in his "Manifesto for Antithetical Criticism," "is the art of knowing the hidden roads that go from
poem to poem."[37]

Straus's strong reader, then, is a controller and a lumper. Bloom's is a resister and a splitter. They could hardly be more antipodean. And that is because, mutatis mutandis, Bloom's is a metaphor for the composer and
Straus's is a metaphor for the academic analyst. The reason for the confusion
is familiar to anyone who knows the intellectual traditions out of which
Straus arrived at his misprision of Bloom; for academic analysts do in fact habitually if untenably identify their activity with composition. This bias informs the whole of Straus's book.

It will therefore occasion no surprise to discover that Straus jettisons
Bloom's revisionary ratios and substitutes his own; that these so-called revisionary ratios do not measure the relationship between particular works but
define general style characteristics and technical procedures amounting to

an asserted common practice; or that while he discusses all kinds of relationships between new music and old, in only two cases out of more than two dozen does Straus discuss what Bloom would recognize as an instance of influence, anxious or not.

The identification of analysis with composition is explicitly asserted in chapter 2, "Analytical Misreadings," in which the analytical writings of several important twentieth-century composers (but mainly Schoenberg, whose influential didactic works contain a wealth of pertinent material) are directly assimilated to the models of compositional practice outlined as "revisionary ratios" in chapter 1. Chapter 3, "Recompositions," describes Schoenberg's arrangements of Bach and Handel, Webern's of Bach, and Stravinsky's of Bach, Chaikovsky, and "Pergolesi." (The irrelevance of this chapter to the question of influence is self-evident, even to Straus; we are not asked to imagine Pergolesi as Laius at the crossroads.) Chapter 4, "Triads," considers the way Berg, Schoenberg, and Stravinsky have handled traditional harmonic configurations. No mention is made of individual precursor-texts or even precursor composers. Nor do they figure in chapter 5, "Sonata Forms," which describes adaptations of that genre in the work of Stravinsky, Bartók, and Schoenberg. Chapter 6, "Six Emblematic Misreadings," treats three familiar quotations (Beethoven's "Heiliger Dankgesang" in Bartók's Third Piano Concerto, Bach's "Es ist genug" chorale in Berg's Violin Concerto, *Tristan* in the *Lyric Suite*); one unfamiliar quotation (the statue scene from *Don Gio vanni* in the graveyard scene from *The Rake's Progress*); and two relationships that could conceivably be called revisionary on Bloom's model: the opening "Hymne" from Stravinsky's Serenade in A is related to Chopin's second Ballade (a genuine surprise and a fruitful discussion); and the first movement of Schoenberg's Third Quartet is related to the corresponding movement of Schubert's Quartet in A Minor, op. 29. A final chapter, "Middleground Misreadings," discusses quasi-tonal coherence in "post-tonal" music by Stravinsky, Bartók, and Schoenberg but again names no precursors.

The strategy of ignoring precursors and admitting to a discussion of influence not only models but also quotations and even arrangements (the last being the musical counterpart to parodies or satires) is consistent with Straus's conceptual swerve away from Bloom. But for the two exceptions noted, Straus casts the past as either depopulated or passive—an object. His "willful" remaker, fully conscious and unworried, is at all times firmly in the driver's seat; his "post-tonal usages" are always granted an easy, indeed an automatic, victory over the tonal practices they suppositionally, and impersonally, confront. Where is the anxiety? There is no contention between rival subjects, no need for psychic defense. There is, in short, no fight at all.

What actual revisionary ratios (or "strategies of reinterpretation," as Straus rechristens them) does his controlling subject wield upon the passive object? Straus identifies eight, but I will limit discussion to the first two, for they are the true subject matter of the book, accounting for the vast preponderance of its argument. The first is *motivicization,* whereby "the motivic content of the earlier work is radically intensified" (17). Here, of course, Straus invokes the dynastic father, whom he will name in the second chapter as the author of the strategy. Schoenberg henceforth displaces Bloom as the author's authentic preceptor.[38]

Motivic saturation ("working with the tones of a motive") is indeed a Schoenbergian sine qua non, since it is that which maximizes self-reference—the *Zweckmässigkeit* that gives the musical art its autonomous *Zweck,* to trace Schoenberg's idealism back to its Kantian roots. It is also what constitutes the special *Inhalt* of *die heil'ge deutsche Kunst* and keeps it *deutsch und echt,* distinct from all its dialectical rivals. Finally, it is the lifeline to tradition that is presumed to maintain the possibility of musical intelligibility in the absence of degree functions and directed harmony. It is what made an atonal practice theoretically viable and legitimate. A large part of the central evolutionary myth of twentieth-century music narrates the growth "in the late nineteenth and early twentieth centuries" of "contextually established motivic associations" to the point where they "come to dominate the structure" (Straus, 22, 23).

Motivicization has also given analysts (Schoenberg prominent among them) plenty to do, which may be one reason it has been valued so highly. Straus's chapter 2 illustrates the way in which Schoenberg sought justifying precedents for his compositional practice in earlier German music, mining the music of Brahms the Progressive for motivic atoms, which he promoted, ignoring harmony or voice leading, as primary agents of musical unity. This bias is convincingly related, in chapter 3, to Webern's atomistic orchestration of the six-part Ricercar from Bach's *Musical Offering,* a more actively interventionist "analytical misreading."

Fair enough, but can the practice be generalized to the point where it not only characterizes Schoenberg and his pupils, but can fulfill Straus's criterion for a revisionary ratio, that is, a *universally shared* musical technique whereby "composers in the first part of the twentieth century, despite their superficial stylistic dissimilarities, [remade] earlier forms, style elements, sonorities, and musical works"? It can, Straus maintains, according to his second "strategy of reinterpretation," straightforwardly called *generalization:* "A motive from the earlier work is generalized into the unordered pitch-class set of which it is a member. That pitch-class set is then deployed in the new work in accordance with the norms of post-tonal usage" (17).

Motives have uncontroversially been part of compositional concept and practice since the eighteenth century. (As analytical premises they have been controversially posited as far back as chant.) Pitch-class sets, while a fairly recent analytical construct (and despite initial formulation in the context of twelve-tone music), name a musical universal.[39] But the operation Straus calls generalization, whereby the concept of motive is identified with that of unordered pitch-class set, may be precisely dated to the year 1963, when Allen Forte published his first "set-theoretic" analysis of an atonal composition. Inevitably, a work of Schoenberg's, his *Sechs kleine Klavierstücke,* op. 19, was chosen for the demonstration.[40]

What Straus calls "the norms of post-tonal usage" were formulated in this context. They depend on assumptions—such as the inversional equivalency of sets, a back-transfer from serial theory—that, while implicit to a degree in Schoenberg's and Webern's "atonal" motivic practice (the only atonal practice that was preserial), were obviously alien to the earlier common practice. There is no reason to assume them to be operative for composers whose concepts and methods were formed outside the preserial orbit. Moreover, only in the rationalistic American twelve-tone theory that occupies a much more recent place in the asserted dynastic succession is the idea implicit that a motive (or "compositional set") could be abstracted to its "total interval content" expressed in terms of "interval classes" (of which there are only six owing to inversional equivalence) and still remain a motive—that is, a compositional apriority.

For Schoenberg, the idea of motive implied a gestalt, a contour or shape; a motive, in other words, was for him (and for everyone else before the "set-theoretic" conceptual innovations of Babbitt and Forte) primarily a configuration of pitches, not pitch classes.[41] Indeed, Schoenberg's concept or doctrine of "developing variation" was downright inimical to the equation of motive with pitch-class set (as defined by specific interval-class content), because developing variation not only allowed, but actually relied on intervallic transformation as a vehicle of that elaborative technique whereby "*different things* can arise from *one thing.*"[42] The converse of Straus's ratio of generalization (indispensable to his analytical practice)—namely, that any recurrently isolable pitch- or interval-class set is entitled to be considered a motive—is thus without historical footing. And so, therefore, are Straus's "norms of post-tonal usage." Even without raising the usual caveats regarding the epistemology of "segmentation" (that is, deciding what pitch-class sets to isolate for purposes of analysis), the relevance of the analyst's concepts and methods to those of the composers for whom he presumes to speak, hence the relevance of his analyses to their compositional practice, is placed severely in doubt.

Straus addresses all questions of relevance, and of proper range of application, in a purely pragmatic way: "Pitch-class set theory provides consistent ways of discussing and relating sonorities of any size or structure in any musical context." All that this means, really, is that the theory offers a way of ignoring size, structure, and context. The last is the crucial worry. "Recent work in music theory has begun to reveal surprising similarities of structure between so-called neoclassical and so-called progressive music," Straus writes (3). But this was inevitable: both "neoclassical" music and "progressive" music are composed of pitch-class sets, as is any other kind of music. The high degree of abstraction implicit in Straus's "generalization" paradigm ensures that similarities of the kind he posits can be "revealed" ad libitum. The paradigm, in other words, is precisely a means not of discovering but of *generating* pitch-structural affinities, both within the individual composition and between compositions regardless of "style." An analyst committed to a value system that privileges motivic saturation will certainly want to bring such similarities to light. Straus's second "strategy of reinterpretation," then, is not a compositional method at all but an analytical machine that levels distinctions and produces an adventitious homogeneity regardless of what is fed into it.

These are familiar objections, embodied by now in a sizable literature.[43] There is no need to rehearse them at any great length here so as to point up yet again the circularity of Straus's methodology or the factitiousness of its revelations. Nor would I ordinarily be eager to raise commonplace intentionalist objections to a method that by now has proved to be of some practical value as an inductive discovery tool.[44]

But Straus makes an openly intentionalist and historiographical appropriation of the method, thereby raising the stakes. By casting set-theoretic operations, under the rubric "generalization," as a revisionary ratio, a composerly strategy of reinterpretation, he declares his "norms of post-tonal usage" to be historical norms of composition. He is in fact the first set-theoretic analyst ever to make the claim explicitly. Bartók and Stravinsky are thus assimilated to Schoenberg—a Schoenberg who is himself anachronistically construed—to define a chimerical "twentieth-century common practice" (17) that recuperates and even reinforces the old evolutionary master narrative. The revisionary ratio arises entirely out of an analytical prejudice, one largely confined by now to a dwindling strain of composers and theorists who persist in upholding the wistful creed that "there is one main way of doing things."[45] What Straus has in effect done is to rewrite Webern's *Der Weg zur neuen Musik,* reviving an old sectarian viewpoint at a time when its claim to universality has been properly discarded, along with all the other historical determinisms that have so bedeviled our unfortunate century.

It is perhaps unnecessary, even bathetical, to remark at this point that nothing could be further from Harold Bloom's purposes than defining a common practice. So why was he ever invoked? Such a tendentious misappropriation of his name, of his theory, and of their joint prestige raises disturbing questions. One has to wonder whether a misprision of this magnitude, on the part of a well-established scholar, could be altogether ingenuous.

These questions come to a head in chapter 3, when Stravinsky's arrangement of Bach's canonic variations on "Vom Himmel hoch" is compared, on the one hand, with his own *Pulcinella* and *Le Baiser de la fée* and, on the other, with the Bach arrangements of Schoenberg and Webern. "For most of his life," Straus observes in conclusion,

> Stravinsky avoided a direct confrontation with the classical mainstream, preferring instead to focus on weaker, more susceptible predecessors like Pergolesi and Tchaikovsky. Through them he would comment on common-practice styles without dealing directly with the true giants of those styles. His turn to serialism, however, marks a new willingness to enter into direct dialogue with the inheritors of the tradition and, through them, with their great contrapuntal predecessors, especially Bach. Stravinsky's turn toward serialism and his late recompositions of Bach and Wolf [the latter actually an orchestration] thus have a common source. In both, Stravinsky confronts the musical mainstream and shows remarkable ability to remake his predecessors in his own image. (70)

Beyond the demeaning implication that Stravinsky became a "strong poet" only upon embracing serialism, what gives offense here is the complacent perpetuation of creaky shibboleths: the impudent identification of *the* classical mainstream with an ad hoc and insularly German tradition (Bach and Wolf, the latter suddenly a giant), and the stale parochial propaganda that casts the New Vienna School and its self-defined legatees on American campuses as the exclusive custodians of this asserted mainstream.[46] It is understandable that Schoenberg might have wished to go on fighting World War I with slogans such as the one that stands as epigraph to this section. For an American scholar of Straus's generation to go on affirming these things is worse than provincial.

What is ignorant, first, is the notion that Chaikovsky and Pergolesi, Stravinsky's demonstratively embraced models, were in fact his objects of contention. That is not a misreading of Bloom; that is sheer incomprehension. The Bloomian question would be, with whom was Stravinsky contending behind the Eliotic mask? But that is unimportant. Momentously ignorant is the evident unawareness of Stravinsky's role, three decades or more before the "confrontation" Straus interprets, in the so-called *retour à Bach* that had such a powerful impact on the music of the 1920s,[47] not excluding German music, and not excluding Schoenberg, in whom it definitely aroused anxieties (or have we repressed der kleine Modernsky?) precisely because it paradoxically portended "the degermanization of music."[48] Stravinsky, not Schoenberg, was touted as "the Bach of today," a hubris that has infuriated German chauvinists, at home and in America, ever since.[49] Straus's forgetting of this episode, if that is what it is, is symptomatic of his programmatic neglect of contexts and circumstances. It annuls his attempt at revising neoclassicism.

.   .   .

Wagner's music was not only the best and most significant of its age . . . but it was also the music of 1870 Germany, who conquered the world of her friends and enemies through all her achievements, not without arousing their envy and resistance.
—SCHOENBERG, "National Music"

When the First World War began, I was proud to be called to arms and as a soldier I did my whole duty enthusiastically as a true believer in the house of Habsburg.
—SCHOENBERG, "My Attitude toward Politics" (1950)

Today I have discovered something which will assure the supremacy of German music for the next hundred years.
—SCHOENBERG TO JOSEF RUFER, 1921 or 1922

So if at the climax of contrapuntal art, in Bach, something quite new simultaneously begins — the art of development through motivic variation — and in our time, at the climax of art based on harmonic relationships, the art of composing with "twelve tones related only to each other" begins, one sees that the epochs are very similar.
—SCHOENBERG, "National Music"

The contexts and circumstances Joseph Straus so studiously ignores offer a rich vein of irony for today's historians and metahistorians to savor. "It was the first time in my career that I lost, for a short time, my influence on youth," Schoenberg complained, adding that "this took place between 1922 and 1930."[50] The reason? "Schönberg is a romantic; our young composers are classic."[51] The German master's complicated response to these divagations and perfidies conditioned the most crucial and influential vicissitude of his career—which, for all the ink that has been spilled over it in the course of seven decades, remains virtually uninterrogated by historians. Dodecaphony has been explored and elucidated from a technical perspective like no other musical innovation in this (or perhaps any) century. As a cultural phenomenon it has not yet begun to be investigated. Such a conspicuous failure betokens reluctance, anxiety, fear of discovery.

Even the most recent studies of Schoenberg dogmatically minimize his own postwar turn—nationalistic and reactionary, alien and antagonistic to "Weimar culture" but oddly akin to Stravinsky's aristocratic Franco-Russian bias—and the concomitant, albeit unexpected, neoclassicizing strain in his own works of the twenties.[52] The enduring power of the modernist (r)evolutionary mythology has put these questions off-limits. Thus Ethan Haimo concludes a laudably meticulous and illuminating technical summary of Schoenberg's path to serialism with a gratuitous disclaimer: "Schoenberg was not engaged in a superficial recycling of classical forms; he was not interested in mere thematic formalism. (Had he been, he could have written classical forms in his contextual period.) On the contrary, although they are cast in seemingly traditional moulds, the forms of the Wind Quintet are quite revolutionary."[53]

There is a tradition for these non sequiturs. Three decades ago Donald Mitchell asserted the existence of "a wide gulf, indeed, between Stravinsky's special sense of the 'past' and Schoenberg's no less special sense of 'immediate tradition.'"[54] Glossing this in the Stravinsky centennial year, Alan Lessem maintained that "if Schoenberg does call into service older form types—sonata, rondo, theme and variations—it is not because he considers them to be 'ideal' . . . but because he sees in them usages which should not be dispensed with until the novel and more difficult aspects of his musical language are better understood."[55]

But the sense of tradition apparent in Schoenberg's works of the twenties is no longer immediate. Like Stravinsky's, it has been put at an ironic distance by the very same end run around an "immediate tradition" that had met with disaster. Haimo's squeamishness is understandable in light of what is by now a lengthy history of attack from the musical left, epitomized in Boulez's infamous squib (recently put back in circulation in a new translation),[56] and also in Adorno's equivocating attitude toward Schoenberg's twelve-tone music. Yet it need not imply endorsement of the "Schoenberg is dead" position to expose the tendentious and tautological nature of Haimo's defense, beginning with the groundless insinuation of the words *superficial, mere,* and *seemingly* as a tactic for prejudicially dichotomizing the radical ("quite revolutionary") and the retrospective. Take out the amulet-words, and Haimo's first sentence becomes false on its face.

As to tautology: if Schoenberg "could have written classical forms in his contextual [that is, "free atonal"] period," then by the same spurious token he could have written progressive, nonthematic forms in his early twelve-tone period (say, up to the *Begleitungsmusik,* op. 34). He did neither, for (not to put it past him) it simply would not have occurred to him to do otherwise than he did, given the historical contexts in which he worked. To imply that formal procedure and compositional method may he mixed and matched at pleasure is another faux-naïf dichotomy. As Haimo devotes his book to demonstrating, the classical forms—with their sectional demarcations and their significantly transposed repetitions—were an essential crucible for working out the twelve-tone discipline; put another way, the development of the twelve-tone method was one of the many coetaneous classicizing tendencies that arose during the first unsteady postwar decade.[57]

The unforeseen metamorphosis of dodecaphony into the scientistic formalism that rose to sudden dominance in the decades following the world's next big conflagration confirms diagnosis of dodecaphony as neoclassicism, despite the vehement disavowal of neoclassicism on the part of the new generation of dodecaphonists. Boulez's stentorian proclamation of Schoenberg's demise is a perfect Bloomian paradigm: the killing of the father and the opportunistic misreading of his legacy, enabling the composers of Boulez's and Babbitt's generation to inherit and rationalize the later Schoenberg's neoclassical technique while at the same time claiming the earlier Schoenberg's patrimony. The misreading has been well ratified in post–World War II academic historiography, newly epitomized by the works of Joseph Straus and Ethan Haimo, in which the serial "discovery" is staunchly represented as the outcome of a straight evolutionary line—perfectly sequent and eminently trackable—rather than as a clinamen, a swerve. The extraordinary privilege accorded serialism as standard-bearer of "the classical mainstream," despite its enormous and obvious break with mainstream composing methods, is a case—a "classic" case, indeed—of victors' history, impressive enough in its day finally to intimidate der alte Modernsky and wring from him the self-pitying if inveterately devious confessions (such as the one discussed in note 46) that the victors and their heirs so love to parade.

But if we are interested in writing history rather than recycling hoary propaganda, we must deconstruct the dear old dualism that casts Schoenberg and his school in heroic opposition to the right deviation and (so far from assimilating the deviation to the "mainstream") learn to see what happened in Vienna as a part of the general swerve. If there is an assimilation to be made, its dynamic has got to be the opposite, the harder, one.

Whatever it was, moreover, the swerve toward (neo)classicism was no agon with the three Bs, let alone "Pergolesi." It conforms to the Bloomian mold at least insofar as it entailed wrestling with threatening fathers, not with benign great-grandfathers. Harold Bloom has spoken to an interviewer of "Hart Crane, with his palpable assertions of Whitmanian influence, but with the poetry's enormous and not-so-covert struggle against the abominable Eliot."[58] J. Hillis Miller, commenting to the same interviewer on Bloom's self-alignment with the "mythological" tradition of criticism associated with Northrop Frye, has observed:

> The real precursor for Bloom is T. S. Eliot: anybody can see that. It's not Frye at all. Part of the strategy of his interview is to name it as Frye, *because that's an easy person to be obligated to.* The real person he was obsessed with at the beginning, and continues to be obsessed with, is the man he calls the abominable Eliot."[59]

It is in this spirit that we ought to be reading Stravinsky's autobiography and conversations, and even (nay, especially) such writings of Schoenberg as "Brahms the Progressive." We should be taking it as axiomatic that acknowledged debts are the easy, discountable ones. We should assume that, just as he concealed his extensive appropriations from folklore in *The Rite of Spring* by confessing to a single one, Stravinsky (like Schoenberg, like the rest of us) confessed his easy debts precisely in order to hide the hard ones. If he tells us that his earliest works were "suspiciously Debussyist" in the eyes of his teacher, it is to conceal his early provincial ignorance of Debussy and his enormous debt to Rimsky-Korsakov. If he tells us (verbally, quotationally, and by dedication) that he was influenced by Debussy in *Zvezdoliki*, it is to conceal his formative, painfully unrequited love of Scriabin, whom he denigrates more vehemently than any other precursor except Wagner, and for the same reason. If, later, he magnifies Chaikovsky and appropriates Handel, it is to obscure and put off the pressing Verdi. If, later still, he claims kinship with Schoenberg and Webern, it is because his music continued, perhaps not so covertly, to swerve away from them, back to the Russia long ago renounced.[60]

If Schoenberg insisted on telling us (and himself) that "my teachers were primarily Bach and Mozart" and that "I also learned much from Schubert and Mahler, Strauss and Reger too. I shut myself off from no one," it was precisely so as to shut himself off from the Debussy who (as Milhaud was so delighted to notice) crowds his way into *Pierrot Lunaire* as soon as the voice part is sung rather than melodramatically declaimed—and it is indeed refreshing to notice this after reading Schoenberg's gloating (if acute) remark that "Debussy's summons to the Latin and Slav peoples, to do battle against Wagner, was indeed successful; but to free *himself* from Wagner—that was beyond him."[61]

But, then, what the abominable Eliot was to Crane and to Bloom, the dread mage of Bayreuth was to everybody, and dread only grew as historical conditions changed. "Brahms the Progressive," which could as easily have been titled "Wagner the Pedant," should be read as a document of its time, when all the world was recoiling from the horrors perpetrated by Wagner's self-designated heirs.[62]

Just as Wagner was everybody's appalling father, so Bach was everyone's handpicked *vecchio genitor*—not a begetting forebear but a begotten one. Once again, overt modeling—and this is surely the Bloomian theory's best precept—is to be read as a displacement from the real anxiety of influence. This central displacement, with its many analogues and corollaries, constituted the essential swerve in the history of classical music in the early twentieth century. Yet for the most part music historians and analysts have been content to treat the avowals of great composers not as testimony but as oracles. Their claims of kinship have been accepted at face value and even reified into unquestionable historical facts; skeptical investigations have been decried.[63]

Here is where Bloom is potentially of greatest use to us. His analysis of the way in which poets make poetic history can be our guide, however, only if we are sensible to its corollary: they *make* history, but they do not *write* it. That remains our job.

NOTES

1. Harold Bloom, *Agon: Towards a Theory of Revisionism* (New York: Oxford University Press, 1982), vii.

2. Harold Bloom, *A Map of Misreading* (New York: Oxford University Press, 1975), 3.

3. Frank Lentricchia, foreword to Harold Bloom, *The Breaking of the Vessels* (Chicago: University of Chicago Press, 1982), x.

4. Leonard B. Mayer, "A Pride of Prejudices; Or, Delight in Diversity," *Music Theory Spectrum* 13 (1991): 241.

5. Bloom, *A Map of Misreading,* 19.

6. Introduction to Vladimir Nabokov, *Lectures on Literature,* ed. Fredson Bowers (New York: Harcourt Brace Jovanovich, 1980), xxiii.

7. All quotations from Bloom in this paragraph and the one above it are from *A Map of Misreading,* 9.

8. Leo Trietler, "History, Criticism, and Beethoven's Ninth Symphony," *19th-Century Music* 3 (1979–80): 204.

9. Bloom, *A Map of Misreading,* 20.

10. Harold Bloom, *Figures of Capable Imagination* (New York: Seabury Press, 1976), 140.

11. Frank Kermode, ed., *Selected Prose of T. S. Eliot* (New York: Harcourt Brace Jovanovich and Farrar, Straus & Giroux, 1975), 40.

12. Donald Francis Tovey, "The Main Stream of Music" (1938), in *The Main Stream of Music and Other Essays* (Oxford: Oxford University Press, 1949), 330–52. "My title," Tovey wrote, "is a metaphor which is useful so long as it is not overworked."

13. John Platoff, "Writing about Influences: *Idomeneo,* A Case Study," in *Explorations in Music, the Arts, and Ideas: Essays in Honor of Leonard B. Meyer,* ed. Eugene Narmour and Ruth A. Solie (Stuyvesant, N.Y.: Pendragon Press, 1988), 43.

14. Ibid.

15. "Poetic influence, in the sense I give to it, has almost nothing to do with the verbal resemblances between one poet and another" (Bloom, *A Map of Misreading,* 19).

16. "An ephebe's best misinterpretations may well be of poems he has never read" (Harold Bloom, *The Anxiety of Influence: A Theory of Poetry* [New York: Oxford University Press, 1973], 70).

17. Cf. Leonard B. Meyer's theory of "Choice, Influence, and Covert Causalism," as set forth in *Style and Music: Theory, History, and Ideology* (Philadelphia: University of Pennsylvania Press, 1989), 142–49. By defining influence as the creation of a "new option" or "a viable alternative," and insisting on (free) choice as "the central issue," Meyer appears to endorse the assimilation of the notion of influence to that of model, hence its virtual elimination.

18. A theory of musical modeling has been most rigorously enunciated with respect to the traditions of the late Middle Ages. See Howard Mayer Brown, "Emulation, Competition, and Homage: Imitation and Theories of Imitation in the Renaissance," *JAMS* 35 (1982): 1–48; Leeman L. Perkins, "The *L'Homme armé* Masses of Busnoys and Okeghem: A Comparison," *Journal of Musicology* 3 (1984): 363–96; J. Peter Burkholder, "Johannes Martini and the Imitation Mass of the Late Fifteenth Century," *JAMS* 38 (1985): 470–523; and, for a contrary view, Rob C. Wegman, "Another 'Imitation' of Busnoys's *Missa L'Homme armé*—and Some Observations on *Imitatio* in Renaissance Music," *Journal of the Royal Musical Association* 114 (1989): 189–202.

19. "No poet, I amend that to no strong poet, can choose his precursor, any more than any person can choose his father" (Bloom, *A Map of Misreading,* 12).

20. Bloom, *A Map of Misreading,* 10.

21. All quotations in this paragraph to this point are from Charles Rosen, "Influence: Plagiarism and Inspiration," *10th Century Music* 4 (1980–81): 93–94.

22. Bloom, *A Map of Misreading*, 11.

23. Bloom, *A Map of Misreading*, 30.

24. Imre Salusinszky, *Criticism in Society* (New York: Methuen, 1987), 49.

25. Bloom, *A Map of Misreading*, 9–10.

26. The map itself is on p. 84, surrounded by a lengthy commentary that recapitulates and reduces much of the argument in the earlier book.

27. In *Agon* he warrants, "I neither want nor urge any 'method' of criticism. It is no concern of mine whether anybody else ever comes to share, or doesn't, my own vocabularies of revisionary ratios, of crossings, of whatever . . . because I don't wish to privilege any vocabularies, my own included" (38).

28. Korsyn, "Towards a New Poetics of Musical Influence," 61. Further references to this source will be made in the text.

29. For ghastly examples of misappropriation, see Alan Street, "Superior Myths, Dogmatic Allegories: The Resistance to Musical Unity," *Music Analysis* 8 (1989): 77–124, esp. 98–101.

30. Indeed, Brahms has figured in most Bloomian applications thus far: see Elaine R. Sisman, "Brahms's Slow Movements: Reinventing the 'Closed' Forms," in *Brahms Studies: Analytical and Historical Perspectives*, ed. George S. Bozarth (New York: Oxford University Press, 1990); and John Daverio, "Brahms, Mozart, and the Anxiety of Influence," an unpublished paper (1988) to which Korsyn refers in a footnote. Korsyn himself has followed up with another study of Brahms and Chopin, as yet unpublished.

31. Theodor W. Adorno, *Philosophy of Modern Music*, trans. Anne G. Mitchell and Wesley V. Blomster (New York: Scabury Press, 1973), 5.

32. The trick is usually done by constructing covertly teleological models in the small, tracing some selected style characteristic between a pair of arbitrarily posited poles, the one representing a *prima prattica,* the other a *seconda.* In Schoenberg's "Brahms the Progressive" (*Style and Idea: Selected Writings of Arnold Schoenberg*, ed. Leonard Stein, trans. Leo Black [Berkeley: University of California Press, 1984], 398–441) the selected style characteristic is phrase structure; in Robert L. Marshall's "Bach the Progressive" (*Musical Quarterly* 62 [1976]: 313–57) it is rhythmic variety.

33. This view was explicitly postulated in German historiography shortly before World War I and has been revived in the German historiography of the past two decades. For an expert summary of this dialectic and an inspired adumbration of its relevance to the future historiography of twentieth-century music, see Karol Berger, review of *A Book about Stravinsky* by Boris Asaf'yev, trans. Richard F. French, *Journal of Music Theory* 28 (1984): 294–302.

34. Alan Street, review of *Remaking the Past* by Joseph Straus, *Tempo*, no. 179 (December 1991): 31–32.

35. Straus, *Remaking the Past*, 12. Further references to this source will be made in the text.

36. Harold Bloom, *Poetry and Repression: Revisionism from Blake to Stevens* (New Haven: Yale University Press, 1976), 3; quoted by Straus on p. 13.

37. Bloom, *The Anxiety of Influence*, 96. Even Korsyn undervalues this most crucial (and attractive) aspect of Bloom's work, quoting Paul de Man's attempt, in reviewing

The Anxiety of Influence, to assimilate the book's message to the infinite regress of deconstructionism as if it were the "wider implication of Bloom's model" rather than a defense against its particularism ("Towards a New Poetics of Musical Influence," 47).

38. To forestall complaint that I am suppressing those places in the book where Straus does invoke Bloom's categories, I hereby list them. Clinamen (the swerve) appears once (134) and is assimilated to Straus's "generalization," discussed below, and to "centralization," defined as the placement of harmonic or contrapuntal events that may occur only incidentally in tonal practice at the structural center of a "post-tonal" piece. Kenosis (emptying-out) is invoked twice (57, 152), equated with an all-purpose antiromanticism (as in Stravinsky's "stripping" Chopin's Ballade "of expressive excess" by abstracting its directed tonal motion into a characteristic tonal and deadlock), and assimilated, once again, to "generalization." Apophrades (return of the dead) is invoked three times (73, 134, 141), not in terms of its mechanism, but in terms of one of its effects as Bloom describes it, that of making it seem as though "the later poet himself had written the precursor's characteristic work." Straus uses the term merely as an encomium, to laud the remaker's triumph over the passive object. (Bloom, meanwhile, associated apophrades with a transparency to the precursor born of mature, if solipsistic, security—but then restimulating anxiety.) The other three revisionary ratios are never invoked. The crudity of these appropriations is epitomized in Straus's strange notion of causality: "Clinamen through the specific musical revisionary strategies by which it is worked out, frequently leads to what Bloom calls *apophrades*" (134).

39. Coinage of the term *pitch class,* as well as *set* in the present usage, is attributed to Milton Babbitt's 1946 PhD dissertation, "The Function of Set Structure in the Twelve-Tone System" (awarded the degree by Princeton in 1992), which circulated for a decade in typescript before seeing its way piecemeal into print (beginning with "Some Aspects of Twelve-Tone Composition," *The Score and I.M.A. Magazine* 12 [1955]: 53–61). The term *pitch class* was apparently first published in Babbitt's article "Twelve-Tone Invariants as Compositional Determinants," *Musical Quarterly* 46 (1960): 246–59. The word *set* was first applied to an unordered collection of fewer than twelve pitch classes by George Perle in *Serial Composition and Atonality: An Introduction to the Music of Schoenberg, Berg, and Webern* (Berkeley: University of California Press, 1962); see Janet Schmalfeldt, *Berg's Wozzeck: Harmonic Language and Dramatic Design* (New Haven: Yale University Press, 1983), 247 n 20.

40. Allen Forte, "Context and Continuity in an Atonal Work: A Set-theoretic Approach," *Perspectives of New Music* 1, no. 2 (Spring 1963): 72—82. In this initial formulation, what Schoenberg called motives are termed "compositional projections" of the "universal" twelve-tone set or aggregate, later simplified to "compositional sets." A year later the method was further generalized and formalized and applied to a composition of Webern's (the fourth of the Five Pieces for String Quartet, op. 5): Allen Forte, "A Theory of Set-Complexes for Music," *Journal of Music Theory* 8 (1964): 136–83.

41. Further on this point with reference to Schoenberg, see Paul Lansky's article "Pitch-Class Consciousness," *Perspectives of New Music* 13, no. 2 (Spring–Summer 1975): 30–56, which proceeds from an analysis of "Vergangenes," the second of the Five Pieces for Orchestra, op. 16. The author begins by complaining that the "analytical use" of such abstracted notions as pitch class, interval class, and the like, "without the interposition of a method of interpretation, or abstraction, may . . . have the

effect of posturing uninterpreted musical ideas as full-blown structural objects," and he goes on to note with some asperity the tendency of noncomposing analysts to "imagine that the rhythmicized pitches of a composition can be so meaningless as to allow their pitch-class abstraction to suffice in an explanation of their musical significance" (31). Neither Lansky nor any other composer could have predicted that such a move might not only be "postured" as an explanatory maneuver, but actually touted (by noncomposers) as a compositional method. "If one steps back into abstracted considerations derived without respect to such concerns" as "the ways in which pitches represent pitch classes, and the ways pitch classes abstract pitch," he warns in conclusion, one cannot "describe any kind of musical sense or progression"; instead, "an understanding of the qualities of musical uniqueness will continue to be suppressed in favor of generalizations" (56). Again, from his composer's perspective he fails to imagine that such suppression and such privileging of generalization, far from the inadvertent analytical flaws he envisions, might be altogether premeditated and essential ploys for constructing revisionist history.

42. "For a Treatise on Composition" (1931), in Schoenberg's *Style and Idea,* 266. Furthermore, Schoenberg wrote, "repetition is the initial stage in music's formal technique, and variation and development its higher developmental stages" (265). The primitive identification of motives and pitch-class sets effectively precludes arrival at the higher stages.

43. See William E. Benjamin, review of *The Structure of Atonal Music* by Allen Forte, *Perspectives of New Music* 13 (1974): 170–90; William E. Benjamin, "Ideas of Order in Motivic Music," *Music Theory Spectrum* 1 (1979): 23–34; Pieter C. van den Toorn, *Stravinsky and "The Rite of Spring": The Beginnings of a Musical Language* (Berkeley: University of California Press, 1987), 207–11; Pieter C. van den Toorn, "What Price Analysis?" *Journal of Music Theory* 33 (1989): 165–89.

44. See especially James M. Baker, *The Music of Alexander Scriabin* (New Haven: Yale University Press, 1986); and Richard Taruskin, review of same, *Music Theory Spectrum* 10 (1988): 143–69.

45. Charles Wuorinen, interviewed by Cole Gagne in Cole Gagne and Tracy Caras, *Soundpieces: Interviews with American Composers* (Metuchen, N.J.: Scarecrow Press, 1982), 394.

46. Straus writes, "Throughout his life Stravinsky was preoccupied by and deeply anxious about his relationship to what he called 'the German stem'" (6). Yet by the time Stravinsky was ready to write about it, he had managed to survive the stem and felt reassured. Straus misses the irony in Stravinsky's reference, elsewhere in the same passage from *Dialogues and a Diary,* to "progressive-evolutionary standards"; he identifies the "German stem" not so much with the tellingly out-of-order list of composers that supposedly constitutes it ("Bach—Haydn—Mozart—Beethoven—Schubert—Brahms—Wagner—Mahler—Schoenberg") as with the teleological critical stance that "evaluates solely in terms of where a thing comes from and where it is going" (Igor Stravinsky and Robert Craft, *Dialogues and a Diary* [Garden City, N.Y.: Doubleday, 1963], 14).

47. Here, too, there were specific "confrontations," not just a generalized stylistic masquerade: for example, Stravinsky's appropriation of Bach's Clavier Concerto in D Minor (BWV 1052) in the first movement of his Concerto for Piano and Winds, described in detail in my essay "The Pastness of the Present and the Presence of the

Past," in *Authenticity and Early Music,* ed. Nicholas Kenyon (Oxford: Oxford University Press, 1988), 169–80—though as modeling this is no more to be construed as anxiety of influence than the arrangements Straus describes.

48. Jean-R. Bloch, "Une Insurrection contre la sensibilité," *Le Monde Musical,* September 1924; quoted in Scott Messing, *Neoclassicism in Music from the Genesis of the Concept through the Schoenberg/Stravinsky Polemic* (Ann Arbor: UMI Research Press, 1988), 135.

49. Edwin Evans, "Igor Stravinsky: Contrapuntal Titan," *Musical America,* 12 February 1921; quoted by Messing on p. 134. Messing calls Evans's comparison "without precedent," yet five years earlier an article on Stravinsky by his Clarens neighbor C. Stanley Wise had included a comparison between the thirty-four-year-old composer of *The Rite of Spring* and "old John Sebastian Bach with his marvellous grasp of counterpoint and delight in setting himself to solve musical puzzles, his never-ceasing experiments in harmony, his domesticity and personal simplicity"—all of which were qualities soon to be canonized in the "neoclassic" ideology ("Impressions of Igor Strawinsky," *Musical Quarterly* 2 [1916]: 250).

50. Arnold Schoenberg, "How One Becomes Lonely" (1937), in *Style and Idea,* 52.

51. Paul Landormy, "Schönberg, Bartók, und die französische Musik," *Musikblätter des Anbruch,* May 1922; quoted in Messing, *Neoclassicism in Music,* 126.

52. See the famous fawning letter of 1924 to Prince Max Egon zu Fürstenberg, the Donaueschingen patron; Arnold Schoenberg, *Letters,* ed. Erwin Stein, trans. Eithne Wilkins and Ernst Kaiser (Berkeley: University of California Press, 1987), 108–9. Only a year before his death in America, Schoenberg reaffirmed his lifelong "superfluous" monarchism (*Style and Idea,* 506).

53. *Schoenberg's Serial Odyssey: The Evolution of His Twelve-Tone Method, 1914–1928* (Oxford: Clarendon Press, 1990), 108. "Seemingly traditional moulds" also characterizes the Suite for piano, op. 25, the Septet Suite, op. 29, and many other works of the period.

54. Donald Mitchell, *The Language of Modern Music* (New York: St. Martin's Press, 1970), 105 (originally published in 1963).

55. Alan Lessem, "Schoenberg, Stravinsky, and Neo-Classicism: The Issues Reexamined," *Musical Quarterly* 68 (1982): 538. Lessem offers in support a quotation from an unpublished essay by Schoenberg titled "Old Forms in New Music": "If comprehensibility is made difficult in one respect, it must be made easier in some other respect. Difficult to comprehend in new music are the chords, the melodic intervals and their progression. Therefore a form should be chosen that will on the other hand reduce difficulties by providing a familiar type of unfolding."

56. "Schoenberg Is Dead," in Pierre Boulez, *Stocktakings from an Apprenticeship,* ed. Paule Thévenin, trans. Stephen Walsh (Oxford: Clarendon Press, 1991), 209–14.

57. Lessem's sustained attempt, in "Schoenberg, Stravinsky, and Neo-Classicism," to distinguish Stravinsky's neo- from Schoenberg's unprefixed classicism is typical special pleading, vitiated by Messing's historical critique of the terms in his *Neoclassicism in Music.* For yet another example of the double standard whereby Schoenberg's *Selbstbildnis* is uncritically accepted while Stravinsky's is aggressively deconstructed, see Mathias Hansen, "Arnold Schönbergs Kompositionsverständnis und seine Auseinandersetzung mit neoklassizistischen Tendenzen in den zwanziger Jahren," *Jahrbuch Peters* 3 (1980): 66–85.

58. Salusinszky, *Criticism in Society,* 50.

59. Ibid., 138; italics added.

60. See my "Stravinsky's *Requiem Canticles* as Russian Music," in *Music Theory and the Exploration of the Past,* ed. Christopher Hatch and David Bernstein (Chicago: University of Chicago Press, 1993), 525–50.

61. All quotations in this paragraph are from "National Music" (1931), in *Style and Idea,* 172–74.

62. The point holds whether one takes as "its time" the year of the essay's publication (1947) or that of its first draft, which was read as a radio lecture in 1933, the year the Nazis came to power.

63. See, on Stravinsky, Claudio Spies, "Conundrums, Conjectures, Construals; or, 5 vs. 3: The Influence of Russian Composers on Stravinsky," in *Stravinsky Retrospectives,* ed. Ethan Haimo and Paul Johnson (Lincoln: University of Nebraska Press, 1987), 76–140. "Brahms the Progressive," of course, has spawned by now a whole critical tradition. Like Bloom, I find reassurance in the vigor with which many of my hypotheses as to Stravinsky's stylistic debts and specific influences have been rejected (see in particular Pieter van den Toorn, "Taruskin's Angle," *In Theory Only* 10, no. 3 [October 1987]: 27–46), and feel confident that Stravinsky would have disapproved of them even more strongly and confirmingly.

39

Back to Whom?

Neoclassicism as Ideology

Scott Messing, *Neoclassicism in Music: From the Genesis of the Concept through the Schoen-berg/Stravinsky Polemic*, Studies in Musicology, no. 101 (Ann Arbor: UMI Research Press, 1988; xvii, 215 pp.)

Stephen Hinton, *The Idea of Gebrauchsmusik: A Study of Musical Aesthetics in the Weimar Republic (1919–1933) with Particular Reference to the Works of Paul Hindemith*, Outstanding Dissertations in Music from British Universities (New York: Garland, 1989; iii, 246 pp.)

Wolfgang Osthoff and Reinhard Wiesend, eds., *Colloquium Klassizität, Klassizismus, Klassik in der Musik 1920–1950 (Würzburg 1985)*, Würzburger Musikhistorische Beiträge, vol. 10 (Tutzing: Hans Schneider Verlag, 1988; 180 pp.)

In their commentary to the Paul Sacher Stiftung facsimile of Stravinsky's *Symphonies d'instruments à vent* (composed in 1920), André Baltensperger and Felix Meyer classify the *Symphonies* as "one of the last works of the composer's 'Russian' period," to be sharply distinguished from "the new 'neoclassical' orientation" around the corner, recognizable by its "complex network of allusions to historical models in art music."[1] Retrospectivism and stylistic allusion—in particular, pastiche or parody of eighteenth-century styles and forms—are indeed the features by which twentieth-century neoclassicism in music is generally identified, but a mere moment's reflection will show their inadequacy to the concept. There are plenty of familiar works that invoke or evoke the eighteenth century (*Der Rosenkavalier*, for one, or *Ariadne auf Naxos*) without their being assimilated to the "neoclassical" model. Strauss's stylistic retrospectivism is usually viewed as a symptom of a more general nostalgia (and nostalgic eighteenth-century pastiche had a considerable nineteenth-century history), whereas the composers usually named as the "neoclassic" ringleaders, chiefly the middle-aged Stravinsky and the young Hindemith, were not stylistically retrospective. (In what way, then, *were* they retrospective?) Unlike the post-*Elektra* Strauss, they did not forfeit their reputations as modernists. Indeed, its proponents have often touted neo-

Originally published in *19th-Century Music* 16, no. 3 (1993): 286–302. Copyright © 1993 by the Regents of the University of California.

classicism as the first truly "modern" twentieth-century style, in that its end run around romanticism signaled a true break with the past rather than maximalization of familiar aims and means.

The origins of neoclassicism are usually located in the disruptions of World War I. Writers hostile to it have often attempted to write it off as a war-bred hysteria, of which the chief outward manifestation, to quote its fiercest antagonist, was "retrogression into the traditional."[2] Many music historians and theorists have ratified this notion, viewing neoclassicism as a sort of salvage operation—a "perestroika," as we have learned to say—by which the doomed "tonal system" was given a superficial preservative restructuring. On this view, neoclassicism was not an authentic modern style but a "right deviation" in defiance of history.

So what was it, hardboiled modernism or futile nostalgia? Can we define it, or can we only know it when we see it? What was its relationship to its own contemporary world, on the one hand, and to the world of the past, on the other? What did it mean to its contemporaries, and what should it mean to us? Should we call it a musical style at all? A concept? A practice? Some recent studies have promoted a fresh approach to these questions by attempting to reconstruct the historical contexts and circumstances out of which the neoclassicizing impulse emerged. The importance of this work lies not only in its contribution to the factual elucidation of the subject but also in its potential for dismantling many of the false premises on which the historiography of twentieth-century music has long been resting. Now that the evils wrought by historical determinism and utopianism have been cathartically acknowledged and disavowed in many areas of life and social thought, the time is right for such a project. Once we begin looking at the neoclassical repertory without teleological or dialectical prejudices, the first thing we learn is that it was an intransigent thing, neither a refuge in the past nor a maintenance of a nervous status quo. Like its collateral descendant, the "historical performance" movement, it was a tendentious journey back to where we had never been.

.   .   .

An art that wishes to be plain, brisk, non-descriptive, and even non-expressive.
—CHARLES KOECHLIN, "Le 'Retour à Bach'"

My Octuor is not an "emotive" work but a musical composition based on objective elements which are sufficient in themselves.
—IGOR STRAVINSKY, "Some Ideas about My Octuor"

Scott Messing is a good digger. In *Neoclassicism in Music,* he successfully unearths the cultural politics out of which *nouveau classicisme* (in German, *Klassizität*) began to emerge—not as nostalgia, and long before the Great War. He reminds us at the very outset that as a musical style category "neoclassicism" is virtually coeval with "classicism" (*classique, Klassik*): hence the futility of trying to gauge the difference between the neo and the real thing; the latter is already a neoclassical construction. He analyzes the cluster of terms habitually mustered to describe the "classic" and the "neoclassic" alike—"clarity, simplicity, objectivity, purity, refinement, constructive logic, concision, sobriety, and so on" (as he lists them on p. xiv)—and shows how they collectively construct national and ethical identities, as well as artistic ones. He demonstrates the connections between (neo)classicism and youth culture, (neo)classicism and cultural elitism, (neo)classicism and authoritarianism, (neo)classicism and the politics of exclusion. He knows how (neo)classicism relates to "decadence." He is aware of the difference between a conservative and a reactionary, and that the latter is a kind of radical. He has investigated the relationship between musicological archaeology and nationalism. And, albeit implicitly, he has a great deal to say about what is now known (after Harold Bloom) as the "anxiety of influence."[3]

His book, in short, is a breakthrough in culturally informed music historiography. That in five years it has not managed to attract interest commensurate with its deserts has to do not only with the author's modest, unassertive diction, and not only with the fact that his offering is a revised dissertation published in a low-prestige series. The unjustified neglect is also, I think, the result of some long-standing academic biases.

Although he has a short and somewhat perfunctory "German" chapter, treating Mann's and Busoni's ideas about *Klassizität* (*neue* for the former and *junge* for the latter), Messing looks at things mainly from the French perspective, training a Gallic lens on Stravinsky (with the late-appearing Schoenberg as the "other" for a change). The author's motivating idea is that "an examination of the critical response to Stravinsky's works as well as the composer's own prose during the period 1914–23 (when the meaning of the term neoclassicism was transformed) can determine the link between his musical style and the aesthetic which attempted to define that style" (88).

In other words, the book intends a discourse that has long been stigmatized and exorcised within the academy as "extramusical." The locus classicus of that dismissal, where neoclassicism is concerned, is Milton Babbitt's edict, in the Stravinsky memorial issue of *Perspectives of New Music*, that "catch words" such as "back to Bach" and "neoclassicism" were only "to be talked about by those who could not and should not talk about the music."[4]

As always with Babbitt, for "talk" read "talk shop"; the reason for dismissing the language of public converse is simply and wholly its lack of "pertinence to professional activity or professional discourse."[5] To equate music, for purposes of discussion, with the techniques of manufacturing music, to regard the manufacturing of music as the only legitimate professional concern of musicians, and to sanction only such locutions as may describe or analogically represent that manufacture is of course merely to practice another politics of exclusion, the "poietic fallacy," as I prefer to call it.[6] It implies a wholly production-oriented model, a model that ought to be as outmoded for cultural history as it has (lately) become in economics. In cultural practice, the production orientation represents the unconscious residue of a romanticism many of its espousers (the "neoclassicists" themselves, for example) have outwardly rejected; and it is the fatal flaw of most twentieth-century theorizing on the arts, including a great deal of ostensibly Marxist theorizing.[7]

"Professional discourse," in any case, is no more transparent a discourse than any other. It does not uncover reality, it merely represents the "interests," on many levels, of "the *[sic]* contemporary composer" (as the young Charles Rosen put it in a jeremiad of long ago), who may or may not be contemporary to the music discoursed about—indeed, who may not exist at all except as a catchphrase.[8] Professional discourse can be, and often is, an instrument of idealization after the fact. As a discourse of entrenched power it is conservative. It is seldom where the cultural action is.

Public discourse, on the other hand, can possess real illocutionary force. It can make things happen. The force and its effects are "historical facts" (as Dahlhaus would say), accounting to a considerable degree for the meaning encoded in artistic products. The whole value of today's revisionary history is the opportunity it offers (read: the obligation it imposes) to problematize the stand pat assumptions of "professional discourse." One of the ways it does this is by recapturing and restoring what Stephen Hinton, in *The Idea of Gebrauchsmusik,* calls the "openness" in which "past events . . . occurred." This is necessary, he says, because "otherwise the very essence of the historical act (as opposed to the scientific fact)—freedom—would be extinguished" (81). Even if one rejects the reason as yet another romantic prejudice (and even if one views as an abuse Hinton's immediate objective, which is to expunge the taint of "ideology" from the "content of art"), one has to approve the de-idealizing objective.

There is no better illustration of the influence of public discourse, and its embodiment in actual music, than the story of the "neoclassical" Stravinsky. What Messing calls "the critical response to Stravinsky's works" and "the aesthetic which attempted to define [his] style" in fact (and to an extent even Messing may not realize) virtually shaped that style.

In France, the actual cognate to the English *neoclassicism* (*néoclassicisme;* cf. the German *Klassizismus*) was at first a pejorative, implying an unimaginative epigonism; French critics at the turn of the century loved to deride Mendelssohn and Brahms, indeed the whole "nineteenth-century German lineage [of symphonists]," as "neoclassic chloroform" (Messing, 12). The concept of "good" classicism—the dialectical adversary of decadence and a force for renewal—was born in phobic reaction to another German, of course, Oedipal antagonist to three generations of French musicians.[9]

The first great flurry of French roots-seeking in the "classical" past came about in the aftermath of the Franco-Prussian War under the aegis of the Société Nationale de Musique. This organization, and the chamber music it presented, could be the subject of a fascinating Bloomian study, since under the motto ARS GALLICA the Société Nationale fostered the greatest rash of Teutonizing *néoclassicisme* in the history of French music. But its 1871 inaugural concert also unveiled the first of many compositions that would appear over the next three decades "dans le style ancien." Much of this repertoire (like the inaugural piece, by Alexis Castillon) consisted of mediocre parlor music, although major composers also contributed to it, among them Saint-Saëns and D'Indy. Even at its fluffiest, though, it was high-minded nationalistic fluff, and its retrospectivism was the result of a Wagner-inspired attempt to circumvent Wagner and everything that had led up to him. Nor ought we forget that some of the earliest swerves toward bona fide "modern music," beginning with Satie's *Trois sarabandes* (1887) and continuing with Debussy's piano suites (*Suite bergamasque*, 1890; *Suite: Pour le piano*, 1894–1901), took place within this ostensibly retrospective domain.

The first musician to whom the word *néoclassique* was applied without irony was, predictably enough, Stravinsky. This happened in 1923, the year of the *Octuor,* but quite a few months before that work actually appeared.[10] The Stravinsky work to which the N-word was first attached, as it happened, was none other than the *Symphonies d'Instruments à vent*—by now, as we have seen, more often viewed in contrast to neoclassicism than as an example of it—and the man who attached it was another Russian émigré, Boris de Schloezer. From the beginning, moreover (and just as predictably), the term characterized Stravinsky in opposition to Schoenberg, whose art "is in its essence Tristanesque, romantic (the same as that of Scriabin)."[11] Nothing could be more critical to our understanding of neoclassicism as term and concept than to recognize these circumstances: the application was made, and the opposition drawn, not with respect to any eighteenth-century stylization but in connection with what is now looked upon as Stravinsky's valedictory to his "Russian period." As a criterion for neoclassicism, retrospection was neither necessary nor sufficient.

What made the *Symphonies* "neoclassical" for Schloezer, thence for many others, was the assumption that it was

> only a system of sounds, which follow one another and group themselves according to purely musical affinities; the thought of the artist places itself only in the musical plan without ever setting foot in the domain of psychology. Emotions, feelings, desires, aspirations—this is the terrain from which he has pushed his work. The art of Stravinsky is nevertheless strongly expressive; he moves us profoundly and his perception is never formularized; but there is one specific emotion, a musical emotion. This art does not pursue feeling or emotion; but it attains grace infallibly by its force and by its perfection. (Quoted in Messing, 130).

These words, quite irrelevant to the poetic conception of the *Symphonies* (a *tombeau* for Debussy that faithfully mimics an Orthodox funeral service),[12] not only characterize reception but also prefigure with uncanny accuracy the most famous Stravinskian pronunciamento of them all—that "over-publicized bit about expression (or non-expression)" from the *Chroniques de ma vie* that the composer would so try to live down in his late years, when he became desperate to forge retroactive links to his "Tristanesque" rival.[13] His initial appropriation of Schloezer's viewpoint shows that Stravinsky invested in (and abetted) it ex post facto.

And despite the fact that this was the judgment of another transplanted Russian, it epitomized that cluster of values—purity, sobriety, objectivity, grace, impersonal precision, and so on—by which the French defined themselves in opposition to the decadently "psychological" Germans, whose art they nervously dismissed with what Messing rightly calls "fashionable anathemas" (59).[14] The great oriental primitive, insofar as he was now suddenly taken to be "the most anti-Wagnerian of musicians," had willy-nilly become the paragon of Frenchness. Until old age—until he made belated peace with "the German stem"[15]—Stravinsky paraded himself as "Wagner's Antichrist."[16]

But it did not happen quite that suddenly. The documents Messing presents depict the culmination of the process by which Stravinsky was co-opted to a long-standing French esthetic program. The initial stages are also worth a look because, contrary to conventional opinion, they relate to the period preceding the war and had as their object *Petrushka* and especially *The Rite of Spring*, works that can now seem even more antithetical than the *Symphonies* to Stravinsky's later stance. The French managed to find in them what they were looking for, though, and this constituted the "intuition" about his music that so impressed Stravinsky at the time, and that he made a point of recalling in a memoir of Jacques Rivière close to five decades later.[17]

Rivière (1886–1925) was the precocious editor of *La Nouvelle Revue française*, the aggressively nationalistic literary forum founded in 1909, the year of Diaghilev's first "saison russe," by a group of seven writers that included André Gide. They adopted, as motto for their program of cultural renewal, something very old indeed: the title of Joachim du Bellay's "pléiade" manifesto of 1549, *Défense et illustration de la langue française*. The inaugural editorial had glossed the slogan as follows:

> *La langue* is not just language, it is culture. . . . *Défense* . . . can mean no more than a psychological reaction, the response or rejoinder of a living organism to all influences, good or bad. . . . The strongest periods are those that react the most vigorously, just as they are the most avid to assimilate. . . . Finally, *illustrer* aspires less here to the sense of rendering illustrious than to that of rendering plain. Genius alone can create glory and he appears only when he appears. But it is for each of us to define him, support him, surround him with an environment of admiration and understanding.[18]

That genius would be Stravinsky, and the explication, bolstering support, and intelligent admiration he received from the *NRF* as by-product of its literary politicking seduced and profoundly influenced him in turn.[19] In his reviews of Stravinsky's ballets, Rivière promoted the composer from the status of mere musician to that of exemplary artist for France. When everyone else was exclaiming at the orgiastic dissonance of *The Rite,* its *âme slave,* its sublime terror, Rivière called it "the first masterpiece we may stack up against those of impressionism," and for the following magnificently expressed reasons:

> The great novelty of *Le Sacre du printemps* is its renunciation of "sauce." *Here is a work that is absolutely pure.* . . . Nothing is blurred, nothing is mitigated by shadows; no veils and no poetic sweeteners; *not a trace of atmosphere.* The work is whole and tough, *its parts remain quite raw;* they are served up without digestive aids; *everything is crisp, intact, clear and crude.* . . . Never have we heard *a music so magnificently limited.* If [Stravinsky] has chosen those instruments that do not sigh, *that say no more than they say,* whose timbres are *without expression* and are *like isolated words,* it is because he wants to *enunciate everything directly, explicitly, and concretely. His voice becomes the object's proxy,* consuming it, replacing it; *instead of evoking it, he utters it.* . . . Thus Stravinsky, with unmatched flair and accomplishment, is bringing about in music the same revolution that is taking place more humbly and tortuously in literature: *he has passed from the sung to the said, from invocation to statement, from poetry to reportage.* (My italics, signaling passages that again herald not just "neoclassicism," but Stravinsky's own esthetic manifestos of the 1920s and 1930s.)[20]

Thus Rivière in 1913. One is tempted to suggest that by misreading Stravinsky so early as a classicist and a positivist, Rivière actually turned him into one. For one is influenced not only by anxiety but also by praise, the more so when the praise is at once so intelligent and so hyperbolic. It is not so hard to understand why, just emerging from a milieu in which he was ranked far below Glazunov (and even behind Maximilian Steinberg, his teacher's son-in-law), Stravinsky should have been susceptible to the blandishments of those who placed him higher than Debussy. He did what was necessary to keep that praise coming.

The retrospective turn was taken, on the way from the *Symphonies* to the *Octuor,* by way of *Mavra* and *Les Cinq doigts,* the latter an insignificant opus but a big milestone. *Pulcinella* had little or nothing to do with it (nor, as Messing points out on p. 112, was it received by the French as "classique"). Strapped for funds, the uprooted Stravinsky was not about to turn down the first paying job Diaghilev had been able to offer him in five years (and only after Falla refused it), but it was not his idea and had little relation to his interests at the time. His defacements of "Pergolesi" were an accommodation between the eighteenth-century *objet trouvé* and the anhemitonic pseudo-folkish harmonizations with which he had been experimenting in *Les Noces,* the project that the *Pulcinella* commission interrupted: the very end of the

"Pergolesi" ballet, with its ersatz dominant chord (a stack of thirds containing every note of the C-major scale except the leading tone), can furnish quick confirmation.

It was the rediscovery of the leading tone, and the reintroduction into his music of the dominant function (very perspicaciously noted, in an early review of *Mavra*, by Poulenc),[21] that proclaimed the self-attachment of Stravinsky's umbilical cord to Western "classical" tradition. To observe the exact moment of its fastening, see the third little piece (Allegretto) in *Les Cinq doigts,* fabulously ironical because it is in fact an unadvertised arrangement of the famous Russian folk tune *Kamárinskaya,* known to all concertgoers from arch-"nationalist" Glinka's *Fantaisie pittoresque* of 1848.

So it was a distanced, ironized past—betokening a stance of highly self-conscious contemporaneity—that Stravinsky evoked, and he accomplished it by the use of an ironized dominant function. Ironized, but not marginalized or denatured: the accompaniment to the "Russian Maiden's Song" in *Mavra,* for example, which became a popular encore item and therefore something of an emblem, consists of nothing but tonics and fully resolving, functional dominants. The harmony and the bass line, however, are misaligned by the use of multileveled ostinati that go in and out of phase. The ear is never allowed to take the V–I cadence for granted. The misalignments continually force renewed attention, achieving precisely the effect that the Russian formalists called *ostraneniye,* "making-strange."

Stravinsky was impelled to a retrospective classicism by what he called the "loss of Russia." In this, by the way, he established belated contact with the original wellsprings of the movement that had fathered the Ballets Russes long before Stravinsky was aboard: *Mir iskusstva* (The World of Art), the self-avowedly classicizing reassertion of aristocratic taste in the face of materialist and utilitarian esthetics that led Diaghilev and Benois in the closing years of the nineteenth century to their rediscovery of the ballet, a classical art that had been preserved in aspic by the Russian autocracy and that now could serve as medium for an artistic and spiritual regeneration. Stravinsky's ironized cultivation of the phonology and morphology of eighteenth-century music was literally a reactionary move,[22] a furious rejection of the horrible new order—Bolsheviks overrunning his native country, proletariats rampant everywhere—that he called "modernism." He went around telling interviewers that "modernists"—the expressionistic "revolutionary" Schoenberg, naturally, above all—"have ruined modern music,"[23] just as modernists of a different stripe had befouled the modern world.

His Chaikovsky ballet, *Le Baiser de la fée,* although externally commissioned, was a relatively unironized pastiche, motivated by disgust with Prokofieff's *Le Pas d' acier,* a flimsy, cacophonous exploitation of Soviet thematics, the "radical chic" of its day. For Stravinsky (especially since Diaghilev's epochal *Sleeping Beauty* of 1921), Chaikovsky, of all nineteenth-century composers the most given to idiosyncratic "eighteenth-century" confections, was above all the paragon of the lost "Imperial" style. Thus, if Stravinsky's music of the 1920s and 1930s was no longer "revolutionary," it was anything but conservative. In the precise meaning of the word, his was a counterrevolutionary art.

With the *Octuor,* Stravinsky joined the *retour à Bach,* and, with his Concerto and Sonate, over the next couple of years he commandeered it. French Bachianism meant purity: the renunciation of all national character in favor of a musical Esperanto with a lexicon heavily laced with self-conscious allusions to the perceived fountainhead of "universal" musical values.[24] French Bachianism was a defense of art against psychopathology: hence all that insistence on objectivity, as in the epigraph above. Above all, French Bachianism was an affirmation of cultural elitism: the craftsman, working at an exalted level of mastery, levitates above the comprehension of the mob. Thus Nadia Boulanger on the *Octuor:*

> Stravinsky appears in the light of the constructivist, of geometry; all of his thought is translated into precise, simple, and classic lines; and the sovereign certainty of his writing, always renewed, here takes on in its dryness and precision an authority without artifice.
>
> No transpositions, all is pure music. . . . The score of the Octet is among those which furnish the satisfaction of the spirit and the eyes which recognize the passions of counterpoint, for those who love to reread the old masters of the Renaissance and Johann Sebastian Bach.[25]

So far from an investment in "the German stem," the *retour à Bach* was an attempt to hijack the Father, to wrest the old contrapuntist from his errant countrymen (who with their abnormal "psychology" had betrayed his purity, his health-giving austerity, his dynamism, his detached and transcendent craft) and restore him to a properly elite station. "I go back to Bach," said Stravinsky in one of those down-with-modernism interviews (Messing, 142), "not Bach as we know him today, but Bach as he really is. You know now they play Bach with a Wagner orchestra and make him sound very pleasant, so people will like him. That isn't the real Bach." It was the original authenticity pitch.

· · ·

Strict polyphonic form . . . requires "performance"; it cannot be "enjoyed"; one has to be part of it.
—ERICH DOFLEIN, "Gegenwart, Gebrauch, Kitsch und Stil" (1929)

After these observations the aim of this book ought to be clear: it is activity.
—PAUL HINDEMITH, *Elementary Training for Musicians*

This can't go on.
—THEODOR W. ADORNO, *Impromptus*

Clarity, sanity, objectivity, elitism . . . Messing stops just short of the dark side, but he hints at it several times, as when he quotes a letter from

Stravinsky to Ansermet, full of praise for the music of "a young gentile German, full of talent, named Paul Hindemith."[26] Chalk up another intransigent binarism, even unlovelier than the rest, to join France/Germany, youthful/decadent, classic/romantic, objective/subjective, authority/identification, reactionary/modernist, Stravinsky/Schoenberg.[27] Had Stravinsky known more about his fair-haired boy, though, he might have been less pleased to greet him.

Messing has speculated that the work Hindemith sent Stravinsky was the Kammermusik No. 1, first performed to a triumphant reception at the Donaueschingen festival just two weeks before Stravinsky wrote to Ansermet. If so, Stravinsky would have been flattered, since the Kammermusik's first movement is "undoubtedly the finest *Petrushka*-derivative of the twentieth century."[28] But making it one of the prime exhibits in *The Idea of Gebrauchsmusik* (where, in a manner recalling Messing's presentation of Stravinsky, it assumes the role of antithesis to Schoenberg's *Kammersymphonie*, op. 9), Hinton points up the crucial differences between the cultural meaning of Hindemith's socially motivated Weimar antiromanticism and Stravinsky's socially detached Parisian elitism. The one challenged the "paradigm of autonomy," the other exalted it. The one was transcendental kitsch, the other transcendental chic.

The concept to which Hinton has devoted his study—together with its companion term, *neue Sachlichkeit*[29]—arose out of what Harold Bloom would call a misprision and what Hinton calls a "fruitful misinterpretation" (24). The fascinating early chapters of Hinton's book, in which these notions are traced to their sources, are his best and most essential contribution to understanding the "right deviation" from the evolutionary straight-and-narrow, which in Germany seemed at first to be more a thing of the left.

Contrary to Hindemith's own claim, in *A Composer's World,* that he had coined the term *Gebrauchsmusik* (which by 1951 he was predictably eager to disavow),[30] the term arose in academic circles. The originator seems to have been Paul Nettl, who used it in a study of seventeenth-century dance music to distinguish dances danced to from dances listened to (*Vortragsmusik*). Heinrich Besseler, whose 1923 dissertation also concerned the origins of the dance suite, not only appropriated the term but also (in a widely disseminated lecture, "Grundfragen des musikalischen Hörens") abstracted it as an esthetic category and sought to ground it in Heidegger's concept of *Faktizität*, the "facticity" of Being (*Dasein*), and in the opposition of *Ding* (thing) and *Zeug* (apparatus). "The less we just stare at the hammer-Thing, and the more we seize hold of it and use it, the more primordial does our relationship to it become," wrote Heidegger in *Sein und Zeit* (Hinton, 13). Besseler, whose research in medieval music had relativized his values, had lost faith in the supremacy of absolute music and its attendant modes of listening. He dreamed of recapturing Heidegger's "primordial" immediacy of experience and the social relevance the music he studied had possessed as an art still un-divorced from life-as-lived. Hence music as *Zeug:* music-for-use, as opposed to music as *Ding* (*eigenständige,* or autonomous, *Musik*). "Gebrauchsmusik represents for the individual something of equal rank to his other activities, something with which he has dealings in the way that one has dealings with things of everyday use, without having to overcome any distance beforehand, that is, *without having to adopt an aesthetic attitude.*"[31]

It is noteworthy that this antiesthetic esthetic of actuality and participa-tion, opposed to the romantic ideal of transcendent genius and the tradition of passive concert-contemplation, should have emerged out of an antiquar-ian milieu. Hinton attributes it to a typically academic generalization: "Besseler's descriptive intentions become normative"; "his academic concern with adequately describing the anthropological and aesthetic context of early music turns into support for a renewal of musical life" (16). It was an-other end run around the nineteenth century, one born not of national as-pirations but of social ones, and inspiring a different sort of musical pseudoretrospectivism. Heidegger apparently intended nothing of the kind. His own esthetics (not explicitly formulated until later) remained firmly tied to the autonomy principles; for him, the music-Thing would always be some-thing to stare at and to sacralize. But Besseler's misreading of his philosophy professor was overdetermined, responsive not only to the perceived impli-cations of Heidegger's thought, but to many other stimuli from what we now call "Weimar culture."

If World War I looms as a great divide even in the historiography of the victor nations, how much more a cataclysm did it seem to the losers, for whom it brought immediate political upheaval and economic chaos, the pal-pable legacy of "decadence." *Gebrauchsmusik* and *neue Sachlichkeit* were not just a reaction to the romantic esthetic of the Sublime, but a reaction to all the forces that were seen to have precipitated the war, forces that notably in-cluded nationalism. Having experienced ruin, German artists—the osten-sible heirs of the "mainstream"—were more suspicious than anyone else of the lie of transcendence, any promise of immortality, permanence, lasting value. Hence the cult of the perishable, the ephemeral, the transient (whence Hindemith's pride in having authored—in the *Lehrstück* of 1929— a piece whose component parts could be rearranged or omitted at plea-sure). Hence, too, the notion of an art that was not merely to be used, but to be used up. Obsolescence—happily planned obsolescence, the consid-ered rejection of "masterpiece culture"—was the corollary (the price) of true contemporaneity. The last movement of Hindemith's Kammermusik No. 1 (Stravinsky may not have thumbed that far) was titled "Finale: 1921" and quoted a foxtrot popularized that year by the Wilm Wilm band. The next year's model, the *Suite '1922'* for piano, sported a "Shimmy" and a

"Boston." The composer's own title-page cartoon shows a chance moment on a bustling thoroughfare.[32]

Antimetaphysics of another sort was embodied in the music Hindemith wrote for himself to perform (epitomized in another product of 1922, the scandalous Sonata for Solo Viola, op. 25, no. 1), an unadulterated *Spielmusik* in which the activity of performance was tantamount to the content of the music. "I composed the first and fifth movements in a buffet car between Frankfurt and Cologne and then went straight on to the platform and played the sonata," Hindemith wrote in his catalog of works (Hinton, 181). Matter-of-factness as high artistic cause is reflected in Hindemith's zealous attempt to insulate his music from "tiresome rubato-playing and 'expression'-art" by the use of sloganeering performance directions (e.g., the famous "Ton-schönheit ist Nebensache"). "Hindemith's achievement," Hinton writes, "was to reintroduce that spontaneity [that had characterized eighteenth-century performance practice] into the composition of sonatas and concerted chamber music against the background of a tradition of romantic autonomy" (186).

The peak of *neue Sachlichkeit* was reached with the *Zeitoper*, epitomized in Hindemith's *Neues vom Tage* (1929), a work whose comic point lay in the incongruity between its canonical (i.e., permanent) genre and its topical (i.e., perishable) content. While sardonic and debunking, and while obviously related to dada and surrealism, this was still not an unserious art. It was after hearing Hindemith's now-lost "Filmmusik" *Felix der Kater im Zirkus* honked out by a mechanical organ at Baden-Baden in 1927 that Aaron Copland was moved to write, "In Hindemith Germany has its first great composer since 1900."[33] By 1932, the last Weimar year, Hindemith's antimetaphysics had taken a self-consciously civic, high-principled turn, epitomized by the *Plöner Musiktag* that earned Stravinsky's outright and undying contempt.[34] This was "Musik als Zeug" with a vengeance, and by paying both spiritual and stylistic homage to the musicologically resurrected *Gebrauchsmusik* (or actual *Dienstmusik*) of the past—*Morgenmusik, Tafelmusik, Kantate,* and *Abendkonzert,* in that order—it managed to be ephemeral *sub specie aeternitatis.*

Casting himself in the role of latter-day *Stadtpfeifer*, Hindemith gave the retrospective turn a new twist: (neo)classicism—"Blockflötenkultur," Krenek would later sniff in disaffection—as ethical imperative. Hindemith had admonished a professional audience in 1927:

A composer should only write nowadays when he knows for what need he is writing. . . . The poor connection in music which exists nowadays between producer and consumer is generally to be regretted. . . . The days of always composing for one-self are perhaps over for ever. (Hinton, 198; cf. Stravinsky: "The trick, of course, is . . . to compose what one wants to compose and to get it commissioned afterward.")[35]

Adorno called this the esthetic of "Gemeinschaftsmusik," antithetical to that of the Vienna school's "neue Musik."[36] It reached an apotheosis at the Baden-Baden festival the same year, for which Hindemith selected the pieces, programming them under four eminently public-spirited categories: *Tonfilme, Musik für Liebhaber, Originalmusik für Rundfunk, Lehrstück.*

Weimarisch notions like these—great artist as good citizen; high art reduced to social transaction; music making as activity, not speculation; classicism as antiestheticism—posed the greatest threat of all to latter-day romantics of the transcendental strain. Modernists of a more ancient esthetic looked nervously to their pedestals. Denunciation was double-barreled. On the one hand, "neue Sachlichkeit" was commercial treason: *Kunstler* fraternizing with *Bürgerthum*. On the other hand, it was political treason, rendering what was God's unto Caesar (or worse, unto the bureaucratic state). Either way, it was no "disinterested" thing. And this is what Schoenberg meant when he accused Hindemith (along with Krenek) of "a lack of conscience" and "a disturbing lack of responsibility."[37] The artist's primary obligation was not to other people but to art. A social conscience was no conscience at all; indeed, lack of a proper contempt for the world and its inhabitants was contemptible. Hindemith's greatest sin, to Schoenberg, was his "nonchalance."[38] (We might prefer to see it now, from the opposite perspective, as noblesse oblige.) And here Schoenberg found himself willy-nilly in agreement with Stravinsky, who had quickly come to suspect the gentile German's promiscuous productivity.[39]

·   ·   ·

The claim that the idea of aesthetic autonomy merely deceives us about the social reality in which nothing exists that does not perform a function, is too crude on the one hand, and too platitudinous on the other, to permit meaningful discussion.
—CARL DAHLHAUS, "The Musical Work as a Subject of Sociology"

So there was a Bach of the right and a Bach of the left. There was the transcendent impersonal artisan whose name came improbably to signify the height of fashion (a fashion that would prove more durable than anyone at first suspected), and there was the old *Gemeinschaftsmusiker,* turning out well-made, socially useful goods to order. Two aspects of a single "classic" creative personality were radically dichotomized to serve contemporary needs, justifying a pair of seemingly antithetical esthetic programs that were nevertheless united in their opposition to the tainted esthetic of "psychology, emotions, feelings, desires, aspirations," and the individualistic subjectivity it glorified. In this shared hostility, both back-to-Bach strains were authentic children of their shattered time; for however else the authoritarian ideologies of the new Europe may have differed, and however they may have clashed rhetorically, they were united in backlash against the arrogant individual whose hubris had brought disaster.

As early as 1913, the year of Jacques Rivière's co-optation of Stravinsky, the critic Henri Clouard asserted that the "classical Renaissance" in French letters was code for regressive political action (Messing, 8). The *NRF,* with its double-barreled elitism combining artistic avant-gardism and reactionary politics was the prototype for many similar ventures, including *Montjoie!* Ricciotto Canudo's riotous protofascist rag (to which Stravinsky was a regular contributor), which reflected the cultural politics of the *NRF* (or of Diaghilev's old *World of Art,* for that matter) as if in a funhouse mirror. By the end of the 1920s, Stravinsky had consciously cast himself as the Mussolini of music—"the dictator of the reaction against the anarchy into which modernism degenerated," in the words of his disciple Arthur Lourié, an early Soviet defector—who wanted to do for modern music what the Duce promised to do for modern Europe.[40] He introduced his famous Charles Eliot Norton Lectures, delivered on the eve of World War II, with an invitation to regard his words as "dogmatic" and "objective" confidences, delivered "under the stern auspices of order and discipline," virtues that are finally associated in the Fourth Lesson with their "best example" in music, a Bach fugue: "A pure form in which the music means nothing outside of itself. Doesn't the fugue imply the composer's submission to the rules? And is it not within those strictures that he finds the full flowering of his freedom as a creator?"[41]

The classic and the romantic are opposed in Stravinsky's exposition under the politically charged rubrics of submission and insubordination. The artist must "submit to the law," to ordained values that transcended individuals, because "Apollo demands it."[42] He had said as much, and said it more eloquently a decade earlier in that great homily known as *Apollon musagète,* the "white ballet" of 1928 that begins (like the *Octuor*) with a polemical cadential trill. *Apollon* wordlessly adumbrated the whole central core of the *Poetics of Music* with its heavy tirade against the Dionysiac hubris of the *Gesammt Kunstwerk.* Apollo versus Dionysus was first of all music vs. drama, thence stasis vs. flux, beauty vs. frenzy, purity vs. mixture, repose vs. desire, containment vs. expression—all easily decoded as classicism vs. romanticism. (As Stravinsky's old mentor and collaborator Alexandre Benois had written, the art of the nineteenth century had been "one great slap in the face of Apollo.")[43] Or rather, that *was* the code for an antiegalitarian message more decorously insinuated by the example of artistic excellence than proclaimed. In *Oedipus rex*—for Stravinsky no family romance but a fable of insubordination and submission—the composer symbolized and ratified the offended universal order by bringing back in glory every stiff traditional convention of the eighteenth-century musical stage, precisely what the Dionysiac Wagnerians in their hubris had tried to abolish in their frenzy for individualistic expression.

Recalling late in life the first staged production of *Oedipus* (Kroll Opera, Berlin, February 1928), Stravinsky focused on the audience, which included both Hindemith ("hingerissen," as Stravinsky recollected) and Schoenberg ("abgekühlt").[44] With a nervous eye on Schoenberg's reputation with the contemporary young, the aged Stravinsky allowed that the German master "must have heard in [*Oedipus*] nothing but empty *ostinato* patterns and primitive harmonies." Indeed, a jotting of Schoenberg's, made the next day but not published until four years after Stravinsky's death, bluntly confirms Stravinsky's apprehensions: "This work is nothing." Period. But with remarkable candor Schoenberg admitted to himself the very same anxiety vis-à-vis Stravinsky that Stravinsky would later feel about Schoenberg: anxiety at his rival's reputation with the contemporary young—which is to say, with Hindemith and Krenek's generation. "I know," Schoenberg wrote, "that the works which in every way arouse one's dislike are precisely those the next generation will in every way like. And the better the jokes one makes about them, the more seriously one will later have to take them."[45]

To disapprove of Stravinsky was by then a Schoenbergian reflex, what with all those "antimodernist" press interviews in which Schoenberg saw himself the butt of Stravinsky's sallies (sallies he had already tried to answer in kind in *Drei Satiren*). And, indeed, who else could Stravinsky have had in mind but the extreme maximalizer of romantic individualism in music, the composer who brought the art of psychopathology to its final shriek in *Erwartung* (which Stravinsky knew only by reputation), and in that virtually clinical study in morbid subjectivity known as *Pierrot lunaire* (which Stravinsky heard in Berlin in 1912 as the composer's guest). To "Bachians" of all persuasions Schoenberg seemed the natural antagonist. To Stravinsky, in particular, Schoenbergian atonality was precisely the degenerate "anarchy" against which he wanted to dictate the Bachian reaction. It must have seemed to a deracinated Russian aristocrat the exact analogue to the "Bolshevik" straits in which the world of his birthright had foundered.

Given the two composers' mutual suspicion, the more is the irony that by the mid-1920s Schoenberg, too, had journeyed back to Bach, joining in the authoritarian reaction against anarchy and psychopathology (a reaction of which, as far as he was concerned, *he* was of course by rights the dictator). The early twelve-tone pieces, through which Schoenberg attempted to introduce a rigorous therapeutic order into atonal music, were cast in the form of Baroque dances—minuets, gavottes, and gigues—as a prelude to the larger sectional forms of the "classical" tradition such as Schoenberg and his pupils had formerly sought to supersede. As "pure" utopian craftsmanship, intricately made but "ohne Zweck," Schoenberg's Bachianism had far more in common with Stravinsky's snooty art than it had with the socially motivated *Gemeinschaftsmusik* of his fellow Germans, toward which his attitude would always remain ironical. Yet because it was largely confined, unlike Stravinsky's, to abstract instrumental genres, Schoenberg's neoclassicism (and Webern's) quickly metamorphosed into technical research and tours de force, foreshadowing the fetishized "professional discourse" espoused by those who later donned the mantle of their authority.

All of this was done, as Stravinsky would say, "under the stern auspices of order and discipline," which is to say, *sub specie patris*. It is no coincidence that Webern's most stringently constrained and dehumanized work, the String Quartet, op. 28, is the one based on a series derived from the B-A-C-H cipher, already impressively invoked in Schoenberg's Orchestral Variations.[46] *Et patriae:* the immediate concern may have been the preservation of a precious heritage at a time of perceived crisis, but it was a heritage dogmatically viewed as supreme, and its supremacy was part and parcel of what had to be preserved.[47] The neoclassicism of Schoenberg and Webern was thus tinged from the outset with chauvinism; their Bach was a third Bach, a national as well as a universal figurehead, asserting one nation's claim to ascendance and forestalling "Latin and Slav hopes of hegemony."[48] "It was mainly through J. S. Bach," Schoenberg alleged, "that German music came to decide the way things developed, as it has for 200 years." And it was precisely Bach's elaboration of the technique of absolute music—"contrapuntal art, i.e., the art of producing every audible figure from one single one"—that vouchsafed German domination.[49]

So, pace Dahlhaus, not even "esthetic autonomy" is unpolitical. It, too, performs a function. Being utopian, it defines itself by what it excludes. Without making essentialist claims about predisposition, one certainly can and should take note of the ease with which utopian formalists have on occasion been seduced by other manifestations of exclusionary politics. Webern's enthusiastic embrace of Hitler has become known by excruciating degrees, likewise the rabidity with which Schenker approved of brownshirt activities from afar in the years before the *Anschluss*.[50]

But so could those who hankered after community fall easy prey to National Socialism's metaphysical organicism.[51] *Gemeinschaft* metamorphosed by easy degrees into *Volksgemeinschaft,* until Krenek could assert the existence of "an unbroken line" leading "from the activist *Wandervogel* (Boy Scout), by way of Hindemith's concerto grosso style, to the Hitler youth, of whom it is told that they give vent to their indomitable spirit of independence by secretly performing Hindemith's *Spielmusik*." With regard to the great Spielmann himself (by then, like Krenek, banned in his homeland as a *Kulturbolschewist*) this was a mean-spirited, envious insinuation; but Hindemith's own subsequent attitudes corroborate this diagnosis of the trends in which he had so conspicuously participated, especially where Krenek writes of the "common . . . tendency to whittle down, a reduction of music from a spiritual art to a professional craft."[52]

"Social-democratic primitive" that he was,[53] Hindemith recoiled not only from this co-optation but from social commitment *tout court,* symbolizing his own withdrawal, and sublimating it, in the figure of "Mathis der Maler," the title character of his opera of 1934, who retreats, spiritually wounded, from the turbulent world of fifteenth-century politics—a world replete with class warfare and book burnings—into the timeless world of art. At the time of the opera's belated première (Zurich, 1938), the expatriated composer identified himself not only with Mathis, who "decides in his work to develop traditional art to its fullest extent," but also, as ever, with "Bach, who two centuries later proves to be a traditionalist in the stream of musical development."[54] A new mission, a new ethos, a new Bach. Hindemith's later writings—like the tepid if cranky Norton lectures he published as *A Composer's World,* delivered exactly a decade (but what a decade!) after Stravinsky's—were as merciless a polemic against his own younger self as was his recomposition of *Das Marienleben.* By then the new ethos of preservation-cum-obligation had degenerated, in his music, into academic complacency and, in his thinking, into a timid housebroken estheticism he nevertheless tried to pass off as the "everlasting values" and the "moral power" of the ancients.[55] In a sentimental bicentennial lecture delivered in Hamburg on 12 September 1950, Hindemith located Bach's crowning achievement precisely in the complete transcendence of the worldly: his "activity has become pure thought, freed from all incidents and frailties of structural manifestation, and he who ascended relentlessly has defeated the realm of substance and penetrated the unlimited region of thought."[56]

An even flabbier esthetic formalism has been the escapism of recent research into the history of music between the wars. To conceive of that history as mere style history is to engage in mythmaking and cosmetics. Recent German writings on neoclassicism have been especially symptomatic: an epitome of sorts is Rudolf Stephan's superficial attempt to equate Stravinsky's neoclassicism in all its particulars with the actual methodology of the Russian formalist school.[57] The Colloquium *Klassizität, Klassizismus, Klassik in der Musik 1920–1950,* held at Würzburg in 1985 and published three years later as the tenth volume in the series Würzburger Musikhistorische Beiträge, is—there is no other way to put it—a shockingly anodyne group of papers and discussions, in which the concept of purity, while inevitably emphasized, is anxiously sentimentalized and construed as benign—as equipoise, calm, serenity, *das Leibhaft-tanzerische,* and so on—even when the products of the National Socialist period (e.g., the musical works and writings by Gerhard Frommel, Stravinsky's foremost disciple in the Third Reich) are under discussion.[58]

Never is the question faced why such qualities were considered exemplary during those turbulent years—and of course Nazi classicism had its enforced Stalinist counterpart, which a glance at Myaskovsky's heap of symphonies will heartsickeningly betray[59]—or why the Bachian Stravinsky was an acceptable model for composers under Hitler. The dichotomization (read: the confusion) of esthetics and politics has never seemed so blind, or, for all its gentle affability, so sinister.

Unfortunately, it is Hinton, a Dahlhaus disciple, who attempts most explicitly to foreclose exploration of the relationship between Weimar esthetics and Nazi esthetics: "It cannot be a historian's task to describe past events using terms defined according to connotations that they have subsequently acquired," he pleads; still less is it appropriate "to take as his point of reference the consequences that are visible now" (81). Hinton's refusal to take ideology and its consequences on board is evenhanded. He wipes the young Hindemith clean of leftist taint by noting blandly that his collaborations with Brecht (*Lehrstück* and *Der Lindberghflug*, the latter a collaboration with Weill as well) "took place at least a year before Brecht's definitive conversion to communism" (203).

We have reached a familiar crux, a mightily fraught one, that haunts contemporary historiography and hermeneutics (as it does even such ostensibly innocent offshoots within the musical academy as "performance practice"), to say nothing of those depressingly familiar debates, such as that sparked by the threat of Wagner performances in Israel, that persist in pitting esthetics against ethics. Is the proper standpoint for a historian or an interpreter the actual contemporary world (one's own *Sachlichkeit*, so to speak) or an idealized, sanitized, purely notional past—the past as refuge, where dreams of a glorious future may be nurtured irresponsibly? Ought we as honest historians to imagine ourselves into the world between the wars as if we did not know what was coming? Or would that be a history without lessons, which is to say, no history at all?

It was precisely its utopian (its "scientific") aspect, as well as the myth of its political suppression, that facilitated serialism's seeming natural selection as the neomodernist lingua franca from out of the ashes of World War II. After the crimes visited on the world by an "organic society," the moral superiority of an art that implied, in Krenek's words, "the loneliness and alienation of humanity" seemed more palpable than ever[60]—especially while the yea-saying bromides of socialist realism were still being enforced with foul rituals of denunciation and contrition in a surviving organic state to the east. But if the dismal history of the twentieth century teaches us anything, it is that utopia, far from a refuge from inhumanity, is itself inescapably inhumane.

Formalism's claim to germ-free moral purity has been tarnished by the disclosure of Webern's political leanings, by the recognition of an officially tolerated school of twelve-tone composers in the Third Reich,[61] and perhaps especially by the self-indicting rhetoric—the purebred rhetoric of *Blut-und-Boden* or agitprop, take your pick—with which a new dialectical monstrosity asserted itself after the war at Darmstadt and Donaueschingen, synthesizing formerly antithetical categories (romantic "megalomania of self-infinitization" and technocratic rationalism) in an orgy of what Adorno would call the "jargon of authenticity," enunciated, appallingly enough, with the aging Adorno's anxious complicity.[62] Meanwhile, one of the Nazi serialists, Paul von Klenau (1883–1946), had openly touted the method as "totalitarian" and claimed that its strict discipline made it "entirely appropriate to the future direction of the 'National Socialist World.'"[63]

The same discipline, among other stock classicizing claims, made the twelve-tone system attractive to Stravinsky—or so the old neoclassicist would tell reporters on his return to the old world after the war: "The twelve-tone composers are the only ones who have a discipline I respect. Whatever else it may be, twelve-tone music is certainly pure music.'"[64] Although he named no names, we know now that he had Schoenberg's Septet Suite (Ouverture—Tanzschritte—Thema mit Variationen—Gigue) foremost in mind and that he was promoting it exactly as he had promoted his own Bachianas thirty years before. Was this "catchphrase journalism" or was it "professional discourse"? Or was it history—a better history than we have had since?

NOTES

1. Igor Strawinsky, *Symphonies d'instruments à vent: Faksimileausgabe des Particells und der Partitur der Erstfassung (1920),* trans. Anne C. Schreffler (Winterthur: Amadeus, 1991), 25. The view of the *Symphonies* as Russian summation is common. Compare Eric Walter White, in whose view Stravinsky's conception shows "a preoccupation with the instrumental development of the Russian popular material already used in many of his vocal compositions, particularly the numerous songs composed during his Swiss exile and *The Wedding,* and also in parts of *The Soldier's Tale.* The new composition can accordingly be looked on as a kind of symphonic summary of some of the musical ideas that had been fermenting in his mind during the previous six years" (*Stravinsky: The Composer and His Works* [Berkeley: University of California Press, 1966], 254–55).

2. Theodor W. Adorno, *Philosophy of Modern Music,* trans. Anne G. Mitchell and Wesley V. Blomster (New York: Seabury Press, 1973), 5.

3. See chapter 38 above.

4. Milton Babbitt, untitled memoir in *Perspectives of New Music* 9, no. 2–10, no. 1 (1971): 106; quoted by Messing, *Neoclassicism in Music,* 193 n 5. Babbitt claimed to be quoting Stravinsky, nor is there any reason to doubt that that is exactly how the octogenarian Stravinsky would have wished to represent his earlier self to an American academic serialist. Yet one has to wonder not only at the relevance but also at the authenticity of the words attributed to the old man when one reads, "to Stravinsky, 'back to Bach' was just . . . an alliteratively catchy slogan." It was that only in a language Stravinsky did not use at the time that the phrase was (thanks to him) "à l'ordre du jour."

5. Babbitt, untitled memoir, 106.

6. See chapters 36 and 40.

7. Adorno launches his *Philosophy,* for example, with the flat assertion that "the state of composition itself" is "at all times the decisive factor influencing the state of music" (xi).

8. See Charles Rosen, "The Proper Study of Music," *Perspectives of New Music* 1 (1962): 80–88 passim.

9. For what is still the most provocative study of anxiety-of-influence in music (and without benefit of Bloom), see Carolyn Abbate, "*Tristan* in the Composition of *Pelléas*," *19th-Century Music* 5 (1981): 117–41. It is eye-opening, considering the many salient echoes of Wagner's opera in the finished work, to learn how strenuously Debussy tried to suppress them. (And then, following the Bloomian paradigm, Debussy—yes, *Pelléas*—became a frightening father in turn: see Larry Stempel, "Not Even Varèse Can Be an Orphan," *Musical Quarterly* 60 [1974]: 46–60.) For a lurid idea of how engulfed in Wagner a less mature or vigilant French composer was likely to be even ten years later, see (or hear) Lili Boulanger's *Prix de Rome* cantata, *Faust et Hélène* (1913), which recommends itself because of the twenty-year-old composer's relative innocence and the imposed speed of contest composition, which precluded much critical reflection. The cantata is an inadvertently hilarious salad of *Tristan, Parsifal*, and the *Siegfried-Idyll*. See also Messing's ex. 1.1 (8–9) for an assortment of involuntary Tristanisms in fin-de-siècle French music, not to be confused with the veritable subgenre of Tristan spoofs that arose in anxious reaction, of which Chabrier's *Souvenir de Munich* (piano four-hands) and Debussy's "Golliwog's Cakewalk" are only the most familiar. (Hinton makes reference to a similar trend in Germany, culminating in Hindemith's *Das Nusch-Nuschi*.)

10. Messing cites a precedent for the interchangeability of *néoclassicisme* and the nonpejorative *nouveau classicisme* in a comment by Diaghilev from 1922: "But no, good heavens, one does not revive. . . . One evolves toward neoclassicism, as Picasso evolves toward Ingres. . . . My god, is it still necessary to explain such things?" (83).

11. Boris de Schloezer, "La musique," *La Revue contemporaine*, 1 February 1923 (Messing, 130).

12. Full details in my *Stravinsky and the Russian Traditions* (Berkeley: University of California Press, 1996), 1486–93.

13. For the famous passage (beginning, "For I consider that music is, by its very nature, essentially powerless to *express* anything at all," but proceeding to posit a "unique," specifically musical emotion that music does convey by its very nature), see Stravinsky, *An Autobiography* (New York: Norton, 1962), 53–54; the disavowal (as "an overpublicized bit," etc.) may be found in Igor Stravinsky and Robert Craft, *Expositions and Developments* (Berkeley: University of California Press, 1981), 101–3.

14. As a construction of national character, this cluster of terms is of course no more "real" than any other essentialism. The land of Racine and Couperin (and Cocteau and Satie) was also the land of Hugo and Berlioz; and Berlioz was a central arbiter (especially as mediated through Schumann, as well as through another non-German, Liszt) of the "German" essence—the discourse of "psychology, emotions, feelings, desires, aspirations"—in opposition to which the French now defined themselves.

15. See Igor Stravinsky and Robert Craft, *Dialogues and a Diary* (Garden City, N.Y.: Doubleday, 1963), 14.

16. Robert Craft, *Present Perspectives* (New York: Knopf, 1984), 220.

17. Igor Stravinsky and Robert Craft, *Conversations with Igor Stravinsky* (Garden City, N.Y.: Doubleday, 1959), 60.

18. Jean Schlumberger, "Considerations," *La Nouvelle Revue française* 1 (1909; rpt. Kraus, 1968), 9–11.

19. For a chronicle of Stravinsky's relations with the journal, see David Bancroft, "Stravinsky and the 'NRF' (1910–20)," *Music & Letters* 53 (1972): 274–88; and "Stravinsky and the 'NRF' (1920–29)," *Music & Letters* 55 (1974): 261–71.

20. Jacques Rivière, "Le Sacre du printemps," *La Nouvelle Revue française,* 1 November 1913 (rpt. in Rivière, *Nouvelles Études* [Paris: Gallimard, 1947], 73, 75–76); trans. adapted from Truman C. Bullard, *The First Performance of Igor Stravinsky's* Sacre du printemps (PhD diss., Eastman School of Music, 1971), 2:269–308.

21. *Feuilles libres* 27 (1922): 223–24. A further extract in translation from the original typescript is given in Stravinsky, *Selected Correspondence,* ed. Robert Craft (New York: Knopf, 1982), 1:158n.

22. Though hardly its "constructive principles," as he represented it one day to Craft (*Conversations,* 18)—for that is precisely the difference between "neoclassicism" and pastiche.

23. *Musical America,* 10 January 1925 (Messing, 141); these interviews were what provoked Schoenberg's *Drei Satiren,* op. 28. See Leonard Stein, "Schoenberg and 'Kleine Modernsky,'" in *Confronting Stravinsky,* ed. Jann Pasler (Berkeley: University of California Press, 1986), 310–24.

24. Some Russians found this hard to swallow: "Stravinsky has delivered himself of a horrifying piano sonata, which he himself performs not without a certain chic," Prokofieff wrote back home to his friend Myaskovsky. "He declares that he is creating a new epoch with this, and that this is the only way to write nowadays, but the music itself sounds like Bach with smallpox (don't get me wrong: I love old Sebastian, but I don't like faking him)" (*S. S. Prokof'yev i N. Ya. Myaskovskiy: Perepiska,* ed. M. G. Kozlova and N. R. Yatsenko [Moscow, 1977], 195, 211, 217–18 [excerpts from three letters conflated]).

25. Nadia Boulanger, "Concerts Koussevitsky," *Le Monde musical,* November 1923 (Messing, 133).

26. Letter of 14 August 1922 (Messing, 124); Stravinsky goes on to say that "this Hindemith is a sort of German Prokofieff, infinitely more sympathetic than *les autres sous-Schoenberg.*"

27. Actually, anti-Semitic sentiments had been built into French (neo)classicism as early as the founding of D'Indy's Schola Cantorum in 1894, the Dreyfus year (see Messing, 19 ff.).

28. Ian Kemp, *Hindemith* (London: Oxford University Press, 1970), 11 (Hinton, 167).

29. Coinage of the term *neue Sachlichkeit* is credited to Gustav Hartlaub, director of the Mannheim Museum; see Jost Hermand, "Unity within Diversity? The History of the Concept 'Neue Sachlichkeit,'" in *Culture and Society in the Weimar Republic,* ed. Keith Bullivant (Manchester: Manchester University Press, 1977), 166–67; also Peter Gay, *Weimar Culture: The Outsider as Insider* (New York: Harper and Row, 1968), 120–22.

30. See Paul Hindemith, *A Composer's World: Horizons and Limitations,* Charles Eliot Norton Lectures, 1949–50 (Cambridge, Mass.: Harvard University Press, 1952), viii.

31. Heinrich Besseler, "Grundfragen des musikalischen Hörens" (Hinton, 14; my italics).

32. It is reproduced in Robert P. Morgan, *Twentieth-Century Music* (New York: W. W. Norton, 1991), 222.

33. Aaron Copland, "Baden-Baden," *Modern Music* 5 (1927): 34 (rpt. in *Copland on Music* [New York: W. W. Norton, 1963], 188).

34. See *Dialogues and a Diary,* 51.

35. Igor Stravinsky and Robert Craft, *Memories and Commentaries* (Garden City, N.Y.: Doubleday, 1960), 86.

36. Theodor W. Adorno, "Zur gesellschaftlichen Lage der Musik" (1932) (Hinton, 72–73).

37. Arnold Schoenberg, "Linear Counterpoint" (1931), in *Style and Idea: Selected Writings of Arnold Schoenberg,* ed. Leonard Stein, trans. Leo Black (Berkeley: University of California Press, 1985), 294.

38. Arnold Schoenberg, "Glosses on the Theories of Others" (1929), in *Style and Idea,* 315.

39. See his letter to Ansermet, 9 September 1923, in which Hindemith is now written off as "a kind of H. Wolf" (*Selected Correspondence,* 1:171; also *Stravinsky in Pictures and Documents,* ed. Vera Stravinsky and Robert Craft [New York: Simon and Schuster, 1978], 250).

40. See Arthur Lourié, *Sergei Koussevitzky and His Epoch* (New York: Knopt, 1931), 196. Stravinsky's worshipful attitude toward the Italian dictator is documented by Robert Craft in "Stravinsky's Politics: Left, Right, Left," in *Stravinsky in Pictures and Documents,* 547–58. For additional information and quotations, see chapter 31 above.

41. Igor Stravinsky, *Poetics of Music in the Form of Six Lessons* (bilingual ed.), trans. Arthur Knodel and Ingolf Dahl (Cambridge, Mass.: Harvard University Press, 1970), 9, 21–23, 99.

42. Ibid., 105.

43. Alexandre Benois, "Vrubel,'" *Mir iskusstva* 10 (1903): 40.

44. *Dialogues and a Diary,* 8–9.

45. "Stravinsky's *Oedipus*" (24 February 1928), in Schoenberg, *Style and Idea,* 483.

46. An essential document of Viennese Back-to-Bachianism is Webern's detailed analysis of op. 28, written at the request of Erwin Stein, the Boosey & Hawkes editor (who, however, did not see fit to publish it in *Tempo*). The essay places equal emphasis on the Quartet's congruence with established tradition, both generally contrapuntal and specifically twelve-tone, and on its successful extensions of traditional technique in both domains. Webern's comments on the derivation of the row, in particular, display the combination of pride in structural density and triumph at its concealment from the uninitiated that has become so familiar in the literature of postwar serialism. The essay, in Zoltan Roman's translation, is given as appendix 2 of Hans Moldenhauer (in collaboration with Rosaleen Moldenhauer), *Anton Webern: A Chronicle of His Life and Work* (New York: Knopf, 1979), 751–56.

47. Schoenberg's remark to Josef Rufer on the significance of his "discovery" of twelve-tone technique is by now so famous that the word *supremacy* has surely brought it to every reader's mind: quotation is superfluous. The dogma of Germanic supremacy in the arts, and in music in particular, is very stimulatingly traced to its romantic roots in Sanna Pederson, "On the Task of the Music Historian: The Myth of the Symphony after Beethoven," *repercussions* 2, no. 1 (Fall 1993): 5–30.

48. "National Music" (1931), in Schoenberg, *Style and Idea,* 173.

49. Ibid., 170, 171.

50. The Moldenhauers presented Webern's Nazism as wartime hysteria (*Anton Webern: A Chronicle,* chap. 30 ["Webern and 'The Third Reich'"], 515–32). Louis Krasner's memoirs of Webern show him a convinced sympathizer as early as 1936: "Some Memories of Anton Webern, the Berg Concerto, and Vienna in the 1930s" (as told to Don C. Siebert), *Fanfare* 11 (1987): 335–47. On Schenker, see William Drabkin, "Felix-Eberhard von Cube and the North-German Tradition of Schenkerism," *Proceedings of the Royal Musical Association* 111 (1984–85): 180–207, esp. the letter of May 1933 (quoted on 189) that gives startling evidence of personal identification with Hitler. Common to these manifestations is the striking faculty of dissociation, the ability to ignore contradictions: Webern maintained good relations with Jews and even deplored Nazi anti-Semitism (though usually ascribing reports of it to anti-German propaganda); Schenker of course was himself a Jew. As Leonardo Sciascia observed (in "Open Doors") of the Italian population under Mussolini, they saw no need to confront the problem of judging fascism as a whole.

51. See Jeffrey Herf, *Reactionary Modernism: Technology, Culture and Politics in Weimar and the Third Reich* (Cambridge: Cambridge University Press, 1984), 30, 36.

52. Quotations from Krenek in this paragraph are from *Music Here and Now,* trans. Barthold Fles (New York: W. W. Norton, 1939), 75.

53. The slur in this case comes not from the right but from the left (Ernst Bloch, "On the Threepenny Opera," in *Erbschaft dieser Zeit* [1935], rpt. in *Marxism and Art,* ed. Maynard Solomon [Detroit: Wayne State University Press, 1979], 576), proving once again that German totalitarian ideologies, whether "left" or "right," were indistinguishably united in their contempt for liberalism.

54. Program note to the première production (28 May 1938), rpt. in the libretto booklet accompanying the Angel recording (SZCX-3869, 1979).

55. See chap. 1 ("The Philosophical Approach") in Hindemith's *A Composer's World,* 1–13.

56. Paul Hindemith, *Johann Sebastian Bach: Heritage and Obligation* (trans. of *J. S. Bach: Ein verpflichtendes Erbe*) (New Haven: Yale University Press, 1952), 40–41.

57. "Zur Deutung von Strawinskys Neoklassizismus," first given as a paper at a Stravinsky centennial conference in Milan and published in the Stravinsky issue of *Musik-Konzepte* 34–35 (1984): 80–88. The same line was followed by Alan Lessem in another centennial piece: "Schoenberg, Stravinsky, and Neo-Classicism: The Issues Reexamined," *Musical Quarterly* 68 (1982): 527–42.

58. For documentation of Stravinsky's efforts to keep himself *persona grata* in the "NS-Staat" even after the Düsseldorf Entartete Musik exhibition of 1938, see the letters to B. Schotts Söhne excerpted in Stravinsky, *Selected Correspondence,* vol. 3 (1985), 217–72. For more on Frommel in relation to Stravinsky, see Wolfgang Osthoff, "Symphonien beim Ende des Zweiten Weltkriegs: Strawinsky—Frommel—Schostakowitsch," *Acta Musicologica* 49 (1987): 62–104.

59. Stalinist neoclassicism can be dated precisely to the Pushkin centenary of 1937—which for Soviet music meant the zealous cultivation of Pushkin settings in a pastiche period style—for it was precisely during the peak of political terror that Soviet composers were first explicitly directed to emulate "russkaya klassika" as a timeless model and as a return to healthy, "normal" musical values after the excesses of early Soviet modernism (see Anna Shteynberg, "Pushkin v tvorchestve sovetskikh kompozitorov," *Sovetskaya muzïka* 1 [1937]: 53). From then until the war, much Soviet

music makes a jarringly tame, incongruously "bourgeois" impression in the context of political exhortation to participate in the turbulence and heroics of "Soviet reality" in the period of the five-year plans. But that is precisely the point. Behind all the activist rhetoric, the arts (and music above all) were under new pressure to provide not stimulus (or not just stimulus) but an anodyne.

60. Obituary, *New York Times,* 24 December 1991.

61. Hans Günter Klein, "Atonalität in den Opern von Paul von Klenau und Winfried Zillig—zur Duldung einer im Nationalsozialismus verfemten Kompositionstechnik," in *Internationaler musikwissenschaftlicher Kongress Bayreuth 1981* (Kassel: Bärenreiter, 1983), 490–94.

62. The term "megalomania of self-infinitization" is Daniel Bell's: see *The Cultural Contradictions of Capitalism* (New York: Basic Books, 1976), 49. For the Adorno concept, see his *The Jargon of Authenticity,* trans. Knut Tarnowski and Frederic Will (Evanston, Ill.: Northwestern University Press, 1973). Darmstadt rhetoric still has its unembarrassed public defenders. Glossing the young Boulez's most notorious apothegm ("Any musician who has not experienced—I do not say understood, but truly experienced—the necessity of dodecaphonic language is USELESS") after forty years, Jonathan Harvey, an English composer, has written: "In our age of tolerant pluralism this could sound like a statement of Erich Honecker. And yet, is it asking so much? To experience this necessity is the gateway to seeing a fresh (!) issue for mainstream European musical language" ("Experiencing Modern Music," *Times Literary Supplement,* 19 June 1992, 16). For a somewhat lurid account of the emergence of this neo-fascist *neuere Sachlichkeit* in postwar Europe, narrated from the perspective of an excluded member of the older generation of serialists, see John L. Stewart, *Ernst Krenek: The Man and His Music* (Berkeley: University of California Press, 1991), 266–71, 296–300.

63. Erik Levi, "Atonality, 12-Tone Music and the Third Reich," *Tempo* 178 (1991): 21. These remarks, made in connection with von Klenau's opera *Michael Kohlhaas* (premièred November 1933), were quoted the next May in the journal *Zeitschrift für Musik,* where the composer further justified dodecaphony as "consistent with Nazi insistence on technical competence" and held it up as an antidote to "individualistic arbitrariness." See Michael Meyer, *The Politics of Music in the Third Reich* (New York: Peter Lang, 1991), 312. For Schoenberg's pained comment, see "Is It Fair?" (1947), in *Style and Idea,* 249–50.

64. "Rencontre avec Stravinsky," *Preuves* 2 (1952): 37.

40

She Do the *Ring*
in Different Voices

Carolyn Abbate, *Unsung Voices: Opera and Musical Narrative in the Nineteenth Century* (Princeton: Princeton University Press, 1991; 288 pp.)

> *What happened today, a narrative.*
>   *We had intended if it were a pleasant day to go to the country it was a very beautiful day and we carried out our intention. We went to places that we had been when we were equally pleased and we found very nearly what we could find and returning saw and heard that after all they were rewarded and likewise. This makes it necessary to go again.*
>   GERTRUDE STEIN, *Four Saints in Three Acts*

The fifth chapter of Carolyn Abbate's *Unsung Voices* opens on a famous narrative, the old comedy of how the *Ring* got written: how Wagner, in an effort to purge his libretto for *Siegfrieds Tod* of its superfluous narratives, preceded it with *Der junge Siegfried;* how, to keep *Der junge Siegfried* from getting bogged down in narrative in its turn, he added *Die Walküre* and, finally, *Das Rheingold;* how, so far from achieving his ostensible purpose, he wound up with four narrative-heavy librettos in place of one (not even ridding the original libretto of its offenders); how he compounded the problem with redundancy and inconsistency—and yet still could boast not only that he had succeeded in his task, but that by these efforts he had made everything "plastic," transparent, involving, and compelling.

"How, then, can we explain the great paradox in the *Ring*'s history," Carolyn Abbate asks, "and what many consider to be the great flaw in its text: that the narratives, despite Wagner's glee over their elimination, were kept, and that in the *Ring*'s final form, these narratives give contradictory accounts of the events we have witnessed?" This question, the great crux of the book, gets asked on page 161. The whole volume—not only the hundred pages or so that follow the question but also the four chapters that precede it—is Abbate's attempt to answer it. Just as Wagner's last *Ring* libretto begat its three

Originally published in *Cambridge Opera Journal* 4 (1992): 187–97. Copyright Cambridge University Press, reprinted with permission.

predecessors, so we may imagine that the four long theoretical chapters that lead up to the big question in *Unsung Voices* sprouted from it and collectively address it, shoring up the author's intuition that there really is no paradox. From the perspective of chapter 5, what had at first appeared a loosely ordered miscellany of somewhat forbidding meditations is suddenly transformed into an intricately plotted and finally thrilling argument poised right on the boundary between critical theory and practical criticism. It is a marvelous epiphany, fully rewarding the faithful reader's labor.

An epiphany, by definition, resists parsing and paraphrasing, but a reviewer has to try. Abbate's basic intuition is that the narratives in the *Ring*'s final form, redundancies, contradictions, and all, are not static but phatic (that is, they monitor relationships among composer, characters, and listeners—both in the house and on the stage), not detached from the action, but a critical part of the work's "plastic" unfolding. They are, as Roland Barthes would put it, catalysts: multivoiced, authored not only by the composer but also by the characters who sing them. Hence they are—the bad news—unreliable as information (musically no less than textually, the well-known critical consensus to the contrary notwithstanding) and also—the good news—reflexive on the work they inhabit, enriching it with dimensions of meaning we as listeners read better than we may know. They achieve this status by playing on the distinction between "phenomenal" music (music heard by stage characters as music) and its opposite, which Abbate Kantishly christens "noumenal" music—the most fundamental of all discriminations to operatic literacy but rarely discussed.[1] This play is the essential, semiotically charged process or agency of musical narration, and remains so when transferred to the instrumental medium. It follows that a narrative is not simply a tale but a telling, requiring a teller (as well as a hearer). Who- or whatsoever is marked as a teller—be it animate or inanimate, be it actual or virtual (sung or "unsung"), be it singer, player, character, instrument, composer, or any of these in combination—is a "voice." And this *voice*, transcending text and action and plot, is the ultimate musical doer, the Lord High Illocutioner.

Each of these points gives rise to long, sometimes chapter-length discussion, theory arising out of a process of generalization. The way the argument is presented, it appears to focus on Wagner as optimal case study. The way it appears on reflection (whether or not the perception mirrors the actual process of its formulation), the case engendered the theory as—to cite a metaphor Abbate invokes somewhere—irritation produces a pearl. The book is thus in essence a work of musical phenomenology, a reception study, resolutely (and happily) centered on esthesis rather than poiesis, to put it à la Nattiez (who is given a big acknowledgment in the preface but rarely cited in the argument). That pits Abbate squarely against traditional students of Wagner, who want to know how the operas were made, thinking that that will tell them what they are and what they do. Abbate, coached not by Wagner but by Brünnhilde, has another way of getting at these primal matters. Her stance also places her athwart conventional musical narratologists, who want to see narrative as an essence (thus recouping formalism) rather than an act. (That she has long pitted herself against seekers—finders, that is—of anodyne unity over rich rupture can go here without saying; in any case she reminds us far too often.) Despite her noted air of sanguinity, Abbate seems a little anxious after all about her esthesic stance. She tries hard to ground her work—or give it an appearance of grounding—in empirical research and postulated intention. She adduces Wagner's sketches for Tannhäuser's Rome Narrative to support her argument, crucial to her notion of musical illocution, that it partakes of the rhetoric of balladry. She even states her thesis as regards the *Ring* in intentionalist terms: "Between the letter to Liszt on 20 November 1851 and the first extensive prose draft for *Walküre* in the spring of 1852, Wagner came to believe that narrative—far from being made expendable by the expansion of *Walküre* and *Rheingold*—was, after all, crucial to the kind of work that he had conceived" (161). But the only evidence of Wagner's belief is the work as Abbate construes it—no evidence of intention at all, then, except in that tautological sense that has rightly given intentionalism its bad name.

Abbate knows this better than I. She is having the problem all of us educated in the heyday of positivism are having with our Mendelian superegos. It gives rise to a persistent tension between what, borrowing from Abbate herself, I will call the "plot-Abbate," an American academic seeking disciplinary turf, and the "voice-Abbate," the possessor of the finest lyric gift among musical critics now writing. I hope she will resolve this tension, for it crimps her style. Plot-Abbate not only looks for redundant empirical grounding; she is also excessively given to positioning herself vis-à-vis other critics—often contentiously, for which she has garnered a measure of ill will (though her targets are nearly always the right ones), but occasionally, it seems, and contrariwise, out of an inflated, ultimately misleading sense of heritage or obligation.

Consider her many references to Edward T. Cone and his well-known book, *The Composer's Voice*. Abbate pays his antiquated arguments excessive attention, as if he had a copyright on the titular word they share. But the voice Cone attended to was the voice of central authority, located in the composer—the "virtual" composer, of course, meaning the one created by the critic as covert locus of his own authority. A rearguard action even in its day, it became openly reactionary in Cone's later article, "The Authority of Music Criticism," aimed at "deconstructionism," by which Cone meant precisely the sort of decentering of interpretive command for which Abbate's concept of "voice" is the instrument. Abbate is now the chief embodiment of everything

Cone wanted to ward off. Her tribute to his "presence in these pages" as a measure of "debt to his unique music-analytical vision" seems naive, even a trifle disingenuous. (Or maybe it's just the superego again. Paradigm shifts can be hard even on nonresisters. Not so long ago, it seems, I was trying to discover just what Musorgsky was trying to accomplish in revising *Boris Godunov*, and trying to determine, though I denied it, just what obligations my discoveries imposed on performers. Where Abbate invokes Cone I aspired even higher up the ladder to objective truth and invoked E. D. Hirsch . . .)

.   .   .

Abbate traces her concept of the "unsung"—the disembodied but still subjective and sensuous arbiter of musical meaning—to Barthes's celebrated "grain of the voice." This is demonstrably a Bloomer: she maintains that Barthes's grain is "something extra in music, . . . conceived as a body vibrating with musical sound—a speaking source—that is not the body of some actual performer." Barthes, meanwhile, had introduced the notion of the grain by describing a "movement from deep down in the cavities, the muscles, the membranes, the cartilages" of a physically present (if for the moment hypothetical) singer—a Russian bass, as it happens—resulting in an impression not of the performer's personality but of "the materiality of the body," standing for everything in an art experience that is not paraphrasable.[2] Abbate thus derives from Barthes the way she derives from Cone: opportunistically, backhandedly, as often as not by inversion. She is a strong critic.

For me there are stronger, more pertinent resonances in Abbate's titular phrase (besides "unsung hero," to be sure, which in this formalist age could well have been its motivation). One is explicitly phenomenological: Roman Ingarden's concept of the nonsounding, covering everything from expression to form to rhythmic or harmonic structure—everything that, while indisputably a part of the experience of the music as music rather than noise, nevertheless is not given in the sounds but has to be constructed by a competent listener.[3] Just so, Abbate's novel formulation names something that informs everyone's musical experience to the point where (I will declare) it has to be regarded as a measure or a test of listening competence. Unless you hear Abbate's unsung voices (I will assert), you aren't hearing music.

But not to worry: you hear them, all right—unless you went to graduate school and learned laboriously to deafen yourself. They live in the disjunctures, the mismatches and misalignments, the "structural dissonances" that we all learn to resolve and routinely discount but that scholars in other humanistic disciplines, unlearning their learning, have recently learned to prize as "hermeneutic windows." "The narrating voice," Abbate writes early on, "is marked by multiple disjunctions with the music surrounding it."

These are signaled by means of "fugitive" signs that can be understood only in their protean contexts. Musical narration, then, is not "an omnipresent phenomenon" (as most narratologists would have it), for then it would be a superfluous concept, "a mere machine for naming any and all music"; in any case, we can describe music as event-sequence perfectly well without invoking it. Instead, it is "a rare and peculiar act, a unique moment . . . within a surrounding music." That is her principal thesis. She will celebrate, throughout, not the general (the "omnipresent") but the particular (the "peculiar," even the unique). That is criticism. *Unsung Voices* is a primer—a vastly needed primer—in heeding musical disjunctions and, resisting our well-schooled urge to finesse them, learning instead to find delight in them and wring meaning from them. Only thus can we hope to accomplish what to a critic should always be the primary objective: to catch at that which cannot be paraphrased.

Problems necessarily begin with vocabulary, which in musicology and music theory has been worked out only for grouping, paraphrase, and reduction (in terms of "genre" or "structure," as topic, mode, sonataform, schenkergraph, pitchclassset, *e tutti quanti*). The only possible recourse is to wholesale coinage (starting with the titular category itself) and plunder (from classical rhetoric, speech-act theory, structuralism, deconstruction). The reader must adapt to a novel and playfully recondite vocabulary (replete with a host of "ordinary" verbs and adjectives unseen since the last Stravinsky-Craft book), and this can inspire resistance. But though occasionally word-drunk, Abbate is rarely inconsiderate of her reader. Nowhere, for example, does she affect the neo-Gallicisms that notoriously stud the discourse of comparative literature, even though at least one of them—Kristeva's *signifi- ance* (the activity of the floating signifier, producing an endless flux of signification)—might have saved her many words in her second chapter ("What the Sorcerer Said," independently famous since its publication several years ago in *19th-Century Music*), where she engages head-on with the problem of fluctuant meaning, one of many hermeneutic terrains where she had been the first musicologist to establish a beachhead. If in the same chapter she trades heavily in structuralist language (primarily via Barthes and his five codes, of which she singles out the "proairetic"—the forwardly progressing—for detailed examination), it is done scrupulously, lucidly, and skeptically—in fact subversively, for Barthes gets quite over his head into musical terms.[4] She interrogates the codes in quest of some means of identifying a tense structure for music, for even the sketchiest verbal narrative is apt to make free with tenses, leaping forward (prolepsis, they call it) and back (analepsis) in a way that one does not immediately think available (except trivially, quotationally) to music. (Have another look at the little paradigm by Gertrude Stein, *structuraliste avant la lettre*, at the top of this chapter.) Not only the structuralist model, but musical narrativity itself is called into question. Ultimately the model is scuttled. A useless ostentation, then? But no: Abbate just wants to clear the field of all the blustering scholasticisms with which literary theorists bombard us poor musicians. She wants to make an end run around pedantic narratology and begin with music—but with music in all its possible richness, not just "the music itself."

.   .   .

Abbate introduces and starts developing her own themes with a specimen of calculated subcanonicity, the Bell Song from Delibes's *Lakmé* ("associated," she reminds us drily, "with such art-deco divas as Lily Pons"—and I can indeed recall Mlle Pons warbling it on the *Ed Sullivan Show*). It is an inspired choice. It tawdrily exemplifies all the "distinctions critical to any interpretation of musical narration: plot and narrating, story and teller, utterance and enunciation," as Abbate first lists them, later adding two more: (strophic) form versus (developing) content and the phenomenal versus the yet-to-be-named noumenal. At the same time it shows how the performing voice (as a "grain") may accomplish—here by a spotlight of cadenzas *sans mesure* and all the rest of the coloratura folderol – something within the action quite at variance with the manifest content of the text, or indeed with the overt plot situation. (Lakmé's singing, ostensibly an entertainment for a holiday crowd, attracts the attention of her forbidden English lover, who does not even understand the words of her narrative, and exposes him to assault by her father.) Plot and voice are thus obviously (and in every sense of the last word) dichotomized. The deceptive triviality of the example seduces: the apparent lowness of the stakes makes acceptance of the author's premises easy. Nobody expects unity or consistency or credibility from Delibes.

And then, in a stunning *coup de théâtre*, this silly tinsel-dissection is redeemed at the other end of the book in a literally blazing peroration, Abbate now subjecting Brünnhilde's stupendous immolation monologue to a virtually duplicate deconstruction that not only lessens our incomprehension of that ultimate aria (an incomprehension Wagner is said to have shared with us), but transfigures the whole last act of *Götterdämmerung*—and thence the *Ring* tetralogy *tout* (ahem) *court*. Voice is played against plot in order to transcend the contradiction—the "hermeneutic crux," as Abbate would have it—between the two images of the Valkyrie, each with its own tradition in legend, that jostle one another in the libretto, at once enriching and confusing it. The one that appears to dominate, so far as plot is concerned, is the pathetic "romantic victim," deceived by Siegfried and now bereft of him. Only in Gutrune's musically insignificant monologue is Brünnhilde described in terms of the other tradition, the one that casts her as a "tragic heroine" who laughs at the news of Siegfried's death "truly and without regret (a queen has avenged a slight to her integrity and her will)." What must be understood as bringing the transformation about is Brünnhilde's nocturnal colloquy with the Rhinemaidens, to which Gutrune also briefly alludes. They sing to Brünnhilde alone, out of our earshot, the one and only all-knowing and all-encompassing narrative of the *Ring* (which for that very reason even Wagner—after all a mortal—could not author), on hearing which the grieving warrior-widow is transformed into the vatic, unsentimental medium who "sets a keystone in the eschatological arch." She reenters our field of audition singing in a new voice—becoming, in Abbate's language, a new "voice-object"—or rather, recapturing the voice through which we first came to know her, the voice of the "eldritch laughter (yes, 'hoijotoho') that ushers her in as both character and voice-object in the first moments of *Walküre* Act II."

This new Brünnhilde, the "voice-Brünnhilde," now wields her instrument like Lakmé (if the bathos can be condoned), transcending text and plot—which still appear to belong to "plot-Brünnhilde"—through her vocalizations and their projections in the orchestra. These include, famously, the one and only recapitulation of Sieglinde's leitmotif (which Wagner—in one of those interesting but ultimately superfluous statements of intention Abbate likes to produce prestidigitator-style to divert attention from where the true trick is done—called "die Verherrlichung Brünnhildens") and of course also her exit line—yes, "hoijotoho"! Thus "Brünnhilde finally rejoins her initial identity as laughter," and Abbate takes leave of her—and of us—with a vision of the clairvoyant Valkyrie as one who "laughs—eternally."

I don't expect that many readers will be satisfied with this insurrectionary reading of Brünnhilde's immolation aria merely on the strength of a précis. The chapter in which it is developed is forty-three pages long (not counting four closely printed pages of endnotes), and Abbate paces her narrative expertly, until by the end the reader is caught up in a compelling musical swirl. That (not the righteousness of the cause, not the torrid rhetoric) is what persuades. Abbate is in the very select company of critics who can truly summon music to their side. Persuasion—transfer of intuition—is all that a critic can seek to achieve by such methods. As Abbate puts it, following René Leibowitz, "verbally couched interpretations of music are performances and can only be more or less convincing." But persuasion—a good performance (not certitude, certainly not "reliability")—is all a good reader will ask for. "I prefer to accept . . . uncertainties as a source of pleasure," Abbate avers, "rather than fear them as inimical to interpretive control." Kinky, some readers will be heard to mutter, but at their frequent best Abbate's performances are more than pleasurable. They are transfixing.

She has not found many good public readers yet. The worst of them, Michael Tanner in the *TLS*,[5] misreads Abbate's most fertile point—that when any narrative is shown to be false or partial, "the reliability of *all* narrating (even that we assume to speak the truth) is impugned"—as if the last word were "denied," then adds, contemptuously: "Only if one is keen that it should be." To this, and to the closed-minded generally, one may (and must) make two rejoinders. First, why is one keen that it not be? (or, What does one protect?); but, second and more substantial, Should one not be keen to see a new idea ring true? (for only then is something gained). What else can it mean to be a keen reader?

Which is not to say that Abbate does not leave herself open to snipers, prone as she is to quiet yet pervasive hyperbole, mainly in the form of gratuitous alls, onlies, and nevers. Had Abbate only omitted the "only" from her description of Brünnhilde's critical insight (after Wotan's self-justifying monologue in *Walküre* act 2) that "no narrative *represents* or stands for past events, that all narratives refer only to themselves as artifice," Tanner would not have been able to deliver his *coup de massue* ("So Brünnhilde was in on poststructuralist clichés from the start").

Far better had Abbate kept to, and developed, her more general introductory account of narrative as being fundamentally not a mimetic but a diegetical (distance-inducing) mode, creating what she calls "discursive disjunction," of which stories, putatively a priori, are the products. Here, to fine effect, she follows film theorists (Kaja Silverman is the one she names), who "draw attention to narrative force as residing not in some realistic depiction of the phenomenal world . . . but rather in inserts, cuts, montages, camera angles, manipulation of soundtrack—all the things that underline arbitrary juxtaposition, that create a distance between the unscrolling film and the events that it depicts." It takes only a moment's reflection to realize that each of the filmic devices Abbate names has counterparts (though she does not venture to catalog them) in standard operatic procedure, narrative being quite obviously allied with insert and flashback, diegetical modes every filmgoer has learned to accommodate without the slightest difficulty.

.   .   .

Yet Abbate's Brünnhilde is poststructuralist for all that, inevitably so. Abbate presents her sybilline heroine as the ultimate listener → reader → critic, the ultimate skeptic—all right, the ultimate deconstructor. She presents her, in fine (like all fine critics), as an alter ego. For her, "the opposition of Gutrune and Brünnhilde" is the opposition of Tanner and Abbate: "the former believes the narratives offered for her consumption; the latter has learned skepticism." But Brünnhilde did not learn her skepticism from Abbate, as Tanner alleges. In fact, as I have already suggested, Abbate learned a properly musical skepticism from Brünnhilde.

She accomplished this by listening, in chapter 5, to Wotan's monologue through Brünnhilde's ears. Listening as a stage character, a technique developed in chapters 3 and 4, the book's theoretical core, she finds that—*Lakmé revient!*—the monologue is "phenomenal" music, discursively disjunct by virtue of its atavistically strophic structure. Wotan, too, exists here not only as character but as voice-object as well. These insights come by way of the most straighforwardly narrated essay in the book (chapter 3), a little potted history of narrative in romantic opera (Mozart→ Marschner → Meyerbeer → *Dutchman*→ *Tannhäuser*), wherein it is shown that the genre is genetically tied to the ballad, a simple, hence capitally phenomenal, strophic song. (The simplicity of the structure and the reflexivity of the genre trace opposite trajectories through Abbate's narrative: dramaturgical complexity and musical complexity grow symbiotically.) When pointed out, the vestigially strophic character of Wotan's monologue is convincingly salient, albeit overgrown with such a thicket of leitmotives and occluded by such a compelling (concurrent) dynamic unfolding from bare recitative through lyric outpouring, that even such knowing Wagnerians as Mann and Dahlhaus could not make it out (nor would they have thought to try, lacking the Abbatian yardstick to take its measure).

To this another sort of smug reader might retort, 'That is the trouble with any criticism which discovers something in a well-known work that no one seems to have noticed before: it is not likely to be important, or to have anything to do with why the work is considered a masterpiece."[6] The trouble with such thinking is that it still takes for granted that what a critic (or a listener) does is to discover meaning, rather than produce it. New meaning is created when old works are asked new questions, questions that arise out of new intellectual climates and concerns. In Abbate's case, as she makes plain in her preface, these contexts are currently "fraught debates on the nature of interpretation," on epistemology. That is the declared poststructuralist standpoint from which she interrogates her objects, and that is why—to her, and through her to us—they offer valuable (not to say "important") commentary on these issues. Thus, at the exact point where, as I read her, Abbate's self-identification with vatic Brünnhilde is most intense, she writes:

> The *Ring* is full of magic tricks—disguising helmets, mysterious liquids, the ring itself—that, as props, are tiny reinscriptions of its larger narrative sleights of hand. Indeed, one central plot-motif in *Götterdämmerung*—Hagen's potion of forgetfulness—overtly projects the *Ring*'s underlying doubts of narration into a stage-object, making a traditional device of sorcery into a sign for epistemological irresolution.

It will not do to complain that the *Ring*, being neither sentient nor sensible, cannot have doubts, cannot perform a sleight of hand (Abbate openly advertises and refuses to apologize for her "prosopopoetical" bent). Nor does it pay to ask whether Wagner could have intended these meanings. He could not have intended them, it goes without saying, any more than he could have foreseen Abbate's interests. But meaning arises—is created—out of a relationship that is forged between subject and object; it is neither "subjective" nor "objective" to the exclusion of the other. Meanings unforeseen by the author (or by anybody else, in the author's day, in our day, or at any time to come) are thus latent in any text, Judge Bork and Professor Rosen notwithstanding. (Rosen's other point, about masterpiece status, is of course pure tautology.)

.   .   .

At last to the core, chapters 3 ("Cherubino Uncovered") and 4 ("Mahler's Deafness"), where Abbate elaborates and finally transcends her phenomenal/noumenal opposition. It is at once the most novel matter she treats and the most old-hat. And the treatment it receives is at once the most original matter in the book and (perhaps in consequence) the most uneven, elegant argumentation jostling against curiously obtuse premises throughout, superb speculation vying with strained. "In opera," chapter 4 begins, "the characters pacing the stage often suffer from deafness; they do not *hear* the music that is the ambient fluid of their music-drowned world." But surely deafness is the inability to hear something one is meant to hear, and these ambient sounds (qua sounds) are meant not for them but for us; thus the many pages Abbate devotes to exploring deafness-anxiety as a source of operatic fascination (though it leads her very smoothly into her excellent Mahler discussion) ring quite false in my ear. She retreats a little: "We must generally assume, in short, that this music is not produced by or within the stage-world, but emanates from other loci as secret commentaries for our ears alone, and that characters are generally unaware that they are singing." But the retreat is unavailing: unawareness, like deafness, implies a defect, and we do not generally assume that operatic characters are defective.

If we are operatically literate we do not wonder whether the characters are "aware" of the music they inhabit. That question will normally come to consciousness only when the convention is flouted, as it occasionally is, facetiously. (Woody Allen, in *Bananas,* opens a closet and finds the harpist whose arpeggios had been accompanying his rapturous thoughts; Stan Freberg, doing Christopher Columbus on a record, sights land: TA-DAA! First Mate: What was that? Columbus: French Horns.) Only the operatically illiterate, moreover, wonder about those "loci," or seriously imagine that they are not "within the stage-world." (Alfred Hitchcock to David Raksin on why there will be no sound track music in *Lifeboat,* a film—a twentieth-century opera—that takes place on the open sea: "Where is the orchestra?" Raksin to Hitchcock: "Where are the cameras?") But the fact that we do not normally wonder about these things only proves Abbate right after all: that is the definition of an assumption—"one," she writes, "that, I would claim, constitutes a basic perceptual code in hearing and viewing opera." *You* would claim? You and everyone else from Count Bardi on down. (But is the ambient music really a "commentary"?)

A thrice-familiar defamiliarizing game, this insistence on "problematizing" assumptions, doggedly bringing unconscious theory into consciousness as a foil to examine the breaches and strains to which conventional operatic etiquette is subjected at the hands of self-conscious composers. Abbate wants to test the borders (and manages to educe a serious, indeed breathtaking counterpart to Allen's and Freberg's tomfoolery in *Tannhäuser;* it forms the capstone to chapter 3), ultimately to see how the phenomenal/noumenal opposition, which she regards as the basic diegetical ploy underlying all musical narration, may be applied to instrumental music. She focuses, very aptly, on the so-called *Todtenfeier,* the tone poem that found its final home as the first movement in the Second Symphony by Gustav Mahler—for Abbate, the most operatic of symphonic composers (for all that he insisted on an irrevocable "parting of the ways" between vocal and instrumental media), because his symphonies "foreground three oscillations" that have their origin in theatrical music (all of them amply prefigured as far back as the *Lakmé* discussion): "that between narrating and enacting, between heard and unheard, and between an intruder and an imperiled terrain."

Such intruders, Abbate demonstrates in chapter 3, announce themselves in romantic opera by means of phenomenal music, marked off dramatically— and, often, reflexively—from the noumenal. In just this way, the E-major theme in the *Todtenfeier* (which Mahler, sketching, actually marked off as a "Gesang") intrudes, and announces itself as a "site of narration," however we may wish to emplot the piece (whether speculatively or through meticulous research such as Stephen Hefling has carried out).[7] The point is, we do so wish if we are musically literate, and we do not have to know the "real" story (a luridly "operatic" farrago by Mickiewicz, as it happens) to know that a story is being told. What creates the narrative necessity is a sense of "fissure," as Abbate names it, "an unmediated juxtaposition of two unrelated musics."[8] With the (self-)dramatizing Mahler, these fissures become "sites of hyperbolic musical disjunction. . . . With the 'Gesang' there is not merely a musical *contrast,* but a registral shift to musical discourse that signals a *singer* and a *song.*" This is a keen insight; and, as often happens, there is a concomitant blindness. Abbate has eyes (that is, ears) for only one member of her narrative-defining pair.

Mahler's musics are disjoint not only by virtue of their keys, their tempi, and (above all) their orchestral voicing, but because the one, being manifestly phenomenal, marks the other as noumenal—the ambient fluid of *our* (temporarily) music-drowned world. We can and do experience music in "real life" the way stage characters experience it, though obviously we are not deaf to it. And so, pace Abbate, neither are they. Her own penetrating remarks on Mahler undo her pet point about what operatic characters hear.

My point about noumenal music, if I will make bold to assert one, is that stage characters do not merely hear it; they live it. That is precisely what makes the music "ambient"; its locus is not "without" but in a supremely literal sense within. (We laugh at Freberg's Columbus not because he hears the

French horns, but because he "merely hears" them.) Just so, listening to Mahler sympathetically, do we live for the moment through him. But there is nothing new in this; it is not "my" point. It is merely another way of stating a familiar intuition that Sessions put memorably well in *Questions about Music:*

> What music conveys to us—and let it be emphasized, this is the *nature of the medium* itself, not the consciously formulated purpose of the composer [though of course it may be so formulated and dramatized, e.g., by Mahler]—is the nature of our existence, as embodied in the movement that constitutes our innermost life: those inner gestures that lie behind not only our emotions, but our every impulse and action, which are in turn set in motion by these, and which in turn determine the ultimate character of life itself.[9]

Where Abbate might like to see the "noumenal" music of opera as the primary locus of this effect, and its adaptation to the symphony as secondary, I would put it just the other way around. It is inherent in the musical experience, as a sizable literature not just in esthetics, but in psychology and anthropology, now attests. When put onstage it becomes a metaphor for what the characters are experiencing, whence opera-conscious symphonists like Mahler can reappropriate the whole operatic complex to dramatize and intensify the emotional experience of concertgoers.

But Abbate's more immediate business is very much to the point. Most conventional music analysis, and even some varieties of "narratology," are determined to heal fissures of every kind, or else conceal them. Abbate, better than any other writer I've read, shows what is at stake in this denial. At the very least, it diminishes: its normalizing tactics "emphasise how self-questioning, richer music (like Mahler's, like all opera) resembles music more ordinary." By focusing so cogently on what a "richer" composer can accomplish through his orchestration, for example, she exposes the pusillanimous, peremptory limits conventional analysts set on musical discourse. (Compare a typical little dictum of Forte's: "One can deal with pitch and disregard orchestration, but the reverse is not, in general, possible.")[10] She points out that discussion of *Todtenfeier*'s form rarely gets beyond the observation—the "factual" observation, she notes, grinning—that the work is "in sonata form," even though that means resolutely ignoring when not deploring its many deviations from that template, the most salient being the redundant returns of the opening group. That, of course, begins to suggest a strophic unfolding (and we know by now what *that* means . . .).

She is hardly less severe with plot-mongers, for all her hermeneutic openness and her noble refusal to regard plots and symbols as "extramusical"—for plot-mongers, too, are limiters. Attempts at "emplotting" works of music inevitably founder, Abbate says, on their "combination of specificity and arbitrariness"—and triviality, I'll add (on the strength of Abbate's fine demonstration in chapter 2), each increasing in direct proportion to the others.

Plot-mongers, too, are analogy-addicts, who constantly forget that analogy is not identity, that analogy entails difference as well as similarity, and that difference (within a context defined by similarity) is ultimately the worthier object of exploration. Abbate is blunt enough, but wishful: "The failure of an analogy may nonetheless serve a purpose, to nudge music critics toward less impressionistic and more skeptical stances regarding the notions that they borrow from literature." Would that they saw the failure! But there is an even larger point at stake, one that might be termed the poietic fallacy: the assumption, already encountered (and countered?), that the meaning of an artwork is wholly an invested meaning, defined and delimited by the process of its manufacture, there to be discovered.

Ultimately Abbate views all of these moves as attempts to quell the "numinous intruder," to whom she had introduced us (through a parade of operatic characters) in chapter 3, the one who

> comes in many guises—as despicable outsider, as revolutionary, as ironic voice, as a carrier from the site of an "unheard" sound. Narrating voices within music, like these strangers who haunt the Romantic tradition, create their own dissonant moments, interrupting the spaces surrounding them.

More than any other writer, as I say, Abbate shows why our postromantic critical and analytical tradition has erected such a fence around "the music itself" to keep that numinous intruder known as "the extramusical" at bay— and why the fence must fall. What we need is less refuge in the antiseptic safety of wholeness and more bold fission expeditions, thus to recapture empathy: "that 'second hearing,'" Abbate calls it, "which reanimates . . . a sense for what is uncanny in music." Nowadays, with music and hearing both so thoroughly canned, there could hardly be a more important project. The aplomb with which the author of *Unsung Voices* has realized her vision of empathic hearing certainly marks her as a virtuoso, in mature command of her idiosyncratic methods, capable of expert musical deconstructions that nowhere succumb to the childish relish in infinite regress that marks the "deconstructionist," and capable of a genuinely feminist hermeneutic that nowhere invokes the shallow reductive categories that serve the already routinized discourse of "feminism."

But virtuosity even her antagonists concede her. For fostering what seems to me the finest symbiosis between theoretical speculation and particular insight yet accomplished on behalf of music, Carolyn Abbate deserves a higher praise. She is more than a virtuoso. She is a heroine.

NOTES

1. And when it is—for example, by Edward T. Cone in "The World of Opera and Its Inhabitants" (reprinted in *Music: A View from Delft* [Chicago: University of Chicago

Press, 1989], 125–37)—the argument is often reduced to an inventory of themes and their provenance that, in its literalism, does justice neither to the richness of the musical discourse nor to the critic's own percipience.

2. Roland Barthes, *Image-Music-Text,* trans. Stephen Heath (New York: Hill and Wang, 1977), 181–82. Later he will index Charles Panzéra's glottis, teeth, mucus membranes, and nose. His whole essay, in fact, could be read as an improbable gloss *au sérieux* on the old radio announcer's blooper, "You've been listening to the mucus of Clyde Lucas."

3. See Roman Ingarden, *The Work of Music and the Problem of Its Identity,* trans. Adam Czerniawski, ed. Jean G. Harrell (Berkeley: University of California Press, 1986), chapter 5: "The Sounding and Nonsounding Elements and Moments of a Musical Work."

4. No one, in fact, is more skeptical than Abbate of facile or uncritical applications of fashionable literary theory to musical texts (perhaps rifest right now among those who are detecting "anxiety of influence" and "revisionary ratios" behind every pitch-class set). She knows how much certain types of literary theory owe to yesteryear's musicography: importing it back, she warns (and shows), results in little more than chic tautology. A special, finely pitched scorn is reserved for presumptuous musical descanting by unqualified literary lions, whatever their mane-spread. Paul de Man's co-opting of music to his deconstructionist program via commentary on Rousseau, for example, is written off as "entrenched and historically limited platitudes" derived from "twentieth-century education in music appreciation." The irony is that, having earned her right to these judgments by mastering discourses other musicologists fear and deride from afar, Abbate is often perceived as one of those who are importing alien and suspect methodology into musicology, subverting it from its truly musical vocation and colonizing it for aggressive neighboring disciplines. Her mastery, enviable and evidently intimidating, is comfortingly confounded with complicity.

5. "The Critic as Virtuoso," *Times Literary Supplement,* 1 November 1991, 19.

6. Charles Rosen, "Radical, Conventional Mozart," *New York Review of Books,* 19 December 1991, 56.

7. See "Mahler's *Todtenfeier* and the Problem of Program Music," *19th-Century Music* 12 (1988–89): 27–53.

8. Here she is close to paraphrasing an insight associated with Anthony Newcomb, that "we, as listeners, create patterns of events in time that will make sense of musical discontinuities; any tear in the musical fabric creates a space into which the constructed story must rush, heading off the vertigo of threatened meaninglessness" (abstracted in Andrew Dell'Antonio, Richard Hill, and Mitchell Morris, "Classic and Romantic Instrumental Music and Narrative" [Report of a colloquium at Stanford University and the University of California, Berkeley, 27–28 May 1988], *Current Musicology* 48 [1991]: 44). The difference, of course, is that Abbate is not nearly so insistent as Newcomb on recuperating the disjunction; in fact, she functions best under threat of vertigo.

9. Roger Sessions, *Question about Music* (New York: W. W. Norton, 1971), 45.

10. Allen Forte, *The Structure of Atonal Music* (New Haven: Yale University Press, 1973), ix.

41

Stravinsky and Us

When, at the dawn of the third millennium, we use the word *Stravinsky,* we no longer merely name a person. We mean a collection of ideas: ideas embodied in, or rather construed out of, a certain body of highly valued musical and literary texts that acquired enormous authority in twentieth-century musical culture. That authority and its consequences are what have been preoccupying my thoughts about Stravinsky since completing *Stravinsky and the Russian Traditions,* which, though published in 1996, was not as recent a study as it seemed. It had spent almost seven years in press, during which time my thinking about "Stravinsky" as a bundle of notions underwent a lot of change.

In keeping with the scholarly tradition in which I was trained, my book was almost wholly concerned with the production of those texts and with determining their place within the historical context contemporaneous with them. My thinking since has been more concerned with the relationship between those texts, and the ideas construed from them, and the contexts in which they have existed since the time of their production, up to their present contexts, including this one. Just as in *Stravinsky and the Russian Traditions* I considered the reciprocal manner in which Stravinsky received influences from his surroundings and influenced those surroundings in turn, so I continue to be interested in that reciprocity of influence in the period since his death.

As I hope to demonstrate, Stravinskian ideas have been so influential that one could almost say that twentieth-century European and Euro-American musical culture has been created in the image of Stravinsky. But at the same time, as Stravinsky reminded us again and again, an influence is (or can be)

Originally delivered as the BBC Inaugural Proms Lecture at the Royal College of Music, London, in August 1996 and published in Jonathan Cross, ed., *The Cambridge Companion to Stravinsky* (Cambridge: Cambridge University Press, 2003), 260–84, 315–16. Reprinted with permission.

something we choose to submit to. And we can be very choosy indeed about what we value and make our own in what is offered to us. So one could say with equal justice that we have created Stravinsky in our image. This reciprocity is what I have taken for my theme: the mutually defining relationship, Stravinsky and Us.

The meanings and values arising out of that relationship fundamentally structured our beliefs and our behavior as twentieth-century musicians, music lovers, and human beings. Some of them, I believe, are overdue for re-examination now that we have become inhabitants of the twenty-first century.

.   .   .

In 1966, which turned out to be the last year of Igor Stravinsky's active creative life, his musical and literary assistant, Robert Craft, summed up the composer's position in the history of twentieth-century music by observing that "he is one of the representative spokesmen of 1966 as he was of '06, '16, '26 and so on."[1] Indeed he was far more than that. By 1966 he did not merely represent the history of twentieth-century music; he practically constituted it. The story of his career had been generalized into the story of twentieth-century music. But in the process of that generalization it had been turned into a myth—or rather, into a congeries of myths, some of them of Stravinsky's own devising, others myths to which he had willingly submitted, still others myths to which his work had been assimilated without his direct participation.

The first work of Stravinsky's to achieve mythical status was of course *The Rite of Spring*, the ballet first performed under the title *Le Sacre du printemps*. Stravinsky conceived the work (as "The Great Sacrifice") in 1910; began composing it in 1911; endured the riotous fiasco of the May 1913 première; experienced through it, shortly before his thirty-second birthday the next year, the triumph of his career ("such as *composers* rarely enjoy," as he bragged in old age);[2] and spent the rest of his long life telling lies about it.

In 1920 he told a reporter that the ballet had been originally conceived as a piece of pure, plotless instrumental music ("une oeuvre architectonique et non anecdotique").[3] In 1931 he told his first authorized biographer that the opening bassoon melody was the only quoted folk song in the score.[4] In 1960 he asserted through Craft that the work was wholly without tradition, the product of intuition alone. "I heard and I wrote what I heard," he declared. "I am the vessel through which *Le Sacre* passed."[5] These allegations and famous words have long since passed into the enduring folklore of twentieth-century music.

Now we know that the ballet's scenario is a highly detailed and (but for the culminating human sacrifice) an ethnographically accurate pair of "Scenes of Pagan Russia," as the ballet's oft-suppressed subtitle proclaims. It was planned in painstaking detail, by the composer in collaboration with the painter and archaeologist Nicholas Roerich, before a note was written. The score contains nine identifiable folk songs, all of them selected with the same eye toward ethnographic authenticity as governed the assembling of the scenario. And finally, in its technique of composition the music magnificently embodied and extended a specific immediate and local tradition—a repertory of harmonic devices based on an "artificial" scale of alternating whole steps and half steps, which Stravinsky's teacher Rimsky-Korsakov had educed from the music of Liszt and passed along to all his pupils.[6]

So the myth of *The Rite of Spring* incorporated at least two big truths at variance with the ascertainable facts: first, that the music was "pure," abstract, unbeholden to any specific time and place for its inspiration; and second, that it represented a violent stylistic rupture with the past, when all the while it was conceived as an exuberantly maximalistic celebration of two pasts—the remote past of its subject and the more recent past of its style.

And yet myths are not merely lies. They are explanatory fictions, higher truths—enabling or empowering narratives that take us *a realibus ad realiora,* "from the real to the more real," to quote Vyacheslav Ivanov, the symbolist poet who was counting on the artists of the early twentieth century, and the musicians above all, to usher in a new mythological age.[7] Stravinsky tacitly acknowledged Ivanov's idea when, in conversation with Robert Craft, he tried to improve on his famous fighting words of the 1930s—you know, that music "is incapable of *expressing* anything at all"—by remarking that "music is suprapersonal and super-real and as such beyond verbal meanings and verbal descriptions" and that instead of depicting ordinary reality, "a new piece of music *is* a new reality."[8] This mythographic or mythopoetic sense of music is one of the essential Stravinskian truths.

In the first instance the myth or "new reality" of *The Rite of Spring* empowered Stravinsky. Having first made his name, courtesy of Sergey Diaghilev and the Ballets Russes, as the protagonist and beneficiary of the greatest craze for Russian music ever to possess the West (as a result of which it was widely if briefly acknowledged that Russia had inherited the musical leadership of Europe), but having renounced Russia in the wake of the 1917 revolution and the ensuing Bolshevik coup d'état, Stravinsky wished frantically not only to attach himself to the Western—or "panromanogermanic"—musical mainstream, as nationalistic émigrés like him understood it,[9] but to maintain his status as its leader. He rejected the parochial lore of his birthright and embraced an aggressively cosmopolitan ideology of absolute music—music without a passport, without a past, without "extramusical" content of any kind.

At the same time this myth of *The Rite* was a powerful enabler for others as well. Detached from their national background and their motivating subject matter, the neoprimitivist musical innovations in *The Rite*—its fragmentedness, its staticness, its radical structural simplifications—provided its legions of imitators with a quick, very necessary bath in the river Lethe at a time when the European tradition seemed over. That is why there *were* so many imitators.

And that, by the way, is what "neoclassicism," at least at first, was all about. It had nothing to do, at first, with stylistic retrospectivism or revivalism, with going "back to Bach" or with vicarious imperial restorations. It had everything to do with a *style dépouillé,* a stripped-down, denuded style, and with the same neoprimitivist, antihumanistic ideals that had already motivated *The Rite* and the other masterworks of Stravinsky's late "Russian period," especially *Svadebka* (The Wedding; first performed as *Les Noces*).

This much we may read in the very first journalistic essay to attach the N-word to Stravinsky—the very first essay, in fact, to apply the word without irony to modern music. It was written in 1923, the year in which Stravinsky's Octet for wind instruments (the first *retour à Bach* piece) was performed, but several months earlier. The man who wrote it was Boris de Schloezer (1881–1969), like Stravinsky a Russian émigré, who is best known for his writings on Scriabin, his brother-in-(common)-law.

The most revealing aspect of Schloezer's early exposition of Stravinsky's neoclassicism, already quoted in chapter 39, is the work that inspired it: not *Pulcinella,* not the Octet, but the *Symphonies d'instruments à vent,* a work we now tend to look upon (and that Stravinsky surely looked upon then) as the composer's valedictory to his Russian period. Nothing could be more critical than this unexpected circumstance to our understanding of Stravinsky's neoclassicism, for Stravinsky lost no time appropriating Schloezer's view. As early as the next year he was looking back on the *Symphonies* as the first of his "so-called classical works."[10] Schloezer had, in effect, revealed to the composer the underlying, indeed profound relationship between his earlier rejection of personal "emotions, feelings, desires, and aspirations" in ritualistic works like *The Rite* and *Svadebka* and the new esthetic of abstraction that attracted not only Stravinsky, but any number of modernist artists to the postwar "call to order" (Cocteau's famous phrase)[11]—a call they heeded in the name of a resurgent, reformulated "classicism."

From this perspective the *Symphonies* was indeed a turning point—or could be one if its memorializing "extramusical" content were purged. And so, in a program note that accompanied performances of the *Symphonies* in the late 1920s and 1930s, Stravinsky described the work as entirely formalist and transcendent: an arrangement of "tonal masses . . . sculptured in marble . . . to be regarded objectively by the ear."[12] The Bachian resonances that we now associate with "neoclassicism" came later, as a metaphor for that transcendence and that objectivity. They have about as much to do with the historical Johann Sebastian Bach as the new line about *The Rite of Spring* had to do with the historical Igor Fyodorovich Stravinsky and his original expressive aims.

But no matter! We are dealing here not with facts but with myths, not with *realia* but with *realiora,* not with the real but with the realer, and the fundamental formalist commitment is the great Stravinsky myth, the great Stravinsky idea, the great Stravinsky truth—the precept or edict (shall we call it the ukase?) that has been regulating the behavior of twentieth-century (and now twenty-first-century) musicians ever since. Ever since the 1920s, in other words, a commitment to formalist esthetics has been the great distinguishing feature of panromanogermanic classical music.

The purity and absoluteness of Stravinsky's music remains an article of faith to many. I have become quite inured over the years to hearing from colleagues and reviewers that the investigations I have made into the sources and backgrounds of Stravinsky's Russian-period work are interesting enough but quite irrelevant esthetically. And it is certainly true, as Pieter van den Toorn says on the very first page of his important book, *Stravinsky and "The Rite of Spring,"* that "for the greater part of this century our knowledge and appreciation of *The Rite of Spring* have come from the concert hall and recordings."[13] To that extent, the myth of *The Rite* has come true, for the music has become quite happily detached from its original scenario and mise-en-scène. For many if not for most spectators visual exposure to the work as a ballet comes after years of tremendous stagings before the mind's eye under the stimulus of the powerful noises that it makes, and seeing it is often disappointing. Even Nicholas Roerich, the original designer and co-scenarist, admitted that "we cannot consider 'Sacre' as Russian, nor even Slavic—it is more ancient and pan-human."[14] To insist that *The Rite* still means what it originally meant—that it is nothing more and nothing less than a pair of "scenes of pagan Russia"—would surely limit and diminish its full human significance, and I for one would never wish my findings about the ballet to diminish it so.

But it may still be worth asking whether that full human significance is well or adequately described by the phrase *architectonique et non anecdotique.* The phrase still sounds like a Pandora's box, and one has to wonder what is being locked up within, just as I still wonder why despite his ample and detailed knowledge of the historical circumstances in which Stravinsky developed his ostensibly radical musical style (knowledge he does not hesitate in the least to share with his reader), Van den Toorn nevertheless subtitled his book *The Beginnings of a Musical Language.* This willed amnesia, I would suggest, is an example of behavior regulated by the Stravinsky myth.

Is there any harm in that? Van den Toorn says no, and in no uncertain terms. He sees nothing but gain. Propositional knowledge, especially historical knowledge, can only interfere, in his view, with esthetic bonding. He quotes (or rather, slightly paraphrases) a remark from one of Stravinsky's books of "conversations" with Craft:

> The composer works through a perceptual, not a conceptual process. He perceives, he selects, he combines, and is not in the least aware at what point meanings of a different sort and significance grow into his works. All he knows or cares about is the apprehension of the contours of form, for form is everything.[15]

There you have it: *form is everything*. You couldn't get more categorical than that in declaring formalist principles. Van den Toorn's move, unanticipated by Stravinsky, perhaps, but clearly regulated by his principles, is to apply the composer's description of composerly behavior to the listener. "One need only substitute listener for composer in the above quotation," he writes, "and the reasoning becomes impregnable."[16] We needn't dwell on distinctions here: what Van den Toorn calls reasoning is pretty clearly a tautology, I think, but what of that? Its purpose and effect are what count for Stravinsky and for Van den Toorn, not its logical status. The purpose, simply, is pleasure, esthetic rapture. "The source of the attraction," Van den Toorn writes,

> the source of our conscious intellectual concerns, is the passionate nature of the relationship that is struck. But this relationship is given immediately in experience and is not open to the inquiry that it inspires. Moments of esthetic rapport, of self-forgetting at-oneness with music, are immediate. The mind, losing itself in contemplation, becomes immersed in the musical object, becomes one with that object.[17]

The trouble is that, as Stravinsky actually concedes, "meanings of a different sort and significance grow into his works" whether or not he knows or cares about them. The esthetic rapture Van den Toorn seeks demands, once again, a willed ignorance, a willed blindness. Directing attention resolutely away from content and focusing entirely on form is hardly an "immediate" response to art. It is no one's first response. (Why else, after all, is a taste for "absolute music" the most notoriously "cultivated" of all artistic tastes?) It is a learned response—learned from Stravinsky. It has its costs.

·　　·　　·

To explore these costs, I want to focus the rest of this discussion on one of Stravinsky's best-known and surely most written-about late works, the *Cantata*, the first composition to follow *The Rake's Progress,* Stravinsky's longest work. At first, it was to have followed quite directly and unproblematically on *The Rake.* It was, in effect, a second collaboration between Stravinsky and W. H. Auden, the *Rake* co-librettist, who had just published, with Norman Holmes Pearson, a five-volume school anthology, *Poets of the English Language* (New York: Viking

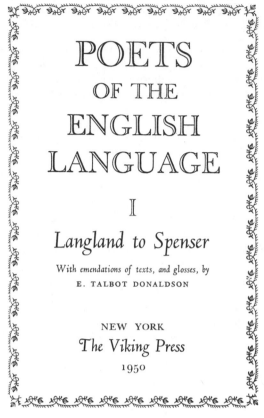

Figure 1. Title page of *Poets of the English Language*, volume 1 (1950). W. H. Auden gave the five-volume set to Stravinsky in 1950.

Press, 1950), and made Stravinsky a present of it (fig. 1). From a letter from Auden to Robert Craft one gathers that Stravinsky was planning a song cycle for mezzo-soprano and small instrumental ensemble on texts from the anthology.[18] In the end, not only the *Cantata* but Stravinsky's next vocal composition as well, *Three Songs from William Shakespeare*, were mined from the contents of Auden's collection. (One can tell that this was Stravinsky's Shakespeare source because he retained all of the quaint spellings that most editors remove but that Auden and his coeditor lovingly restored.)

The first item from *Poets of the English Language* to be set, in July 1951, was "The Maidens Came," one of six poems grouped under the rubric "Anonymous Lyrics and Songs" in volume 1 (fig. 2). The setting is in a sort of period style, both as regards prosody and as regards texture. Stravinsky had been hearing a

CONTENTS	xi
STEPHEN HAWES (1474–1523)	326
FROM The Pastime of Pleasure	
Dame Music	326
The Seven Deadly Sins	328
Time and Eternity	332
EVERYMAN (1510)	336
JOHN SKELTON (1460?–1529)	368
The auncient acquaintance, madam	368
Lullay, lullay	370
Philip Sparrow	371
FROM Speak, Parrot: Parrot's Soliloquy	414
FROM The Garland of Laurel	
To Mistress Isabel Pennell	423
To Mistress Margaret Hussey	424
ANONYMOUS LYRICS AND SONGS	
Westron winde, when will thou blow	426
Benedicite, what dremid I this night	426
Who shall have my faire lady	427
The maidens came	427
A Lyke-Wake Dirge	428
Tomorrow shall be my dancing day	430
ANONYMOUS BALLADS	
The Wife of Usher's Well	432
Edward	433
The Unquiet Grave	435
Sir Patrick Spens	436
The Three Ravens	438
The Laily Worm and the Machrel of the Sea	439
The Riddling Knight	441
SIR THOMAS WYATT (1503?–1542)	443
Who so list to hount	443
The Lover Compareth his State to a Shippe in Perilous Storme Tossed on the Sea	443
The Lover Sheweth How He is Forsaken of Such as He Sometime Enjoyed	444
Ys yt possible	445
What shulde I saye	446
The Lover Complayneth the Unkindness of His Love	447

Figure 2. "Anonymous Lyrics and Songs" as listed in the contents of *Poets of the English Language.*

lot of Renaissance and Baroque music at the so-called Evenings on the Roof Concerts in Los Angeles, at which Craft had become a frequent conductor. At the first such concert he attended, in 1944 (four years Before Craft), he heard Elizabethan virginals music and some keyboard works of Purcell, both for the first time.[19] Later he heard Dowland lute songs and Elizabethan madrigals and much more. "The Maidens Came" is full of the Lombard or "Scotch snap" rhythms characteristic of Purcellian text declamation. They must have struck Stravinsky's ear as especially fresh, even though he did not grasp—or characteristically chose to ignore—the distinctive relationship of the Lombard pattern to the English short stress. The setting is also full of short stretches of canonic writing, often by inversion, such as one finds in early keyboard and consort fantasias.

In his letter of September 1951, Auden sent Craft a rather long list of additional suggestions from his anthology for inclusion in the cycle, mainly Elizabethans like Sidney, Jonson, and Campion, but also Pope, Blake, Burns, even Christina Rossetti. By the time Stravinsky returned to the composition, however, in February 1952, he had decided to cast the work for a more complex medium, including a small women's chorus and two singers, the original mezzo and also a tenor, each of whom sing solos, now called "Ricercars," and then combine for a duet. And, possibly because he wanted to maintain the archaic period flavor of the original setting, he decided to confine the texts to the little group of anonymous lyrics from which he had taken "The Maidens Came," setting the group to music practically in toto (omitting only the second and third items as listed), as many readers will already have noticed after glancing at figure 2. He gave the *Cantata* an elegant overall shape by using one of the longer items, "A Lyke-Wake Dirge," as a kind of choral refrain, its successive verses intercalated around and between the solo items.

The longest item in the group, the carol "Tomorrow shall be my dancing day," was set as a tenor solo to form the *Cantata*'s centerpiece. Now "Tomorrow shall be my dancing day" is not only the longest and most elaborately composed piece in the *Cantata*. It is also one of the most revered items in the later Stravinsky catalog, owing to the circumstances of its creation, which entail an important creative crisis. No biography of the composer or critical study of his work fails to cite it, usually with at least one musical example.

On the face of it, the setting does not seem very different from "The Maidens Came." Like its predecessor it uses canonic textures of a rather archaic sort, admitting *cancrizans,* or reversed order, alongside contour-inversion to its repertoire of contrapuntal devices. Unlike "The Maidens Came," however, and especially in view of its length, the composition is severely limited in its melodic material. The eleven-note canonic subject on which the entire piece is based is a complex derivation from a phrase, seemingly selected at random, from "The Maidens Came" (ex. 1).

Example 1. Transformation of a phrase from "The Maidens Came" into the canonic subject of Ricercar II.

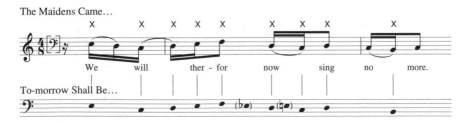

Example 2. Stravinsky's row-chart for Ricercar II. Used by permission of the Paul Sacher Foundation.

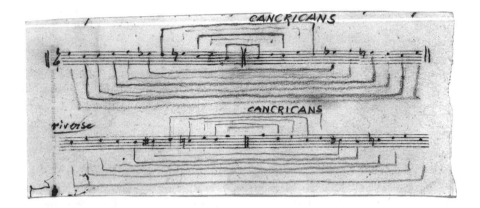

As Craft has testified, immediately on fashioning this little theme, Stravinsky drew a chart on the back of a sheet of stationery from La Boutique, his wife's art gallery on La Cienega Boulevard in Los Angeles, which shows, as Craft put it, "the four orders—original, retrograde, inverted, retrograde inverted—of his eleven-note 'series.'"[20] As you can see from this chart (ex. 2), the *cancrizans* is so arranged as to produce a harmonic closure on its starting point—a traditional pendular (there-and-back) motion with an implied tonic-dominant/dominant-tonic harmony, the old "binary form" we've all studied in school. The inversion is contrived so as to produce the same progression. Its pitch level is chosen so that its opening pair of notes reproduces the pitches of the original phrase with exchanged positions. In formal terms this would be described as a transposition down a major third (in more formal terms, transposition by eight semitones, or—in still more formal terms, those of the theory journals—"t8"), but I'm sure that Stravinsky did not think of it as a transposition at all—quite the opposite, in fact. He must have thought of it not in purely pitch or intervallic terms but in harmonic terms, according to which the inversion changes as little as possible.

Now, although the material in the second Ricercar, and its handling, might well seem just as archaistic as in the first ("The Maidens Came"), the second Ricercar is radically separated in the historical, biographical, analytical, and critical literatures from the rest of the *Cantata* and attached to a different story altogether. Craft put it very succinctly when he wrote that the second Ricercar in the *Cantata* "marks the first effect on Stravinsky of Schoenberg's serial principle," and most of the succeeding literature on the piece has been more or less a gloss on that little sentence.[21]

Realizing that the internal evidence for such an assertion is slim, Craft elaborated with some historical reportage of a kind that he, not only a witness but also an actual participant on the scene, was uniquely qualified to give: "Although cancrizans of the kind found in this Ricercar were *[sic]* employed centuries before," he wrote, "Stravinsky came to them there by way of his contemporary"—his recently deceased contemporary and neighbor, one should add, Schoenberg having died in Los Angeles the year before, as it happened, while Stravinsky was hard at work on "The Maidens Came"— and Craft added as further corroboration that Stravinsky "heard some of the Viennese master's music, as well as much discussion about it, in Europe in the autumn of 1951" when he returned to the old world for the first time after the war to conduct the *Rake* première.

Craft went on to record the fact that while working on the second Ricercar, Stravinsky attended several rehearsals of a performance Craft was then preparing at UCLA of Schoenberg's Septet-Suite, op. 29, and was full of questions about Schoenberg's technique. Once one knows this it makes some sense to relate the manipulations of the eleven-note motive in the second Ricercar to the so-called twelve-tone technique, since like a tone row the motive is treated as an entirely abstract ordered succession of pitches—or rather, pitch classes, as Milton Babbitt would christen them a few years later. Unlike the canons in "The Maidens Came," the ones in the second Ricercar are entirely free as to rhythm and octave register.

Evidence of another sort comes from a touching entry in Craft's diary, describing an occurrence Craft first made public in a centennial lecture published in the *Atlantic Monthly* and, in characteristic fashion, retold subsequently with a great deal of exasperating variation in the details.[22] I quote it here in its latest, and in some ways most plausible (because least sensational), incarnation, from the revised *Chronicle of a Friendship* (72–73). The date is 8 March 1952, four days after the second Ricercar had been completed:

> We drive to Palmdale for lunch, spareribs in a cowboy-style restaurant, Bordeaux from I. S.'s thermos. A powdering of snow is in the air, and, at higher altitudes, on the ground: Angelenos stop their cars and go out to touch it. During the return, I. S. startles us, saying he fears he can no longer compose; for a moment he actually seems ready to weep. V. gently, expertly, assures him that whatever the difficulties, they will soon pass. He refers obliquely to the Schoenberg Septet and the powerful impression it has made on him. After 40 years of dismissing Schoenberg as "experimental," "theoretical," "*démodé*," he is suffering the shock of recognition that Schoenberg's music is richer in substance than his own.

Craft's interpretation here is a little different from those he has offered elsewhere, which have centered on the perhaps more telling fact that Stravinsky was becoming aware that younger musicians, especially in Europe, were more interested just then in Schoenberg than in himself. At any rate, it is clear that Stravinsky was suffering a crisis of confidence, one brought on, as far as I can read the circumstances, precisely because he realized that, as the second Ricercar demonstrated, even when emulating Schoenberg's serial procedures he found himself still tied willy-nilly to his older harmonic thinking, his deeply ingrained habits of the ear. He was evidently afraid that he himself might be becoming "démodé." It was a frightening thought indeed to one who had become so used to the role of defining, at times fairly dictatorially, what would be à la mode.

More evidence of Stravinsky's crisis mentality can be found in the printed documents surrounding the *Cantata*—namely, the published score and a program note that Stravinsky wrote (or at least signed) for the première performance in Los Angeles, in November 1952. Let me quote a bit from the latter. First, Stravinsky notes the general circumstances of the composition: "After finishing *The Rake's Progress* I was persuaded by a strong desire to compose another work in which the problems of setting English words to music would reappear, but this time in a purer, non-dramatic form." Following a description of the Dirge and the first Ricercar, he comes to "Tomorrow shall be my dancing day." It is, he says,

> also a Ricercar in the sense that it is a canonic composition. Its structure is more elaborate than that of "The Maidens Came." The piece begins with a one-bar introduction by the flutes and cello, the statement of the canonic subject which is the subject of the whole piece. This subject is repeated by the tenor, over a recitative style accompaniment of oboes and cello, in original form, retrograde (or cancrizans, which means that its notes are heard in reverse order—in this case, in a different rhythm), inverted form, and finally, in retrograde inversion.

Then comes a musical example showing the voice part of the opening stanza with the four forms, taken as if exactly from example 2, marked off with brackets as in example 3. What is truly surprising is that the published

Example 3. Example accompanying Stravinsky's program note to the *Cantata* in 1952.

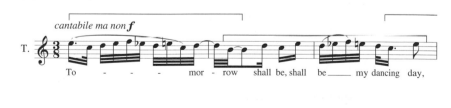

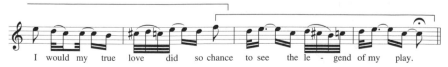

score incorporates these brackets, not only in the opening or expository section Stravinsky quoted in the note, but throughout the piece, showing every single permutation of the eleven-note motive, as Stravinsky cumbersomely attempted to describe them in prose, as the note continues:

> The fourth and sixth canons are nine bars long, the others are twelve bars long. The instrumentation of all the canons is two oboes and cello. In the first canon, the second oboe proposes the original subject and the first oboe takes it up at the minor third above, while the tenor sings it in inverted form. The second canon begins with the voice singing the Cantus in cancrizans form, a minor third below; the cello is in original form a fourth below. The third canon is identical with the first. In the fourth canon the first oboe follows the second at the interval of a second while the voice transposes the Cantus in inverted form down a minor third to A. In the three last bars, the cello, which has been accompanying with a new rhythmic figure, plays the Cantus in F, original form, while the voice and first oboe play it in A, original form. The fifth canon is identical with the first. The sixth begins with the Cantus in the voice in original form . . .[23]

And so on—and on and on. And what makes this program note particularly noteworthy, over and above what I believe it is fair to call its obsession with technical detail, is the fact that this was only the second time in his career that Stravinsky ever offered a technical analysis of any of his compositions. (The other, very brief, concerned *The Firebird*, composed forty-two years earlier.)[24] One begins to get a feel for what Craft described in his memoir as the "substance" that Stravinsky had begun to envy in Schoenberg, and the way it jibed with the older versions of the Stravinsky myth.

A more explicit indication of this tie-in, and of its relationship to the cold-war artistic temper, came in an interview Stravinsky gave a Paris reporter on 28 April 1952, about seven weeks after that tense moment in the car that Craft so hauntingly described. Craft's description of this occasion is very droll.[25] Stravinsky was returning to Europe for the first time since *The Rake* and was touching down in Paris, his home for almost twenty years, for the first time since before the war. It was just a touching-down: Stravinsky was actually on his way to Geneva, and the plane was refueling. His friend Nicolas Nabokov, the newly appointed secretary-general of the Congress for Cultural Freedom, was waiting with a gaggle of paparazzi, whom he hustled into the waiting room for what we would now call a photo op. What Stravinsky told the reporter from the congress's own organ, *Preuves*, during that hectic stopover, in response to what was by then an inevitable question, has already been quoted in part at the end of chapter 39:

> The twelve-tone system? Personally I have enough to do with seven tones. But the twelve-tone composers are the only ones who have a discipline I respect. Whatever else it may be, twelve-tone music is certainly pure music.[26]

Of course, he was describing his second Ricercar, which appropriated the twelve-tone discipline and applied it to seven (well, eight) tones. The discipline was what he wished to claim, and relate to his old notions of "pure" music—something that Schoenberg never did, because he never had that notion. Quite the contrary: Schoenberg always refused to offer technical descriptions of his music, and claimed to despise them. To Rudolf Kolisch, his brother-in-law, who had worked out an exemplary formalistic analysis of Schoenberg's Third Quartet very much on the order of Stravinsky's analysis of his *Cantata,* Schoenberg addressed one of his most famous missives: "I can't utter too many warnings against overrating these analyses, since after all they only lead to what I have always been dead set against: seeing how it is *done;* whereas I have always helped people to see: what it *is!*"[27]

Stravinsky, on the contrary, seemed only to be interested in showing how it was done. And so have been almost all the later commentators on the *Cantata,* of whom there have been so many. Meanwhile, he embarked on the task of expanding from seven to twelve. He did it the way countless other students were doing it at the time. He got hold of *Studies in Counterpoint* (1940) by Ernst Krenek, one of his California neighbors, only the second practical primer in twelve-tone composition ever published, and began working his way through the exercises in it. You can see some of them right on the surface of *Threni,* Stravinsky's first completely dodecaphonic construction, composed in 1957–58. On the way to that piece there had been several others that used rows containing more or fewer than twelve tones and a couple of larger works that were intermittently twelve-tone (*Canticum sacrum, Agon*). The trajectory by which Stravinsky zeroed in on the new discipline is one of the most orderly and trackable processes of its kind in the history of music, and so of course it has been traced very frequently in the literature, especially after Milton Babbitt's seminal exposition, "Remarks on the Recent Stravinsky," first given as "a lecture under the auspices of the Santa Fe Opera as part of its Festival in honor of Igor Stravinsky's 80th birthday," that is, in 1962, and published two years later in *Perspectives of New Music.*

Babbitt set the tone for these surveys by looking back on Stravinsky's quest from the perspective of its completion, thus comparing Stravinsky's serial practice at every stage with the fully elaborated twelve-tone technique he finally embraced—which made for some very tortuous descriptions. Here is how the analysis of the second Ricercar from the *Cantata* begins:

> The serial unit here consists of eleven ordered pitch elements, but only six different pitch elements. Since there are, then, non-immediate repetitions of pitch elements within the unit, the serial characterization, in terms of the relation of temporal precedence among pitches, requires that each occurrence of a pitch element which occurs multiply be differentiated ordinally; more concisely, if it is agreed to represent a pitch element of a serial unit by an ordered

pair signifying the element's order number and pitch number, then the collection of such ordered pairs associated with the twelve-tone set necessarily defines a biunique, one-to-one function, while that of a serial order with repetitions cannot. This latter collection defines a function, but not a biunique one, and the inverse, therefore, is not a single-valued function.[28]

And here is another pertinent excerpt:

> Whereas the operations in the twelve-tone system necessarily result in permutations of the elements of the set, in a non twelve-tone serial unit, they do not. Indeed, if the serial unit is not inversionally symmetrical, as it is not in the Cantata, the effect of inversion can never be to permute, but rather to adjoin pitches which are not present in the original unit. So, whereas an inversion of a twelve-tone set can be so identified only by virtue of order, in the case of such a serial structure as that of the Cantata, it can be identified by pitch content alone. Here, then, is combinational rather than permutational serialism, since each form of the serial unit represents a selection from the twelve pitch classes rather than a particular ordering of these classes. A significant criterion of similarity, of hierarchization, among such serial forms, then, is the number of pitch classes shared between and among set forms; and this, in turn, depends entirely upon the exact intervallic content of the serial unit constructed by the composer as a contextual norm.[29]

I said that these were pertinent excerpts, and I meant it, but what are they pertinent to? Not the *Cantata*, because Babbitt is saying only what Stravinsky did not do in composing that piece and sheds no light at all on what he did do. Why then, despite that impertinence and despite its extreme tortuousness, has Babbitt's telling of this tale become so influential? It has been influential because it effectively turns the story of Stravinsky's late career into a teleology, a quest narrative, and in so doing it assimilates the story to yet another myth, one of the great myths of the twentieth century, that of the general teleology according to which the structure of music and the compositional practices that produce that structure have been said to evolve by stages, and inevitably, from tonal to atonal, finally to serial.

Because Stravinsky underwent this evolution late, presumably, he was allowed to bypass the middle term and evolve directly from tonal to serial. But this discrepancy does not prevent his career from assuming a kind of paradigmatic status, by which his ontogeny recapitulates the phylogeny of twentieth-century music. In doing so, Stravinsky's career can be subsumed into a progress narrative, progress being the most potent form that myth has taken in the nineteenth and twentieth centuries. So we end up with an assimilation of one powerful myth, the Stravinskian myth of purity, to an even more powerful myth, the positivistic myth of progress. Like any myth, but doubly so, this double myth has functioned as a regulator of belief and behavior. It has immense authority, an authority that has only recently, with great difficulty and against strong resistance, begun to be challenged.

What has been the chief regulation? I've already hinted at it: the resolute deflection of musical consciousness from "what it is," as Schoenberg would say, to "how it's done." Often, and very misleadingly, it is expressed as an exclusion of "extramusical" ideas from consideration of "the music itself." And this taboo, to reiterate, has cost us very dear.

To return to the second Ricercar: it can hardly have escaped notice that Stravinsky's description, to say nothing of Babbitt's, has entirely avoided any mention of what the piece *is*. At its most basic level, it is a setting of a carol that narrates the life of Christ. How is it that this fact is thought to be irrelevant to a description of the piece, especially as we know Stravinsky to have been, or at any rate to have professed being, a religious believer? Could the subject really have played no part in the selection of the text? Was it only "problems of setting English words" that mattered to Stravinsky, not the words he set?

Let us look closely at a part of the piece, the last part for which I have already quoted Stravinsky's description, namely, the fourth canon (ex. 4). We may see all the things to which Stravinsky called attention, underscored by his use of brackets to which I have added identifications of the serial forms employed using the standard music theory representational mode. First there is the beautifully worked out canon in the voice and the two oboes in which three different transpositions of the inverted form of the theme are combined. Then the voice shifts over to the original form of the "riverso cancrizans," as Stravinsky called it on his chart (ex. 2), or the retrograde inversion, as it is called in standard terminology. Finally, as Stravinsky pointed out, the original eleven-note "serial unit," as Babbitt puts it, is enunciated by the voice and first oboe in A major while the cello plays it in F major. All of this is worked out ingeniously and beautifully. Contemplating the musical construction one can indeed experience, with Pieter van den Toorn, a "moment of esthetic rapport, of self-forgetting at-oneness with music," in which "the mind, losing itself in contemplation, becomes immersed in the musical object, becomes one with that object."

But there is something else in example 4 besides what Stravinsky, Babbitt, or Van den Toorn would recognize as the "musical object." There is something "extramusical" as well—something never alluded to by Stravinsky, by Babbitt, by Van den Toorn, by Colin Mason, by Heinrich Lindlar, by Henry Cowell, by André Boucourechliev, by Robert Morgan, by Paul Griffiths, by Louis Andriessen and Elmer Schönberger, by Stephen Walsh, by Joseph Straus, or by any of the other musician-commentators who have offered detailed descriptions of the *Cantata* in print. There is also this, which never failed to take audiences by surprise when I delivered this chapter as a lecture, even though example 4 had by then been staring them in the face for about three minutes:

Example 4. Ricercar II, ritornello and fourth canon.

> The Jews on me they made great suit,
> And with me made great variance;
> Because they lov'd darkness rather than light.

Is it necessary to point out that this is a deplorable text, even if a venerable one, rehearsing as it does the old guilt-libel against the Jews as children of darkness and as deicides, a libel that has caused rivers of Jewish blood to be spilled? And does it surprise you that it could strike someone like me, your academic colleague, as incomprehensible that a great composer, whose prestige must inevitably lend it respectability, would choose such a text to set, seven years after Hitler?

But I want to emphasize at the outset, and as forcefully as I know how, that Stravinsky's motives in setting this text are not the issue I am addressing. His anti-Semitism is not my present subject, nor is anyone's. My subject today is blindness to its presence, a blindness that innumerable performers and commentators have shared with Stravinsky and that is the most urgent aspect of what I see as the issue of Stravinsky and Us—taking "Stravinsky" now in the sense I originally announced, to mean a set of regulative ideas and premises, and taking "Us" to mean those whose beliefs and behaviors have been so regulated.

For purposes of the present discussion, I am perfectly willing to grant that Stravinsky was blind—or, if you prefer, insensitive—to the import of the words he was setting. This for him was a long-standing habit. From his earliest modernist days he claimed to be interested in words only for their sounds, not their meaning. There is evidence that this was the case in the *Cantata,* both in his explicit remark that the verses he chose for it "attracted me not only for their great beauty and their compelling syllabification, but for their construction which suggested musical construction,"[30] and in a hilarious entry in Craft's diary in which Auden, after the *Cantata* has been performed and is in process of publication, finally explains to Craft and Stravinsky what the words of the "Lyke-Wake Dirge" actually mean.[31] Stravinsky set them without knowing, probably without caring.

It was not the first time. More than one piece from the Russian period—*Svadebka,* for example, or (for a particularly piquant instance) the "Zapevnaya," or "counting game," from the *Quatre chants russes* of 1919—contain Russian peasant words and phrases that even Pyotr Kireyevsky, the compiler of the anthology of folk verses on which Stravinsky relied, and a legendary connoisseur, found incomprehensible. He marked such texts in his anthology with little question marks and ellipses that seem to have attracted Stravinsky to them as honey attracts a bear.

More evidence of Stravinsky's lack of concern for the words in his second Ricercar is the fact that he was inattentive to the form of the poem even as he

To-morrow shall be my dancing day

To-morrow shall be my dancing day,
   I would my true love did so chance
To see the legend of my play,
   To call my true love to my dance.
Sing, oh! my love, oh! my love, my love, my love,
This have I done for my true love.

Then was I born of a Virgin pure,
   Of her I took fleshly substance;
Thus was I knit to man's nature,
   To call my true love to my dance.
Sing, oh! etc.

In a manger laid and wrapp'd I was,
   So very poor, this was my chance,
Betwixt an ox and a silly poor ass,
   To call my true love to my dance.

Then afterwards baptized I was,
   The Holy Ghost on me did glance,
My Father's voice heard from above,
   To call my true love to my dance.

Into the desert I was led,
   Where I fasted without substance;
The Devil bade me make stones my bread,
   To have me break my true love's dance.

The Jews on me they made great suit,
   And with me made great variance,
Because they lov'd darkness rather than light,
   To call my true love to my dance.

For thirty pence Judas me sold,
   His covetousness for to advance;
Mark whom I kiss, the same do hold,
   The same is he shall lead the dance.

Before Pilate the Jews me brought,
   Where Barabbas had deliverance,
They scourg'd me and set me at nought,
   Judged me to die to lead the dance.

Then on the cross hanged I was,
   Where a spear to my heart did glance;
There issued forth both water and blood,
   To call my true love to my dance.

Then down to Hell I took my way
   For my true love's deliverance,
And rose again on the third day
   Up to my true love and the dance.

Then up to Heaven I did ascend,
   Where now I dwell in sure substance,
On the right hand of God, that man
   May come unto the general dance.

(*As printed in Sandys' Christmas Carols, London, 1833*)

Figure 3. Text layout of "To-morrow shall be my dancing day," from *Poets of the English Language.*

was setting it. As you can see in the text that Auden printed (fig. 3), the poem is a carol, and like all carols it has a burden, which Auden printed once in full and once abbreviated to show that it should follow every stanza. Stravinsky set the poem exactly as it was printed, not the way it should be performed. (No, he didn't actually set the words "Sing, oh! etc.," but he set the burden only the two times Auden printed it.) Yet more evidence of his unconcern: he gave an inscribed copy of the *Cantata* score to Otto Klemperer, a Hitler refugee, whom I cannot think he meant to insult.[32] So it was not that Stravinsky sought out a text libeling the Jews to set. It simply did not matter to him.

    Other people's texts, however, did matter to him at times. About Schoenberg he once remarked, "Nearly all of his texts are appallingly bad, some of them so bad as to discourage performance of the music."[33] He no doubt had *Die glückliche Hand* in mind, or some other embarrassing expressionistic effusion like that. But all that this shows is that Stravinsky's artistic sensibilities were more acute than his moral ones. Here is another manifestation of the dichotomy. It is a letter from Stravinsky to Craft, or rather a passage from a letter from Stravinsky to Craft, dated 8 October 1948, that has been silently expunged from both purportedly complete documentary publications of the letters.[34] The subject of comment is a demonstration against Serge Lifar, Diaghilev's last *premier danseur,* on account of his wartime collaboration with the Germans in occupied Paris. Stravinsky writes:

> If there were some intelligent Jews picketing before Lifar not for his "fascism" (or, later on, "communism," about which they are silent of course), but for his quite obvious want of talent, I would gladly change my mind about Jews.

The expression here is gratuitously vulgar and malicious, and for that reason repellent on its face, but the actual sentiments expressed are not unrelated, I would argue, to the blindnesses and exclusions that I have been describing and that we all practice to some extent, even those of us who are trying to shed them. We all operate under pressure to put what we call "artistic" considerations front and center in any discussion of art, and to resist—indeed, to disdain—considerations of any other kind.

Nowadays that pressure and that resistance are most easily seen, in the musical world, in the ongoing debate about Wagner. Not content to print one, the editors of the *Musical Times* recently printed two separate hostile critiques of a single book, Marc Weiner's *Richard Wagner and the Anti-Semitic Imagination,* in a single issue. The one that shocked and depressed me was the one that prefaced any consideration of the author's arguments with an elaborate ritual in which the reviewer crossed himself, spat in all directions, and calumniated in advance all who raise the very issue of "Richard Wagner's racist and antisemitic theories" in the context of his art. Such people are prejudged as "careerist journalists and musicologists" who "pander" to fashion and aim merely to present themselves as "trendily antiestablishment."[35]

In the critique that followed, much was made of the fact that Prof. Weiner and others who have tackled these problems are not professional musicians and are therefore unqualified to write about music. But of course it is inevitable that these "extramusical" questions will be broached from the standpoint of disciplines that are not regulated by the Stravinsky myth.

And that, of course, is the reason why the only discussion I have ever seen of the anti-Semitic text in Stravinsky's *Cantata* appeared not in a musical or musicological publication but in a Jewish-interest periodical, *Midstream.* The author, a painter and literary anthologist named Jacob Drachler, described his persistent efforts to lodge an effective protest at Stravinsky's setting of lines so offensive to Jews, efforts that culminated in a letter to Robert Craft, posted on April 15, 1971 (the date was poorly chosen, being that of Stravinsky's funeral). The reply came not from Craft but from Lillian Libman, Stravinsky's personal manager:

[Mr. Craft] says that Mr. Stravinsky, of course, was not thinking about "the holocaust of modern European Jewry" when he set those lines of 15th century verse. In fact, he got quite a jolt from the lines himself when he first heard the piece, and he had changed the text, substituting, I think, "my foes" or "my enemies" (we can't remember exactly)—but in any case the words were definitely changed, and the music amended, but again we don't know exactly when.

    If and when a new edition of the score comes out, Mr. Craft will see to it personally that the change is made.[36]

It will probably not surprise you to learn that this was never done, and I think it is clear that Ms. Libman's letter was just an offhand attempt to dispose of a nuisance.[37] But how should we deal with the question, if we agree that there is a problem? Ought moral sensibilities, as much as artistic ones, discourage performance of excellent music? Stravinsky's answer, I believe, has been sufficiently implied. What should ours be? The dichotomy normally invoked in such discussions, between "the music itself" and "the extramusical," can be easily unmasked in this case. For if the music itself—what Van den Toorn calls "the musical object"—is alone what engages "esthetic rapport," and the extramusical is altogether to be excluded from a proper esthetic response, then we should have no problem with the second Ricercar. We can perform and enjoy it as an instrumental solo, or a vocalise.

    But of course this would not be an acceptable solution. Why? Because it would violate the integrity of the musical text as the composer left it. In more casual language, it would make the performance "unauthentic." The composer's intentions, as we normally construe them, would not be carried out, and that would breach the most fundamental ethical obligation of "classical music" as practiced in the twentieth century.

    Of course, this, too, is an ethical constraint we owe in large part to the mythmaking authority of Stravinsky, who inveighed constantly against the performer's right to any exercise of subjective judgment. The snooty "neoclassical" sermon in the last of his Harvard lectures of 1939, published under the title *Poetics of Music*, transfers the objectivist esthetic identified by Schloezer in Stravinsky's composerly attitudes to a performance practice, the most influential set of performerly precepts ever explicitly enunciated in the twentieth century. The insistence in that lecture on the distinction between *execution*—selfless submission to "an explicit will that contains nothing beyond what it specifically commands"—and *interpretation,* which lies "at the root of all the errors, all the sins, all the misunderstandings that interpose themselves between the musical work and the listener," has been, much more than any earlier historical precedent, the driving force behind "authentic" performance, manifested not only in early music, but in all performances that adhere to the ethic of scrupulous submission, which means just about all performances of classical music that one will hear today.[38]

But how ethical are such ethics, if they cause us to value the integrity of works of art above humane concerns? How ethical is an ethic that obliges us, when the *Cantata* is on the program, to lend our unprotesting presence to an execration of the Jews, and thus become complicit in it, and even more than that, to maintain a pretense that nothing of the sort is taking place? How ethical is an ethic implying that artistic excellence or beautiful form redeems ugly or objectionable content, as so many have argued of late in the case of T. S. Eliot? What is the difference between saying that and saying that artistic excellence excuses objectionable content of any kind? And if we allow this much, then what prevents art from becoming for all of us, as it undoubtedly is for some of us, a means for secretly gratifying our inner bigot?

How ethical, finally, is an ethic that holds artists and art lovers to be entitled, by virtue of their artistic commitment to moral indifference, and that *the greater the artist, the greater the entitlement*? The truth of this last, most painful, corollary, I think, can be confirmed by a thought experiment. As many readers will recall, Gustav Holst also made a setting, in his case for mixed chorus, of "Tomorrow shall be my dancing day," the carol that furnished the text for Stravinsky's second Ricercar. It is an attractive piece. Unlike Stravinsky's setting, it was written long before the Holocaust, in 1916. I would wager, though, that performers would be far more likely to think twice before performing Holst's setting than they evidently are before performing Stravinsky's, and that audiences hearing Holst's setting would be far more likely to notice and protest the meaning of the words. The only reason I can think of for the difference is the differing stature of the composers. It is Stravinsky, not Holst, who has been classified as an unassailable great. Hence the dispensation he is granted, and hence the distress my words may be causing some readers.[39]

But is great art ennobled by this attitude? Are we? Or are we not debased and diminished, both as artists and as human beings, by such a commitment to "abstract" musical worth? And for a final disquieting thought, has that commitment got nothing to do with the catastrophic decline that the prestige of classical music—and of high art in general—has suffered in our time?

So what, you may finally wonder, do I think we should do about the *Cantata*? Certainly not suppress it; although I personally would not be opposed to instrumental performance of the second Ricercar or some modification of the text, especially if it is not done "silently," à la Dr. Bowdler, which evades the problem, but rather with an accompanying announcement or explanation that exposes and confronts it.[40] I hope and trust that it is clear to one and all that inviting performers to consider such a course is not the same as decreeing that they do and that an appeal to discretion is a far cry from censorship, which is in any case a legal, not a moral, category.

But even without modification, exposure of the problem is very much to be encouraged, I believe; and that is what I have sought to make of the opportunity of addressing you. In an unfortunately acidulous exchange with me about the *Cantata* in the *New York Review of Books* some years ago, Robert Craft made the claim (later included in the expanded *Chronicle of a Friendship*) that in his own first Los Angeles performance he substituted "my enemies" for "the Jews on me" in the first line of Canon Four and that for this he was reproached by Auden.[41] "'By any definition *The Merchant of Venice* is anti-Semitic,' [Auden] said, 'but we can't change it.'"

Why not? Modifying a performance does not permanently alter the work; and in any case we are not called upon to change it. But we *are* called upon to face the issue and talk about it, I believe; and we had better. That is the very least we can do if we want to escape from the counterproductive complacency on which the Stravinsky myth insists, and keep high art kosher.

POSTSCRIPT, 2008

Before publishing it, I delivered this lecture more than two dozen times, over a period of six years, and on four continents. Almost invariably, and despite my express disclaimer that Stravinsky's anti-Semitism was not the issue I was addressing (this time, anyway), members of the audience tried at question time to exonerate him of the charge I seemed to be making, or at least to argue that the text of "Tomorrow shall be my dancing day" did not have to be construed as anti-Semitic. I regarded these interventions as further examples of behavior regulated by the Stravinsky myth, hence as evidence in support of my thesis, and confirmation of its urgency. More confirmation came in March 2004, when the *BBC Music Magazine* and *The Gramophone* carried reviews of *The Cambridge Companion to Stravinsky*, both of them singling out my chapter therein for harsh disparagement. In the former, Bayan Northcott found it "depressing" that anyone would publish my "much-pedalled *[sic!]* thesis . . . that Stravinsky managed to impose his formalist values so totally on modernism that when he set a line of anti-Semitic medieval verse six *[sic]* years after the Holocaust, nobody protested or even noticed. He entitles this tissue of tendentious generalizations and tricky logic 'Stravinsky and Us.' Us? Speak for yourself, Professor Taruskin."

And so I do. But at least Northcott, even if he—trickily or tendentiously—exaggerated it, got my thesis right. In *The Gramophone*, Stephen Walsh, Stravinsky's latest biographer, pooh-poohed my attempt "to get us to close our ears to the anti-Semitic line in Stravinsky's *Cantata*." How obtuse is that? I adduce these topsy-turvy responses to my efforts to get listeners to open their ears as proof that (to answer another common objection) I am not arguing with straw men. Northcott's and Walsh's responses give depressing evidence that many if not most professional writers on music simply cannot cope intellectually with an argument that calls for the ethical or political evaluation of a work of art. I would like to think that "ordinary" listeners are by now less encumbered by the Stravinsky myth.

Meanwhile, my contention that Stravinsky set the offensive text not necessarily with malice but in an esthetically justified indifference to the fate of the Jews has received some unexpected confirmation from Robert Craft in his volume of memoirs, *An Improbable Life* (Nashville: Vanderbilt University Press, 2002), published after my talk had itself gone to press. There it is revealed that after Stravinsky conducted the première performance of the *Cantata* at a Los Angeles Chamber Symphony concert in November 1952,

> [t]he piece was savaged by Mildred Norton, a Los Angeles reviewer, because of the line. . . . Stravinsky contended that the offending line amounted to dogma at the time it was written, and that the poem was an untouchable classic. . . . Lawrence [Morton] wished to program the Cantata in one of his 1953 [Evenings on the Roof] concerts and asked me to discuss with him the possibility of changing the line and of convincing Stravinsky to accept it. After much thought and a slight adjustment of the musical rhythm, we agreed to substitute the phrase "My enemies on me made great suit." I took him to see Stravinsky, whom he did not know, and, who said that he had no intended to hurt or affront anyone and that the reaction had surprised him. By this time he had received a letter from Alexandre Tansman, his biographer in the early California years, then living in Paris, criticizing him for having set such a text only seven years after the opening of the death camps. Stravinsky did not answer and never spoke to Tansman again. (137–38)

Indeed, Craft reports that four years later, on coming unexpectedly face-to-face with Tansman, "his close friend in Hollywood during the war years, . . . Stravinsky cut him dead, ignored his outstretched hand, and did not utter a word in response to his welcome," so resentful was he over Tansman's criticism of his indifference to the fate of the Jews (180). Nevertheless, Craft continues, Stravinsky "consented to my Evenings on the Roof performance with the emended text." Still, when Stravinsky recorded the *Cantata*, first in 1953 and again in 1965, the original text was restored, possibly because a recording, being "permanent," has a higher cultural standing, and is subject to more exigent esthetic constraint, than a live performance. According to Craft, Stravinsky invited the performer in the 1965 recording, the British tenor Alexander Young, to use the altered text, but the latter refused, as he put it, "to desecrate [!] one of the most beautiful poems in the language," even with the composer's consent (138). By then, evidently, the Stravinsky myth could overrule Stravinsky.

NOTES

1. Robert Craft, "Introduction: A Master at Work," in Igor Stravinsky and Robert Craft, *Retrospectives and Conclusions* (New York: Knopf, 1969), 3.

2. Igor Stravinsky and Robert Craft, *Expositions and Developments* (Garden City, N.Y.: Doubleday, 1962), 164.

3. Michel Georges-Michel, "Les deux Sacres du printemps," *Comoedia*, 11 December 1920. Cited in Truman C. Bullard, "The First Performance of Igor Stravinsky's *Sacre du printemps*" (PhD diss., University of Rochester, 1971), 1:3.

4. See André Schaeffner, *Strawinsky* (Paris: Éditions Rieder, 1931), 43 n 1; also "Table des planches" (p. 217), pl. 21.

5. Stravinsky and Craft, *Expositions and Developments*, 169.

6. See Richard Taruskin, *Stravinsky and the Russian Traditions* (Berkeley: University of California Press, 1996), chaps. 4, 12.

7. See Bernice Glatzer Rosenthal, "The Transmutation of the Symbolist Ethos: Mystical Anarchism and the Revolution of 1905," *Slavic Review* 36 (1977): 616.

8. Stravinsky and Craft, *Expositions and Developments*, 114–15; the original "over-publicized bit about expression" (as it is described there) is from Stravinsky's autobiography *(Chroniques de ma vie)* in its anonymous English translation (New York: Simon and Schuster, 1936), 83.

9. The term *panromanogermanic* comes from Prince Nikolai Sergeyevich Trubetskoy's Eurasianist tract, *Yevropa i chelovechestvo* (Sofia: Rossiysko-Bolgarskoye Knigoizdatel'stvo, 1920), a book published by Stravinsky's friend Pyotr Suvchinsky (Pierre Souvtchinsky).

10. Letter to Charles-Ferdinand Ramuz, 23 July 1924; Robert Craft, ed., *Stravinsky: Selected Correspondence*, vol. 3 (New York: Knopf, 1985), 83.

11. As embodied in the title to his collected essays, *A Call to Order*, trans. Rollo H. Myers (London: Faber and Gwyer, 1926).

12. Quoted in Deems Taylor, "Sound—and a Little Fury" (review of the American première under Leopold Stokowski), reprinted in *Of Men and Music* (New York: Simon and Schuster, 1937), 89–90.

13. Pieter C. van den Toorn, *Stravinsky and "The Rite of Spring": The Beginnings of a Musical Language* (Berkeley: University of California Press, 1987), 1.

14. "Sacre," in N. K. Roerich, *Realm of Light* (New York: Roerich Museum Press, 1931), 188.

15. Stravinsky and Craft, *Expositions and Developments*, 115; quoted in Van den Toorn, *Stravinsky and "The Rite of Spring,"* 18. In the last sentence, where Van den Toorn quotes Stravinsky as saying "form," the original text, both times, has "the form."

16. Van den Toorn, *Stravinsky and "The Rite of Spring,"* 19.

17. Pieter C. van den Toorn, "Politics, Feminism, and Music Theory," *Journal of Musicology* 9 (1991): 276.

18. Letter received 20 September 1951; printed in Robert Craft, *Stravinsky: Chronicle of a Friendship*, rev. and expanded ed. (Nashville: Vanderbilt University Press, 1994), 65.

19. Dorothy Lamb Crawford, *Evenings on and off the Roof: Pioneering Concerts in Los Angeles, 1939–1971* (Berkeley: University of California Press, 1995), 64.

20. Vera Stravinsky and Robert Craft, *Stravinsky in Pictures and Documents* (New York: Simon and Schuster, 1978), 422.

21. Ibid.

22. The lecture was first published in *Atlantic Monthly* (December 1982) under the title "On a Misunderstood Collaboration: Assisting Stravinsky"; this version was reprinted (under the title "Influence or Assistance?") in Robert Craft, *Present Perspectives* (New York: Knopf, 1984), 246–64 (the anecdote in question appears on 252–53). A second version, set down in a letter to Joan Peyser, was published by the latter in "Stravinsky-Craft, Inc.," *American Scholar* 52 (1983): 513–22.

23. As reprinted in Eric Walter White, *Stravinsky: The Composer and His Works* (Berkeley: University of California Press, 1966), 430–31.

24. First published in 1928 directly on the Aeolian piano roll of the ballet, this analysis is discussed in Taruskin, *Stravinsky and the Russian Traditions,* 587–98.

25. Craft, *Chronicle of a Friendship,* 75.

26. "Rencontre avec Stravinsky," *Preuves* 2 (1952): no. 16, p. 37.

27. Letter of 27 July 1932; Arnold Schoenberg, *Letters,* ed. Erwin Stein, trans. Eithne Wilkins and Ernst Kaiser (Berkeley: University of California Press, 1987), 164.

28. Milton Babbitt, "Remarks on the Recent Stravinsky," as reprinted in Benjamin Boretz and Edward T. Cone, eds., *Perspectives on Schoenberg and Stravinsky* (Princeton, N.J.: Princeton University Press, 1968), 171.

29. Ibid.

30. Program note to the *Cantata,* as reprinted in White, *Stravinsky,* 429. These words are a virtual paraphrase of Stravinsky's explanation, in *Chroniques de ma vie,* of his fascination with Russian folk verses during the years of World War I: "What fascinated me in this verse was not so much the stories, which were often crude, or the pictures and metaphors, always so deliciously unexpected, as the sequence of the words and syllables, and the cadence they create, which produces an effect on one's sensibilities very closely akin to that of music" (Stravinsky, *An Autobiography,* 83). These are the words that immediately precede the famous sermon ("that overpublicized bit") on music and expression.

31. Craft, *Chronicle of a Friendship,* 89 (entry for 26 December 1952).

32. See the Alain Nicolas auction catalogue, *Autographes-Livres-Documents* (Paris: Librairie les neuf Muses, 1993), lot no. 196.

33. Igor Stravinsky and Robert Craft, *Conversations with Igor Stravinsky* (Garden City, N.Y.: Doubleday, 1959), 78.

34. "'Dear Bob (sky)' (Stravinsky's Letters to Robert Craft, 1944–49)," *Musical Quarterly* 65 (1979): 412–13; Robert Craft, ed., *Stravinsky: Selected Correspondence* (New York: Knopf, 1982), 1:346–47. A facsimile of the uncensored letter was displayed, and the quoted passage read aloud, by Charles M. Joseph, in "Ellipses, Exclusions, Expurgations: What Do Stravinsky's Letters Really Say?" paper presented at the 58th annual meeting of the American Musicological Society, Pittsburgh, 7 November 1992.

35. David Allenby, "Judge for Yourselves," *Musical Times* (June 1996): 25.

36. Quoted in Jacob Drachler, "The Case of the Stravinsky Cantata," *Midstream,* August–September 1971, 37. In the second volume of his Stravinsky biography, Stephen Walsh cites—superciliously, I regret to say—some other protests by Jewish lis-

teners, including the pianist Jakob Gimpel. See S. Walsh, *Stravinsky: The Second Exile: France and America, 1934–1971* (New York: Knopf, 2006), 95–96.

37. Its substance was incorporated into a footnote on p. 304 of Lillian Libman, *And Music at the Close: Stravinsky's Last Years* (New York: W. W. Norton, 1972). Pieter van den Toorn relied on this evidence (and this evidence alone), as well as the passage to which it was appended, in which Ms. Libman characterized reports of Stravinsky's anti-Semitism as "ridiculous fiction" that "could hardly have entered the scope of his thought," in declaring the matter excluded from further scholarly consideration. See Pieter C. van den Toorn, "Will Stravinsky Survive Postmodernism?" *Music Theory Spectrum* 22 (2000): 121. I know of no comparable case, at least in the refereed professional literature, in which the word of a press agent is invoked in order to justify the foreclosure of academic inquiry. Such subscholarly credulity is impressive testimony to the continuing regulative force of the Stravinsky myth and its deleterious effect on scholarship.

38. See Igor Stravinsky, *Poetics of Music in the Form of Six Lessons* (Cambridge, Mass.: Harvard University Press, 1970), 163.

39. The situation is admittedly somewhat complicated by the fact that Holst's setting, unlike Stravinsky's, is used in Anglican services, where a different set of audience expectations and a different set of premises regulating audience behavior are in force. For a discussion of them, see Harold Copeman, *Singing the Meaning* (Oxford: published by the author, 1996). But at an Anglican service there would also presumably be no Jewish ears to offend.

40. In his 1995 recording of the *Cantata* for Music Masters, Robert Craft did change "The Jews on me" to "My enemies," according to the suggestion embodied in Lillian Libman's letter to Jacob Drachler. The change was silent, however, and the problem unaddressed.

41. See "Jews and Geniuses: An Exchange," *New York Review of Books*, 15 June 1989, 58; Craft, *Chronicle of a Friendship*, 107–8 (entry for 16 March 1954).

42

Setting Limits

As the son and brother of lawyers, I couldn't be more delighted to be asked to address this symposium as a keynoter. But I have some misgivings, too. A keynoter, as I have always understood the term, is an agenda-setter, and I am uncomfortable in that role. In my own field, my reputation is more that of an agenda *up*setter, and that is one of the reasons why my work attracted the attention of your conveners, hence one of the reasons why I am here. But I am unaware of having an agenda where the topic of this meeting is concerned, and no idea of what yours might be. I will use my time, instead, to pose a question and propose an answer that, if we're lucky, will lead to some discussion.

But firstly, if the time you'll not begrudge, as the Judge says in your favorite operetta, I'll tell you how I came to be your keynoter—or at least how I think I did. About ten years ago I received out of the blue an offprint of an article from the *University of Pennsylvania Law Review* called "Law, Music, and Other Performing Arts," by Professors Sanford Levinson of the University of Texas and Jack Balkin of Yale. It was ostensibly a review of *Authenticity and Early Music,* a collection of essays edited by Nicholas Kenyon, then the editor of *Early Music* magazine, and published by Oxford University Press in 1988, to which I had contributed. I read it with fascination and gratitude, the latter simply because the authors had so well understood the position I had taken in the debates about what was then known as authentic performance practice in music. My musical and musicological colleagues seemed unable to hear what I was really saying when I said that their ideas of historical performance practice, on which the claim of authenticity was based, derived from

Originally delivered as the keynote address at the conference "Law, Music, and Other Performing Arts," University of Texas at Austin, 4 March 2002. This is its first publication.

a selective reading of history in the service of a modern—or, more strongly, a modernist—ideology. They thought I was claiming that what they were doing was incorrect or misguided or deceitful; but what I meant to imply (and even said outright on occasion) was that their accomplishment was actually far more important and authentic than they claimed or even realized, since it made them the authentic voice of their time, which was our time.

It is true that I contended that mimicking obsolete historical styles of performance was of no intrinsic esthetic value. Since "authentic" performers thought that they were accurately mimicking such styles and that that was where the value of their work lay, they concluded that I was denying the value of their work. But in fact my theory was that the "mainstream" or "modern" performers, whose hegemony the "authenticists" were challenging, were the ones who were mimicking obsolete historical styles (the ones in which they had been trained), and that those who *claimed* to be mimicking obsolete historical styles were in fact creating something new and vital, and much to be preferred. I only wished they would call their accomplishment by its right name, because that might have freed them to go further and be bolder, and emancipate themselves even more completely from unthinking obeisance to received wisdom and constraint. But somehow they heard me saying the opposite, and I acquired a reputation as an enemy of historical performance when I had meant to be its best (or at least its truest) friend. A whole literature of futile debate had grown up in the wake of this misunderstanding.

Levinson and Balkin heard my message loud and clear and related authentic performance practice, as I had analyzed it, with theories of what they called legal modernism—theories that are doubtless familiar to many of you attending this conference but that were as yet unknown to me or, as far as I knew, to any musicologist. The interdisciplinary resonances their review disclosed to me were the most powerful confirmation my theories had received and opened up some new vistas to me. I acknowledged this debt in the introduction to a book called *Text and Act* (Oxford: Oxford University Press, 1995), in which I collected some of my essays on the subject of musical performance, including the one that Levinson and Balkin had reviewed, and also made some efforts to broaden the scope of my analysis into a more interdisciplinary terrain encompassing not only the legal issues they had raised but also issues coming from anthropology, sociology, and cognitive psychology.

David Hunter, the music librarian at the University of Texas at Austin, and thus a colleague of Prof. Levinson, was at the time the book review editor of *Notes,* the journal of the Music Library Association, and he had the happy idea to commission from Professors Levinson and Balkin a review of *Text and Act.* I got no prizes for writing that book, I can tell you, but they got a prize for reviewing it, and it was very well deserved. (I've always wanted to ask them, though, how it felt for two law professors to divide a check for $50.)

Again they amazed me with their quick and profound comprehension, aided no doubt by their outsider perspective, of issues that too many musicians and musicologists still had difficulty grasping, and I am glad to use this opportunity to add yet another round to our exchange of public compliments.

In their review Levinson and Balkin focused on the claim of privilege to which proponents of "authenticity" felt themselves entitled by virtue of their superior knowledge (or so they claimed) of composers' intentions. The law professors understood that my strictures were not addressed only to this particular claim of privilege, but to any and all such claims that sought to circumvent the judgment and preferences of listeners—that is, those most immediately affected by performance decisions. They understood and endorsed my equation of the authenticists' claim to objective knowledge of history with the modernist claim to objective knowledge of musical structure, and my contentions, first, that no one's knowledge of cultural artifacts can be the product of anything other than interpretation; second, that all interpretations are to be judged on a continuum; and third, that the only proper judges are living listeners, not dead authorities, be they composers, theorists, or instrument builders.

All works of art, I argued (and they agreed), are subject to social mediation. It is, indeed, the price of living. Social mediation is what renders works of art intelligible, and it is what gives them continuing relevance. And social mediation inevitably changes whatever it mediates. There can be no appeal to a higher authority, I said (and they agreed), and any attempt at such an appeal is in fact a covert assertion of the appellant's own authority. I wanted to hug them when I read the sentence I am about to quote, which so succinctly encapsulated everything I had been trying to say: "His complaint is that authenticists, like other ideologues, try to discredit competing presentations as 'incorrect' or, indeed, incompetent, when the proper focus should be on whether the performances are more or less enjoyable and artistically effective." Yes indeed, and doesn't it seem obvious? Ought it to require a musicologist and a pair of legal scholars to come up with such a truism? Maybe not, but apparently it does.

So I was altogether unprepared for the authors' parting shot, in which they in effect asked me to go a little further in my theorizing and make more explicit the criteria of judgment that I advocate against the fraudulently exigent claims of the authenticists. "The real theoretical question," they assert, implying that I had not sufficiently answered it, "is what accounts for our ability to construct boundaries of interpretive possibility and to denounce some musical or legal performances as fraudulent." "The world," they continued,

> can be divided into those who look for algorithms, formal criteria, and determinate procedures to answer this question, and those who denounce the search for such mechanisms as fruitless (and even as a potential harbinger of tyranny). Like Taruskin, we doubt that such algorithms exist, and we believe

that the evaluation of performance must necessarily rest on pragmatic grounds. The lack of algorithms does not mean that we must throw up our hands and pronounce ourselves unable to assess the merits of different performances. . . . Taruskin certainly has no hesitation in doing that in regard to music, nor do we in regard to law. Standards of assessment cannot be reduced to formal criteria or decision procedures.[1]

But somehow they are left unsatisfied with my tolerance, or pragmatic flexibility, or whatever it is. "We are left curious," they write, "as to what it would take for Taruskin to say of a performance, 'this just doesn't count as an even minimally faithful rendition of Beethoven.' At what point would he invoke the authority of the score, for example, as limiting the liberties available to the performer?"[2]

I am astonished at these questions, and at my reviewers' assumption that I could possibly answer them within the premises of my book. I am particularly astonished at the notion of there being some "point" that I could define a priori at which authority would somehow kick in despite all they and I have said against invoking authority as a critical yardstick. And I am even more astonished at their assumption that I would locate that authority in the score, when I have been devoting my entire career as a critic to combating the fetishizing of texts. There is no such point at which I would invoke the authority of the score as limiting the liberties available to the performer. Nor can there be; for its existence would imply that there must be some a priori standard or principle to which I would appeal, and I cannot see the difference between such a standard and the "algorithms, formal criteria, and determinate procedures" that both Professors Levinson and Balkin and I had (I thought) forsworn. Am I right in detecting in these final questions of theirs some residual faith in algorithms after all? If so, I deplore it not merely because it is inconsistent with the positions that they otherwise maintain (a little inconsistency hardly mattering among friends, or at least among pragmatists), but because it smacks—dare I say it?—of prior restraint.

The critical faculty, if it is to be respectable in my sight, can only be exercised after the fact, and there must always be the possibility that the performance will change the critic's mind. Prejudgments are simply prejudices—isn't that what the word means?—and they are indeed harbingers, if not already embodiments, of tyranny. The performers' liberties are potentially the critic's liberties as well, and to me the word *liberty* has no pejorative side. Taking liberties is absolutely all right with me, if it leads to a result I like. Of course there is always the danger of error and excess in the exercise of liberty, but the same dangers inhere in the exercise of restraint.

One case that my critique has made notorious was that of Andrew Porter, the longtime music critic of the *New Yorker* magazine, who was held in high esteem by musicologists and who announced an impending series of recitals, at which two prominent New York musicians would perform the Beethoven sonatas for piano and cello, by sniffing, "They are fine artists, *but* they play modern instruments. I look forward to their recitals but will know them for what they are: transcriptions, in effect, in which Beethoven's tone colors, textures, attacks, and sonic durations are inevitably altered."[3] Did Beethoven have tone colors? Did he have attacks, other than sciatica (or on his landlady)? Did he have sonic durations? I don't even know what a sonic duration is, but I do know that Mr. Porter was advocating bigotry, as was Malcolm Bilson when he declared, just as notoriously (if somewhat ambivalently), "Perhaps it is wrong to put the instrument before the artist, but I have begun to feel that it must be done."[4]

In any case, I see no difference except in degree of obnoxiousness between, on the one hand, my reviewers' assumption that when push comes to shove (and may that day never come) authority will somehow save the day and, on the other hand, snobberies and bigotries like the ones put forth by Andrew Porter and Malcolm Bilson—or even the notorious theory of the nominalist philosopher Nelson Goodman, according to which a performance of a Bach Brandenburg Concerto that contains a wrong note is not a performance of a Bach Brandenburg Concerto at all.[5] Goodman's stipulation puts his philosophy of performance (or, as he calls it, his theory of notation) entirely outside the realm of human transactions, along with most theories of musical performance hatched by analytical philosophers, who inhabit a world much simpler than ours, where objective authenticity is possible and perfect consistency rules. With respect to Professors Levinson and Balkin and the field they plow, I am certainly willing to grant that there may be reasons to have limits up one's sleeve in the field of law that do not apply to the field of music. In law the stakes can be infinitely higher than in music criticism, where only reputations and careers are threatened, not life or limb or property. But the idea that there are—or should be—tacit limits, preferably uninvoked yet reassuringly there to be invoked, still pervades the real world of music and musicology, and it demands renewed scrutiny.

·   ·   ·

Interestingly, Professors Levinson and Balkin tried to entice a theory of limits out of me by dangling before me the related field of dramatic performance, where (they write) "producers and directors sometimes take such liberties with the text that audiences wonder whether to ask for their money back."[6] This field intersects most obviously with musical performance in the case of opera, and my reviewers followed the two questions I have already quoted with a third. "In particular," they wrote, "it would be interesting to hear his thoughts on some of the more daring opera productions of recent times," perhaps thinking of Jonathan Miller, our other keynoter this afternoon. Do I sense a staged confrontation?

If so, it has failed. My tolerance of human foibles is indeed without limit, even when it comes to producers and directors. But I can do better than just give you my own thoughts on the matter. I can report to you on a recent conference we had in Berkeley in connection with last year's Verdi centennial. Convened by my colleague Mary Ann Smart under the general rubric "Primal Scenes," it focused on the relationship between interpretation and performance, or (more precisely) the relationship between the sort of interpretation that critics do and the sort that performers do. Most of the papers subjected a scene from one of Verdi's operas to an *explication de texte* and then either speculated or demonstrated how the reading thus arrived at might be embodied in a staging of the work. Inevitably, questions of rights and proprieties arose, like the ones we are considering at this conference, but they were rarely met head-on.

One exception was a paper by Roger Parker, Great Britain's leading Verdi scholar, which focused on a scene from *Don Carlos* (or *Don Carlo,* if you prefer). The discrepancy in names reflects the complicated history of the work, which was created for the Paris Opera in 1867 but revised for the Italian stage in 1884. There are four recognized authorial (that is, authentic) versions of the work: namely, the original Paris version as written, the version actually performed there, a preliminary revision dating from 1872, and the thoroughgoing overhaul a dozen years later. The efforts of musical philologists have mainly been devoted to the mechanical tasks of restoring and distinguishing between the various layers of authorial revision, and also to more ideologically driven arguments in favor of this or that version, implying a defense of its integrity.

Prof. Parker took a different tack. His paper concerned the duet between Philip II of Spain and Rodrigue, Marquis of Posa, in act 2, the most heavily revised number in the score, which exists in four discrete redactions, one per version.[7] His main exhibit was not one or another of the canonical versions but rather a new recording of the scene in which the four versions were freely conflated according to no other criterion, it seemed, than the performers' (or, presumably, the conductor's, that is, Antonio Pappano's) moment-by-moment musical or dramatic preferences. What surprised most listeners, and (as you can imagine) greatly gratified me, was that Prof. Parker praised the approach taken in the recording and said that now that a complete critical edition of the opera, containing all the music of all the versions, is available, he both expected conflation to become the rule and welcomed it, because it would afford listeners and critics an endless prospect of new versions to savor and compare. Where most critics would lament the freedom, equating it in advance with abuse, Prof. Parker saw fit to emphasize the best possible outcome: new versions that would equal or even surpass the merits of the authorial versions.

I was thrilled both to hear such an authoritative musicological voice come down on the side of imagination and liberty—and for all the right reasons, too—and to hear a connoisseur of connoisseurs maintain openness to new impressions and the possibility of being convinced by them. It was extraordinary to hear Prof. Parker actually (if tacitly) allow the possibility that a nonauthorial version of the opera might be better than any of the authorial ones.

Well, what's "better"? I can't give you Prof. Parker's answer, but I can give you one of my own. The only opera that rivals *Don Carlos* for a checkered creative history is Musorgsky's *Boris Godunov*. It has two complete authorial versions—one finished in 1869, the other in 1872—and a host of authorial variants. One of the biggest differences between the two main versions involves the role of the Holy Fool or Simpleton (in Russian, the *yurodivïy*). In the version of 1869 he appears in the penultimate scene of the opera, one taken directly from Pushkin's historical play of the same name, in which the Holy Fool sings a crazy song about Russia's misfortunes, is tortured by a gang of street urchins, and finally confronts the title character directly with his crime of regicide and refuses to pray for him. In 1872 Musorgsky replaced that scene with one that had no analogue in Pushkin's play and that now ended the opera. Unlike the scene from Pushkin, which shows the crowd submissive and suppliant, it followed more recent historians by showing the crowd in open revolt against the tsar-usurper. The composer transferred part of the episode with the Holy Fool into the new scene, and ended the whole opera with a heartrendingly expanded version of the Fool's demented lament.

The two scenes are mutually exclusive. They have a considerable amount of music in common, and they embody contradictory conceptions of the historical conditions on which the drama is based. And yet in 1939, the year of the composer's birth centennial, the Bolshoi Theater in Moscow put on a production of *Boris Godunov* that included both scenes, redundancy and contradiction be damned, using them to flank the scene of the title character's death. One cannot make a coherent logical case for such a conflation, and there is good reason to think it was motivated in the first instance by a Stalinist view of the opera's role as a political commentary on the illegitimacy of tsarist rule, each scene contributing its mite to that propagandistic task. And yet both scenes are searingly effective musical and dramatic achievements. Both bring tears to the eyes of the audience, and the reprise of the Fool's lament (which is not a reprise unless both of the scenes are included) is perhaps the crowning stroke of musicodramatic genius. No wonder the version of the opera concocted in Moscow possibly for political purposes became canonical in the Soviet Union, and remains so in post-Soviet Russia. Although unforeseen and seemingly disallowed by the author (even though it uses only material he composed), it is, I believe, a greater work than either of the two authorial versions.

But greater on what basis? If you measure greatness the modernist way, in terms of internal unity and elegant form, it is a travesty. If you measure greatness the way audiences measure greatness, in terms of what it does to them, it is a masterpiece. Modernists, for whom the very first principle of art is "the customer is always wrong," cannot be expected to respect such a definition of greatness, and that is exactly where I differ with them (though whether to call that difference premodern or postmodern I leave to you). My sympathy, as a member of the audience, is finally with my own kind. Does an evil message (say, the Stalinism to which I have already called attention, or the anti-Semitism of Bach's *St. John Passion,* or the German chauvinism of Wagner's *Die Meistersinger*) prevent a work from achieving the status of a masterpiece? Obviously not, except by the sort of spurious critical fiat that declares evil masterpieces to be a contradiction in terms that must be resolved either by proving that they are not evil or by proving that they are not masterpieces. We all know that is a spurious solution. That is exactly why we are having this conference.

To return to Roger Parker and his evaluation of *Don Carlos,* it will not surprise you to learn that the first question he received at discussion time was the question Professors Levinson and Balkin addressed to me: where would you draw the line? Prof. Parker, God bless him, said that he was not prepared to draw one. The questions got more specific and pointed. What if a director (or even a singer) insisted on importing into the scene an aria that was not from *Don Carlos,* or not even by Verdi? Prof. Parker stood his ground, knowing full well (as did the questioners, also good historians) that such importations were the standard practice of the eighteenth century, and lasted well into the nineteenth; and that when the practice died out it was as a result of an ideological change that had nothing to do with the audience.

Finally somebody threw out the old standby, "So, anything goes then?" and Prof. Parker hedged a little. He said he welcomed all conflations and experiments so long as they were seriously motivated and not merely commercial. That, of course, created an opening for me. How, I asked him, could he tell the difference if all he had to go on was the result? At this, Prof. Parker said, "Well, of course, I'd read your program notes, Richard," and the discussion dissolved in friendly laughter. But the point hung in the air, and I want to have it hang here, too. If motive counts above result, we are still modernists (or, if you prefer, romantics) and still bigots.

·   ·   ·

One of Prof. Parker's interlocutors, the one who asked if he would accept a non-Verdian interpolation, was Philip Gossett, a textual critic who until the recent conference at Berkeley had enjoyed a special reputation for philological vigilance. He was among the intrepid group of scholars who in the 1970s won academic respectability for Italian opera, until then regarded as performers' music rather than scholars' music (or as we say in the trade, music of the repertory rather than the canon). That academic respectability, however, was won on fairly paradoxical grounds. Those grounds were textual. Prof. Gossett labored to restore the text of Rossini's operas to their original authorial state and then became a self-proclaimed "crusader" on behalf of the texts he had restored, insisting on their authority in preference to the socially mediated versions prevalent in the repertory.[8] Turning Rossini's texts—that is, Gossett's texts—into fetish objects comparable with Beethoven's texts amounted to turning Rossini into a composer comparable with Beethoven, at least insofar as academic practice was concerned, and that is what got Rossini through the door.

Prof. Gossett himself observed in one of his earliest Rossini studies that "an Italian opera in the first half of the nineteenth century was treated as a collection of individual units that could be rearranged, substituted or omitted depending on local conditions of performance, local taste or, on many occasions, whim."[9] The new academic view of Rossini operas as inviolable works was thus altogether unhistorical. But that did not deter Prof. Gossett from excoriating performers who departed from what he called the "fully authentic" versions of Rossini's operas, namely, the versions (reconstructed by Gossett) that the composer, acting as impresario, had prepared for performance at the theaters where, at various times, Rossini had found employment.

Prof. Gossett fully lived up to his calling as crusader in the tone of high moral dudgeon he habitually adopted as reviewer. The piece that established his reputation as a critic, a review of the Angel recording of Rossini's *The Siege of Corinth* with Thomas Schippers conducting and Beverly Sills as Pamira, was timed to coincide with the performance of the same work with the same conductor and prima donna that marked Mme Sills's highly touted debut at the Metropolitan Opera in 1975. Maestro Schippers's textual choices were characterized as "indefensible licenses, crimes, so to speak, against the composer," a charge that the exacting historian backed up with a patently unhistorical thesis. "The argument," he wrote,

> that crimes were committed in Rossini's life is no argument at all for their perpetuation, though most of the offenses I am about to describe are without precedent in contemporary performance. Nor should the atrocities Rossini himself occasionally committed be considered central to the discussion. That a composer acting as arranger may feel compelled by reasons beyond his control to submit parts of his scores to emasculation is no reason for us to transform "the little knife," as the Italians used to call it, into a machete.[10]

"Licenses," "crimes," "offenses"—even "atrocities," a term normally reserved for Nazis or Bosnian Serbs. Leaving "emasculation" for another day—to do that one justice would require a whole other keynote address—we still have a wonderful world of coercive rhetoric to explore. But I will confine myself to noting that although Prof. Gossett claimed to derive his authority from the composer, he in fact held it above the composer's authority as soon as the composer left his composing desk (or, in Rossini's case, his bed) and entered the socially mediated world of performance.

Gossett founded his claim of authority on scientific method, a method dramatically asserted over the course of the review by a process of purportedly objective classification set out in five impressive "tables." The first of these was a tabulation of "The Musical Units in *The Siege of Corinth*," sixteen in all. Table 2 listed four "Pieces Recorded with Insignificant or Acceptable Alterations, If Any." Table 3 listed five "Pieces Recorded with More Substantial but Generally Acceptable Alterations." Table 4 detailed "Two Numbers with Unacceptable Alterations in the Recorded Version," and table 5 listed the six "Remaining Solo Arias," all of which were found to embody indefensible licenses attributable as much to Mme Sills as to the conductor, for "always lurking in the background is the prima donna, with the demands prima donnas have made since opera first emerged."[11] Down with her, the reviewer implies. Away with the conductor. Away with all the other mediators who stand between us and the score. "Rossini can speak to us in his own language," Prof. Gossett concluded. "We need only give him the opportunity."

The idea that a composer "speaks in his own language" is another idea that is worth a more extended look than we can give it today. It suggests the proper historical context for Prof. Gossett's harangue. That context is German romanticism and its modernist transformations, according to which the role of the artist is to embody his unique individuality—that is, his personal integrity and authenticity—in his art with a minimum of interference from social convention. It is the view that dichotomizes the interests of artists and audience, and has led high art (and classical music above all) into the cul de sac that, in the period since 1975, has led to all the agonizing reappraisals, recriminations, and attempts at reconciliation that constitute one strain of what we rather inadequately call "postmodernism." Among its effects has been the repudiation of exigently puritanical stances like Prof. Gossett's, and a penchant for radical "revisionary" stagings of operatic classics that attempt to reengage the interest of the operatic public by attaching those classics to issues of contemporary social and political concern.

One might have expected Philip Gossett to be in the forefront of opposition to such radical stagings, of the kind known as *Regietheater* or *Regieoper* (director's theater or director's opera) in Germany, where they have been rifest. But at the Berkeley Verdi conference Prof. Gossett surprised us almost as much as did Prof. Parker, when he took the opportunity, in the course of a paper otherwise devoted as usual to sketches and texts, to inveigh, almost as thunderously as I have just inveighed at him, at a *New Yorker* essay by Alex Ross in which the critic claimed that Verdi uniquely resists "directorial brainstorms and interpretive ego trips" and makes monkeys of the arrogant know-nothings who update or recontextualize or otherwise distort his works.[12] Still using the morally charged language he habitually employs, Prof. Gossett assailed this as an intolerable infringement on the rights of creative artists.

Oddest of all, when I ventured to congratulate him at question time on his newly liberalized views, Prof. Gossett indignantly declared that his views had not changed in the least and that he had always upheld directorial insurgency no matter how radical, thinking it a necessary preservative that prevents old operas from going stale. He trained his sights not only on what he took to be conservative critics such as Alex Ross but also—and I have to say, predictably—on the resistant *loggionisti,* the Italian opera fans who, he implied, understood the aims neither of the radical directors nor of the Verdi they claimed to love.[13]

He seemed to believe what he was saying, and I was left with a paradox. It was later on in the conference that the paradox resolved itself for me, albeit far from reassuringly. A young German scholar, Clemens Risi, gave a report from the *Regietheater* battlefield. He called it "Shedding Light on the Audience: Strategies of Verdi Stagings and Performance Analysis."[14] It featured videotapes of some particularly aggressive German productions—the notorious Frankfurt *Aida* directed by Hans Neuenfels in 1981 and a 1994 production of the same opera from Graz, Austria, staged by Peter Konwitschny—that notably provoked their audiences. It turned out, among other things, that the first phrase of the paper's title was not only a metaphor but also a literal description: one of Konwitschny's strategies was actually to raise the house lights during the Triumphal March so that the audience itself, surrounded by Verdi's trumpets, became the viewed object. On an almost barren stage one saw not the familiar procession of camels, Ethiopian prisoners, and whatnot, but rather the Egyptian royals having what looked like a New Year's party, while Aida, their black maid, swept up.

The image of Aida wielding a broom was borrowed directly from Neuenfels's production, in which the curtain went up at the sound of the Triumphal March to reveal another audience—the original La Scala audience of 1872 in period dress—watching the Frankfurt audience of 1981 as it looked in vain for the spectacular procession it had paid to see. Each audience became the object of the other's gaze. It was the spectators, in Mr. Risi's words, "bored and sated with luxuries, who [were] at the center of attention." Finally the Ethiopian prisoners did appear, and, as Mr. Risi described them, they "were led to a laid table and forced to use knives and forks in order to eat roasted chicken." This "failed experiment in civilization" ended in an open revolt and a savage repression.

The videotaped excerpts that Risi showed from both productions included many shots of the respective audiences, as they reacted with the mounting indignation that it was obviously the directors' primary purpose to arouse. Or rather, we observed the audiences dividing into pro and contra factions, whose jeers and grimaces gradually veered away from the stage and toward each other. The directors had succeeded in engineering a social division between the insulted bourgeois and the taunting avant-garde.

So what else is new in the gray-bearded realm of high modernism? Of all possible approaches to staging an opera, this one is by now perhaps the very biggest cliché.

Or at least that was my jaded reaction. Young Mr. Risi seemed very impressed with what he took to be its postmodernity, and with its social engineering. He touted the confrontational stagings for, as he put it, stripping the audience, including himself, "of our own feeling of superiority and our own arrogance towards the Other." But what they chiefly exposed for me was the two directors' altogether unchallenged feeling of superiority and their arrogance toward their other, namely, the audience, the perennial modernist other. It is a stance by now expected, well rewarded, and hence the very opposite of risky. Nothing nowadays could be more cozy or smug.

Seemingly strangest of all, yet on reflection all too predictable, was Mr. Risi's contention (echoed by Prof. Gossett at discussion time) that the radical stagings were in fact attempts to restore the original power of the operas, dulled by overfamiliarity, to achieve the effects at which Verdi was aiming. As Mr. Risi put it, "Why should we believe that a 'uomo di teatro'" like Verdi "would refuse strategies to pull the audience out of its lethargy and lead them to an active participation?" In short, the strategies of Herren Neuenfels and Konwitschny were in effect professions of solidarity with Verdi's true intentions.

Well, now we were on familiar territory. As usual, the claim of fidelity to the author's intentions was tiresomely easy to puncture. Verdi's solidarity, from the beginning of his career to the end, was always with the audience. He had nothing but scorn for the idealistic social contempt of German romantics, and he never evinced the slightest aggression toward the public on whose approval his livelihood depended. Invoking the authority of original intentions was in this case, as it always is, only a cover for asserting the invoker's authority. (And of course it is here that issues of musical and legal interpretation most obviously intersect.) But again, Mr. Risi and Prof. Gossett were apparently sincere in their belief that these willfully disfigured productions were in fact faithful ones, and therefore not to be faulted on grounds of authenticity.

On what grounds could such a claim be defended? On the most banal and obvious grounds: the new German productions were radical only in their visual aspects. In both cases, the performances of the score were scrupulously compliant with what the composer had written, although occasionally the noise made by the 1981 Frankfurt audience caused the conductor to stop the music and wait for the hubbub to subside. This, however, was not an intentional alteration to the score, only an attempt to cope with conditions outside of the musicians' control.

And in fact, with the single exception of Peter Brooks's 1984 adaptation of Bizet's *Carmen* as *La Tragédie de Carmen,* I cannot think of a single "radical" operatic staging, no matter how outlandish the concept, in which the music is subjected to the least alteration or distortion beyond what is considered normal in opera houses, namely, cuts and transpositions to accommodate singers. In Jonathan Miller's famous English National Opera *Rigoletto* of twenty years ago, for example, the Duke of Mantua, now a Mafia don, may play *La donna è mobile* through a jukebox, but the sounds that come out of it are not jukebox sounds but the vocal and orchestral sounds that Verdi notated some 130 years earlier.

Indeed, the possibility occurs to me that "normal" musical alterations are actually less likely to occur in *Regieoper* than in traditional stagings. Peter Sellars's Mozart productions —you remember, *Don Giovanni* in East Harlem, *The Marriage of Figaro* in Trump Tower, and *Così fan tutte* in a neon-lit diner—were actually accompanied by period instrument bands, at a time when such a practice still connoted "authenticity." His earlier newsmakers had involved Handel operas, likewise given fastidious period performances by specialist musicians. As I pointed out at the time, updating the stage action while embalming the pit noises in period timbres accomplished a double defamiliarization, and this must have been at least part of Sellars's intention. But a double defamiliarization could also have been accomplished by updating the timbres and embalming the stage action in period conventions. That, however, is a road as yet untraveled. How come?

The most that Sellars—who is described by the *New Grove Dictionary of Opera* as "iconoclastically untraditional"—has ever tampered with a score, to my knowledge, was in his Glyndebourne *Magic Flute* of 1990, in which he cut out the spoken dialogue (to unanimous disapproval, leading to a rare instance of backing down). Even here, however, not a note of Mozart was touched, only the words of his librettist Schikaneder; and the musical settings, despite the fact that the locale of the opera had been transposed to contemporary Los Angeles, were punctiliously sung in German. It seems never to have occurred to any director, no matter how "radical," to update the music along with the mise-en-scène, even though that would remove, at least for me, the most serious roadblock to the suspension of disbelief in updated opera.

Why no Mozart on rock guitars or Verdi in tinny prerecorded jukebox timbres? Why no techno Traviatas or R&B Götterdämmerungs? Why didn't Neuenfels or Konwitschny have Verdi's Triumphal March performed as an electronic collage or by an Egyptian cabaret orchestra? Clearly a double standard is at work—and it is a necessary double standard. It underwrites the spurious claims on which the directors stake their authority. If the music is rendered without distortion, fidelity to the composer's intentions—his "true" or latent intentions—may be claimed, and that claim may then be generalized to justify (or validate) the whole production. So it transpires that no operatic director has yet dared to be "iconoclastically untraditional." The chief icon—the composer—has been left intact, and the traditional power relations of our musical culture remain unchallenged. That is why *Regieoper* has been so eminently acceptable to opera house managements. They know that no real threat is being mounted, and they also know that controversy is always good for business. Neuenfels, Konwitschny, Sellars, and the rest may congratulate themselves on their daring, but they have acted in craven collusion with the business interests they make a pretense of opposing.

. . .

When a double standard is so bald, so arbitrary, and so easily unmasked, one has to ask why so many intelligent people have upheld it. The reason, as I see it, is that no one, or very few, really want to exercise their intelligence. Or rather, they do not want to exercise real judgment, or make real decisions for which they will have to take responsibility. Granting unlimited license in one dimension of operatic practice but granting no freedom at all in the other dimension is a mindless dodge. Submit to it, and you'll never have to think again.

That is why we set limits. It is a perfect escape from freedom, as perfect in its way as submission to religious discipline, or to the discipline of a totalitarian political party. And it is a perfect analogue to Nelson Goodman's mindlessly simplified definition of a musical work. I've already mentioned that in Goodman's world a performance of a Bach concerto that contains a wrong note is not a performance of that concerto at all. Now I will add that a performance of the concerto that lasts all day is perfectly acceptable to Goodman's theory, as long as all the rhythms in the score are correctly executed at the chosen tempo, however far that tempo may be from anything that Bach could have reasonably intended. That is because pitches and rhythms are "notational" in Goodmanian terms. That is, they are exactly specified as quantities, while Italian tempo designations are not. Similarly, in our modern world of musical performance, the score of an opera is held to be "notational" and therefore binding, while everything pertaining to the visual realization is not. The one requires utter fidelity, zealously policed by the likes of Prof. Gossett. The other allows utter, and often cynical, freedom.

That mindless commitment to textuality, and the dull sameness it enforces, is killing. The boredom of endlessly reproducing fetishized texts is what invites, and even demands, the compensatory excesses of *Regieoper*. It is the only area of classical musical performance today in which executant creativity is not stifled, but only because of the devil's bargain the directors have struck with the conductors. The few classical musicians who have lately tried to reintroduce creative performing practices are as yet confined to the ghetto of the avant-garde. Or else, like Robert Levin (the one living pianist

who can perform a Mozart concerto the way Mozart did, with improvised cadenzas and florid embellishments throughout), they continue to meet with
stiff opposition from an entrenched academic orthodoxy spearheaded by
Christoph Wolff of Harvard and Neal Zaslaw of Cornell.[15] These historians
persist in minimizing, or denying outright, the most fundamental historical
realities, on the basis not of research or knowledge but rather on that of a
contemporary and wholly ahistorical ideology.

The ideology of mindlessness has recently been given comprehensive and
militant expression by a prominent and influential musical polymath only
tangentially affiliated but wholly allied with, and highly respected within, the
academic community. Gunther Schuller, equally distinguished as a composer, a performer, a jazz historian, a music educator, a music editor, a music
publisher, and a recording executive, published a book called *The Compleat
Conductor* in 1997 that amounted to a 571-page kvetch that the custodians of
our musical museum have not entirely given up the exercise of subjective
judgment and as a result commit the kind of thing Philip Gossett calls
"crimes against the composer" in virtually their every performance and
recording. Among the indicted were not only the usual suspects like Artur
Nikisch, Wilhelm Furtwängler, Hans Knappertsbusch, Leopold Stokowski,
Serge Koussevitzky, Willem Mengelberg, Leonard Bernstein, George Solti,
and other "romantics" known for taking liberties in the name of expression.
They included all the famous literalists of the past as well, beginning with Arturo Toscanini himself, the first to proclaim the *com'è scritto* (play it as writ-
ten) faith, and going on from there with names like Felix Weingartner, Fritz
Reiner, George Szell, Eugen Jochum, and even René Leibowitz, who before
Schuller was the most prominent high-modernist puritan. And they included
all the self-proclaimed authenticists of the early-music movement, like Frans
Brüggen (who advertises his "obedience" to the composer), Roger Norrington (the metronome man), John Eliot Gardiner, and Nikolaus Harnoncourt.
Schuller backed up his charges with an unbelievably compulsive and
tedious—and, let's face it, inane—game of "gotcha," comparing everybody's
recordings atomistically with the scores—which is why the book was so long
and (I'll bet) unread by anybody straight through. But he certainly had the
goods. No matter how distinguished the name, Schuller was able to cite endless misdemeanors: metronome settings not adhered to; markings ignored,
even contradicted; departures from the notated rhythm; and unmarked dynamics, fermatas, accents, and tempo changes galore.

Most of the conductors whom Schuller berates would probably describe
themselves as faithful to the scores from which they conduct, although some
might choose to characterize their fidelity (like the modern stage directors
we have been looking at) in terms of the effect or spirit of their performances
rather than in terms of text or letter. Schuller, however, is a fundamentalist
who will brook no extenuating circumstances. Departure from the letter of

the text is inexcusable vainglory, no matter who does it or why; and this categorical prejudice is supported by something very like the doctrine of papal infallibility. Composers and performers, you see, belong to different species. Their endowments are not to be located on a continuum, but on separate planes of existence. "The composer and his score," Schuller writes,

> *have* to be respected, especially when that composer is a Beethoven, a Tchaikovsky, a Wagner, a Brahms, a Stravinsky, or any of the other fifty to a hundred composers whose masterpieces make up the bulk of our repertory. To answer the question even more provocatively—and to answer it with another question: Are conductors X and Y, both world famous and popular, really better musicians than Brahms or Beethoven? Are they such fantastic musicians that they have the right to disregard or override most of the basic information contained in a composer's score? The answer is an unequivocal no; they aren't; and they don't have that right![16]

You may have thought that I speak figuratively when I speak of mindlessness. But you see, I mean it quite literally. According to Schuller's tautological philosophy, there can be no success in performance other than success in submission, as Stravinsky once notoriously put it, to an explicit will that intends no more than it commands.[17] "If an interpretation," Schuller writes, "no matter how compelling, how exciting, no matter how sublime at certain moments, is achieved from outside the score's basic information, to the extent that it ignores this core, it is to that extent invalid."[18]

Cui bono? one has to ask at this point. Who benefits from a dispensation in which to be compelling, exciting, or sublime is less important than to be correct? Who benefits from such a dogmatically uncritical viewpoint? I cannot think, after all, that it is the composer, unless it is a composer, and we have certainly known plenty of these (especially in Gunther Schuller's generation), who is also concerned less with being compelling or sublime than with being correct. There is the source of our mindless limits. It is the price of that pusillanimous overvaluation of correctness, of all virtues surely the paltriest. And that is why classical music is dying. The Schullers are killing it off. Or trying to.

But here is the good news. Not even Schuller practices what he preaches. His book is riddled with contradictions. Deep down, like everyone else, he respects the score only insofar as he agrees with it. Noting that few conductors observe the first movement repeat via the first ending in Brahms's First Symphony, he derides the few who do observe it as "historically informed authenticists," even though the composer's intentions in this case could not be clearer—or to put it more carefully, as Schuller might at his most severe, even though the first ending is part of "the score's basic information." But Schuller doesn't like the first ending. And he advises those who elect to play it to alter it—replacing a D-flat with a D-natural—to remove what Schuller considers its "awkwardness" and "an abruptness in the harmonic progression which I can't quite analyze."[19]

All of a sudden the composer is no longer infallible. All of a sudden the exercise of subjective judgment is called for. Well and good. I agree. But as Paul Griffiths observed (with respect to a different contradiction) in his review of Schuller's book, "Here, in one line, Schuller has blown the whistle on his own game (though that does not stop him going on playing it for another 350 pages)."[20]

Or consider Schuller's remarks on the conductor Carlos Kleiber:

> Kleiber is so unique, so remarkable, so outstanding that one can only describe him as a phenomenon. This does not mean that he is a "perfect" conductor—perhaps no one can be that—but he has so many extraordinary attributes that make him a great and important representative of the art of recreation and performance.

And what are these attributes? He "goes in for the grand line, the large shape, and the clarification of inherent structure," Schuller writes. And as a result:

> I find that he is not (or elects not to be) conscious of every detail in a score, even details which others would rightly consider very important. Like many maestri, he is selective in what he chooses to point out (by his gestures) to the orchestra and the audience. And like many others, he has some questionable musical habits, such as almost always crescendoing much too early—he loves to drive orchestras to a climax—conducting too often only the primary melodic or thematic lines, frequently neglecting to make the orchestra really play the softer dynamics, occasionally indulging in unnecessary over-conducting. But whatever he does, he does with such consummate control, gesturally and intellectually, and with such a joy of music-making, ranging from complete confidence-building relaxation in front of an orchestra to passionate, almost ecstatic outbursts, that one can only be compelled to admire in awe—even if one does not always agree with every aspect of his performances. Kleiber is a virtuoso in the best sense, a virtuoso with a mind.[21]

You could hardly hope to find a better rebuttal to the mindless—and, in the first instance, to Schuller himself. In the end it is the exercise of subjective judgment by a properly qualified judge and not mindless submission to the score (or to the use of the "correct" version or the "right" instrument) that produces performances that benefit listeners. I was about to write "composers and listeners," but truly we owe nothing to composers, at least the dead ones who overwhelmingly populate our performing repertory. Schuller harps interminably about "respect for the dead," but our obligations are to the living. Schuller's unwitting yet endearing self-rebuttal is life-affirming. It puts to shame the text-fetishism that continues to dominate contemporary theories of musical interpretation, with their arbitrary limits and their hatred of freedom. Schuller shows that we strive hard for perfect mindlessness, but, being human, we inevitably fall short of perfection. I devoutly hope and optimistically trust that we will always continue to do so.

NOTES

1. Sanford Levinson and Jack Balkin, review of Richard Taruskin, *Text and Act: Essays on Music and Performance, Music Library Association Notes* 53 (1995–96): 422.

2. Ibid., 422–23.

3. Andrew Porter, "Musical Events," *New Yorker,* 3 November 1986; italics added. This is one of the few *New Yorker* reviews by Porter that has not been collected for reprinting in book form.

4. Malcolm Bilson, "The Viennese Fortepiano of the Late Eighteenth Century," *Early Music* 8 (1980): 162.

5. See Nelson Goodman, *Languages of Art* (Indianapolis: Hackett, 1976), 120n.

6. Levinson and Balkin, review of *Text and Act,* 422.

7. A revised version of Parker's paper is published as "Philippe and Posa, Act II: The Shock of the New," *Cambridge Opera Journal* 14 (2002): 133–48.

8. Philip Gossett, remarks made to the Central Opera Service on the occasion of the performance of Rossini's *Tancredi* by the Houston Grand Opera, 17 November 1977; reprinted in *Current Musicology,* no. 26 (1978): 40: "The crusade for *Tancredi* is part of a larger crusade which has as its goal replacing in opera houses throughout the world, both large and small, the editions being used today of Italian nineteenth-century opera (the operas of Rossini, Bellini, Donizetti, and Verdi) with new critical editions."

9. Philip Gossett, "The Operas of Rossini: Problems of Textual Criticism in Nineteenth-Century Opera" (PhD diss., Princeton University, 1970), 21.

10. Philip Gossett, review of Rossini, *The Siege of Corinth* (Angel SCLX 3819), *Musical Quarterly* 61 (1975): 627.

11. Ibid., 634.

12. Alex Ross, "Verdi's Grip," *New Yorker,* 24 September 2001, 84.

13. Gossett's views on the *loggionisti* are set forth at length in "Scandal and Scholarship," *New Republic,* 2 July 2001, 23–32.

14. A revised version is published as "Shedding Light on the Audience: Hans Neuenfels and Peter Konwitschny Stage Verdi (and Verdians)," *Cambridge Opera Journal* 14 (2002): 201–10.

15. For Wolff's arguments, see "Cadenzas and Styles of Improvisation in Mozart's Piano Concertos," in *Perspectives on Mozart Performance,* ed. R. Larry Todd and Peter Williams (Cambridge: Cambridge University Press, 1991), 215–38. Zaslaw's can be found in his notes accompanying the Deutsche Grammophon Archiv recording of the complete Mozart piano concertos by Malcolm Bilson and the English Baroque Soloists under John Eliot Gardiner (11 CDs, recorded 1983–88).

16. Gunther Schuller, *The Compleat Conductor* (New York: Oxford University Press, 1997), 29–30.

17. See Igor Stravinsky, *Poetics of Music in the Form of Six Lessons,* trans. Arthur Knodel and Ingolf Dahl (Cambridge, Mass.: Harvard University Press), Lesson Six, "The Performance of Music and Epilogue."

18. Schuller, *The Compleat Conductor,* 106.

19. Ibid., 308 n 1.

20. Paul Griffiths, "What's the Score?" (review of Schuller, *The Compleat Conductor*), *New York Times Book Review,* 24 August 1997, 11.

21. Schuller, *The Compleat Conductor,* 193–94.

INDEX

Text:	10/12 Baskerville
Display:	Baskerville
Compositor:	Binghamton Valley Composition
Music Engraver:	Mansfield Music Graphics
Printer/Binder:	Sheridan Books, Inc.